Globalization & Growth

Case Studies in National Economic Strategies

2nd Edition

Richard H. K. Vietor
Harvard Business School

THOMSON

SOUTH-WESTERN

Australia · Canada · Mexico · Singapore · Spain · United Kingdom · United States

THOMSON

SOUTH-WESTERN

Globalization & Growth:

Case Studies in National Economic Strategies, 2e

Richard H. K. Vietor

VP/Editorial Director:
Jack W. Calhoun

VP/Editor-in-Chief:
Michael P. Roche

Publisher:
Michael B. Mercier

Sr. Acquisitions Editor:
Peter Adams

Sr. Developmental Editor:
Trish Taylor

Sr. Marketing Manager:
John Carey

Production Editor:
Emily S. Gross

Manufacturing Coordinator:
Sandee Milewski

Technology Project Editor:
Peggy Buskey

Media Editor:
Pam Wallace

Design Project Manager:
Chris Miller

Cover Designer:
Chris Miller

Cover Image:
© Corbis

Compositor:
HeartWood Designs, Inc.

Printer:
West Group
Eagan, MN

For more information
contact South-Western,
5191 Natorp Boulevard,
Mason, Ohio, 45040.
Or you can visit our Internet site at:
http://www.swlearning.com

Globalization is the historic process of economic integration that has occurred since World War II. Trade in goods and services, investments in equities and debt, tourism, development of intellectual property, and financial transactions have become thoroughly internationalized. This is the context for business. Thus, for those who would understand economic development, it is more important than ever to have a thorough, current knowledge of the political-economic strategies deployed in major areas of the world.

The cases in this book were developed for use in teaching international political economy at the Harvard Business School. They represent the major developmental trajectories that have defined the recent history of economic growth. These cases empirically describe the strategies of Singapore, China, India, Russia, Mexico, Brazil, South Africa, Saudi Arabia, Europe, Italy, Japan and the United States. As a group, these countries represent more than half the world's population and nearly two-thirds of its gross domestic product.

The cases are as much political and institutional as economic. This is intentional. At Harvard, we teach an analytical methodology for managers called "country analysis." This is a method of identifying the economic performance, social and political context, and national development strategy of a country (or region) and of assessing the strategy in terms of its effects on performance and its fit with context. Once mastered, this form of analysis allows managers to assess international environments and issues themselves and confidently draw conclusions about market growth, labor costs, inflation and exchange rate stability, and direct investment opportunities in the near-term future. We believe that all business and governmental managers should be able to perform this sort of analysis effectively.

AUTHOR

Richard Vietor is the Senator John Heinz Professor of Environmental Management at the Harvard Graduate School of Business Administration and Senior Associate Dean. He teaches courses on regulation of business, the environment, and the international political economy. He received a B.A. in economics from Union College (1967), an M.A. in history from Hofstra University (1971), and a Ph.D. in history from the University of Pittsburgh (1975).

Before coming to the Business School in 1978, Professor Vietor held faculty appointments at Virginia Polytechnic Institute and the University of Missouri at Columbia. He is the recipient of a National Endowment of the Humanities Fellowship and Harvard's Newcomen Fellowship. In 1981 he received the Newcomen Award in business history. In 1993-94 he served as president of the Business History Conference.

Professor Vietor's research on business and government has been published in more than seventy cases and in numerous journals and books. He has contributed chapters to *America versus Japan* (1986), *Wallstreet and Regulation* (1987), *Future Competition in Telecommunications* (1989), and *Beyond Free Trade* (1993), His books include *Environmental Politics and the Coal Coalition* (1980), *Energy Policy in America Since 1945* (1984), *Telecommunications in Transition* (1986), *Strategic Management in the Regulated Environment* (1989), *Contrived Competition: Regulation and Deregulation in America* (1994), and *Business Management and the Natural Environment* (1996).

CONTRIBUTORS

Rawi Abdelal is Assistant Professor of Business Administration at the Harvard Business School. Professor Abdelal has a B.S. degree in economics from Georgia Institute of Technology (1993), an M.A. (1997) and a Ph.D. (1999) in government from Cornell University. Professor Abdelal teaches Business, Government and the International Economy in Harvard's MBA curriculum. He is author of several cases on Russia, South Africa and Malaysia, articles in *East European Politics and Societies* and *Journal of Communist and Transition Politics,* and an award-winning book entitled *National Purpose in the World Economy: Post-Soviet States in Comparative Perspective* (2001).

Laura Alfaro is Assistant Professor of Business Administration at the Harvard Business School. Professor Alfaro has a B.A. degree in economics from Pontifica Universidad in Chile, an M.A. (1996) and a Ph.D. (1999) in economics from the University of California, Los Angeles. Professor Alfaro teaches Business, Government and the International Economy in Harvard's MBA curriculum. She is author of several cases, on Brazil, Malaysia and Botswana, and has published articles in *The Journal of Applied Economics, Eco`nomia, Economics and Politics, Review of International Economics,* and *Journal of International Economics.*

Robert Kennedy is Professor of Business Administration at the University of Michigan Business School and Associate Director of the William Davidson Institute. He teaches courses on international business and the global economy. Professor Kennedy holds a B.A. in economics from Stanford, an M.S. in management from M.I.T., and a Ph.D. in business economics from Harvard. Professor Kennedy has written dozens of cases on business operating in developing countries, has worked as a venture capitalist in East Europe and as a marketing manager at Microsoft, and has published several articles on industrial organization and economic liberalization in *The Journal of Economics and Management Strategy, Journal of Industrial Economics, World Development* and *The International Journal of Industrial Organization.*

CONTENTS

Introduction   vi

CHAPTER 1   Savings, Productivity, and Structured Growth   1
Case Study   Singapore Inc.   2

CHAPTER 2   Gradual Transition from a Planned Economy   29
Case Study   China: Facing the 21st Century   31

CHAPTER 3   Import Substitution to Washington Consensus   58
Case Study   India on the Move   59

CHAPTER 4   State Socialism's Disintegration   86
Case Study   Russia: The End of a Time of Troubles?   87
Conceptual Note   The State   112

CHAPTER 5   Structural Adjustment beyond the Washington Consensus   118
Case Study   Mexico: The Unfinished Agenda   119

CHAPTER 6   Regional Free Trade amidst Instability   151
Case Study   Brazil: Embracing Globalization?   152

CHAPTER 7   The African Renaissance   180
Case Study   South Africa: Getting in GEAR   181

CHAPTER 8   Islamic Resurgence   208
Case Study   Saudi Arabia: Getting the House in Order   209
Industry Note   World Oil Markets   233

CHAPTER 9   Regional Integration   251
Case Study   European Monetary Union   252

CHAPTER 10   Monetary Union and Microeconomic Competitiveness   284
Case Study   Italy: A New Commitment to Growth   285

CHAPTER 11   The Limits of Managed Growth   315
Case Study   Japan: Beyond the Bubble   316

CHAPTER 12   Deficits, Debt, and Defense   345
Case Study   Excerpts from Economic Report of the President, 2003   346

South Africa's currency, the rand, falls from 8 to 13 and then recovers in less than one year. Following the U.S. Federal Reserve, the European Central Bank lowers interest rates to ward off deflation. Three of Japan's big banks—Dai-Ichi Kangyo, Fuji and IBJ—merge to form Mizuho Holdings, the world's largest bank. China enters the World Trade Organization, while Mexican farmers protest further tariff reduction as scheduled by the North American Free Trade Agreement (NAFTA). Each of these seemingly diverse events is part of the globalization process that unceasingly shapes the conditions of national economic development.

This casebook presents twelve cases of national economic strategies that represent the major developmental trajectories in the era of globalization. The cases are used in the MBA curriculum and in executive programs at the Harvard Business School to teach the issues and problems in economic development today. This is an applied, empirical approach to learning about macroeconomic management, economic development, international trade, and the cross-border flows of goods, services and capital. The country cases provide both description and data on a particular situation facing the national leadership. The class discussion covers both concepts and decision points, with the intention of helping students to develop useful frameworks for analyzing political-economic conditions and possibly acting on that understanding.

The book begins with this brief introduction that defines globalization, describes the important trajectories of economic development, and summarizes our "country analysis" methodology. The rest of the book contains twelve chapters, each focusing on a country (or regional) case: (1) Singapore, (2) China, (3) India, (4) Russia, (5) Mexico, (6) Brazil, (7) South Africa, (8) Saudi Arabia, (9) Europe, (10) Italy, (11) Japan, and (12) the United States.

Globalization is a historic process of economic integration and cultural homogenization across national borders fostered by significant advances in transportation and communication technologies after World War II and a new commitment to global cooperation and peace. The process was hastened by eight rounds of GATT (General Agreements on Tariffs and Trade) negotiations that liberalized trade between 1947 and 1993 and helped trade grow twice as quickly as the world economy.

Floating exchange rates, cross-border energy dependences, and sovereign lending during the 1970s and 1980s facilitated cross-border ownership of debt and the reciprocal obligations of interest payments. Subsequently, this led to a series of debt crises, from which key multilateral institutions (the IMF and the World Bank) gained enhanced responsibilities. The crisis-rent countries, meanwhile, liberalized during the 1980s and 1990s, embracing globalization through floating exchange rates, lower tariffs and more open capital markets. This was accompanied by financial services deregulation and privatization, where firms took significant cross-border equity positions in developed and developing countries.

Throughout this period, large firms were striving to achieve scale and scope economies across more and more international markets. This caused a burst of cross-border equity investments after 1985, giving rise to more than 70,000 multinational corporations with more than 830,000 foreign subsidiaries. Finally, a bevy of regional initiatives, such as the Single Europe Act, Mercosur, and NAFTA, removed the remaining barriers to trade and the movement of goods and capital. The extreme form of these developments is the creation in 1999 of the European Union, designed to fully coordinate monetary, fiscal and perhaps social and political policies.

Thus, the global economy has undergone a vast transformation in the past half-century—a degree of economic integration never before experienced. And this process of globalization has momentum. Barring unforeseen circumstances, it will likely continue.

Development trajectories are the growth paths defined by economic, political and social policies that sweep countries forward for years or decades, before bending, often sharply, towards some new direction. To some extent, a country can influence its trajectory through its choice of policies. But the trajectory is also influenced by other factors, including culture, resources, institutions and developments elsewhere in the global economy. One could define any number of trajectories—from broad regions to specific, small-nation choices. I have chosen eight such paths around which to base this book. These eight are, I believe, the most important paths driving global development into the twenty-first century. Managers who understand them can make more informed decisions about doing business in a particular regional or national context

Asian High Growth is the trajectory that has most affected the greatest number of people in the past 40 years. Japan pioneered this model between 1953 and 1971, growing at 10.1 percent annually in real terms. The "Asian Tigers"—Korea, Taiwan, Hong Kong and Singapore—emulated pieces of the model and likewise achieved extraordinary growth. But at the heart of Asian high growth are the two giants—China and India—with more than one-third of the earth's population. Both have experienced rapid growth. The former maintains a strong, centralized communist government, while the latter operates under the world's largest democracy.

These two giant cases are followed by an equally important one on Russia that illustrates a second important trajectory—that of *State Socialism's Disintegration* in East Europe and the Soviet Union. Russia, unlike either China or India, attempted both "glasnost" and "perestroika" simultaneously, and utterly failed. Its economy shrank by 54% between 1991and 1999, until finally a new leader—Vladimir Putin—attempted to begin rebuilding economic and political institutions.

Debt Crisis and Recovery is the third trajectory that will be examined through two important lenses—Mexico and Brazil. Here we see massive borrowing during the 1970s and early 1980s, followed by two decades of structural adjustment and liberalization. Difficult microeconomic issues have now become the focus of reformers' attention.

The fourth trajectory is the *African Renaissance*—the resumption of economic growth after almost a century of colonial and post-colonial stagnation. Sub-Saharan Africa is coming alive economically, as governments throw out mean dictators and begin liberalizing both political and economic institutions. And leading this charge, in many ways, is South Africa—the most developed of Africa's economies.

Islamic Resurgence is the theme of the fifth trajectory treated in this volume. The Islamic world, fuelled in large measure by its oil wealth, has been trying to establish Islam as a significant political and economic, as well as religious, force. With about 1.2 billion Muslims worldwide, this religious culture has the potential to play a significant role in the world. Saudi Arabia, with the world's largest petroleum reserves as the protector of Islam's two holiest shrines—Mecca and Medina—provides a fascinating view of extraordinary issues facing an Islamic State.

The *Advanced Economic Integration* of Europe is the sixth important trajectory of globalization. Western Europe is far ahead of the rest of the world in the process of integration. Having started in 1951 with iron and steel, Europe has formed a common, integrated market with a single currency—the European Union. As of this writing, its fifteen members are in the process of drafting a new constitution and on the verge of integrating six to eight new members from Eastern Europe. Voluntary unification, to this degree, is perhaps unique in world history—but remains full of uniquely difficult challenges. Italy, one of the Unions' larger members, is struggling to adjust to integrated competition without controlling its own monetary or fiscal policy.

A seventh trajectory, the *Limits to Managed Growth,* examines the stagnation of Japan's economy since 1991. After years of miracle growth, during which its economy grew from less than $2000 to $39,000 per capita, Japan collapsed into recession in 1991 from which it has scarcely recovered during the past twelve years. Monetary policy doesn't work, fiscal policy doesn't work, and what little growth Japan has comes from exports to the West. Somehow, Japan must find a way to remake its institutions to effectively deal with a globalized world.

The United States, which represents about 28 percent of world output, has been plagued by huge fiscal and balance of payments deficits since 1981. During that time, government debt has surged, and foreigners have made net purchases of $2.8 trillion in U.S. assets. Presently, the Bush administration's preoccupation with security issues and tax cutting seems only to exacerbate the force of this final trajectory *Deficits, Debt and Defense.*

Country analysis is a framework for studying countries' economic strategies. First developed at the Harvard Business School in the late 1970s, the approach designed by Bruce Scott combines elements of business strategy and Alfred Chandler's work linking strategy and structure. When used as a tool to understand country performance, the framework organizes information into three groups for cross-analysis: performance, context, and strategy. Performance generally includes economic outcomes, such as growth, inflation, unemployment, etc. Context includes important social and political conditions, institutions, natural resources and demographics, industry structure, law, government, etc. Finally, strategy represents the goals and policies of the nation state. These include fiscal and monetary policy, trade policy, and various structural policies such as privatization, foreign direct investment, price controls, industrial policy, etc.

Once the relevant and important data are organized into these bins, the analysis shifts to understanding how the various elements fit together. For example, how does culture or demography affect a country's strategy? How does geography determine which strategies are even viable? Or, how does strategy affect performance?

The cases in this textbook include a number of fairly standard indicators of economic performance. Among these are national income accounts, balance of payments accounts, inflation and unemployment, fiscal balances, monetary measures (money supply and interest rates), exchange rates, and often productivity and unit labor costs. What other data are presented depend on the case: data on resource extraction, foreign direct investment, banking data, debt, oil production and prices, tax details, tariff details, corruption, income distribution, environmental performance, etc.

Even more important is the salient context. In China, for example, the absence of the rule of law is crucial. In India, contracts are in English and are typically negotiated by lawyers. In Japan, the system of permanent employment and the structure of keiretsu groups are crucial to the nation's past successes and to its present difficulties. In Brazil and South Africa, unequal income distribution is a vital political reality. In Europe, price variations say much about unfulfilled integration, while in Saudi Arabia, religious fundamentalism defines much of the domestic, political, and cultural condition.

Among the important ideas and concepts students should try to derive from these cases are strategy, structural adjustment, institutional reform, motivations and conditions for foreign direct investment and the sources of productivity and economic growth. In several of these cases, countries are struggling to develop a viable economic development strategy or to change strategies to move forward to the next level of development. Students should think about the feasibility of these choices, in terms both of implementation and of effectiveness for the new millennium. Several countries are trying to adjust their economic structures to fit better with the new terms of trade in global commerce. In every case, implementing strategic choices requires fiscal resources and institutional reform. The latter includes efforts to fix the banks and state-owned enterprises in China, to streamline bureaucracies in Japan, to legitimate privatization in Russia, or to improve higher education in Singapore.

We often ask our students, and encourage the reader to think about, whether multinational firms should invest in the country being considered. That is, are the political circumstances conducive to investment? Is the investment secure? Is the government secure? Will economic growth, inflation and exchange rate stability allow the manager to build a strong business? Is the market growing? Are wages low enough and stable enough to make this a competitive export platform? Are incomes high enough to provide sufficient purchasing power for local customers? Is the regulatory environment stable? Are contracts secure? Above all, can one expect to make money in this environment?

These are some of the important ideas to bear in mind as you work through these cases. It is hoped they provide a better understanding of how countries develop, how they are responding to globalization, and how globalization is changing the environment of business.

Savings, Productivity, and Structured Growth

On New Year's Day 2003, Prime Minister Goh Chok Tong is reviewing his annual speech on public economic policy. His government has adopted a new strategy, including macroeconomic stimulus and a microeconomic refocusing on higher value-added sectors—particularly biomedical sciences. He hopes to get Singapore growing again as it had from 1965 through the late 1990s, to catch up with the U.S.A. in GDP per capita.

Given Southeast Asia's difficulties since the Asia Crisis in 1997, this was an ambitious goal. Excess capacity in the region, combined with slow growth in the West and stagnation in Japan, had led to intense competition, deflation, and shrinking export growth. Singapore's extraordinary platform for foreign-direct investment and assembly was being challenged by lower-cost locations in Malaysia and China. In high value-added sectors, such as software and biomedical research, India was becoming an imposing challenge.

Singapore, however, had several huge strengths. Its government, which owned more than a quarter of the economy, was efficiently run, stable, honest, and widely supported. Its savings levels were extraordinary, providing more than enough money for the high levels of domestic investment. And productivity, including total factor productivity, was explicitly managed. The Economic Development Board, meanwhile, structured and implemented industrial policy.

But was this enough? As effective as it sounded, with low expenditures, low taxes, and strong institutions, did Singapore's strategy add up to a winning strategy in a region that had become intensely competitive?

CASE STUDY   **SINGAPORE INC.**

RICHARD H. K. VIETOR

EMILY J. THOMPSON

> *We have become rich in one generation—a miracle perhaps—but too quickly and hence not deep-rooted enough. Will we decline in the next generation?*
> —Prime Minister Goh Chok Tong[1]

Introduction

On January 1, 2003, Singapore's prime minister, Goh Chok Tong, sat down to breakfast to review his notes for the New Year's speech he would give later that afternoon. After 40 years of remarkable growth, Singapore had gone from a per capita income of US$427 in 1960 to one of US$20,748 in 2002. But thanks to the global economic downturn of the previous two years, Singapore had experienced one of the worst recessions and levels of unemployment in its history. In contrast to its 10.3% growth in 2000, Singapore's economy shrank by 2.2% in 2001.[2] After contracting by more than 10% on an annualized basis in the third quarter, Singapore's growth expectations of 2% to 2.5% for 2002 did not look much brighter.[3]

Goh and his party, the People's Action Party (PAP), confronted the task of returning the economy to a sustainable level of growth. The Economic Review Committee (ERC) had convened in December 2001 to evaluate government policies to make the country more competitive. Chaired by the deputy prime minister (DPM) and finance minister, Lee Hsien Loong,[4] the ERC released its first recommendations in April of 2002. To promote Singapore as a hub for global business and to diversify the economy, the ERC recommended a variety of tax cuts and incentives to attract both foreign investment and talent. To balance the loss in revenues, the ERC recommended an increase in the goods and services tax (GST).

Falling in line with the ERC's recommendations to decrease Singapore's dependence on the U.S. economy and the electronics industry, the Economic Development Board (EDB), the government's industry-development agency, had developed an "ecosystem" strategy to foster innovation and diversify the economy. By investing in and promoting new science and technology "clusters," Singapore planned to move its economy up the value chain toward knowledge-based sectors.

Goh would be announcing implementation of the first stage of the tax reforms in his speech. As he looked over his outline, he pondered whether or not the strategy was beneficial to the country as a whole. By cutting corporate and personal income taxes while increasing the GST, the burden of the reforms would be shouldered by Singapore's lower-income group. Furthermore, by focusing on a scientific knowledge-based economy, Singapore would be depending heavily upon its nascent education system while running the risk of leaving a large percentage of its population behind if it failed at increasing the country's skill base.

Country Background

Singapore is located one degree north of the equator between the tip of Malaysia and the islands of Indonesia [see **Exhibit 1.1**]. Slightly smaller than New York City, the city-state has a total landmass of 692.7 square kilometers consisting of one main island (42 by 23 kilometers) and more than 30 smaller surrounding islands.[5] With 3,378,300 residents in 2002, Singapore's population is composed of three main ethnicities—Chinese (76.5%), Malay (13.8%), and Indian (8%)—and spoke four official languages: English, Mandarin, Malay, and Tamil.[6]

Colony to Republic

Sir Stamford Raffles arrived in Singapore in 1819 in search of a trading port and base to secure British trade routes in the region. Seeing the value of the island's unique location and natural harbor, he remarked, "It has been my

---

Professor Richard H. K. Vietor and Research Associate Emily J. Thompson prepared this case. HBS cases are developed solely as the basis for class discussion. Cases are not intended to serve as endorsements, sources of primary data, or illustrations of effective or ineffective management.

good fortune to establish this station in a position combining every possible advantage, geographical and local."[7] At the time, Singapore had a population of 150 and was ruled by a Johor sultanate under Dutch influence. Ownership was later transferred to the British East India Company through cash payments to the sultanate and the Anglo-Dutch Treaty of 1824. As a part of the British Straits Settlements that included Malacca and Penang, the multicultural fishing village of Singapore became a thriving port. The opening of the Suez Canal in 1869 established Singapore as a port of call on the Europe-East Asia trade route. Its ever-increasing prosperity attracted immigrants from China, India, Malaysia, and Europe.

During World War II, the British surrendered Singapore to the Japanese in February of 1942. The colony suffered greatly under harsh Japanese rule. Residents of Singapore died from malnutrition and disease or were executed. Having regained colonial control in 1945, the British decided against reuniting Singapore with the Malayan peninsula and proclaimed Singapore a separate crown colony.

Conceding to requests for government representation by Singapore's merchant class, the British instituted, in 1948, a legislative council of Singaporeans to advise the governor. Five years later, the British further loosened control and appointed a commission to redraft Singapore's constitution for limited self-rule. Although Britain retained control of the colony's defense, security, and foreign affairs, Singapore held its first elections for the legislative assembly. Labor and student unrest, however, continued in the face of the limitations.

A delegation sent to London succeeded in persuading Britain to grant the state of Singapore political autonomy and to schedule elections. A member of the delegation, 35-year-old Lee Kuan Yew, was named prime minister after his party, the PAP, took 41 of the 53 seats. United with the communists against the colonial British authority, the PAP sought to obtain complete independence from Britain as part of the noncommunist Federation of Malaya. Singapore joined with Malaya, Sarawak, and North Borneo to form the Federation of Malaysia in September of 1963.

Almost immediately, however, problems developed between the Malay central government and the Singaporean government over the issues of revenues, common markets, and political control. Political tensions were acted out on the streets of Singapore in a series of riots between Malay and Chinese ethnic groups. Worried that the Chinese Singaporeans and communist elements might take over the central government, Malaysia voted to expel Singapore. On August 9, 1965, Singapore became an independent nation. Reflecting upon the separation, the tearful Lee stated, "For me it is a moment of anguish. All my life, my whole adult life, I have believed in merger and unity of the two territories."[8]

Early Years of Republic

Educated in law at Cambridge University in England, Lee founded the PAP in 1954. Over the years, the PAP shifted from being part of a moderately left, anti-colonial front with the communists to a further right, socialist party. Lee, credited by many as the designer of "Singapore Inc.," served as the world's longest-running prime minister ever, from 1959 to 1990. After 1990, he served as a senior minister in the cabinet and advisor to the prime minister. During his time in power, Lee modeled Singapore and its values after his own, stressing the importance of education, discipline, a strong work ethic, and ethnic tolerance.

With the departure of the British on the horizon and no natural resources of its own, Singapore, Lee noted, "faced tremendous odds with an improbable chance of survival. Singapore was not a natural country but man-made, a trading post the British had developed into a nodal point in their worldwide maritime empire. We inherited the island without its hinterland, a heart without a body."[9] Wrote one student on the subject, "Not until after 1965 was the word 'Singaporean' used as a description of identity. Thus much of the culture of Singapore was created in the years after independence."[10]

The government, headed by Lee, prioritized its most pressing needs. First, it had to secure its independence by strengthening its defenses and gaining international recognition with a seat in the United Nations. The unstable environment resulting from Singapore's traumatic break from Malaysia also demanded a quick establishment of law and order. The cabinet immediately formed the Ministry of Interior and Defense to build both police and army forces.

The second most pressing issue was the economy. At its independence in 1959, Singapore had a 14% unemployment rate.[11] With the impending withdrawal of the British, whose military-base operations contributed 20% of gross domestic product (GDP), Singapore had to find a new source of employment for its people.[12] In an effort both to create jobs and to secure its political standing, the PAP set up the Housing Development Board (HDB) in 1960. The HDB's primary objective was to build basic public housing units quickly, providing jobs and homes for Singaporeans at subsidized rates. Within its first 18 months of operation, the HDB built enough housing to accommodate 30,000 people.[13] Public housing soon became the norm in Singapore. By 2001, over 85% of the population lived in HDB-affiliated housing.[14]

After an unsuccessful attempt at import substitution between 1959 and 1965, the government concluded that its future lay with American multinational corporations (MNCs).[15] Singapore's new economy was built upon a two-part strategy. First, because of hostile regional relations, Singapore would have to "leapfrog" its neighbors as trading partners and attract foreign companies to manufacture in Singapore for export back to the developed world.[16] Second, Singapore sought to define itself as a "First World Oasis in a Third World Region."[17] As Lee emphasized in his memoirs, "We had one guiding principle for survival, that Singapore had to be more rugged, better organized, and more efficient than others in the region."[18]

Political System

Singapore was governed by a parliamentary system consisting of 84 elected members (9 elected directly and 75 elected in teams of 4–6 to represent the 14 group representation constituencies and ensure at least one racial minority member per team).[19] Members of Parliament (MPs) were voted into office in general elections every five years. Voting was compulsory for all elections. The president was elected directly as the constitutional head of state. Choosing among MPs with the majority of the Parliament's support, the president formally appointed the country's prime minister. Advised by the prime minister, the president also appointed the cabinet from the Parliament. The cabinet consisted of the prime minister and 14–16 elected ministers responsible for the affairs of state. As well as these elected officials, each meritocratic ministry had a senior permanent secretary or senior civil servant. Exposing Singapore's leaders to the overall shared strategy, lateral job switching in senior positions was a common practice. Having worked in ministries ranging from Defense to Manpower, the permanent secretary in the Ministry of Information Technology and the Arts (MITA), Tan Chin Nam, explained, "The initial start is a challenge, but it keeps our perspective fresh and the government flexible."[20]

Control

From the beginning of the PAP's rule in 1959, the government required sufficient control to push through the reforms necessary to transform Singapore into an attractive site for foreign investment. Led by trade unions, labor strikes were a common event in post-independence Singapore. Realizing that labor unrest threatened Singapore's ability to attract foreign firms, President Yusof bin Ishak stated, "The excesses of irresponsible trade unions . . . are luxuries which we can no longer afford."[21] After its landslide victory in the 1968 election, the PAP used its power to deal swiftly with the labor unions. Unions that broke the laws were banned, and many of their leaders were arrested. Under the new legislation, the government would regulate wages through the National Wages Council and employers would be given greater freedom over hiring and firing. Furthermore, the National Trades Union Congress was set up to represent worker interests in accordance with the PAP's philosophy.

As benefits were usually tied to the PAP's remaining in power, opposition was almost non-existent. For example, the PAP used the HDB to build and maintain its political base. When the PAP's power showed signs of weakening in the early 1990s, renovation priority was given to constituencies that voted heavily for the party.[22] "I think they [Singaporeans] know that the way they vote will influence their own personal well-being—their town, their neighborhood, their property values," explained DPM Lee.[23] Singapore's laws also reinforced the PAP's power. The Internal Security Act, left over from colonial days, allowed the government to detain political opponents indefinitely, without trial.

Rigid public-office requirements and government censorship of the media further bolstered the PAP's authority. Under Singapore's Newspaper and Printing Presses Act, MITA could limit the circulation of publications judged to be "engaging in the domestic politics of Singapore."[24] In 1993, for example, the government reduced *The Economist's* circulation for refusing to publish its response to an article detailing the difficulties faced by Singapore's opposition candidates. MITA promised to continue reducing the circulation progressively until the magazine published the government's complete response. The government defended censorship on the grounds that it was necessary to maintain the country's delicate racial harmony. After the government determined that censorship was suppressing the arts, a Censorship Review Committee was established in 2002 to consider loosening restrictions. Furthermore, the ubiquity of the Internet made many censorship laws more symbolic than restrictive.

From anti-spitting campaigns in the early 1960s to a ban on the sale of chewing gum, the "Nanny State" maintained tight control over the social and physical environment of the island. To improve the standard of living, distinguish itself for investment, and improve its prospects as a destination for tourism, Singapore instituted the "clean and green" movement to beautify its surroundings.[25] Millions of trees, palms, and shrubs were planted, and the Singapore River was completely cleaned up. Each November, Singapore's leaders, including its prime minister, planted saplings for National Tree Planting Day. By improving the island's drainage systems and reducing the insect population, the entire population benefited. As Lee reflected, "Greening is the most cost-effective project I have launched."[26] To reinforce the beautification efforts, heavy fines were levied for littering and damaging public areas. A system of electronic cordon pricing that charged higher rates for driving into the central business district at peak times substantially resolved traffic congestion from as early as the 1970s. Personal vehicle ownership was also sharply curtailed by taxation and the high costs associated with bidding for the limited number of certificates of entitlement (COEs). For example, a buyer of a $20,000 car in 2002 would not only have to pay $10,000 (50%) in taxes but would also have to bid as much as $30,000 or more to receive a COE.[27]

Crime rates remained extremely low due to strictly enforced penalties. Amnesty International estimated Singapore to have the highest per capita execution rate in the world.[28] In 1994, the 18-year-old American Michael Fay brought Singapore's justice system into the world spotlight. Found guilty of vandalism, Fay was sentenced to six strokes of the cane. Out of respect for President Clinton and his plea for leniency, the penalty was eventually reduced to four strokes. Although many considered Singaporean authority to be repressive and overbearing, as a *Straits Times* columnist surmised, "Singaporeans appear(ed) willing to overlook the sacrifice of civil liberties for the practical benefits of an orderly and comfortable society."[29]

Anticorruption

> If we believe that we are immune to it (corruption), we are really risking our future. It is a worldwide disease and especially endemic in Asia, and we can be easily stricken by it. Only constant vigilance has kept it down.
> —Prime Minister Goh Chok Tong[30]

Ranked number five out of 102 on the 2002 Transparency International Corruption Perceptions Index, the authoritarian Singapore government was renowned for its honesty and transparency.[31] The Corrupt Practices Investigation Board (CPIB), an independent group that reported directly to the prime minister, was set up in 1952 to enforce anticorruption laws in both the private and public sector. According to the CPIB, any person found guilty of corruption could be fined up to S$100,000 (US$54,000), imprisoned for five years, or both. Making corruption even less tempting, Singaporean government officials' salaries were higher than those of most other countries. The prime minister's 2000 salary was a little more than US$1.1 million; his most junior minister earned approximately US$550,000.[32] Responding to criticism of the 2000 salary hike, the government argued it was necessary for retaining talent. Lee defended the ministers' high pay, stating, "See it in proportion to what is at stake."[33] Goh further reasoned, "The damage we had prevented to the economy from the Asian financial crisis is more than enough to pay the ministers and the other political office-holders for the rest of their political lives and in fact over many lifetimes."[34]

To keep salaries competitive with those of the business world, a formula determined government pay scales. For example, an entry-level minister or senior permanent secretary earned a salary equal to 60% of the median salary of the top eight earners in six professions ranging from bankers to multinational CEOs.[35] To help justify the high salaries, senior government officials' bonuses and many departmental budgets were tied to the country's GDP performance. "We are 100% government, but in terms of operational discipline, we are run like the private industry," explained a senior director at EDB.[36] In 2002, senior ministers suffered appropriately.

External Relations

ASEAN

In an effort to promote regional trade and stability, Singapore joined with Thailand, Malaysia, Indonesia, and the Philippines to form The Association of Southeast Asian Nations (ASEAN) in August of 1967. ASEAN's primary purpose was to provide individual members with leverage in negotiating international trade issues for the region as a whole. In the early twenty-first century, however, Singapore upset many of ASEAN's members by pursuing its own bilateral trade agreements with the United States, Japan, New Zealand, Australia, and Mexico. In defending Singapore's actions as necessary for access to freer markets and diversification, the minister of Trade and Industry, George Yeo (HBS MBA 1985), stated, "Singapore has no plans to abandon the region. Over 70% of all inter-ASEAN trade moves through Singapore. If the region thrives, we benefit even more."[37]

ASEAN also provided a forum for resolving regional relationship disputes. Beginning with its expulsion in 1965, Singapore experienced continuously difficult relations with Malaysia. Malaysia, a direct competitor for investment and trade, provided Singapore with the majority of its water supply. In September 2001, Lee and Prime Minister Mahathir Mohamad of Malaysia agreed to extend the standing water-supply contract. Relations soured, however, in 2002 when Malaysia announced that it would increase water prices. In an effort to lessen its future dependence upon Malaysia, Singaporean scientists developed "NEWater," which was potable water recycled from sewage. Citizens had their first taste of it in August of 2002, and the government planned to introduce it into the municipal water supply in February of 2003.

China

Our biggest challenge is . . . to secure a niche for ourselves as China swamps the world with her high-quality but cheaper products.[38]
—Prime Minister Goh Chok Tong

Like the rest of the world in 2002, Singapore looked to China as both its next great market opportunity and a considerable threat. In 1997, China surpassed Malaysia as Singapore's top destination for investment abroad.[39] In addition to its financial investment, Singapore hoped to leverage its unique administrative skills and infrastructure knowledge in a partnership with China to industrialize Singapore. Graduating 400,000 engineers in 2001, China could provide Singapore with valuable human capital.[40]

Described by one senior Singaporean executive as a "black hole" for low-end operations, China threatened to take away much of Singapore's manufacturing business. Attracting over US$52 billion in 2002, China drew 70% of foreign investment in the region.[41] Shanghai threatened to jeopardize Singapore's position as the global financial services hub for the region. Singapore planned to defend itself economically by staying one step ahead of China in moving up the value-added chain while benefiting from China's growth at the same time. As Yeo explained, "China's competitiveness will have a deflationary effect in many sectors. The only way for us to compete is to take advantage of it. We can't fight it, but we must turn it into a strength by making use of cheaper Chinese inputs. In the future, China will be an investor in Southeast Asia, and Singapore will be an important facility for China as its companies internationalize."[42]

Security

Surrounded by antagonistic neighbors, the tiny city-state took its defense seriously. In 2002, Singapore spent 5.3% of its GDP on its defense budget [see **Exhibit 1.7**]. In addition to a defense agreement as part of the British Commonwealth, Singapore had more than 250,000 reservists and a technologically sophisticated arsenal of more than 350 tanks and 150 combat aircraft.[43] As former Brigadier-General Yeo acknowledged, "Whatever happens in the region, we know we live in a difficult neighborhood and could get gobbled up. We exist because we take our defense seriously."[44] With the detention of 13 Singaporean Jemaah Islamiyah operatives (purportedly linked to al Qaeda) in December 2001 and the Bali bomb blast in October of 2002, domestic as well as regional security became a major concern for Singapore. Remembering Singapore's history of racial riots in the 1960s and well aware of Singapore's still-fragile racial comity in 2002, Goh stated, "The most pressing concern for us . . . is not the economy. The recession, though painful, is a short-term problem. . . . Our greater worry is the threat to our security, and to our racial and religious harmony, following the discovery of terrorist activities in our country."[45]

Economic Growth

For most of its recent history, Singapore maintained tight control over its economy while concentrating on six policies: investment in the state, active encouragement of foreign investment, a pro-business environment, free trade, a tight monetary policy, and high savings. Upon the recommendation of a United Nations development program committee, the Ministry of Trade and Industry (MTI) had established the Economic Development Board (EDB) in 1961 to act as a "one-stop shop" for the foreign investor.[46] Going directly to the customer in his home country, the EDB's primary job was to woo foreign investors by not only meeting but surpassing the needs of their business. The EDB's initial goal in the 1960s was to drive investment into the four labor-intensive industries of ship refitting and repair, metal engineering, chemicals, and electrical equipment and appliances.[47]

Government-Owned Companies

Having a weak private sector in its post-independence days, Singapore formed government-linked companies and statutory boards to provide the infrastructure necessary both to improve living conditions and to make the country attractive for foreign investment. Initially responsible for the essential utilities (Public Utilities Board), banking (Development Bank of Singapore), port operations (Port of Singapore Authority), construction (Jurong Town Corporation), public housing (HDB), airline (Singapore Airlines), and defense

industries (Singapore Technologies), the government soon had stakes in almost all areas of the economy including such industries as food supply and travel.

Many of the government-linked companies were supervised through the government's investment arm, Temasek Holdings. In 2002, Temasek owned more than 40 firms, or 20% of Singapore's market capitalization, accounting for 13% of Singapore's annual product.[48]*Although Temasek often had large stakes in specific companies, each company was supervised by its own board. Defending its large stake in the economy, Temasek argued that it was a separate entity from the government. A government-owned firm did not mean it had to answer to the government; rather, it was run like any other business, keeping the goal of the greatest return on investment in mind.[49] When critics called for more competition, Temasek responded by stating that it would only divest when entities were deemed to be no longer of strategic importance to the economy, viable market alternatives existed, and the necessary regulatory structures were in place.[50]

An example of Singapore's successful government-linked companies, Singapore Airlines (SIA) grew from a small regional airline to one of the world's leading passenger carriers. Splitting from the joint-venture Malaysian-Singapore Airlines in 1972, SIA focused on meeting superior standards of quality and service. SIA's chairman explained, "We cultivate a culture of service and even look for it when recruiting. We train our stewardesses for four to five months before they ever come into contact with a live passenger. We also take our customer feedback very seriously."[51] In 2002, Singapore Airlines was again the most highly rated and one of the most profitable airlines in the world.

Foreign Direct Investment

With no capital of its own in the 1960s, the Singaporean government saw the importance of foreign direct investment as one route to growth. Singapore had very few restrictions relating to foreign investment and charged no capital gains tax. By attracting MNCs, Singapore could benefit by gaining employment, technology, managerial expertise, and human capital for the country. MNCs, in turn, would be attracted to

---

* The rest of the public sector accounted for an additional 9% of Singapore's GDP.

Singapore's stable and open economy, efficient government, tax incentives, and docile labor supply. By the end of 2000, cumulative foreign direct investment into Singapore stood at US$114 billion[52] [see **Exhibit 1.11a**].

Efficiency and infrastructure Focusing first on attracting the labor-intensive manufacturing industry, the government invested heavily in developing industrial estates to house foreign firms. In 1968, Jurong Town Corporation (JTC) was incorporated to construct ready-built factories and industrial estates. JTC's first major project was the transformation of swampland on Singapore's southern coast into the Jurong Industrial Estate for manufacturing firms. Later, in 1991, after the chemical industry was targeted as a key cluster for growth, JTC began the Jurong Island project, an intensive S$23 billion reclamation of land between seven small islands [see **Exhibit 1.1**].

The EDB had proved in 1968 that it could provide a quick-start environment for manufacturers. In only two months, the EDB enabled National Semiconductor to begin production.[53] As one former EDB employee explained, "[Y]ou could just walk into the EDB office, discuss your project, and lease a factory site or standard building on the spot."[54] Soon thereafter, other MNCs, including Texas Instruments and Hewlett-Packard, relocated operations to Singapore. More recently, the American head of Citibank Singapore ranked Singapore, with its accessible and efficient government, the top place for his company to do business in Asia. He remarked, "If I have a problem, I have complete access to the government. When we have problems, they deal with them with speed. There is no bureaucracy to cut through. The government works as a fluid and highly lubricated machine."[55]

Tax incentives In 1967, the government had passed the first Economic Expansion Incentives Act to attract manufacturing firms by providing tax relief. Singapore continued to use tax incentives to attract particular industries deemed vital to Singapore's economic strategy. "Pioneer" status, tax exemption for a period of five to ten years, was given to both start-up companies and MNCs making significant investments in Singapore. From manufacturing firms during the late 1960s and 1970s to financial services firms during the 1980s and technology companies during the 1990s, tax incentives were used to help move Singapore up the value chain as its economy matured.

Educated labor Achieving a GDP growth rate of 13.6% in 1968, Singapore's economy continued to grow throughout the 1970s[56] [see **Exhibit 1.2**]. In light of the global oil shock of 1979 and a growing labor shortage, Singapore recognized a need to move toward more technology and capital-intensive industries. Launching a "second industrial revolution," the EDB turned its focus in the early 1980s to restructuring the economy and moving it up the value chain. As the minister of MTI declared in 1981, "The prime objective of the plan is to develop Singapore into a modern industrial economy based on science, technology, skills, and knowledge."[57] Parliament established the Skills Development Fund in 1979 to improve the skill base of Singapore's workers. The fund provided financial incentives to employers to train their employees through a grant scheme. The government attempted to discourage low-cost industries by raising wage levels while increasing the skill base of the worker population. As a result, Singapore's economy contracted 1.4% in 1985. The government reacted quickly, however, by freezing wages and reducing employer taxes to return growth to 2.1% in 1986.[58] By 1988, Singapore was growing again at a rate of 11.3%, the highest economic growth rate in the world.[59]

Pro-Business Mind-Set

Labor The Singaporean government considered itself to be in a unique partnership with business. One senior civil service officer went further, describing business as the government's "customer." Not only meeting its customer's present needs, the government strived to anticipate future needs by preparing the infrastructure and educating workers years in advance.[60] Even the labor union, or National Trade Union Congress (NTUC), was a partner of business. Early on, Lee created a seat in the cabinet for the secretary general of the NTUC. The unions would be aware of the reasons behind government policies and, as a member of the cabinet, the minister could support workers' rights. As secretary of the NTUC, Lim Boon Heng, put it, "The unions realize that much of what is good for business is also good for the workers. In Singapore, having a job is the most important thing. The unions must help create the necessary conditions to help encourage companies to come invest in Singapore."[61] Retrenchment policies were almost completely at the will of the management. Singaporeans, known for their strong work ethic, were expected "to pull their weight and make themselves relevant to their employer."[62]

"In the 1970s, EDB was so successful in attracting local as well as foreign investors to set up labor-intensive projects in Singapore that we literally ran out of workers," recalled one EDB official.[63] Foreign labor eventually supplemented both skilled and unskilled labor forces. Working in the industries of construction, ship repair, and domestic work, unskilled workers were issued short-term work permits. In general, the higher the level of skill required, the easier it was to attain a work permit. Closely watching the country's unemployment levels, the government used the issuance of work permits as a macroeconomic tool to regulate unemployment and thus wages and inflation. Although it remained attractive to unskilled laborers, Singapore often had difficulty retaining its skilled workforce. In a 2002 ACNielsen survey, 20% of Singaporeans considered leaving the country, citing factors such as the high cost of living, the stressful education system, and the unresponsive, overbearing government.[64] Reacting to news of the trend, Goh stated, "Fair-weather Singaporeans will run away whenever the country runs into stormy weather. I call them quitters."[65]

Productivity   The secretary general of the NTUC was also the chairman of Singapore's productivity agency, SPRING (Standards, Productivity and Innovation Board). "We believe in promoting productivity," said Secretary Lim, "because if we increase this, we can negotiate for sustainable increase in wages. Instead of just concentrating on sharing the cake, we concentrate on making a bigger cake. We each get the same slice, but it's a bigger slice."[66] Union leaders took a mandatory module on the subject of total-factor productivity (TFP).

To meet the needs of investors and improve the quality of its workforce, Singapore had launched the productivity movement in 1981 as a key part of its economic restructuring program. The Productivity Standards Board (later renamed SPRING) made productivity issues a key priority for all areas of government. From releasing the motivational song "Good, Better, Best" on the radio and printing slogans such as "Come On Singapore—Let's All Do a Little Bit More" to establishing the Quality Control Circle College, SPRING worked hard to highlight the importance of productivity to the country and its workforce.

Despite the launch of this productivity movement, Singapore's growth of TFP had recently dipped sharply.[67] TFP accounted for the portion of GDP growth attributable to efficiency gains above and beyond capital accumulation and labor growth. The productivity movement's efforts to improve the skills of the workforce and the quality of capital investments, however, showed some signs of paying off. Singapore's TFP growth rate improved from an average of less than zero from 1980 to 1985 to an estimated 3.8% between 1985 and 1990[68] [see **Exhibit 1.9b**]. In April of 1992, Alwyn Young, an MIT economist, released a study purporting that Singapore's TFP growth had been slightly negative between the years of 1970 and 1990. (See "Accounting for Productivity Growth," HBS No. 794-051.)[69] He argued that Singapore's economic growth was almost completely due to capital accumulation. MTI economists later responded by noting that Young's paper did not take into account certain characteristics unique to Singapore.[70] They argued that if Singapore's unique subsidized housing policies and transient, unskilled worker population were accounted for differently, Singapore's TFP for the period would be closer to 1.6%.[71]

Nonetheless, after publication of Young's study, the government stepped up its efforts by setting an aggressive goal of 4% TFP growth per year to meet its 7% annual GDP growth target.[72] Due to the Asian financial crisis of 1997–1998 and the later global economic downturn, however, growth rates proved erratic through 2001 [see **Exhibit 1.10b**]. After productivity fell by 5.4% in 2001, the government refocused its efforts. In April of 2002, to complement the country's shift toward a knowledge-based economy, SPRING repositioned itself to promote additional innovation as an engine for future productivity growth. Its CEO stressed, "We need to move from being an efficiency city to being an innovation nation."[73]

Free Trade

Originally serving as an *entrepôt* for regional trade, Singapore became a major global exporter as its industries grew. Trade served as a key engine of growth. Singapore's trade volume was two to three times its GDP, one of the highest ratios in the world [see **Exhibit 1.2**]. Singapore had experimented briefly with import substitution but realized that its domestic market and natural resources were simply too small. The government then implemented an export-oriented growth strategy.

Over the next few years, the government gradually removed almost all tariffs and invested in improving infrastructure and the efficiency of its ports. The abandoned British naval bases were turned into ship-repair sites. By 1975, Singapore was the third-busiest container port in the world.[74] As one analyst put it, "The government viewed the port as its lifeline, devoting as much capital to the facilities as it could afford. The result was a perpetual state of expansion and upgrading."[75]

The government set up the Trade Development Board (later International Enterprise Singapore) in 1983 to promote the export of goods from Singapore and establish Singapore as a major international trading hub. TradeNet, the first e-trade processing system, was launched in 1989 by the Trade Development Board. It drastically improved efficiency and turnaround time for businesses.

Moving into the early twenty-first century, Singapore remained highly dependent upon the external environment, with total trade making up 277% of its GDP in 2001 [see **Exhibit 1.11**]. The current account balance, which was negative into the 1980s, turned positive in 1985 and has remained so ever since. At US$17.9 billion in 2001, the current account balance was 27% of GDP [see **Exhibit 1.8**]. Excluding the years of economic downturn, Singapore's external trade grew often in double-digit percentages. As many of the American MNCs used Singapore as a site for manufacturing product components, Singapore's second-largest trading partner was the United States. In 2000, 22.3% of all nonoil exports went to the United States[76] [see **Exhibit 1.12**].

Monetary Policy

A vital part of "Singapore Inc.," the Monetary Authority of Singapore (MAS) maintained tight control over monetary policy as the country's de facto central bank. Complementing Singapore's efforts to provide a stable environment for investment, MAS was created by an act of Parliament in 1970 "to regulate all elements of monetary, banking and financial aspects of Singapore."[77] The government later granted MAS additional authority over the insurance and securities industries. The main domestic banks set commercial lending and deposit rates. MAS's primary objective was to sustain a continuously competitive economy. Through an exchange rate-centered policy, MAS maintained a low inflation rate and kept interest rates on a par with foreign rates [see **Exhibit 1.4**]. With a managed float, MAS regulated the Singapore dollar against a trade-weighted basket of currencies. Although restrictions on lending and trading of the Singapore dollar existed as part of MAS's currency controls, some restrictions were relaxed in 2002 to help boost the financial sector and increase capital flows.

High Savings

The Central Provident Fund (CPF), as a publicly managed, mandatory savings program, served to provide social security for Singaporeans. First established in 1955 under colonial rule, CPF operated on a fully funded basis. Upon retirement, Singaporeans received tax-exempt benefits on the basis of past contributions plus interest.[78] The rates of interest were based upon fixed-deposit and savings-deposit rates of major banks and were guaranteed to pay at least 2.5% per annum.[79] Contribution rates varied according to the age of participants. Members could only begin making retirement withdrawals at the age of 55, while setting aside a minimum sum to provide for basic needs. Upon a member's death, savings were redistributed among his beneficiaries.

The percentage rate contributed by the employer and withheld from the employee's salary was linked to the country's macroeconomic objectives. Maintaining a high rate of savings made it possible for Singapore to finance its own development without having to depend on foreign loans. The government could borrow from the fund at a low rate of interest and invest the capital in infrastructure and new economic ventures. For example, to finance Singapore's economic move up the value chain in the early 1980s, the contribution rate was raised to 50% (25% by employer) [see **Exhibit 1.6a**]. However, after the recession hit in 1986, the employer's contribution rate was immediately lowered to 10% to ease the economic burden without drastically reducing employee wages. The ERC was responsible for setting the fund's long-term rate. Working closely with the MAS, the financially autonomous CPF board, representing members of the employer, employee, and government sectors, determined short-term adjustments.

Originally, the CPF was set up as a worker retirement plan requiring only a 10% total contribution. In 1968, the government broadened the fund to provide home-ownership benefits through the Public Housing Scheme. The contribution rate was raised to 13%, and Singaporeans could use their CPF savings to buy their HDB flats. Later, in 1981, the Residential Properties Scheme was implemented to make it possible for members to purchase private properties. In both instances, if members later sold their property, the principal amount withdrawn and interest accrued would return to their CPF fund for future use. As the nation developed, the CPF was expanded to look after the health-care (Medisave/MediShield), insurance (Family Protection), and investment (Asset Enhancement) needs of the nation. Willie Tan, CPF general manager, explained, "Today, CPF serves more than just the financial needs of old age. It also provides for the home-ownership and health-care needs of its members."[80] Each CPF member contributed to an Ordinary, Medisave, and Special Account. The ordinary account included savings that could be used for housing, insurance, education, approved investments, and family member "top-ups" (members could choose to add additional money to family members' accounts). As the name implied, the Medisave account, in combination with the national health plan, covered members' and their dependents' medical expenses. The special account was reserved for selected investment, old age, and contingency purposes.[81] Accounts received different percentages of the total contribution according to the member's age [see **Exhibit 1.6c**].

Special and Ordinary Account investments, as part of the Asset Enhancement benefit, gave members more responsibility for their retirement and a chance to gain a higher return as long as they accepted the higher risks.[82] In 2001, members could invest 100% of their accounts into low-risk, professionally managed products, including Singapore government bonds, unit trusts, and fixed deposits.[83] Thirty-five percent of investable[84] savings, however, could be invested into stocks on the Singapore Exchange. CPF funds for the most part remained in low-risk investments; in December 2001, S$89 billion of

the CPF's total S$92 billion was invested in Singapore government bonds.[85] With 2.92 million members at the end of 2001, Singapore had one of the highest domestic savings rates in the world—46% of GDP[86] [see **Exhibit 1.5**].

Enterprise Ecosystem

As we continue striving to overcome new challenges, EDB will endeavor to do even better to entrench Singapore as a compelling hub for business and investment. The linchpin of our new approach rests on building a vibrant enterprise ecosystem—a total environment bringing together companies big and small, foreign and local, thriving in synergy and symbiosis.
—Teo Ming Kian, chairman, EDB[87]

Realizing it could no longer compete on cost alone in the ever-competitive global marketplace, Singapore focused on further diversifying its economy and moving toward a knowledge-based world. In order to become a "compelling global hub for business and investment," the EDB had devised a dual approach: continue to focus on the already strong "clusters" of chemicals, electronics and precision engineering, logistics and transport services, and infocomms and media while encouraging innovation and entrepreneurship in all existing and new sectors of growth. "We know that what we have been doing well is our cash cow. We don't intend to throw that away, but we are aware that competition is increasing, and we need to be ready for it," reasoned the EDB's assistant managing director, Chua Taik Him. Singapore's transformation would be carried out not just by the EDB but by the country as a whole. "We want to encourage innovation and entrepreneurship throughout the economy," said Chua. "We'll do this by investing in our human capital, technology, and infrastructure. This will be done by Singapore, not just EDB. We have a *national* mind-set."[88]

Biomedical Sciences—The Next "Big Thing?"

An example of Singapore's commitment to diversifying the economy, the new biomedical sciences (BMS) cluster encompassed the pharmaceutical, medical technology, biotechnology, and health-care services industries.[89] The chairman of the EDB explained:

> When we first became concerned about diversifying the economy further, we tried to determine the next big thing that could leverage our advantages and competencies built up over the years. Biomedical sciences is an industry that amply suits Singapore. It is not labor and land intensive. It requires a well-trusted system of operation. It is intellectual capital intensive, and intellectual property is well protected. We don't have much in the way of resources to offer, but what we do have is brains![90]

To build on Singapore's competitive advantage of its infrastructure, intellectual property laws, and health-care system, the government set aside S$1 billion to transform Singapore into a "biopolis" of Asia. The government sought to both foster start-up firms and entice established biomedical companies into locating their manufacturing, research and development (R&D), clinical development, and Asian headquarters operations in Singapore. As it had done to attract MNCs, the EDB strove to provide a "one-stop" service for biomedical companies and investors. The EDB Biomedical Services Group was organized to assist companies in the planning, investment, and marketing aspects of the biomedical sector. Through a combination of efforts by its government agencies, Singapore planned to provide the infrastructure along with the financial and intellectual capital necessary to make biomedical services an important and sustainable part of the economy.

Infrastructure As it had done earlier in chemicals and electronics, Singapore invested in building the infrastructure necessary for the research and manufacturing needs of BMS companies. One North, a visionary industrial park for both start-up and established companies, housed the 18-acre complex ("Biopolis"), devoted exclusively to biomedical R&D efforts. Located near the National University of Singapore and the National University Hospital, Biopolis expected to meet both the residential and research needs of 2,000 scientists and professionals.[91] The government had begun the first seven buildings of the complex in 2002 and planned to have the private sector complete the future construction. For clinical trial requirements, Singapore's extensive hospital and health-care system served as a convenient and suitable site for testing in Asia. Meeting the manufacturing needs of pharmaceutical companies, the Tuas Biomedical Park was constructed in 1998 on 160 hectares of reclaimed land. After initially setting the goal of housing 15 global life-science manufacturing firms by 2010, by 2002 Singapore had already attracted more than half, including Merck, Pfizer, and Wyeth.[92]

Financial capital In addition to providing economic office space to start-up companies, the EDB set up the S$1 billion Biomedical Sciences Investment Fund (BMSIF) to assist in funding new ventures. The fund would invest directly into promising private companies, coinvest in Singapore-based ventures, invest in homegrown ventures, and make investments into other overseas BMS funds.[93] The EDB's managing director, Chua, explained,

> The government now serves as a facilitator and catalyst to the private sector. In the past, the government would become very involved in the details. In a new scheme started to help seed new enterprises, we let a third-party investor do the due diligence and we, in EDB, will match dollar for dollar up to a certain amount in the investment if requested to help. Many regional start-ups are being attracted to Singapore, and many local and foreign incubators have been set up. Investors in start-ups that fail can also deduct the capital loss from their taxable income. We have become very start-up friendly.[94]

Several of Singapore's social controls were relaxed to promote this entrepreneurship. Stem-cell research, for example, was supervised and supported by the government. "We want to make Singapore the friendliest place to start a company and grow. In the past, we didn't let people use their subsidized public housing for business. Now, we have removed that restriction and allow people to work at home so long as they don't bother their neighbors," Chua explained.[95] Already a highly efficient system, government bureaucracy was also modernized to meet the needs of entrepreneurs. In 2002, a new company could incorporate online in less than 24 hours.[96]

Intellectual capital   If Singapore's enterprise ecosystem strategy were to have a chance of success, Singapore's education system would have to fully foster and support it. Believed by many to stifle creativity and entrepreneurial thinking, Singapore's traditional rote-learning method had come under criticism. The government made significant investments in promoting new ways to teach while encouraging innovation with scholarships and awards. To strengthen its higher education, the EDB planned to attract at least 10 "world-class education institutions" by 2008.[97] By 2003, schools including INSEAD, Johns Hopkins, Wharton, and MIT had set up satellite campuses or educational joint ventures in Singapore. Although all forms of education were addressed in improving Singapore's innovation mind-set, a special focus was placed on building the country's scientific knowledge base.

Established in 1991, the National Science and Technology Board (NSTB) had as its primary mission to "raise the level of science and technology in Singapore."[98] The NSTB, later renamed the Agency for Science, Technology and Research (A*STAR), built Singapore's scientific knowledge base through a series of five-year plans.[*] Headed by Philip Yeo (HBS MBA 1976) since 2001, A*STAR's third five-year plan (2001–2005) was given a budget of S$7 billion. A*STAR governed four divisions: the Biomedical Research Council (BMRC), the Science and Engineering Research Council (SERC), the Exploit Technology Pte Ltd. (ETPL), and the Corporate Planning and Administration Division (CPAD). The research councils promoted and oversaw all R&D efforts in the Singapore public sector, with BMRC responsible for Singapore's BMS industry and SERC supervising research efforts in Singapore's traditional industries of chemicals, electronics, infocomms, and engineering. ETPL, the commercial arm of A*STAR, worked to identify, protect, and market intellectual property created in any of A*STAR's programs. Finally, CPAD served as the administrative arm of A*STAR's operations.

---

[*] According to the EDB, the number of research scientists and engineers per 10,000 workers grew from 27.7 to over 80 in the first 10 years.

Each of the four divisions worked to fund and promote scientific research and education with the goal of creating the "Boston of the East." A*STAR supported most of the country's public-sector research through grants and assistance in finding funds. In addition to helping start the Genome Institute of Singapore, Institute of Molecular and Cell Biology, and Institute of Bioengineering, A*STAR together with the government and corporate sponsors awarded research and education grants to promising students. In addition to awarding scholarships at both its local universities, Nanyang Technological University and National University of Singapore, A*STAR also awarded students with grants to study abroad at top foreign universities, with the obligation of returning to Singapore to work for a set number of years after graduation.

ERC Recommendations

In late 2001, Prime Minister Goh established the ERC to develop a new macroeconomic policy to further diversify Singapore's economy, attract more foreign businesses, and develop the entrepreneurial, innovative, and science-focused environment necessary for a knowledge-based economy. DPM Lee Hsien Loong was chosen to chair the new committee. With wages rising and countries such as Hong Kong and Ireland offering competitive income tax rates, officials feared that businesses and workers might leave Singapore for cheaper locations. Tax incentives would therefore play a key part in attracting the biomedical, pharmaceutical, health-care, education, and telecommunications sectors to Singapore's shores.

In April of 2002, Lee recommended that the government cut corporate taxes from 24.5% to 22% and personal income taxes from 26% to 22%, with the aim of reducing both to 20% before 2005. To encourage diversification into knowledge-based industries, the budget included additional tax breaks for research and development. The Monetary Authority of Singapore estimated that the tax cuts could boost real GDP by 1.2% and investment by more than 10% between 2004 and 2007.[99]

Although the government generally ran budget surpluses, it expected to run a slight deficit during the near term. Some of the tax cuts, however, would be offset by a rise in the goods and services tax from 3% to 5% by the end of 2003. Reflecting the strong Singaporean work ethic, the ERC favored raising taxes on goods and services: "GST preserves the incentive to work and encourages enterprise. As people's income increases, income tax will push them into higher tax brackets, which take larger proportions of their income. GST will not."[100] The ERC expected the tax hike to raise an additional S$1.3 billion, slightly lower than the forecast S$1.32 billion loss from the cuts.[101] In an effort to mitigate the negative effects of the tax hike on the lower-income groups, the ERC recommended the tax increase be phased over two years and that the government "implement a comprehensive offset package to help Singaporeans adjust."[102] The package would consist of a special type of redeemable government bond, or "New Singapore Share."

The ERC recommended increasing competition to help build a more entrepreneurial and vibrant culture. Specifically, the government should gradually divest itself from all "nonstrategic" businesses when it commercially made sense to do so.[103] Emphasizing that Singapore's restructuring plans were long term, Lee stated, "You can change taxes, you can change policies quickly, but if you want to change mind-sets, promote entrepreneurship or innovation, or cause people to be less risk averse, those are not changes you can cause overnight."[104] He added, "This package is a critical element of our strategy to make Singapore more competitive and to create more jobs and prosperity for Singaporeans."[105]

Decision

Finishing his coffee and kaya toast, Prime Minister Goh gathered his notes. Before finalizing his speech, he had to be sure that the ERC's fiscal changes were best for the country as it faced another economic downturn. Would the focused microstrategy of enterprise ecosystem combined with the government's macrostrategy of tax incentives be enough to keep Singapore afloat in the face of competition from China, a weak U.S. economy, and the country's continued shortage of natural and human capital resources?[106]

EXHIBIT 1.1   MAPS OF SINGAPORE AND SURROUNDING COUNTRIES

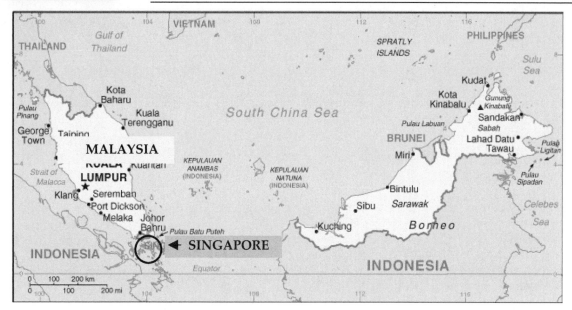

SOURCE: CIA World Factbook 2002.

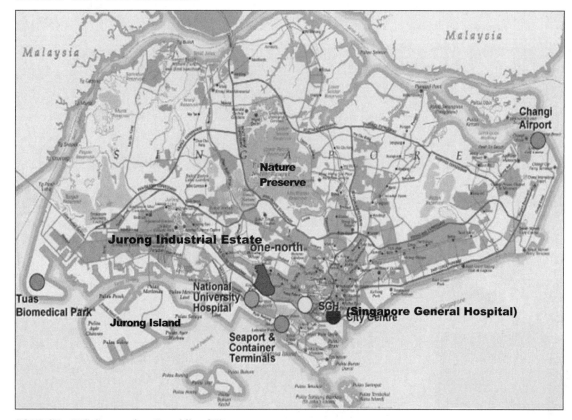

SOURCE: JTC Corporation, Republic of Singapore.

EXHIBIT 1.2	GDP AND COMPONENTS																			
	1970	1975	1980	1985	1990	1991	1992	1993	1994	1995	1996	1997	1998	1999	2000	2001
Nominal GDP (S$m, current market price)	5,804	13,443	25,091	38,924	66,885	74,613	81,224	94,289	107,851	118,963	129,506	141,438	136,801	138,763	159,216	153,572
Real GDP Growth (%) [a]	12.8	9.3	8.5	6.4	8.4	6.8	6.7	12.3	11.4	8.0	8.3	8.5	-0.8	6.4	9.9	-2.1
Per Capita GDP (US$ at current market prices)	914	2,505	4,854	6,466	12,110	13,773	15,427	17,601	20,640	23,806	25,022	25,109	20,841	20,722	22,988	20,748
Per Capita GDP (purchasing power parity in US$)	n/a	2,860	5,471	8,088	13,768	14,867	16,275	18,368	20,427	22,270	23,748	24,917	24,210	27,024	24,970	24,910
Private Consumption (% of GDP)	67.5	60.4	51.5	45.1	46.4	45.3	45.6	45.3	44.2	41.5	41.3	40.1	39.1	41.1	40.1	42.2
Government Spending (% of GDP)	11.9	10.6	9.8	14.3	10.2	9.9	9.3	9.4	8.4	8.6	9.5	9.4	10.1	10.1	10.5	11.9
Gross Fixed Investment (% of GDP)	32.5	35.9	40.7	42.2	32.5	33.9	36.0	35.2	33.9	33.9	38.5	38.7	37.4	33.7	29.4	29.2
Exports (% of GDP)	n/a	n/a	138.0	132.0	179.0	184.0	186.0	198.0	212.0	219.0	214.0	212.0	200.0	202.0	205.0	196.0
Imports (% of GDP)	n/a	n/a	144.0	135.0	174.0	175.0	177.0	189.0	198.0	205.0	204.0	202.0	183.0	184.0	189.0	174.0
Deflator (1995=100)	n/a	52.4	65.3	75.0	87.3	90.8	92.0	95.2	97.8	100.0	101.2	101.9	100.1	95.3	98.6	96.6
Annual Inflation Rate (%)	n/a	n/a	4.5	2.8	3.1	4	1.3	3.5	2.7	2.2	1.2	<1	-1.8	-4.8	3.5	2

SOURCE: Singapore Department of Statistics; International Monetary Fund.

[a]Five-year moving averages, 1970–1990.

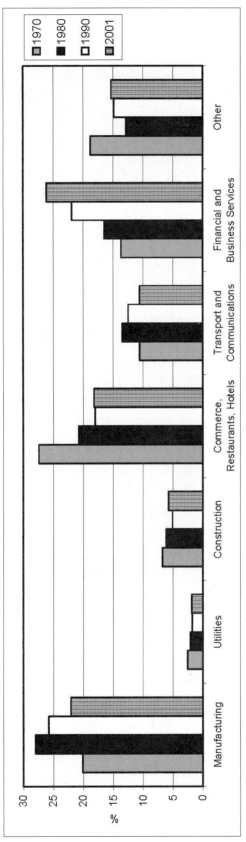

EXHIBIT 1.3   **GDP BY SECTOR**

Legend: 1970, 1980, 1990, 2001

Sectors: Manufacturing, Utilities, Construction, Commerce, Restaurants, Hotels, Transport and Communications, Financial and Business Services, Other

SOURCE: Singapore Department of Statistics.

EXHIBIT 1.4   **MONETARY POLICY**

	1980	1985	1990	1991	1992	1993	1994	1995	1996	1997	1998	1999	2000	2001
Exchange Rate (S$/US$avg/yr)	2.14	2.20	1.81	1.73	1.63	1.62	1.53	1.42	1.41	1.48	1.67	1.69	1.72	1.79
Consumer Price Index (Nov. 1997–Oct. 1998=100)	68.4	80	85.2	88.1	90.1	92.2	95.1	96.7	98	100	99.7	99.8	101.1	102.1
CPI (%) change per year	8.4	0.5	3.4	3.4	2.3	2.3	3.1	1.7	1.4	2.0	-0.3	0	1.3	1
Deposit Rate	9.4	5.0	4.7	4.6	2.9	2.3	3	3.5	3.41	3.47	4.6	1.7	1.7	1.54
Lending Rate	11.7	7.9	7.4	7.6	6.0	5.4	5.9	6.4	6.3	6.3	7.4	5.8	5.8	5.7
M2 (millions S$)	16,065	28,148	61,845	69,542	75,728	82,130	93,980	101,968	111,951	123,444	160,784	174,474	170,898	180,909
M2 Growth Rate (%)	n/a	11.9	17.1	12.4	8.9	8.5	14.4	8.5	9.8	10.3	30.2	8.5	-2.0	5.9

SOURCE: Singapore Department of Statistics; International Monetary Fund.

EXHIBIT 1.5	SAVINGS AND INVESTMENT (IN BILLIONS OF S$)										
	1970	1975	1980	1985	1990	1996	1997	1998	1999	2000	2001
Savings											
GDP	5.8	13.4	25.1	38.9	63.7	128.2	140.3	137.6	140.1	159.9	153.4
Consumption (Gov't & Private)	4.6	9.5	15.4	23.1	34.8	65.1	69.4	67.8	71.6	81	83.1
Statistical Discrepancy	-0.1	0.1	-0.3	-0.2	-0.1	1.8	2.8	2.7	2.8	0.3	0.2
Gross Domestic Saving	**1.1**	**4**	**9.4**	**15.6**	**28.8**	**64.9**	**73.7**	**72.5**	**71.2**	**79.2**	**70.6**
% of GDP	18.3	29.6	37.5	40.1	28.9	50.6	52.5	52.7	50.8	49.5	46.0
Gross National Saving	**1.1**	**4**	**8.3**	**16.5**	**28.9**	**65.3**	**81.0**	**78.8**	**72.7**	**78.0**	**69.3**
Investment											
Gross National Saving	1.1	4	8.3	16.5	28.9	65.3	81.0	78.8	72.7	78.0	69.3
Net Funds from Abroad	1.1	1.4	3.3	0	-3.9	-17.7	-26.9	-33.0	-28.0	-27.4	-32.0
Gross Capital Formation	**2.2**	**5.4**	**11.6**	**16.5**	**24.9**	**47.6**	**54.2**	**45.8**	**44.7**	**50.5**	**37.2**

SOURCE: Years 1970–1990, HBS No. 793-096; Years 1996–2001, Singapore Department of Statistics.

EXHIBIT 1.6A	HISTORICAL RATES OF CONTRIBUTION TO CENTRAL PROVIDENT FUND (1955–2001)													
	1955	1968	1970	1973	1975	1980	1985	1986	1988[a]	1990	1995	1999	2000	2001
Employer (%)	5	6.5	8	15	15	20.5	25	10	12	16.5	20	10	12	16
Employee (%)	5	6.5	8	11	15	18	25	25	24	23	20	20	20	20
Total (%)	10	13	16	26	30	38.5	50	35	36	39.5	40	30	32	36

SOURCE: 2001 CPF Annual Report.

[a] After 1988, rates varied according to worker age. The rates for 55 and under are shown.

EXHIBIT 1.6B	CENTRAL PROVIDENT FUND CONTRIBUTION RATES (2001)			
Age	Employer Share (%)	Employee Share (%)	2001 Rates (%)	Long-Term Goal (%)
55 and Below	16.0	20.0	36.0	40.0
55-60	6.0	12.5	18.5	20.0
60-65	3.5	7.5	11.0	11.5
65+	3.5	5.0	8.5	9.0

SOURCE: 2001 CPF Annual Report.

EXHIBIT 1.6C	**CENTRAL PROVIDENT FUND CONTRIBUTION BREAKDOWN**

Age	Ordinary Account (%)	Special Account (%)	Medisave Account (%)	Total (%)
35 and below	26	4	6	36
25-45	23	6	7	36
45-55	22	6	8	36
55-60	10.5	0	8	18.5
60-65	2.5	0	8.5	11
65+	0	0	8.5	8.5

SOURCE: 2001 CPF Annual Report.

EXHIBIT 1.6D	**2001 CENTRAL PROVIDENT FUND DISTRIBUTION OF BALANCES**

Age	# of Members	Balance (S$bn)
35 and below	877,531	20.4
35-45	823,353	32.6
45-55	626,934	31.4
55-60	148,726	4.0
60+	416,647	3.6
Unspecified	29,482	0.1
Total	2,922,673	92.2

SOURCE: 2001 CPF Annual Report

EXHIBIT 1.7	GOVERNMENT REVENUES AND EXPENDITURES (IN MILLIONS S$) (FINANCIAL YEAR BEGINNING APRIL 1)							
	1991	**1996**	**1997**	**1998**	**1999**	**2000**	**2001**	**2002 (Budgeted)**
Operating Revenue	**15,697.4**	**28,929.7**	**29,181.4**	**27,911.0**	**30,645.1**	**33,726.3**	**29,871.2**	**29,214.0**
Tax Revenue of which	12,466.1	23,205.3	23,011.1	21,551.1	22,623.5	25,627.6	24,172.4	22,905.0
Income tax [a]	6,035.5	10,950.7	10,195.3	11,331.2	11,747.9	13,538.4	13,231.0	12,303.2
Assets taxes	1,361.5	1,823.5	2,335.3	1,529.4	1,314.1	1,605.7	1,517.5	1,410.3
Taxes on motor vehicles [b]	1,379.7	1,998.2	1,743.0	1,204.7	1,719.3	2,505.8	1,972.1	2,249.3
Other tax revenue [c]	3,689.4	8,432.9	8,737.5	7,485.8	7,842.2	7,977.7	7,451.8	6,942.2
Other Operating Revenue [d]	3,231.3	5,724.4	6,170.3	6,360.0	8,021.7	8,098.7	5,698.8	6,309.0
Total Expenditures	**11,774.5**	**23,286.4**	**23,042.7**	**26,933.9**	**25,079.0**	**27,908.5**	**27,305.3**	**28,328.5**
Security and External Relations	4,206.6	7,157.7	8,559.5	9,307.6	9,303.0	9,626.1	10,227.3	10,640.3
Social Development								
Operating [e]	3,568.0	4,952.4	5,479.6	5,433.3	5,409.5	6,653.8	7,769.9	8,023.1
Development [f]	2004.1	2,857.6	3,306.4	5,277.8	5,141.4	4,517.1	4,169.7	4,585.9
Economic Development								
Operating	173.7	688.7	707.7	893.3	865.3	2,908.4	1,113.3	1,175.2
Development	961.7	1,913.9	3,565.3	4,488.4	2,881.6	3,146.9	2,906.3	2,327.5
Government Administration	578.4	4,216.0	1,424.2	1,533.6	1,478.1	1,056.2	1,118.8	1,576.4
Pension	282.5	n/a	n/a	n/a	n/a	n/a	n/a	n/a
Financial Transfers	n/a	1,500.0[g]	n/a	n/a	n/a	n/a	n/a	n/a
Surplus	**3,922.9**	**5,643.4**	**6,138.8**	**977.2**	**5,566.1**	**5,817.9**	**2,565.9**	**885.5**
Less Special Transfers [h]	n/a	3,365.6	886.9	52.2	681.6	1,834.6	5,263.8	n/a
Budget Surplus (Deficit)	**3,922.9**	**2,277.8**	**5,251.8**	**925.0**	**4,884.5**	**3,983.3**	**(2,697.9)**	**885.5**

SOURCE: Ministry of Finance, Republic of Singapore.

[a] Income tax includes contributions by statutory boards.

[b] Taxes on motor vehicles comprise additional registration fees, road tax, special tax on heavy-oil engines, passenger vehicle seating fees, and nonmotor vehicle licenses but exclude import duties on motor vehicles that are classified under customs and excise duties.

[c] Other tax revenue includes property tax, estate duty, customs and excise duties, GST, betting taxes, stamp duty, selective consumption taxes, and other taxes.

[d] Other operating revenue includes fees and charges collected, net investment income (NII) contribution, and other operating revenue. Contribution from NII was introduced in FY2000.

[e] Government operating expenditure refers to expenditure on manpower, other operating expenditure (excluding expenses on investment and agency fees on land sales), and grants-in-aid.

[f] Government development expenditure excludes loans to statutory boards and industrial and commercial enterprises. From FY2001, land-related expenditure items are no longer classified under development expenditures. These expenditures are therefore excluded from the period April 2001 onwards.

[g] One-off compensation payment for early termination of monopoly rights in basic telecommunication services.

[h] Special transfers include New Singapore Shares, CPF top-up, and funds for eldercare, lifelong learning, etc.

Notes: Refinements have been made to the sectoral classification of ministries from FY2001. The Ministry of Foreign Affairs has been shifted to the newly renamed "Security & External Relations" sector, while the Ministry of National Development has been transferred to the "Social Development" sector. These changes have been made to better reflect the main functions of the two ministries. For the same reason, the sector "General Services" has been renamed "Government Administration."

EXHIBIT 1.8	BALANCE OF PAYMENTS (IN MILLIONS US$)													
	1970	1980	1990	1991	1992	1993	1994	1995	1996	1997	1998	1999	2000	2001
Current Account Balance	**(572)**	**(1,563)**	**3,122**	**4,880**	**5,915**	**4,211**	**11,400**	**14,900**	**12,823**	**17,927**	**19,706**	**16,527**	**15,921**	**17,885**
Trade balance	(855)	(4,200)	(1,633)	(110)	(1,821)	(2,724)	1,354	976	2,225	1,118	14,907	11,227	11,571	12,872
Exports of goods	1,447	18,200	54,679	61,333	66,565	77,858	97,919	118,456	126,010	125,746	110,591	115,514	138,931	122,478
Imports of goods	(2,302)	(22,400)	(56,311)	(61,443)	(68,387)	(80,582)	(96,565)	(117,480)	(123,786)	(124,628)	(95,685)	(104,287)	(127,483)	(109,605)
Net services	253	3,173	4,169	4,699	6,663	7,276	9,146	12,282	10,225	11,512	1,054	4,455	5,068	5,725
Services—credit	489	6,085	12,811	13,823	16,200	18,597	23,044	29,649	29,958	30,493	18,125	23,690	26,761	26,168
Services—debit	(236)	(2,912)	(8,642)	(9,124)	(9,537)	(11,321)	(13,898)	(17,367)	(19,733)	(18,981)	(17,071)	(19,235)	(21,693)	(20,443)
Net income	38	(429)	1,006	757	1,548	195	1,561	2,528	1,441	6,465	4,932	2,027	595	664
Income—credit	67	953	6,508	7,558	8,214	8,075	9,783	12,958	12,534	13,893	12,665	16,184	16,295	14,920
Income—debit	(29)	(1,382)	(5,502)	(6,801)	(6,666)	(7,880)	(8,222)	(10,430)	(11,093)	(7,428)	(7,733)	(14,157)	(15,700)	(14,256)
Net transfers	(8)	(107)	(421)	(466)	(475)	(536)	(661)	(886)	(1,067)	(1,168)	(1,187)	(1,183)	(1,314)	(1,378)
Transfers—credit	n/a	n/a	123	129	172	140	145	156	157	151	130	134	127	123
Transfers—debit	n/a	n/a	(544)	(595)	(647)	(676)	(806)	(1,042)	(1,224)	(1,319)	(1,317)	(1,317)	(1,441)	(1,501)
Capital Account [a]	**n/a**	**n/a**	**(22)**	**(34)**	**(38)**	**(71)**	**(84)**	**(71)**	**(139)**	**(173)**	**(226)**	**(191)**	**(163)**	**(161)**
Financial Account [b]	**173**	**1,583**	**3,947**	**2,346**	**1,793**	**(1,212)**	**(8,841)**	**(878)**	**(4,825)**	**(10,976)**	**(21,008)**	**(22,718)**	**(10,836)**	**(18,768)**
Direct Investment Outflow		21	(2,034)	(526)	(1,317)	(2,152)	(4,577)	(3,442)	(6,827)	(9,360)	(795)	(4,277)	(4,966)	(10,216)
Direct Investment Inflow	93 (net)	1,117	5,575	4,887	2,204	4,686	8,550	8,788	10,372	12,967	6,389	11,803	5,407	8,609
Portfolio Investment Assets			(1,610)	(665)	1,091	(7,833)	(7,840)	(7,769)	(12,625)	(13,088)	(10,860)	(7,938)	(7,867)	(5,256)
Portfolio Investment Liabilities	0 (net)	13 (net)	573	(242)	1,398	2,867	114	410	938	82	929	2,311	(2,034)	720
Other Investment Assets			(220)	1,831	(6,685)	(7,104)	(10,999)	(12,150)	(13,538)	(41,692)	127	(20,002)	(5,974)	(15,472)
Other Investment Liabilities	80 (net)	432 (net)	1,664	(2,940)	5,101	8,324	5,911	13,285	16,856	40,114	(16,800)	6,743	4,598	2,847
Net Errors & Omissions	**583**	**643**	**(1,616)**	**(2,995)**	**(1,570)**	**4,650**	**2,261**	**(5,352)**	**(464)**	**1,162**	**4,494**	**(783)**	**1,884**	**184**
Change in Reserves [c]	**184**	**663**	**5,431**	**4,197**	**6,100**	**7,578**	**4,736**	**8,599**	**7,396**	**7,940**	**2,965**	**4,194**	**6,806**	**(860)**

SOURCE: Years 1970–1980, HBS No 9-793-086; 1990–1997, *International Financial Statistics Yearbook 2001*, International Monetary Fund; Years 1998–2001, *International Financial Statistics, January 2003*, International Monetary Fund.

[a] All transactions that involve capital transfers and acquisition or disposal of nonproduced, nonfinancial assets.

[b] All transactions in the external financial assets and liabilities of an economy.

[c] Positive numbers indicate additions to reserves.

EXHIBIT 1.9A	**EMPLOYMENT / PRODUCTIVITY**										
	1991	**1992**	**1993**	**1994**	**1995**	**1996**	**1997**	**1998**	**1999**	**2000**	**2001**
Labor Force ('000)	1,554	1,619	1,635	1,693	1,749	1,802	1,876	1,932	1,976	2,192	2,119
Unemployment (%)	2.7	2.7	2.7	2.6	2.7	3.0	2.4	3.2	4.6	4.4	3.4
Average Nominal Monthly Earnings (S$)	1,669	1,804	1,918	2,086	2,219	2,347	2,480	2,740	2,813	3,063	3,134
Average Real Monthly Earnings[a] (S$)	1,894	2,002	2,080	2,193	2,295	2,395	2,480	2,748	2,819	3,030	3,070
Real Wage Growth (%)	6.0	6.0	4.0	5.0	5.0	4.0	4.0	11.0	3.0	7.0	1.0
Unit Labor Cost (%)	6.7	3.4	(0.9)	2.3	2.5	2.6	0.7	4.0	(10.4)	(0.2)	7.3
Labor Productivity Growth (%)	1.9	3.2	9.2	6.6	2.9	1.4	2.3	(2.8)	7.4	5.9	(5.4)
Total Factor Productivity Growth (%)	0.9	1.1	6.5	4.7	1.1	(0.7)	0.3	(5.2)	2.7	4.2	(6.4)

SOURCE: "Productivity Statistics 2002," SPRING Singapore.

[a] CPI is deflator.

EXHIBIT 1.9B	**PRODUCTIVITY AND GDP GROWTH**

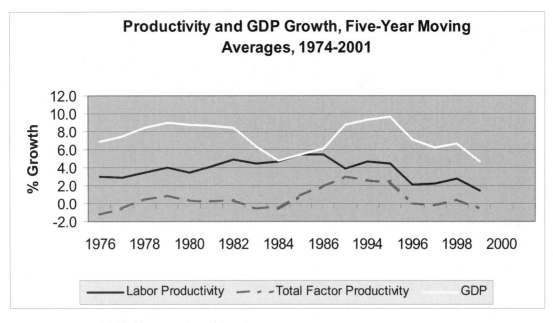

SOURCE: 2001 SPRING, Singapore Annual Report.

EXHIBIT 1.10A	CONTRIBUTIONS TO GROWTH IN GDP AND PRODUCTIVITY (% PER ANNUM)					
	1990-1995	**%**	**1995-2000**	**%**	**1990-2000**	**%**
Change in GDP	8.7	(100)	6.1	(100)	7.4	(100)
Attributed to:						
Productivity	4.6	(53)	2.5	(41)	3.6	(48)
Employment	4.1	(47)	3.6	(59)	3.9	(52)
Change in Productivity	4.6	(100)	2.5	(100)	3.6	(100)
Attributed to:						
Capital Intensity	1.8	(38)	2.2	(88)	2.0	(56)
Total Factor Productivity	2.9	(62)	0.3	(12)	1.6	(44)

SOURCE: "Productivity Statistics 2002," SPRING Singapore.

EXHIBIT 1.10B	SOURCES OF GDP GROWTH

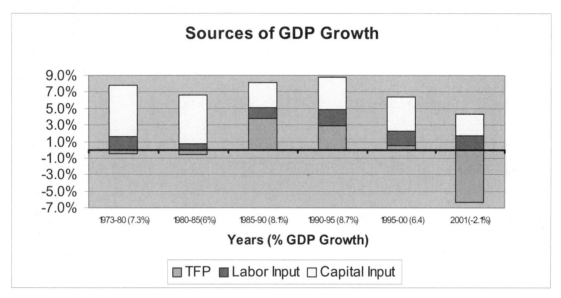

SOURCE: 2001 SPRING, Singapore Annual Report.

EXHIBIT 1.10C	TFP GROWTH FOR SELECTED COUNTRIES

	1975-1985	**1985-1990**	**1990-1995**	**1995-2001**
Singapore	-0.1	3.8	2.9	-0.6
Austria	1.3	1.9	1.5	1.5
Finland	1.5	2	1.8	3.3
Ireland	1.8	2.9	2.6	4
Sweden	0.5	0.8	1.7	1.9
EU-15	1.4	1.5	1.1	1
United States	1	0.9	0.9	1.5
Taiwan	n/a	5.4	3.5	1.7
Malaysia	n/a	n/a	2.4	0.9

SOURCE: 2001 SPRING, Singapore Annual Report.

| EXHIBIT 1.11A | **CUMULATIVE FOREIGN INVESTMENT IN SINGAPORE BY COUNTRY (%)** | | | | | | | |

	1989	1994	1995	1996	1997	1998	1999	2000
United States	20%	17%	17%	17%	19%	16%	16%	19%
Netherlands	7%	6%	5%	7%	6%	7%	14%	16%
Japan	21%	20%	19%	19%	17%	17%	15%	13%
Switzerland	5%	7%	8%	8%	8%	10%	10%	9%
United Kingdom	9%	10%	10%	11%	11%	12%	7%	5%
Hong Kong	7%	5%	5%	5%	4%	3%	3%	3%
Malaysia	4%	4%	4%	4%	4%	4%	3%	3%
Australia	7%	4%	4%	3%	3%	3%	2%	2%
Canada	5%	3%	3%	3%	3%	2%	3%	2%
France	1%	2%	2%	2%	3%	3%	2%	3%
Others	13%	21%	22%	20%	23%	23%	25%	26%
Total Direct Investment (S$M)	**41,063.0**	**80,163.8**	**92,840.7**	**105,015.1**	**125,274.3**	**139,905.4**	**157,593.8**	**181,939.8**
Portfolio Equity Investment	5,967.1	2,867.4	1,269.0	2,839.4	4,118.5	5,774.3	7,028.1	6,736.0
Total Equity Investment	**47,030.1**	**83,031.2**	**94,109.7**	**107,854.5**	**129,392.8**	**145,679.7**	**164,621.9**	**188,675.8**

SOURCE: Singapore Department of Statistics.

| EXHIBIT 1.11B | **SINGAPORE'S CUMULATIVE EQUITY INVESTMENT ABROAD BY COUNTRY (%)** | | | | | | |

	1994	1995	1996	1997	1998	1999	2000
United States	6%	5%	5%	5%	5%	6%	8%
Europe	7%	10%	13%	14%	7%	7%	6%
Australia	3%	3%	3%	2%	2%	3%	3%
Japan	1%	1%	1%	1%	2%	2%	1%
Hong Kong	17%	14%	11%	10%	10%	11%	7%
China	5%	8%	12%	14%	18%	17%	17%
Malaysia	22%	20%	16%	11%	11%	10%	11%
Indonesia	7%	8%	7%	9%	6%	6%	5%
Thailand	2%	2%	2%	1%	2%	4%	4%
India	0%	0%	1%	0%	1%	1%	1%
Taiwan	2%	1%	1%	2%	2%	3%	4%
Others	28%	26%	27%	31%	34%	32%	35%
Total Direct Investment Abroad (S$M)	**29,765.4**	**39,145.3**	**42,224.1**	**57,191.5**	**53,210.6**	**65,071.5**	**68,810.8**
Portfolio Equity Investment	7,289.3	10,936.6	15,640.8	14,034.1	11,656.0	16,427.5	18,717.1
Total Equity Investment	**37,054.7**	**50,081.9**	**57,864.9**	**71,225.6**	**64,866.6**	**81,499.0**	**87,527.9**

SOURCE: Singapore Department of Statistics.

EXHIBIT 1.12 **EXTERNAL TRADE**

	1997	1998	1999	2000	2001
Growth in Trade (% at 1995 prices)	10.9	-6.7	7.4	15.8	-10.4
Exports	11.6	-0.3	5.4	16.8	-8.6
Imports	10.2	-12.9	9.5	14.8	-12.4
Total Trade (S$M)	382,218	353,627	382,432	470,001	425,718

Exports by Major Country (%)	1997	1998	1999	2000	2001
United States	18%	20%	19%	17%	15%
Hong Kong	10%	8%	8%	8%	9%
China	3%	4%	3%	4%	4%
Japan	7%	7%	7%	8%	8%
South Korea	3%	2%	3%	4%	4%
Malaysia	17%	15%	17%	18%	17%
Philippines	2%	2%	2%	2%	3%
Taiwan	5%	4%	5%	6%	5%
Thailand	5%	4%	4%	4%	4%
India	2%	2%	2%	2%	2%
Europe	15%	18%	16%	15%	15%
Australia & New Zealand	3%	4%	4%	3%	4%
Africa	1%	1%	1%	1%	1%
Other	8%	8%	8%	8%	9%
Total (S$M)	185,613	183,763	194,290	237,826	218,026

Imports by Major Country (%)	1997	1998	1999	2000	2001
United States	17%	18%	17%	15%	16%
Hong Kong	3%	3%	3%	3%	2%
China	4%	5%	5%	5%	6%
Japan	18%	17%	17%	17%	14%
South Korea	3%	3%	4%	4%	3%
Malaysia	15%	15%	16%	17%	17%
Philippines	2%	2%	3%	2%	2%
Taiwan	4%	4%	4%	4%	4%
Thailand	5%	5%	5%	4%	4%
India	1%	1%	1%	1%	1%
Europe	16%	16%	15%	14%	15%
Australia & New Zealand	2%	1%	2%	2%	2%
Africa	0%	1%	1%	1%	1%
Other	10%	9%	10%	11%	11%
Total (S$M)	196,605	169,864	188,142	232,175	207,692

Exports by Commodity (%)	1997	1998	1999	2000	2001
Oil	9%	7%	8%	10%	10%
Non-Oil	91%	93%	92%	90%	90%
Food, Beverage, & Tobacco	3%	3%	3%	2%	2%
Crude Materials	1%	1%	1%	1%	1%
Chemicals and Chemical Products	6%	6%	8%	7%	8%
Manufactured Goods	6%	5%	4%	4%	4%
Machinery and Transport Equipment	66%	66%	66%	67%	64%
Miscellaneous Manufactured Articles	8%	8%	8%	8%	9%
Other	2%	4%	2%	1%	1%
Total	100%	100%	100%	100%	100%

SOURCE: Singapore Department of Statistics.

ENDNOTES

1   Speech by Prime Minister Goh Chok Tong, "National Day Rally 2001" (The University Cultural Centre, National University of Singapore, August 19, 2001).

2   "Economic Survey of Singapore 3rd Quarter, 2002," Ministry of Trade and Industry, p. 14.

3   Ibid., p. 41.

4   Lee Hsien Loong was the eldest son of former Prime Minister Lee Kuan Yew.

5   "The World Factbook 2002, Singapore," Central Intelligence Agency Web site, <http://www.cia.gov/cia/publications/factbook/geos/sn.html>.

6   Singapore Department of Statistics Web site, <http://www.singstat.gov.sg/keystats/mqstats/mds/mds21a.pdf>.

7   Lady Raffles, "Memoir of the Life and Public Services of Sir Thomas Raffles," in W.G. Huff, *The Economic Development of Singapore* (Cambridge, UK: Cambridge University Press, 1994), p.8.

8   "Singapore Is Out," *Straits Times*, August 10, 1965, on *Our Story Asia* Web site, <http://ourstory.asia1.com.sg/merger/headline/mpledge.html>.

9   Lee Kuan Yew, *From Third World to First: The Singapore Story 1965-2000* (New York, NY: HarperCollins, 2000), p. 3.

10 Forest Reinhardt and Edward Prewitt, "Singapore" (Boston, MA: Harvard Business School Publishing, 1993), p.6.

11 Chan Chin Bock, *Heart Work: Stories of How EDB Steered the Singapore Economy from 1961 into the 21st Century* (Singapore: Singapore Economic Development Board, 2002), p.15.

12 Lee Kuan Yew, *From Third World to First*, p. 33.

13 Lee Kuan Yew, *The Singapore Story: Memoirs of Lee Kuan Yew* (Singapore: Times Editions Pte, 1998), p. 344.

14 Statistics Singapore Web site, <http://www.singstat.gov.sg/keystats>.

15 Lee Kuan Yew, *From Third World to First*, p.57.

16 Ibid.

17 Ibid.

18 Ibid.

19 "Singapore: Political Structure," Economic Intelligence Unit, *EIU Business Asia*, March 25, 2002.

20 Interview with Tan Chim Nam, permanent secretary, Ministry of Information, Communications and the Arts, Republic of Singapore.

21 "Singapore: A Country Study," Library of Congress Web site, <http://memory.loc.gov/cgi-bin/query/r?frd/cstdy:@field(DOCID+sg0035)>.

22 "Vote Will Decide Upgrading Priority," *Straits Times*, April 18, 1992, in W.G. Huff, *The Economic Development of Singapore* (Cambridge, UK: Cambridge University Press, 1994), p. 354.

23 Sumiko Tan, "PM: Your Vote Will Have Immediate Impact on Your Life," *Straits Times*, December 24, 1996.

24 Moses Naim, "Singapore's Big Gamble," *Foreign Policy* (May/June 2002): 35.

25 Lee Kuan Yew, *From Third World to First*, p 175.

26 Ibid., p. 178.

27 Hadi Soedarsono and Leow Ju Len, "Prices Down, but Pricier to Own," *Straits Times*, June 1, 2002.

28 "Country Profile: Singapore, 2002," Economic Intelligence Unit.

29 Cherian George, *Singapore: The Air Conditioned Nation* (Singapore: Landmark Books, 2000), p. 21.

30 Anna Teo and Audrey Tan, "PM Goh—Pay Hikes for Ministers, Civil Servants Are Fair," *Business Times Singapore*, July 1, 2000.

31 Transparency International Web site, <http://www.transparency.org>.

32 Cherian George, *Singapore: The Air Conditioned Nation*, p. 76.

33 Irene Ng, "Fact of Life Today—Government No Longer Has Pick of Scholars," *Straits Times*, July 1, 2000.

34 Chua Mui Hoong, "Judge My Government by Its Results, says PM," *Straits Times*, July 1, 2000.

35 "Paying What It Takes for a First-Class Civil Service," *Straits Times*, June 30, 2000.

36 Interview with Chua Taik Him, assistant managing director, Economic Development Board, Republic of Singapore.

37 Interview with George Yeo, minister for Trade and Industry, Republic of Singapore.

38 Roger Mitton, "Asia Looks to Itself," *Asiaweek*, August 24, 2001.

39 *Singapore Investment Abroad 1999-2000*, Singapore Department of Statistics, August 2002.

40 Sue Herera, "Profile: Highly Competitive Educational System in China," *CNBC: Business Center*, November 15, 2002.

41 World Economic Forum Web site, <http://www.weforum.org/site/homepublic.nsf/Content/Growing+Chinese+Economy+to+Benefit+Neighbors>.

42 Interview with George Yeo, minister for Trade and Industry, Republic of Singapore.

43 "Country Profile: Singapore, 2002," Economist Intelligence Unit.

44 Interview with George Yeo, minister for Trade and Industry, Republic of Singapore.

45 "Terror Threats, Racial Harmony Are Singapore's Main Worries," *Agence France Presse*, February 11, 2002.

46 Tan Sek Toh in Chan Chin Bock, *Heart Work: Stories of How EDB Steered the Singapore Economy from 1961 into the 21st Century* (Singapore: Singapore Economic Development Board, 2002), p. 38.

47 Lee Kuan Yew, *From Third World to First,* p. 59.

48 Richard Hubbard, "No Big Singapore Inc. Sale as It Focuses Overseas," *Reuters*, August 28, 2002.

49 Interview with executive, Temasek Holdings.

50 "Temasek Announces New Charter," Temasek Press Release, July 3, 2002.

51 Interview with Koh Boon Hwee, chairman, Singapore Airlines.

52 Singapore Department of Statistics Web site, <http://www.singstat.gov.sg/keystats/surveys/fei2000.pdf>.

53 Tan Sek Toh in Chan Chin Bock, *Heart Work: Stories of How EDB Steered the Singapore Economy from 1961 into the 21st Century* (Singapore: Singapore Economic Development Board, 2002), p. 45.

54 Ibid., p. 38.

55 Interview with Sunil Sreenivasan, country corporate officer, Citibank, N.A.

56 Singapore Dept of Statistics Web site, <http://www.singstat.gov.sg/keystats/hist/gdp1.html >.

57 Economic Development Board Web site, <http://www.sedb.com/edbcorp/aboutedbhistory>.

58 Singapore Department of Statistics Web site, <http://www.singstat.gov.sg/keystats/economy.html>.

59 Ibid.

60 Lee Kuan Yew, *From Third World to First,* p. 66.

61 Interview with Lim Boon Heng, secretary-general, NTUC, chairman, SPRING, Singapore, and minister, Prime Minister's Office, Republic of Singapore.

62 Ibid.

63 Tan Sek Toh in Chan Chin Bock, *Heart Work: Stories of How EDB Steered the Singapore Economy from 1961 into the 21st Century* (Singapore: Singapore Economic Development Board, 2002), p. 39.

64 "Growing Numbers of Singaporeans Want to Quit the Country," *Agence France-Presse*, September 4, 2002.

65 Ibid.

66 Interview with Lim Boon Heng, secretary-general, NTUC, chairman, SPRING, Singapore, and minister, Prime Minister's Office, Republic of Singapore.

67 Forest Reinhardt, "Accounting for Productivity Growth" (Boston, MA: Harvard Business School Publishing, 1993), p. 3.

68 SPRING Singapore, 2001 Annual Report, p. 42.

69 Forest Reinhardt, "Accounting for Productivity Growth" (Boston, MA: Harvard Business School Publishing, 1993), p. 5.

70 "Economic Survey 3rd Quarter 2002," Economist Intelligence Unit, p. 46.

71 Ibid., p. 53.

72 "Country Profile: Singapore, 2001," Economist Intelligence Unit.

73 Interview with Lee Suan Hiang, chief executive, SPRING Singapore, Republic of Singapore.

74 WGBH Web site, <http://www.pbs.org/wgbh/commandingheights/lo/countries/sg/sg_overview.html>.

75   Reinhardt and Prewitt, "Singapore" (Boston, MA: Harvard Business School Publishing, 1993), p.11

76   "Economic Survey of Singapore: 3rd Quarter, 2002," Ministry of Trade and Industry, p. 141.

77   Monetary Authority of Singapore Web site, <http://www.mas.gov.sg/>.

78   W.G. Huff, *The Economic Development of Singapore* (Cambridge, UK: Cambridge University Press, 1994), p. 334.

79   Interview with Central Provident Fund Board, Republic of Singapore.

80   Ibid.

81   Central Provident Fund, 2001 Annual Report, p. 15.

82   Ibid., p. 35

83   Interview with Central Provident Fund Board, Republic of Singapore.

84   According to the 2001 CPF Annual Report, "investable savings" were defined as "the ordinary account balance plus net amounts withdrawn for education and investments."

85   Central Provident Fund, 2001 Annual Report, p. 48.

86   Department of Statistics, *Yearbook of Statistics Singapore, 2002*, p. 62.

87   Interview with Chua Taik Him, assistant managing director, Economic Development Board, Republic of Singapore.

88   Ibid.

89   Economic Development Board, 2001 Annual Report, p. 23.

90   Economic Development Board, 2001 Annual Report, p. 1.

91   Interview with Sally Tan Meow Ling, Manager, One North Development Group, JTC Corporation.

92   "Country Commerce: Singapore," Economist Intelligence Unit, June 2002.

93   Biomed Singapore Web site, <http://www.biomed-singapore.com/bms/inv_bmsif.jsp#>.

94   Interview with Chua Taik Him, assistant managing director, Economic Development Board, Republic of Singapore.

95   Ibid.

96   Ibid.

97   Republic of Singapore, "Bites of the Week," *MITA News*, February 1–7, 2003.

98   A*STAR Web site, <http://www.a-star.edu.sg>.

99   Singapore US Embassy Web site, <http://singapore.usembassy.gov/ep/2002/Budget2002.html>.

100   Channel NewsAsia Web site, <http://www.channelnewsasia.com/cna/parliament/erc/report8.htm>.

101   Anna Teo, "Singapore Ushers in Bold, New Tax Regime," *Business Times Singapore*, May, 4, 2002.

102   Economic Review Committee Web site, <http://www.erc.gov.sg/frm_ERC_TaxPackage.htm>.

103   Economic Review Committee Web site, <http://www.erc.gov.sg/frm_ERC_ExecutiveSumm.htm>.

104   "State of the Economy: Looking Back on 2001, What's Ahead in 2002," *Singapore: A Monthly Update from the Singapore Embassy* (January 2002): 2.

105   Anna Teo, "Singapore Ushers in Bold, New Tax Regime," *Business Times Singapore*, May 4, 2002.

106   The authors wish to acknowledge the invaluable research assistance provided by Pak Sing Lee and the Economic Development Board of Singapore.

Gradual Transition from a Planned Economy

Since its revolution in 1949, China has experienced 50 years of economic and political turmoil. This case focuses on China's development strategy since 1978 and the challenges the country faces at the end of the century. Although China's economic transformation has been astounding, continued rapid growth is by no means assured.

Gaining some understanding of China is important for several reasons. First, it is the world's most populous country, with more than 1.3 billion people. Second, it also has a huge economy when measured according to purchasing power—the third largest in the world. Finally, China's strategy has been unique. While borrowing from its high-growth Asian neighbors, its policies are not neatly categorized into standard developmental frameworks.

This case is organized into four broad sections, the first two of which are introductory. The first section provides a very brief introduction to China's history, dating to 2200 BC. The second section discusses the Mao era, during which the country experienced a series of abrupt and arbitrary economic and political transitions.

The third section, which is the heart of the case, discusses the market-oriented economic reforms implemented by Deng Xiaoping following Mao's death. Unlike the economic reforms implemented by governments in East Europe or Latin America, Deng had no grand design. His reforms were experimental and sequential, took place at the margin, and generally bubbled up from the provinces. Taken together, these initiatives amount to an implicit, derived strategy.

The final section of the case discusses a series of challenges facing China as the century ends. These include the reform of state-owned enterprises, rising unemployment, financial-sector reform, relations between the provinces and the central government, pressure for political liberalization and human rights, unemployment and environmental degradation, and the process of globalization while not being a member of the World Trade Organization (until 2002).

This is a challenging case. Unlike that of Singapore, China's development strategy is not always logical or consistent. Likewise, the challenges that this country faces are complex and, in many cases, efforts to address one problem make the others worse. Despite these issues, China's performance has been so extraordinary, occupying such a central place in the world economy that its general managers must grapple with these issues.

| CASE STUDY | CHINA: FACING THE 21ST CENTURY |

ROBERT E. KENNEDY

Introduction

As 1997 drew to a close, economic czar Zhu Rongji considered the economic and political challenges that China would face in the next decade. It had been a tumultuous year. Long-time paramount leader Deng Xiaoping had died in February, trade tensions with the United States escalated when the U.S. blocked China's membership in the World Trade Organization (WTO), and a series of currency crises in Asia threatened regional recession and the competitiveness of Chinese exports. Perhaps most important, there was widespread concern that China's vigorous growth was threatened by several long-neglected issues. Should China alter its development strategy, especially in light of the leadership change?

Since Deng had initiated China's program of economic reform in 1978, China had experienced a stunning transformation. GDP had grown at a 9.5% annual rate, per capita income had more than quadrupled, foreign direct investment had boomed, and trade had increased from 10% to 45% of GDP—making China the world's seventh-largest exporter.[1] Although per capita GDP was still only $600 when measured at official exchange rates, China's economy had become the world's third-largest when adjusted for purchasing power.[2] Most observers were awed by the magnitude of the transformation; the World Bank referred to the reforms as "spectacularly successful."[3]

Deng's death had settled a long-simmering dispute over succession for the top positions of the Communist party and the country. After seven years of grooming, President Jiang Zemin, Zhu's patron and a cautious reformer, had emerged as the top leader. Zhu was currently number three in the hierarchy and was expected to become the prime minister when the current prime minister, Li Peng, retired in March 1998.

Deng's death and the political ascendancy of the reformers provided an opportunity to reassess China's economic strategy. Deng's primary goals had been political stability and rapid economic growth. But the focus on short-term growth had left many issues unaddressed. Losses at state-owned enterprises and banks were growing, posing a potential threat to China's fiscal health. Trade tensions with the United States were increasing on both political and economic fronts. The Communist party's political legitimacy was threatened by corruption and a shift of power to the provinces. Pollution was a growing danger to public health. Finally, and perhaps most threatening in the long run, China's market institutions remained underdeveloped.

As economic czar, Zhu was charged with addressing these issues. He was inclined to think strategically, but radical action would be difficult. Nearly everyone agreed that China had great economic potential, but that potential might remain unrealized unless Zhu found a way to address the factors that threatened long-term growth.

Historical Background

Dynastic China

China claims one of the longest histories of any civilization, dating from at least 2200 BC, when farming clans began to form in the Yellow River valley. Central government first arose in approximately 1120 BC, when the Zhou clan established control over the Yellow River valley. The Zhou ruled the region until 480 BC, when China splintered during the Warring States period (480 BC–221 BC). During this period, Confucius, one of China's greatest philosopher-sages, tried to convince the rulers of the virtues of order and the ways of maintaining it. China's first emperor, Qin Shi Huang, unified the country in 221 BC, creating its first dynasty. Qin is credited with laying the foundation for the birth of the Chinese state. He standardized the Chinese currency, weights and measures, and the written language. He also created a national

Professor Robert E. Kennedy and Research Associate Katherine Marquis prepared this case. This case was developed from published sources. HBS cases are developed solely as the basis for class discussion. Cases are not intended to serve as endorsements, sources of primary data, or illustrations of effective or ineffective management. We are grateful for substantial input from Professor Yasheng Huang and Research Associate Teresita Ramos.

army and established a centralized political apparatus that ruled much of China's present territory. Qin died in 210 BC and his empire quickly disintegrated. Following Qin, China was ruled by a series of dynasties that all used the imperial system he created. Confucianism became the official state ideology under the Han dynasty (206 BC–220 AD).

Three basic pillars sustained China's imperial system. The first was the emperor, who sat at the pinnacle of power and enjoyed the "Mandate of Heaven." This mandate gave the emperor the divine right to rule but was contingent upon good conduct. Chinese history contains many examples of peasants rising against an emperor whose conduct was perceived as a sign that he had lost the mandate of heaven. The second pillar was the imperial bureaucracy. The Chinese invented the art of bureaucracy, along with sophisticated procedures to reward, monitor, and control these bureaucrats. The bureaucracy was selected using arduous, multi-tiered and multi-year civil service examinations, which were quite well developed by the seventh century.* The third pillar was Confucianism, a philosophy that stressed three bonds: between subject and ruler, between son and father, and between husband and wife. The idea was that rulers should govern their countries as patriarchs governed a family. This moralistic approach had a profound impact on the development of Chinese political institutions and has influenced China through modern times. Because it viewed the rulers as moral beings, Confucianism downplayed the need to create institutions to "check and balance" the ambition of rulers. Confucianism's view of society as a network of relationships also led to the practice of *guanxi*, the cultivation of relationships to help make one's way in the world, which was still important in contemporary China.

Dynastic China has been credited with some of the world's greatest technological inventions. The Chinese invented paper, printing, the compass, iron casting, mechanical clocks, and gunpowder, in each case centuries before these items were introduced in the West. In addition to its technological lead, imperial China seemed to have many of the ingredients required for rapid development. The currency was unified, production was quite specialized, and the cities housed great markets. Thus, China's subsequent economic stagnation was one of the great paradoxes of economic history. As historian R. H. Tawney commented, Chinese peasants "ploughed with iron when Europe used wood, and continued to plough with it when Europe used steel."[4]

China's last dynasty, the Qing (1644–1911), collapsed under both internal and external forces. Probably the single most important internal factor was the unprecedented population growth between the mid-eighteenth and mid-nineteenth centuries, when China's population increased from 143 million to 423 million. This growth strained food supplies and led to widespread malnutrition. In addition, the dynasty refused to allow the bureaucracy to grow along with the population. This increased the competition for coveted civil service positions, leading to bribery and corruption that ultimately undermined the imperial examination system.[5]

A second important factor was Western penetration of China starting in the nineteenth century. The first opium war with the British (1839–1842) led to the Treaty of Nanking, signed in 1842. The treaty forced China to open five port cities to British trade, ceded Hong Kong to the British, established extraterritoriality (where foreign nationals were exempted from Chinese law), and surrendered substantial economic sovereignty to foreigners. The treaties undermined the legitimacy of the Qing emperor and inspired Chinese nationalism against the Manchu regime.† The dynasty was overthrown in 1911 by the army in the hinterland city of Wuchang. Given the enormity of the event, the mutiny was relatively small, involving only a few thousand soldiers and was largely nonviolent.

---

* There were three rounds of qualifying examinations: one at the county level, one at the prefectural level, and then the qualifying examination itself. The actual examination then was offered at three levels—in the provincial capitals, in Beijing, and then at the imperial palace. Typically, a man started preparing for these examinations at the age of seven and, if successful, finished all of them around the age of 35.

---

† The Qing emperors were ethnically Manchu, a tribe that had traditionally been on the fringe of Chinese civilization and outside China proper. For that reason, the manchu dynasty was never fully accepted by the Han Chinese—the ethnically dominant racial group—even though the Manchus were completely absorbed into Chinese culture.

The Republican Era

After the demise of the Qing, the country descended into chaos. Regional warlords established fiefdoms throughout the country and the central government became inoperative. Throughout the 1910s, the warlords fought among themselves while Chinese intellectuals debated what direction the country should move. This changed abruptly when the Versailles Peace Conference, which brought World War I to a close, awarded German holdings in China's Shangdong province to Japan instead of returning them to China. Students in Beijing rioted, burning down government buildings and assaulting the Japanese ambassador. The riots soon spread and brought the country to a standstill. The riots, which came to be known as the "May Fourth Incident," introduced a new form of violent "mass politics" to China.[6]

Two broad political efforts emerged from the May Fourth Movement: the Guomindang (GMD), a nationalist party that had been founded by anti-imperial revolutionaries; and the Chinese Communist Party (CCP), founded by leftist students, academics, and other urban intellectuals. In the early 1920s, the GMD gained control of several southern provinces, most notably Guangdong. The CCP had a following in the cities, but did not control any provinces. Both groups had close ties to the Soviet Union, which convinced them to join forces in 1924 in an effort to reunify the country.

GMD/CCP cooperation ended in 1927 when GMD leader Chiang Kai-shek launched a surprise attack that killed nearly 90% of the CCP's members. The surviving Communists fled to the rural areas in the south and began building support among the peasantry. Between 1927 and 1934, the CCP rebuilt itself as a rural party. It was during this period that Mao Zedong, a young peasant from the central province of Hunan, developed his thinking on four crucial issues: land reform, how to develop and sustain political activity among peasants, how to govern territory under the CCP's control, and how to use military force effectively in the countryside. In 1927, Mao wrote that peasants' "political activity tends to rise up like a storm that unleashes tremendous violence and passion, but then quickly exhausts itself."[7] This view shaped Mao's political thinking until his death, and did much to change modern China.

The Communists were eventually forced to move north in the fantastic "Long March" from Jiangxi to Shaanxi, a year-long trek that took them through vast reaches of inhospitable terrain. More than 80% of the marchers died and, for decades, participation in the Long March was a powerful legitimizing force for surviving political leaders.

External events again intruded when Japan invaded China in 1931. The Japanese occupation prompted a second alliance between the GMD and CCP that lasted until the early 1940s. The CCP remained in the northern provinces while the GMD retreated to China's southwest. When the Allied Forces defeated Japan, the United States recognized the GMD as the legitimate government of China and airlifted GMD officials to China's leading cities. Chiang launched another effort to exterminate the CCP in the winter of 1946, prompting a full-scale civil war. By late 1949, the CCP had routed the GMD, which fled to Taiwan. On October 1, 1949, Mao stood atop the Tiananmen "Gate of Heavenly Peace" and proclaimed the formation of the People's Republic of China.

The Maoist Era

When the CCP came to power, China had been in decline for nearly a century, and by one estimate, since 1400.[*] Between 1949 and his death in 1976, Mao directed a radical transformation of the country. He appears to have been driven by two goals: achieving a peasant-led socialist revolution and rapid economic development. As his focus shifted from one goal to the other, policy followed, often abruptly. The Maoist period can be divided into four eras: political consolidation and economic reconstruction (1949–1957); the Great Leap Forward (1958–1960); economic recovery (1961–1965); and the Cultural Revolution (1966–1976).

After expelling the GMD to Taiwan, Mao moved quickly to establish political control and rebuild the economy. He deployed the People's Liberation Army throughout the country and set up provincial governments under CCP control. He also targeted potential opponents with mass

---

[*] In 1820, China had been the world's largest economy, with a 30% share of world GDP. By 1950, its share had fallen to only 7%. A. Maddison, *Monitoring the World Economy* (Paris: OECD, 1995). Elsewhere, Maddison (1991) estimates that China's per-capita GDP declined from $500 in 1400 to $454 in 1950, measured in constant 1985 prices.

political campaigns. These included land reform (which targeted land-owners and rich peasants), the "Suppression of Counterrevolutionaries" campaign (former GMD officials), the "Thought Reform of Intellectuals" campaign (non-CCP intellectuals), and the "Anti-Rightist" campaign (intellectuals and some party officials). These campaigns employed the techniques Mao had developed in the countryside, including mass action, violence, and forced public "confessions." During the period of consolidation, the CCP looked to the Soviet Union for guidance on how to rebuild the economy. Thus, the first five-year plan (1953–1957) emphasized central planning, capital accumulation, and investment in heavy industry. The strategy led to GDP growth of nearly nine percent* and by 1957 Mao had consolidated his power.

Mao became increasingly disillusioned with Soviet guidance in the late-1950s and sought to establish a distinctive Chinese approach to development. He was particularly incensed by a 1956 speech in which Soviet Premier Nikita Khrushchev attacked Joseph Stalin's legacy, cautioning against granting too much power to a willful leader. As Mao searched for another approach, he became convinced that mass action by the peasantry would allow China to leap over the normal stages of economic development. This led to a program referred to as the "Great Leap Forward." Land that had been distributed to peasants was reclaimed and granted to rural communes. Communes were directed to mobilize peasants in order to increase agricultural production, build rural infrastructure, and establish an industrial base in the countryside—with a special emphasis on steel production. Ambitious targets were set and initial reports from the countryside were promising. More than a million "backyard" iron smelters were constructed in the first year and the state statistical bureau claimed that the production of food and cotton doubled. But the gains were largely fictitious. Local officials, eager to report that the masses had responded enthusiastically to the program, falsified

production figures. Most steel was of such low quality that it could not be used. But this was not apparent to the planners, who instructed the communes to shift more labor from farming to industry. Agricultural output plummeted and 20 million–30 million people—mostly the elderly and people in poor health—starved to death. Kenneth Lieberthal, a well-known political scientist, observed that the Great Leap was "in the final analysis, a tremendous, willful leap away from reality."[8]

As the extent of the Great Leap disaster became clear,† Mao quietly shifted strategies. He withdrew from day-to-day decision making and recalled the country's well-trained bureaucracy. Mao's longtime lieutenant, Deng Xiaoping, was asked to stabilize the economy. Deng quickly reversed much of the Great Leap—breaking communes into smaller units, reorganizing economic reporting, bringing back technical experts, and forcing peasants to return to farming. The economy quickly recovered and, by 1965, output had returned to pre-Great Leap levels.

Mao apparently found it difficult to remain in the background. He grew increasingly suspicious of the government bureaucracy and of intellectuals in the CCP, whom he suspected were exploiting the countryside, just as the imperial elites had done. Mao launched a stunning attack on the establishment in 1966, declaring a Cultural Revolution to "destroy the old and establish the new." His goal was to rekindle the spirit of the Long March, throwing China into a state of permanent revolution. Mao encouraged youthful Red Guards to destroy the "four olds" (e.g., old ideas, old culture, old customs, and old habits). In practice, this meant widespread beatings, denunciations and mob-instigated "trials." Red Guards roamed the country attacking establishment elites, including government officials, managers, intellectuals, and former members of the bourgeois class. Even high government officials were not immune; Mao denounced Deng Xiaoping, and he was "sent down" to the countryside. Deng's son was permanently disabled when he was thrown out of a window by Red Guards.

---

* During the first five-year plan, national income grew at an 8.9% annual rate and agricultural output grew by 3.8%. Fairbank, p. 358. Maddison (1991) estimates that this growth was due almost entirely to capital accumulation. The capital stock grew at an annual rate of 9.2% between 1950 and 1973, while total factor productivity grew by only 0.49%.

† Estimates put the GDP decline at more than 30%, approximately the same decline experienced in the United States during the Great Depression. See Fairbank and Reischauer, *China: Tradition and Transformation*, p. 500.

China turned inward during this period. All ambassadors were recalled from abroad, and students attacked the British, Soviet, and Indonesian embassies. Mao eventually realized that the Cultural Revolution had spun out of control and ordered the army to reestablish control in 1969. The violence continued sporadically, especially in the countryside. When Mao began to experience health problems in the early 1970s, political infighting between "moderates" (headed by Zhou Enlai) and "radicals" (led by Mao's wife, Jiang Qing) took center stage. Deng was rehabilitated in 1973 and became the leading moderate when Zhou died in January 1976. Mao died on September 9, 1976. After a two-year struggle between the rival camps, Deng emerged as the paramount leader in mid-1978.

Institutions of Social Control

The CCP exercised a tremendous degree of control over the Chinese population, primarily though four layers of administration: the central government, provinces, local authorities (either counties or cities), and "units" (*danwei*). Although the economy was centrally planned, it was less rigidly hierarchical than in the Soviet Union. The central government set broad goals, but allowed the provinces and local authorities a high degree of autonomy regarding how to reach these goals. Political control was tight, however, and the locus of this control was the unit. All citizens were required to belong to a unit. For most, the unit was their employer; for students it was their school; and for farmers, their commune. The *danwei* were multi-purpose bodies. They were responsible for providing housing, primary and secondary schooling, pensions, and ration coupons for food, clothing, and furniture. The units also administered birth control programs, approved marriages and divorces, and resolved personal disputes. The key to the unit's importance was that few individuals were given permission to transfer from one unit to another. Workers were guaranteed lifetime employment, but were not free to switch jobs or move to another city. Each unit, even within cities, was an isolated political and social organization, with little communication between members of different units.

The Era of Economic Reform

Compared to the upheaval China had experienced since 1949, the situation that Deng inherited in 1978 was relatively stable. The moderate faction of the CCP had gained control of the party but did not enjoy the unchecked power that Mao had possessed. Political interactions between the reformers and hard-liners would dictate the pace and thrusts of the reform effort throughout the 1980s. Deng was wary of political manipulation and mass upheaval and shifted away from ideological exhortations, using material incentives instead. His strategy involved two simple principles: "reform measures were legitimate if they promoted rapid economic growth and if they did not weaken the Party's control of the political system [and]; everything else was subject to compromise."[9] Deng was known for his pragmatism, perhaps best summed up in his slogan "Who cares if a cat is black or white, as long as it catches mice." In practice, this meant both the marketization and internationalization of the economy. Deng also moved to depoliticize society, creating a sphere of private activity beyond the reach of politics. But political reform was relative. There would be no move toward democracy and the CCP would retain its monopoly on power.

While the economy had stabilized, Deng still faced a great challenge. China's territory was nearly identical to that of the United States, but it had four times the population and just one-quarter of the arable land with which to feed them.[10] Eighty-two percent of the population lived in rural areas, but rural incomes had been stagnant for more than a decade. The Great Leap and Cultural Revolution had inflicted lasting damage on the economy,* and more than 60% of the population lived on less than one dollar a day, the international poverty line. There was no rule of law in the Western sense.[11] Famine was an ever-present concern—mass starvation had occurred just 15 years before and population growth had outstripped grain production since the early 1950s.[12] Still, China did have several factors working in its favor. Its workforce was

---

* One study estimates that the damage done by the GLF and Cultural Revolution had reduced China's 1978 GDP by at least 50%. G. Chow and Y. Kwan, 1996, "Estimating Economic Effects of the Political Movements in China," *Journal of Comparative Economics* 23(2): 192-208.

skilled and disciplined. Millions of overseas Chinese were willing to trade with and invest in China. And China's neighbors in Asia had demonstrated the potential for high growth.

One of Deng's first steps was to tighten controls on population growth. The country had long been the most populous in the world, and opinion among the leadership was divided about whether this was a national asset or liability. Mao had considered a large population an asset, as "every person added two more hands to work." During the first 20 years of the People's Republic, no effort was made to restrict births, and the birth rate was consistently above 30 per thousand population. Zhou Enlai had come to believe that controlling population growth was a precondition for economic development and had initiated a two-child policy in 1971—with the goal of reducing the birth rate to 20 per thousand by 1980. The campaign's slogan was "late, sparse, and few."[13] Zhou's policy had limited success, as the birth rate declined to 23 per thousand by 1975. Deng launched a one-child policy in 1978. Women were required to obtain permission to have more than one child, with monitoring and enforcement provided by the units. A variety of rewards and punishments were used to enforce the policy, including subsidies, social sanctions, destruction of property, and occasionally, forced abortions. The program was fairly successful in the cities, where the average number of children declined to one per family. The program was, however, fiercely resisted in the countryside where the average number of children was still 2.3 per family. In an effort to maintain social peace, the government relaxed the one-child policy where resistance was greatest. Ethnic minorities were exempted, and most counties granted permission for a second child if the first was a girl.

While Deng was clearly responsible for the economic reforms initiated since 1978, only a few policies were imposed from the center. Beijing, with the support of the Peoples Liberation Army, was responsible for maintaining political stability. Further, the high savings rate and exchange rate policy were also due to central government policies. Most other reforms bubbled up from below. Deng created space for experimentation and local officials responded enthusiastically. Successful innovations were duplicated and eventually endorsed by the central government; unsuccessful experiments were discarded. The

reforms can be divided into four broad categories. These were rural reform, trade and investment reform, SOE/urban reform, and institutional reform.

Reform in the Countryside

The first wave of reforms took place in the countryside. In 1978, most peasants still lived in rural communes and were instructed to produce fixed quantities of agricultural products to meet the plan. In some areas, local officials had begun to allow peasants to retain production above their contracted amount and often looked the other way when this production was sold on local markets. Prompted by officials in drought-ravaged provinces, Deng undertook several measures to increase crop production and raise rural incomes. He instructed local officials to increase procurement prices for central plan quotas and to allow above-quota output to be freely sold.[14] This created a "dual price" system, in which a fixed amount of output was delivered to meet the plan and all incremental output was sold at market-determined prices. Deng also increased state investment in agriculture and relaxed restrictions on interprovincial trade in agricultural products.[15]

A related innovation was the "Household Responsibility System." Although officially prohibited by the central government, many communes began to lease plots of land to individual households. As payment, the family was responsible for managing production and delivering a fixed quota of output to the commune. The system shifted control of production decisions from communes to households, and thus led to very different behavior. The Household Responsibility System spread quickly after 1979. In 1981, when the central government officially approved the system, 45% of rural households were already participating. By 1983, the system had spread to 98% of farming households.

The reforms had an immediate impact and production of all types jumped sharply. The most rapid gains in agricultural output occurred between 1978 and 1984, when grain yields grew at a 5.7% rate, the production of oilseeds doubled, and cotton output tripled.[16] Pork, beef, and mutton production all grew by at least 80%.[17] After 1984, growth slowed to its long-term average of about 2%.

The changes in the countryside led to a virtuous cycle. Increased production and procurement prices raised rural incomes and led to a sharp increase in savings.* Higher incomes created demand for consumer goods that were in short supply. To meet this demand, local governments began to direct savings into collectively-owned firms, known as "Township and Village Enterprises" (TVE), many of which were actually established during the Great Leap Forward to promote rural industrialization.† Increases in agricultural productivity freed up surplus labor in the countryside.‡ Industrial output in the countryside boomed. By the time the central government officially approved rural industrial development in 1984, Township and Village Enterprises' share of industrial output had grown from 22% to 30%. It grew to 36% in 1988, and has stayed at about that level since. Throughout the 1980s, TVE output grew at an average rate of 30% a year.[18] By 1995, 23 million TVEs employed 129 million people.[19]

Trade and Investment Reforms

China's self-imposed isolation during the Cultural Revolution had come at a time when other Asian economies were taking off. Hong Kong, Japan, Singapore, South Korea, and Taiwan had all combined technology imports with export promotion to drive rapid growth. Deng believed a similar strategy would work for China, but the country had a long way to go. The economy was extremely isolated, with a trade to GDP ratio of only 10% and no stock of foreign direct investment. Internationalization was also needed for less philosophical reasons. Reform in the countryside had led to strong demand for imports, primarily fertilizer and capital equipment, and foreign exchange reserves had fallen dangerously low. Despite these factors,

internationalization proved to be quite controversial. Hard-liners resisted because of worries about foreign influence.

As with other elements of Deng's reforms, events quickly overtook the planners' deliberations and reform proceeded along three distinct paths. The first was piecemeal trade reform, which started in 1979 and continued through the mid-1990s. Prior to 1979, all trade had flowed through 12 foreign trade corporations (FTCs). After that, local officials started to license their own FTCs and allowed local firms to bypass central government FTCs. By 1988, the number of registered FTCs had grown to 5,075. In addition, the number of domestic firms with foreign trade rights mushroomed, reaching nearly 10,000 in the mid-1990s.[20] In the early 1980s, the central government also began a slow reduction in import tariffs, but many nontariff barriers remained.[21]

The liberalization of foreign direct investment (FDI) was much more controversial than trade reform. Neighboring high-growth countries had pursued different strategies with regard to FDI. Foreign direct investment had played an important role in Hong Kong and Singapore but little role in Japan and South Korea. FDI troubled hard-liners because it involved much closer foreign ties than simple trade. To the hardliners, foreign investment implied foreign control of Chinese assets and a dilution of the socialist character of the economy. Given China's history, this was an especially sensitive issue. A compromise was reached where foreign investment would be restricted to just a few geographic areas, thereby isolating foreigners' influence while the costs and benefits of FDI could be studied. Four coastal cities were designated Special Economic Zones in 1980 and granted permission to experiment with new institutions, such as tax rates and approval procedures for foreign investment.§ Enterprises operating in the Special Economic Zones were exempted from the central plan, labor regulations, and many taxes.**

---

* The annual rural household income increased from 133.6 yuan in 1978 to 397.6 yuan in 1985. Gross savings by rural households increased from 55.7 billion yuan to 438.1bn between 1978 and 1984. China Statistical Bureau.

† Most TVEs were owned by rural *danwei* (units) and enjoyed much more freedom than SOEs. They could generally produce anything they chose, within geographical limits, and retained their own earnings. After the disastrous experience during the Great Leap Forward, most TVEs produced agricultural equipment and simple manufactured products.

‡ By the mid-1980s, more than 100 million adults had given up farming and were working in villages and townships across China. Lieberthal, p. 148.

---

§ Three SEZs were located in Guangdong province (Shenzhen, across from Hong Kong's New Territories; Zhuhai, next to the Portuguese colony of Macao; and Shantou, in the northern part of the province). The fourth (Xiamin) was located in Fujan province, near Taiwan.

** The most ambitious of the SEZs was Shenzhen, a small town on the border of Hong Kong's New Territories. The location was chosen to take advantage

A third set of reforms involved foreign currency. The inflation-adjusted (i.e., "real") value of the yuan was steadily lowered, starting in 1980 and continuing through 1993. Several microeconomic reforms were also implemented. Until the mid-1980s, foreign currency transactions were tightly regulated. All capital transactions required central bank approval, while the treatment of trade transactions varied according to firm ownership. Enterprises with foreign capital that were located in Special Economic Zones were generally allowed to retain foreign currency and to import and export freely. Domestic firms required regulatory approval and foreign-currency allowances to import and were forced to turn over all export earnings to the state banking system. In the mid-1980s, the government introduced a complex system in which domestic firms could retain a portion of the foreign exchange they generated. In 1986, the government introduced a dual exchange rate system on which domestic firms could buy and sell limited amounts of foreign currency (this will be discussed in greater detail below).

The reforms led to a dramatic transformation of China's links to the outside world. Merchandise exports grew from $11 billion in 1978 to $24 billion in 1984, a 14% growth rate. By 1996, exports had reached $154 billion. During this same period, exports increased from 4.9% to 18% of GDP. The response to liberalization of FDI was much slower. Foreign direct investment flows grew from $57 million in 1980 to $2.7 billion in 1990. It exploded after 1993, jumping from $7.2 billion in 1992 to $42 billion in 1996. Since 1993, China has been the world's largest developing-country recipient of

FDI. In the mid-1990s, large trade surpluses and inbound-capital flows put upward pressure on the yuan and led to a rapid accumulation of foreign reserves.

The reforms led to some severe distortions, however. Naughton concluded that by 1987, China had established, in essence, two separate trading regimes. One was an export processing regime. Although it was extremely open, access was controlled: most domestic firms were excluded, while most foreign-invested firms could participate. The other was the traditional, but increasingly reformed, [domestic] Chinese regime, which is basically an import-substitution regime.[22]

Much of the export processing regime revolved around simple, labor-intensive assembly. In this system, components were imported duty-free, an enterprise in China assembled them, and the goods were then re-exported. In many cases, the Chinese firm simply provided assembly work on a contract basis—it never took title to the imported materials. The export processing regime was fairly small until the early 1990s, never accounting for as much as 10% of total Chinese exports. But as inbound-FDI increased and economic growth in the Special Economic Zones reached a fever pitch in the mid-1990s, foreign invested enterprises' share of exports increased rapidly, reaching 31% in 1995, and more than 40% for the first six months of 1996 [see **Exhibit 2.9**]. Exports from the rest of the economy had grown but at a much slower pace.

State-Owned Enterprise Reform

The reforms in the countryside and the Special Economic Zones fueled sharp increases in production and incomes, but they also increased pressure on state-owned enterprises—the backbone of the urban economy. The SOEs had been nurtured under central planning and accounted for 78% of industrial output and 19% of total employment in 1978 (vs. 72% of employment in agriculture). SOEs in key sectors (such as heavy industry, mineral extraction, energy production, and banking) reported to the central government. Others reported to provincial or local governments. Enterprises purchased inputs and sold their output at state-determined prices, produced to a quota, and turned all of their profits over to the state, which also covered operating losses. As of 1978, SOEs were also the primary source of government

---

of the Hong Kong economy, which was beginning to transfer labor-intensive industry offshore. Shenzhen had almost no industrial base, but the local government moved quickly to upgrade the infrastructure and create a friendly legal environment. The results were immediate and quite astonishing. Industrial output grew at an annual rate of 56% between 1979 and 1983 and increased to 100% in both 1983 and 1984. In 1984, 14 more SEZs were opened along the coast and in major cities. One persistent problem during the early years of investment until 1986 was the issue of currency conversion, but foreign trade continued to increase in the second half of the decade after the expansion of the SEZ experiment. Joint Economic Committee, 1986, *China's Economy Looks toward the Year 2000* (Washington: U.S. Government Printing Office), p. 355.

revenues—they paid income taxes equal to 19% of GDP and remitted profits equal to an additional 19% of GDP.[23] Like most SOEs elsewhere, state-owned enterprises in China were considered overstaffed, inefficient, and poorly managed. The World Bank estimates that manufacturing productivity in SOEs declined at an annual rate of 1.2% from 1978 to 1983.[24] SOEs were, however, the primary conduit for social services in urban areas. They provided housing, education, health care, and lifetime employment for their workers. In many cases children inherited their parents' jobs. This system was known as the "iron rice bowl."

In the early 1980s, some local officials began to experiment with an ad hoc "Management Responsibility System," a counterpart to the Household Responsibility System used in agriculture. New freedoms were negotiated on a firm-by-firm basis and fell into three categories: increased autonomy over production and investment decisions, the right to retain a portion of profits, and the right to sell above-plan output at market prices. By 1984, profit retention and production autonomy were in widespread use, but formal permission to produce above the plan was still rare [see **Exhibit 2.10**]. In October 1984, the central government formally approved these practices, which then spread quickly. Price controls for (above-plan) final goods were loosened starting in 1980, and dual-track prices were introduced for intermediate goods in 1985.

Unlike the rural and trade reforms, initiatives designed to improve the performance of SOEs had limited success. SOEs' share of industrial output continued to fall, from 78% in 1978 to 55% in 1990. Despite this drop in their share of output, SOEs' share of total employment showed only a small decline, from 19% to 18%. As non-state firms gained competitiveness, SOEs' monopoly positions were eroded and their combined contributions to the central government fell sharply (from 38% of GDP in 1978, to only 3.6% in 1990).[*] About two-thirds of SOEs lost money in 1992 and government subsidies to loss-making enterprises increased from 2.0% of GDP in 1985 to 3.1% in

1990.[25] The data are mixed about whether productivity in SOEs increased following the reforms, but most analysts agree that productivity growth in SOEs lagged that in TVEs and the private sector.[26]

While the Management Responsibility System did little to improve SOE performance, it provided opportunities for corruption. Enterprise directors used their personal relationships (*guanxi*[†]) with local and national leaders to negotiate prices for industrial inputs. Directors often used their lowest-quality inputs for goods bound for the state and focused their efforts and resources on above-plan production. The dual-price system created the opportunity to earn high profits by diverting plan-output to the unregulated market. Because state-delivery quotas were negotiated, SOE managers had an incentive to bribe local officials. International surveys rated China as one of the most corrupt countries in the world.

Institutional Reform

In addition to the rural, trade, and urban reforms, China implemented a series of institutional reforms between 1978 and 1995. Four were particularly important: increased provincial autonomy, fiscal reform, financial sector reform, and currency reforms.

As part of Deng's impulse toward experimentation, the central government granted provincial governments increased autonomy with regard to taxation and industrial development in 1984. Local governments were granted significant tax collection authority in what was known as the "tax contract system." Under this system, the local government collected taxes and turned over a tax quota to the central government, retaining a high proportion of any above-quota tax revenue. Provincial authorities used this freedom to allocate funds to local SOEs and TVEs. The new system led to a sharp decline in central government revenue, which fell from 9.6% to only 6.0% of GDP between 1986 and 1992. The central leadership viewed this development with alarm as the fiscal contraction at the center eroded the government's ability to stabilize the economy and to affect income transfers across regions.

---

[*] This figure, while accurate, overstates the extent of SOE's relative decline. Taxes as a share of GDP were declining sharply during this period, and the central government's share of total tax revenues was also declining (see exhibits). Both of these issues are discussed below.

[†] Guanxi was an integral part of Chinese culture and business. Some viewed *guanxi* as a social lubricant that helped to establish trust and reciprocity. Others viewed it as mere corruption.

In 1994, the central government implemented an extensive tax reform. It established a National Tax Service that was responsible for direct collection of national taxes, making central tax collection largely independent of local officials. The 1994 reform also reduced the number of taxes from 32 to 18 and introduced a value-added tax. Finally, it moved the system toward more uniform treatment for domestic and foreign-invested firms. Prior to reform, income tax rates had varied by ownership type and because of bargaining between firms and various tax collection authorities. After the reforms there was a single income tax applied to all domestic firms and the government announced that it planned to unify the tax treatment of foreign-invested firms.[27] The new system reversed fiscal contraction, and the central government's share of consolidated revenue rose dramatically from 22% in 1993 to 50% in 1996.[28]

The dispersal of economic power to the provinces also had an adverse effect on the conduct of monetary policy. Because local governments often appointed the directors of regional branches of the People's Bank of China, they could pressure local branches to overextend credit and to direct loans to politically-favored projects, rather than to those that were economically viable or which the central government wished to support.* This led to excessive credit expansion and a rising share of bad loans. In response, the central government moved to strengthen the monetary functions of the People's Bank of China. In 1995, the central government established a new Central Bank Law that prohibited overdrafts to government agencies and recentralized monetary control in the central bank.

Although the main thrust of institutional reforms in the 1990s was to recentralize fiscal and monetary controls, there had also been a quiet move away from China's rigid political centralization. During the Maoist period, the commune system served both economic and political functions such as tax collection and enforcing population controls. As the commune system was dismantled, the reformist leaders began to fear that a political vacuum was forming in the countryside. To fill this void, reformist leaders began to introduce competitive elections for village-level officials in the late-1980s. By the mid-1990s, four-fifths of Chinese villages had held at least one such election. Studies show that village elections improved governance. For example, in areas where village elections were held, there was more compliance with tax collection and population controls.[29]

The final set of institutional reforms involved currency convertibility. Prior to 1986, the yuan was largely inconvertible. Domestic exporters were allowed to retain only a small percentage of their export earnings,† and importers had to petition the Bank of China for currency. In an effort to decentralize decision making while still retaining some control, the central government introduced a dual exchange rate system. Under this system, the central bank fixed the official exchange rate but allowed limited free exchange on a parallel "swap market." The exchange rate on the swap market was set by market forces and was generally much lower than the official rate. Domestic enterprises were forced to turn over the bulk of their foreign receipts to the central bank at the official rate but could trade a small portion on the swap markets. Enterprises with foreign capital were allowed to trade all of their export receipts. The treatment of domestic enterprises served as a tax on domestic exports while subsidizing imports.[30]

In 1994, the authorities abolished the dual exchange rate and merged the market and official rates at the market rate. This amounted to an effective devaluation of the yuan by about 50%. The action gave a large boost to Chinese exports. The merchandise trade balance was in surplus every year from 1993, rising to $18.1 billion in 1995. With the exception of 1993, the current account was in surplus every year since 1990. These surpluses, combined with large FDI inflows, led to a huge buildup of foreign exchange reserves.[31]

Economic Strategy in the Mid-1990s

China's ninth five-year plan (1996–2000) outlined the country's economic strategy at the end of the century. It established a goal of 8% GDP growth and noted the necessity of completing two fundamental transitions: from a

---

* The local influences on money creation came out when the central government needed to print money to meet the credit shortfalls created by the actions of these local governments.

---

† Special allowances were made for foreign producers operating in SEZs.

traditional, planned economy to a "socialist-market economy," and from extensive growth (based on increases in inputs) to intensive growth (driven by improvements in efficiency).

The plan consisted of five (sometimes contradictory) initiatives. The first was to continue the fight against inflation through fiscal and monetary restraint. Inflation had peaked at 24% in 1994, but had fallen to 3% by 1997. Second, the reform of state-owned enterprises was to be refocused and accelerated. The effort was narrowed to the 1,000 largest state-owned firms. Smaller firms were to be privatized or shut down.

The third initiative involved strengthening China's integration with the international economy. In order to achieve its growth objectives, China needed unfettered access to international export and capital markets. But tensions created by China's import restrictions, rapid growth in exports, and the large bi-lateral trade surplus with the United States had led to China's exclusion from the newly formed World Trade Organization. WTO membership would have guaranteed access to export markets. Without it, China would be forced to rely on bi-lateral negotiations.

The fourth initiative was designed to increase productivity growth. Science and technology funding was increased and the central government announced that it would focus industrial policy on five "pillar" industries. These industries (machinery, electronics, petrochemicals, automobiles, and construction) were to receive increased investment appropriations and special protection from international competition. Proposals to protect these industries had led to some of the sharpest conflicts with China's trading partners. Finally, the plan reiterated the need for economic and political stability.

Challenges on the Eve of a New Millennium

China experienced a stunning transformation in the Deng era. Although highest in the coastal provinces, growth was widespread. If China's 30 provinces had been counted as individual economies, the 20 fastest-growing economies in the world between 1978 and 1995 would have been Chinese.[32] The share of the labor force employed in agriculture declined from 71% to 50%, a shift that took 59 years in Japan. China's economic transformation was matched by improvements in social indicators. The birth rate fell by 25%. Infant mortality declined from 85 per 1,000 births in 1975 to 45 in 1990—compared with 127 for India and 111 for Indonesia, both measured in 1990.[33] Various estimates put the number of people who were lifted above absolute poverty in the 1980s at around 100 million.

Despite these impressive achievements, Zhu faced a series of unresolved issues that threatened to derail future growth. SOE losses were mounting and rising unemployment threatened social stability. The banking system was in danger of collapse. Relations between the central government and the provinces remained tense. Further integration with the world trading system was threatened by China's exclusion from the WTO. And unchecked development had caused serious environmental damage.

SOE Reform

Despite vigorous reform efforts since 1984, the financial performance of SOEs continued to deteriorate. As TVEs, private firms, and foreign-invested enterprises flourished in the 1990s, state-owned enterprises had been in steady retreat. By 1994, SOEs produced the majority of output in just nine sectors.* These sectors were protected by regulatory or technological barriers to entry, and thus provided a safe harbor for struggling state firms. In 1996, half of SOEs were losing money, and the government estimated that 30% were effectively bankrupt.

In 1996, Vice-Premier Zhu expressed pessimism about SOE performance: "The current problems of SOEs are excessive investments in fixed assets with very low rates of returns and a low sales-to-production ratio, giving rise to mounting inventories. The end result is that the state has to inject an increasing amount of working capital through the banking sector into the state enterprises."[34]

The politics of SOE reform had always been much more difficult than the economics of reform. The SOEs were considered the backbone of socialism, thus making an explicit privatization policy difficult. Surveys suggested

---

* Sectors dominated by SOEs include: resource extraction, utilities (water, power, and gas supply), tobacco, machinery, petrochemicals, automobiles, and construction.

that about one-third of the 100 million SOE workers could be laid off with no effect on output, but liquidating insolvent SOEs could easily lead to political and social instability.

Beginning in 1994, the Chinese government adopted a three-pronged new approach toward SOEs, summarized in the slogan, "Grasping the big ones and letting go of the small ones." The first prong was to preserve government control of the largest SOEs, while attempting to reform these enterprises by combining them into Chaebol-type conglomerates and by altering their governance structures.[35] The second prong was to permit outright privatization of the small SOEs controlled by local governments.* The third prong was to allow bankruptcies and mergers of the truly nonperforming SOEs. In September 1997, at the 15th Party Congress, the Chinese leadership formally affirmed this policy.

Unemployment

China's intense focus on rapid growth was driven by the need to create jobs for the country's vast population. Even with a highly effective birth-control program in place, China's population continued to increase by approximately 14 million people per year—equivalent to adding another Texas or Australia annually. In addition to this natural population growth, several factors heightened the need to create jobs. Large numbers of workers continued to leave farming. Chinese experts predicted that as many as 180 million working-age adults would be under- or unemployed in rural areas by 2005.[36] Further, there was vast overemployment in the state-sector. Finally, the reforms since 1978 had loosened political control of the population. As the power of the units (*danwei*) declined, many workers left their home counties, creating an estimated 100 million "floating workers" who moved from city to city seeking temporary employment.

The Financial Sector

The poor financial performance of SOEs was reflected in the deteriorating finances of the financial sector. In the late 1980s, in an effort to

contain fiscal deficits, the central government directed state banks to cover SOE losses with loans. By the mid-1990s, SOEs absorbed more than 70% of the loans granted by state banks. The Chinese government estimated that loans at state banks equal to 8%–10% of GDP would have to be written off, but international analysts put the figure much higher—at 25% to 35%. By contrast, the costs associated with the savings and loan crisis in the United States amounted to only 2% of GDP.[37]

To deal with this issue, the political and policy functions of Chinese banks were separated from their commercial functions. Three new policy banks were established in 1994 for the purpose of policy lending. This allowed other banks, primarily the four large state banks, to specialize in commercial lending activities.† Over time, the commercial banks were to transfer their policy lending portfolio to the policy banks.[38]

In addition, the authorities opened two stock exchanges in Shanghai and Shenzhen and allowed the establishment of nonbank financial institutions to engage in limited financial intermediation. Several foreign banks opened representative offices, although their operations were strictly limited.

Provincial-Center and Province-Province Tensions

The moves toward fiscal recentralization helped to stabilize the central government's fiscal situation, but significant tensions remained. The income gap between the booming coastal provinces and the interior regions continued to grow [see **Exhibit 2.14**], and the central government's attempts to transfer resources to poorer regions were resisted by the wealthier provinces. As coastal provinces became fiscally self-sufficient, the central government's influence over them was sharply curtailed. Senior officials in Guangdong have noted that central austerity efforts have little effect on them, because they were net contributors to the central budget.[39]

The rich coastal provinces had nearly independent industrial policies—they provided

---

* Because of the ideological sensitivity of the issue, the Chinese government does not use the term *privatization* explicitly. Instead, euphemisms such as *ownership change* and *nonpublic ownership* are used to refer to what functionally is a privatization process.

---

† The policy banks are the State Development Bank, the Agricultural Development Bank, and the Export-Import Bank. The four main state banks are the Industrial and Commercial Bank, the Agricultural Bank, the Bank of China, and the People's Construction Bank

tax breaks to investors, built infrastructure, and subsidized key sectors. Many provinces had erected trade barriers against neighboring provinces, and the transportation infrastructure often petered out at provincial borders. Despite China's huge size, little regional specialization had occurred. Alwyn Young, who analyzed trade patterns and inter-regional variation in production patterns, concluded that, instead of specializing, most provinces attempted to enter the same industries. This led to excessive industrial duplication, large opportunity costs, and growing regional tensions.[40]

Political Liberalization and Human Rights

China's economic reforms had not been matched by political liberalization. While many villages had held contested elections for local positions, the CCP maintained its monopoly on all provincial and national positions. There was disagreement among economists and political scientists about whether sustained economic growth required political freedom.[*] The CCP clearly believed it was not.

Grassroots calls for democracy and local autonomy led to several incidents that heightened tensions with other countries. Two events in 1989 brought these issues to a head. In March of that year, demonstrations protesting China's control of Tibet led to PLA intervention and the imposition of martial law in the region. Two months later, tanks were used to clear democracy demonstrators from Tiananmen Square, leading to several hundred deaths.[†] These incidents, as well as other disagreements over human rights—such as the use of prison labor and forced sterilizations—led to periodic calls for economic sanctions against China. These issues were raised annually when the United States Congress reviewed China's most-favored-nation status.

---

[*] Some economists suggested that political freedom was a luxury good—that is, one for which demand grew rapidly as living standards rose.

[†] There remains much disagreement about the number of deaths that occurred in Tiananmen Square. The Chinese government denies that any students died. *The New York Times* cites "a minimum of several hundred killed." *The Times* continues: "It is possible that the true number of deaths might be 1,500 or more." *The New York Times*, June 6, 1989, page A1.

Economic Integration

China's economic strategy depended on continued access to international markets, but its trading partners had become increasingly concerned about their levels of access to the Chinese market. China's exporters could be assured of continued access to foreign markets only if China joined the World Trade Organization and conformed to its fair trade principles. But the United States had blocked China's ascension to the WTO because of a dispute about the pace of import liberalization. The United States promised to veto China's entry to the WTO until it agreed to join as a "developed country." China was unwilling to join without "developing country" status. "Developed" countries were expected to meet WTO standards quickly, while "developing" countries were allowed an extended transition period, as well as an exemption for "concessions that are inconsistent with their development, financial, and trade needs."[41]

China's status upon entry to the WTO would determine the pace of further import liberalization, particularly in "pillar" industries and those dominated by SOEs. Abrupt import liberalization would place further pressure on SOEs and state-owned banks, perhaps further complicating the reform process.

In spite of the WTO dispute, China had undertaken several policies designed to encourage closer integration with the world economy. The yuan was fully convertible for current account transactions, although not for capital account operations. The government had implemented a series of tariff reductions, with the average tariff level declining from 40% in 1991 to 23% in 1996. The government announced that it planned further reductions, to 15%, by 1998. Nontariff barriers had been reduced—the number of items with import quotas was cut from 660 to 384 in 1996—but still covered a large portion of trade, including many agricultural products, machinery, and electronic products. Finally, the central government had cut back on import tariff rebates and VAT rebates for exports by enterprises with foreign capital.[‡]

[‡] Both measures have produced an outcry among foreign companies. Although the tax equalization is meant to level the playing field, foreigners believe that domestic firms have many other advantages including lower land rentals and lower prices for many essentials.

The dispute over China's WTO entry was exacerbated by a disagreement over the size of the U.S.-China bilateral balance. The United States reported a $39.5 billion deficit with China in 1996, while China claimed its surplus was only $10.5 billion.[*] The primary source of conflict was over how to account for the value of goods that passed through Hong Kong. When calculating the bilateral trade balance, the United States attributed to China the full value of all goods shipped through Hong Kong. China counted only the value of goods leaving China whose final destination was known when they left the country. At heart, the dispute centered around how to account for the value added to these goods in Hong Kong. One group of economists put the true bilateral imbalance at $16 billion–$22 billion for 1995 (compared with the U.S. estimate of $33.7 billion and the Chinese claim of $8.6 billion).[42]

The Environment

Rapid economic growth had led to extensive environmental damage in China. The country's air and water were among the most polluted in the world, especially in urban areas. In addition to aesthetic losses, the economic costs of pollution were extremely high. The World Bank estimated that the total economic costs of pollution were between 3% and 8% of GDP, and that more than 20% of deaths in China were pollution-related.[43]

At least three factors contributed to the high levels of pollution in China. First, energy use had grown rapidly, and nearly 80% of China's energy was generated using coal—a pollution-intensive energy source. Second, rapid urbanization had overtaxed waste disposal systems and exposed high numbers of people to

pollutants. More than 200 million people had moved to urban areas since 1978, but the waste infrastructure had not kept pace. Seventy-seven percent of industrial waste was treated, compared with only 7% of municipal waste.[44] Third, deforestation and the loss of arable land had reduced the environment's ability to absorb pollution. Deforestation averaged 0.7% per year in the 1980s, and approximately 0.35% of farmland was lost each year to urbanization and construction. Total cropland in China declined from 105 million hectares in 1961 to only 96 million in 1990, while the population doubled.

Despite high levels of pollution, several positive trends had emerged. Growth in the emission of major pollutants grew more slowly than GDP, and the government indicated that it would raise energy prices and invest in pollution control.[45] Still, the magnitude of the required investment was disputed. China spent approximately 0.6% of GDP on environmental control and planned to increase this to 0.85%.[†] The World Bank recommended that China invest at least 3.1% of GDP in pollution abatement—as compared with 2.2% in the United States. World Bank economists estimated that these investments would lead to benefits totaling 8.8% of GDP.

Whither China?

In late 1997, the Asian financial crisis highlighted the severity of the issues facing China. Starting with several bank defaults in Thailand, the crisis had spread quickly to Malaysia, Indonesia, the Philippines, and South Korea. Each was forced to close insolvent financial institutions, devalue its currency, and ask the International Monetary Fund for assistance. The Asian crisis was of great concern for two reasons. It revealed weaknesses in the "Asian" development model China had been pursuing. In addition, the large devaluation by China's neighbors threatened its export markets, potentially cutting into export growth just as domestic demand was slowing.

Zhu had recently received his year-end economic projections for 1997. The good news

---

Lower tax burdens are viewed as offsetting these disadvantages on the part of foreign-invested enterprises (FIEs). The scrapping of the tariff exemptions is expected to increase the business costs for the FIEs. The US-China Business Council estimates that the business cost will rise by 28%. "How and Why to Survive Chinese Tax Torture," *The Economist* (1995): 63-64.

[*] If the U.S. figure is correct, then China has the second highest bilateral surplus with the United States (after Japan's $59 billion). If the Chinese figure is correct, China's surplus with the United States would be lower than those of Japan, Canada, Mexico, Germany, and Taiwan.

[†] The Chinese government estimates that higher expenditures are needed, and that it would take at least 1.5% of GDP just to control environmental degradation. *World Resources: A Guide to the Global Environment*, World Resources Institutes, 1994, p. 62.

was that GDP had increased by 8.8%, while inflation had declined to less than 3%. But these figures masked several troubling developments. Foreign investment had grown only 3%, retail sales had slowed, and inventories had piled up.

Although China's growth rate since 1978 was extraordinary, the structural impediments to reform were becoming more severe. It was not difficult to design isolated policies to address SOE restructuring, job creation, relations with the provinces, international trade relations, or the environment. The difficulty arose when the individual policies came into conflict.

Could China continue to muddle through—relying on incremental reform, spontaneous innovation in the provinces, and annual U.S. approval of MFN? Or was it time for a fundamental rethink of China's strategy, perhaps leading to faster and more comprehensive reform?

EXHIBIT 2.1   MAP OF CHINA

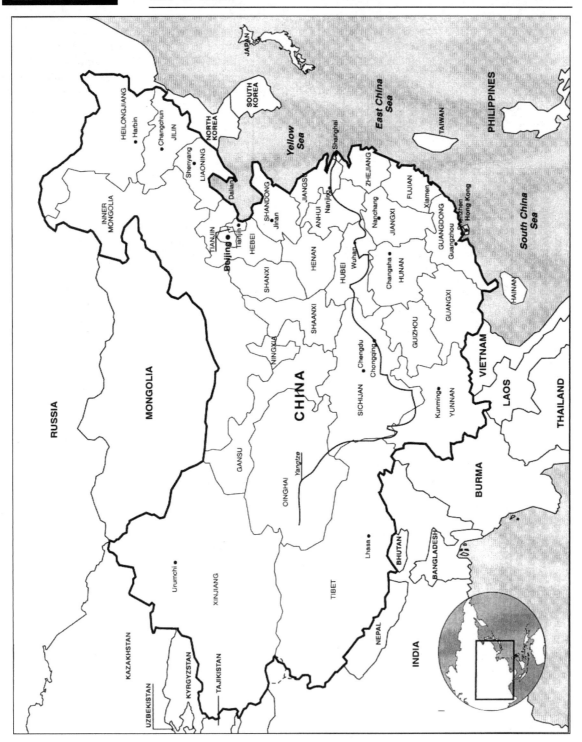

SOURCE: Case writer.

EXHIBIT 2.2 — NATIONAL INCOME ACCOUNTS (BILLIONS OF YUAN AT CURRENT PRICES)

Year	1978	1982	1986	1990	1991	1992	1993	1994	1995	1996
Private Consumption	204.4	320.9	522.9	911.3	1,031.6	1,246.0	1,568.2	2,123.0	2,634.3	3,257.9
Investment	119.0	157.5	419.8	644.4	751.7	963.6	1,499.8	1,859.2	2,278.7	2,686.7
Government Consumption	26.3	43.8	85.2	225.2	283.0	349.2	450.0	598.6	697.3	759.2
Exports	17.2	40.5	79.0	297.0	382.8	468.4	524.2	1,043.3	1,242.7	
Imports	17.9	32.5	77.8	255.2	339.6	444.4	594.0	997.0	1,078.3	
Net Exports										145.9
GDP[a]	349.1	530.2	1,029.1	1,854.8	2,161.8	2,663.8	3,463.4	4,662.2	5,826.1	6,849.8
Real GDP Growth (%)	--	9.0	8.8	8.3	13.5	14.2	13.4	11.2	10.7	9.7
Govt. Consumption as % of GDP	7.5	8.3	8.3	12.1	13.1	13.1	13.0	12.8	12.0	11.6
Gross Savings as % of GDP	36.5	28.2	34.7	37.4	--	37.2	40.3	43.6	41.0	42.9
Inflation (%)	1.9	2.1	8.9	3.1	3.5	6.3	14.6	24.2	16.9	8.3

SOURCE: Adapted from International Financial Statistics, Chinese Statistical Yearbook. --: Data not available.

[a] GDP as reported by the Chinese government includes the value of subsidies paid to agriculture, industry, and the service sector in addition to the factor costs of production.

EXHIBIT 2.3 — GROSS OUTPUT VALUE BY SECTOR AND OWNERSHIP[a] (BILLIONS OF YUAN AT CURRENT PRICES)

Year	1978	1982	1986	1990	1992	1994	1995	1996
Total	563.4	829.4	1,520.7	3,158.6	4,615.0	9,266.0	11,223.4	12,302.3
Agriculture	139.7	248.3	401.3	766.2	908.5	1,575.0	2,034.1	2,342.8
Industry, of which	423.7	581.1	1,119.4	2,392.4	3,706.6	7,690.9	9,189.4	9,959.5
State-owned	328.9	432.6	697.1	1,306.4	1,782.4	2,620.1	3,122.0	2,838
Collective-owned	94.8	144.2	375.1	852.3	1,410.1	3,143.4	3,362.3	3,924
Individual-owned	--	0.3	30.9	129.0	250.7	885.3	1,182.1	1,544
Other	--	3.9	16.3	104.8	263.4	1,042.1	1,523.1	1,653
Agriculture as % of Total	24.8	29.9	26.4	24.3	19.7	17.0	18.1	19.0
SOEs as % of Total Industrial Output	77.6	74.4	62.3	54.6	48.1	34.1	34.0	28.5
COEs as % of Industrial Output[b]	22.4	24.8	33.5	35.6	38.0	40.9	36.6	39.4
COEs as % of Total Agricultural and Industrial Output[b]	16.8	17.4	24.7	27.0	30.6	33.9	30.0	31.9

SOURCE: Adapted from *Chinese Statistical Yearbook*.

[a] These figures exceed the GDP figures because they report Gross Output Value, not value added, by sector. Gross Output Value for a sector is equal to the sum of output value (list price multiplied by quantity produced) for each enterprise in the sector. This methodology leads to double counting of intermediate goods. The government does not provide the data required to calculate value added by sector.

[b] COEs are collectively-owned enterprises. The category includes Township and Village Enterprises, Urban Enterprises, and Cooperative Enterprises.

EXHIBIT 2.4 CONSOLIDATED GOVERNMENT REVENUE AND EXPENDITURES (BILLIONS OF YUAN AT CURRENT PRICES)

Year	1970	1975	1980	1985	1989	1990	1991	1992	1993	1994	1995	1996
Revenue from Enterprises [a]	37.9	40.0	43.5	63.9	64.6	68.2	70.2	68.4	63.1	60.9	75.9	82.2
Industrial and Commercial Taxes	24.2	35.8	51.0	109.7	176.0	185.8	198.1	224.4	319.4	391.4	458.9	527.0
Tariffs	0.7	1.5	3.3	20.5	18.1	15.9	18.7	21.2	25.6	27.2	29.1	30.1
Other	3.3	4.1	18.0	56.8	67.2	81.4	78.7	78.6	67.5	78.6	92.8	135.0
Total Revenues	**66.1**	**81.4**	**115.8**	**250.9**	**325.9**	**351.3**	**365.7**	**392.6**	**475.6**	**558.1**	**656.7**	**774.3**
Construction	39.3	48.2	71.5	112.8	129.2	136.8	142.8	161.3	183.5	239.3	285.5	c
Culture and Education	5.2	10.3	19.9	40.8	66.8	73.8	88.5	97.0	117.8	150.2	175.6	c
National Defense	14.5	14.2	19.4	19.2	25.1	29.0	33.0	37.8	42.6	55.1	63.7	c
Government Administration	3.2	4.2	7.6	17.1	38.6	41.4	41.4	46.3	63.4	847	99.7	c
Subsidies to SOEs				50.7	59.8	57.8	51.0	44.4	41.1	36.6	32.7	c
Other	2.7	5.1	4.4	10.5	22.6	27.3	36.4	31.8	56.9	49.9	57.8	c
Expenditures [b]	**64.9**	**82.0**	**122.8**	**251.1**	**342.1**	**366.1**	**389.5**	**418.6**	**505.3**	**615.8**	**715.0**	**827.4**
Deficit/Surplus	**1.2**	**-0.6**	**-7.0**	**-0.2**	**-16.2**	**-14.8**	**-23.8**	**-26.0**	**-29.7**	**-57.7**	**-58.3**	**-53.1**
Surplus/Deficit as % of GDP			-1.5	0.0	-1.0	-0.8	-1.1	-1.0	-0.9	-1.2	-1.0	-0.8
Central Govt. Revenue as % of Total Rev.	28	12	25	31	25	28	26	25	20	52	50	47
Central Govt. Spending as % of Total Spending	59	50	54	32	26	27	28	28	26	29	28	c

SOURCE: Adapted from *Chinese Statistical Yearbook*.

a Includes profit remissions and income taxes from SOEs.

b Excludes interest payments on government debt. This means that expenses and the deficit are understated. The Chinese government reports only consolidated principal and interest payments.

c Data not available.

EXHIBIT 2.5   BALANCE OF PAYMENTS[a] (MILLIONS OF US DOLLARS)

Year	1978	1980	1982	1984	1986	1988	1990	1991	1992	1993	1994	1995	1996
Merchandise exports		18,188	21,125	23,905	25,756	41,054	51,519	58,919	69,568	75,659	102,561	128,110	151,077
Merchandise imports		-18,294	-16,876	-23,891	-34,896	-46,369	-42,354	-50,176	-64,385	-86,313	-95,271	-110,060	-131,542
Trade balance		**-106**	**4,249**	**14**	**-9,140**	**-5,315**	**9,165**	**8,743**	**5,183**	**-10,654**	**7,290**	**18,050**	**19,535**
Net services		241	488	-46	1,551	1,220	1,451	2,784	-225	-868	302	-6,093	-1,984
Net factor payments		195	451	1,620	176	-126	1,107	914	288	-1,259	-1,019	-11,774	-12,437
Net transfers		570	486	442	379	419	274	831	1,155	1,172	335	1,435	2,130
Current account	c	**900**	**5,674**	**2,030**	**-7,034**	**-3,802**	**11,997**	**13,272**	**6,401**	**-11,609**	**6,908**	**1,618**	**7,243**
Capital account items													
Net FDI		57	386	1,124	1,425	2,344	2,657	3,453	7,156	23,115	31,787	33,849	38,066
Net portfolio flows		c	21	-1,638	1,568	876	-241	235	-57	3,049	3,543	631	1,744
Mon. & bank transactions		-290	-69	-489	2,951	3,913	839	4,344	-7,433	-2,690	2,685	4,035	156
Errors and omissions	c	c	293	-889	-958	-957	-3,205	-6,767	-8,211	-10,096	-9,100	-17,822	-15,504
Overall balance		561	6,305	138	-2,048	2,374	12,047	14,537	-2,060	1,769	30,453	22,469	31,705
Current acct. balance, % of GDP		0.3	2.1	0.7	-2.4	-0.9	3.1	3.3	1.3	-1.9	1.3	0.2	0.9
Avg. exchange rate (yuan/$)	1.68	1.50	1.89	2.32	3.45	3.72	4.78	5.32	5.51	5.76	8.62	8.35	8.31
Real exchange rate (Inflation adjusted, 1978 = 100)[b]	100	96	68	54	39	43	37	32	32	34	28	31	33
Foreign currency and gold reserves	c	3,116	11,840	17,801	11,994	19,135	30,209	44,308	21,230	22,999	53,560	76,037	107,676
Total foreign debt	c	4,504	c	c	c	42,439	55,301	60,259	72,428	85,928	100,457	118,090	c
Inflation (CPI, %)	1.9	2.6	2.1	11.6	8.9	16.3	3.1	3.5	6.3	14.6	24.2	16.9	8.3
Credit growth (%)	11.2	18.4	10.4	31.6	34.1	18.9	23.3	20.0	22.3	14.6	23.8	22.8	c

SOURCE: Adapted from *Balance of Payments Statistics Yearbook* and *International Finance Statistics Yearbook*. 1980 information from World Bank, *World Tables*, 1991, as reported in *China: The Great Awakening*, Harvard Case Study, number 9-794-019.

a The trade figures in this table differ from those which follow because of differences in the way China and the IMF account for goods transhipped through Hong Kong. This table is based on IMF data. The tables that follow are based on Chinese government data.

b Measured against the U.S. dollar. A decline in the index indicates a *depreciation* of the yuan.

c Data not available.

EXHIBIT 2.6   EXPORTS BY DESTINATION

Exports (millions of US dollars)

	1978	1980	1985	1990	1992	1994	1996
Total	9,955	18,099	27,327	62,091	84,940	121,047	151,197
Hong Kong	2,533	4,354	7,148	27,163	37,511	32,365	32,904
Japan	1,719	4,032	6,091	9,210	11,699	21,490	30,888
Taiwan	a	a	a	320	697	2,242	2,804
Other Asia	479	1,734	1,493	4,076	6,740	11,462	16,959
United States	271	983	2,336	5,314	8,599	21,421	26,731
Germany	330	771	746	2,062	2,447	4,762	5,852
Other EU	843	1,543	1,537	4,213	5,557	10,656	14,016
Other	3,780	4,682	7,976	9,733	11,690	16,649	21,043

Exports (as percent of total)

	1978	1980	1985	1990	1992	1994	1996
Hong Kong	25.4	24.1	26.2	43.7	44.2	26.7	21.8
Japan	17.3	22.3	22.3	14.8	13.8	17.8	20.4
Taiwan	a	a	a	0.5	0.8	1.9	1.9
Other Asia	4.8	9.6	5.5	6.6	7.9	9.5	11.2
United States	2.7	5.4	8.5	8.6	10.1	17.7	17.7
Germany	3.3	4.3	2.7	3.3	2.9	3.9	3.9
Other EU	8.5	8.5	5.6	6.8	6.5	8.8	9.2
Other	38	25.8	29.2	15.7	13.8	13.8	13.9

SOURCE: Adapted from *Direction of Trade Statistics Yearbook.*

a Data not available.

EXHIBIT 2.7   TRADE BALANCE WITH SELECTED COUNTRIES[a] (MILLION OF US DOLLARS)

	1978	1980	1985	1990	1992	1994	1996
Total	-1,140	-1,900	-1,490	8,740	4,350	5,400	12,200
Hong Kong	2,458	3,784	2,386	12,598	16,972	22,877	25,065
Japan	-1,386	-1,137	-9,087	1,554	-1,987	-4,829	1,698
Taiwan	b	b	b	-1,934	-5,193	-11,842	-13,382
Other Asia	93	808	-600	1,173	200	-1,340	-4,108
United States	-450	-2,847	-2,863	-1,277	-304	7,444	10,552
Germany	-700	-562	-1,701	-918	-1,576	-2,374	-1,473
Other EU	-97	132	-2,167	-1,954	-1,283	-812	1,458

SOURCE: Adapted from *Direction of Trade Statistics Yearbook.*

a Chinese trade statistics vary from some of its trading partners' particularly the industrial countries. See the text for a short discussion of the disagreement with the United States on this issue.

b Data not available.

| EXHIBIT 2.8 | UTILIZATION OF FOREIGN CAPITAL[a] (BILLIONS OF US DOLLARS) |

	1979–1983	1984	1985	1986	1987	1988	1989	1990	1991	1992	1993	1994	1995	1996
Foreign loans	11.8	1.3	2.7	5.0	5.8	6.5	6.3	6.5	6.9	7.9	11.2	9.3	10.3	12.6
Foreign direct investment	1.9	1.6	1.7	2.0	2.3	3.2	3.4	3.5	4.4	11.0	27.5	33.8	37.5	41.7
Other foreign investments	0.9	0.2	0.3	0.4	0.3	0.6	0.4	0.3	0.3	0.3	0.3	0.2	0.3	0.4
Total	14.5	3.1	4.7	7.3	8.4	10.3	10.1	10.3	11.6	19.2	39.0	44.3	48.1	54.7

SOURCE: Adapted from *Chinese Statistical Yearbook.*

a This table reports total *inbound* FDI. The balance of payments [see **Exhibit 2.5**] reports *net* FDI.

EXHIBIT 2.9A	EXPORTS BY ENTERPRISES WITH FOREIGN CAPITAL (%)	
Year	**Exports**	**Share in total exports**
1985	0.3	1.1
1986	0.6	1.9
1987	1.2	3.1
1988	2.5	5.2
1989	4.9	9.4
1990	7.8	12.6
1991	12.0	16.8
1992	17.4	20.4
1993	25.2	25.8
1994	34.7	28.7
1995	46.9	31.5
1996 (first six months)	26.2	40.8

SOURCE: Adapted from China, SSB; China, General Administration of Customs, China Customs Statistics, as reported in Barry Naughton, "China's Emergence and Prospects as a Trading Nation," *Brookings Papers on Economic Activity* 2: 1996. p. 299.

EXHIBIT 2.9B	PRINCIPAL IMPORTS AND EXPORTS FOR CHINA (1996)		
Principal Exports	**$ billion**	**Principal Imports**	**$ billion**
Clothing and Textiles	37.1	Machinery and Elect Equip.	54.8
Machinery and Elect. Equip	35.3	Chemicals	18.1
Foodstuffs	11.6	Textiles	12.0
Chemicals	8.9	Iron and Steel	7.2
Footwear	7.1	Mineral Fuels	6.9
Mineral Fuels	5.9		

SOURCE: Adapted from *Economist Intelligence Unit: Country Report: China*, 3rd Quarter 1997.

EXHIBIT 2.10	DECENTRALIZATION OF DECISION-MAKING IN STATE-OWNED FIRMS									
	1980	**1981**	**1982**	**1983**	**1984**	**1985**	**1986**	**1987**	**1988**	**1989**
Marginal retention rate (%)[a]	11	12	11	14	17	17	19	23	26	27
Autonomy in production decisions (% firms)	7	8	10	14	25	35	40	53	64	67
Management responsibility system (% firms)	0	0	0	1	2	4	8	42	83	88
New management appointed after 1980 (% firms)	9	9	15	25	40	40	61	75	85	94

SOURCE: China The World Bank, *China 2020: Development Challenges in the Next Century*, 1992.

a Portion of profits that could be retained if profits exceeded the base level.

Note: Based on a 1991 retrospective sample survey of state enterprises.

EXHIBIT 2.11	POPULATION			
	Total Population (millions)	**Urban Population as % of Total**	**Rural Population as % of Total**	**Population Growth Rate (%)**
1975	924.2	17.3	82.7	1.57
1980	987.0	19.4	80.6	1.19
1986	1,075.0	24.5	75.5	1.55
1988	1,110.2	25.8	74.2	1.58
1990	1,143.3	26.4	73.6	1.44
1991	1,158.2	26.4	73.6	1.30
1992	1,171.7	27.6	72.4	1.16
1993	1,185.1	28.1	71.9	1.15
1994	1,198.5	28.6	71.4	1.12
1995	1,211.2	29.0	71.0	1.05
2000[a]	1,255.1	[b]	[b]	0.93
2010[a]	1,348.0	[b]	[b]	0.70
2020[a]	1,434.3	[b]	[b]	0.60
2030[a]	1,500.6	[b]	[b]	0.39

SOURCE: Adapted from *Chinese Statistical Yearbook*. World Bank, *World Population Projections*.

a Projections

b Data not available.

EXHIBIT 2.12	INDICATORS OF ECONOMIC DEVELOPMENT								
Country	Population in 1995 (millions)	Population Density (people/km²)	GNP per Capita ($, 1995)	Average GDP Growth (1990-95)	External Debt as % of GDP (1995)	Trade as % of GDP	Labor Force in Agriculture (%, 1990)	Population Below $1/day (%, 1985 prices)	Average Inflation (%, 1990-95)
Asia									
China	1,200.2	125	620	12.8	17.2	40	74	29.4	9.3
India	929.4	282	340	4.6	28.2	27	64	52.5	9.8
Indonesia	193.3	101	980	7.6	56.9	53	57	14.5	8.8
Korea	44.9	454	9,700	7.2	a	67	18	a	6.7
Malaysia	20.1	61	3,890	8.7	42.6	194	27	5.6	3.3
Philippines	68.6	229	1,050	2.3	51.5	80	45	27.5	9.8
Thailand	58.2	113	2,740	8.4	34.9	90	64	0.1	5.0
Vietnam	73.5	221	240	8.3	130.2	83	72	a	88.3
Other Developing									
Chile	14.2	19	4,160	7.3	43.4	54	19	15.0	17.9
Poland	38.6	123	2,790	2.4	36.1	53	27	6.8	91.8
Russia	148.2	9	2,240	-9.8	37.6	44	14	1.1	148.9
South Africa	41.5	35	3,160	0.6	a	44	14	23.7	13.9
Developed									
Canada	29.6	3	19,380	1.8		71	3	a	2.9
Japan	125.2	331	39,640	1.0		17	7	a	1.4
Germany	81.9	230	27,510	a		46	4	a	a
United Kingdom	58.5	238	18,700	1.4		57	2	a	5.1
United States	263.1	28	26,980	2.6		24	3	a	3.2

SOURCE: Adapted from *World Development Indicators*, 1997.

a Data not available or not reported.

EXHIBIT 2.13 INDICATORS OF SOCIAL DEVELOPMENT

Country	Life Expectancy at Birth (years)	Fertility Rate (1995)[a]	Adult Illiteracy Rate (% males)	Adult Illiteracy Rate (% females)	Labor Force (millions, 1995)	Annual Deforestation[b] (1,000 km²)	Average Annual Deforestation[b] (%, 1980-90)	Population with Safe Access to Water (%)	Malnutrition (% under age 5)
Asia									
China	69	1.9	10	27	709	8.8	0.7	83	17
India	62	3.2	35	62	398	3.4	.6	63	63
Indonesia	64	2.7	10	22	89	12.1	1.1	63	39
Korea	72	1.8	1	c	22	0.1	0.1	89	c
Malaysia	71	3.4	11	22	8	4.0	2.1	90	23
Philippines	66	3.7	5	6	28	3.2	3.4	84	30
Thailand	69	1.8	4	8	34	5.2	3.5	81	13
Vietnam	68	3.1	4	9	37	1.4	1.5	38	45
Other Developing									
Chile	72	2.3	5	5	6	-0.1	-0.1	96	1
Poland	70	1.6	c		19	-0.1	-0.1	c	c
Russia	65	1.4	c		77	15.5	0.2	c	c
South Africa	64	3.9	18	18	16	-0.4	-0.8	c	c
Developed									
Canada	78	1.7	c	c	15	-47.1	-1.1	100	c
Japan	80	1.5	c	c	66	0	0	c	3
Germany	76	1.2	c	c	40	-0.5	-0.4	c	c
United Kingdom	77	1.7	c	c	29	-0.2	-1.1	c	c
United States	77	2.1	c	c	133	3.2	0.1	90	c

SOURCE: Adapted from *World Development Indicators*, 1997.

a Fertility rate is the number of children that would be born to a woman if she were to live to the end of her childbearing years.

b Annual deforestation refers to the permanent conversion of natural forest area to other uses as a percentage of forested land. Includes shifting cultivation, permanent agriculture, ranching, or infrastructure development. These areas do not include areas logged but intended for regeneration or areas degraded by human or natural disasters. Negative numbers indicate an increase in forest area.

c Data not available or not reported.

EXHIBIT 2.14A	INCOME INEQUALITY: NET INCOME OF RURAL HOUSEHOLDS IN SELECTED PROVINCES (YUAN/CAPITA, CURRENT PRICES)

| | GDP or National Income per Capita[a] | | | Index (all China = 100) | | |
Province	1978	1985	1995	1978	1985	1995
All China Total	133.57	397.6	1,577.7	100	100	100
Selected High Income Provinces						
Beijing	224.8	775.1	3,223.7	168.3	195.0	204.3
Shanghai	290.0	805.9	4,245.6	217.1	202.7	269.1
Jiangsu	152.1	492.6	2,456.9	113.9	123.9	155.7
Zhejiang	[b]	548.6	2,966.2	[b]	138.0	188.0
Guangdong	182.3	495.3	2,699.2	136.5	124.6	171.1
Selected Low Income Provinces						
Yunnan	123.9	338.3	1,011.0	92.8	85.1	64.1
Shaanxi	133	295.3	962.8	99.6	74.3	61.0
Gansu	98.4	255.2	880.3	73.7	64.2	55.8
Qinghai	[b]	343.0	1,029.8	[b]	86.3	65.3
Ningxia	115.9	321.2	998.7	86.8	80.8	63.3
Standard Deviation from Index— Calculated using all 30 Provinces				35.2	32.2	49.3

SOURCE: Adapted from *Chinese Statistical Yearbook*.

a 1978 column reports national income per capita; 1985 and 1995 report GDP per capita.

b Data not available.

EXHIBIT 2.14B	INCOME INEQUALITY: RURAL AND URBAN GDP PER HEAD (YUAN, CURRENT PRICES)

	1978	1980	1985	1990	1992	1994	1995	1996
Rural household income	133.6	191.3	397.6	686.3	784.0	1,221.0	1,577.7	1,926.1
Urban household income	316.0	439.4	685.3	1,387.3	1,826.1	3,179.2	3,892.9	4,377.2
Rural income as % of urban income	42.3	43.5	58.0	49.5	42.9	38.4	40.5	44.0

SOURCE: Adapted from *Chinese Statistical Yearbook*.

ENDNOTES

1   Sachs and Woo, 1977, "Understanding China's Economic Performance," NBER working paper 5935.

2   "How Big Is Asia?" *The Economist*, February 7, 1998, page 72, and *International Financial Statistics Yearbook*.

3   *China 2020: Development Challenges in the New Century*, The World Bank, 1997, p. *ix*.

4   Eckstein, A., 1981, *China's Economic Revolution* (Cambridge: Cambridge University Press).

5   Fairbank, John King, 1987, *The Great Chinese Revolution, 1800-1985* (New York: Harper & Row).

6   Lieberthal, Kenneth, 1995, *Governing China* (New York: W.W. Norton and Company).

7   Lieberthal, p. 45.

8   Lieberthal, p. 102.

9   Quoted from John Bryan Starr, 1997, *Understanding China* (New York: Hill and Wang), p. 79.

10   *Ibid.*, p. 19.

11   Lieberthal, p. 150.

12   Grain yields had grown at a 1.8% annual rate between 1952 and 1978. Population had grown at a 2.0% rate. Bruce L. Reynolds, ed., 1998, *Chinese Economic Policy* (New York: Paragon House), p. 214.

13   John Bryan Starr, 1997, *Understanding China: A Guide to China's Economy, History, and Political Structure* (New York: Hill and Wang).

14   Procurement prices for quota-production increased an average of 17%. Above-quota production could be sold for 30%-50% more than the new quota prices. J.Y. Lin, "Rural Reforms and Agricultural Growth in China," *American Economic Review* 82(1): 34-51.

15   Michael Ying-Mao Kau and Susan H. Marsh, eds., 1993, *China in the Era of Deng Xiaoping: A Decade of Reform* (Armonk: M.E. Sharpe, Inc.), p. 107.

16   World Bank, 1997, *China 2020: Development Challenges in the New Century*

17   Kau and Marsh, p 106.

18   *The Economist*, China Survey, November 28, 1992, p. 12.

19   *China Statistical Yearbook*, 1997.

20   Naughton, 1996, "China's Emergence as a Trading Nation," Brookings Papers on Economic Activity, p. 273-344.

21   Naughton, p. 297.

22   Naughton, 1996, p. 298.

23   Sachs and Woo, 1997, p. 27.

24   Kau and Marsh, p. 108.

25   *China 2020: Development Challenges in the New Century*, The World Bank, 1997, Tables 19-22.

26   *Ibid.*

27   World Bank, 1995 #1697, pp. 61-63.

28   The tax figures are from State Statistical Bureau. *Zhongguo tongji nianjian 1997 [China Statistical Yearbook 1997]*. Beijing: Zhongguo tongji chubanshe, 1997.

29   Yasheng Huang, 1995 #1128.

30   Walter Tseng, et alia, *Economic Reform in China: A New Phase* (Washington, D.C.: The International Monetary Fund, 1994), pp. 5-6.

31   "Emerging Market Indicators." *The Economist* (1997): 108.

32   *China 2020: Development Challenges in the New Century*, World Bank, 1997, p. 3.

33   Infant mortality is measured as deaths before age five. "China's Growth Path to the 21st Century: Recommendations from the World Bank." *Transition* 8.5 (1997): 5-7.

34   *People's Daily, Overseas Edition*, March 11, 1996. Quoted from Sachs and Woo, 1997.

35   See "China and the Chaebol." *The Economist*, 1997: 97-98.

36   Lieberthal, p. 245.

37   *The Economist*, March 8, 1997, "Survey China: The Death of Gradualism," p. S16.

38   See *The Chinese Economy: Fighting Inflation, Deepening Reforms* (Washington, DC: The World Bank, 1996) for a detailed discussion.

39   Country Profile: China, *Economist Intelligence Unit*, 1996-1997, page 30.

40   Alwyn Young, "The Razor's Edge: Distortions and Incremental Reform in the People's Republic of China," University of Chicago working paper.

41   Office of the United States Trade Representative, "A Summary of the Final Act of the Uruguay Round,", http://www.wto.org/wto/ursum_wpf.html.

42   Feenstra, R., W. Hai, W. Woo, J. Sachs, and S. Yao, "The U.S.-China Bilateral Trade Balance: Its Size and Determinants." Research presented at the UNDP-HIID Conference on China's integration with the World Economy.

43   *Clear Water, Blue Skies*, The World Bank, 1997.

44   *Clear Water, Blue Skies*, The World Bank, 1997, page 12.

45   *Clear Water, Blue Skies*, The World Bank, 1997, page 9.

Import Substitution to Washington Consensus

India is the world's largest democracy and it is the second most populous country.

This case introduces this vast country and explores its economic strategy during two distinct eras—the era of import substitution (1947–1991) and the liberalization era (post-1991).

The first sections describe the cultural and political diversity of India—multiple languages, ethnic groups, religions, and castes. Understanding this diversity is important, as it relates directly to developmental problems and political stability.

The next section describes India's development strategy—import substitution—between independence and 1991. This section provides students with a good opportunity to see, in the extreme, the problems with such a strategy as well as the reasons for its ultimate failure.

Imposition of an IMF bailout in 1991, combined with a relatively stable government mandate for the Congress Party, gave rise to the gradual implementation of policies described as the "Washington Consensus." The third section describes the political issues of implementation as well as the institutional problems associated with this gradual liberalization. It highlights tremendous success in Bangalore, where service outsourcing and information technology have become India's competitive advantage. But it also dwells on India's disastrous budget deficit and political problems with Pakistan.

The case poses several questions: Is India's choice of strategies adequate? That is, will it be politically feasible and will it make India grow at rates close to China's growth rates? Should the government be doing things differently, or does political instability mandate caution? And is this a good place to invest? Can India hope to win foreign direct investment in competition with the likes of Singapore, China, South Africa, Mexico, and Brazil?

[handwritten notes at top:]
problems 1) corruption
2) land disputes w/ Kashmire
3) poor infrastructure
4) nuclear program
36% of the world's poor live in India

CASE STUDY   INDIA ON THE MOVE

RICHARD H. K. VIETOR

EMILY J. THOMPSON

This Budget is of an "India that is on the move." An India that now rapidly advances to prosperity. It is about an India that banishes poverty and builds on its great resource base, the strength of its human capital, and the immense reservoir of its knowledge.
—Opening Statement, 2003–2004 Budget

Introduction

In late February of 2003, Jaswant Singh, India's newly appointed finance minister, looked carefully over the latest draft of the 2003–2004 Union Budget. A member of the Bharatiya Janata Party (BJP), Singh faced the difficult task of crafting a budget that would ensure his party's political control while achieving the goals set forth in the recently approved 10th Five-Year Plan. Although the government faced a fiscal deficit as high as 5.6%, any drastic cuts in expenditure could cost his party the upcoming 2004 general election. More importantly, the upcoming budget would serve as the government's first major statement concerning whether it planned to back up the strategic vision set forth in the 10th Plan.

Chaired by Prime Minister Vajpayee, the Planning Commission had set forth India's vision statement for its economic and social *[handwritten: India's goals]* growth for 2002–2007 [see **Exhibit 3.10b**]. Among the highlights, the plan targeted increasing India's growth rate of 5.4% (9th Plan) to 8%. The growth rate would need to continue to increase to 9.3% during the 11th Plan in order to create 100 million new jobs for India's growing population. The country's per capita income (US$453 in 2002), according to the plan, would double by 2012. Agriculture would remain a significant engine of growth, still employing more than half the population. To address environmental concerns while meeting the needs of the growing population, however,

agricultural productivity would have to increase. More efficient contract farming would be encouraged. Futures trading in all commodities would be allowed. Finally, for India's states to take advantage of comparative advantage in their agricultural sectors, interstate barriers to trade and commerce would be removed.

India's official unemployment in 2002 was 9%, or roughly 35 million people.[1] But because more than 90% of India's workforce worked in the "unorganized sector," exact unemployment figures were difficult to calculate. Some analysts estimated it to be higher than 20%.[2] In order to provide jobs, India would have to expand its industrial and services sectors. The government planned to raise private-sector investment by increasing the inflow of foreign direct investment to US$7.5 billion and speeding up "disinvestment"—privatization of the public sector—setting a goal of 780 billion rupees (Rs) by 2007.

In addition to raising money through privatization receipts, the plan recommended more efficient fiscal management. The finance minister's advisor, Vijay Kelkar, had made similar recommendations earlier that same year: downsize the government, widen the tax base, remove many of the tax exemptions and incentives, and cut subsidies.

India's level of human development was a key focus of the 10th Plan. As the economy developed, the plan envisaged a reduction in the poverty ratio from 26% to 21% of the population, potable drinking water in all villages, and a cleanup of all major polluted rivers by the end of the 10th Plan. Reducing India's population growth rate and increasing the country's literacy rate to 75% would play key roles in achieving a higher standard of living [see **Exhibits 3.2a** and **3.2b**].

As it had been throughout much of its history, India in 2003 remained embroiled in social, political, and religious conflicts. Singh had to consider carefully the political ramifications of making the necessary changes recommended by the Planning Commission and Kelkar's committee. The risk would be

---

worthwhile if the extensive goals of the 10th Plan were reached. But, could they be attained in only 5 to 10 years? What measures would the new budget have to take to ensure the 10th Plan became a reality, rather than mere words on paper?

Country Background

At 3.3 million square miles, India is slightly bigger than one third of the United States and bordered by Pakistan, China, Nepal, Bhutan, Myanmar, and Bangladesh [see **Exhibit 3.1**]. The Indian subcontinent is a fertile and mineral-rich region. In addition to iron ore, bauxite, and natural gas, India has the fourth-largest coal reserve in the world. While India has some oil reserves, it remains highly dependent upon imported petroleum. Seven major ports along India's 7,000 kilometers of coastline serve the Indian Ocean trade routes.

Demography

Growing at 1.5%, India's population reached 1.05 billion in 2002 and was expected to surpass China's population by 2018.[3] The Indian government, under Indira Gandhi, had made a brief effort to slow population growth through forced sterilization in the early 1970s. The highly unpopular program, however, was soon abandoned. The ratio of women to men in 2002 was 933 to 1,000 as a result of female infanticide, feticide, and neglect.[4] Life expectancy had increased to 62 in 2002 from 32 in 1951.[5] The country's literacy rate was 65% in 2001 but varied greatly by region and gender. For example, the state of Kerala had a 90% literacy rate, while the state of Bihar was lower than 50% [see **Exhibit 3.5**]. While 76% of India's males were literate, only 54% of its females could read.

Even though an urbanization trend was doubtlessly under way, India's population remained highly dependent upon agriculture; 72% of its population resided in rural regions in 2001.[6] Poor weather could severely affect a quarter of India's gross domestic product (GDP). For example, the lack of monsoons in 2002 threatened India's agricultural output and thus its economic growth. Using the $1 a day poverty line, the World Bank estimated that 36% of the world's poor lived in India in 2001. A total of 433 million people, or 44% of India's population, were poor. Fifty percent of the country's poor were concentrated within the states of Uttar Pradesh, Bihar, and Madhya Pradesh.[7]

An extremely diverse country with more than 650 dialects and numerous religions, India had 18 official languages. Hindi was the most prevalent language and was spoken by roughly 30% of the population. English, while only spoken by 2% of the population and not considered an official language, remained the dominant language of government and business.[8] Hindu was the largest religious group in 2002 (81.3%), followed by Muslim (12%), Christian (2.3%), Sikh (1.9%), and various others (2.5%).[9] A polytheistic religion, Hindus are born into a specific "caste" of a structured hierarchy. The highest caste is the Brahmin (priest), followed by the Kshatria (warrior), Vaishya (merchant), and Sudra (peasant) castes. Each caste is broken into sub castes with varying restrictions placed on both social and professional activities. The "untouchable" underclass lies at the bottom of the hierarchy and is traditionally destined to a life of poverty and menial work.

By the end of the 20th century, caste had become less of an issue in urban society. Discrimination, however, continued. Partly to gain political support and partly to improve conditions for "scheduled castes" and minorities, the Indian government instituted the world's first affirmative action program of "reservations" in its constitution. Similar to quotas, reservations required that a certain number of positions in government and educational institutions be made available for members of the underclass.

History

India's history is rich in tales of invasions by empires ranging from Alexander the Great to the Moghuls. Until the British arrived in the nineteenth century, the Indian subcontinent was a fragmented land of feudal kingdoms. British influence first came to India in 1600 with the establishment of the East India Company. The British later abolished the East India Company after a bloody mutiny. India was made a crown colony with the India Act of 1858. Under the leadership of a viceroy, the British established the Indian Civil Service to help administer the colony but gave little authority to the Indians.

Although most of its efforts were self-serving, Britain did provide some benefits to the region. The British instituted a legal and educational system based on English standards. They also united the fragmented region by teaching a common language (English) and building a network of railroads and highways. Britain's arrogant exploitation and governance without representation of the Indian people, however, angered the populace. The father of independent India, Mahatma Gandhi, led a tireless campaign of civil disobedience against British rule. Under Gandhi's leadership, the Indians promoted the ideals of "swadeshi," or self-sufficiency, and boycotted British goods and services. After more than 25 years of pressure by Gandhi's movement, Britain granted India full independence in 1947.

Beginning in the 1930s, bitter disputes developed between the Muslim League and the largely Hindu Indian National Congress. Upon its independence, India was partitioned into two states: the secular, democratic India and the Islamic East and West Pakistan. Believing in one unified, secular country, Gandhi declared, "Even if the whole of India, ranged on one side, were to declare that Hindu-Muslim unity is impossible, I will declare that it is perfectly possible."[10] Gandhi's protests, however, fell on deaf ears. Ten to fifteen million Hindu and Muslim refugees moved either to or from India amidst extreme violence that eventually claimed more than 600,000 lives.[11] Agreeing that Jawaharal Nehru should be elected India's first prime minister, Gandhi accepted no official role in government. He continued to focus on easing tensions in the newly partitioned regions. In January of 1948, Gandhi was assassinated by a Hindu extremist.

Troubles with Pakistan

Shortly after the partitioning, the Hindu ruler of Jammu-Kashmir signed his state over to India. Pakistan believed that because the region was predominantly Muslim, it should be a part of Pakistan. India, however, argued that it had a legal right to Kashmir. The countries fought two major wars over the region. The United Nations stepped in after the first war in 1948 and established a "line of control" that gave Pakistan control over the northern part of the region. India later refused the UN's resolution to allow Kashmiri self-determination. India believed that if it permitted Kashmir to secede, "balkanization" of its highly fragmented country would result. A second major war over the

region was fought in 1965 and ended in another stalemate.

After Pakistan accused India of supporting Bengali separatists in East Pakistan, India and Pakistan entered a third war in 1971 that resulted in the sovereign state of Bangladesh. India tested its first nuclear device in 1974. Pakistan immediately followed suit with its own nuclear program. A bitter arms race ensued. India continued to accuse Pakistan of funding the Muslim militants in Kashmir. Pakistan, in turn, denied the accusations and declared that it only "morally" supported the cause of the Kashmiri separatists. The arms race culminated in the detonation of nuclear devices by both countries in 1998. In 2002, a U.S. defense agency estimated that between 8 million and 12 million people would die instantly if a nuclear war took place on the subcontinent.[12]

Domestic Issues

In addition to foreign relations difficulties, domestic strife was a common occurrence in India. For example, two of India's prime ministers, Indira Gandhi and her son Rajiv (daughter and grandson of Nehru), became the most famous victims of such tensions. In 1984, Indira Gandhi attempted to crush a secessionist movement in the state of Punjab. Troops were sent in to break up a militant group housed in the Sikh "Golden Temple." The troops not only killed the Sikh terrorists but also greatly damaged the sacred shrine. In November of the same year, Indira Gandhi's own Sikh bodyguards assassinated her to avenge her regime's assault on their religion

Regional violence continued after Gandhi's death. Indira's son, Rajiv Gandhi, became prime minister in 1984. After violence broke out in Sri Lanka between the Tamil separatists and the Sinhalese government, Gandhi sent in Indian peacekeeping troops to put an end to the dispute. The situation, however, went unresolved. After losing his reelection in 1989, Gandhi began a new campaign for re-election. Resenting the Indian government's earlier interference under Gandhi and wanting to make sure it could not happen again, a Tamil suicide bomber assassinated Gandhi at a 1991 election rally.

Government Structure

Less than three years after independence, India declared itself a republic. A constitution established India as a secular, parliamentary democracy modeled after the British system. Run by a large central bureaucracy, India was divided into 28 states and seven union territories. Executive, judicial, and legislative branches governed India at both the central and state levels. The states had the exclusive right to directly tax agricultural income and land and to regulate property ownership. Given that agriculture made up much of India's GDP, the central government was denied a large source of tax revenue.

The president and the Cabinet of Ministers represented the executive branch. Elected through an electoral college system for a five-year term, the president had no constitutional powers. The Raiya Sabha (Council of States) and the Lok Sabha (House of the People) served as a bicameral parliament. The Rayia Sabha was made up of no more than 250 members and included 12 members nominated by the president. The Lok Sabha consisted of 530 directly elected members from the states, 13 members from the union territories, and 2 members nominated by the president. The president appointed whoever had the majority support of the Lok Sabha as prime minister. The prime minister only remained in office for as long as he maintained majority support. Independent of all other branches, the judiciary interpreted the constitution and was represented by the Supreme Court at the central level and the High Courts at the state level.

Politics

Led by the Nehru-Gandhi dynasty, the Congress Party had uninterrupted control of the government for 33 of the 44 years following independence. The Party's power, however, began to weaken after scandals were revealed. The first outrage involved Indira Gandhi's declaring a state of emergency in 1975 and imprisoning her opponents. A second scandal linked her son Rajiv to corrupt activities involving kickbacks from foreign investors.

After Rajiv Gandhi's assassination in 1991, the Congress Party lacked a prominent leader. The aged P. V. Narasimha Rao led the Congress Party from 1991–1996 and was responsible for much of India's free market reforms in the early to mid-1990s. After the Congress Party's defeat in 1996, Sonia Gandhi, the Italian-born widow of Rajiv, entered the political arena as the new leader of the Congress Party. The Congress Party had drawn its support in the past by remaining in the center on issues. This neutral stance, however, eventually hurt its image. Sonia Gandhi's foreign origin also limited her popularity among several groups. Jairam Ramesh, the advisor to the Congress Party, explained, "The more educated and urban the crowd, the greater is the salience of the foreign factor. The less educated care less about her foreign birth. It is the educated elite who are more against her on the grounds that they figure we should be able to find at least one good candidate out of our one billion."[13]

As the Congress Party's power waned, the Indian electorate fractured into regional and caste groups. With more than eight national and two dozen regional parties, coalition governments became a norm in India [see **Exhibit 3.14**]. Staying in power for any significant amount of time proved difficult for many coalition members. Ramesh explained, "Indians vote out governments; they don't vote in governments. They don't care about who you are, they just care about voting whoever is in power out."[14] The BJP first appeared as a major party in 1991 when it won control of four states. The BJP served as the political wing of the traditionally Hindu religious group Rashtriya Swayamsevak Sangh (RSS), which was criticized for its fundamentalism. Its most famous members included the prime minister and deputy prime minister in 2003 and the convicted assassin of Mahatma Gandhi.

To gain majority control of the government, the BJP had to join 25 other parties to form the coalition of the National Democratic Alliance. Although the sheer number of disparate interests moderated the extremist elements of the BJP somewhat, efforts to reform the government amidst constant disorder proved difficult. In one account, "Opposition members sabotaged proceedings by crowding round the speaker's chair and shouting slogans until an adjournment was granted for the day." In 2002, *The Financial Times* estimated that almost half of Parliament's days in session were forced to adjourn for reasons of parliamentary rowdiness.[15]

Economic History

Import Substitution

[handwritten: Structuralist (Lenin)]

[handwritten margin note: barriers toward imports — force themselves to build industries]

Impressed by the Soviet Union's centrally planned industrialization of an agrarian, fragmented land, Nehru dreamed of building India into a similarly industrialized, socialist state. The government issued the Industrial Policy Resolution (IPR) in 1948 to give the government exclusive authority over infrastructure operations such as railroads, telecommunications, and the post.[16] To determine India's economic objectives, Nehru chaired and established the first Planning Commission in 1951. Accused by some of suffering from the "East India Syndrome," India's nationalist leaders had a deeply rooted fear of entering into the servile relationships created by a dependency on foreign capital. The first Five-Year Plan, therefore, focused upon remaining independent through the promotion of Gandhi's ideals of *swadeshi*.

Combining Nehru's industrialization dreams with Gandhi's rural ideology, India would strengthen its agricultural and power sectors while increasing investment from 5% to 7% of the national income. As 72% of the country was employed in agriculture, the plan allocated 45% of its resources to the agricultural sector while industry received less than 5%.[17] By the end of the first five years, India had increased its agricultural production level and raised its GDP by 3.6% [see **Exhibit 3.10a**].

India's second Five-Year (1956–61) Plan sought "to rebuild rural India, to lay the foundations of industrial progress, and to secure to the greatest extent feasible, opportunities for weaker and under-privileged sections of our people and the balanced development of all parts of the country."[18] After a foreign exchange crisis in 1957, the government sought to limit outflow of foreign currency and to implement a strategy of import substitution, replacing imports with domestic production. India would continue to model itself after the seemingly successful Soviet Union by further industrializing while remaining isolated from foreign investment and trade. In theory, by creating a wall of protective measures, imports would be made uncompetitive, and India's domestic industry would be given the opportunity to flourish.

"Permit Raj"

[handwritten: licensing from fed gove — publicly owned]

To encourage India's self-sufficiency with respect to all products including raw materials, capital, and consumer goods, the government instituted a number of controls in the form of licensing and highly protective trade and investment restrictions. Nicknamed the "Permit Raj," the colossal Indian bureaucracy created a complex system of licensing that fostered both inefficiency and corruption. Former Finance Minister Manmohan Singh explained,

> It [the Permit Raj] was inevitable, because in an economy where resources are scarce [and] demands are too many, you need rationing, you need controls, and therefore you need permit license rights. In the initial stages, these controls were introduced in the name of introducing greater rationality into the allocation process. But after a period of time, they became instruments of corruption. They became instruments of delay. They became instruments of uncertainty, and the economy simply could not get a clear sense of direction.[19]

Special permission in the form of licenses had to be obtained through a complicated set of procedures, usually involving several ministries. If they chose to follow the rules, private-sector firms faced substantial delays and barriers to entry in the form of bureaucratic procedures. To import an item, a company had to prove an item essential and impossible to manufacture in India within "a reasonable time period."[20] In some cases, importing a restricted item could take up to four years and involve negotiating 16 separate procedures. Severely limiting their competitiveness, the tight import policy often forced Indian companies to buy poorer-quality and more expensive domestic goods.

A combination of high tariffs and quantitative restrictions (quotas) were placed on all goods coming into the country. Almost 60% of tariffs were subject to rates in the range of 110%–140%.[21] The restrictive quotas, in particular, placed serious limitations on private-sector companies in terms of the technology made available for running their businesses. For example, Ambassador, India's largest car manufacturer, inefficiently manufactured cars of the same design for 50 years. Additionally, the government placed price and distribution controls on many commodities including coal, steel, sugar, and light bulbs. Specific consumer goods were reserved for small-enterprise production, thus further limiting the quantities produced. Extremely high tariffs were placed on the import of capital goods. One economist estimated India's protection of the capital goods sector to be in excess of 200% in 1962.[22]

Planned Development

Having severely burdened the private sector, the Indian government expanded its reach by issuing a second Industrial Policy Resolution in 1956. The government now had control of 12 more sectors, including commercial banking, insurance, fertilizer, mining, steel, chemical, and oil. With a continued focus on investing in agriculture and heavy industry, the Planning Commission directly determined all public-sector investment. A complicated industrial licensing program was implemented to monitor the sectors and prevent "unnecessary" competition or duplication of efforts.

By nationalizing the financial sector and tightly controlling the capital markets, the government strongly influenced private investment decisions. In addition to equity ownership, the Congress Party's close relationship with the large, family-owned conglomerates (business houses) that dominated the private sector of India gave the government almost complete control over the Indian economy. For example, Tata and Birla, the two top business houses, controlled one-fifth of all private corporate assets in India in 1973. Collectively, the 75 major business houses controlled approximately 45% of the private (formal) sector.[23]

Not only did the government determine who could operate in specific industries, but the government also regulated where companies could be located, how much they could produce, what specific machinery they could purchase, and whom they could fire. All private-sector firms valued at Rs 750,000 or more had to obtain additional licenses for increasing their capacity beyond 125%.[24] Larger companies often had to first be approved by the Monopolies Control Commission before being granted expansion licenses. In some instances, companies could expand only if they did not increase the

percentage of imported goods required for production.[25]

As a key part of its measures to limit unemployment, the government actively subsidized failing public-sector companies deemed "sick units." Instead of going bankrupt, failing companies received loans from government-owned banks. Companies first needed permission from the government before they could lay off any workers. Fostering inefficiency and complacency, permission was only granted after the companies met a number of complex requirements. By the 1980s, the government owned nearly half of India's industrial assets and was subsidizing 90,000 sick units.[26] And it had nationalized 100% of the banks.

Agriculture remained a primary focus of investment in the third and fourth Five-Year Plans. Despite the government's continued efforts, however, food shortages still occurred into the 1970s. Both plans fell short of reaching their goals amidst the distractions of three major wars with China (1962) and Pakistan (1965 and 1971). Beginning in 1967 under Indira Gandhi, India launched its "Green Revolution." New fertilizers and strains of high-yield seeds were developed along with advanced methods of irrigation and farming. By 1979, India was exporting a portion of its record 131 million tons of grain produced.[27]

Export Policy

In contrast to its growth in agriculture, India's export growth declined over time, dropping from 6.5% of its GDP in 1950 to 3.6% in 1970.[28] Realizing the need for increased trade to alleviate India's balance-of-payments shortfalls, the government had made some efforts to stimulate exports in the late 1960s and early 1970s. Making India's exports more competitive, the rupee was devalued by over 57% in 1966. Two important incentive schemes, the Cash Assistance Scheme, which compensated exporters for indirect taxes, and the Registered Exporters Policy, which permitted exporters to import otherwise restricted imports for use in their products, were also enacted to help relieve some of the burden.

Hoping to bring in foreign currency, technology, and expertise, the government made an effort in the late 1960s to encourage joint ventures with multinational firms. After the 1973 oil shock, however, a 40% cap was placed on foreign equity ownership. Multinationals including IBM, Mobil Oil, and Coca-Cola were forced to liquidate their assets and leave the country on financially unfavorable terms. Although the restrictions were later relaxed after a second balance-of-payments crisis in the late 1970s, few of the foreign firms returned.

In 1971, India went to war against the U.S.-supported Pakistan. As a measure of defense against U.S. action, India entered into a treaty with the Soviet Union shortly before going to war. For the next 20 years, India formed both a military and economic partnership with the Soviet Union. In addition to supplying India with arms and economic aid, the Soviet Union served as an important trade partner in India's efforts to achieve export-led growth. The eastern European region constituted 22.2% of India's export trade in 1980 and 19.3% in 1989.[29]

Path to Globalization

Gradual "Washington Consensus"

The collapse of the Soviet Union in 1991 issued a clear warning to the world that the ideas behind central planning needed to be reconsidered. Adding to the turmoil caused by the loss of its major trading partner, India faced tremendous political and social instability in 1990. Various coalitions had formed in Parliament to challenge the standing of the Prime Minister, V.P. Singh. Seeking support from the populous underclass, V.P. Singh released the Mandal Commission report on "Other Backward Castes." The report recommended instituting "reservations" or quotas as high as 27.5% for both jobs in government and admissions to public universities for members of backward castes (purportedly representing 50% of the Indian population).[30] Students and members of the middle class protested loudly through a series of demonstrations that included one at which a student defiantly lit himself on fire.

After two governments fell amidst the 1990–1991 unrest, the newly elected Indian government of Prime Minister Narasimha Rao (Congress Party) faced a severe balance-of-payments crisis. As a result of high oil prices and its stagnant export industry, India's current account deficit had risen above 3% of its GDP and its reserves had depleted to less than US$1 billion. With only enough reserves to last two weeks, India was forced to turn to the International Monetary Fund (IMF) for assistance. The IMF granted the loans but only on the condition that India begin making major economic reforms consistent with the recently nicknamed "Washington Consensus" policies. First coined by the economist John Williamson in 1989, the Washington Consensus prescribed 10 policies for market reform: fiscal discipline, increased public expenditure on health and education, tax reform, interest rate liberalization, a competitive exchange rate, the removal of barriers to trade and barriers to foreign investment, privatization, deregulation, and secure property rights.[31]

Under the leadership of Rao and Finance Minister Manmohan Singh, India embarked upon a plan of gradual liberalization toward a more market-oriented economy. Although some reforms had been attempted under Rajiv Gandhi in the late 1980s, Rao's regime would greatly accelerate the pace of the reforms. The primary focus of the reforms would revolve around reducing the government bureaucracy while stabilizing the country's macro economic balance. In terms of convincing MPs to support the reforms, former Finance Minster and HBS 1968 graduate P. Chidambaram noted, "[We] presented them the hard facts that unless all this was done the economy would simply collapse."[32]

In an effort to move towards an economy more regulated by the discipline of market competition, India removed almost all import- and capacity-licensing restrictions. Subsidies were restricted and tariffs were simplified and lowered. For example, the average tariff rate was reduced from a peak rate of 300% in 1990–1991 to 110% by 1992–1993.[33] A disinvestment commission (later the Ministry of Disinvestment) was set up to plan and supervise the gradual reduction of the public sector. Rao stipulated, however, that the government retain a controlling ownership stake and only sell its "nonstrategic" interests. The 40% cap on foreign ownership was removed, and the Reserve Bank of India (RBI) granted automatic approval for investments up to 51%. To open the financial sector, the government made allowances for private banks and a limited number of foreign bank branches. Approved foreign institutional investors (FII) were licensed and controls governing takeovers were relaxed through the passage of the Takeover Act of 1994. Total holdings of FIIs, however, could not exceed 24%

(10% limit for each single FII).[34] Finally, the Securities and Exchange Board was established to regulate India's reopened capital markets.

On the macroeconomic front, Rao attempted to reduce the country's massive fiscal deficit by broadening the tax base and reducing expenditure. India's monetary policy was tightened to reduce inflation. At the same time, the rupee was devalued 22% against the U.S. dollar in 1993 and became convertible on the current account in 1994.

Success and Failure of "Consensus" Reform: 1995–2003

In hard economic terms, yes, growth rate has moved up to a 6% path. That is significant but not dramatic. I would use the word dramatic once we moved to an 8% path. The result is that many sectors of India's economy are still not opened. The unreformed sectors are as large as the reformed sectors and this is what is holding back growth. But clearly a 6% growth is a sharp improvement on a 3.5% growth or a 5% growth, and at least for about five or six years in the '90s, we were generating a large number of jobs. Inflation has been at a historical low for many, many months in this decade, compared to the average of 8% to 10%. The average has been only about 5% to 6% here. And today, there is a sense of hope and confidence about the future among the young generation. And we no longer penalize efficiency or enterprise; in fact, we reward it.

—P. Chidambaram, Finance Minister
1996–1998[35]

As Chidambaram acknowledged, Rao's reforms had an immediate, although not dramatic, effect on India's economy. Surpassing the growth achieved under Rajiv Gandhi, the reformed economy grew at a respectable rate of 6% in an environment of reasonably low inflation and interest rates [see **Exhibits 3.2** and **3.3**]. India's investments in its higher education appeared to pay off in the growth of its technology sector. An entrepreneurial spirit took root in parts of India as private and foreign investment increased. The largest change, however, was in the mind-set of

the people. Reform was now looked upon in a positive light by much of the country. The pace of reform, however, slowed once the country seemed free of its initial crisis. Additionally, problems of the past in terms of corruption, fiscal imbalances, and domestic/external conflict continued to distract India's leaders from pushing through the necessary reforms.

Growth of IT

Although India's 10th Plan made allotments for improving the country's primary education system, in the past the focus of education had been on higher education. Rooted in its efforts to industrialize, the government realized it had to promote engineering colleges in order to build India's technical knowledge base. Perhaps to the detriment of India's primary education system, the government funded 16 central universities made up of more than 12,000 colleges. The state maintained a complete monopoly on higher education; private universities were prohibited. In later years, India proved unable to recover much of its higher-education expenses. The 2001 U.N. Human Development Report estimated that India lost US$2 billion per year in resources due to the emigration of computer professionals.[36] As government finances continued to be scarce, questions were raised as to whether or not India's underfunded education system favored quantity over quality of graduates. The director of the Indian Institute of Information Technology, Bangalore, explained, "[T]he quality of teachers and teaching has fallen to abysmal levels in many colleges."[37]

There was no discounting, however, the benefit of the sheer volume of educated workers in India. With over 7 million enrolled students in 2000, India produced more college graduates than almost any other country in the world. Although it lost close to 100,000 professionals per year to the United States, India still had more than 1 million students enrolled in technical programs in 2001.[38] India's slowly opening economy coincided with the global boom in the technology sector and thus provided a valuable source of cheap, educated labor for the world market. By 2002, software exports and services made up 2% of India's GDP. Some analysts expected the sector to grow above 7% of GDP by 2008 and make up 30% of India's foreign exchange inflows.[39]

Taking advantage of the technology-savvy, English-speaking workforce, American companies began outsourcing information technology (IT) and back-office operations to India. More than 40% of the world's *Fortune* 500 companies outsourced a portion of their services operations to India in 2002.[40] Often answering the phones with assumed American names, Indian customer service agents replaced U.S. counterparts for a fraction of the price. Having the advantage of a nine-hour time difference, Indian operations made 24-hour service possible. As an example of tremendous cost savings, Ernst & Young began outsourcing tax return services to India in 2002. Sharda Cherwoo, Ernst & Young's Shared Services CEO, explained, "We hire fresh-out-of-college graduates with bachelors degrees in accounting or math. On an average, we pay them from US$3,000 to US$5,000 per year, including benefits. We can do this at a significantly lower cost compared to doing the same returns in the U.S."[41]

Likewise, General Electric had more than 11,000 Indian employees involved in back-office and call-center operations in 2002. Looking beyond back-office operations, General Electric saw great research potential in India. Pramod Bhasin, head of GE Capital India, explained, "We just realized that the biggest thing India gives us is its intellect."[42] Home to the prestigious Indian Institute of Management and Indian Institute of Science, Bangalore, the "Silicon Valley of India," offered an ideal location for quality research at tremendous cost savings. After investing more than US$80 million, GE India opened the John F. Welch Technology Center in 2000. Complete with an amphitheater and cricket pitch, the technology center offered an ideal place for outsourcing GE's high-level appliance, medical, and aerospace designs.

Rise of Indian Entrepreneurs

Encouraged by the loosening restrictions on the import of technology and the absence of taxes on software exports, Indian entrepreneurs began building their own IT firms, including such notable firms as Wipro, Tata Consultancy Services, and Infosys. Publicly listed on the NASDAQ exchange in 1999, Infosys grew from US$2.2 million in revenues in 1991 to $545 million in 2002. Explaining how his business

could flourish in India, Infosys' CEO, Nandan Nilekani, stated, "The IT industry is not impeded by government policy issues but encouraged. Ninety-eight percent of our revenue comes from the global markets. Our business does not exist in the physical world so we don't have to worry about such factors as ports, roads, airports, etc. We also do not have labor problems. We are a unique set of businesspeople."[43]

Foreign Direct Investment

Foreign direct investment (FDI) was slow to enter India. In comparison to the US$50 billion invested in China in 2002, analysts estimated India's inflow of FDI to be at US$4.4 billion [see **Exhibit 3.8**]. India measured its FDI in different terms than most other countries. Excluding any reinvested foreign profits and proceeds from foreign equity listings, India's comparable level of FDI was perhaps closer to US$8 billion in 2002.[44]

As India's economy slowly opened, many major multinational companies entered the Indian market. Most companies, however, had limited presences in the form of joint ventures with local companies due to the continuing restrictions on foreign ownership. India's substandard infrastructure proved to be a large deterrent to foreign investors. The 1998 Global Competitiveness Report of the World Economic Forum ranked India at the very bottom of the 53 countries studied. In particular, India failed to provide adequate power, transportation, and communications. Well aware of the country's range of problems, many foreign investors remained wary of committing large sums of money to projects in India. For example, one prominent foreign investor explained, "The infrastructure in terms of power, roads, seaports, and airports is not here. The economy's slow growth and the slow progress of privatization are also deterrents. Companies can't take advantage of the low-cost labor if the free trade and necessary infrastructure are not available to support it. You combine all of this together and it is no wonder why more foreign investors are not here."

Greatly restraining the movement of goods throughout the country, India's highway system hindered both domestic and foreign operations. For example, it took eight days for a truck to travel from Delhi to Mumbai (1,407 kilometers).[45] Although plans were made to create a "golden quadrilateral" of highways to connect Delhi, Calcutta, Chennai, and Mumbai, India's underfunded highway system remained in poor condition. Of the 3.3 million kilometers of roads in India in 2000, 1.6% of the roads carried 40% of the country's traffic.[46]

India's bureaucracy continued to be a headache for foreign investors. GE India's president explained that, "The reason our office is in Delhi and not Bangalore or Hyderabad is because of the necessity of an interface with the government. You simply can't do business in India without it."[47] The cities of Bangalore and Hydrabad became the capital cities of India's growing technology sector because their respective state governments made efforts to facilitate the country's complex bureaucratic processes. Comparing the southern states' efforts to minimize bureaucracy to the lack of efforts in the north, one Delhi lobbyist stated, "[Y]ou are contrasting emerging market best practice with emerging market worst practice . . . . That is why the South is attracting such large IT and even manufacturing investments."[48]

Serving as a primary example for foreign investors to remain wary of doing business in India, Enron's majority stake in the Enron/GE/Bechtel's US$2.9 billion Dabhol Power Plant became the largest FDI project and public relations disaster in the post-reform era. Accusing the Maharashta state of reneging on its payment contract, Enron's CEO, Kenneth Lay, threatened, "If they try to squeeze us down to something less than cost then it basically becomes an expropriation by the Indian government, and that would send an incredibly damaging signal to the international capital markets and investment community as to making any future investments in India."[49] Controversy surrounded the lack of transparency involved in the negotiations by all parties of the Dabhol project. Alluding to a scandalous "education" fund, Enron employee Linda Powers testified before the U.S. House of Representatives that Enron had spent US$20 million on "educating" Indians in the workings of capitalist business.[50]

Corruption

Embedded within India's bloated bureaucracy, corruption continued to pervade all branches and ranks of the Indian government. From paying traffic cops to look the other way to theft of almost 40% of the country's electricity output,

corruption was a significant part of life in India.[51] Corruption hit India's poor the hardest. While some of the poor received low-quality, insect-infested food subsidies, up to 40% of India's famine relief stock often ended up for sale on the black market.[52] Transparency International ranked India 72nd on its Corruption Perception Index in 2002.[53]

Referring to India's continuing moral issues, Minister of Disinvestment Arun Shourie commented, "It [corruption] is how you bring down governments . . . the declining quality of our leadership is a real part of it. Problems stem from the weakness and the third-rateness of the political class in general. The reason is simple. Second-rate persons select third-rate persons. You do this for 50 years and you have serious problems." Shourie continued, "Candidates with criminal backgrounds should not be able to stand for election. Many of the people who have to vote this legislation through are the very same people who have such a background."[54] The legislation referred to by Shourie required candidates to disclose their financial assets and criminal backgrounds. The bill was rejected by the Parliament in July of 2002; roughly 20% of the MPs were believed to have criminal backgrounds as serious as kidnapping, rape, and murder.[55]

Privatization

> Post WTO, we can only survive if we are competitive. Profit-making companies need to improve performance. The entire world has privatized profit-making companies. We cannot survive without this strategy.
> —Ministry of Disinvestment[56]

To many members of India's elite, privatization seemed the answer to both reducing corruption and improving economic growth. Aroon Purie, the chief editor of *India Today*, commented, "You only have to worry about corruption when you have to interact with the government. Corruption is a function of regulation . . . it is a factor of the current infrastructure. The less you have to do with government, the less that corruption is a problem."[57] Despite reform efforts to reduce the public sector, government-controlled entities still accounted for 43% of capital stock in India and 15% of nonagricultural employment in 2001.[58] India's 10th Five-Year

Plan specifically focused on promoting privatization in order to gain US$20 billion in revenues. In 2002, the first year of the 10th Five-Year Plan, the government had received US$3 billion in privatization receipts.

"Our privatization policy is clear. Other than defense, railway, and atomic energy, all sectors are being privatized," explained Secretary of Disinvestment Pradip Baijal. The government's privatization track record was mixed. From 1991 through 2000, 48 companies had been privatized to some degree for a total receipt of Rs 30,917 crore.[59] The first major effort was the Common Economic Program. Launched in 1996, it called for an increase in foreign investment and the privatization of "non-core" and "terminally sick" public enterprises. While the BJP tended to exclude foreign investment in the consumer goods industry, it encouraged multinationals to invest in export and high-technology activities.

Under pressure from the IMF, liberalization proceeded in fits and starts in the early 1990s. It picked up some momentum in the latter half of the decade. In 1998, the government doubled the stake foreign investors could own in Indian banks to 40%. A year later, reforms opened up the pharmaceutical and mining sectors to foreign investment. To further accelerate the process, the government made its pricing more competitive by moving from a predetermined prices band system to a market-determined competitive bidding system. Shares would be sold to retail investors at a discount. In 1999, the government opened the insurance sector to private competition and allowed 26% foreign ownership in joint ventures. The government also planned to reduce state ownership of banks to below 33%. Among the "fast-track divestments" was the sale of 25% of the state's ownership and management control of the telecom company Videsh Sanchar Nigam Ltd. (VSNL) to the industrial conglomerate Tata Group. In January of 2003, the government announced that it would be offering a 34% stake in India's national oil companies.

Despite strong privatization efforts, few state enterprises were placed in private hands. Instead, most minority shares were sold to other state corporations. When private companies did successfully purchase stakes, the vast majority were domestic. Explaining the reasons behind the predominance of Indian buyers, Shourie explained, "All acquisitions are done through competitive bidding. Foreign companies never

thought this process would go through, so they aren't always willing to fully commit. It is not such a bad thing. If foreign companies were buying everything, there would be immediate backlash throughout the country. It is better that most of it comes from green-field investments."[60]

Shourie, who was principally responsible for increasing the pace of privatization, was appointed minister of disinvestment in 2000. Since coming to office, Shourie had privatized 22 more companies, for US$2.2 billion by mid-2002.[61] Several of the companies sold became examples to the country of the benefits of privatization. The bakery Modern Foods had doubled its production within the first year after being sold to Hindustan Lever in 2000. A second example, Hindustan Zinc Ltd., had increased its sales by 29% and its production by 17% when compared with the corresponding quarter of the previous year.[62]

Although a strong consensus was building in favor of privatization, the speed of the reform process appeared to have slowed with the approach of the 2004 general election. Many politicians feared that their parties would lose the electoral support of special-interest groups if they pushed through the necessary reforms. Protests by politicians, unions, and the media stalled privatization plans. "I'm disposing of bleeding ulcers . . . but the allegation is that I'm selling crown jewels," related Shourie.[63] "Sick-unit" designation and other government subsidies had protected jobs in the past. Often guaranteed a job for life by the government, employees feared they would lose their job security if their companies were transferred to the more efficient private sector. The upper management of public-sector companies also had a strong vested interest. Baijal explained, "The top management are against it [privatization]. They are currently benefiting from subsidies. The public sector puts equity investments into these failing companies. Who gets the benefits of this equity? The rent seekers."[64] Discussing the necessity of reform, Shourie reinforced, "Through privatization, the state institutions are weakened, but society is made healthier. We need to transfer power from the state to society. The state becoming leaner will result in greater nimbleness and dedication by all."[65]

Fiscal Deficit

With a history of high fiscal deficits, the central government ran a deficit equal to 5.9% of the country's GDP in 2002–2003 [see **Exhibit 3.11**]. When combined with the deficits of the states, the fiscal red ink was believed to exceed 10% of GDP [see **Exhibit 3.12**]. Debt servicing made up half of the government's expenditure and thereby prevented both the state and central governments from investing in the infrastructure and sorely needed social welfare programs. In addition to diverting the government's money from essential programs, the burdensome deficit crowded out private investment by raising interest rates to levels as high as 12% in 2002.

Although the government announced plans to reduce the deficit to 5.6% during the 2003–2004 period, challenging obstacles remained in its path. Reining in expenditure proved particularly difficult in light of continuing difficulties with Pakistan. India's military expenditure rose to 10% of total expenditure in 2002. Furthermore, natural disasters ranging from droughts to the 2001 Gujarat earthquake required additional government expenses. Agriculture and energy subsidies additionally made up 11% of the government's expenditure and could be difficult to reduce without risking the loss of electoral support. Fertilizer subsidies alone made up 0.7% of GDP in 2001.[66] A report by the McKinsey Global Institute estimated that privatizing the state electricity boards would save the government from paying subsidies amounting to almost 1.5% of India's 2001 GDP.[67]

As the states retained the right to tax the agriculture and property sectors, the central government could not easily broaden its tax base to increase revenues. Additionally, the central government excluded all of the IT industry and small-scale manufacturers from taxes. The deputy governor of the RBI related, "We have shot ourselves in the foot in terms of the number of exemptions given. The direct taxes that the government actually assesses, people are just not paying. Our tax base has gone up, but so has tax avoidance . . . in many cases, it is the rich who are not paying their taxes."[68] Less than 2% of the Indian population paid income tax.

The states, equally, had a difficult time collecting revenue. McKinsey estimated that Mumbai's revenues from its property tax amounted to only 0.002% of the estimated value of the city's buildings.[*] Unable to collect sufficient taxes, the government could not recover costs spent on infrastructure. For example, Delhi supplied water to the city at a price one-tenth its cost.[69]

Social and Political Conflict

In late May 1999, a quasi-war erupted between India and Pakistan over the disputed state of Kashmir. After two months of intense fighting, military leaders from both countries agreed to withdraw. The conflict resumed in December, when Pakistani rebels held 154 Indian Airlines passengers hostage for eight days. In March 2000, a cease-fire was ordered. Vajpayee and Pakistan's General Musharaff met in July 2001, hoping to resolve the Kashmir issue. The leaders, however, failed to reach a consensus.

Tensions flared again in December. Terrorists belonging to a Pakistani militant group stormed the Parliament of India, leaving 12 dead. Following the attack, there was talk of war. Musharaff promised to crack down on terrorist groups, but many of his efforts proved ineffective. While more than 2,000 Islamic militants were arrested in Pakistan in January, three-quarters of them were released by March. In May 2002, militants killed 34 soldiers and civilians on a Kashmir army base and heightened tensions further. More than one million troops from both countries lined up along the shared border and the Kashmir Line of Control. Worried about the chance of a nuclear war breaking out, the United States put serious diplomatic pressure on both countries to avert war. Unlike the rest of the world and even the country's own media, India's leaders downplayed the likelihood of a nuclear war. One Indian corporate executive stated, "Pakistan is completely irrelevant in the daily life of India. Neither side is going to fire a missile, so long as an extremist is not in power."[70] Or as India's external affairs minister, Yashwant Sinha, further exclaimed, "Were we about to unleash nuclear weapons on each other? Total bunkum!"[71]

Adding to India's strife, religious tensions continued to boil to the surface of Indian political life. Harkening back to India's partition, one of the most violent periods in history, the Ayodhya temple dispute, caused intense unrest. Before a group of hardline supporters from Hindu Parishad (VHP), the Shiv Sena Party, and

---

[*] The ratio in developed countries is around 1%–2%.

BHP stormed the Ayodhya site and tore it down in 1992, a sixteenth-century Babri mosque had stood on the grounds. The Hindus believed the site to be the birthplace of the Hindu god Rama. They believed that Muslim invaders had destroyed the previous temple devoted to him. Riots broke out following the destruction of the temple, resulting in the deaths of an estimated 2,000 people.

Ten years later, religious violence once again broke out in the state of Gujarat and put in doubt the secularity of India's government leaders. In March of 2002, Muslim militants firebombed a train, killing 58 Hindu activists who were returning from the Ayodhya site. In retaliation, extremist Hindus slaughtered an estimated 2,000 Muslims and left tens of thousands of people homeless in the state of Gujarat.[72] As ownership of the site had been disputed since 1853, following the 2002 riots the Supreme Court banned all religious activities on the site.

The state government and police were criticized for their lack of action in ending the riots. During the horrific bloodshed, Gujarat's BJP Chief Minister Modi remarked, "The five crore people of Gujarat have shown remarkable restraint under grave provocation."[73] Making matters worse for the government, a British government report found evidence of the "ethnic cleansing" having been planned months beforehand by right-wing Hindu officials.[74] The central government, too, appeared at fault. Though pressured by the opposition to end the violence, Vajpayee feared losing the support of the VHP and initially did nothing. After losing the February state elections in Uttar Pradesh, Punjab, and Manipur, the BJP did not want to risk losing its coalition support as it headed into the 2004 general election. Arguing it owed its power to the Ayodhya temple campaign, far-right elements of the BJP pushed for the government to publicly back the building of the Hindu temple. Caving to demands in early 2003, the government planned to petition the Supreme Court to allow the building of a Hindu temple.

First Step to 8% Growth?

Singh surveyed the piles of reports stacked on his desk. The Planning Commission had provided a road map for achieving growth, but to achieve its priorities, significant reforms would have to be passed. During the 1990s, a balance-of-payments crisis, caused in part by the Gulf War oil shock, had pushed India into reforms. Although another war in the Persian Gulf threatened to raise oil prices, India's economy was reasonably stable in 2003, with the exception of a burgeoning fiscal deficit. India had comfortable reserves and a positive current account balance for the first time in 24 years. Although its economy was not meeting its targets, India was still one of the fastest growing economies in the world, growing at close to 6% from 1992 to 2002.

If Singh decided to follow the Planning Commission's guidelines, the new budget would be the first step toward making the plan's vision a reality. On the one hand, Kelkar's reports had made a strong argument for firm fiscal discipline. Cutting back on expenditures, however, could prove highly unpopular. Many of India's citizens had become highly dependent upon government subsidies and employment. Politics having polarized, India existed in a constant state of domestic and external unrest. Right-wing factions pushed for "saffronization"—the promotion of traditional Hindu values—and gained more power with each election. Would the India of the future continue to be receptive to change? Could it afford not to be?

EXHIBIT 1.11A **MAP OF INDIA**

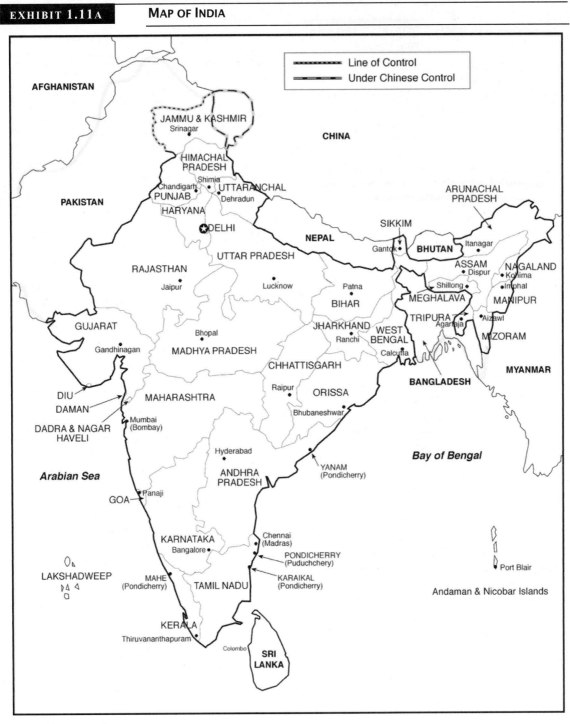

SOURCE: Case writer.

EXHIBIT 3.2A	2002 HUMAN DEVELOPMENT RANKINGS[A]

High Human Development

1	Norway
20	Italy
40	Uruguay

Medium Human Development

54	Mexico
60	Russian Federation
82	Peru
96	China
110	Indonesia
120	Guatemala
123	Morocco
124	India
125	Swaziland
130	Cambodia

Low Human Development

138	Pakistan
140	Bhutan
160	Gambia
173	Sierra Leone

SOURCE: United Nations Development Program (UNDP), *Human Development Report 2002*.

[a]Based upon the factors of life expectancy, educational attainment, and adjusted income.

EXHIBIT 3.2B	INDICATORS OF HUMAN DEVELOPMENT IN INDIA

Life Expectancy at Birth, 2001–2006		Infant Mortality Rate, 2000	
Male	63.87	Male	67
Female	66.91	Female	69

Birth rate (per 1,000), 2000	25.8
Death rate (per 1,000), 2000	8.5
Total fertility rate, 1995–2000 (per woman)	3.3
Annual population growth rate (%), 1975–2000	1.9
Annual population growth rate (%), 2000–2015	1.3
Population using adequate sanitation facilities (%)	31
Contraceptive prevalence (%), 1995–2000	48
Physicians (per 100,000 people), 1990–1999	48
Children underweight for age (% under age 5), 1995–2000	47
People living with HIV/AIDS, adults (% age 15–49), 2001	0.79
Public education expenditure (as % of GNP), 1995–1997	3.2
Public education expenditure (as % of government expenditure), 1995–1997	11.6
Telephone mainlines (per 1,000 people), 1990	6
Telephone mainlines (per 1,000 people), 2000	32
Cellular mobile subscribers (per 1,000 people), 1990	0
Cellular mobile subscribers (per 1,000 people), 2000	4

SOURCE: Ministry of Finance, Government of India; UNDP, *Human Development Report 2002*.

EXHIBIT 3.3	NATIONAL INCOME ACCOUNTS (YEAR BEGINNING APRIL 1)													
	1975	1980	1985	1991	1992	1993	1994	1995	1996	1997	1998	1999	2000	2001[a]	2002[a]
Gross national product (Rs bn)	754.5	1,305.2	2,481.1	5,790.1	6,615.8	7,692.7	9,039.8	10,597.9	12,304.6	13,769.4	15,831.1	17,402.1	19,031.0	20,813.5	22,361.0
Real GNP growth over previous year (%)	9.1%	7.3%	4.5%	1.1%	5.1%	5.9%	7.2%	7.5%	8.2%	4.8%	6.4%	6.2%	4.3%	6.0%	4.4%
Gross domestic product (Rs bn)	787.6	1,438.0	2,780.0	6,531.0	7,484.0	8,592.0	10,127.7	11,880.1	13,682.1	15,225.5	17,409.4	19,369.0	20,590.0	22,961.0	24,583.0
Private consumption (% of GDP)	73.4%	69.0%	63.6%	68.3%	66.9%	66.9%	65.6%	64.5%	66.0%	64.0%	65.6%	65.3%	65.1%	65.0%	66.0%
Government consumption (% of GDP)	9.7%	10.0%	11.8%	12.8%	12.7%	12.7%	12.0%	12.2%	11.8%	12.5%	13.4%	14.3%	14.5%	14.2%	13.0%
Gross fixed capital (% of GDP)	16.9%	18.3%	19.5%	22.0%	22.4%	21.4%	21.9%	24.4%	22.8%	21.7%	21.5%	21.5%	22.2%	21.7%	22.0%
Exports (% of GDP)	5.1%	4.7%	3.9%	6.7%	7.2%	8.1%	8.2%	9.0%	8.7%	8.5%	8.0%	8.2%	9.9%	9.1%	n/a
Imports (% of GDP)	6.7%	8.7%	7.1%	7.3%	8.5%	8.5%	8.9%	10.3%	10.2%	10.1%	10.2%	11.1%	11.2%	10.7%	n/a
Population (millions)	600.7	675.0	750.9	851.9	868.9	886.3	903.9	922.0	939.5	955.2	970.9	986.6	1,002.1	1,017.5	1,045.8
Per capita GNP (Rs)	1,256.0	1,933.6	3,304.3	6,796.7	7,614.0	8,680.1	10,000.4	11,494.6	13,096.4	14,414.9	16,305.1	17,638.3	18,990.4	20,454.7	21,381.7
Per capita GNP(US$)	150.0	245.9	267.1	298.9	334.8	334.9	328.0	366.4	403.9	406.8	449.0	427.5	441.1	455.1	453.1
GDP deflator (1995 = 100)	17.5	25.9	38.5	70.3	76.5	83.8	91.8	100	107.4	114.4	123.4	127.8	133	138.5	n/a
Inflation rate (%)	n/a	8.2%	8.3%	10.6%	8.8%	9.5%	9.5%	8.9%	7.4%	6.5%	7.9%	3.6%	4.1%	4.1%	n/a
Gross domestic saving (% of GDP)	**17.2%**	**18.9%**	**19.5%**	**22.0%**	**21.8%**	**22.5%**	**24.8%**	**25.1%**	**23.2%**	**23.1%**	**21.7%**	**23.2%**	**23.4%**	**24.0%**	**n/a**
Household sector savings (% of GDP)	11.7%	13.8%	14.3%	17.0%	17.5%	18.4%	19.7%	18.2%	17.0%	17.6%	18.9%	20.3%	20.9%	22.5%	n/a
Industry of origin (% of GDP)															
Agriculture, forestry, mining, etc.	46%	42%	39%	34%	34%	34%	33%	31%	31%	29%	29%	27%	26%	26%	n/a
Manufacturing, construction, and utilities	20%	22%	23%	24%	24%	24%	24%	25%	25%	25%	25%	24%	25%	24%	n/a
Trade, transport, and storage	17%	18%	19%	19%	19%	19%	20%	21%	21%	22%	22%	22%	23%	23%	n/a
Financing, real estate, and business services	6%	7%	8%	11%	11%	12%	11%	11%	11%	12%	12%	13%	13%	12%	n/a
Public administration, defense, and other services	11%	12%	12%	12%	12%	12%	12%	12%	11%	12%	13%	13%	14%	14%	n/a

SOURCE: International Monetary Fund, *International Financial Statistics Yearbook 2002*; Ministry of Finance, Government of India, *Economic Survey of India 2001–2002*; Economic Intelligence Unit, *Country Data 2000–2003*.

[a]Estimates.

EXHIBIT 3.4	FINANCIAL INDICATORS																
	1975	1980	1985	1990	1991[a]	1992	1993	1994	1995	1996	1997	1998	1999	2000	2001	2002
Exchange rate (Rs/US$ period average)	8.38	7.86	12.37	17.50	22.74	25.92	30.49	31.37	32.43	35.43	36.31	41.26	43.06	44.94	47.19	48.61
M2 growth rate (%)	n/a	20%	17%	17%	18%	17%	17%	20%	11%	19%	18%	18%	17%	15%	14%	n/a
Consumer price index	21.4	26	40.6	60.8	69.2	77.4	82.3	90.7	100	109	116.8	132.2	138.4	144	149.3	n/a
CPI (% change)	--	4%	9%	8%	14%	12%	6%	10%	10%	9%	7%	13%	5%	4%	4%	n/a
Interest rates:																
Bank rate	9.0	9.0	10.0	10.0	12.0	12.0	12.0	12.0	12.0	12.0	9.0	9.0	8.0	8.0	6.5	n/a
Lending rate	n/a	16.5	16.5	16.5	17.88	18.92	16.25	14.75	15.46	15.96	13.83	13.54	12.54	12.29	12.08	n/a
Reserves[b]																
Total reserves (US$ billion)	2.25	7.05	6.32	6.52	10.49	11.86	19.81	25.29	22.93	26.79	31.92	33.45	38.54	43.88	n/a	n/a

SOURCE: International Monetary Fund, *International Financial Statistics Yearbook 2002*; Reserve Bank of India, Ministry of Finance, Government of India, *Economic Survey of India 2001–2002; 2002–2003*.

[a]Figures for 1991 onward are not comparable with earlier periods due to downward adjustment of rupee effected in July 1991.

[b]Foreign exchange includes foreign assets of RBI and government balances held abroad up to 1955–1956.

EXHIBIT 3.5	LITERACY AND POPULATION VARIATIONS BY STATE[A]												
	Literacy Rates, 1951–2001 (%)						2001 Literacy (%)		('000)	2001 Population		1991–2001 Growth	Income by State[b] 2000 (US$)
State	1951	1961	1971	1981	1991	2001	Male	Female		Rural	Urban		
Andaman & Nicobar Islands	25.8	40.1	43.6	51.6	73.0	81.2	86.1	75.3	356	67%	33%	27%	459.3
Andhra Pradesh	13.2	24.6	24.6	29.9	44.1	61.1	70.9	51.2	75,728	73%	27%	14%	364.3
Arunachal Pradesh	n/a	47.9	11.3	20.8	41.6	54.7	64.1	44.2	1,091	80%	20%	26%	324.6
Assam	18.3	33.0	28.7	n/a	52.9	64.3	71.9	56.0	26,638	87%	13%	19%	226.9
Bihar	12.2	21.8	19.9	26.2	38.5	47.5	60.3	33.6	82,879	90%	10%	-4%	113.7
Chandigarh	n/a	55.1	61.6	64.8	77.8	81.8	85.7	76.7	901	10%	90%	40%	987.9
Chatisgarh	n/a	n/a	n/a	n/a	n/a	65.2	77.9	52.4	20,796	80%	20%	n/a	241.7
Dadra & Nagar Haveli	4.0	11.6	15.0	26.7	40.7	60.3	73.3	52.4	220	77%	23%	59%	n/a
Daman & Diu	22.9	34.9	44.8	56.7	71.2	81.1	88.4	70.4	158	64%	36%	55%	n/a
Delhi	38.4	62.0	56.6	61.5	75.3	81.8	87.4	75.0	13,783	7%	93%	46%	864.8
Goa	23.0	36.2	n/a	n/a	75.5	82.3	88.9	75.5	1,344	50%	50%	15%	1,003.6
Gujarat	n/a	n/a	35.8	43.7	61.3	70.0	80.5	58.6	50,597	63%	37%	22%	427.8
Haryana	n/a	24.1	26.9	36.1	55.8	68.6	79.3	56.3	21,083	71%	29%	28%	528.3
Himachal Pradesh	7.7	24.9	32.0	42.5	63.9	77.1	86.0	68.1	6,077	90%	10%	18%	421.0
Jammu & Kashmir	n/a	13.0	18.6	26.7	n/a	54.5	65.7	41.8	10,070	75%	25%	30%	275.9
Jharkhand	n/a	n/a	n/a	n/a	n/a	54.1	67.9	39.4	26,909	78%	22%	n/a	214.4
Karnataka	19.3	29.8	31.5	38.5	56.0	67.0	76.3	57.5	52,734	66%	34%	17%	401.4
Kerala	40.7	55.1	60.4	70.4	89.8	90.9	94.2	87.9	31,839	74%	26%	9%	433.1
Lakshadweep	15.2	27.2	43.7	55.1	81.8	87.5	93.2	81.6	60	57%	45%	15%	n/a
Madhya Pradesh	9.8	20.5	22.1	27.9	44.2	64.1	76.8	50.3	60,385	73%	27%	-9%	240.4
Maharashtra	20.9	35.1	39.2	47.2	64.9	77.3	86.3	67.5	96,752	58%	42%	23%	527.9
Manipur	11.4	36.0	32.9	41.4	59.9	68.9	77.8	59.7	2,389	76%	24%	30%	285.3
Meghalaya	n/a	n/a	29.5	34.1	49.1	63.3	66.1	60.4	2,306	80%	20%	30%	291.8
Mizoram	n/a	n/a	n/a	59.9	82.3	88.5	90.7	86.1	891	51%	49%	29%	346.3
Nagaland	10.4	20.4	27.4	42.6	61.6	67.1	71.7	61.9	1,989	82%	18%	64%	292.5
Orissa	15.8	25.2	26.2	34.2	49.1	63.3	76.0	51.0	36,707	85%	15%	16%	190.2
Pondicherry	n/a	43.7	46.0	55.9	74.7	81.5	88.9	74.1	973	34%	67%	20%	697.7
Punjab	15.2	31.5	33.7	40.9	58.5	70.0	75.6	63.6	24,289	66%	34%	20%	557.3
Rajasthan	8.9	18.1	19.1	24.4	38.6	61.0	76.5	44.3	56,473	77%	23%	28%	266.7
Sikkim	7.3	14.2	17.7	34.1	56.9	69.7	76.7	61.5	540	89%	11%	33%	346.0
Tamil Nadu	20.8	36.4	39.5	46.8	62.7	73.5	82.3	64.6	62,111	56%	44%	11%	442.5
Tripura	15.5	24.3	31.0	42.1	60.4	73.7	81.5	65.4	3,191	83%	17%	16%	319.3
Uttaranchal	n/a	n/a	n/a	n/a	n/a	72.3	84.0	60.3	8,480	74%	26%	n/a	n/a
Uttar Pradesh	10.8	20.7	21.7	27.2	41.6	57.4	70.2	43.0	166,053	79%	21%	19%	216.3
West Bengal	24.0	34.5	33.2	40.9	57.7	69.2	77.6	60.2	80,221	72%	28%	18%	357.6
All India	**18.3**	**28.3**	**34.5**	**43.6**	**52.2**	**65.4**	**76.0**	**54.3**	**1,027,013**	**72%**	**28%**	**21%**	**413.5**

SOURCE: Office of the Registrar General of India, *Census of India 2001*.
[a]Census could not be conducted in certain areas due to natural calamities and domestic disturbances. Projected figures.
[b]Per capital net state domestic product (at current prices). Year 1999 data used for Jkarkhand, Chattisgarh, Mizoram, Nagaland, and Andaman and Nicobar Islands.

EXHIBIT 3.6	ESTIMATES OF EMPLOYMENT IN ORGANIZED PUBLIC AND PRIVATE SECTORS											
	1990	1991	1992	1993	1994	1995	1996	1997	1998	1999	2000	2001
Public sector (millions)	18.8	19.1	19.2	19.3	19.4	19.5	19.4	19.6	19.4	19.4	19.3	19.1
Male	16.5	16.7	16.8	16.8	16.9	16.9	16.8	16.8	16.7	16.6	16.5	16.3
Female	2.2	2.3	2.4	2.5	2.6	2.6	2.6	2.7	1.8	2.8	2.9	2.9
Private sector (millions)	7.6	7.6	7.9	7.9	7.9	8.0	8.5	8.7	8.7	8.7	8.6	8.7
Male	6.2	6.2	6.4	6.3	6.3	6.4	6.7	6.8	6.7	6.7	6.6	6.6
Female	1.4	1.4	1.5	1.6	1.6	1.6	1.8	1.9	2.0	2.0	2.1	2.1
Total (millions)	26.4	26.7	27.1	27.2	27.3	27.5	27.9	28.3.	28.1	28.1	27.9	27.8

SOURCE: Ministry of Finance, Government of India, *Economic Survey of India 2002–2003.*

EXHIBIT 3.7A	GOVERNMENT OWNERSHIP AND PRODUCTIVITY

Indexed to U.S. = 100 in 1998

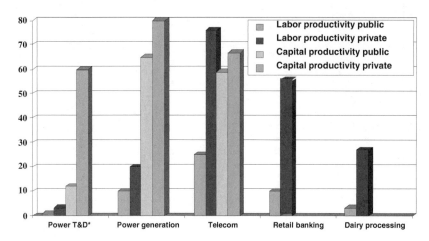

*Transmission and distribution

SOURCE: Case writer created using data from "India: The Growth Imperative," McKinsey Global Institute, September 2001.

EXHIBIT 3.7B	LABOR PRODUCTIVITY BY INDUSTRY, 2001

Sector	Industry	Labor Productivity (Index: U.S. = 100)	% of Employment
Agricultural	Dairy Farming	0.6	2.0
	Wheat Farming	1.3	0.1
	Sector Average[a]	1.2	14.6
Transition	Construction (mud)	1.7	0.6
	Wheat Milling	2.2	0.1
	Street Vendors	3.5	3.0
	Rural Stores	6.0	1.0
	Tailors	12.0	0.7
	Sector Average[a]	6.9	5.6
Modern	Power (T&D)	1.0	0.2
	Wheat Milling	7.0	0.01
	Power Generation	9.0	0.1
	Steel	11.0	0.1
	Retail	12.0	2.0
	Retail Banking	12.0	0.3
	Housing Construction	15.0	1.0
	Dairy Processing (organized sector)	16.0	0.1
	Automotive	24.0	0.1
	Telecom	25.0	0.1
	Apparel	26.0	0.4
	Software	44.0	0.1
	Sector Average[a]	15.0	4.51

SOURCE: Case writer created using data from "India: The Growth Imperative," McKinsey Global Institute, September 2001.

[a]Grossed up to overall economy.

EXHIBIT 3.8	BALANCE OF PAYMENTS (US$ MILLIONS)														
	1975	1980	1985	1991	1992	1993	1994	1995	1996	1997	1998	1999	2000	2001	2002ᵃ
Current Account Balance	**(148)**	**(1,785)**	**(4,177)**	**(4,292)**	**(4,485)**	**(1,876)**	**(1,676)**	**(5,563)**	**(5,956)**	**(2,965)**	**(6,903)**	**(3,228)**	**(4,198)**	**1,351**	**3,665**
Export of goods	4,666	8,303	9,465	18,095	20,019	22,016	25,523	31,239	33,737	35,702	34,076	36,877	43,132	44,915	49,968
Import of goods	(4,952)	(13,947)	(15,081)	(21,087)	(22,931)	(24,108)	(29,673)	(37,957)	(43,789)	(45,730)	(44,828)	(45,556)	(55,325)	(57,618)	(62,656)
Trade balance	*(286)*	*(5,644)*	*(5,616)*	*(2,992)*	*(2,911)*	*(2,092)*	*(4,150)*	*(6,718)*	*(10,052)*	*(10,028)*	*(10,752)*	*(8,679)*	*(12,193)*	*(12,703)*	*(12,688)*
Services—credit	841	2,971	3,384	4,925	4,934	5,107	6,038	6,775	7,238	9,111	11,691	14,509	18,331	20,286	23,345
Services—debit	(1,054)	(2,981)	(3,903)	(5,945)	(6,735)	(6,497)	(8,200)	(10,268)	(11,171)	(12,443)	(14,540)	(17,271)	(19,913)	(16,087)	(17,828)
Net services	*(213)*	*(10)*	*(519)*	*(1,020)*	*(1,801)*	*(1,390)*	*(2,162)*	*(3,493)*	*(3,933)*	*(3,332)*	*(2,849)*	*(2,762)*	*(1,582)*	*4,199*	*5,517*
Income—credit	130	1,058	528	232	377	375	821	1,486	1,411	1,484	1,806	1,919	2,280	2,749	2,237
Income—debit	(388)	(523)	(1,347)	(4,235)	(4,289)	(4,121)	(4,370)	(5,219)	(4,667)	(5,002)	(5,443)	(5,629)	(6,156)	(5,403)	(5,721)
Net income	*(258)*	*535*	*(819)*	*(4,003)*	*(3,912)*	*(3,746)*	*(3,549)*	*(3,733)*	*(3,256)*	*(3,518)*	*(3,637)*	*(3,710)*	*(3,876)*	*(2,654)*	*(3,484)*
Transfers—credit	636	3,347	2,799	3,736	4,157	5,375	8,208	8,410	11,350	13,975	10,402	11,958	12,577	12,577	14,583
Transfers—debit	(26)	(14)	(23)	(13)	(18)	(23)	(23)	(27)	(66)	(62)	(67)	(35)	(68)	(68)	(264)
Net transfers	*610*	*3,333*	*2,776*	*3,723*	*4,139*	*5,352*	*8,185*	*8,383*	*11,284*	*13,913*	*10,335*	*11,923*	*12,509*	*12,509*	*14,320*
Financial Account	**944**	**483**	**3,281**	**3,450**	**4,075**	**7,074**	**10,576**	**3,861**	**11,848**	**9,635**	**8,584**	**9,579**	**9,616**	**9,545**	**12,678**
Direct investment outflow	--	--	--	--	--	--	(83)	(117)	(239)	(113)	(48)	(79)	(335)	(5)	(16)
Direct investment inflow	(10)	--	--	74	277	550	973	2,144	2,426	3,577	2,635	2,169	2,315	3,910	2,950
Portfolio investment liabilities	--	--	--	5	284	1,369	5,491	1,590	3,958	2,556	(601)	2,317	1,619	2,100	n/a
Other investment assets	3	(318)	53	(808)	929	1,830	1,170	(1,179)	(4,710)	(4,743)	(3,239)	(450)	(1,136)	n/a	n/a
Other investment liabilities	952	802	3,228	4,180	2,587	3,325	3,024	1,423	10,413	8,357	9,837	5,623	7,152	n/a	n/a
Net other investment	*955*	*484*	*3,281*	*3,372*	*3,516*	*5,155*	*4,194*	*244*	*5,703*	*3,614*	*6,598*	*5,173*	*6,016*	*4,300*	*n/a*
Errors & omissions	(439)	(361)	500	607	1,482	(987)	1,492	970	(1,934)	(1,348)	1,390	313	670	861	172
Reservesᵇ	**(357)**	**1,663**	**397**	**235**	**(1,072)**	**(4,211)**	**(10,391)**	**733**	**(3,958)**	**(5,321)**	**(3,071)**	**(6,664)**	**(6,087)**	**(11,757)**	**(16,514)**

SOURCE: International Financial Statistics Yearbook 2002; Economic Intelligence Unit, India Country Report, December 2002.

ᵃApril–December 2002 data—annualized.

ᵇNegative numbers represent additions to reserves.

MAJOR SOURCES OF INVISIBLE RECEIPTS IN INDIA'S BALANCE OF PAYMENTS

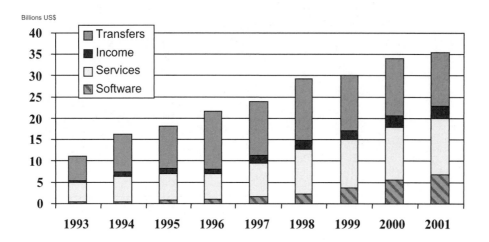

SOURCE: Reserve Bank of India, *Annual Report 2001–2002.*

GROWTH PERFORMANCE IN FIVE-YEAR PLANS

Plan	Years	Target (%)	Actual (%)
1ˢᵗ Plan	1951–1956	2.1	3.60
2nd Plan	1956–1961	4.5	4.21
3rd Plan	1961–1966	5.6	2.72
4th Plan	1969–1974	5.7	2.05
5th Plan	1974–1979	4.4	4.83
6th Plan	1980–1985	5.2	5.54
7th Plan	1985–1990	5.0	6.02
8th Plan	1992–1997	5.5	6.68
9th Plan	1997–2002	6.5	5.35

SOURCE: Planning Commission, Government of India.

[a]First three plans measure GNP. Fourth through ninth measure GDP at factor cost.

EXHIBIT 3.10B   HIGHLIGHTS OF 10TH FIVE-YEAR PLAN

Economic	Social	Political
Annual 8% GDP growth during 2002–2007	Reduction in poverty ratio to 21% from 26% by 2007 and 11% by 2012	Reduction of central government staff
Annual FDI flows of US$7.5 billion	Increase of literacy rate to 75% by 2007	Reduction in subsidies and administrative overheads
Divestment target of Rs 780 billion in five years	Reduction of infant mortality to 45 per 1,000 by 2007 and 28 [per 1,000] by 2012	Eliminating interstate barriers to trade and commerce
Fifty million jobs in five years	Halving of maternal mortality ratio to 2 by 2007	Amendment of Essential Commodities Act
Public sector outlay at Rs 1.59 billion	Increase in forest/tree cover to 25% in 2007 and 33% by 2012	Amending Agriculture Produce Marketing Act
Central plan outlay at Rs 9.21 billion	Potable drinking water in all villages	Liberalizing agri-trading, agri-industry, and exports
States and UT outlay at Rs 6.71billion	Cleaning of all major polluted rivers	Encouraging contract farming
Central Budgetary support at Rs 7.06 billion	Decadal population growth to reduce from 21.3% in 1991–2001 to 16.2% in 2001–2011	Futures trading in all commodities
Incremental capital-output ratio at 3.6%	All children in school by 2003 and all children to complete five-year schooling by 2007	Strengthening of bankruptcy and foreclosure laws
Investment rate of 28.4% of GDP		Labor reforms
Domestic savings rate of 26.8% of GDP		Policy reforms for small scale, including "deresevation"
External savings of 1.6%		Decontrol of private road transport passenger services
Reduction in Government dis-savings to -0.5%		
Increase in tax-GDP ratio to 10.3% by 2007		
Widening of tax base and improving collections		
Removing tax incentives and concessions		
Introducing an integrated central and state VAT		

SOURCE: Planning Commission, Government of India, *Tenth Five-Year Plan 2002–2007*; Shahid K. Abbas, "10th Plan Okayed," <http://rediff.com>, accessed October 5, 2002.

EXHIBIT 3.11A	PAST UNION BUDGETS (RS CRORE)			
	1998–1999	**1999–2000**	**2000–2001**	**2001–2002**
Revenue	149,510	181,513	192,624	201,449
Tax revenue	104,652	128,271	136,916	133,662
Nontax revenue	44,858	53,242	55,708	67,787
Capital receipts	16,507	11,854	14,171	20,049
Recoveries of loans	10,633	10,131	12,046	16,403
Other receipts	5,874	1,723	2,125	3,646
Total receipts	166,017	193,367	206,795	221,498
Nonplan expenditure[a]	212,548	221,902	242,942	261,259
Plan expenditure[b]	66,818	76,182	82,669	101,194
Total expenditure	279,366	298,084	325,611	362,453
Fiscal deficit	113,348	104,717	118,816	140,955
% of GDP	6.5%	5.4%	5.7%	6.1%

SOURCE: Ministry of Finance, Government of India; Aparajita Saha, "What Is the Union Budget," <http://rediff.com>.

[a] "Plan" expenditures are estimated after discussions between respective ministries and the Planning Commission.

[b] "Nonplan" expenditure accounts for the budgets of central government ministries, including interest payments, subsidies, government employee salaries, grants to states and union territories governments, pensions, police, economic services in various sectors, other general services, social services, and grants to foreign governments. Nonplan capital expenditure mainly includes defense, loans to public enterprises, loans to states, union territories, and foreign governments.

EXHIBIT 3.11B	ESTIMATED 2002–2003 AND 2003–2004 UNION BUDGETS (RS CRORE)	
	2002–2003 Revised Estimates	2003–2004 Estimates
Revenue:	236,936	253,935
Gross tax	221,918	251,527
Excise	87,383	96,791
Customs	45,500	49,350
Corporation tax	44,700	51,499
Income tax	37,300	44,070
Service tax	5,000	8,000
Taxes on union territories	540	557
Other	1,495	1,260
Less surcharges to Calamity Fund	1,600	3,600
Less states' share	56,141	63,758
Net tax revenue	164,177	184,169
Nontax revenue	72,759	69,766
Capital receipts	21,611	31,223
Total receipts	258,547	285,158
Nonplan expenditure:	289,924	317,821
Interest payments	115,663	123,223
Defense	41,088	44,347
Subsidies	44,618	49,907
Pensions	14,231	15,466
Social services	6,679	6,829
Economic services (agriculture, industry, power, etc.)	11,670	11,241
Other	35,030	38,371
Plan expenditure	114,089	120,974
Total expenditure	404,013	438,795
Fiscal deficit	(145,466)	(153,637)
% of GDP	5.9%	5.6%

SOURCE: Ministry of Finance, Government of India.

EXHIBIT 3.12	COMBINED FISCAL DEFICITS FOR CENTER AND STATES

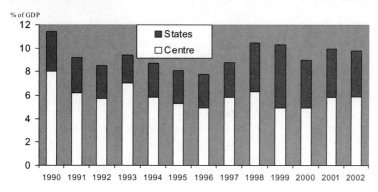

SOURCE: Reserve Bank of India, *Annual Report 2001–2002.*

EXHIBIT 3.13A	COMPOSITION OF GROSS CAPITAL FORMATION

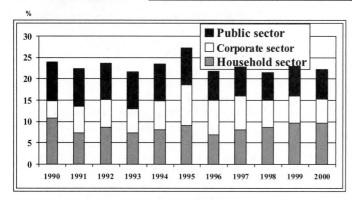

SOURCE: Reserve Bank of India, *Annual Report 2001–2002.*

EXHIBIT 3.13B	INDIAN DEMOCRACY PROFUSION OF PARTIES

Seats in India's Lower House, 1998 Election[a]

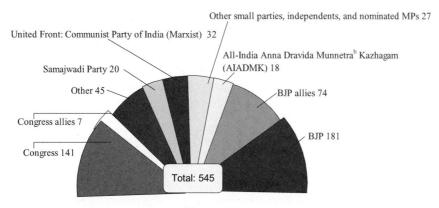

SOURCE: Richard Vietor.

[a]Some parties realigned after election.   [b]Defected from the government on April 17, 1999.

ENDNOTES

1 "10th Five-Year Plan (2002–2007)," India Planning Commission, p. 144.

2 "Deep Cracks in India's Ruling Coalition," *Business Week Online*, <http://www.businessweek.com>, accessed April 2, 2002.

3 Gautam Naik, "A Global Journal Report: Global Population Boom Goes Bust," *The Asian Wall Street Journal*, January 27, 2003.

4 "Country Profile: India 2002," Economist Intelligence Unit, p.16.

5 "Country Profile: India 2002," Economist Intelligence Unit, p.17.

6 Census of India 2001 Web site, <http://www.censusindia.net/>.

7 "India: Country Assistance Plan 2001," The World Bank Group, June 2001, p.11.

8 "Teaching English the Indian Way," BBC Online, <http://news.bbc.co.uk>, May 17, 2000.

9 "Country Profile: India 2002," Economist Intelligence Unit, p.17.

10 D. G. Tendulkar, *Mahatma* (Delhi: Government of India, 1960), Volume 2, p. 236.

11 "India Partitioned as Raj Withdraws," History Today (August 1997), Vol. 47, No. 8.

12 "Casualties in Nuclear Exchange Could Be between 8 and 12 Million," *Associated Press Newswires*, May 28, 2002.

13 Interview with Jairam Ramesh, secretary, Economic Affairs Department, All India Congress Committee.

14 Ibid.

15 Edward Luce, "Rowdies Lower the Tone in World's Most Populous Democracy," *The Financial Times*, April 20, 2002.

16 Robert Kennedy, "India in 1996," HBS Case No. 798-065 (Boston: Harvard Business School Publishing, 1998), p. 5.

17 "First Five-Year Plan," India Infoline Web site, <http://www.indiainfoline.com>.

18 "2nd Five-Year Plan," Planning Commission of India Web site, <http://planningcommission.nic.in>.

19 "Commanding Heights: Interview with Manmohan Singh," WGBH Web site, <http://www.pbs.org/wgbh/commandingheights>.

20 Richard Vietor, Max Weston, and Waleed Iskander, "India (A)," HBS Case No. 793-112 (Boston: Harvard Business School Publishing, 1993), p. 5.

21 Arvind Panagariya, "India's Economic Reforms," Asian Development Bank: ERD Policy Brief Series, Number 2, February 2002, p. 5.

22 Jagdish Bhagwati and P. Desai, *India: Planning for Industrialisation* (London: Oxford University Press, 1970), p. 363.

23 Much of paragraph taken from page 7 of "India (A)," HBS Case No. 793-112.

24 Anne Krueger, *The Benefits and Costs of Import Substitution in India* (Don Mills, Ontario: Burns and Machern, 1975), p. 23.

25 Ibid., p. 127.

26 Robert Kennedy, "India in 1996," HBS Case No. 798-065, p. 5.

27 "The Green Revolution," India Onestop Web site, <http://www.indiaonestop.com>.

28 Pradeep Agarwal, Subir Gokarn, Veena Mishra, Kirit Parikh, and Kunal Sen, *Policy, Regimes and Industrial Competitiveness* (London: Macmillan Press, 2000), p. 252.

29 Arvind Virmani, "India's BOP Crisis and External Reform: Two Paradoxes," *Chintan Occasional Paper*, September 2001, p. 12.

30 Ashok Malik, "Reservations: How Do We Untangle the Knot?" *India Today*, October 7, 2002.

31 John Williamson, "What Washington Means by Policy Reform," in *Latin American Adjustment: How Much Has Happened?* (Washington, DC: Institute for International Economics, 1990), Chapter 2.

32 "Commanding Heights: 2/6/01 Interview with P. Chidambaram, Finance Minister of India, 1996–1998," WGBH Web site, <http://www.pbs.org/wgbh/commandingheights>.

33 Arvind Virmani, p. 20.

34 Tim Callen and Paul Cashin, "Assessing India's External Position," Reynolds and Towe, *India at the Crossroads: Sustaining Growth and Reducing Poverty* (Washington DC: IMF, 2001), p. 35.

35 "Commanding Heights: 2/6/01 Interview with P. Chidambaram, Finance Minister of India, 1996–1998," WGBH Web site.

36 United Nations Development Programme, *Human Development Report 2001* (New York: Oxford University Press, 2001), p. 91.

37 Raj Chengappa, et al., "Higher Education: The Need for Radical Surgery," *India Today*, September 30, 2002, p. 5.

38 United Nations Development Programme, *Human Development Report* 2001, p. 91.

39 "Study Sees IT Sector Growing at 34%," *Business Line*, June 11, 2002.

40 Edwin Luce, "India Stirs," *The Financial Times*, August 29, 2002.

41 Interview with Sharda Cherwoo, CEO, Ernst & Young Pvt. Ltd., Shared Service Location.

42 Joanna Slater, "Outsourcing—GE Reinvents Itself in India," *Far Eastern Economic Review*, March 27, 2003.

43 Ibid.

44 Edwin Luce, "India Stirs."

45 "Combined Fiscal Deficit of 11–12% Not Sustainable: Claude Smadja," Confederation of Indian Industry Press Releases, November 2000.

46 "India To Upgrade Highways Network with US$516 Million from World Bank," The World Bank Group Press Release, June 9, 2000.

47 Interview with executive, GE India.

48 Edwin Luce, "India Stirs."

49 Sheila McNulty and Khozem Merchant, "Enron Issues Veiled Sanction Threat to India," *The Financial Times*, August 24, 2001.

50 Khozem Merchant and Robert Shrimsley, "The Enron Affair," *The Financial Times,* January 12, 2002.

51 "India: The Growth Imperative," *McKinsey Global Institute*, September 2001, p. 5.

52 Edward Luce, "Hands-On Politics: Integrity Has Given Way to Greed and Criminality in India's Public Life," *The Financial Times*, October 12, 2002.

53 Transparency International Web site, <www.transparency.org>.

54 Interview with Arun Shourie, minister, Ministry of Disinvestment, Government of India.

55 Edward Luce, "Rowdies Lower the Tone in World's Most Populous Democracy," *The Financial Times*, April 20, 2002.

56 Lok Sabha, "Presentation on Disinvestment to Committee on Petitions," Ministry of Disinvestment, October 2002.

57 Interview with Aroon Purie, editor-in-chief, *The India Today* Group.

58 "India: The Growth Imperative," p. 5.

59 Lok Sabha, "Presentation on Disinvestment to Committee on Petitions."

60 Interview with Arun Shourie.

61 "A Passion For Privatizing," *Business Week*, July 8, 2002, p. 58.

62 Lok Sabha, "Presentation on Disinvestment to Committee on Petitions," p. 29.

63 "A Passion For Privatizing," *Business Week*, July 8, 2002, p. 58.

64 Interview with Pradip Baijpal, secretary, Ministry of Disinvestment, Government of India.

65 Interview with Arun Shourie, minister.

66 Arvind Panagariya, "India's Economic Reforms," Asian Development Bank: ERD Policy Brief Series, February 2002, 2, p. 8.

67 "India: The Growth Imperative," *McKinsey Global Institute,* September 2001, p. 6.

68 Interview with Rakesh Mohan, deputy governor, Reserve Bank of India.

69 "India: The Growth Imperative," *McKinsey Global Institute,* September 2001, p. 4.

70 Interview with M. S. Banga, chairman, Hindustan Lever Ltd.

71 Interview with Yashwant Sinha, External Affairs Minister, Government of India.

72 "'We Have No Orders to Save You:' State Participation and Complicity in Communal Violence in India," *Human Rights Watch*, Volume 14, No. 3, April 2002, p. 4.

73 Ibid., p.7.

74 BBC News Web site, <http://news.bbc.co.uk/2/hi/south_asia/1951471.stm>, accessed April 25, 2002.

State Socialism's Disintegration

This case examines the challenges facing Russian President Vladimir Putin in 2000. President Putin has inherited a deeply troubled Russian economy. The transition from socialism to capitalism, begun in 1991, has been fraught with difficulty. This case explores the recent history of Russia's transition, attempts to identify the sources of Russia's economic troubles, and evaluates President Putin's political and economic plans.

The first section provides a brief synopsis of liberalization, stabilization, and privatization under President Boris Yeltsin. The second section describes the economic difficulties Russia experienced during the 1990s, involving demonetization, federalism, taxes, contract enforcement, the legal system, the 1998 financial crisis, and public health. The final section surveys the government's plans to improve Russia's economic performance.

It has now become common among journalists and scholars to blame the "weakness," "incoherence," and "incapacity" of the Russian state for Russia's economic problems during the 1990s. More importantly, Russia's leaders themselves now also believe that their central problem is a dysfunctional state, and they hope to undertake *gosudarstvo stroitel'stvo*, or state-building. The case is designed to teach this basic point about the relationship between Russia's state and its troubled economic transformation and, in general, to emphasize the importance of coherent political institutions for a capitalist economic system.

CASE STUDY   **RUSSIA: THE END OF A TIME OF TROUBLES?**

RAWI ABDELAL

> *lomat'—ne stroit' (to tear down is not to build)*
>
> —Russian proverb

Introduction

On December 31, 1999, Boris Yeltsin, who had taken office in 1991 as the first democratically elected president in Russia's history, resigned. In a poignant farewell speech, he asked the forgiveness of Russian citizens, "For the fact that many of the dreams that we shared did not come true. And for the fact that what seemed simple to us turned out to be tormentingly difficult." Yeltsin once had believed that Russia "at one stroke, in one spurt, could leap from the gray, stagnant, totalitarian past into the bright, rich, civilized future," a view he now considered "naïve." The aging, frequently ill leader argued that Russia's difficulties required a new generation of leaders; he had one in mind. Yeltsin appointed Prime Minister Vladimir Putin the acting president, a post he would hold for three months, until a new election could be held in March 2000. Always "certain of the surprising wisdom of Russians," Yeltsin urged Russian voters to elect Putin to a four-year term as president.[1]

Russian voters did indeed choose Putin, who easily defeated ten other candidates in the first round of voting with 53 percent of the vote, 20 percent more than his nearest rival, the Communist Gennady Zyuganov.

Putin's rise to power and popularity, from relative obscurity to the country's highest office in less than a year, had been dramatic and rapid. On August 9, 1999, he became Prime Minister. That fall, after a series of unclaimed bombings terrorized Moscow and led to 300 deaths, Putin solidified his power base and became even more popular during his prosecution of the second Chechen War. When he assumed office on May 7, 2000, President Putin appeared to have a significant mandate from the Russian people to do *something* to solve Russia's political, economic, and military problems.

President Putin inherited an unenviable role, however, for Russia's problems were enormous. There were no obvious solutions. The years after December 1991, when the Soviet Union disintegrated, had once been called *chudesnye*, or miraculous. By 1999, some Russians declared that their country was in the midst of a new *smutnoe vremia*, or Time of Troubles, a phrase that referred to a legendary period of political upheaval and instability in the early seventeenth century.

Certainly, the 1990s were a decade of economic troubles. In 1998, the Russian economy seemed to have reached its nadir. GDP had fallen to 55 percent of its 1989 level. [See **Exhibits 4.7a** to **d, 4.8, 4.9**.] Between 1988 and 1995, the proportion of Russians living below the poverty line increased from 2 to 50 percent.[2] A few Russians made fortunes during these years of economic transformation, but the overall benefits of change were uneven. Russia's Gini coefficient, a measure of income inequality, nearly doubled between 1989 and 1995, rising from .27 to .48.[3] Popular opinion held that 100 families owned 60 percent of the country's wealth. If true, this would have been a remarkable development for a country in which the institution of private property was merely a decade old.

What could President Putin do to turn Russia around? Advice from Western advisors was just as plentiful as when Russia began its economic transformation during the early 1990s. But many Russians no longer trusted Western advisors, whom they associated with the economic collapse. Although many observers agreed on the desirability of a well-functioning market economy, there was no consensus about how to create one. Within Russia, the reformist agenda was hotly contested; many Russians still rejected capitalism and supported the Communist Party.

What had gone wrong with Russia's economic reforms? Analysts disagreed about that as well. Russia's still-influential Communist

---

Professor Rawi Abdelal with the assistance of Research Associate Kimberly Haddad prepared this case. HBS cases are developed solely as the basis for class discussion. Cases are not intended to serve as endorsements, sources of primary data, or illustrations of effective or ineffective management.

Party believed that economic reform had gone too far too quickly.[4] Some Western economists complained that the Russian government had not implemented economic reform completely or quickly enough.[5] Still other analysts emphasized that the problem was not the amount of reform (too much or too little), nor its speed (too fast or too slow), but some other, unforeseen difficulty of the reform process.[6] To understand what went wrong in Russian economic reform, analysts invoked a list of possibilities: the lack of trust in Russian culture and civil society, corruption, "Eastern" civilization, Orthodox religion, the persistence of Communist ideology, the naivete of the reformers, an unwieldy federal political system, and, most vaguely, "politics." But those who sought to solve Russia's problems needed to understand exactly what had happened.

Russia's Economic Reform, 1991–

Between 1917 and 1991, the Union of Soviet Socialist Republics (USSR) existed as one state. Just as the Soviet political system was a dramatic experiment in organization, so too was the Soviet economic system. The Soviet economy was based on state ownership of the means of production, administrative hierarchy, command planning and production targets, and collectivized agriculture. Managers of firms, all state-owned, were concerned primarily with meeting production targets set by state planners. Because the state allocated credit and resources, budget constraints were soft. The state also coordinated inputs and outputs and set prices, which played a passive role in the economy. Decisions about what to produce were made by institutions of the state, particularly the *Politburo*, *Gosplan*, and various government ministries.[7]

The Soviet system achieved rapid economic growth between the 1920s and the 1950s and created a formidable industrial and military power. By the middle of the 1980s, however, the Soviet Union's once remarkable economic growth had disappeared. Growth rates had been in decline since the 1960s, leading eventually to a crisis of legitimacy for both the Soviet state and the Communist regime. Soviet economic growth had been based on a massive mobilization of resources for industrial and military development. Soviet planners rapidly expanded employment and invested enormously in physical capital. Ultimately, however, growth based on resource mobilization experienced diminishing returns: Soviet productivity eventually began a long secular decline from which it never recovered. Technological innovation stagnated as well: Soviet planners found it easier to mandate increased production in heavy industrial sectors such as steel (Soviet leader Nikita Khrushchev once remarked that the planners demanded so much that they must be "steel-eaters") than to create incentives for high-technology and consumer products. In 1985, to save the system and the Union amidst economic stagnation and a pervasive sense of crisis, Mikhail Gorbachev, head of the Soviet Communist Party, initiated *perestroika* (a restructuring of the economy).

In late October 1991, Boris Yeltsin, who had been elected the President of Russia the previous June, announced that his administration would radically reform the economy of the republic, despite the fact that the Soviet Union, of which the Russian republic was a part, still existed. Yeltsin sought not to save the Soviet economic system, as Gorbachev had done, but to destroy it. Russia's Congress of People's Deputies gave Yeltsin the authority to reform the republic's administration for a period of one year, between November 1991 and December 1992. During this year, Yeltsin was authorized to mandate components of his economic reform program by decree, change the structure of government, and appoint all cabinet ministers without parliamentary approval. Yeltsin seized the opportunity and promised that although the transition would be painful, it would at least be rapid: "It will be worse for everybody for about half a year."

Yeltsin entrusted the reform process not to politicians but, in his words, to "professionals." This turned out to be an ideologically committed group that came to be known in Russia as the "young reformers." They were professional economists all under the age of 40, and they guided Yeltsin's attempt to create a market economy. Some Russians interpreted the youth and political inexperience of the reform team ungenerously. Vice President Aleksandr Rutskoi, for example, called them "small boys in pink shorts and yellow boots."[8] The ranks of the young reformers included Anatoly Chubais, who became known for his relentless commitment to the reforms; Yegor Gaidar, the intellectual leader of the group; and Alfred Kokh, who would play an important role in the privatization process.[9]

The reformers planned to free most prices, three quarters of which were still state-controlled, liberalize imports, overhaul the tax system, eliminate the budget deficit, tighten monetary policy, and privatize the majority of state-owned firms. Overall, their plans fell into three categories: price and trade liberalization, macroeconomic stabilization, and privatization. Several features of their approach led to its being called "Shock Therapy," after a similar program in Poland. These features included the speed with which the plan was supposed to be implemented, as well as the administration of the plan by a small, politically insulated reform team.[10]

The economic reforms were quite controversial and generated significant opposition from some members of parliament, bureaucrats, and directors of industrial firms—the so-called "red directors." In the autumn of 1993, when Yeltsin ordered the dissolution of parliament and called for new parliamentary elections, acrimonious politics became violent. A number of members refused to leave the parliamentary building, an act that led to a two-week standoff between the president and legislature. On October 3–4, 1993, Yeltsin used military force to end the confrontation. In November 1993, he issued a new constitution, which was ratified by a referendum the following month.

In December, elections were held for a new bicameral legislature. This legislature consisted of a Federation Council, composed of two representatives from each of Russia's 89 regions, and a more powerful State Duma, composed of 450 members, half of whom were allocated to parties based on voter support, and the other half of whom were elected directly. Russian voters did not support the parties of economic reform, Russia's Choice and Yabloko, which won little more than a third of the seats in the Russian Duma. Centrist parties, ambivalent about reform, won approximately 40 percent of the seats. The biggest blow to the young reformers was the success of parties explicitly against capitalist reform of any kind, including the Communist and Agrarian Parties [see **Exhibits 4.10a** to **f**].

Liberalization and Stabilization

With the help of the International Monetary Fund (IMF), the reform team implemented its liberalization and stabilization plans. The government freed most prices on January 2,

1992.[11] At the same time, the reformers sought tight monetary policy to rein in inflation, some of which was inevitable as a result of allowing prices to rise to market-clearing levels. The reform team also intended to balance Russia's budget.

For the first few months of 1992, the reformers achieved some success. In April 1992, however, as powerful political and economic forces increasingly opposed the tight monetary and fiscal policies, both were progressively relaxed. Then, the Russian central bank itself complicated the reform efforts with its liberal credit policy. In June 1992, President Yeltsin nominated Viktor Gerashchenko to be chairman of the Central Bank of Russia (CBR). Gerashchenko, who had been the head of *Gosbank*, the Soviet central bank, did not agree with the reformers' approach to monetary policy. Instead of tight monetary policy, Gerashchenko generously offered the CBR's credit to Russia's struggling industrial enterprises. With Gerashchenko's role at the CBR in the hands of the parliament, half of whose members opposed the reformers' shock therapy approach, the Yeltsin government was unable to impose monetary discipline and a hard budget constraint on Russian firms.

Finally, beginning in January 1995, the government apparently managed to stabilize the macroeconomic environment, or at least to reduce inflation. Although the government's fiscal imbalance persisted, by July 1995 inflation had fallen below 5 percent per month, a level it maintained until the financial crisis of August 1998.[12]

Privatization, 1992–1994: Vouchers and Auctions

The young reformers proceeded under the assumptions that any private owner of Russian assets and companies would manage more efficiently than the state, and that new private owners would demand the appropriate institutional foundations of markets. As two American economists who had advised the Russian reform team observed, "the reformers predicted that institutions would follow private property rather than the other way around."[13] In the long run, the young Russian reformers argued, owners of privatized firms, no matter who they were or how they acquired ownership rights, would have incentives to increase the value of their firms, to seek profits, to compete, and to generate efficiency and growth for the economy as a whole. Anatoly Chubais, the reformer most responsible for Russia's several rounds of privatization, once remarked of Russia's emerging business elite: "They steal and steal and steal. They are stealing absolutely everything, and it is impossible to stop them. But let them steal and take their property. They will then become owners and decent administrators of this property."[14]

The reformers began the privatization process by giving away public assets to those who, in principle, had always owned them: the public. Every Russian citizen was offered a "voucher," which could be exchanged for stock in privatized firms, invested in a voucher fund, or sold for cash. The direct exchange for stock was supposed to take place at a "voucher auction," during which holders of vouchers bid for shares. In December 1992, beginning with the Bolshevik Biscuit Company, the Russian government began auctioning off stock in state-owned firms. The reformers achieved their goal of rapidly privatizing a large number of firms. Between January 1992 and June 1994, the government privatized 16,500 firms, shares of which were held by over 41 million Russians, either directly or through voucher investment funds. However, the very speed of the privatization process limited the ability of citizens to understand and participate fully in the process. Auctions happened quickly all over the country, and many were underpublicized.

The directors of Russia's large industrial enterprises generally opposed both restructuring and privatization, which threatened their control over much of the economic structure Russia had inherited from Soviet industrialization. As a compromise, the government offered, through three separate programs, the current workers and managers preferential access to their firm's shares. By far the most popular of the three programs was the so-called "Option 2," with which workers and managers received 51 percent of the voting shares in their firms at a nominal price. Through a variety of complex schemes, many not legal, some managers acquired even greater control over their firms' assets. Thus, "insiders" received more control than the reformers originally had hoped, and many of the newly private firms did not restructure quickly and efficiently.[15]

Privatization, 1995–1999: Pledge Auctions

Russia's most valuable and highly prized public assets—the natural gas, oil, and mineral deposits with which the country is abundantly endowed—were excluded from the process of mass privatization. Instead, these "strategic" industries were the subject of a number of presidential decrees issued during late 1992. The GKI (*Gosudarstvenny Kommitet Imushchestvo,* or State Property Committee) was to deal with those sectors later. Between 1995 and 1997, when it did privatize those resource sectors, the GKI created a controversy that continued into the next decade and undermined public support for the reform process. The background of these later privatizations was the fiscal crisis faced by Boris Yeltsin and the reformers in 1995. The budget was in deep trouble because expenditures continued to outpace revenues by a large margin. [See **Exhibits 4.2a and 4.2b**.]

In March 1995, Oneksimbank, chaired by Vladimir Potanin, proposed a solution to Yeltsin's fiscal problems. In consultation with the leaders of several other powerful banks, Menatep, Inkombank, Imperial, and Stolichny, Potanin suggested that the banks offer the Russian government a large loan for one year. As collateral, the banks would hold and manage the state's blocks of shares in 29 large Russian firms, most of which were state-owned oil and minerals assets. The block of shares in each firm was to be distributed to a specific bank to hold in trust after an open and competitive auction, or "pledge auction," as the government called it. The proceeds of each auction were "loaned" to the Russian government. If, at the end of the year, on September 1, 1996 (after the summer's presidential elections), the Russian government elected not to repay the loan, ownership of the blocks of shares would be transferred to the winners of the pledge auctions, who would have been holding and managing the shares.[16] Details of the plan, approved by President Yeltsin, were codified on August 31, 1995, in Decree No. 889: "On the Procedure for Pledging Stock Held in Federal Ownership for the Year 1995." The GKI authorized Oneksimbank and the other banks to organize the pledge auctions.

For the most part, the banks agreed among themselves in advance which bank would bid for each block of shares. According to Leonid Nevzlin, a business partner of Menatep's Mikhail Khodorkovsky, "We reached an agreement of who would take what. We agreed not to get in each other's way."[17] Because the auctions were public, outside financial groups also could bid—a fact that created some difficulties for the arrangement. In each case, however, the GKI, led by the reformer Alfred Kokh, disqualified the outside bidder on technical grounds. Foreign bidders were excluded from seven auctions, including the potentially most lucrative oil companies (Lukoil, Sidanko, Yukos, and Sibneft) as well as the main mineral and metals firm (Norilsk Nickel). Ultimately, the government held 12 pledge auctions only.

One of the more controversial cases involved Norilsk Nickel, a conglomerate whose holdings included a factory at Norilsk; refining works in southern Siberia; two nickel factories on the Kola Peninsula near Norway, which produce 20 percent of the world's nickel; and Krasnoiarsk Non-Ferrous Metallurgical Works, which extracts 40 percent of the world's platinum production. The Norilsk Nickel pledge auction took place on November 17, 1995. Oneksimbank, the auctioneer, won the auction and paid the Russian government $170.1 million, up from a starting price of $170 million set by the GKI. Rossiiski Kredit, another large bank not involved in the arrangement with the government, intended to contest Oneksimbank's bid for Norilsk Nickel, an attractive prospect because of its annual profits of $400 million. However, Alfred Kokh of the GKI discovered a procedural irregularity in Rossiiski Kredit's bid. As Kokh recalls, "As I examined the bids closely, I smelled a rat."[18] On the day of the auction, Kokh informed Rossiiski Kredit that its bid would be excluded, although the rules required that potential bidders be notified of any procedural problems before the auction. Outraged, Vitaly Malkin, the chairman of Rossiiski Kredit, tore open the envelope containing his bank's bid and announced that it was $355 million, more than double Oneksimbank's bid. Thus Potanin, the creator of the pledge auctions plan, received one of its largest prizes at what appeared to be a considerable discount. By some estimates, Norilsk Nickel earned Potanin's financial-industrial empire $100 million per month.

The other bankers who had organized the pledge auctions achieved similar success in their efforts to acquire the blocks of shares on which they planned to bid.[19] No outside bidders won any of 12 pledge auctions held in late 1995. The government received $800 million in loans from the auctions, a welcome inflow into the federal budget. The Western media called it the "loans-for-shares" deal.

After the pledge auctions, the pace of privatization slowed considerably. During 1997 and 1998, the government sold its stake in eight major enterprises only. In 1999, privatization practically ceased.

The Rise of the "Oligarchs," 1995–1997

During the mid-1990s, Russians began to refer to a handful of powerful businessmen as "the oligarchs," a term that reflected Russians' perception that the businessmen's wealth had given them political influence.[20] As Russians began to suspect that privatization mostly benefited a privileged few, a new word entered the vernacular to describe what had happened to the most valuable assets of the state. The Russian verb *prikhvatit'* means "to grab." Russians punned that *privatizatsiia*—privatization—had instead been *prikhvatizatsiia*—grab-ization. It was widely believed that the oligarchs had done much of the grabbing.

The 1996 presidential election was the defining moment of the oligarchs' image in Russian society. The Yeltsin administration and the young reformers had, until 1995, kept their distance from these already powerful businessmen. The pledge auctions reflected a deal that the Yeltsin administration and the reformers were, by their own estimation, forced to make. Because of the inability of the state to meet its fiscal obligations, the government needed the funds the oligarchs offered.

The government faced a larger problem as well: Yeltsin's unpopularity and the upcoming presidential election. The president's popularity ratings had plummeted into the single digits, falling at times to 5 percent. Meanwhile, public support for Gennady Zyuganov, the head of Russia's Communist Party, seemed to increase in proportion to the difficulties of economic transition. In early 1996, many analysts believed Zyuganov was almost certain to defeat Yeltsin. In January 1996, mere months before the election, Zyuganov led the polls by a substantial margin, followed by Yeltsin in fifth place, with only 8 percent of the population intending to support the incumbent president.[21]

For a number of reasons, the oligarchs were worried about a possible Zyuganov presidency. Many feared Zyuganov would end Russia's experiment with markets and democracy. The oligarchs also were fairly certain that Zyuganov would not honor the pledge auctions arrangement. Without this arrangement, the oligarchs stood to lose not only millions of rubles but political power as well. To prevent this from happening, Zyuganov's political ambitions had to be derailed. As Yegor Gaidar, a committed reformer, put it, "I understood the loans-for-shares program perfectly well. The loans for shares created a political pact. They helped to ensure that Zyuganov did not come to the Kremlin. It was a necessary pact."[22]

At the World Economic Forum in Davos, Switzerland, in February 1996, Russia's most powerful businessmen, along with Anatoly Chubais, one of the reformers, agreed to cooperate to support Yeltsin's reelection bid. In addition, the businessmen hired Chubais to organize Yeltsin's campaign, for which they also promised substantial financial support. The Davos Pact, as it came to be called, included Boris Berezovsky, Vladimir Gusinsky, Mikhail Khodorkovsky, Vladimir Potanin, and Aleksandr Smolensky, all of whom had been involved in the pledge auctions, as well as two critics of the pledge auctions, Mikhail Fridman and Piotr Aven, who were convinced that the Zyuganov threat was serious enough to support Yeltsin's reelection bid.[23] Yeltsin recalls his "first-ever meeting with representatives of the major banks and media groups: Boris Berezovsky, Vladimir Gusinsky, Mikhail Khodorkovsy, Vladimir Potanin, [and] Mikhail Fridman. ... They offered all their resources—media, regional contacts, and funding."[24] Although Russian law limits presidential candidates to $3 million in campaign spending, Yeltsin's campaign team admitted that more than $100 million was spent on the president's reelection bid. Estimates from other sources were higher, ranging from $500 million to $1 billion.[25]

Apart from their financial backing, the oligarchs held considerable influence over much of Russia's popular media.[26] Four banks controlled by the oligarchs were part of a consortium that owned a controlling stake of the ORT television station: the Alfa group (controlled by Mikhail Fridman and Piotr Aven);

Logovaz (connected to Boris Berezovsky); Menatep (associated with Mikhail Khodorkovsky); and Stolichny (run by Aleksandr Smolensky). As chairman of the board of ORT, and with an additional block of ORT shares, Berezovsky delivered his influence over the station, as well as his newspapers, *Nezavisimaia gazeta*, *Novaia izvestiia*, and *Kommersant*. Vladimir Potanin's Oneksimbank owned *Izvestiia*, *Komsomolskaia pravda*, *Russkii telegraf*, and *Ekspert*, which supported Yeltsin's reelection. Most remarkable was the change in the coverage of the Yeltsin administration by the NTV television station, owned by Vladimir Gusinksy's Media-Most group. NTV had been highly critical of the Yeltsin administration's handling of the Chechen war, but during the election campaign rallied behind the president. Igor Malashenko, NTV's president, joined the campaign officially as Yeltsin's media adviser. *Segodnia* and *Itogi*, Media-Most's newspapers, also supported President Yeltsin openly.[27]

All of this led Yeltsin's rival, Gennady Zyuganov, to complain: "The mass media are being used to conduct an extravagant campaign in support of Mr. Yeltsin and at the same time to attack national-patriotic forces and to promote hysteria and psychosis."[28] His communist colleagues in the Duma also dealt Zyuganov's presidential campaign a blow. In March, they passed two resolutions denouncing the December 1991 Belovezhskaia accords, which had officially dissolved the Soviet Union. The Russian parliament thus announced in the middle of the campaign that, as far as it was concerned, the Soviet Union still legally existed.

Ultimately, the Yeltsin re-election campaign was successful, and the incumbent president defeated Zyuganov in the second round of voting on July 3, 1996. In August, Yeltsin named Vladimir Potanin of Oneksimbank Deputy Prime Minister. Then, in September, the Yeltsin administration decided not to repay the pledge-auction loans. Ownership of the state's shares of the natural resource firms, therefore, was transferred to the banks that had been holding those shares as collateral. Many analysts believe, however, that the oligarchs were not good managers of their new property.[29]

Russia's Economic Troubles, 1991–1999

The Ruble, Barter, and Demonetization

Russia's currency troubles during the decade were complex.[30] One problem was that the currency Russia inherited in December 1991 was the Soviet ruble, the currency used by all 15 former Soviet states. Although only Russia's central bank could actually print new rubles (all the printing presses were in Russia), the central banks of the other new states could issue ruble credit. As a result, Russia's central bank did not have complete control over the country's money supply until July 1993, when the central bank issued a new currency that was truly a Russian ruble.

The consolidation of Russia's money was made even more complex by developments within Russia. Although by 1993 rubles came from only one central bank, many Russian firms began to use rubles less frequently to complete transactions with one another. Instead, Russian business-to-business transactions were increasingly based on barter. During Soviet times, barter had been common because the state set prices. After prices were freed in January 1992, barter became much less common. But beginning in 1994, barter increased, as did new, uniquely post-Soviet forms of barter. [See **Exhibit 4.5**.]

Estimates of barter varied, but everyone knew it was increasing. In January 1992, less then 10 percent of industrial sales were completed by barter. But in January 1999, almost 50 percent of industrial sales involved barter. Some estimates of barter in industrial sales ranged as high as 70 percent. Seizing the opportunity, professional intermediaries began to organize complex chains of deliveries involving a number of firms.

As these barter relationships expanded, they created a number of problems for the Russian economy. Without cash revenues, for example, firms were unable to pay salaries. The federal government could not effectively tax industries that relied on barter because it was unable to evaluate accurately the value of a firm's assets and transactions. Of more consequence was that so many firms relied so much on barter that few firms had cash to pay taxes at all. Provincial governments began to tax in kind, and eventually the federal government was forced to tax in kind

as well. Some analysts believed that barter allowed Russian firms, which essentially were bankrupt, to avoid bankruptcy itself, and also to avoid restructuring or laying off employees.[31]

In addition to direct barter among firms, new monetary surrogates emerged, primarily as local currencies. Several kinds of these quasi-monies appeared in Russia's regions. Sometimes regional governments, such as Tatarstan's, issued their own money substitutes to supplement a supply of rubles they considered insufficient. Local commercial banks and firms, especially influential fuel and power companies and railroads, issued promissory notes called *vekselia*, or wechsels (from the German word meaning bill of exchange), that began to circulate as independent local currencies.

The Regions, Federal Authority, and Taxes

Russia, as the territorial state it was in 2000, never existed before 1991. Prior to 1917, "Russia" was Tsarist Russia, a vast empire ruled by the Romanov dynasty. The Tsarist Empire covered most of the territory that, after the Russian Revolution, later became part of the Soviet Union. The "Russia" that existed in Soviet times was one of 15 constituent Soviet republics, all of which became independent states during 1991.

Since 1991, post-Soviet "Russia" is, officially, the Russian Federation, which has its own complex federal system inherited from Soviet authorities. There are 89 federal units, or "subjects," of the Russian Federation, organized into six legal categories. There are 21 "republics," each of which bears the name of a non-Russian ethnic group.[32] Then there are 49 *oblasts* and 6 *krais*, populated primarily by ethnic Russians. Moscow and St. Petersburg have special status as "federal cities," but are treated functionally as *oblasts*. Finally, there are 10 autonomous *okrugs* and 1 autonomous *oblast*, whose populations are predominantly non-Russian. Russians referred to these administrative units collectively as "the regions."

In June 1990, even before the 1991 collapse of the Soviet Union, the newly elected parliament of the Russian republic had declared "sovereignty" from the Soviet Union. In response, 16 autonomous republics within the Russian republic offered their own declarations of sovereignty, in an attempt to recast the balance of power between federal government and the regions within Russia. At the time, Boris

Yeltsin, then chairman of the parliament, encouraged this action. Yeltsin was engaged in his own struggle with Soviet leader Mikhail Gorbachev. Gorbachev sought to hold the Soviet Union together, whereas Yeltsin sought more power for himself as the leader of Russia. Because he was eager not to set a Russian precedent for re-centralizing federal authority within the Soviet Union, Yeltsin told the leaders of Russia's regions to "take as much sovereignty as you can swallow."[33]

Russia's regional leaders swallowed a great deal of sovereignty during the early 1990s, and they did not give it back. A few adopted their own "regional" constitutions, and claimed that their laws took precedence over federal law. At least a dozen regions actually violated federal laws; the Kremlin's count was 30. Sixteen claimed the right to conduct an independent foreign economic policy. Nine claimed the right to control the natural resources on their territory. According to the Ministry of Justice, between 25 and 35 percent of regional legislation did not conform to federal laws or the constitution.[34] Although the 1993 Constitution was supposed to have definitively settled the balance of power between the federal government and the regions, President Yeltsin, in his attempt to hold the fragile federation together, signed a number of bilateral treaties with various republics and *oblasti*. By 2000, Yeltsin's government had signed 50 treaties with various administrative units of the Federation, each redefining authority that was supposed to have been settled in the Constitution. A number of these bilateral treaties rearranged authority over taxes [see **Exhibit 4.4**].

The federal government's inability to impose its authority on all of Russian territory or all of Russia's regional and local governments created a number of problems for the economy. For example, Russia was only nominally a customs union, since goods could not always move freely across regional borders. Russia's fiscal system was troubled as well. Although the federal government was unable to collect its taxes effectively, regional and local governments seemed to fare much better. Apparently the federal government became unable to acquire its share of tax receipts from regional and local authorities.[35] [See **Exhibit 4.5**.]

Russia's tax laws, enormously complex and confiscatory, led to other tax collection problems unrelated to Russia's federalism. According to one prominent executive, Robert Sheppard of the Sidanko Oil Company, firms in Russia were faced with a difficult problem of "tax management." In Sidanko's case, the firm was subject to 17 different taxes that added up to 110 percent of revenue.[36] As a result, even honestly run firms simply could not pay everything the tax authorities demanded. The government taxed gross revenues rather than profits; limited the deductibility of items generally considered to be standard business expenses, such as insurance and advertising; and required frequent reporting.[37] Therefore, many Russian firms and citizens felt justified avoiding some of their official tax burden. Many of Russia's smaller firms, unregistered with the government and unvisited by tax inspectors, operated on a cash-only basis. Even some larger, more visible firms avoided many tax obligations—40 percent of all tax arrears were owed by the 100 largest Russian companies.[38] Russian citizens used a variety of methods to avoid personal income taxes, including simply not reporting income, as well as complex arrangements with their employers to receive salary in the form of stock options.[39]

During the 1990s, Russia's efforts to crack down on tax evasion produced mixed results. The government created a Tax Police, complete with guns and significant executive authority. As the government became more aggressive, however, Russian citizens and firms sought other ways to evade taxes.[40] Because tax authorities lacked a database of taxpayer information, they enforced collection based on incomplete, sometimes incorrect information at their disposal. To Russian firms and citizens, the method seemed simply arbitrary.[41] In a few cases, tax collectors were treated harshly: in 1996, 26 tax collectors were murdered, 74 injured, and 6 kidnapped. Another 41 had their homes burned down.[42] Late in 2000, Russia's Orthodox Church sought to improve the agency's popularity when it named the apostle Matthew patron saint of the Tax Police.[43]

Together, these problems meant the Russian government had a difficult time meeting its budgetary obligations—to provide basic social services, to pay the salaries of its employees and of the military, and to pay the pensions of Russia's retirees. Russia's fiscal woes were persistent, and Russia's political leaders worried publicly about the consequences. In June 1998, Prime Minister Sergei Kirienko observed, "If the state does not learn to collect taxes, it will cease to exist."[44]

Contracts, "Violent Entrepreneurship," and the Law

The results of Russia's legal reforms also were mixed. Western advisors aided the Russian government's attempts to place the economy on a sound legal foundation. These efforts included a 1993 Bankruptcy Law (superseded in 1998), a 1995 Securities Law (and Securities Commission created in 1996), and a 1995–1996 Civil Code, enacted in parts, which included many ideas from the Anglo-Saxon model of company law, with wide-ranging protection for minority shareholders. By the middle of the 1990s, Russia seemed at least to have appropriate laws on the books.

When it came time to apply and enforce these "transplanted" laws, however, difficulties arose.[45] Russia did not have an effective court system. It needed to establish an independent judiciary and appropriately trained judges to interpret these laws in the Russian context. Courts needed a way to enforce their decisions as well. More generally, after several generations of arbitrariness and corruption in Soviet law, Russian society had to learn to trust the law and the legal system. Progress on these matters came more slowly than Russia's legal reformers hoped.

In 1991, *arbitrazh* courts, which hold jurisdiction over business disputes involving legal entities, became the institutional successor to the Soviet *Gosarbitrazh*.[46] Analysts have disagreed about the evolving role of *arbitrazh* courts in the Russian economy. Some have found that the slowness of the courts and their inability to enforce decisions led Russian managers to rely primarily on extra-legal means to resolve business disputes.[47] According to one recent survey, only 56 percent of Russian managers felt that courts could enforce contracts, compared with 73 percent of Polish managers and 87 percent of Romanian managers, who were also operating in the context of a transitional economy.[48] Others have found that Russian managers do rely on the *arbitrazh* courts, as well as the threat to use them, to negotiate agreements with business partners, but primarily as a last resort when face-to-face discussions break down.[49]

In Russia's regions, powerful political and business interests frequently controlled *arbitrazh* courts. During the 1990s, the federal government simply could not and therefore did not pay regional judges or significantly support the court system. As a result, regional governors, among others, often took the task of maintaining the courts upon themselves, with unsurprising results for how the courts functioned. This situation led to the rise of so-called "hostile takeovers" in Russia, a phrase that came to refer to the manipulation of bankruptcy laws rather than to the acquisition of equity. Because bankruptcy proceedings were initiated and resolved in regional courts, firms sometimes managed to acquire the lucrative assets of competitors' firms through their influence in the courts. A well-publicized struggle between the Sidanko Oil Company and a rival firm was a case in point.[50] The rival, the Tiumen Oil Company (TNK), purchased the debt of a Sidanko subsidiary, Chernogoneft, and then sued Chernogoneft in a local bankruptcy court. TNK eventually acquired Chernogoneft, and its valuable Siberian oil field, at a bankruptcy auction in 1999. In the end, a deal was made. TNK returned Chernogoneft in exchange for 25 percent of Sidanko's stock. The episode caught the attention of the Western press because BP Amoco, the largest foreign direct investor in Russia, was a minority shareholder in Sidanko, having acquired a 10 percent stake for $571 million in 1997.[51] Similarly, although the Securities Commission technically was an institution of federal authority, regional and local courts frequently overruled its decisions and thus limited its attempts to improve corporate governance.[52]

Several niches in the new Russian economy that entrepreneurs filled successfully and profitably were private security, contract enforcement, dispute settlement, and transaction insurance. Many Russian managers claimed they received insufficient protection from public authorities, such as the police. There was, therefore, significant demand for private services, according to Russian firms, because of high entrepreneurial risks associated with the failure of business partners to observe contracts or pay debts. This "privatization of protection" was linked to the perception that *arbitrazh* courts were slow to rule and unable to enforce decisions [see **Exhibit 4.6**].

According to Russian sociologist Vadim Volkov, there were three basic types of entrepreneurial activity in the market for private protection and contract enforcement. First, there were units of police and security forces that also sold their services privately, and illegally, to Russian firms. Second, and also illegal, were organized criminal groups, the so-called Russian *mafiia*, that offered similar services. Finally, there were private protection agencies, whose numbers grew quickly during the 1990s after their activity was made legal in March 1992. By the beginning of 1999, approximately 11,000 private security agencies had registered with government authorities. They employed more than 160,000 licensed workers armed with 71,000 registered firearms. Estimates of the activity of private activity of police and of the Russian *mafiia* vary widely, but analysts generally consider both to be significant.

An important part of the activity of all three types of entrepreneurs was their credible threat to use force to resolve disputes, just as the protection offered by public actors, like police, relies on the organization of force. These "violent entrepreneurial agencies" offered an important service to Russian firms. Although the costs of those services varied, the industry standard by the end of the decade was 20 to 30 percent of profits for most business transactions, but up to 50 percent for collecting bad debts.[53]

The August 1998 Crisis

Russians refer to the August 1998 financial crisis as "the decisions of August 17," the day Prime Minister Kirienko announced that the government was forced to default on its domestic debt, devalue the ruble, and impose a moratorium on repaying foreign private debt.

Although Russia's 1995 macroeconomic stabilization program brought down levels of inflation, it did not resolve the government's tax collection problems. The government essentially replaced monetary financing of the budget deficit with borrowing on a newly created government bond market and on international capital markets. [See **Exhibit 4.14**.] Government bonds paid generous rates of return (generally 30 to 40 percent per year) to a relatively small number of domestic banks licensed to operate in the market. Many of these banks borrowed heavily in dollars, which they exchanged for rubles in order to purchase more of the government's debt, thus increasing foreign lenders' exposure to the Russian government's default risk. In addition, the government eventually opened the domestic

government bond market to foreigners, who could then directly hold Russian debt.[54] By the summer of 1998, foreigners, either directly or indirectly, held 40 to 50 percent of the government's domestic debt.[55]

The consequences of the 1998 crisis for Russia's economy, and the economies of Russia's neighbors, were enormous. Russians experienced a sharp drop in real income, living standards, and employment. The crisis caused a temporary paralysis of the payments and settlements system and ruined the balance sheets of the large private banks whose holdings were primarily government bonds. The government defaulted on $40 billion in ruble-denominated bonds—heavy losses for private investors.

The August crisis was blamed on a number of factors, some external to Russia, others internal. The Russian government tended to blame falling oil prices [see **Exhibit 4.13**]. Russians also pointed out that the Asian financial crisis of the summer of 1997 seemed to have made foreign investors in emerging markets skittish. Although the IMF supported the Russian government's attempt to maintain its currency peg to the dollar, others argued that the ruble, after having experienced several years of real appreciation of the exchange rate, was overvalued. Some critics suggested that the government's borrowing had been excessive, and that the government's debt was too costly and too short-term. The months leading up to August 1998 also had been tough for the Russian stock market, which had declined 90 percent by July 1998 after its 1997 high.[56]

A Demographic Crisis

By the end of the 1990s, Russia's public health was clearly in crisis.[57] In 6 of those 10 years, the life expectancy of Russians had fallen. The average Russian woman could expect to live 72 years, but the average Russian man failed to reach 60. Between 1990 and 2000, death rates rose by almost a third, whereas birth rates plummeted nearly 40 percent. Russia's population shrank every year, falling from 148 million in 1992 to 146 million in 1999.

The country's public health infrastructure, seriously underfunded, was collapsing. Cases of infectious diseases that had once been under control increased alarmingly. All of this led the United Nations to estimate that Russia's population could shrink to 120 million over the next 50 years. According to Rafael Oganov, of

Russia's National Center for Preventive Medicine, "In the Soviet Union, we used to have a good system of health care. The quality wasn't good, of course, but the system was accessible to everyone and free. When the Soviet Union collapsed, they began reforms. These reforms have mostly destroyed what existed before, and nothing replaced it."[58] Soviet firms themselves had played an important role in the provision of social security, but their own post-1991 crises, as well as rising unemployment, changed the structure of the health care system. The failure to replace Soviet public health institutions was not for a lack of trying to design new rules from scratch. Russian leaders revised the formal rules governing the country's health care system a number of times during the 1990s. According to the *New York Times*, "Russia has decentralized its Soviet health bureaucracy, then tried to recentralize it; thrown the door open to private health insurers, then moved to close it; guaranteed free medicine to those who needed it, then limited free medicine to the neediest. Eight different health ministers have tried to run the system during the last 10 years."[59]

President Putin in 2000

Such was the context that President Putin inherited in 2000. Many analysts wondered what Putin *could* possibly do to resolve Russia's crisis. Others debated what Putin *would* actually do.

On December 29, 1999, two days before Yeltsin resigned the presidency, Vladimir Putin published an essay, *Russia at the Turn of the Millennium*. Then on February 25, 2000, in the middle of his campaign for the presidency, Putin published an *Open Letter to the Russian Voters*. These two documents illustrate that Putin had his own sense of what had gone wrong in Russia's transition, and they offer insight into his political philosophy.

In *Russia at the Turn of the Millennium*, Putin concluded that "Russia needs strong state power," and that "Russians are alarmed by the obvious weakening of state power." According to Putin, policy implementation was difficult: "We are at a stage where even the most correct economic and social policies can start misfiring because of the weakness of the state and managerial bodies."

In a similar vein, his *Open Letter* emphasized the need for law and order: "...the

supremacy of legality, a dictatorship of the law that is equal to all." Order was central to the acting president's vision for the future. He wrote of, "...the absence of firm and generally recognized rules. As well as any individual, society cannot do without them. As applied to the state, these rules are the law, constitutional discipline, and order. This means the security of a citizen's family and property, his or her personal safety, as well as his or her confidence in the immutability of the established rules of the game." "The stronger the state," Putin concluded, "the freer the individual."

The *Open Letter* highlighted the failings of public authority and found the source of some of those failings in Russian society itself: "Look what happens. You are not sure of the stability of your business because you cannot rely on the force of the law or the honesty of the officials. So, you are dissatisfied with the services offered by the state and you refuse to pay all the taxes due. What's more, you can live pretty comfortably while doing this. And the state fails to get sufficient revenues to keep an impartial judicial system, it pays small salaries to its officials, and they take bribes. The result is a vicious circle."

One of President Putin's first initiatives upon taking office was to reorganize Russia's federal system by adding an additional layer of political authority between the center and the regions. Putin issued a decree on May 13, 2000, that created seven federal super-regions headed by presidential appointees (the *polpredy*, of whom two were former generals and two others former KGB officers). Their responsibility included implementing federal law and presidential decrees in the regions. In addition, President Putin sponsored legislation in the Duma to allow Russia's president to dismiss the legislative and executive authorities in the regions, if their laws contradicted federal laws or the Constitution. Finally, after 2001, Russia's regional governors no longer will be allowed to hold seats in the Federation Council.[60]

The administration reportedly also planned to amalgamate the regional branches of the CBR, the tax inspectorate, and the Customs Committee. The administration made plans for Putin to annul the bilateral treaties that created special tax privileges for several of Russia's regions, including Tatarstan.[61] A Ministry of Finance official predicted, however, that Tatarstan would not accede without a fight to the president's revision of the power balance between federal and regional authority.[62] Insiders reported that the presidential administration was drafting a new constitution, despite the existence of substantial opposition to the formal strengthening of federal authority.[63] According to one official at the Ministry for Economic Development and Trade, "In Russia, we need to strengthen the state in order to improve the functioning of the market."[64]

President Putin also sought to change the state's relationship with the oligarchs. On May 12, heavily armed and masked officers of the tax police and Federal Security Service conducted an armed raid of Vladimir Gusinsky's Media-Most headquarters. Gusinsky was imprisoned for three nights. The reason for the investigation was $380 million that Gazprom, the government-controlled natural gas monopoly, had loaned to NTV, Media-Most's television station. Gusinsky complained publicly about his and NTV's rough treatment, and called Putin's motives into question, since NTV was the only country-wide television station to have criticized Putin openly during the Chechen War and presidential campaign. Eventually, Gusinsky was allowed to leave the country, but not before he acceded to a deal transferring all of Media-Most to Gazprom in exchange for writing off the Gazprom debt. Outside of the country, Gusinsky claimed that he had been coerced into signing away Media-Most and argued that the Putin administration was essentially eliminating the freedom of the press.[65]

Putin's administration also began tax investigations into other oligarchs and their firms. On July 17, Boris Berezovsky resigned his seat in the Duma in protest of the government's policies "aimed at eliminating major independent businesses in Russia."[66] Finally, on July 28, Putin met with 21 of Russia's wealthiest and influential businesspeople, not including Gusinsky and Berezovsky, to "redefine the relationship between the state and big business."

For their part, the oligarchs showed little sign of retreating quietly. Boris Berezovsky wrote an op-ed for the *New York Times* in which he complained about President Putin: "If asked to describe myself, I say, rightly, that I am a businessman who turned to politics, an entrepreneur, a communications executive. But in Russia and in the West, I have been called an oligarch, someone who wielded unknown power in the Yeltsin years and who does not believe in democracy. This was an unfair portrayal, but I never felt seriously compelled to refute it until recently. The current situation in Russia has made it necessary for me to tell the world of concerns I have for the future of democracy there. Actions against me and against my main rival in the media business, Vladimir Gusinsky, are only the most visible signs of authoritarian retrenchment."[67]

Some observers, both inside and outside Russia, suggested that President Putin should deal with the oligarchs more aggressively. One prominent and controversial argument was that Putin should renationalize and reprivatize Russia's most valuable firms.[68] Mikhail Fridman, another "oligarch," commented, "I think the best plan would be if Putin were to declare an amnesty on everything that happened in the past. There were breaches of the law, but to open all that up again, to undo privatizations three or four years after they happened, it's crazy."[69]

Thus, in 2000, President Putin proposed both a diagnosis and a cure for Russia's political-economic problems. But many analysts disagreed with the diagnosis, and many powerful Russians themselves opposed Putin's cure. There were two big questions remaining. Was Putin right? Even if he were right, could he implement the cure?

| EXHIBIT 4.1 | MAP OF RUSSIA |

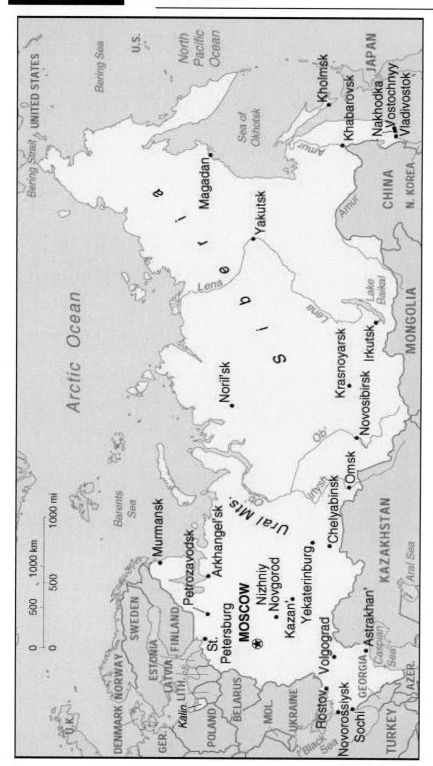

SOURCE: Courtesy of The General Libraries, The University of Texas at Austin.

| EXHIBIT 4.2A | FEDERAL GOVERNMENT BUDGET EXECUTION, 1994–99 (IN BILLIONS OF RUBLES) |

	1994	1995	1996	1997	1998	1999
Revenue	72.1	198.1	268.1	310.4	296.3	608.0
VAT	31.4	78.0	115.4	117.9	117.4	218.8
Other taxes on goods and services	4.5	17.7	51.4	53.4	58.1	90.6
Profit taxes	17.1	41.0	34.8	33.1	32.3	79.1
Personal income taxes	0.1	3.3	5.1	1.7	0.0	19.8
Natural resource taxes	1.0	3.0	4.5	7.0	3.3	10.5
Taxes on trade	9.6	29.7	27.6	30.1	45.3	86.3
Budgetary funds	3.0	15.4	22.9	38.3	26.3	55.2
Other	5.4	10.0	6.4	28.8	13.5	47.8
Expenditure	141.8	286.7	447.7	490.2	454.9	822.3
Non-interest expenditure	129.8	231.9	320.9	372.2	332.4	534.7
Government administration	14.4	4.5	5.4	9.7	10.3	14.8
International activity	---	21.5	20.6	4.3	9.0	36.1
Defense	28.0	47.6	63.9	79.7	60.6	116.1
Law enforcement and public order	10.8	19.2	28.5	43.7	35.3	60.4
Science	---	4.8	6.6	9.5	5.7	11.2
Education	5.5	8.6	11.4	14.4	13.7	20.9
Health and emergency management	2.3	5.9	8.3	15.5	13.4	17.5
Social policy	1.0	3.8	9.9	22.7	36.7	49.1
Environment	---	1.3	2.0	2.5	2.2	2.9
Culture and mass media	1.7	2.8	2.0	2.5	2.3	4.9
Industry, energy and construction	18.2	25.7	26.2	26.6	13.3	16.9
Agriculture and fishing	---	6.2	8.5	12.1	4.0	9.1
Transportation and communication	---	0.5	0.7	3.8	1.1	0.9
Net lending	14.0	22.8	19.6	18.3	9.5	9.4
Inter-government Transfers	25.1	31.0	55.2	55.9	51.4	71.1
Budgetary funds	3.0	14.1	16.5	29.1	24.0	55.3
Other	5.8	11.7	35.7	21.8	40.0	37.9
o/w accumulation of arrears	---	---	---	10.4	12.1	23.3
Interest Payments	12.0	54.7	126.8	118.0	122.4	287.6
External debt	3.1	16.9	22.8	23.8	41.7	88.9
Accumulation of external arrears	0.0	0.0	0.0	0.0	15.0	124.8
Domestic debt	8.9	37.8	104.0	94.2	65.7	73.9
Overall Balance (deficit -)	-69.7	-88.5	-179.8	-179.8	-158.5	-214.3

SOURCE: IMF, *IMF Staff Country Report: Russian Federation*, No. 00/150 (November 2000): 80.

| EXHIBIT 4.2B | FEDERAL GOVERNMENT BUDGET EXECUTION, 1994–99 (IN PERCENT OF GDP) |

	1994	1995	1996	1997	1998	1999
Revenue	11.8	12.9	12.5	12.3	11.0	13.4
Cash	11.4	11.0	9.1	10.0	9.0	13.4
Non-cash	0.4	1.9	3.4	2.3	2.0	0.0
Expenditure	23.2	18.6	20.9	19.4	16.9	18.1
Interest	2.0	3.6	5.9	4.7	4.5	6.3
Non-interest	21.2	15.1	15.0	14.8	12.3	11.8
Overall balance	-11.4	-5.7	-8.4	-7.1	-5.9	-4.7

SOURCE: IMF, *IMF Staff Country Report: Russian Federation*, No. 00/150 (November 2000): 80.

EXHIBIT 4.3	DECENTRALIZATION IN RUSSIAN STATE FINANCE

Tax Revenues as Percent of GDP

	Total	Federal	Subnational
1992	28	16	12
1993	25	10	15
1994	27	12	15
1995	25	14	11
1996	27	14	13
1997	24	10	14
1998	22	9	13

SOURCE: OECD, *OECD Economic Surveys, 1999–2000: Russian Federation* (Paris: OECD, 2000): 124.

EXHIBIT 4.4	AGREEMENTS BETWEEN THE FEDERAL GOVERNMENT AND REGIONAL ADMINISTRATIONS ON INTERGOVERNMENTAL RELATIONS

Following the Agreements (*Soglasheniia*) on Intergovernmental Fiscal Relations of 1994 and early 1995, which granted a special privileged status to Tatarstan, Bashkortostan, and Sakha (Yakutia), several other Subjects of the Federation have sought to conclude similar special bilateral arrangements. In general, these arrangements are in conflict both with the Constitution and the basic policy strategy of guaranteeing uniform rules of the game for all Subjects of the Federation.

Region	Date Signed	1	2	3	4	5	6	7	8	9	10	11	12
Republic Tatarstan	02/15/94	•	•										
Republic Bashkortostan	08/03/94	•											
Republic Sakha (Yakutia)	06/28/95		•	•									
Udmurt republic	10/17/95			•			•						
Sverdlovsk oblast	01/12/96			•	•	•					•	•		•
Krasnodar kray	01/30/96			•									
Komi republic	03/20/96			•	•						•	•	
Khabarovsk kray	04/24/96						•				•		
Irkutsk oblast	05/27/96						•	•	•		•		•
Nizhny Novgorod oblast	06/08/96										•		
Rostov oblast	05/29/96						•						
St. Petersburg	06/13/96	•	•	•	•	•	•		•	•	•	•	•
Vologda oblast	07/02/97										•		
Murmansk oblast	10/30/97								•		•		•
Yaroslav oblast	10/30/97										•		
Chelyabinsk oblast	07/04/97								•		•		

SOURCE: OECD, *OECD Economic Surveys, 1999–2000; Russian Federation* (Paris: OECD, 2000): 122.

Key for the principal clauses:
1. Regions can keep 100 per cent of some federal taxes collected in the region.
2. Individual agreements over tax-sharing rates.
3. Federal expenditures in a region are financed by retaining federal taxes collected in the region.
4. Rights to conduct individual offsets between the region and the federal budget.
5. Gold guarantee fund for region's obligations.
6. Individual agreements over transfers and the data used to calculate them.
7. Agreements over "minimal" budgets and tax-sharing to finance them.
8. Compensation from the federal budget for federal mandates.
9. Special center-region funds to finance "targeted expenditures."
10. Financing federal expenditures in a region by the Federal Treasury from federal taxes collected in the region.
11. Financing regional programs from the federal budget.
12. Authority over revenue and expenditures of the regional part of federal extra-budgetary funds and, in some cases, to approve appointments of their heads.

| EXHIBIT 4.5 | **BARTER AS PERCENT OF INDUSTRIAL SALES, 1992–99** |

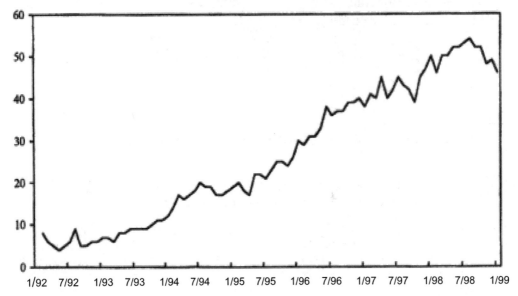

SOURCE: IMF, *IMF Country Staff Report: Russian Federation*, No. 99/100 (September 1999): 141.

| EXHIBIT 4.6 | **THE GROWTH OF RUSSIA'S PRIVATE SECURITY INDUSTRY, 1992–98** |

	1992	1993	1994	1995	1996	1997	1998
Private Protection Companies	0	1,237	1,586	3,247	4,434	4,705	5,650
Private Security Services	0	2,356	2,931	4,591	5,247	4,973	4,720
Private Detective Agencies	0	947	2,088	149	182	809	434
Total Number of Agencies	0	4,540	6,605	7,987	9,863	10,487	10,804

SOURCE: Vadim Volkov, "Security and Rule-Enforcement in Russian Business: The Role of the 'Mafia' and the State," Program on New Approaches to Russian Security (PONARS) Policy Memo Series, No.79 CSIS (October1999): 2.

| EXHIBIT 4.7A | **GDP BY EXPENDITURE, 1991–99** |

	(Annual Percentage Change at Constant Prices)								
	1991	1992	1993	1994	1995	1996	1997	1998	1999
Gross domestic product	-4.6	-14.6	-7.6	-11.7	-4.5	-6.7	0.9	-5.5	3.2
Consumption	-6.1	-5.2	-1.0	-3.1	-2.7	-3.1	3.0	-2.3	-3.5
Households	-4.6	-3.0	1.2	1.2	-2.8	-4.7	5.4	-3.6	-5.3
General government	-11.3	-11.8	-6.4	-2.9	1.1	0.8	-2.4	0.6	0.9
Nonprofit institutions	34.5	-1.0	0.2	-35.9	-30.5	-0.5	-1.8	-1.6	0.0
Gross Investment	-2.3	-36.9	-29.4	-31.2	-10.8	-20.6	-3.6	-31.3	9.3
Capital formation	-15.5	-41.5	-25.8	-26.0	-7.5	-19.3	-5.7	-11.2	2.4
Changes in inventory	264.1	-29.2	-37.4	-47.1	-30.4	-27.3	8.9	---	-55.7
Net exports of goods and services	171.4	717.1	23.2	-13.0	3.2	21.2	-8.8	111.0	60.2

SOURCE: IMF, *IMF Staff Country Report: Russian Federation*, No. 00/150 (November 2000): 29.

EXHIBIT 4.7B	GDP BY EXPENDITURE, 1991–99

	(In Percent of GDP at Current Prices)								
	1991	1992	1993	1994	1995	1996	1997	1998	1999
Consumption	63	50	64	70	71	71	75	77	69
Households	41	34	41	44	49	49	50	54	50
General government	17	14	18	23	19	20	21	19	15
Non-profit institutions	4	2	5	3	2	2	3	3	3
Gross Investment	37	36	28	26	25	24	22	15	15
Capital formation	24	25	21	22	21	21	19	17	16
Changes in inventory	13	11	7	4	4	3	3	-2	-1
Net exports of goods and services	0	15	8	5	3	4	3	7	16

SOURCE: IMF, *IMF Staff Country Report: Russian Federation*, No. 00/150 (November 2000): 29.

EXHIBIT 4.7C	GDP BY SECTOR, 1991–99

	(In Percent of GDP)								
	1991	1992	1993	1994	1995	1996	1997	1998	1999
Agriculture	14.0	7.2	8.2	6.5	7.2	7.3	6.5	5.8	6.9
Industry	38.2	33.7	34.4	32.8	29.0	29.5	28.3	29.0	31.9
Construction	9.4	6.3	7.9	9.1	8.5	8.4	7.9	7.1	5.9
Wholesale, retail, foreign trade, public catering, procurement	12.2	29.1	19.0	18.3	19.6	18.3	17.6	19.0	22.1
Transportation and communications	7.5	7.4	8.6	9.9	11.9	12.4	12.1	11.1	10.2
Finance, credit, insurance, real estate operations, science and research, housing, geology, subsoil resources, exploration, meteorology computer services, others	8.7	8.2	10.8	9.6	9.0	8.0	8.9	9.1	8.3
State administration and defense	2.5	2.1	3.1	4.7	5.2	5.2	6.2	6.7	4.8
Education, culture, art, health care, physical education, social security, utilities, people's associations, non-production services to households	7.5	6.0	8.0	9.1	9.6	10.9	12.5	12.2	9.9

SOURCE: IMF, *IMF Staff Country Report: Russian Federation*, No. 00/150 (November 2000): 30.

EXHIBIT 4.7D	CONSUMER PRICE INFLATION, 1992–99

(Percentage Changes from December to December)							
1992	1993	1994	1995	1996	1997	1998	1999
2,508.8	839.9	213.7	131.4	21.8	11.0	84.5	36.6

SOURCE: IMF, *IMF Staff Country Report: Russian Federation*, No. 00/150 (November 2000): 43.

EXHIBIT 4.8	BALANCE OF PAYMENTS, 1994–99 (MILLIONS OF CURRENT U.S. DOLLARS)					
	1994	**1995**	**1996**	**1997**	**1998**	**1999**
Current Account	8,850	8,025	12,448	2,545	1,040	24,961
Goods and Services	10,958	11,323	17,809	11,611	13,250	32,058
Exports	76,250	93,481	103,844	103,088	87,255	84,346
Imports	-65,292	-82,158	-86,035	-91,476	-74,005	-52,288
Investment income and compensation of employees	-1,802	-3,371	-5,434	-8,706	-11,801	-7,631
Compensation of employees	-114	-303	-406	-342	-164	221
Investment income	-1,688	-3,068	-5,028	-8,365	-11,637	-7,852
Current transfers	-306	73	72	-360	-409	534
Capital and Financial Account	-8,612	730	-6,774	5,480	8,193	-17,403
Capital account	2,410	-347	-463	-797	-382	-328
Financial account	-11,022	1,077	-6,311	6,277	8,575	-17,075
Direct investment	538	1,658	1,708	4,036	1,734	1,164
Abroad	-101	-358	-771	-2,603	-1,027	-2,145
In Russia	640	2,016	2,479	6,639	2,761	3,309
Portfolio investment	21	-2,444	4,410	45,807	8,619	-614
Assets	114	-1,705	-172	-156	-257	254
Liabilities	-93	-738	4,583	45,963	8,876	-868
Other investment	-11,634	11,173	-13,786	-41,610	-7,032	-15,672
Assets	-17,522	5,186	-29,074	-26,608	-16,003	-15,124
Changes in the stock of non-repatriated export proceeds and non-repatriated import advances	-3,860	-4,928	-9,773	-11,458	-8,879	-5,384
Liabilities	5,889	5,987	15,288	-15,002	8,971	-548
Reserve Assets	1,896	-10,386	2,841	-1,936	5,305	-1,778
Adjustment to reserve assets[a]	-1,844	1,076	-1,484	-20	-50	-176
Net errors and omissions	-238	-8,755	-5,674	-8,025	-9,234	-7,558

SOURCE: Central Bank of Russia.

[a]The item "Adjustments to reserve assets" is meant to reconcile the balance of payments and international investment position data that are prepared in accordance with the 5th edition of IMF's Balance of Payments Manual, and also with international reserves data, which have national differences. The methodology of preparation of official reserves has the following differences from that of the Manual: 1-up to the 3rd quarter, 1999 short-term foreign currency deposits in resident banks were included in the international reserves. 2-started from the 3rd quarter, 1999 reserve assets are determined net of counterpart of foreign exchange funds placed on the resident banks' accounts with the Bank of Russia (excluding funds extended by the Bank of Russia for the servicing of the official foreign debt).

EXHIBIT 4.9	EXCHANGE RATE MOVEMENTS, 1994–99 (RUBLES/US$)						
Exchange Rates	**1993**	**1994**	**1995**	**1996**	**1997**	**1998**	**1999**
Official rate (ae)	1.25	3.55	4.64	5.56	5.96	20.65	27.00
Real effective exchange rate (rec)	---	91.12	100.00	122.07	128.92	114.15	80.90

SOURCE: IMF, *International Financial Statistics*, July 2000, pp. 654–655.

Key to notation:
ae = end-of-period
rec = real effective exchange rate index is derived from the nominal effective exchange rate index, adjusted for relative changes in consumer price

EXHIBIT 4.10A   **PRESIDENTIAL ELECTION RESULTS, 1991**

Boris Yeltsin elected the President of the RSFSR (with Aleksandr Rutskoi as vice president) for five-year term. Assumed office on July 10, 1991.

Candidate(s)	Percent of Vote	Millions of Votes
Yeltsin and Rutskoi	57.3	45.6
Ryzhkov and Gromov	16.9	13.4
Zhirinovsky and Zavidiya	7.8	6.2
Tuleyev and Bocharov	6.8	5.4
Makashov and Sergeyev	3.7	3.0
Bakatin and Abdulatipov	3.4	2.7
Against all	1.9	1.5
Invalid Votes	2.2	1.7

SOURCE: Case writer.

EXHIBIT 4.10B   **PRESIDENTIAL ELECTION RESULTS, 1996**

	First Round, June 16, 1996		Second Round, July 3, 1996	
Candidate	Percent of Vote	Millions of Votes	Percent of Vote	Millions of Votes
Yeltsin	35.3	26.7	53.8	40.2
Zyuganov	32.0	24.2	40.3	30.1
Lebed	14.5	11.0		
Yavlinsky	7.3	5.6		
Zhirinovsky	5.7	4.3		
Others	2.2	1.6		
Against all	1.5	1.2	4.8	3.6
Total Valid Votes		74.5		73.9

SOURCE: Case writer.

EXHIBIT 4.10C   **PRESIDENTIAL ELECTION RESULTS, 2000**

Candidate	Percent of Vote	Millions of Votes
Vladimir Putin	52.9	39.7
Gennady Zyuganov, Communist	29.2	21.9
Grigory Yavlinsky, Yabloko	5.8	4.4
Aman-Geldy Tuleev	3.0	2.2
Vladimir Zhirinovsky, Liberal Democratic Party of Russia (LDPR)	2.7	2.0
Others	3.5	2.7
Against all	1.9	1.4
Total Valid Votes	68.0	74.4

SOURCE: Case writer.

EXHIBIT 4.10D	**DUMA FINAL ELECTION RESULTS, DECEMBER 1993**

The Duma election result consists of the 225 seats allocated in the nationwide proportional representation (PR) ballot and the seats allocated in 225 single-member districts (SMD). In 1993, there were only 219 deputies elected in 225 single-member districts.

Party	PR Seats	SMD Seats	Total Seats	Percent of total
Liberal Democratic Party of Russia (Zhirinovsky)	59	5	64	14.4
Russia's Choice (Gaidar)	40	24	64	14.4
Communist Party (Zyuganov)	32	10	42	9.5
Women of Russia (Lakhova)	21	2	23	5.2
Agrarian Party of Russia (Lapshin)	21	16	37	8.3
'Yavlinsky-Boldyrev-Lukin' Bloc	20	7	27	6.1
Party of Russian Unity and Concord (Shakhrai)	18	4	22	5.0
Other Parties	14	21	35	7.9
Independent Candidates	0	130	130	29.3
Total	225	219	444	100.0

SOURCE: Case writer.

EXHIBIT 4.10E	**DUMA FINAL ELECTION RESULTS, DECEMBER 1995**

Party	PR Seats	SMD Seats	Total Seats	Percent of total
Communist Party (Zyuganov)	99	58	157	34.9
Liberal Democratic Party of Russia (Zhirinovsky)	50	1	51	11.3
Our Home is Russia (Chernomyrdin)	45	10	55	12.2
Yabloko (Yavlinsky)	31	14	45	10.0
Agrarian Party of Russia (Lapshin)	0	20	20	4.4
Democratic Choice of Russia (Gaidar)	0	9	9	2.0
Power-to the people! (Ryzhkov-Baburin)	0	9	9	2.0
Congress of Russian Communities (Skokov-Lebed)	0	5	5	1.1
Other Parties	0	22	22	4.9
Independent Candidates	0	77	77	17.1
Total	225	225	450	100.0

SOURCE: Case writer.

EXHIBIT 4.10F	**DUMA FINAL ELECTION RESULTS, DECEMBER 1999**

Party	PR Seats	SMD Seats	Total Seats	Percent of Total
Communists (Zyuganov)	67	47	114	25.4
Unity (Putin)	64	9	73	16.3
Fatherland (Primakov)	37	29	66	14.7
Right Forces	24	5	29	6.5
Yabloko (Yavlinsky)	16	5	21	4.7
Zhirinovsky Bloc	17	0	17	3.8
Our Home is Russia	0	8	8	1.8
Minor Parties	0	9	9	2.0
Independents	0	112	112	25.4
Total	225	224	449	100.0

SOURCE: Case writer.

EXHIBIT 4.11	EXPORTS AND IMPORTS BY PARTNER, 1993–99 (MILLIONS OF U.S. DOLLARS)

	1992	1993	1994	1995	1996	1997	1998	1999
Exports								
U.S.	694	1,998	3,748	5,092	4,584	4,951	4,808	6,433
EU	20,226	19,672	22,412	26,054	26,977	28,000	22,826	24,022
CIS	---	---	13,574	14,366	15,310	16,584	13,369	10,690
Other	18,822	22,377	23,344	32,083	34,567	34,619	28,727	31,938
Imports								
U.S.	2,885	2,304	2,071	2,651	2,231	4,061	3,992	2,387
EU	15,953	11,198	15,383	18,005	15,669	19,578	15,427	11,102
CIS	---	---	10,309	13,450	13,935	14,081	11,015	8,339
Other	15,895	13,249	10,837	12,293	11,483	14,409	12,042	8,484

SOURCE: IMF, *Direction of Trade Statistics* (Washington, D.C.: IMF, 1997–2000).

EXHIBIT 4.12	EXTERNAL GOVERNMENT DEBT (BILLIONS OF U.S. DOLLARS)

	1991	1992	1993	1994	1995	1996	1997	1998
Federal Government	96.8	107.7	112.7	119.9	120.4	125.0	123.5	147.1
Former USSR debt	96.8	104.9	103.7	108.6	103.0	100.8	91.4	95.2
– To official creditors	62.2	69.2	68.1	69.9	62.6	61.9	56.9	59.5
– To commercial creditors	32.9	34.0	34.0	37.0	39.3	38.8	33.9	35.2
– Bonds	1.7	1.7	1.6	1.7	1.1	0.1	0.1	0.0
Debt accumulated by the Russian Federation	0.0	2.8	9.0	11.3	17.4	24.2	32.1	51.9
– To multilateral creditors	0.0	1.0	3.5	5.4	11.4	15.3	18.7	26.0
– To official creditors	0.0	1.8	5.5	5.9	6.0	7.9	7.6	9.7
– Bonds	0.0	0.0	0.0	0.0	0.0	1.0	4.5	16.0
Sub-national governments	0.0	0.0	0.0	0.0	0.0	0.0	1.1	2.2
Total	96.8	107.7	112.7	119.9	120.4	125.0	124.6	149.3

SOURCE: OECD, *OECD Economic Surveys, 1999–2000: Russian Federation* (Paris: OECD, 2000): 67.

EXHIBIT 4.13	INTERNATIONAL CRUDE OIL PRICES, 1992–2000 (US$/BARREL)

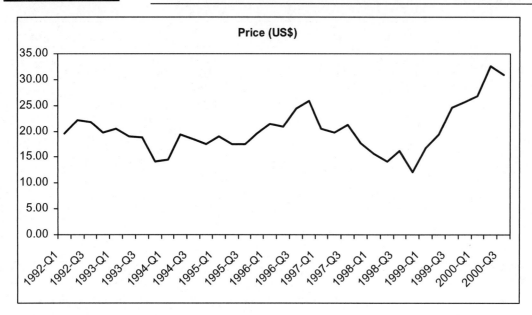

SOURCE: Thomson Financial; Name: West Texas Int.; Code: CRUDOIL.

EXHIBIT 4.14	INTEREST RATES

Annual Percentage Rates, Period Average

	CBR Refinance Rate	Overnight Interbank Rate	GKO Average Secondary Market Yield, All Maturities
1995	185	190	162
1996	110	48	86
1997	32	21	26
1998	60	51	NA
1999	57	15	NA

SOURCE: Russian-European Centre for Economic Policy, *Russian Economic Trends: Monthly Update* (SITE 11 October 2000).

ENDNOTES

1 "Yeltsin Resigns," *New York Times*, January 1, 2000.

2 The GDP data are in European Bank for Reconstruction and Development (EBRD), *Transition Report 1999: Ten Years of Transition* (London: EBRD, 1999), p. 63. The poverty data are in Branko Milanovic, *Income, Inequality, and Poverty During the Transition from Planned to Market Economy* (Washington, D.C.: World Bank, 1998), pp. 68-69. The World Bank estimated that more than 30 percent of Russians lived below the poverty line in 1994. See World Bank, *World Development Report 2000/2001* (Washington, D.C.: World Bank, 2000), p. 281.

3 UNICEF, TransMONEE database, 2000. A Gini coefficient of 0 represents complete equality, while 1 represents complete inequality.

4 Gennady Zyuganov, *My Russia: The Political Autobiography of Gennady Zyuganov* (Armonk, N.Y.: M. E. Sharpe, 1997), especially pp. 139-168.

5 See, for example, Anders Åslund, "Russia's Collapse," *Foreign Affairs*, vol. 78, no. 5 (1999): 64-77.

6 See, for example, Joseph Stiglitz, "Whither Reform? Ten Years of the Transition," presented at the Annual Bank Conference on Development Economics (ABCDE), World Bank, April 28-30, 1999; and Yoshiko Herrera, "Russian Economic Reform, 1991-98," in *Challenges of Russian Democratization*, ed. Robert Moser and Zultan Barany (Cambridge: Cambridge University Press, 2001).

7 On the organization of the Soviet economic system, see Alexander Dyck, "The USSR 1988: The Search for Growth," Harvard Business School Case No. 795-060.

8 Quoted in John Lloyd, "Yeltsin Deputy Attacks Government," *Financial Times*, December 19, 1991.

9 On the Russian reforms of the early 1990s, see Alexander Dyck, "Russia 1994," Harvard Business School Case No. 795-089.

10 See Robert E. Kennedy and Amy L. Sandler, "Shock Therapy in Eastern Europe: The Polish and Czechoslovak Reforms," Harvard Business School Case No. 797-068; and Robert E. Kennedy and Amy L. Sandler, "Transition to a Market Economy: The Components of Reform," Harvard Business School Note No. 797-080. Also see Peter Murrell, "What Is Shock Therapy? What Did It Do in Poland and Russia?" *Post-Soviet Affairs*, vol. 9, no. 2 (1993): 111-140.

11 The government still controlled prices for basic foods, energy, housing, and transportation, and raised them administratively.

12 See Daniel S. Treisman, "Fighting Inflation in a Transitional Regime: Russia's Anomalous Stabilization," *World Politics*, vol. 50, no. 2 (1998): 235-265; and Andrei Shleifer and Daniel Treisman, *Without a Map: Political Tactics and Economic Reform in Russia* (Cambridge, Mass.: MIT Press, 2000), chs. 3-4.

13 Andrei Shleifer and Robert Vishny, *The Grabbing Hand: Government Pathologies and Their Cures* (Cambridge, Mass.: Harvard University Press, 1998), p. 11. See also, for example, Maxim Boycko, Andrei Shleifer, and Robert Vishny, *Privatizing Russia* (Cambridge, Mass.: MIT Press, 1995).

14 Quoted by Sergei Kovaliev in Chrystia Freeland, *Sale of the Century: Russia's Wild Ride from Communism to Capitalism* (New York: Crown Business, 2000), p. 70.

15 Gustafson, *Capitalism Russian-Style*, ch. 2. Also see Andrew Spicer, Gerald A. McDermott, and Bruce Kogut, "Entrepreneurship and Privatization in Central Europe: The Tenuous Balance between Destruction and Creation," *Academy of Management Review*, vol. 25, no. 3 (2000): 630-649.

16 Technically, the pledgees then had the right to sell the shares through another auction. The Western media called this arrangement "loans for shares." The details are now widely available. See, for example, Ira W. Lieberman and Rogi Veimetra, "The Rush for State Shares in the "Klondyke" of Wild East Capitalism," *George Washington Journal of International Law and Economics*, vol. 29, no. 3 (1996): 737-768; and Bernard Black, Reinier Kraakman, and Anna Tarassova, "Russian Privatization and Corporate Governance: What Went Wrong?" *Stanford Law Review*, vol. 52 (forthcoming 2000).

17 Quoted in Freeland, *Sale of the Century*, p. 174.

18 Alfred Kokh, *The Selling of the Soviet Empire: Politics and Economics of Russia's Privatization— Revelations of the Principal Insider* (New York: S.P.I. Books, 1998), p. 121, and pp. 115-123 for more on Norilsk Nickel. Ch. 4, "The Pledge Plan," outlines the so-called "loans-for-shares" arrangements in candid detail.

19 Menatep, which was led by Mikhail Khodorkovsky, acquired a 45 percent block of shares of the Yukos oil company for $159 million (up from a starting price of $150 million) and then another 33 percent block for $150.1 million (up

from a starting price of $150 million). Firms associated with Boris Berezovsky acquired a controlling block of shares in the Sibneft oil company for $100.3 million (up from a starting price of $100 million), after a competing bid of $175 million was disqualified because the bank guarantee was not properly signed.

20 See Hans-Henning Schröder, "El'tsin and the Oligarchs: The Role of Financial Groups in Russian Politics between 1993 and 1998," *Europe-Asia Studies*, vol. 51, no. 6 (1999): 957-988.

21 See Lilia Shevtsova, *Yeltsin's Russia: Myths and Reality* (Washington, D.C.: Carnegie Endowment for International Peace, 1999), p. 156.

22 Quoted in Freeland, *Sale of the Century*, p. 171.

23 Chrystia Freeland, John Thornhill, and Andrew Gowers, "Wealthy Clique Emerges from Kremlin Gloom," *Financial Times*, October 31, 1996; Chrystia Freeland, John Thornhill, and Andrew Gowers, "Moscow's Group of Seven," *Financial Times*, November 1, 1996.

24 Boris Yeltsin, *Midnight Diaries*, trans. Catherine A. Fitzpatrick (New York: PublicAffairs, 2000), pp. 20-21.

25 See Juliet Johnson, "Russia's Emerging Financial-Industrial Groups," *Post-Soviet Affairs*, vol. 13, no. 4 (1997): 333-365, at p. 349; and Lee Hockstader and David Hoffman, "Yeltsin Campaign Rose from Tears to Triumph: Money, Advertising Turned Fortunes Around," *Washington Post*, July 7, 1996.

26 For example, see David Remnick, "The War for the Kremlin," *New Yorker*, July 22, 1996; Aleksei Zudin, "Biznes i politika v prezidentskoi kampanii 1996 goda (Business and Politics in the Presidential Campaigns of 1996), *Pro et Contra*, vol. 1, no. 1 (1996): 46-60; and Michael McFaul, *Russia's 1996 Presidential Election: The End of Polarized Politics* (Stanford: Hoover Institution Press, 1997), ch. 3.

27 See, for example, John Lloyd, "The Russian Devolution," *New York Times*, August 15, 1999.

28 Quoted from Zyuganov's "Letter to the Central Electoral Commission," June 27, 1996, reprinted in his *My Russia*, pp. 171-173.

29 Black, Kraakman, and Tarassova, "Russian Privatization and Corporate Governance."

30 See especially David Woodruff, *Money Unmade: Barter and the Fate of Russian Capitalism* (Ithaca, N.Y.: Cornell University Press, 1999).

31 Clifford G. Gaddy and Barry W. Ickes, "Russia's Virtual Economy," *Foreign Affairs*, vol. 77, no. 5 (1998): 53-67.

32 In the Russian language there is a distinction between civic and ethnic conceptions of "Russian" that does not exist in English. In Russian, *rossiiskii* connotes a relation to the Russian state, while *russkii* implies Russian ethnicity. So, while all Russian citizens are *rossiiskii*, not all citizens are considered *russkii*.

33 Yeltsin initially directed the comment to the leadership of the oil-rich republic of Tatarstan in August 1990. He repeated the remark in an interview with *Komsomolskaia pravda* in March 1991.

34 Yoshiko Herrera, "Imagined Economies: Regionalism in Sverdlovsk, Russia," Paper Presented at the Annual Meeting of the American Political Science Association, Washington, D.C., August 31 - September 3, 2000.

35 Daniel S. Treisman, "Russia's Taxing Problem," *Foreign Policy*, no. 112 (1998): 55-67.

36 Author's interview with Robert Sheppard, President of Sidanko, Moscow, November 21, 2000.

37 Thane Gustafson, *Capitalism Russian-Style* (Cambridge: Cambridge University Press, 1999), pp. 196-198.

38 *Russian Economic Trends*, no. 3 (1997): 15.

39 Jennifer Franklin, "Tax Avoidance by Citizens of the Russian Federation," *Duke Journal of Comparative and International Law*, no. 8 (fall 1997): 135-173.

40 See Frank Gregory and Gerald Brooke, "Policing Economic Transition and Increasing Revenue: A Case Study of the Federal Tax Police Service of the Russian Federation, 1992-98," *Europe-Asia Studies*, vol. 52, no. 3 (2000): 433-455.

41 Franklin, "Tax Avoidance by Citizens of the Russian Federation."

42 "Disappearing Taxes: The Tap Runs Dry," *Economist*, May 31, 1997.

43 "Church Names Patron Saint of Tax Police," *Reuters*, December 12, 2000.

44 Quoted in David Hoffman, "Yeltsin Demands Action on Economy," *Washington Post*, June 24, 1998.

45 On problems of "transplanted" laws, see Katharina Pistor, Martin Raiser, and Stanislaw Gelfer, "Law and Finance in Transition Economies," *Economics of Transition*, vol. 8, no. 2 (2000): 325-368.

46 Russia has a dual court system. All non-business legal matters are heard in general jurisdiction courts. See Kathryn Hendley, "Remaking an

Institution: The Transition in Russia from State *Arbitrazh* to *Arbitrazh* Courts," *American Journal of Comparative Law*, vol. 46, no. 1 (1998): 93-127.

47 See Jonathan R. Hay and Andrei Shleifer, "Private Enforcement of Public Laws: A Theory of Legal Reform," *American Economic Review*, vol. 88, no. 2 (1998): 398-402.

48 Simon Johnson, John McMillan, and Christopher Woodruff, "Contract Enforcement in Transition," EBRD Working Paper No. 45, October 1999.

49 Kathryn Hendley, Barry W. Ickes, Peter Murrell, and Randi Ryterman, "Observations on the Use of Law by Russian Enterprises," *Post-Soviet Affairs*, vol. 13, no. 1 (1997): 19-41; and Kathryn Hendley, Peter Murrell, and Randi Ryterman, "Law, Relationships, and Private Enforcement: Transactional Strategies of Russian Enterprises," *Europe-Asia Studies*, vol. 52, no. 4 (2000): 627-656.

50 Author's interview with Robert Sheppard, President of Sidanko, Moscow, November 21, 2000.

51 For more on this episode, see "Russia: Rules of War," *Economist*, December 4, 1999; Jeanne Whalen and Bhushan Bahree, "How Siberian Oil Field Turned into a Minefield—BP Amoco Learns Bruising Lesson on Investing in Russia," *Wall Street Journal*, February 9, 2000; and Andrea Chipman, "Russia's Sidanko Battles to Stay Afloat, Regain Units Lost to Rival—With Bankruptcy behind It, Oil Firm Hopes to Strike a Deal with Tiumen," *Wall Street Journal Europe*, November 17, 2000.

52 Author's interview with Marlen D. Manassov, Managing Director, Brunswick UBS Warburg, Moscow, November 27, 2000.

53 Vadim Volkov, "Violent Entrepreneurship in Post-Communist Russia," *Europe-Asia Studies*, vol. 51, no. 5 (1999): 741-754.

54 Paul Krugman, "The Other Bear Market: The Run on Russia," *Slate*, September 10, 1998.

55 Thierry Malleret, Natalia Orlova, and Vladimir Romanov, "What Loaded and Triggered the Russian Crisis?" *Post-Soviet Affairs*, vol. 15, no. 2 (1999): 107-129, p. 115.

56 For a review of these explanations, see Andrei Illarionov, "The Roots of the Economic Crisis," *Journal of Democracy*, vol. 10, no. 2 (1999): 68-82.

57 The following paragraphs are drawn from information in the following articles: Michael Wines, "An Ailing Russia Lives a Tough Life That's Getting Shorter," *New York Times*, December 3, 2000; Michael Wines with Abigail Zuger, "In Russia, the Ill and the Infirm Include

Health Care Itself," *New York Times*, December 4, 2000; and Abigail Zuger, "Russia Has Few Weapons as Infectious Diseases Surge," *New York Times*, December 5, 2000.

58 Quoted in Wines and Zuger, "In Russia, the Ill and the Infirm Include Health Care Itself."

59 Wines and Zuger, "In Russia, the Ill and the Infirm Include Health Care Itself."

60 See "Beyond the Kremlin's Walls: President Vladimir Putin Is Trying to Bring Russia's Regions Back into Line," *Economist*, May 20, 2000; and "The Bridling of Russia's Regions," *Economist*, November 11, 2000. Also see Michael Wines, "Putin's Move on Governors Would Bolster His Role," *New York Times*, May 22, 2000; "Putin's Plan to Increase Central Power Wins Support," *New York Times*, July 20, 2000; and Michael Wines, "Russia's Powerful Regional Chiefs Yield Meekly to Putin," *New York Times*, July 27, 2000.

61 Author's interview with Alexander Zhukov, Chairman of the Committee of the State Duma on Budget and Taxes, Moscow, November 21, 2000.

62 Author's interview, Ministry of Finance of the Russian Federation, Moscow, November 24, 2000.

63 Author's interview, Legal Department of the State Duma, Moscow, November 20, 2000.

64 Author's interview, Ministry of Economic Development and Trade of the Russian Federation, Moscow, November 28, 2000.

65 David Hoffman, "Russians Drop Charges against Media Tycoon," *Washington Post*, July 28, 2000; Michael Wines, "Russian Puzzle: What Does War on Tycoons Mean?" *New York Times*, July 15, 2000; and Daniel Williams, "Putin Makes Mark in First 100 Days," *Washington Post*, August 15, 2000.

66 John Lloyd, "The Autumn of the Oligarchs," *New York Times*, October 8, 2000; Sharon La Franiere, "Tax Police Accuse Russia's Largest Carmaker of Fraud," *Washington Post*, July 13, 2000; and Charles Clover and Stefan Wagstyl, "Kremlin Widens Probe Into Tax Evasion," *Financial Times*, July 13, 2000.

67 Boris A. Berezovsky, "Putin Reins in Russia, at a Price," *New York Times*, September 22, 2000.

68 For a proposal that Putin renationalize and then reprivatize Russia's oil and gas companies, see Lee S. Wolosky, "Putin's Plutocrat Problem," *Foreign Affairs*, vol. 79, no. 2 (2000): 18-31.

69 Quoted in Lloyd, "The Autumn of the Oligarchs."

CONCEPTUAL NOTE   THE STATE

RAWI ABDELAL

> *In framing a government which is to be administered by men over men, the great difficulty lies in this: you must first enable the government to control the governed; and in the next place oblige it to control itself.*
> —The Federalist, No. 51

The state is a fundamental institutional foundation of modern capitalism. States both create and enforce laws, and the legal underpinnings of economic activity vary substantially from place to place, with significant consequences for growth and distribution.[1] The character of state authority is, therefore, a central feature of the country context within which firms operate.[2] In practice, states are vital to the organization of economic activity throughout the world.

The importance of states does not mean, however, that "the state" is easy to understand and analyze. This analytical note summarizes several conclusions from social science scholarship on the nature of the state. It describes several key conceptual variables that can be used to analyze specific states, and outlines various theoretical approaches to the state that underpin analyses of the role of public authority in the economy.

Understanding the State

The German sociologist Max Weber (1864-1920) provided the classic definition of the state: a set of institutions that link public authority and society, "an administrative and legal order." The Weberian concept of the state is an administrative apparatus, an organization of public institutions. For Weber, a state has three main elements: a regularized "administrative staff," or bureaucracy; a successful claim of a monopoly on the legitimate use of force; and the projection of its administrative authority and monopoly of legitimate force within a specific territory.[3] In other words, a state is more than the sum of its parts, because a state is also the particular configuration of a society"s public institutions.

Weber distinguished various functions of the state, as well as the institutions that performed them. According to Weber, a few basic functions are central to every state: "...the enactment of law (legislative function); the protection of personal safety and public order (police); the protection of vested rights (administration of justice); the cultivation of hygienic, educational, social-welfare, and other cultural interests (the various branches of administration); and, last but not least, the organized armed protection against outside attack (military administration)."[4] Thus, the state as a whole is made up of: a legislature, administrative agencies that collect taxes and enforce laws, courts that interpret laws, and police and military that exert coercive authority.

The importance of military force and territory to the Weberian definition also reveals that the state is Janus-faced: each state exists in a system of other states, some of which rule within neighboring territories.[5] Each state simultaneously faces inward, toward the society it governs, and outward, representing that society in the wider world. Indeed, the task of war making, the defense of territorial sovereignty and society, was one of the fundamental historical forces that shaped the creation of modern states.[6]

Concepts Related to the State

The state is a particularly modern form of political organization whose historical development dates from the sixteenth and seventeenth centuries. Pre-modern forms of political organization, such as the tribe, the city-state, and the dynastic empire were gradually displaced by the modern state. Social scientists generally distinguish the concept of the state from similar concepts. A *country* is a place, a defined territorial space, but it is not a set of institutions. Germany, for example, *is* a country, and it *has* a state. *Society* refers to people, the citizens of a state, as well as the people"s private institutions and organizations. Firms, for example, exist as a part of society in capitalist

Professor Rawi Abdelal prepared this note as the basis for class discussion rather than to illustrate either effective or ineffective handling of an administrative situation.

economies. A *nation* is a concept that refers to a group of people: the people of Japan compose a nation; the Japanese nation lives in the country of Japan, which is governed by the Japanese state. A *government* is an agent of public authority that acts within the institutional context of the state. Although we may occasionally refer to countries, societies, nations, and states as shorthand for the same idea, sometimes it is useful to distinguish them for the purposes of analyzing the political-economic environments that firms encounter around the world.

The State, Order, and Property

Coercion is a crucial element of state authority, because the state"s credible threat to enforce laws by force underlies its maintenance of domestic order. As the English political philosopher Thomas Hobbes (1588-1679) wrote, "The Office of the Sovereign (be it a Monarch, or an Assembly) consisteth in the end, for which he was trusted with Sovereign Power, namely the procuration of *the safety of the people*."[7] For Hobbes, who had lived through the exceptionally bloody English Civil War, the breakdown of sovereign authority was a disaster to be avoided at all costs.

For the political philosopher John Locke (1632-1704), who was an important intellectual influence on the authors of the constitution of the United States, the protection of private property was a central function of state authority: "The great and chief end, therefore, of men"s uniting into commonwealths, and putting themselves under government, is the preservation of their property."[8] A stable institutional order is a foundation for regularized economic activity, particularly for investing in and improving property, processes that require long time horizons.

Locke"s insight into the importance of the state for secure property rights forms the foundation of much recent scholarship on the economic functions of the state. Property rights, a complex economic institution, encompass much more than control over physical assets. A share of stock, for example, is an ownership claim, but it is useful only insofar as it is recognized by others and by law. Ownership consists of the right to use an asset, to change it, and to transfer it through sale or gift. The use, or control, of an asset implies security into the future. And the transfer of an asset requires a contract, which must be enforced either by social norms or public authority. For secure property rights to extend across social groups, and not just within them, public authority is generally a necessary background condition. Thus, as the economic historian and Nobel laureate Douglass North summarizes, "The basic services that the state provides are the underlying rules of the game."[9]

In addition to monopolizing the legitimate use of force, modern states have almost always attempted to maintain a monopoly on the definition of money within their economies. The vast majority of states have assumed the sole responsibility of issuing currency as well.[10]

These economic functions of the state—order, property, money—are basic to even the most minimal conception of the state, including that of Adam Smith.[11] In today"s world economy, states often take upon themselves much more expansive and daunting tasks. They routinely regulate and attempt to shape markets. The economic *goals* of states may vary substantially from country to country, and certainly in ways that matter for how their economies function. But, to a large extent, the basic economic *functions* of states in capitalist economies remain constant. States must be effective in order to allow markets to operate.

How States Vary

When analyzing states, scholars generally assess three variables: autonomy, capacity, and legitimacy. These concepts define the relation between public authority and society.

State Autonomy

State autonomy, then, is a concept that describes the independence of state institutions from societal pressure. According to sociologists Karen Barkey and Sunita Parikh, "Autonomy refers to the state's ability to formulate interests of its own, independent of or against the will of divergent societal interests."[12]

A high degree of state autonomy, in itself, is neither necessarily good nor bad, but it does affect how states make policy and enforce laws. A good example is the difference between French and U.S. state-society relations.[13] Traditionally, the French state has remained relatively autonomous from societal actors. It has formulated ambitious goals that sometimes seemed to contradict the preferences of societal actors. In the 1970s, when the leaders at the top of the insulated French bureaucracy decided to expand the civilian use of nuclear power, the French state pursued their goal vigorously and effectively, despite strong ecological protests. In contrast, the U.S. state is characterized by more diffuse institutional power, and more openness to societal influences on the formulation of policy goals. In 1993, when the administration of President Bill Clinton tried to formulate a complex set of policies to reorganize the U.S. health care system it failed completely. In this case, even the highest executive power was unable to define the interests of the state autonomously from influential societal forces—including a large number of insurance companies, health maintenance organizations, and physicians" associations that opposed the goal.

State Capacity

State capacity denotes the ability and effectiveness of the state to perform its basic political and economic functions. Samuel Huntington, a Harvard political scientist, offered this classic formulation: "The most important political distinction among countries concerns not their form of government but their degree of government."[14]

In general, most societies seem to prefer to be governed by a capacious state. The French-U.S. comparison is again illustrative. With regard to basic state functions (enforcing laws, collecting taxes, providing basic social services and infrastructure, paying the salaries of the bureaucracy and the military), both the French and U.S. states exhibit a high capacity, as do the other advanced industrial states. Thus, despite the distrust of the state in the American political tradition, and despite the considerable restraints on public authority defined by the U.S constitution, the American state performs its limited functions effectively. In addition to the state"s control over its own territory, the state"s fiscal capacity is often a useful indicator of its effectiveness. Harvard sociologist Theda Skocpol argues: "A state"s means of raising and deploying financial resources tells us more than could any other single factor about its existing (and immediate potential) capacities to create or strengthen state organizations, to employ personnel, to co-opt political support, to

subsidize economic enterprises, and to fund social programs."[15]

Legitimacy

Legitimacy is about society"s belief in the state and its leaders. Legitimacy is also about society"s consent about the state"s social purpose. States seek legitimacy in the eyes of the society they seek to govern.[16] Indeed, legitimacy makes the process of government easier, if not simply possible. The compliance of societal actors with the laws of the state cannot result just from routine capitulation or even from careful cost-benefit calculations about the probability of punishment. For one thing, no state has enough coercive power—police and military—to *force* the entirety of a society to obey laws. When a state is legitimate, people obey laws because they believe it is *right* to obey them.

Theories of the State

For centuries, scholars have debated with each other about the nature of the state, and they have proposed theories to describe and explain state behavior. A passing familiarity with the differences among the various approaches to the state is useful primarily because most people implicitly assume some particular theory of the state when they analyze the political environment of business or offer policy recommendations. It is important to make these assumptions explicit, and sometimes to question them, in order to analyze a particular political-economic situation more effectively. For example, many economists recommend against an activist industrial policy because they implicitly assume a pluralist or predatory theory of the state. That is, they believe that the state would either be captured by societal interests or be selfish in its implementation.

The Marxist Theory of the State

According to Karl Marx and Friedrich Engels, "The executive of the modern state is but a committee for managing the common affairs of the whole bourgeoisie."[17] The basic idea in the Marxist theory of the state is that the most important impetus for public policy comes from societal actors, and in particular a single class—the bourgeoisie—in capitalist economic systems.[18] The Marxist conception of the state is one with essentially no autonomy from society, while state capacity, understood as the effectiveness of the state in achieving the interests of the bourgeoisie, is high. However, the legitimacy of the state, in this theory, is quite low, particularly within the working class.

The Pluralist Theory of the State

The pluralist theory of the state sees it as an arena in which interest groups struggle and compromise. State autonomy, in this conception, is low, and state capacity is left as an open question. Given the history of American politics, it is not surprising that the pluralist theory finds its most coherent expression in American political science and the history of American political thought. Thus, the policies of the state in traditional pluralist analysis are the outcome of a struggle among interest groups.[19] In the pluralist conception, politics are about allocation, rather than rule or control. The state is just a collection of individuals in legislative, executive, and judicial roles, rather than comprising an administrative apparatus or legal order. The state"s legitimacy, in pluralist theory, is taken as given. But the pluralist theory is similar to the Marxist understanding of public policy in that societal interests are the main source of public policy and the goals of political authority.

The "Statist" Theory of the State

Political scientist Stephen Krasner attempted to distinguish a "statist" view from both the Marxist and pluralist theoretical traditions. According to Krasner, the state is "a set of roles and institutions having peculiar drives, compulsions, and aims of their own that are separate and distinct from the interests of any particular societal group."[20] In other words, the state could be understood as an actor in its own right, and could be strong or weak in relation to its own society. The goals of the state, in this conception, are left open. For example, Krasner discussed the concept of the "national interest," but did not deduce it. In this "statist" theory of the state, both autonomy and capacity are understood to be high, as is legitimacy.

The Predatory Theory of the State

Political scientist Margaret Levi formulated what she called "The Theory of Predatory Rule." In this "predatory" conception, the state is the coercive apparatus of rulers who seek to maximize revenue subject to the constraints of their bargaining power relative to society, their transaction costs, and discount rates.[21] The state's goals are given by assumption: states want, in a word, more—tax revenue, primarily. In the predatory conception, the state is completely autonomous from society, while its capacity and legitimacy vary.

ENDNOTES

1   See, for example, Debora Spar, "Note on Rules," Harvard Business School Note No. 799-013.

2   Alexander Dyck, "Country Analysis: A Framework to Identify and Evaluate the National Business Environment," Harvard Business School Note No. 797-092.

3   Max Weber, *Economy and Society*, ed. Guenther Roth and Claus Wittich, 2 vols. (Berkeley: University of California Press, [1922] 1978), especially vol. 2, chs. 9-13. For Weber's other writings on the state, see "The Fundamental Concepts of Sociology," in *Max Weber: The Theory of Social and Economic Organization*, ed. Talcott Parsons (Oxford: Oxford University Press, 1950); and "Politics as Vocation," in *From Max Weber: Essays in Sociology*, ed. H. H. Gerth and C. Wright Mills (Oxford: Oxford University Press, 1958). For contemporary Weberian interpretations of the state, see also Peter J. Katzenstein, ed., *Between Power and Plenty* (Madison: University of Wisconsin Press, 1978); Peter J. Katzenstein, *Small States in World Markets* (Ithaca, N.Y.: Cornell University Press, 1985); Joel S. Migdal, *Strong Societies and Weak States* (Princeton, N.J.: Princeton University Press, 1988); and Gianfranco Poggi, *The State: Its Nature, Development, and Prospects* (Stanford: Stanford University Press, 1990).

4   Weber, *Economy and Society*, p. 905.

5   Janus was the god of gates and doorways in Roman mythology, and he was often depicted with two faces looking in opposite directions. On the state as Janus-faced, see J. P. Nettl, "The State as a Conceptual Variable," *World Politics*, vol. 20, no. 4 (1968): 559-592.

6   Joseph Schumpeter, "The Crisis of the Tax State," in *Joseph A. Schumpeter: The Economics and Sociology of Capitalism*, ed. Richard Swedberg (Princeton, N.J.: Princeton University Press, [1918] 1991); Charles Tilly, "Reflections on the History of European State-Building," in *The Formation of National States in Western Europe*, ed. Charles Tilly (Princeton, N.J.: Princeton University Press, 1975). Also see Otto Hintze, "The State in Historical Perspective," in *State and Society*, ed. Reinhard Bendix (Berkeley: University of California Press, 1973).

7   Thomas Hobbes, *The Leviathan*, ed. C. B. Macpherson (New York: Penguin, [1651] 1985), p. 376, emphasis in original.

8   John Locke, "An Essay Concerning the True Original, Extent and End of Civil Government," in *Treatise of Civil Government and a Letter Concerning Toleration*, ed. Charles L. Sherman (New York:

Irvington, [1689] 1979), p. 82. More generally, see ch. 5, "Of Property," and ch. 9, "On the Ends of Political Society and Government."

9   Douglass North, *Structure and Change in Economic History* (New York: W. W. Norton, 1981), p. 24.

10 Weber, *Economy and Society*, vol. 1, pp. 166-168.

11 Adam Smith, *An Inquiry into the Nature and Causes of the Wealth of Nations* (London: T. Nelson and Sons, [1776] 1891), Book V, especially pp. 289-342.

12 Karen Barkey and Sunita Parikh, "Comparative Perspectives on the State," *Annual Review of Sociology*, vol. 17 (1991): 523-549, p. 525.

13 Peter J. Katzenstein, "International Relations and Domestic Structures: Foreign Economic Policies of Advanced Industrial States," *International Organization*, vol. 30. no. 1 (1976): 1-45.

14 Samuel P. Huntington, *Political Order in Changing Societies* (New Haven, Conn.: Yale University Press, 1978), p. 1.

15 Theda Skocpol, "Bringing the State Back In," in *Bringing the State Back In*, ed. Peter B. Evans, Dietrich Rueschemeyer, and Theda Skocpol (Cambridge: Cambridge University Press, 1985), p. 17.

16 Weber, *Economy and Society*, vol. 1, pp. 212 ff., especially "Legal Legitimacy."

17 Karl Marx and Friedrich Engels, "Manifesto of the Communist Party," in *The Marx-Engels Reader*, 2nd ed., ed. Robert C. Tucker (New York: W. W. Norton, 1978), p. 475.

18 This reflects what has been called an "instrumental" Marxist approach to the state. There are also more sophisticated Marxist approaches, for example, that of Nicos Poulantzas, "The Problem of the Capitalist State," *New Left Review*, no. 58 (1969): 67-78. On Marxist approaches to the state, see James A. Caporaso and David P. Levine, *Theories of Political Economy* (Cambridge: Cambridge University Press, 1992), pp. 186-188; and Martin Carnoy, *The State and Political Theory* (Princeton, N.J.: Princeton University Press, 1984).

19 See, for example, David Truman, *The Governmental Process: Political Interests and Public Opinion* (New York: Knopf, 1951); and Robert Dahl, *Who Governs?* (New Haven, Conn.: Yale University Press, 1963). The classic statement of pluralism is Arthur Bentley, *The Process of Government: A Study of Social Pressures* (Chicago: University of Chicago Press, 1908). For a review, see Stephen Krasner,

"Approaches to the State: Alternative Conceptions and Historical Dynamics," *Comparative Politics*, vol. 16, no. 4 (1984): 223-246.

20 Stephen Krasner, *Defending the National Interest: Raw Materials Investments and U.S. Foreign Policy* (Princeton, N.J.: Princeton University Press, 1978), p. 10. For more on statist approaches to political economy, see Caporaso and Levine, *Theories of Political Economy*, pp. 188-191.

21 Margaret Levi, *Of Rule and Revenue* (Berkeley: University of California Press, 1988), ch. 2.

C H A P T E R

Structural Adjustment beyond the Washington Consensus

After 71 years of one-party rule, Mexico experienced a political revolution in 2000. Vincente Fox, representing a minority party, was elected president. During the previous 30 years, Mexico's rocky development strategy had shifted from import substitution, to debt-leveraged oil development to structural adjustment.

In 1982, Mexico was the first developing country to lapse into debt crisis, unable to pay the interest and amortization of its foreign debt, in dollars. Faced with IMF conditionality, the government of Miguel de la Madrid began the long, agonizing process of structural adjustment—reducing deficits; radically devaluing the currency; controlling wages; and opening up to foreign direct investment, international trade, and privatization. De la Madrid was succeeded by Carlos Salinas, who appeared as a savior but left office under a cloud of corruption on the cusp of the Tequila Crisis. His successor, Ernesto Zedillo, spent his first year bailing Mexico out of its worst debt crisis yet. But with U.S. help, Zedillo got Mexico growing again and also opened its political system to a more open, democratic form that finally gave rise to Vincente Fox.

With the macroeconomy under control, Fox is committed to repairing a deeper crisis—"the human crisis of people sunk in poverty." He is intent on helping the poor; repairing health care, education, and labor law; dealing with immense environmental problems; rebuilding Pemex, Mexico's state oil company; and establishing a stronger, more durable relationship with the United States. To do so, however, Fox needs funds from a population historically unwilling to pay taxes.

CASE STUDY MEXICO: THE UNFINISHED AGENDA

RICHARD H. K. VIETOR

REBECCA EVANS

It is certainly valuable not to have to talk about a financial crisis; but it is sad to have to speak of a much more important and deeper crisis, the human crisis of the people sunk in poverty; the social crisis of those who have been excluded from development.
—President Vicente Fox Quesada

Introduction

On July 7, 1997, Vicente Fox Quesada, the charismatic governor of the Mexican State of Guanajuato, stood in line to cast his vote in the mid-term national elections. When questioned by reporters, Fox announced his surprise bid for the 2000 presidency. In just a few days, Fox and his five-man team launched a nationwide campaign. Three years later, the team waited anxiously for the call that would determine whether or not Fox, the National Action Party's (PAN) candidate, would steal the presidency from the predicted winner, Francisco Labastida of the Institutional Revolutionary Party (PRI). At 1:30 a.m. on July 3, 2000, President Zedillo called to congratulate Fox on becoming Mexico's first non-PRI president in 70 years.[1]

During his campaign, Fox, a former Coca-Cola executive, had proposed an ambitious economic and social reform agenda that included widening of the tax base, liberalization of the electricity sector, increased education spending, poverty relief, a renewed fight against crime and corruption, and the formation of a North American common market (where goods and people could move freely). Above all, Fox promised to boost GDP growth to an annual rate of 7% by the end of his six-year term.

After his inauguration on December 1, Fox unveiled his cabinet, which included a mix of technocrats and liberals committed to his reform agenda. Fox chose Francisco Gil Díaz, a University of Chicago-trained economist and former CEO of Avantel SA, as his Finance

Minister. Luis Ernesto Derbez, a former World Bank executive, was appointed Economic Minister, and Eduardo Sojo Garza-Aldape, who had acted as Fox's economic cabinet coordinator in Guanajuato, was chosen to be the new economic czar. Other key appointments included Carlos Abascal Carranza as Labor Minister, Ernesto Martens Rebolledo as Energy Minister, Josefina Vázquez Mota as Social Development Minister, and Victor Lichtinger as Environment Minister.

In his first 100 days in office, Fox moved quickly to purge the government of the corruption and inefficiencies that had plagued the Mexican political system for years. Fox and his ministers worked around the clock to restructure existing government agencies and to create new offices for migrants, disabled citizens, and other underrepresented groups. After pushing an austere budget through Congress, Fox introduced legislation, which included bills to increase the autonomy of Mexico's indigenous people and improve their standard of living; to impose a 15% VAT (Value-Added Tax) tax on food and medicine; and to privatize new generation of electricity. In March, Fox met with U.S. President George W. Bush and lobbied for increased immigration quotas for Mexican workers.

With an early approval rating of 70%, it appeared that Fox would have no trouble restoring the Mexican people's faith in democracy. However, not everyone was convinced that Fox would be able to deliver on his campaign promises. "The big problem in Mexico is that there are three powers that influence government: religion, economics, and politics. A man can't represent all these interests, but Fox is pretending he can," stated Gregorio Urías Germán of the Party of the Democratic Revolution (PRD).[2] With a divided Congress, Fox lacked the political support he would need to enact necessary economic and social reform. The center-right PAN held only 41% of the seats in the Chamber of Deputies and 36% in the Senate [see **Exhibit 5.5**]. As he neared the end of his honeymoon, Fox remained confident, "Many people say I'm optimistic, but I deliver. I delivered results in Guanajuato and that, I will say, is my best ability—to deliver."[3]

Country Information

Located in North America, Mexico shares a 1,950-mile border with the United States in the north and a small border with Guatemala and Belize in the south [see **Exhibit 5.1**]. The varied terrain includes plains, deserts, rain forests, and mountains. The climate in northern Mexico is hot and dry, while in the southern states, it is tropical. Rich in natural resources, Mexico has oil reserves that were estimated at 45.7 billion barrels in 2000.

With a population of 101.9 million, Mexico is ranked the eleventh most populated country in world. In 1997, 34.7% of the population was below the age of 15. Nearly 70% of the population lived in urban areas, and close to 89% of Mexicans were Catholic.[4] Mexico City, with an estimated population of 20 million, was one of the most populated cities in the world. About 60% of Mexicans were "mestizo," a mix of Spanish and native descent, while 10% were indigenous. Most of the country's indigenous people lived in remote villages that lacked electricity, schools, and basic health services. With their unique customs and numerous dialects, the indigenous communities resisted the government's assimilation efforts.

Mexico was divided into two main socioeconomic regions. The northern region boasted higher wages, more industry, and better infrastructure than the south. In the southern region, there were greater indigenous and rural populations, more poverty, higher illiteracy rates, and lower productivity.[5] "The North is a more developed world which is influenced tremendously by the United States. Their culture, values and environment are very similar to the United States, but in the South it is completely different," explained Alberto Ortega Venzor, coordinator of the Presidential Office for Public Policy.[6]

Modern History[7]

In 1910, Mexican peasants and middle-class progressives had joined forces and revolted against the 30-year dictatorship of Porfirio Díaz. The bloody rebellion lasted for 10 years and helped shape the conscience of modern Mexico. The new 1917 Constitution established a federal republic and granted separate powers to the executive, legislative, and judicial branches, although primacy was given to the executive. Power was vested in the president, who was elected to a six-year term or *sexenio* but was prohibited from running for successive terms of office.

The nation's first official political party was formed during the devastating aftermath of the Revolution. In the hope of resolving future political conflicts more peacefully, President Plutarco Elías Calles centralized political power under the National Revolution Party (PNR) in 1929. The PNR, which later renamed itself the Institutional Revolutionary Party (PRI), went on to dominate Mexican politics for the next seven decades.

The Mexican oil industry, which was nationalized in 1938, was dominated by the state-owned oil and natural gas monopoly, Pemex or Petróleos Mexicanos. A great source of national pride, Pemex stood as a symbol of Mexican independence. The strong public support for Pemex made it nearly impossible for politicians to discuss the privatization of the energy sector.

After World War II, Mexico enjoyed many years of steady economic growth. Officials followed a policy of import-substitution industrialization, which greatly reduced the country's dependence on raw material exports and imported manufactured goods. Foreign direct investment increased five-fold from 1950 to 1970, with the United States taking the lead. During his presidency from 1952 to 1958, Adolfo Ruiz Cortines adopted a "stabilized development" (*desarrollo estabilizador)* model, which called for tight fiscal policies. These austerity measures led to a period of sustained, low-inflation growth throughout the 1950s and 1960s. However, economic growth faltered in the late 1960s. Political unrest climaxed with the 1968 Tlateloco Massacre, a student-led rebellion, which was violently suppressed by the government.

The 1976 Peso Crash

Under the leadership of President Luis Echeverría Álvarez (1970–1976), the country switched to a policy of shared development, which expanded the role of the state in the economy. In an unsuccessful attempt to stimulate growth and improve infrastructure, the state increased investment and encouraged import substitution in intermediate and capital goods. As a result, fiscal and current account deficits widened and inflation increased to a rate of 30%. In 1973, foreign investment was severely restricted. By September 1976, the situation reached crisis proportions; for the first time since 1954, the central bank was forced to devalue the peso by more than 40%, from 12 to 19 old pesos per dollar. This collapse launched a 24-year-long period of economic crises that severely hampered development in Mexico.

José López Portillo of the PRI took office at the end of 1976 and quickly instituted an austerity program that improved the balance of payments. Vast oil reserves were discovered in Mexico during the late 1970s, which greatly increased foreign exchange earnings and allowed external borrowing at low interest rates. The government began to finance its current account deficit through external debt, and revenue from oil exports was spent on other fiscal expenditures.[8] This sparked a development boom known as the "Mexican Miracle," and the government continued to increase spending on oil, agriculture, and tourism. Still, the economic miracle failed to reach many Mexicans. At the end of the 1970s, 35%–40% of all households earned a total income below the prevailing minimum wage; nearly 20% of the population in 1979 suffered from malnutrition; and 45% did not receive adequate health care.[9]

Although economic growth surged in the early 1980s, trouble brewed beneath the surface. Imports were growing at a faster pace than exports as the fixed exchange rate became overvalued. In the last year of the López Portillo administration, the budget deficit ballooned to 17% of GDP. Public external debt nearly doubled from US$40bn to US$78bn in just two years. Still, the government, blinded by the strength of its oil reserves, refused to address the nation's growing macroeconomic imbalances. As the private sector grew wary of the overvalued peso, investors began selling pesos and by June 1982, capital was leaving the country at a rate as high as US$400m per day. Yet even as inflation rates soared and oil prices started to fall in the second half of 1981, López Portillo vowed to "defend the peso like a dog."

By the summer of 1982, the deterioration of the Mexican economy was impossible to ignore: the outstanding stock of external debt had grown at an annual rate of 30% since 1973, creating a huge burden on debt service. By 1982, interest payments on external debt represented 35.4% of exports.[10] On August 12, 1982, the so-called Mexdollar accounts, dollar-denominated deposits held in Mexican banks, were frozen. Three days later, the world reeled with the news that Mexico could no longer meet interest payments on its foreign debt. López Portillo was forced to devalue the peso and the country plunged into its worst recession since the Great Depression.[11]

On September 1, López Portillo nationalized the banking system and inaugurated exchange controls. This unexpected move aggravated capital flight and ruptured the implicit contract between the private sector and the government. In early December, Mexico signed a strict agreement with the IMF in which it pledged to reduce the deficit, restrict growth in the money supply, devalue the peso, and privatize state-owned companies.

President Miguel de la Madrid (1982–1988) was elected amidst the chaos of the 1982 economic crisis. He had before him the huge tasks of effecting structural economic reform and repairing the fissure between the private and public sectors. The PRI's de la Madrid was a 47-year-old Harvard Kennedy School graduate who had spent most of his career in the treasury and central bank. At the behest of the IMF, he invoked strict austerity measures to reduce the fiscal deficit. Intense budget cutting, an increase in public sector prices, and a higher value-added tax helped bring the deficit under control during the first two years. De la Madrid devalued the peso and cut real wages. Nominal minimum wages, which had been indexed to rates of past inflation, were tied to expected inflation rates in 1983, but were severely underestimated during this period. Tight fiscal and monetary policies were maintained until 1985, when the budget was loosened for the mid-term elections.

The mid-1980s brought a series of crises that shook the Mexican economy: a devastating earthquake in Mexico City killed thousands and caused at least US$5bn in damages; the IMF suspended payment on its Extended Fund Facility agreement; low employment growth forced Mexicans to seek jobs in the informal sector and in the U.S.; oil prices took a nose-dive, falling as low as US$8.54 barrel in July 1986; then the Mexican stock market crashed in October 1987. The market crash triggered a new wave of capital flight and another major peso devaluation. Inflation hit an annual rate of 159%.

Desperate for a new macroeconomic stabilization program, the government negotiated a *Pacto*, an agreement between government and representatives of business, unions, and agriculture to cooperate and coordinate wage bargaining and price setting in order to combat inflation. In addition to wage and price adjustments, the peso was devalued by 22% more and tariffs on imports were reduced from 40% to 20%. Restrictions on foreign direct investment were eased, allowing IBM and Hewlett-Packard to set up wholly owned subsidiaries. For the first time, 100% foreign ownership of Mexico's *maquiladoras,* or assembly factories, was allowed. (By the end of 1986, 90% of the *maquiladoras* were U.S.-owned.) With its entry into GATT in August 1986, Mexico further reduced tariff rates from 23% to 12.5% over the next three years, signifying a new commitment to liberalized trade. De la Madrid also initiated the privatization of state-owned firms; by 1988, the sale of 117 firms had raised close to US$700m.

The 1988 Elections

As the 1988 elections approached, voters remained frustrated with slow growth and high unemployment. Opposition parties gathered strength, and after defecting from the PRI and forming a new party, Cuauhtémoc Cárdenas challenged the PRI's candidate, Carlos Salinas, for the next presidency. The election results were delayed for a week, during which Cárdenas ballots were found "floating down rivers and smoldering in roadside bonfires." When the official results were released, Salinas had won only 50.7% of the vote.

Salinas devoted his first months in office to a restoration of the government's legitimacy. Despite his party's close ties with the Oil Workers Union, Salinas began by arresting its leader, Joaquín Hernández, on charges of assassination, job peddling, and fraud. Next, he locked up financier Eduardo Legorreta and four associates for securities fraud surrounding the stock market crash of 1987. He finished the crusade with the arrest of the notorious drug trafficker, Miguel Félix Gallardo. In an effort to show his commitment to the opening up of the political process, Salinas attended the inauguration of the PAN's Ernesto Ruffo Appel as governor of Baja California Norte.

Continuing with de la Madrid's economic reforms, Salinas renewed the *Pacto*, maintained wage and price controls and fixed the peso, allowing it to devalue by one peso per day. He also expanded the privatization program by selling Telmex. Hoping to generate foreign exchange, Salinas further eased foreign investment regulations, allowing 100% ownership in the tourism sector.

In February 1990, Mexico reached an agreement with its foreign bank creditors that would convert bank debt into "Brady Bonds," 30-year zero-coupon bonds guaranteed by the U.S. Treasury on the collateral of Mexican oil reserves. The agreement decreased the debt burden by as much as 20%. It also cut annual payments by US$3bn over the next four years.

In 1989, Salinas, another graduate of Harvard University with a Ph.D. in political economy, appeared in *Fortune* magazine's list of the top 25 business leaders. In a poll conducted by the *Los Angeles Times,* he received a 79% presidential approval rating. By the end of the year, economic growth had reached 3% and inflation had fallen to about 20% (from 159% in 1987.) Pleased with the prospects for Mexico's economic reform, foreign investors were sending money into the country during the early 1990s, stimulating both domestic consumption and investment. Confined to fluctuate within a band since 1991, the peso/dollar exchange rate seemed to be appreciating in the early 1990s. Although the bottom of the band allowed for a gradual depreciation, the magnitude of capital inflows kept the rate at the top of the band. And from late 1992 on, the peso's exchange rate demonstrated remarkable stability, evidence in the government's eyes of the success of its structural reforms.

Despite the appearance of a prosperous economy, some critics argued that the peso's strength was actually evidence of macroeconomic mismanagement. In reality, a steady *nominal* exchange rate had produced an appreciating *real* rate. An overvalued currency made for inexpensive imports, causing consumption and imports to rise more quickly than income. Meanwhile, the spending boom of the late 1980s and early 1990s had caused private savings to collapse, plunging from 21.8% of GDP in 1983 to 12.1% in 1994. In addition, economic growth had been declining steadily since 1990, slipping from a rate of 5.1% in 1990 to 3.6% in 1992. By the end of 1993, the country was experiencing no growth and job creation remained stagnant.[12]

The Political Shocks of 1994

As New Year's Day 1994 approached, Mexicans were eager to usher in a new era of economic and political stability. A year earlier, Salinas had signed the historic North American Free Trade Agreement (NAFTA), a treaty between Mexico, the United States, and Canada that converted all quotas between the countries to tariffs and removed all tariffs on trade over a 10- to 15-year period. Salinas believed that the agreement would ensure Mexico's competitiveness in the world economy.

Instead of celebrating the first day of NAFTA on January 1, 1994, Salinas was forced to deal with a peasant uprising in the southern state of Chiapas. In the first hour of the new year, the Zapatista National Liberation Army, a group of Indian rebels who objected to NAFTA, seized the city of San Cristóbal de las Casas and declared war on the government. Salinas sent the Mexican Army to Chiapas to squash the rebellion. By the end of the week, the Zapatistas had retreated to the jungle. More than 100 people were killed in the insurrection.

On March 23, 1994, Luis Donaldo Colosio, the PRI candidate for president, was assassinated at a campaign rally in Tijuana. It was speculated that those in the PRI that opposed Colosio's promise to continue Salinas' reforms had conspired to kill Colosio. In response to the growing political violence, foreign confidence dwindled, and investors sold peso securities. Fearing devaluation, Mexican investors quickly moved their savings offshore to safe dollar accounts. Faced with major reserve losses, Mexican authorities decided to raise interest rates and use reserves held at the central bank to maintain the value of the peso. To maintain the gross level of reserves, the government issued *tesobonos*, short-term Mexican government debt instruments indexed to the dollar, which enabled them to borrow more dollars from abroad. The peso declined from 3.1 to 3.4 new pesos/dollar (the new peso was one-thousandth of the old peso), the bottom of the allowable band.

The Zedillo Years[13]

Salinas' efforts to eliminate electoral fraud (he had granted autonomy to the electoral authority) helped make the 1994 national elections the cleanest to date. The PRI's Ernesto Zedillo Ponce de León was sworn into office on December 1, 1994. Having inherited the economic and political difficulties experienced by the Salinas administration, the Yale-trained economist focused his attention on restoring confidence and establishing his authority. However, three weeks into Zedillo's term, with no sign of a clear economic plan, the peso plummeted from 3.4 new pesos to the dollar on December 20 to 5.7 on January 9. Capital markets lost confidence, and reserves hit rock bottom as the country faced US$28bn in *tesobono* liabilities.

The delayed announcement of Zedillo's "emergency economic program" (rescheduled seven times) fueled concerns that the new government was incapable of formulating a coherent economic strategy. In his January 3, 1995, national address, Zedillo announced an international aid package of $18 billion, quickly arranged in the two weeks following devaluation. The new economic program aimed to cut the current account deficit with unions accepting a 7% limit on wage increases for 199,5 and with business leaders promising to hold down prices. The government pledged a spending cut of 1.3% of GDP to achieve a year-end budget surplus of 0.5% of GDP, but it was unwilling to forego continued flexibility in the exchange rate regime. Investors were not reassured by the president's speech and continued to pull money out of Mexico.

On January 5, Zedillo sent Guillermo Ortiz Martinez, the new Minister of Finance, to New York in order to reassure anxious investors of Mexico's ability to honor its debt. If Mexico defaulted on its obligations it would certainly plunge into a depression. A Mexican default might also trigger massive capital flight from other Latin American and developing countries, eventually hitting the United States, which depended on those areas for about 40% of its exports. To prevent such a disaster, the Clinton administration joined with the U.S. Exchange Stabilization Fund and the IMF to provide a $50 billion relief package in March.

The bailout provoked sharp reactions in the United States and in Mexico, but the peso's free fall was halted; the Mexican stock market stabilized and began rising again. Ortiz spent most of 1995 removing billions of dollars of bad loans from bank balance sheets and arranging restructuring programs for mortgage holders and other small debtors. After posting negative GDP growth in 1995, the economy quickly rebounded, growing 5.1% in 1996 and a spectacular 6.8% in 1997 [see **Exhibit 5.2**]. By the end of the year, private investment had increased to 25.7%; the fiscal budget was balanced; the current account deficit had fallen to 1.8% of GDP; and foreign direct investment, which was pouring in, reached a record high of U.S.$12.8bn [14] [see **Exhibits 5.3 and 5.4**].

After revitalizing the economy, Zedillo concentrated his efforts on the opening up of the PRI-dominated political system. In July 1996, Zedillo convinced Congress to adopt new election rules. When the new rules were tested in the July 1997 midterm elections, the PRI lost its majority in Congress for the first time in seven decades. Perhaps more surprising was the victory of the PRD's twice-defeated candidate, Cuauhtemoc Cárdenas, for the governorship of Mexico City. The PAN also captured governorships in the important states of Querétaro and Nuevo León. In the years following, the opposition parties formed a shaky alliance in Congress, but the competing ideologies of the PAN and the PRD prevented the formation of a formal alliance. Still, Zedillo's efforts at political reform had changed Mexican politics forever.

The Fall of the PRI

The 71-year-long reign of the PRI ended abruptly on July 2, 2000, when the PAN's Vicente Fox defeated Francisco Labastida by a vote of 42.7% to 35.8%. Voters likened Fox's stunning victory to the collapse of the Berlin Wall and appeared optimistic that the new president would carry Mexico into a new era of clean politics and economic prosperity. "The election of Fox was an important transition for Mexico. The common thought had been that if the economy was growing at a fast rate and the debt structure was in line, then people would want the existing party to rule. But the 2000 elections showed a different line of thinking. If the macroeconomy was strong, then the country could afford to take a risk and vote for a new party," explained Eduardo Sojo Garza-Aldape, chief of the Presidential Office. [15]

With a peaceful election and what appeared to be a stable macroeconomy, the country anticipated its smoothest transition in decades. In early October, Fox announced a conservative economic agenda for 2001 that targeted economic growth of 4.5% (down from 6.9% in 2000), a fiscal deficit of 0.5%, foreign direct investment aimed at $14bn, inflation of 7%, and a current account deficit of 3.6% of GDP. [16] Confident that the proposed fiscal agenda would keep the macroeconomy in good shape, the Fox administration aimed to tackle the more-pressing microeconomic issues. In his December inaugural speech, Fox stated, "Although the macroeconomic variables are stable, we have not yet fulfilled the long-held desire to moderate wealth and extreme poverty." He went on to outline a myriad of issues that he would address during his *sexenio*. Among them were plans to open the electricity sector to privatization, to transform the state-owned oil monopoly into an efficient company, to update labor legislation, to create jobs in the marginalized regions of the South, to improve educational infrastructure and teacher training, to eradicate police corruption, to fight drug trafficking, to protect water and forests, and to eliminate poverty.

Mexico's Economic Problems

Income Inequality and Its Causes

Mexico ranked fifty-fifth in the human development index and had the thirteenth-largest economy in the world. [17] More than half of the country's 100 million inhabitants lived in poverty, while 24 million lived in extreme poverty. [18] The poverty gap between northern and southern Mexico was expanding. Nearly 50% of those living in extreme poverty were concentrated in Mexico's 10 poorest states: Veracruz, Chiapas, Puebla, Michoacán, México, Jalisco, Hildago, Guanajuato, Guerrero, and Oaxaca. [19] [See "Map of Mexico," **Exhibit 5.1**.] Poverty was more acute in rural areas and isolated municipalities where poor infrastructure, inadequate health services, and weak product and labor markets lowered the standard of living. The National Statistics Institute (INEGI) revealed in its 2000 study that 70% of homes in the poorest municipalities had dirt floors, 37% lacked bathrooms, 87.2% lacked refrigerators, and 69.4% lacked televisions [20] [see **Exhibit 5.6**]. While average life expectancy and infant mortality rates had improved over the last decade, there were still severe regional imbalances.

Although income distribution in Mexico had improved during the 1970s, it had worsened considerably in the 1980s. Income inequality had remained at high levels during the 1990s despite a surge in economic growth. By 2000, Mexico had one of the highest gini coefficients in Latin America [see **Exhibit 5.7**]. The income share of the top 20% of the population was 60.0%, while the bottom 20% held only 3.3%. Much of the income inequality stemmed from wage inequality, which was influenced by schooling, urbanization, family tradition, and the informal sector. The minimum wage in Mexico was equivalent to US$4 per day; however a third of working Mexicans received less than the minimum wage.[21] Meanwhile, 42% of the workforce earned just twice the minimum salary per day.[22]

Mexico had one of the most pronounced education gaps in Latin America. On average, there was a nine-year schooling gap between the richest decile and the bottom 30% of the population. "The main element of poverty is undoubtedly the vicious education system that preserves and makes poverty permanent," remarked Dr. Luis Rubio of CIDAC.[23] The average Mexican child received only 7.7 years of education, though schooling levels varied by region [see **Exhibit 5.10**]. While attendance in primary schools was high, many low-income children dropped out of school at an early age, while wealthier children went on to attend secondary schools and universities [see **Exhibit 5.8a**]. Many lower-income families didn't have the resources to finance the private costs (transportation, food, books, clothing, etc.) of keeping their children in school.[24] Wage increases associated with early years of schooling were much lower than those from higher education [see **Exhibit 5.8b**]. In rural areas, where access to education was limited, returns were less than those in urban centers. In fact, workers with the same education level earned 44% less in rural Mexico than in urban Mexico. The quality of education also contributed to income inequality. Private schools provided a much better education than public schools, but only 10% of the country could afford private institutions.[25]

Mexican households were characterized by strong family ties. Nearly 84% of Mexican children lived in nuclear or extended families.[26] Family traditions and decisions affected income levels. Rural-dwelling families tended to have more children, in part because children could work to support the family at an earlier age.

These families earned far less than urban-dwelling families [see **Exhibits 5.9a** and **5.9b**]. The female labor participation rate in Mexico was unusually low [see **Exhibit 5.11**]. Mexico's *macho* culture influenced many women's decisions to stay at home, though progressive women's organizations had denounced Labor Minister Carlos Abascal's remarks that women should serve their traditional roles as housewives and mothers.[27] Poor women were less likely to work because they had more children. They also lacked access to modern conveniences that made housekeeping chores more efficient. Although there were some job opportunities in the informal sector, low wages and a lack of benefits discouraged many women from entering the labor force. Parents' education levels could explain much of the educational attainment gap in Mexico. Since education directly influenced earnings, a parent's education level determined if the family could afford to keep children in school. Many children dropped out of school after observing how the labor market rewarded their parents' education[28] [see **Exhibit 5.14**].

Mexico's underdeveloped financial markets prevented many citizens from taking advantage of high returns. Inadequate land titling and weak credit institutions blocked low-income individuals and small businesses from gaining access to credit. According to the Inter-American Development Bank, deeper credit markets would increase the availability of capital to both the formal and informal sectors and eventually lead to increased productivity and higher wages[29] [see **Exhibits 5.13a** and **5.13b**].

Mexico's geography and natural resource endowments seemed to augment the income imbalance. The oil industry absorbed most of Mexico's capital and offered few employment opportunities. As a result, development and wages slumped in other economic sectors. Although increased government spending of oil revenues created a rise in inflation, the high value of oil buoyed the currency. With an often-overvalued currency, the non-oil industries were less successful at competing with imports.

Volatility, trade liberalization, and globalization might also contribute to income inequality in Mexico. Frequent periods of economic instability limited capital accumulation, interfered with childhood education, and lowered productivity. Volatility hit low-income groups the hardest as they had fewer means to protect themselves from economic shocks. In a debate over the benefits of NAFTA, most studies concluded that trade liberalization hurt income inequality in Mexico. In an essay on welfare reform, Guillermo Trejo and Claudio Jones wrote, "Preliminary evidence suggests that economic and trade liberalization have had contrasting effects across regions: with relatively high levels of infrastructure and human capital, along with their proximity to the United States, most northern states have been able to benefit form the rapid and unilateral opening of the Mexican economy, whereas large portions of the rural and backward south have been affected negatively."[30] Some argued that globalization also reinforced income inequality because it drove down the price of unskilled labor so that Mexico could compete with China, India, and other developing countries.

Meanwhile, technological advances raised the wages of skilled workers, further widening the income gap [see **Exhibits 5.20** and **5.21**].

For the next two decades, the ratio of children to workers was predicted to decline in Mexico. This might provide the country with an opportunity to increase the resources available for education, health services, and other social reforms. With fewer dependent children and elders, workers would be able to increase their savings. Mexico had changed from a pay-as-you-go pension system to a fully funded pension system in 1997, so increased savings should allow workers to provide for their own retirement, releasing the burden from their children's generation. There was hope that if the government took advantage of the demographic opportunity, income distribution might be improved.[31]

Critics argued that the social welfare programs of previous administrations had failed to reduce poverty. Trejo and Jones wrote, "López Portillo and Salinas launched massive antipoverty programs; centralized and free of institutional checks, these programs became policy tools to generate political support for the presidency and the PRI and had little, if any, effect on poverty reduction."[32] In fact, research economist Dr. Miguel Székely speculated, "Maybe countries should not have a separate set of social policies. Instead, they should incorporate social development into their overall economic development strategies, so that the overall strategy is only put forward if it helps to improve the social conditions of the population."[33]

Fox had appointed Josefina Vázquez Mota, previously a PAN congresswoman, as the new Minister for Social Development. Sedesol, the Ministry of Social Development, had 20,000 employees and a new budget of $14b pesos. Although the 2001 budget was 4% greater than the 2000 budget in nominal terms, it was 5% less than the old budget in real terms. Most Mexicans were confident that the new minister would try to devise an effective social development strategy. "Josefina has shifted the way we think about poverty. She's said, 'Let's stop arguing about the causes of poverty, and instead, focus on the causes of wealth.' I think her new focus is fantastic," commented Dr. Luis Rubio.[34]

The newly structured ministry drafted a strategy that would attack poverty on three different fronts. First, it focused on building social capital by restoring confidence in the political system (by eliminating corruption), increasing participation in the labor force, and encouraging indigenous people to modernize. The next step involved building human capital by improving the education system. Lastly, it aimed to improve infrastructure in poor municipalities.[35]

Sedesol also planned to continue Zedillos' successful Progresa program. This food, health, and education program provided 400,000 rural families living in extreme poverty conditions in eleven regions with a monthly stipend of US$37. Instead of traditional food subsidies of milk and tortillas, Progresa linked social security payments to school attendance. The stipend was contingent on children's school attendance and regular visits to health clinics. An independent study found that children from Progresa-sponsored families were likely to stay in school for one more year than those not sponsored by Progresa. In Mexico, this extra year of education translated into an average increase of 8% in income over a lifetime.[36] Fox had also proposed expanding Progresa to cover urban families living in poverty[37] [see **Exhibit 5.15**].

A Weak Education System

The Ministry of Public Education (SEP) was established in 1921 to provide support and structure for the Mexican education system. In the early 1940s, local teachers' unions came together to form the National Union of Education Workers (SNTE), a PRI union. Together, the SEP and SNTE controlled educational policy and decision-making until

1992, when Salinas introduced a series of reforms that decentralized basic education. The reforms gave states control over basic and teacher education, limited the SEP's functions to coordination and compensatory actions, and redesigned the primary education curriculum. In 1996, Zedillo introduced a new teacher evaluation and training system, but the SNTE's involvement threatened the legitimacy of the evaluations.[38]

Nearly 10% of the Mexican population over the age of 14 was illiterate. In the southern states, the illiteracy rate was closer to 40%.[39] Primary education for children aged 6 to 14 was free and compulsory, yet statistics revealed that only 6 out of 10 children completed primary education.[40] One study showed that only 14 out of 100 Mexican students who completed first grade went on to finish high school.[41] Higher education participation rates were equally low with only 1,730 students per 100,000 population seeking advanced degrees.[42] "Most children drop out of school because they have to work. Some students who are talented scholars or athletes don't get enough support from schools. Their morale goes down and they quit," reflected Agustin Carmona, a second-grade teacher in Mexico City.[43]

Public school teachers were overworked, underpaid, and underskilled. Many teachers worked two shifts: the first shift ran from 8:00 a.m. to 12:30 p.m. and the second shift ran from 2:00 p.m. until 6:00 p.m. Class size ranged from 20 students per class in the city to 50 students per class in the suburbs. Although teachers were required to attend "normal" or teacher training schools for four years, many teachers had only one year of post-high school training.[44] Teacher's salaries ranged from US$300 to US$600 per month. "The problem with teachers is that a lot of them lack commitment and preparation. I think that the government should pay more attention and force teachers to take more education courses," suggested Carmona. "They should offer full-time positions where teachers can teach in the morning and prepare lessons in the afternoon."[45]

Many public schools also suffered from a lack of infrastructure. In Ciudad Juárez, for example, several children attended classes in old school buses, while others studied in classrooms without electricity.[46] Most schools endured shortages of chairs, desks, lamps, books, chalk, and erasers. Malnourished students had difficulty concentrating, and few schools had cafeterias or hot lunch programs.

President Fox had promised to increase education spending (which equaled 4.5% of GDP in 2000) to 7.5% of GDP in 2001. He had also announced his goal to raise the average level of schooling to nine years by the end of his administration.[47] Fox's plans for education reform included a system of need-based scholarships and student loans that would help poor students receive high school and university degrees.[48] The Fox administration recognized that overcoming the SNTE would be a huge hurdle. "The union is very strong, and in the past it was used as a political tool. About half of them are administrators, and the other half are teachers. This is awful, we should have more teachers and fewer administrators," commented Ortega.[49]

The Labor Dilemma

Mexican workers grew frustrated with the lack of real wage gains. Wages had 60% less purchasing power than they did in 1982.[50] In early 2001, the National Minimum Salary Commission agreed to raise the minimum wage by 6.99%. However, the raise marked only a 0.49% increase over the targeted 6.5% inflation rate for 2001. Despite complaints from labor activists, businesses applauded the raise, arguing that it would help create 800,000 new jobs.[51] Mexico's partial unemployment rate of 18%, which measured underutilized workers, was a more accurate measure than the 2.6% open unemployment rate. An estimated 9.3 million Mexicans worked in the informal sector, contributing 13% to GDP[52] [see **Exhibit 5.12**].

During his campaign, Fox had pledged to restore purchasing power by linking wages to productivity increases. He chose Carlos Abascal, a former businessman, as the new secretary of the Labor and Social Welfare Ministry. Within three months, Abascal had announced a new labor council to replace the 14-year-old *Pacto* system of wage bargaining and price controls. "I am changing the way of doing dialogue with labor. We had 12 years of the *Pacto*. Although it was successful at the beginning, it became very routine under Zedillo," said Abascal.[53] The new Council for Productive Sector Dialogue would bring together representatives from businesses, labor organizations, and government ministries to make labor reform.

Abascal hoped to create a new labor culture between unions and businesses. "We need to make changes in this country, changes within the existing leadership, not with new union leaders but with the current ones. Business leaders and union leaders need to work together and face the same reality," said Abascal.[54] In Mexico, 40% of the workforce was unionized.[55] Most workers belonged to one of nine large national unions that were closely linked to the PRI. The Confederation of Mexican Workers (CTM) remained the largest and most influential union. In the past, the CTM had colluded with the PRI to keep wages down and had made little effort to improve workers' rights. More recently, smaller independent unions had been formed in some of the high-tech industries, and some pointed out that they were better paid and more productive.[56] Abascal believed that the "new unionism" would lead to more jobs, increased productivity, better training, and a higher standard of living for Mexicans.[57]

The Labor and Social Development Ministry planned to work closely with Congress to amend the existing labor law. The 1970 law regulated labor contracts, minimum wages, hours of work, official holidays, paid vacations, trade unions, and strikes.[58] The rigid law also required employers to offer large severance packages, which prevented many businesses from hiring and firing employees. Abascal planned to modernize the public administration, to separate the unions from the PRI's influence, and to create an international treaty on labor issues. "We realize that we can't do all this in one sexenio, but we need to set a base. Changes will be noticeable because the bar is so low," observed Abascal.[59]

Migration to the United States

Motivated by large wage differentials (the average Mexican worker could earn 10 times more per day in the United States), an estimated 300,000 undocumented Mexicans crossed the border each year.[60] High security at the border forced migrants to risk their lives crossing deserts and crawling through sewerage pipes to reach the United States. An estimated 400 migrants had died while trying to cross the border in 2000.[61] Once safely in the United States, Mexicans found jobs in the agricultural, service, and construction industries and sent an average US$6bn back home each year.

Fox urged the United States to open its borders to Mexican workers and proposed the formation of a North American common market. "We must have a long-term vision . . . to open the borders to the free flow of people. By the time of that vision, we should have narrowed the gap in the fundamentals of our economies," said Fox.[62] Disgusted with the increasing violence along the border, Fox implored the United States to stop building border walls and barbed wire fences. In December, he traveled to the border to shake hands with the "Mexican heroes" who were returning home for Christmas.

In the United States, some Congressmen lobbied for a guest worker program, which would increase temporary work visas for Mexican workers from 40,000 in 2000 to 150,000 by 2005.[63] Others pushed for legislation that would grant legal residency to the 5 million undocumented Mexicans living in the United States. A White House official told *The New York Times,* "While the president does not believe that amnesty is the only means by which humane treatment and the status of migrants can be addressed, I can assure you that we believe that the issues of migration are going to be an ongoing discussion between the two countries."[64]

Crime and Corruption

Mexico's soaring crime rates threatened lives and discouraged foreign investment. In 1997, 17,000 people were murdered in Mexico. Bank robberies, abductions, and shootings had become a part of daily life in Mexico City, where an average of eight murders occurred each day. In Tijuana, there were 323 homicides in 1999, and criminal organizations involved in the drug trade were growing increasingly powerful. Foreign businesses with operations in Mexico considered moving to safer countries. Several wives and children of top executives had been kidnapped and held for ransom. Corporations faced escalating crime-prevention costs, which included background checks, bullet-proof vehicles, and police escort services. In 1999, security spending for Sony's Mexican operation doubled to US$1m.[65]

Corruption also plagued Mexico's police and judicial system. Mexico was ranked fifty-ninth out of 90 countries in a corruption index compiled by Transparency International.[66] Few Mexicans trusted police officers, who often joined criminal activity rather than fighting it.

Severely underpaid and poorly trained, Mexican police would often take bribes instead of enforcing the law. Some policemen argued that accepting these bribes was the only way they could afford to feed their families. Eager to fight crime, Fox declared, "We must also take all the necessary steps to end corruption, which is the evil of all evils. As long as we have corruption, crime will continue on the streets. As long as there is impunity, organized crime will continue on the streets."[67] After taking office, Fox announced a nationwide Crusade Against Corruption. He established a new Security and Police Ministry and fired police officers in droves. New officers were required to have at least 12 years of schooling, and their salaries were doubled.

Many Mexicans were skeptical of Fox's ability to rid the country of graft. After decades of corrupt government, cheating and bribery had become a common aspect of Mexican life. "Eighty percent of the population would be willing to violate the law if nobody noticed. It's more comfortable for them to live under the current system than to live under enforced legal practices," explained Abascal.[68]

Drug Trafficking

Drug trafficking organizations continued to corrupt Mexico's law enforcement agents. Key members of the Arellano Felix Organization (AFO), one of Mexico's two major drug cartels, had described a criminal empire that paid Mexican police to help with assassinations and guard drug shipments. In 1997, authorities had arrested General Jesus Gutierrez Rebollo, Mexico's chief drug enforcer, charging he was on the payroll of the nation's largest drug cartel. In January 2001, Joaquin "El Chapo" Guzman, a Sinaloa drug lord, escaped from a maximum-security prison after allegedly bribing prison guards. Five days later, President Fox announced a crusade against narcotics trafficking and organized crime. Pledging to eradicate corruption, Fox said, "Today I reaffirm our war without mercy against the pernicious criminal mafias . . . so every family can sleep peacefully, so we can all live without fear of going out into the street."[69]

In March 2001, the United States certified Mexico and 19 other countries in its annual antidrug report. The U.S. government applauded the Mexican government's latest achievements in the war against drugs: two more AFO members were arrested; opium poppy production was greatly reduced; and in a precedent-setting decision, the Mexican Supreme Court ruled that Arturo Páez Martínez, a Mexican accused of smuggling more than 2,200 pounds of cocaine into the United States, could be extradited to California.[70] Still, the United States admitted that the Mexican government "lack[ed] the broad institutional capability to fully implement its antidrug legislation and national drug strategy"[71] [see **Exhibit 5.16**].

During his February 2001 visit with Fox, Bush had acknowledged that the United States played a significant role in the Mexican drug problem. "One of the reasons why drugs are shipped is because U.S. citizens use drugs," stated Bush.[72] The two presidents discussed the need to coordinate efforts to reduce drug production, trafficking, and consumption. "Only by joining forces with strategic coordination and by sharing information can we face and defeat this situation," said Fox.[73]

Environmental Degradation

Mexico's pervasive environmental destruction resulted in an estimated annual loss equivalent to 11% of GDP.[74] Air pollution, deforestation, water contamination, and improper disposal of hazardous wastes threatened Mexico's natural environment. Mexico City, Guadalajara, Monterrey, Minatitlán, Coatzacoalcos, Tampico, and Salamanca were among Mexico's most polluted cities. And lower-income groups, of course, carried much of the burden of environmental degradation. As desertification destroyed an average of 870 square miles of arable land each year, poor farmers were forced to abandon their farms and move into the slums of crowded cities.[75] Studies revealed that seven out of eight infant deaths among indigenous people were linked to water pollution.[76]

The environmental movement in Mexico evolved slowly. While the United States passed clean air and water acts during the 1970s, Mexico struggled to keep its economy afloat. Mexico's environmental conscience bloomed only during the de la Madrid administration. De la Madrid established the country's first independent Environment Ministry (SEMARNAT) in the early 1980s. However, enforcement and pollution control remained weak until the NAFTA negotiations of the early 1990s. The treaty forced Mexico to adopt strict environmental regulations modeled after those of the U.S.'s Environmental Protection Agency.[77] Still, environmental groups struggled to make the Mexican people care about the environment. Many Mexicans remained ignorant of the pollution around them. "It's a problem when you feel it, but when you don't have direct contact with it, it doesn't bother you," explained Rodolfo Lacy Tomayo of SEMARNAT. "Even if you see a forest being cut down, you don't get the big picture of deforestation unless you go up in a helicopter."[78]

In 2001, SEMARNAT employed 32,000 people (15,000 worked for the independent Water Commission) and had a budget of US$1.4bn. Working to create a Mexico with an "environmental conscience," Fox appointed Victor Lichtinger as the new Secretary of the Environment. Lichtinger, an economist with doctoral studies in agricultural and natural resource economics at Stanford, had directed the Commission for Environmental Cooperation in Montreal. After restructuring the ministry, Lichtinger would focus on Mexico's most pressing environmental issues: deforestation, water, and hazardous wastes. However, Lichtinger admitted that macroeconomic restraints would inhibit environmental reform. Although the 2001 budget had increased in nominal terms, the budget allocated to SEMARNAT and its related organizations had decreased by 3.4% in real terms. "Even if I received grant money from the World Bank," explained Lichtinger, "Díaz would just subtract that amount from my budget and use it for another part of the government."[79]

Encircled by the mountains of a closed valley, Mexico City suffered from a constant blanket of air pollutants. By 2001, pollution levels had stabilized in response to strong efforts to curb emissions: regular car inspections were mandatory; trains switched from oil to natural gas; and industries could burn only natural gas. Although air pollution levels remained dangerously high, the federal government decentralized air quality control to state governments and turned its attention to the country's more serious environmental problems. "We've done about all we can for now. The air will never be clean, there are just too many people," explained Lichtinger.[80]

With a loss of 600,000 hectares of forest each year, Mexico had one of the highest deforestation rates in the world.[81] The government estimated that 30% of trees were cut

for fuel burning, 40% for agriculture cultivation and cattle grazing, and 30% were lost to illegal logging and slash-and-burn practices.[82] Besides threatening biodiversity, deforestation led to erosion of topsoil and contributed to the depletion of the water supply. As a result, arable land in southern Mexico declined at an alarming pace. SEMARNAT was in the process of developing a national commission for forestry that would be modeled after the National Water Commission. Lichtinger planned to reduce deforestation rates by deregulating forestry activity and assigning property rights to individuals.[83]

With a rapidly declining water supply, water was Mexico's most threatening environmental problem [see **Exhibit 5.17**]. Nearly 50% of the water supply was lost through leaky pipes during distribution. Agribusiness, cattle ranchers, and mining firms consumed an estimated 70% of the water supply at no cost.[84] Industrial waste and sewage contaminated the supply; government statistics showed that only 17% of wastewater was treated. The remaining untreated water flowed directly into rivers and lakes. Although many municipalities had built treatment plants, most lacked the money to train workers and operate the plants.[85] Lichtinger made plans to charge businesses for water consumption and hoped to involve the private sector in the building and operation of proper water treatment plants.[86]

Improper waste disposal threatened public health. Mexico lacked the proper institutions, organizations, and facilities for waste disposal. The country's only hazardous waste site was located in Monterrey, and its high monopolist prices caused many companies to dump water illegally. "We have a very bad hazardous waste situation in Mexico. Some of the businesses are disposing hazardous waste with their trash," noted Lacy.[87] Statistics showed that by 2005, Mexico City would run out of space to dispose garbage, which accumulated at a rate of 12,000 tons per day.[88] Lichtinger hoped that an incentive-based program would encourage companies to properly dispose of hazardous waste.[89]

Pemex contributed to both air and water pollution. In 1996, Pemex established the Corporate Direction for Industrial Safety and Environmental Protection (SIASPA) to implement safety and environmental protection practices. By 1999, the company's air emissions had fallen by 13.7%, water pollutants had dropped by 21.7%, and generation of hazardous wastes was lowered by 47.9%. Pemex had aimed to reduce total emissions and discharges by 16% more in 2000.[90] "We are working very hard to protect the environment by changing our drilling and exploration operations so that they are more environmentally friendly," said Rafael Fernandez de la Garza, director of Industrial Safety and Environmental Protection at Pemex. "We are also making an effort to protect natural areas. My feeling is that if we want to work in a naturally protected environment, we have to first understand the way the ecology works in that area."[91]

Corruption within the Environment Ministry had contributed to lax enforcement of environmental standards. The country's 300 environmental inspectors each earned an average salary of US$350 per month.[92] Business executives would often bribe inspectors to pass their companies when they failed to meet the environmental standards. Lichtinger intended to eliminate corruption by motivating inspectors with rewards. In addition, the Ministry aimed to make its Environmental Impact Assessment (EIA) process more transparent. "In the past, the system was very corrupt. You passed in your application, and if you offered someone enough money, they would allow you to go ahead with the project," explained Lichtinger.[93]

In March 2001, Fox and Lichtinger announced the National Crusade for Water and Forests. The new plan included incentives for local communities to help protect the environment and a new policy to educate people on the environment.[94] The plan required each government agency to introduce environmental considerations into its economic decisions. "Every sectoral plan will have a sustainability component with indicators on how to use alternative sources of energy or how to use water efficiently," said Lichtinger.[95] Not everyone believed that the crusade would improve Mexico's environment. "I am optimistic of the action and decisions that the new government will take in regards to the environment. But, I am pessimistic about the results for forests, water, and hazardous waste. There just isn't enough money," commented Hernando Guerrero, director of the Mexico Liasion Office of the Commission for Environmental Cooperation.[96]

A Closed Energy Sector

State-owned Pemex, which produced and distributed refined oil and petrochemical products, was the fifth-largest oil company in the world. In 2000, Mexico produced 3 million barrels of oil per day and exported 1.4 million barrels per day[97] [see **Exhibit 5.18**]. Pemex was composed of four separate divisions: Pemex Exploración and Producción (PEP) explored and developed oil and natural gas reserves, which were concentrated in the northeast, southeast, and offshore in the Gulf of Mexico. Pemex Refinación (PR) converted crude oil into gasoline, diesel, and liquefied gas and distributed these products throughout Mexico. Pemex Gas y Petroquímica Básica (PGPB) processed, transported, distributed, and commercialized natural and liquid gas. In addition, PGPB produced and commercialized basic petrochemical products. Pemex Petroquímica produced and commercialized various petrochemical products such as ammonia, methanol, and polyethylene.[98]

Oil revenues, which accounted for a third of total government revenue, had financed social reforms for many years. With the government's collection of two-thirds of Pemex's earnings, management lacked sufficient capital to reinvest in the company. Pemex had also grown into a somewhat bloated and inefficient bureaucracy. Officials estimated that the modernization of Pemex's ailing facilities would require an enormous investment. Recognizing that the privatization of Pemex was politically infeasible, President Fox pledged to keep the state-owned company but planned to restructure and modernize its operations. "Pemex has to become a competitive and integral company whose purpose is to maximize oil revenue, contribute to the nation's development, and satisfy the needs of its clients," declared Fox.[99] In early March, Raul Munoz Leos, the newly appointed general director of Pemex and a former DuPont executive, announced a restructuring plan that would include US$3bn in cost cuts and major layoffs from its 120,000 workers.[100]

For decades, Pemex's management team had included bureaucrats and politicians. These directors had been accused of corruption and mismanagement. Eager to transform Pemex into a sleek multinational company, Fox had proposed a new board of directors. He planned to appoint four highly successful business leaders to the board: Carlos Slim Helu, chairman of Telefonos de Mexico and its wireless spin-off,

America Mobil; Lorenzo Zambrano, president of Cemex, a leading cement maker; Alfonso Romo Garza, chairman of Grupo Pulsar, which had interests in insurance and biotechnology; and Rogelio Rebolledo, a former Pepsi-Cola executive. Other board members would include Finance Minister Francisco Gil Diaz, Energy Minister Ernesto Martens Robolledo, and five representatives from the Pemex labor union. Many skeptics questioned whether conflicting interests among the board members would lead to mismanagement. "The game is just now starting. We are still unsure if we'll be able to work well with the union members," admitted Juan Antonio Barges Mestres, Subsecretary of the Energy Policy and Investment Ministry.[101]

Electricity Mexico's two state-owned electricity companies, the Federal Electricity Commission (CFE) and Light & Power (LFC), generated 94% of the country's electricity. Oil-fired plants generated the most electricity, although the government intended to convert many plants to natural gas by 2005. Thermal power plants accounted for 65% of energy production. Hydroelectric plants produced 25%, and Mexico's only nuclear power plant generated close to 4%.[102]

Government studies estimated that the demand for electricity in Mexico would increase by a third over the next six years. Meeting the demand could cost close to US$25bn.[103] Existing legislation allowed limited involvement of the private sector in electricity generation while the transmission and distribution of electricity remained completely closed. Fox recognized that further privatization of the electricity industry would be essential to keep the economy growing at 7%. He planned to submit an electricity sector reform bill that would allow for more private participation in the sector, however many PRI Congressmen were opposed to it. If the energy bill failed to pass, the government would need to spend up to US$5bn per year to meet electricity demand.[104] Already, the government spent US$3.5bn annually to subsidize electricity for domestic use.[105] Although it cost about 14 cents to produce one kilowatt-hour, the government charged residents only 6 cents[106] [see **Exhibit 5.19**]. "The subsidy comes out of the federal budget," explained Nicéforo Guerrero Reynoso, the Subsecretary of Energy Operations. "We want to get the price up to the real cost in 6 to 10 years."[107]

Natural gas Natural gas was the most liberalized energy sector. The 1995 Natural Gas Law allowed the private sector to build, operate, and own facilities for gas transportation, storage, and distribution, while exploration and production operations were reserved for the public sector.[108] Despite Mexico's abundant natural gas reserves, most had yet to be explored. The Energy Ministry planned to move more aggressively into exploration, but expected that it would take at least three years before this could be developed.

Demand for natural gas was expected to increase as new power plants were built to meet the growing need for electricity. With its rapid industrial growth and clean air provisions, northeastern Mexico would also increase the demand for natural gas in the future. "Pemex's resources will not be enough to exploit and explore natural gas reserves, and I need gas!" exclaimed Barges. "We will have to double production in the next six years in order to supply the growing demand."[109] Barges urged Congress to change the Constitution so that the private sector could get involved in dry gas.[110]

Petrochemicals Mexico's 61 petrochemical plants produced 13 different types of petrochemicals. In 1996, the government approved legislation that restricted the state's production rights to only 8 petrochemicals. The new law enabled the private sector to produce petrochemicals with 100% of the equity. Since private companies could hold only 49% of the equity in Pemex's plants, few investors showed interest in the privatization of public petrochemical complexes in 1999.[111]

Instead of privatizing petrochemical facilities, the Ministry planned to invite private companies to form joint ventures with Pemex. The two parties would combine their assets to establish a new company and each would receive stock. An IPO would soon follow, and Pemex would sell the majority of its shares, leaving the new company in private hands. BASF-Shell and Pemex, for example, were in the process of forming a new fertilizer company.

A Start

With non-oil tax revenues equal to only 11% of GDP, Mexico had the lowest tax take of the 29 members of the Organization of Economic Cooperation and Development (OECD).[112]

Loopholes in the complex tax system enabled many businesses and consumers to evade taxes, while goods in the informal economy avoided taxation altogether. Weak enforcement and a general distrust of the government also contributed to Mexico's 30% tax evasion rate. Disillusioned by years of political corruption, many Mexicans equated tax collection with robbery. "Mexicans see themselves as citizens with rights but no obligations," explained Dr. Luis Rubio, Director of the Center for Development. "They don't see themselves as having to pay taxes, and this mentality will have to change."[113]

Macroeconomic stability and microeconomic reform rested on the government's ability to increase revenues. In March 2001, Finance Minister Francisco Gil warned that the fiscal deficit was grossly underestimated. Although Congress had passed a budget with a targeted deficit of 0.65%, Gil explained that the deficit could grow to as much as 4% if all budgetary spending items were included.[114] Government spending in the oil and electricity sectors, known as *Pidiregas,* and liabilities incurred from bank bailouts had been omitted from the original account. Faced with a large fiscal deficit and a cooling economy, the government needed to boost revenues in order to finance its social programs.

Hoping to reduce Mexico's dependence on oil revenues, Fox planned to restructure the tax system. "We are going to address fiscal reform on the consumer side of taxes. We have to increase government income and take strong actions against tax evasion and begin to bring the informal market above ground," stated Fox.[115] In late March, he sent a controversial fiscal reform bill to Congress. The bill proposed a new 15% value added tax that would unify the four existing rates. Foodstuffs and medicines would no longer be tax exempt. The plan aimed to simplify the existing system by eliminating exemptions and inclusions. In addition to reducing the number of tax brackets, the personal income tax was to be cut from 40% to 20%. The corporate tax would be lowered from 35% to 32%, with discounts for companies that reinvested profits.[116] Fox hoped that the lower taxes would lead to a wider tax base and greater revenues.

Fox would have to lobby hard to win approval for his new tax plan. "The VAT tax on food and medicine will be a tough political obstacle for Fox," commented Ortega. "Right now, the Mexican people won't pay taxes because they feel the government has no legitimacy. Fox will have to convince them that the new VAT tax will help the government have more resources to spend on social services."[117] In Congress, Fox faced an even larger battle. The PRD criticized the VAT tax, arguing that it forced the poor to carry the burden of fiscal reform. "We don't agree with Fox's proposal to tax food and medicines," asserted a PRD Congressman. "We won't support it when the bill goes through Congress."[118]

The Next 100 Days

With his first 100 days behind him, Fox braced himself for the opening of the next congressional session. The coming months would reveal whether or not the divided Congress would come together to support his ambitious reform agenda. The Mexican people's hopes for poverty relief, education reform, and political transparency rested on the shoulders of the country's first non-PRI leader. Already Fox had been unable to deliver on his promise to resolve the Chiapas conflict in the first "15 minutes" of his presidency. Fox had met the Zapatistas' demands to free jailed rebels and shut down military bases in Chiapas. But Congress continued to oppose Fox's bill to increase indigenous rights, even after meeting with Zapatista rebels who had marched for 40 days from Chiapas to Mexico City.

Even though Mexico had successfully avoided an economic crisis during the transition, fiscal austerity remained a priority. Growing trade and fiscal deficits, scarce consumer credit, falling oil prices, and slow industrial growth threatened to destabilize the economy. In an attempt to reduce its dependence on the U.S. market, Mexico had signed trade agreements with Israel, Guatemala, Honduras, El Salvador, and the European Union. Still, export growth slumped in response to the U.S. economic slowdown. Despite the cooling global economy, the peso continued to strengthen. Noting that the peso, which was then floating, had appreciated 4% against the dollar in early 2001, Mexican businessmen warned that the peso was overvalued. While new cabinet members busily restructured their ministries and announced crusades against poverty, crime, and environmental degradation, critics insisted that the government lacked the funding to achieve Fox's lofty social goals. Still, Fox maintained that increased privatization and efficiency in the energy sector and the passage of the fiscal reform bill could augment the government's coffers. "I think these political and economic adjustments are absolutely necessary, but it will be complicated to make Congress realize this. It will be a bumpy road," concluded Dr. Rubio, "but I believe Fox will be successful in the long run."[119]

EXHIBIT 5.1　　　　　**MAP OF MEXICO**

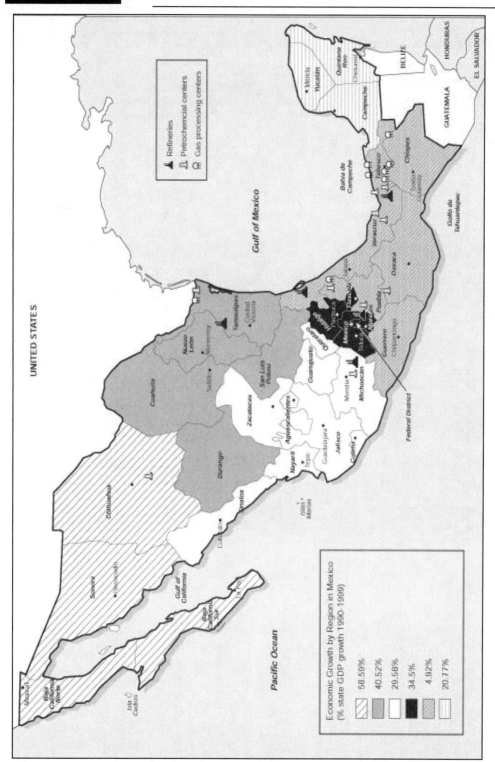

SOURCE: Source for Regional Economic Data: IPADE.

EXHIBIT 5.2   HISTORICAL SUMMARY, 1989–2000

	1989	1990	1991	1992	1993	1994	1995	1996	1997	1998	1999	2000
GDP and Components:												
Nominal GDP (mil MXP, current market prices)	549,000	739,000	949,000	1,125,000	1,256,000	1,420,000	1,837,000	2,504,000	3,179,000	3,791,000	4,623,000	5,322,900
Real GDP (mil MXP, constant 1993 prices)	1,085,815	1,140,848	1,189,017	1,232,162	1,256,196	1,312,201	1,230,608	1,293,859	1,381,525	1,448,135	1,501,008	1,609,100
Real GDP per capita (mil of MXP)	13,624	14,033	13,795	14,634	14,641	15,031	13,377	13,827	14,521	14,981	15,296	16,156
Real GDP growth rate (%)	4.2	5.1	4.2	3.6	2.0	4.5	-6.2	5.1	6.8	4.8	3.7	6.9
Private Consumption (% of GDP)	68.9	69.6	70.5	71.8	71.9	71.5	67.1	64.9	64.1	68.2	68.0	69.6
Government Consumption (% of GDP)	8.2	8.4	9.1	10.0	11.1	11.5	10.5	9.7	9.9	9.4	10.0	9.9
Gross Fixed Investment (% of GDP)	17.2	17.9	18.7	19.6	18.6	19.4	16.2	18.0	19.5	21.3	21.0	21.0
Exports (% of GDP)	18.9	18.5	16.3	15.2	15.3	16.8	30.4	32.5	30.3	31.3	30.8	33.8
Imports (% of GDP)	19.1	19.8	19.3	20.3	19.2	21.6	27.8	30.3	30.4	33.2	32.1	36.3
Employment, Wages, and Other:												
Employment (millions)	n/a	n/a	30.5	n/a	32.8	33.9	35.2	37.4	38.6	38.6	39.1	n/a
Labor Force Participation Rate (%)	n/a	60.9	60.8	60.8	60.8	60.8	61.0	n/a	n/a	64.4	n/a	n/a
Open Unemployment Rate (%)	3.0	2.8	2.6	2.8	3.4	3.7	6.3	5.5	3.8	3.2	2.5	2.2
Recorded Unemployment Rate[a] (%)	21.0	20.5	20.8	21.7	23.2	22.1	25.3	25.3	23.3	21.8	19.1	18.5
Average Nominal Wages (% change)	n/a	n/a	25.0	20.9	11.3	1.8	13.8	20.0	18.0	19.3	17.0	13.5
Average Real Wages (% change)	n/a	n/a	1.9	4.7	1.4	-4.8	-15.7	-10.7	-2.2	2.9	0.4	3.7
Unit Labor Costs (% change)	n/a	n/a	15.2	17.2	11.1	1.2	-41.5	-7.4	6.4	1.4	9.6	12.4
Gross National Savings (% GDP)	20.3	20.3	18.6	16.6	15.2	14.7	19.3	22.6	24.2	20.2	20.3	20.0
Population (millions)	n/a	81.2	n/a	n/a	n/a	n/a	91.2	n/a	94.7	96.3	98.1	n/a
Population Growth Rate (% change)	n/a	2.0	n/a	n/a	n/a	n/a	1.8	n/a	1.7	1.6	1.8	n/a
Financial Indicators:												
U.S. CPI (% change)	4.8	5.4	4.2	3.0	3.0	2.6	2.8	2.9	2.3	1.5	2.2	3.4
Exchange Rate (MXP/dollar)	2.64	2.95	3.07	3.12	3.11	5.33	7.64	7.85	8.08	9.87	9.51	9.46
Stock of M1 (mil of MXP)	29,087	47,439	106,227	122,220	143,902	145,429	150,572	206,180	267,113	308,135	395,475	505,277
M1 growth rate (%)	37.3	63.1	123.9	15.1	17.7	1.1	3.5	36.9	29.6	15.4	28.3	27.8
CPI (% change)	20	26.7	22.7	15.5	9.8	7.0	35.0	34.4	20.6	15.9	16.6	9.5
28-day Cetes (nominal interest rate)	n/a	34.8	19.3	15.6	15.0	14.1	48.4	31.4	19.8	24.8	21.4	15.3

SOURCE: Banco de México; Inter-American Development Bank.

MXP = new Mexican pesos; *Italics represent estimates*; n/a = not available.

[a]Recorded official unemployment and partial employment as a percentage of total labor force.

EXHIBIT 5.3	BALANCE OF PAYMENTS, 1900–2000 (MILLIONS OF U.S. DOLLARS)										
	1990	1991	1992	1993	1994	1995	1996	1997	1998	1999	2000
Current account balance	**-7,451**	**-14,888**	**-24,442**	**-23,400**	**-29,663**	**-1,575**	**-2,328**	**-7,454**	**-15,724**	**-14,253**	**-16,941**
Trade balance	-881	-7,279	-15,934	-13,481	-18,464	7,089	6,531	623	-7,915	-5,668	-7,795
Exports of goods	40,711	42,687	46,196	51,885	60,882	79,542	96,000	110,431	117,459	136,391	166,469
Imports of goods	-41,592	-49,966	-62,130	-65,366	-79,346	-72,453	-89,469	-109,808	-125,374	-142,059	-174,264
Net services	-2,229	-2,090	-2,684	-2,529	-2,722	65	83	-1,216	-1,002	-2,562	-2,846
Services—credit	8,094	8,869	9,275	9,517	10,321	9,780	10,899	11,400	12,065	11,733	12,717
Services—debit	-10,323	-10,959	-11,959	-12,046	-13,043	-9,715	-10,816	-12,616	-13,067	-14,295	-15,563
Net income	-8,316	-8,265	-9,209	-11,030	-12,259	-12,689	-13,472	-12,108	-12,821	-12,337	-12,844
Income—credit	3,273	3,523	2,789	2,694	3,347	3,713	4,033	4,430	4,911	4,890	6,510
Income—debit	-11,589	-11,788	-11,998	-13,724	-15,606	-16,402	-17,505	-16,538	-17,732	-17,227	-19,354
Net transfers	3,975	2,746	3,385	3,640	3,782	3,960	4,530	5,247	6,014	6,314	6,544
Transfers—credit	3,990	2,765	3,404	3,656	3,822	3,995	4,560	5,272	6,042	6,341	6,570
Transfers—debit	-15	-19	-19	-16	-40	-35	-30	-25	-28	-27	-26
Capital account balance	**8,327**	**24,508**	**26,419**	**32,483**	**14,584**	**15,404**	**4,070**	**15,762**	**17,464**	**14,141**	**17,920**
Liabilities	17,027	25,507	20,867	36,085	20,255	22,762	10,412	9,047	17,033	16,781	10,377
Indebtedness	12,369	11,007	3,544	13,573	7,423	26,577	-2,483	-7,583	6,174	1,313	n/a
Foreign direct investment	2,663	4,762	4,393	4,389	10,973	9,526	9,186	12,830	11,311	11,568	13,162
Portfolio investment	1,995	6,332	4,783	10,717	4,084	519	2,801	3,215	-666	3,769	-2,225
Money market	0	3,406	8,147	7,406	-2,225	-13,860	908	585	214	131	n/a
Assets	-8,700	-999	5,552	-3,602	-5,671	-7,358	-6,342	6,715	431	-2,640	7,544
In foreign banks	761	921	2,186	-1,280	-3,714	-3,164	-6,055	4,860	155	-1,672	n/a
Credits granted abroad	-530	19	63	-281	-41	-276	-625	-114	330	425	n/a
External debt guarantees	-7,354	-604	1,165	-564	-615	-662	544	-708	-769	-836	n/a
Other	-1,577	-1,335	2,138	-1,477	-1,301	-3,256	-206	2,677	715	-557	n/a
Errors & Omissions	**2,520**	**-2,167**	**-961**	**-3,142**	**-314**	**-4,238**	**35**	**2,197**	**400**	**463**	**2,595**
Net Change in International Reserves[a]	**-3,396**	**-7,453**	**-1,016**	**-5,941**	**15,393**	**-9,591**	**-1,777**	**-10,505**	**-2,140**	**-351**	**-3,574**

SOURCE: *Economist Intelligence Unit*; Banco de México; International Monetary Fund.

[a](+) indicates a decrease in reserves; (-) indicates an increase in reserves.

EXHIBIT 5.4A **FEDERAL GOVERNMENT FINANCES, 1995–2000 (BILLIONS OF MXP)**

	1995	1996	1997	1998	1999	2000[a]
Revenue	280.1	392.6	503.5	545.3	674.4	866.0
Taxes	170.3	226.0	312.1	404.3	521.7	578.8
Income	73.7	97.2	135.1	169.5	216.1	254.1
VAT	51.8	72.1	97.7	119.9	151.2	190.7
Excise taxes	24.7	29.7	45.4	76.6	106.7	82.0
Foreign trade	11.2	14.9	18.1	21.5	27.3	33.3
Others	8.9	12.1	15.8	16.8	20.4	18.7
Nontax revenue	109.8	166.6	191.4	141.0	152.7	287.2
Oil	72.3	112.8	122.7	88.8	*90.2*	n/a
Expenditures	293.1	403.1	543.7	610.3	752.1	945.9
Current expenditure	259.1	355.2	481.7	545.3	*677.7*	n/a
Wages, purchases and services	47.9	64.3	69.0	74.9	*82.7*	n/a
Revenue sharing and transfers	138.1	192.0	292.7	368.4	*446.5*	n/a
Interest payments	70.3	94.3	114.2	95.7	*144.8*	177.6
Capital expenditure	34.0	47.9	62.0	65.0	*74.4*	n/a
Government Deficit	-13.0	-10.5	-40.2	-65.0	-77.7	-79.9
Government Deficit (% of GDP)	0.7	0.4	1.3	1.7	1.7	1.0

SOURCE: The Economist Intelligence Unit; Secretariat of Finance & Public Credit.

[a]Estimates.

EXHIBIT 5.4B **TOTAL NET PUBLIC DEBT (AS % OF GDP)**

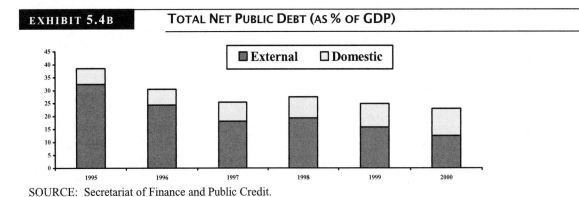

SOURCE: Secretariat of Finance and Public Credit.

EXHIBIT 5.4C **INSTITUTE FOR THE PROTECTION OF BANK SAVINGS OBLIGATIONS PAYMENTS FOR 2000 (MILLIONS OF MXP)**

I.	**Balance of IPAB's Gross Liabilities**	**844,160**
II.	**Balance for interest computing**[a]	**725,260**
	a) real interest rate %	7.0
	b) IPAB spread %	1.2
III.	**IPAB interest rate (a+b) %**	**8.2**
IV.	**Real interest payments (II*III)**	**59,471**
V.	**IPAB revenues**	**59,500**
	c) Budgetary transferences	35,000
	d) Asset sales	20,000
	e) Bank quotas	4,500

SOURCE: Institute for the Protection of Bank Savings (IPAB).

[a]The excluded obligations are: IPAB's obligations with Nafin and Banxico (76,390 mil MXP), which, according with the Bank Savings Law, will be covered by those institutions; loss-sharing obligations of banks (23,280 mil MXP); and the liabilities associated to the debtors support programs (19,230 mil MXP), which are allocated in a separate item of the budget.

EXHIBIT 5.5	LEGISLATIVE ELECTION RESULTS, JULY 2, 2000

	Deputies			Senators			
	FPP[a]	PR[b]	Total	FPP	FM[c]	PR	Total
Partido Revolucionario Institucional (PRI)	131	78	209	32	15	13	60
Alianza por el Cambio	141	82	223	28	10	13	51
Partido Acción Nacional (PAN)	136	72	208	N/A	N/A	N/A	46
Partido Verde Ecologista de Mexico (PVEM)	5	10	15	N/A	N/A	N/A	5
Alianza por Mexico	28	40	68	4	7	6	17
Partido de la Revolucion Democrática (PRD)	26	27	53	N/A	N/A	N/A	15
Partido del Trabajo (PT)	2	6	8	N/A	N/A	N/A	1
Convergencia por la Democracia (CD)	0	3	3	N/A	N/A	N/A	1
Partido de la Sociedad Nacionalista (PSN)	0	3	2	0	0	0	0
Partido Alianza Social (PAS)	0	2	2	0	0	0	0
Total	**300**	**200**	**500**	**64**	**32**	**32**	**128**

SOURCE: *The Economist*, EIU Country Report—July 2000 (London, U.K.).

[a]First-past-the-post. [b]Proportional representation. [c]First minority.

EXHIBIT 5.6	SOCIAL INDICATORS, 1998

Country	Human Development Rank[a]	Infant Mortality per 1,000 Live Births	Main Telephone Lines per 1,000 People[b]	Televisions per 1,000 People[b]
United States	3	7	661	847
Argentina	35	19	203	289
Mexico	**55**	**28**	**104**	**261**
Brazil	74	36	121	316

SOURCE: *The Economist*.

[a]Out of 174; 1 = high levels of development, 174 = low levels of development. [b]1996–98.

EXHIBIT 5.7	INCOME DISTRIBUTION (%)

					Deciles						
	1	2	3	4	5	6	7	8	9	10	Gini coefficient
Argentina	1.5	2.8	3.8	4.8	5.4	7.3	9.0	11.8	17.0	35.9	0.48
Bolivia	1.5	2.6	3.4	4.2	5.2	6.3	7.9	10.5	15.6	42.1	0.53
Brazil	0.8	1.7	2.5	3.4	4.5	5.7	7.6	10.5	16.4	47.0	0.59
Chile	1.3	2.2	3.0	3.8	4.7	5.9	7.5	10.1	15.3	45.8	0.56
Costa Rica	1.4	2.9	4.0	5.2	6.3	7.7	9.6	12.1	16.4	34.2	0.46
Ecuador	0.6	1.7	2.8	3.9	5.2	6.5	8.3	10.9	15.6	44.0	0.57
El Salvador	1.0	2.4	3.4	4.5	5.7	7.1	8.9	11.4	16.2	39.4	0.51
Mexico	**1.1**	**2.2**	**3.0**	**3.9**	**5.0**	**6.2**	**7.9**	**10.5**	**15.6**	**44.4**	**0.55**
Panama	0.6	1.7	2.7	3.8	5.0	6.5	8.5	11.6	16.9	42.7	0.56
Paraguay	0.7	1.6	2.4	3.5	4.6	6.1	8.0	10.7	15.8	46.5	0.59
Peru	1.5	2.9	3.9	5.1	6.4	7.7	9.4	11.8	15.9	35.4	0.46
Uruguay	1.8	3.2	4.3	5.4	6.6	8.0	9.7	12.2	16.4	32.3	0.43
Venezuela	1.6	2.9	3.9	4.9	6.1	7.5	9.3	11.8	16.2	35.8	0.47

SOURCE: Inter-American Development Bank.

Note: 1 = poorest decile, 10 = richest decile.

| EXHIBIT 5.8A | SCHOOL ATTENDANCE BY INCOME LEVEL (IN PERCENT) |

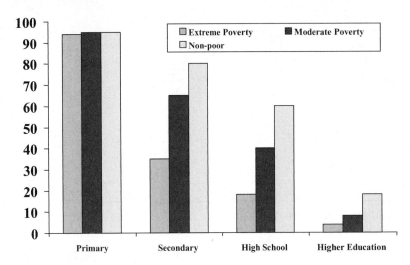

SOURCE: Miguel Székely.

| EXHIBIT 5.8B | WAGE INCREASE PER ADDITIONAL YEAR OF SCHOOLING AT DIFFERENT SCHOOLING LEVELS |

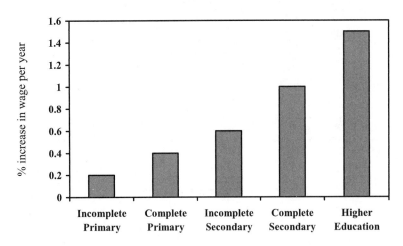

SOURCE: Miguel Székely.

EXHIBIT 5.9A   **URBAN-RURAL INCOME GAP**

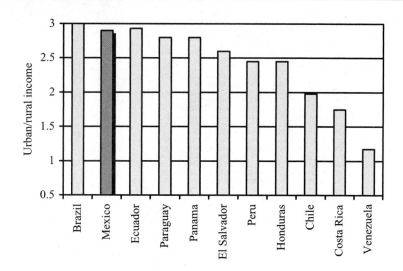

SOURCE: Inter-American Development Bank.

EXHIBIT 5.9B   **LABOR INCOME GAP BETWEEN RURAL AND URBAN AREAS**

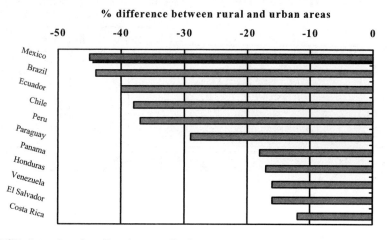

SOURCE: Inter-American Development Bank.

| EXHIBIT 5.10 | REGIONAL DIFFERENCES IN SCHOOLING |

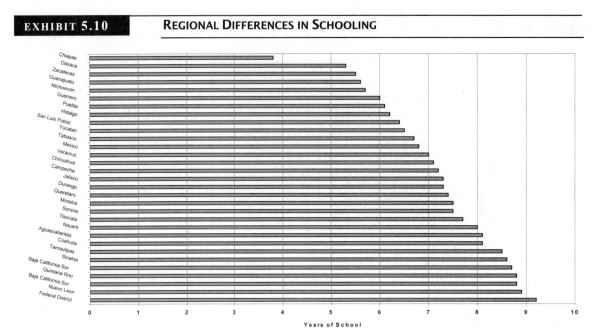

SOURCE: Miguel Székely.

| EXHIBIT 5.11 | FEMALE LABOR PARTICIPATION RATE IN THE 1980s AND 1990s |

SOURCE: Inter-American Development Bank.

*Countries with urban data only.

| EXHIBIT 5.12 | HOURLY COMPENSATION COST FOR PRODUCTION WORKERS IN MANUFACTURING (US$) |

	1975	1980	1985	1990	1995	1996	1997	1998	1999
United States	6.36	9.87	13.01	14.91	17.19	17.70	18.27	18.66	19.20
Canada	5.96	8.67	10.95	15.95	16.10	16.64	16.47	15.60	15.60
Mexico	1.47	2.21	1.59	1.58	1.51	1.54	1.78	1.84	2.12

SOURCE: U.S. Department of Labor, Bureau of Labor Statistics, September 2000.

EXHIBIT 5.13A	HOUSEHOLD SAVINGS RATE

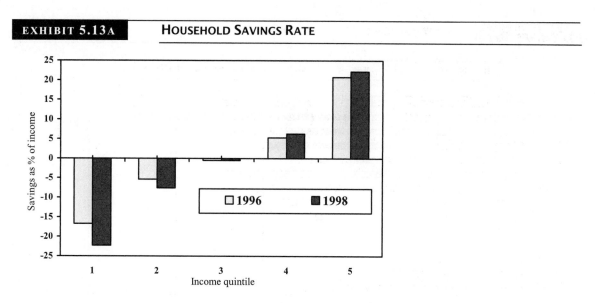

SOURCE: Miguel Székely.

EXHIBIT 5.13B	HOUSEHOLD DISTRIBUTION WITH ACCESS TO FORMAL CREDIT

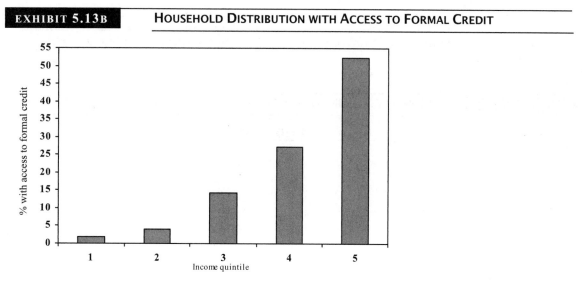

SOURCE: Miguel Székely.

| EXHIBIT 5.14 | EDUCATIONAL ATTAINMENT GAP[A] |

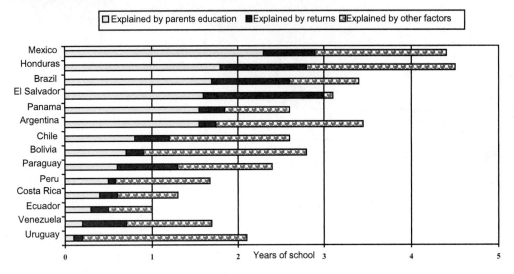

SOURCE: Inter-American Development Bank

[a]The gap shows how much of the difference in educational attainment of high- and low-income children is due to the fact that their parents have different educational levels. Inter-American Development Bank estimated that, on average, the variations in the parent's level of education explain about 30% of the predicted difference in their children's educational attainment.

| EXHIBIT 5.15 | MONTHLY AMOUNT OF PROGRESA MONETARY SUPPORT PER CHILD (MXP) |

Type of Benefit	1998 (1)	1998 (2)	1999 (1)	1999 (2)
Nutrition Support	95	100	115	125
Primary School	65	70	75	80
3	65	70	75	80
4	95	100	115	125
5	95	100	115	125
6	130	135	150	165
Secondary School				
First year				
Boys	190	200	220	240
Girls	200	210	235	250
Second year				
Boys	200	210	235	250
Girls	220	235	260	280
Third year				
Boys	210	220	245	265
Girls	240	255	285	305
Maximum support[a]	585	625	695	750

SOURCE: SEDESOL.   [a]Maximum support for each family.

Note: 1= January-June, 2= July-December. Progresa monetary supports are given directly to the female of the beneficiary families. The supports are given in cash every two months. The monetary supports are indexed to the inflation rate and adjusted every six months to retain their purchasing power.

EXHIBIT 5.16	DRUG STATISTICS	

	2000	1995
Seizures		
Opium (mt)[a]	0.27	0.22
Heroin (mt)[a]	0.268	0.203
Cocaine (mt)[a]	18.3	22.2
Cannabis (mt)[a]	1,619	780
Methamphetamine (mt)[a]	0.555	0.496
Arrests		
Nationals	10,771	9,728
Foreigners	233	173
Total arrests	11,004	9,901

SOURCE: U.S. Department of State.   [a]mt = metric ton.

EXHIBIT 5.17	WATER SUPPLY AND DEMAND IN THE VALLEY OF MEXICO

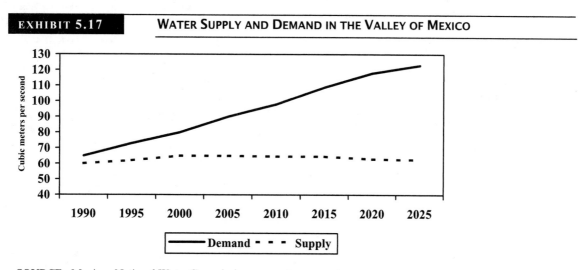

SOURCE: Mexican National Water Commission.

EXHIBIT 5.18	OIL AND GAS PRODUCTION AND EXPORTS

	1995	1996	1997	1998	1999	2000
Crude oil production (m barrels)	955.2	1,043.2	1,103.0	1,120.6	1,086.2	1,095.0
Daily average (m barrels)	2.6	2.9	3.0	3.1	3.0	3.0
Oil reserves (bn barrels)	62.1	60.9	60.2	58.7	58.2	45.7
Gas production (m cu ft/day)	3,759.0	4,195.0	4,467.0	4,791.0	4,791.0	4,679.1
Gas reserves (bn barrels equivalent)	13,262.0	12,428.0	12,338.0	12,093.0	11,994.0	10,700.0
Oil exports ($US m)	8,422.6	11,653.7	11,323.2	7,134.3	9,920.4	16,380.0
Crude oil	7,419.6	10,705.3	10,333.8	6,367.9	8,851.0	n/a
Other	1,003.0	948.4	989.4	766.4	1,069.4	n/a

SOURCE: The Economist Intelligence Unit.

EXHIBIT 5.19	ELECTRICITY PRICES ($US)		
	Residential	**Industrial**	**Agriculture**
Mexico			
Subsidized price/kilowatt-hour	0.06	0.04	0.04
Fully-loaded cost/kilowatt-hour	0.14	0.14	0.11
United States			
Price/kilowatt-hour	0.08	0.04	n/a

SOURCE: Energy Ministry.

EXHIBIT 5.20	MAIN TRADING PARTNERS (% OF TOTAL)									
	1995		1996		1997		1998		1999[a]	
	Exports[b]	Imports[c]	Exports	Imports	Exports	Imports	Exports	Imports	Exports	Imports
United States	83.6	74.5	84.0	75.6	85.6	74.8	87.9	74.5	88.4	74.3
European Union	4.3	8.0	3.7	8.0	3.6	8.4	3.3	7.9	3.9	9.0
Latin America & Caribbean	6.1	2.7	6.5	2.0	6.0	2.2	5.0	2.1	3.9	2.3
Canada	2.5	1.5	2.3	1.7	2.0	1.7	1.3	1.6	1.7	1.9
Japan	1.2	4.7	1.4	4.4	1.0	3.9	0.7	2.8	0.6	3.3

SOURCE: The Economist Intelligence Unit.

[a]Estimate.

[b]Exports from Mexico.

[c]Imports to Mexico.

EXHIBIT 5.21	DIRECTION AND COMPOSITION OF TRADE, 1998 ($USM)			
	U.S.	Canada	Germany	Total
EXPORTS				
Animals for food	212	0	0	212
Meat and fish and preparations	707	0	0	858
Fruit, vegetables, and preparations	2,863	30	3	3,211
Coffee, cocoa, tea, spices, and manufactures	682	24	2	840
Crude petroleum	5,036	113	0	6,399
Chemicals	3,277	211	51	5,598
Textile fibers, yarn, cloth and manufactures	1,775	75	9	2,381
Nonmetallic mineral manufactures	2,048	59	22	2,503
Metals and manufactures	5,153	93	64	6,462
Iron and steel and manufactures	3,008	82	48	4,014
Machinery	12,703	434	267	15,334
Electrical and electronic equipment	30,585	295	89	31,830
Road vehicles	17,611	369	392	19,486
Other transport	1,288	4	0	1,313
Furniture, lighting, prefab buildings	2,221	11	21	2,361
Clothing and footwear	6,623	37	8	6,897
Scientific instruments	3,340	31	65	3,718
Total, including others	101,927	1,716	1,112	117,325
IMPORTS				
Food	4,172	54	3	5,279
Meat and fish and preparations	1,052	0	1	1,180
Cereals and preparations	1,555	24	0	1,820
Oilseeds	977	14	1	1,362
Mineral fuels and lubricants	2,062	10	8	2,678
Chemicals	11,676	529	1,164	15,457
Paper etc and manufactures	2,492	26	11	2,771
Textile fibers, yarn, cloth and manufactures	3,368	67	27	4,203
Metals and manufactures	7,272	449	410	11,810
Iron and steel and manufactures	4,591	300	339	6,867
Nonferrous metals and manufactures	2,681	49	24	3,370
Machinery	12,417	1,480	1,127	19,002
Electrical and electronic equipment	24,068	516	1,190	29,914
Road vehicles	7,929	836	441	10,067
Other transport	898	4	2	1,006
Clothing	3,333	7	2	3,649
Scientific instruments	2,727	190	284	3,958
Total, including others	93,237	4,558	4,553	125,193

SOURCE: The Economist Intelligence Unit.

ENDNOTES

1 IPADE arranged interviews with government officials, academics, and business leaders and provided economic information that was essential to the development of this case.

2 Interview with Dr. Luis Rubio F., Director General, Centro de Investigacion para el Desarrollo, A.C.

3 "Fox Breaks Presidential Mold to Woo Support." *The News.* Mexico City, March 12, 2001.

4 *EIU Country Profile-Mexico*, The Economist Intelligence Unit, 2000.

5 "After the Revolution: A Survey of Mexico." *The Economist,* October 28, 2000.

6 Interview with Alberto Ortega Venzor, Coordinator, Presidential Office of Public Policy.

7 This section draws heavily on the case "Mexico in Debt" by Research Associate Eilene Zimmerman, HBS case no. 9-797-110.

8 Jonathan Heath, *Mexico and the Sexenio Curse,* Washington, D.C.: CSIS Press, 1999.

9 World Bank, *World Bank Report*, 1997.

10 Jonathan Heath. *Mexico and the Sexenio Curse,* Washington, D.C.: CSIS Press, 1999, pg. 22.

11 Donald E. Schulz, *Mexico in Crisis,* Strategic Studies Institute at the U.S. Army War College, 1995.

12 Ibid.

13 This portion of the case draws heavily on the "Mexico in Debt Supplement," HBS Case #9-700-051.

14 Jonathan Heath, *Mexico and the Sexenio Curse,* Washington, D.C.: CSIS Press, 1999, pg. 21.

15 Interview with Eduardo Sojo Garza-Aldape, Chief of the Presidential Office, Presidential Office of Public Policy.

16 Peter Fritsch, "Fox Sets Conservative Targets for Mexico's Economic Growth." *The Wall Street Journal,* October 11, 2000.

17 "Rich Is Rich and Poor Is Poor" *The Economist,* October 28, 2000.

18 EFE News Service, "Mexico-Poverty Zedillo Administration Acknowledges Failure to Curb Poverty." September 22, 2000.

19 SEDESOL

20 Dow Jones International News, "Mexico Poverty Study Shows Significant Contrasts." January 31, 2001.

21 "Rich Is Rich and Poor Is Poor" *The Economist,* October 28, 2000.

22 Dow Jones International News, "Mexico Poverty Study Shows Significant Contrasts." January 31, 2001.

23 Interview with Dr. Luis Rubio F., Director General, Centro de Investigacion para el Desarrollo, A.C.

24 Dr. Miguel Székely's presentation, "A New Social Development Strategy for Latin America: The Case of Mexico."

25 Inter-American Development Bank, *Facing Up to Inequality in Latin America, 1998–1999 Report.*

26 Ibid.,pg.67.

27 EFE News Service, "Mexico-Women, PRI-Women Accuse Fox Administration of Misogyny."

28 Inter-American Development Bank, *Facing Up to Inequality in Latin America, 1998–1999 Report.*

29 Ibid., pg. 6.

30 Guillermo Trejo and Claudio Jones, "Political Dilemmas of Welfare Reform: Poverty and Inequality in Mexico," *Mexico Under Zedillo*, edited by Susan Kaufman Purcell and Luis Rubio. London: Lynne Rienner Publishers, 1998.

31 Inter-American Development Bank, *Facing Up to Inequality in Latin America, 1998–1999 Report,* pgs. 115–116.

32 Guillermo Trejo and Claudio Jones, "Political Dilemmas of Welfare Reform: Poverty and Inequality in Mexico," *Mexico Under Zedillo*, edited by Susan Kaufman Purcell and Luis Rubio. London: Lynne Rienner Publishers, 1998.

33 Dr. Miguel Székely's presentation , "A New Social Development Strategy for Latin America: The Case of Mexico."

34 Interview with Dr. Luis Rubio F., Director General, Centro de Investigacion para el Desarrollo, A.C.

35 Interview with Gonzolo Robles, SEDESOL

36 "An Improvement but Not By Much," *Financial Times Mexico Survey.* December 14, 2000.

37 Guillermo Trejo and Claudio Jones, "Political Dilemmas of Welfare Reform: Poverty and Inequality in Mexico," *Mexico Under Zedillo*, edited

by Susan Kaufman Purcell and Luis Rubio. London: Lynne Rienner Publishers, 1998.

38 Ibid.

39 Interview with Gonozolo Robles, SEDESOL

40 *EIU Country Profile-Mexico,* The Economist Intelligence Unit, 2000.

41 Dudley Althaus, "Mexico's Education System Needs Rebuilding, Revenue, and Resuscitation." *Houston Chronicle.* November 26, 2000.

42 *EIU Country Profile-Mexico,* The Economist Intelligence Unit, 2000.

43 Interview with Agustin Carmona, second grade teacher.

44 Ibid.

45 Ibid.

46 Ginger Thompson, "Chasing Mexico's Dream into Squalor," *New York Times,* February 11, 2001.

47 "The Fox Experiment Begins," *The Economist,* December 2, 2000.

48 Dudley Althaus, "Mexico's Education System Needs Rebuilding, Revenue, and Resuscitation," *Houston Chronicle,* November 26, 2000.

49 Interview with Alberto Ortega Venzor, Coordinator, Presidential Office of Public Policy.

50 *Country Commerce Report: Mexico.* The Economist Intelligence Unit, September 2000.

51 "Minimum Wage Raise" *Business Mexico.* February, 2001.

52 "Survey Mexico." *The Economist,* October 28, 2000.

53 Interview with Carlos Abascal Carranza, Secretary of Labor.

54 Ibid.

55 *Country Commerce Report: Mexico.* The Economist Intelligence Unit, September 2000.

56 "Survey Mexico." *The Economist,* October 28, 2000.

57 Interview with Carlos Abascal Carranza, Secretary of Labor.

58 *Country Commerce Report: Mexico.* The Economist Intelligence Unit, September 2000.

59 Interview with Carlos Abascal Carranza, Secretary of Labor.

60 Pamela S. Falk, "Easing Up at the Border." *The New York Times.* February 15, 2001.

61 Mary Jordan, "Immigration on Mexican Agenda." *Washington Post,* February 16, 2001.

62 Transcript of Washington Post Online's discussion with Mexican President Vicente Fox, February 15, 2001.

63 Ginger Thompson, "U.S. and Mexico to Open Talks on Freer Migration for Workers." *The New York Times,* February 16, 2001.

64 Ibid.

65 Elisabeth Malkin, "Sounding the Alarm in Mexico." *BusinessWeek.* June 26, 2000.

66 Tim Gaynor, "Facing Endemic Graft, Fox's Crusade May Fail." *The News.* March 1, 2001.

67 Transcript of Washington Post Online's discussion with Mexican President Vicente Fox, February 15, 2001.

68 Interview with Carlos Abascal Carranza, Secretary of Labor.

69 Kevin Sullivan, "Mexicans Question Escape of Drug Lord." *Washington Post.* January 25, 2001.

70 Tim Weiner, "Mexico Agrees to Extradite Drug Suspect to California." *The New York Times.* January 17, 2001; U.S. Department of State, Narcotics Control Report 2000.

71 "Narcotics Control Report." U.S. Department of State, 2000.

72 Julie Weise, "Drug Certification at the Crux." *The News.* March 2, 2001.

73 Transcript of Washington Post Online's discussion with Mexican President Vicente Fox, February 15, 2001.

74 Diego Cevallos, "Environment-Mexico: The High Cost of Environmental Destruction." *Inter Press Service. March 8, 2001.*

75 Julie Watson, "In Mexico, the Very Land Is Dying." *The Seattle Times.* July 30, 2000.

76 Interview with Victor Lichtinger, Environment Minister, SEMARNAT.

77 Interview with Hernando Guerrero, Director of Mexico Liaison Office, Commission for Environmental Cooperation.

78 Interview with Rodolfo Lacy Tomayo, Coordinador de Asesores del C. Secretario, SEMARNAT.

79 Interview with Victor Lichtinger, Environment Minister, SEMARNAT.

80 Ibid.

81 Jo Tuckman, "Mexico's New Environment Secretary Visits Jailed Environmentalists." *Associated Press.* March 2, 2001.

82   Interview with Victor Lichtinger, Environment Minister, SEMARNAT.

83   Ibid.

84   Tim Weiner, "Mexico Grows Parched, with Pollution and Politics." *The New York Times*. April 14, 2001.

85   Interview with Ing. Rodolfo Lacy Tomayo, Coordinador de Asesores del C. Secretario, SEMARNAT.

86   Interview with Victor Lichtinger, Environment Minister, SEMARNAT.

87   Interview with Rodolfo Lacy Tomayo, Coordinador de Asesores del C. Secretario, SEMARNAT.

88   Michael J. Mazarr, *Mexico 2005*. Washington, D.C.: Center for Strategic and International Studies, 1999.

89   Interview with Victor Lichtinger, Environment Minister, SEMARNAT.

90   *Pemex Safety, Health, and Environment Report*, 1999.

91   Interview with Rafael Fernandez de la Garza, Director, SIASPA.

92   Interview with Victor Lichtinger, Environment Minister, SEMARNAT.

93   Ibid.

94   Diego Cevallos. "Environment-Mexico: The High Cost of Environmental Destruction." *Inter Press Service*. March 8, 2001.

95   Interview with Victor Lichtinger, Environment Minister, SEMARNAT.

96   Interview with Hernando Guerrero, Director of Mexico Liaison Office, Commission for Environmental Cooperation.

97   "Mexico." Energy Information Administration, October 2000.

98   *Pemex Safety, Health, and Environment Report*, 1999

99   Graham Gori, "New Directors for Mexico Oil Monopoly." *The New York Times*. February 15,2001.

100 Chris Kraul, "Mexico Unveils Restructuring Plan" *Los Angeles Times*. March 23, 2001.

101 Interview with Juan Antonio Barges Mestres, Subsecretary of the Energy Ministry.

102 "An Energy Overview of Mexico." United States Department of Energy. November 2000.

103 "Survey Mexico." *The Economist*. October 28, 2000.

104 Mayela Cordoba, "Mexico: CFE Director on Need for Electricity Reforms." *World News Connection*. March 27, 2001.

105 Tim Weiner, "Roadblocks Right and Left for Mexican President." *The New York Times*. January 22, 2001.

106 Interview with Niceforo Guerrero Reynoso, Subsecretary of Energy Operations.

107 Ibid.

108 "An Energy Overview of Mexico." United States Department of Energy. November 2000.

109 Interview with Juan Antonio Barges Mestres, Subsecretario de Politica y Desarrollo de Energeticos, Secretaria de Energia

110 Interview with Juan Antonio Barges Mestres, Subsecretario de Politica y Desarrollo de Energeticos, Secretaria de Energia

111 *Mexico: Country Profile*, 2000, The Economist Intelligence Union.

112 "A System That Needs Some Simplifying." *Financial Times Survey on Mexico*. December 14, 2000.

113 Interview with Dr. Luis Rubio F., Director General, Centro de Investigacion para el Desarrollo, A.C.

114 Rodrigo Martinez, "Deficit May Soar, but Analysts Unfazed." *The News*. March 3. 2001.

115 Peter Fritsch, "Tax Trauma Awaits Mexico's New Leader." *The Wall Street Journal*. October 23, 2000.

116 Traci Carl, "Fox's Mexico Tax Plan Draws Critics." *The Associated Press*. March 15, 2001.

117 Interview with Alberto Ortega Venzor, Coordinador, Oficina de la Presidencia para Las Politicas Publicas.

118 Interview with Dip. Gregorio Urías Germán, Vicecoordinador General Grupo Parlamentario P.R.D.

119 Interview with Dr. Luis Rubio F., Director General, Centro de Investigacion para el Desarrollo, A.C.

Regional Free Trade amidst Instability

This case examines Brazil's development strategy since World War II, that of import substitution, and its shift after debt crisis to a model of monetary control and export-led growth. By 2001, Brazil seems to be emerging from decades of economic stagnation and uncertainty. Yet despite optimistic forecasts, its economic situation is fragile and the external sector remains a concern. Its leaders, however, are grappling with a choice between regional integration and globalization. They must find a way to deal wit the rules of the World Trade Organization that Brazil and other developing countries feel favor the interests of industrialized nations, to their detriment. Alternatively, Brazil's leaders must decide whether or not the country's future rests with closer links with Mercosur—the regional trade agreement between Brazil, Argentina, Uruguay, and Paraguay.

In addition to the classic trade diversion-creation argument by Jacob Viner, four alternative views have emerged on regionalism. Some economists argue that regionalism accelerates the multilateral political process. Others argue that regionalism offers "quicker and more certain" trade results. Another view is that multilateralism (WTO) is "dead," leaving regionalism as the best alternative. A final view is that regionalism is the reaction of developing countries to the formation of other trade blocks (e.g., European Union and NAFTA).

CASE STUDY   BRAZIL: EMBRACING GLOBALIZATION?

LAURA ALFARO

Introduction

For more than a century, Brazil was referred to as the country of the future. Analysts had always predicted that this sleeping giant, blessed with natural resources and a large internal market, would become a world power. But the prediction never materialized. The road to development for Brazil had not been easy. The Great Depression of the 1930s was disastrous for an economy that was extremely dependent on coffee exports. Later, for almost 40 years, Brazil followed an import substitution strategy characterized by massive government investment, targeting of key industries, and protection against competition with high tariff walls. For decades, the strategy appeared to be successful: Brazil grew by 7% per year between 1950 and 1980 and created a large and diversified industrial sector. But during the "lost decade" of the 1980s disaster struck again. Inflation soared, investment collapsed, foreign investors ran for cover, and growth stagnated as the country was haunted by the largest external debt in the developing world [see **Exhibits 6.2** to **6.7**].

In 1994, President Fernando Henrique Cardoso took office with a new development strategy: to privatize state-owned firms, deregulate the economy, lower trade barriers, and become competitive in the world economy—in short, to embrace globalization. In many ways, his strategy was a success. The economy grew and inflation rates hit record lows. Doubts re-emerged, however, in 1998 when Brazil was threatened by the Asian financial crisis. The economy slowed and investors attacked the real by selling their Brazilian currency. In 1999, after Brazil devalued its currency, the economy was stagnant. But by the year 2000, the economy seemed to have recovered from the currency crisis, and the country was expected to grow once again.

Despite optimistic forecasts, the external sector remained a concern, as it had been since the Great Depression. Trade and current account deficits persisted. Exchange-rate stability, as well as the external perception of the country, depended on the current account. Accordingly, one of the government's major priorities was to increase exports. To do so, however, the government had to overcome two sets of problems. The first set included internal factors—high tax burden and inadequate infrastructure—that together were known as the "Brazilian cost." The second set was external—a wide variety of barriers that kept Brazilian products out of world markets.

One option for Brazil was to put its faith in the World Trade Organization's (WTO) quest to reduce trade barriers around the world and to use that forum to fight against practices that damaged Brazilian interests. Unfortunately, hopes that the WTO could fulfill this promise were dimmed by the failure of the WTO's 1999 Seattle Conference to set an agenda for the next round of trade negotiations.

An alternative was to strengthen the Mercosur union.[1] During the 1990s, Mercosur, the regional integration area that included Brazil, Argentina, Paraguay, and Uruguay, had become the fastest growing market for Brazilian goods. In addition, many observers argued that Mercosur had become a strong force in negotiations with other trading blocs and countries. However, Brazil's 1999 devaluation had strained its relations with the Mercosur countries, particularly Argentina, which was having its own economic difficulties. After the devaluation, trade disputes increased. Brazilian economist Jose Roberto Mendonça de Barros pronounced Mercosur "dead." "The differences between the exchange rate regimes mean that Argentina and Brazil cannot live together," he said.[2]

Indeed, in line with this view, many critics thought Brazil had already gained all it could from Mercosur and instead should concentrate its efforts on gaining market access in the United States and Europe by pursuing bilateral trade agreements with its major trade partners.

Professor Laura Alfaro prepared this case with the assistance of Ernesto Leme (MBA 2001). HBS cases are developed solely as the basis for class discussion. Cases are not intended to serve as endorsements, sources of primary data, or illustrations of effective or ineffective management.

Now the question became: What trade strategy—global, regional, or bilateral—was best for the future? Could Brazil pursue all these strategies at once? Or did Brazil have to choose?

Brazil: The Country

With an area of 3.27 million square miles covering 47% of South America, Brazil is the fifth-largest country in the world—it is 18,500 square miles larger than continental United States—sharing its borders with 10 of the 12 other South American countries [see **Exhibit 6.1**]. In addition, with more than 166 million people, Brazil is the world's fifth most populated country. As the world's ninth-largest national economy in terms of purchasing power, Brazil dominates the Latin American region, producing over a third of its output.[3]

Amazonia, which makes up one-third of the Earth's tropical forest, has the highest level of biodiversity in the world, with nearly two million animal and plant species. Brazilian environmental problems, with widespread pollution and deforestation of the Amazon region, have attracted international attention.

Economic Structure

Because of its tropical and subtropical climate, vast arable land, and ample natural resources, Brazil is a natural exporter of many products. It is the world's largest tobacco and sugar exporter, the producer of 85% of the world's orange juice concentrate, and it has been the world's largest coffee producer for over a century. In addition, the country is the second-largest exporter of soy and the third-largest exporter of beef and chicken. With one-third of the world's total iron reserves, Brazil rivals Australia as the world's major iron exporter, with 30% of world exports. It is also the world's second-largest producer of tin, the sixth-largest producer of aluminum, and the tenth-largest producer of gold.[4] Remarkably, although Brazil is the fifth-largest agricultural producer in the world, only about one-third of the country's export earnings derive from primary products [see **Exhibit 6.7b**]. Brazil's main exports include transportation equipment (planes and autos) and metallurgical and chemical products.

Political Institutions

In 1985, after 21 years of military rule, Brazil returned to democracy as a federal republic with a presidential system. The president was elected for a maximum of two terms of four years each. Congress was bicameral, comprising a 513-member Chamber of Deputies and an 81-member Senate. Regional representation in Congress favored the less developed states of the north, northeast, and center-west. Brazil's highly fragmented political system included 18 political parties represented in Congress.

The Brazilians

Until the latter part of the nineteenth century, the population was made up mainly of descendants of Portuguese, African, and indigenous peoples. At the end of the nineteenth century and in the first decade of the twentieth century, Brazil attracted a large wave of immigrants from Italy, Germany, Poland, the Middle East, and Japan. "There is a strong and deep feeling among Brazilians of all racial backgrounds and national origins that they form a 'people' and a nation."[5] A national poll found that Brazilians were optimistic about the future, and most of them thought Brazil would become a superpower some day.[6]

In 1999, 35% of Brazilians were under the poverty line.[7] Poverty was most severe in northeast Brazil, where income per capita in many states was half that of the national average. In 1999, the richest 10% of Brazilians earned 47.9% of income and the lowest 20% only 5.7%. With a Gini coefficient of 0.6, Brazilians had one of the most unequal distributions of income in the world [see **Exhibits 6.10a** and **6.10b**]. Behind Brazil's vast inequality lay a neglected system of mass education, but stagnation, unemployment, and chronic inflation further aggravated the inequality[8]. According to a study by the Ministry of Justice, homicides in Brazil increased by 6.81% a year (annualized rate) from 1979 to 1998; whereas, population growth during the same period was only 1.67%. The report attributed the increase in homicides to a lack of police enforcement and social inequalities. Other reports claimed that one of the reasons Brazil did not develop a tourist industry, despite the country's great natural appeal, was the increase in violent crime.

Social mobility was constrained by disparities in education, income, and power.

Education was unevenly distributed in terms of quality both across rural and urban areas as well as across regions (north-south). Illiteracy rates among seven-year-olds and above, estimated at 11.5% in urban areas, reached 33.3% in rural areas. In 1996, less than one-third of the population had 7 years or more of school. Ironically, at 18.0 % of GDP (1996 data), Brazil had one of the highest social spending levels in Latin America. However, 41% of social spending went to pensions, whereas education and culture received only 22%. In addition, a disproportionate share of public spending was directed to universities, which, despite being free, were attended primarily by middle- or upper-class students. Diane Jean Schemo wrote in the *New York Times,* "In terms of globalization and competitiveness, education and job training are absolutely critical and Brazil falls way behind. It's the lack of investment in basic education that is holding and will hold Brazil back."[9]

Historical Background: Reshaping the Economic Structure

Discovered by the Portuguese in 1500, Brazil derived its name from the first product exploited by the Portuguese colonizers, *pau brasil (*Brazil-wood).[10] From the colonial era through the twentieth century, Brazil's economic growth was driven by the economic cycles of its products: sugar, gold, and, perhaps most importantly, coffee.[11]

Coffee, introduced into Brazil in the early part of the eighteenth century, became a major growth industry during the nineteenth century and the first decades of the twentieth century. By the 1920s, coffee represented more than 70% of total exports and accounted for approximately 10% of Brazil's GDP.[12] When the Great Depression hit, however, plunging coffee prices took a tremendous toll. Exports fell from $445.9 million in 1929 to $180.6 million in 1932, forcing the government to devalue the currency, impose exchange controls, and offer credit and tax exemptions to domestic manufacturers.[13] These policies, together with the lack of competition from imports, favored the expansion of the industrial sector. By 1931 industrial output had fully recovered to 1928 levels. In the following years, it more than doubled, becoming for the first time the economy's leading sector.

By the 1950s, industrialization and import substitution no longer represented a defensive reaction to external events. Rather, they had become "the principal method for the government to modernize and raise the rate of growth of the economy."[14] Along with many Latin American counterparts, Brazilian leaders believed developing countries had a potential comparative advantage in manufacturing. Initially, however, they could not compete against well-established manufacturing in other more developed countries. The theory was that manufacturing could develop only if governments supported new industries until they became strong enough to compete in the international market.[15]

The Brazilian strategy was to protect the domestic market with tariffs, non-tariff barriers, exchange rate controls, and import licensing. Additionally, the government offered credit through the National Bank of Economic Development (BNDE).[16] The government also used various incentives to attract foreign direct investment (FDI) and created state enterprises in basic industries and public utilities. Effective tariffs averaged over 250% for manufactured goods.[17] The maximum expression of these policies was President Kubitschek's (1956–1961) "Plano de Metas" (Program of Targets), which included industries such as steel, automobiles, aluminum, cement, heavy machinery, and chemicals. These industries were considered "growing points" that could create "backward" and "forward" linkages and externalities to the rest of the economy.[18]

Although the economy grew at nearly 7% per year between 1950 and 1963, the economic strategy had negative side effects. Inflation began to rise and, because of the high import content of investments, the economy started to experience balance of payments problems. Some analysts argued that the inefficient industrial structure and the failure to diversify exports were behind these difficulties.[19] In April 1964, economic stagnation, increasing labor agitation, and fears of communism eventually led to the overthrow of the government. Thereafter came a 21-year period of military rule.

The Military Government

During the early years, the military government focused on controlling inflation and reducing macroeconomic imbalances.[20] The balance of payments problem was addressed by devaluing the currency and attracting foreign capital. In addition, the government once again took the lead role in economic development by undertaking infrastructure projects, enlarging the role of state owned enterprises (SOEs), and stimulating private initiatives through credit and fiscal incentives. State enterprises dominated in steel, mining, and petrochemicals. It had been estimated that of the 100 largest firms (in value of assets), 74% belonged to the government.[21] During "the Brazilian Economic Miracle" of 1968 to 1973, the economy grew at more than 10% per year. Rapid growth and industrialization lent credence to the military's vision of "*grandeza*" or superpower status worthy of Brazil's size and potential.[22] However, in the words of Jorge Dominguez, "it was not growth without tears... The peak years of the boom matched the regime's harshest repression, which included imprisonment and torture, censorship, and other restraints of civil liberties."[23]

During the first oil shock of 1973, the price of oil quadrupled. At that time, Brazil was importing 80% of its oil. Faced with this crisis, the incoming administration of President Ernesto Geisel (1974 to 1979) had two options: devalue the currency and attempt to reduce the country's non-oil import bill, or push for higher growth rates by intensifying the import substitution strategy. The latter, which Brazil chose, would require a reduction in foreign reserves or an increase in foreign debt. In 1975, the government introduced an ambitious National Development Plan that included a huge investment program and widespread incentives designed to intensify import substitution. Referring to this period, Antônio Delfim Neto, Finance Minister from 1968 to 1973, said: "The government was megalomaniac. We became '*Brasil Imperial*'. They wanted to build atomic bombs and rockets... If you took a project of size X, the government would not finance it... if it was 3X they would."[24] For the moment, the policies seemed to have worked. The economy grew around 6% for the rest of the decade.

As expected, the government plan led to a dramatic increase in both foreign debt and inflation. In 1979, debt servicing amounted to over 63% of the country's exports. Foreign debt rose from $6.4 billion in 1973 to $54 billion in 1980. The public sector conducted most foreign borrowing. By 1981, state firms accounted for almost half of the country's foreign debt.

The Second Oil Shock and Transition to Democracy

In March 1979, Brazil's last military president took office. The government soon faced even higher oil prices. As a result of the United States' restrictive monetary policy, interest rates shot up. Because most of Brazil's debt had been contracted on floating interest rates, the hike in international interest rates automatically increased the cost of new borrowings and servicing the outstanding debt. These events hit a vulnerable economy with an unsustainable public sector. Brazil, with the largest external debt in the developing world, had to pay as much as 5% of annual GDP for debt servicing. The results were domestic recession, inflation, devaluation, rising interest rates, and real wage reductions. In 1981, GDP fell by more than 4% while fiscal deficits increased, inflation skyrocketed, and public and private investment fell [see **Exhibits 6.2 to 6.7**]. The "miracle" had vanished.

By the mid-eighties, Brazil returned to democracy and hopes rose anew. A series of newly elected governments turned first to the problem of inflation, which had grown to over three digits by the end of the decade [see **Exhibit 6.3**]. During this time, however, a series of stabilization programs failed to discourage the public sector's deficit spending. With each failure, inflation soared. The general mood became deep disillusionment. Referring to this time, *The Economist* wrote, "...to outsiders, Brazil—to be frank—was a joke.... This was a country with huge potential, outsiders agreed. But a serious one? No."[25]

In May 1993, matters finally began to improve when President Itamar Franco appointed Senator Fernando Henrique Cardoso, a former left wing, internationally respected sociologist, as his fourth finance minister. Cardoso announced his economic plan—the "Real Plan"—in December 1993. The "Plano Real" included a brief fiscal adjustment, which, in 1994, allowed the government to achieve a small fiscal primary surplus and introduced a new currency at a semi-fixed parity with the dollar: the real. Inflation dropped from 50% per month in June 1994 to about 2% per month in the fourth quarter of 1994. The plan's success helped Cardoso win the election of October 1994 with an overwhelming 54% of the votes.

Brazil under President Cardoso

The Cardoso administration believed that the triumph over inflation required a new development model.[26] The Brazilian Central Bank President during that period, Gustavo Franco, said, "'Openness' represents a real challenge to Brazilian industry; it forces managers to look for ways of reducing costs and improving quality and efficiency. The axis of transformation must be privatization and productivity."[27]

Consequently, after taking office Cardoso sent Congress several proposed amendments to the Constitution in order to modernize the economy and improve the fiscal accounts. He quickly won approval to deregulate the economy and to end exclusive market access for national companies in certain sectors of the economy. But his plans to restructure the public sector and reform the tax and social security systems met with strong resistance in Congress. Public sector employees, who had a strong lobby in congress, stood to lose the most. It took almost four more years (until April 1998) to repeal the constitutional provision that prohibited government employees from being fired.

Meanwhile, Cardoso and his administrative team also moved to open Brazil's economy to the outside world. They intensified trade liberalization efforts, lowered average import tariffs from 32% in 1990 to 14% in 1994, and removed non-tariff barriers. To stimulate investment, which had fallen to 18% of GDP by 1992, the new administration widened the privatization program, which had been initiated during the preceding government by privatizing the steel company, electricity assets, banks, railways, and other state-owned firms.[28] Between 1991 and 1999, privatization receipts amounted to more than $73 billion.

As these changes rippled through the economy, the impact of the "Plano Real" brought what an entire generation of Brazilians had never before experienced—price stability. Low-income workers no longer needed to rush to the supermarket on payday to buy food before prices increased. In 1994, 33% of those living in Brazil's six largest cities were officially deemed poor; by 1996, the number had fallen to 25%. Meanwhile, cheap imports resulted in lower prices and, consequently, consumption soared. Spurred on by international competition, some businesses began to cut costs and invest in new technologies, while others went bankrupt. FDI increased as multinationals decided that Brazil was an emerging market they could not afford to ignore. Economic growth was strong, although interest rates remained high.

Unfortunately, the proposals to balance the budget, such as abolishing tenure of public servants, readjusting the retirement age, and reforming the tax system, remained stuck in Congress. The slow pace of fiscal reform meant that government expenditures continued to rise [see **Exhibit 6.6**].[29] In the aftermath of the Mexican financial crisis, concerns about the fiscal imbalances, the real appreciation of Brazil's currency, and increasing current account deficits emerged. The external imbalance was partly financed by FDI (most notably in 1998), medium- and long-term debt via the international bond markets, and substantial inflows of short-term portfolio capital attracted by high interest rates. By 1998 foreign debt was around $243 billion. Brazil, once again, had become highly vulnerable to volatility in global capital markets [see **Exhibit 6.7**].[30]

After the Russian crisis of mid-1998, the Central Bank sharply increased interest rates. Price stability had enabled Cardoso to win a constitutional amendment that allowed him to stand for re-election. Fearful of losing the gains achieved under the Real Plan, on October 4, 1998, Brazilians elected Cardoso to lead the country for four more years. A $41.5 billion assistance package from the IMF temporarily calmed the markets in the second half of November. But the IMF help came with a demand for higher revenues and cuts in government expenditures. In December 1998, when the government failed to gain sufficient Congressional support for the IMF austerity package, doubts soared about further fiscal adjustments. Reserves left the country at the rate of one billion dollars per day, and even renewed hikes in interest rates seemed unlikely to stop capital flight. After replacing the President of the Central Bank, Cardoso took what *The Economist* called, "...the most traumatic decision of his political career." He ordered the devaluation of the real.[31] On January 12, 1999, the Central Bank devalued the currency by 8%. After two days of substantial Central Bank intervention in the foreign-exchange market, the real was allowed to float. It fell as low as R2.14:$1 in early March (compared with R1.21:$1 prior to the devaluation). The appointment of Arminio Fraga as president of the Central Bank calmed the markets. Fraga, an experienced economist and associate of George Soros, kept interest rates high despite the possibility of recession.

Although there were initial fears of a return to soaring prices, not only was inflation contained, but Brazil's economic performance in the second quarter of 1999 was remarkable. Contrary to expectations, the annual contraction in GDP in the first half of 1999 was less than 0.5%. During the first half of 2000, GDP grew about 4%. The government was confident that Brazil again would be on the path to long-term sustainable growth. The agriculture sector benefited from lower import tariffs, increased investments, and new technologies. Lower import tariffs also reduced the cost of inputs and machinery, promoting new investments in the consumer goods sector.

Despite the improved economic prospects, there were concerns about Brazil's future engine of growth and the vulnerability of the external sector. According to Brazilian economist Jose Roberto Mendonça de Barros: "Brazil is growing again. But for this growth to be sustainable over the long term, it is necessary to create trade surpluses in order to reduce the current account deficits. The external sector is still our major vulnerability."[32]

The External Challenge

Between 1988 and 1997, Brazilian exports rose from $33.8 billion to $53 billion—an average annual growth rate of 4.6%. During the same period, imports quadrupled, growing by an average of 15.4% to reach $60 billion, thereby turning the initial trade surplus into a trade deficit [see **Exhibit 6.7a**]. Although trade accounts improved after the 1999 devaluation, the results fell short of market expectations. Traditional labor-intensive industries, such as textiles and shoes, lost ground to producers in Asia. Capital goods, raw materials, and oil still dominated imports [see **Exhibit 6.7b**]. With a growing GDP and optimistic forecasts for 2001 and 2002, the import bill was expected to grow. The current account deficit was still above 4% of GDP, and the external debt remained about $231 billion in November 2000.

The National Confederation of Industries coined the term "*Custo Brasil*" to refer to the type of costs that originate outside the firm such as those caused by a lack of infrastructure,

excessive taxation, and high financing costs. Brazilian producers complained that the "Brazilian cost" negatively affected their competitiveness in the global arena.

The tax burden in Brazil was estimated to be about 29% of GDP. In the United States, it was close to 28% of GDP, in Korea 21%, in Mexico 17%, and in China only around 8% of GDP.[33] Furthermore, the business community argued that Brazil's highly regulated system of labor relations had led to increasingly high costs to employ workers. Compulsory benefits to wages of full-time employees were said to almost double the cost of labor.[34] These benefits included a contribution of 20% of employee wages to the National Institute for Social Security, a mandatory bonus of one-month's pay (called the 13th salary), paid vacations of 30 calendar days, medical assistance, unemployment benefits, and a monthly minimum wage.[35] All these labor rights were guaranteed in the 1988 Constitution, which legalized unions, collective bargaining negotiations, and the right to strike in both the private and public sectors.

After the re-emergence of unions in the 1970s, the labor movement gained a relatively strong influence on elections and on shaping legislation. Virtually all professions were represented by unions and union contributions were deducted from wages. The strongest unions were in the metallurgy and automotive sectors. In fact, Brazil's strongest opposition force, the Worker's Party (Partido dos Trabalhadores–PT), was born in the midst of a huge strike movement in the late 1970s in São Paolo, the most important region for the country's automotive industry. However, those who seemed to benefit from the unions were middle-class workers and workers in the formal sector.[36] Approximately 50% of workers in Brazil were informal wage laborers.[37]

Finally, interest rates, though declining, were still high compared to international standards, thus limiting credit, local demand, and investments. Brazil's Foreign Minister Luiz Felipe Lampreia commented that "without lower interest rates and tax reform, opening the markets could be very dangerous for the Brazilian productive sector."[38]

On the other hand, critics argued that there were additional explanations for Brazil's poor trade performance. They pointed to the fact that Brazilian products, such as steel-related products, oranges, and sugar—all goods in which the country had a clear comparative advantage—faced high trade barriers in the United States and Europe. Furthermore, the country was constantly subject to trade investigations. Most recently, the Brazilian government had been accused by Canada of subsidizing Empresa Brasileira de Aeronáutica SA, Embraer, a producer of small jets.

Although the country had few high-tech industries, Embraer had become Brazil's "Hot Commodity," as the headline of a *New York Times* article read, and "...was on the verge of displacing Canada's Bombardier as the world's third largest manufacturer of commercial aircraft."[39] Embraer's foreign sales, supported by subsidized interest rates through the Export-Financing Program (Proex), allowed the company to borrow cheaply. Proex was an important source for Brazilian companies seeking to equalize local and international interest rates for exporters.[40] Canadian officials claimed that the subsidies unfairly allowed Embraer to gain market share. Brazilian officials responded that Canadian firms received similar support. In July 2000, the WTO gave Canada permission to impose as much as $226 million per year in trade sanctions against Brazilian goods. Referring to this incident, Brazilian Foreign Minister Luiz Felipe Lampreia said the WTO regulations, "...were made to benefit developed countries and do not offer emerging economies the chance to reduce the gap between the two blocs."[41]

In February 2001, in a move that Canadian officials said was not related to the Embraer-WTO ruling, Canada temporarily banned Brazilian beef imports. Canadian officials argued that Brazil had failed to provide required information to determine whether the country was free of mad-cow disease. The Brazilian government claimed to have provided such information.[42] Although Canada lifted the ban one month later, Brazilian officials were frustrated by Canada's arbitrary action and by the lack of clear WTO rules in relation to sanitary restrictions.[43]

For the Brazilian Government, reduced trade barriers and increased exports were top priorities. One way to achieve these goals was to try to push its views through the WTO. In addition, the country could try to negotiate bilaterally with the United States and Europe, or it could concentrate its effort in consolidating Mercosur. After all, Brazilian external trade during the 1990s had

benefited from the Mercosur regional integration initiative.

Mercosur, the Common Market of South America[44]

In 1986, Brazil and Argentina began to negotiate the Mercosur project, in spite of the failure of previous trade integration attempts. This project was an effort to increase growth and competitiveness after a period of sharp trade contraction between the two countries. Moreover, the political leadership in both countries saw regional integration as a way to diminish traditional geopolitical rivalries, to weaken respective military establishments, and to consolidate the emerging democracies.[45] Argentina and Brazil had long been divided by ambitions to become regional powers—a goal that dated back to the early days of their independence. During the 1970s, both countries had military governments that engaged in arms races of their own, which encompassed the production of weaponry as well as the development of nuclear power capability. Argentina's defeat in its war with Britain over the Malvinas/Falkland Islands (1982) and the subsequent withdrawal of the armed forces from power in both Argentina and Brazil made security concerns based on military considerations a very low priority. For the civilian administrations that ensued, security took on a new meaning: the preservation of regional peace and democracy.[46]

However, the negotiations stalled, primarily due to continued economic instability in both counties. But the project was revived in 1989 when the end of the Cold War brought the threat that Eastern Europe would draw investments away from Latin America. Furthermore, the region faced what seemed to be a world of strengthening trading blocs and bilateral agreements. Close to home, for example, the United States, Canada, and Mexico negotiated a free trade area (NAFTA). Changing international conditions coincided with political changes in Brazil and Argentina as Fernando Collor de Mello and Carlos Menem, both elected in 1989, pushed their countries towards liberalization and free markets.[47] In August of that year, Uruguay and Paraguay were invited to become members of Mercosur.

The Mercosur integration process became official in March 1991 with the signing of the

Asuncion Treaty. The treaty envisioned the creation of a common market between Brazil, Argentina, Uruguay, and Paraguay by December 31, 1994, and the gradual coordination of macroeconomic policies.

After January 1, 1995, 90% of intra-regional trade circulated free of tariffs and quotas. Each country agreed to a "transition list" of products considered to be "sensitive" to foreign competition as needing protection until 2006.

In addition, member countries adopted a common external tariff (CET) and quotas with non-member countries. The CET was set between 0% and 23% of an import's value for some 90% of the products, with the remaining 10% included on a list of exceptions. The objective of this list was to allow the countries to adapt to the new competitive conditions of the international market. Tariffs were high on imports considered to be a threat to domestic production and low on goods used in the production of export products or not produced in the domestic market. Uruguay's list contained 212 products, such as milk products, chemicals, textiles, and steel products; Paraguay's 210-product list included chemicals, agriculture, and textiles; and Argentina's 232 products included chemicals, paper, and footwear. Brazil's 175-product list ranged from machines for industry (subject to a 20% tariff in 1998) to consumer goods such as cassette players (32%), hairdryers (29%), and cardiac pacemakers (10%). Capital goods confronted different rates among countries. In Brazil, the rate was 20%, in Argentina 10%, and in Paraguay and Uruguay 0%.

"Rules of origin" were created to avoid a "triangular circulation" of goods from countries outside the bloc: i.e., importing a good through a lower-tariff country within Mercosur and selling it later in a higher-tariff country. Goods sold within the four countries were exempt from tariffs only if at least 60% of their raw materials were produced in the region. However, a number of exceptions were permitted, in accordance with the specific situation of each country. For example, Paraguay was allowed a national content level of 50% for certain products. The automobile sector was excluded from the regional agreement, and the tariff was set at 35% and the local-content requirement at 30%.

In a common market, not only goods, services, and capital circulate without restrictions between member states, but labor is also supposed to move freely. Within Mercosur, however, immigration procedures remained complex. There was a lack of coordination of legislation on pensions and business practices.

In 1996, Chile became an associate member of the union.[48] This led to a nearly one-third reduction in the average tariff rate on Mercosur/Chilean trade. Chile's associate status allowed it to maintain a flat external tariff of about 11% on imports from non-Mercosur countries. In 1997, after negotiating a similar agreement, Bolivia also became an associate member.

After the creation of Mercosur, trade among the member countries increased rapidly, making Mercosur the fastest growing trade region in the world. From 1991 to 1997, exports within the region rose from $5.1 billion to $20 billion. Bilateral trade between Brazil and Argentina represented approximately 75% of total trade flows within the region.[49] Argentina became Brazil's second trading partner after the United States, although the European Union was still the main destination of Brazilian goods [see **Exhibit 6.7e**].

Gains from Mercosur?[50]

Many observers criticized Mercosur on grounds that the member countries were simply too dissimilar and unstable. There were huge differences in population and territory [see **Exhibits 6.9** and **6.11**]. More importantly, the Mercosur economies had different productive structures. To cope with differences in the degree of openness and protection desired by each member and by each sector within each country, sensitive products had been excluded. This meant that Mercosur became only a partial customs union and intra-Mercosur integration had never been completed.[51] Trade conflicts among the four countries over a wide range of products, such as autos, sugar, milk, and chicken, were common.

Despite these differences, some experts regarded Mercosur as a success, and the increase in trade was a clear example that there was no need to further harmonize policies. Others argued that Mercosur survived because of exceptional conditions since free trade had started from an unusually low level.

Economists noted that it was remarkable that the regional integration had succeeded despite the macroeconomic turbulence in the member countries. [52] Just after Mercosur was formed,

Argentina launched its Convertibility Plan and pegged its currency to the U.S. dollar. Inflation came down and growth picked up. But the Argentinean real exchange rate appreciated against the Brazilian currency, and their market was flooded with Brazilian goods. In November 1992, Argentina imposed a tax on imports, which targeted, in particular, Brazilian exports. But by 1994, the problems had ended as Brazil launched the Real Plan. The Brazilian economy boomed, and now the real appreciated against the peso. In 1995, Brazil imposed import quotas and other measures to curb the surge in Argentine imports. As problems began to spread in East Asia, Argentina and Brazil increased the CET by 3%, while Paraguay and Uruguay only implemented it selectively.

A series of bilateral agreements signed between individual Mercosur members and third parties, such as the Argentina-Mexico Trade-Accord in 1998 and the Brazil-Andean Community agreement in 1999, raised doubts about the consolidation of the custom union planned for 2006.[53]

After the 1999 real devaluation, roles changed once again—the Brazilian real depreciated against the Argentinean peso and Brazilian products became more competitive. However, this time the Brazilian economy boomed while Argentina sank into deep recession. Argentina raised barriers against Brazilian goods. Brazil struck back by imposing restrictions against Argentina's imports.[54]

Some economists, pointing to the European Union example, argued that Mercosur's future would be bleak, unless there was better macroeconomic coordination and even adoption of a single currency. However, as others pointed out, it was not clear that the Mercosur countries formed an optimal currency area, or that Brazil wanted to return to a fixed rate. Additionally, adopting a single currency, or even an intermediate step, such as an exchange rate band, would require an unprecedented degree of coordination between Latin American economies. In addition, the fiscal and monetary reforms required for a single currency would incur social costs due to the likelihood of an increase in unemployment that tends to accompany such adjustments. These social costs would, of course, limit political support for the unification process.[55] Critics argued that Brazil already had gained what it could from Mercosur.

To pursue further regional integration would be a waste of diplomatic time.

In any event, to bring Mercosur's integration scheme back on track, members needed to reduce trade tensions, eliminate restrictions on free trade and the CET, and coordinate macroeconomic policy. The final objective of a common market required greater interdependence. The resulting loss of autonomy would be acceptable only with great support from the unions, the business community, and the major political parties. It was not clear whether Mercosur had such support. According to a survey carried out by the National Association of Financial, Management and Accounting Executives in 1998, 58% of 267 entrepreneurs interviewed in Brazil claimed that Mercosur had not led to any significant increase in their business volumes; 41% claimed the opposite. Only 34% thought Mercosur could increase their business volumes by up to 5%.

On the other hand, some experts as well as government officials argued that Mercosur had brought substantial economic and political benefits to Brazil. Intra-regional trade had created opportunities for economies of scale mostly in the manufacturing sectors without a major displacement of local production in the Brazilian economy. The inter-sectorial specialization pattern favored Brazil, whose exports were chiefly electric and mechanical machinery and equipment and automobiles [see **Exhibit 6.7d**]. Mercosur allowed Brazil some flexibility to protect and expand industries considered important to the country.

In addition, specialists involved in international negotiations viewed the strengthening of Mercosur as imperative for Brazil. Mercosur was the South American response to the demands of the New World economy and the resentment against multilateral organizations, such as the WTO, in dealing with requests from developing countries. By negotiating as a bloc, especially if other South American countries joined, Brazil would have a greater voice in defending its interests against the European Union and the United States.

Mercosur: A United Voice?

In November 2000 Mercosur was dealt a significant blow when Chile announced that it would begin bilateral trade talks with the United States. Chile's announcement was perceived to weaken Brazil's efforts to strengthen and expand

Mercosur and to boost its negotiating power by presenting a united front. With the Chilean shift, Brazil now faced the prospect that its other South American partners, in particular Argentina, would be tempted to defect and begin bilateral negotiations with the United States as well.

Thus, Brazil also had to consider the possibility of pursuing bilateral agreements with its major trade partners.

The European Union

In 1999 the European Union, Brazil's major consumer market, accounted for about 29% of all Brazilian exports. The European Union also imposed the most commercial barriers on Brazilian products, such as tariffs, non-tariff barriers, quotas, and anti-subsidy measures.[56] For example, orange juice and meat were subject to a 36.4% and 20% tariff, respectively, in addition to non-tariff barriers.[57] Among the non-tariff barriers, the most notable were the restrictions allowed within the WTO, like the multilateral quotas for textile imports, as well as sanitary and environmental restrictions, which adversely affected Brazilian exports of primary products. A major threat was the strengthening of diplomatic and commercial ties between the European Union and countries in Eastern Europe, such as Poland and Hungary, which directly competed with Brazil.[58] Economists in Brazil highlighted the importance of eliminating the obstacles imposed by the Europeans.[59] According to some calculations, GDP would grow by 5.05% with the creation of a free trade area with the European Union, although this would bring greater benefits to the agricultural sector than to Brazil's manufacturing industry [see **Exhibit 6.7c**].

Free-Trade Area of the Americas (FTAA)[60]

The FTAA project, which included the 34 countries of the hemisphere with the exception of Cuba, began in June 1990 with the "Initiative for the Americas" launched by President George Bush. Following this proposal, the first major step was taken toward formatting the FTAA at the Presidential Summit in Miami (December 1994). The 34 presidents agreed to increase cooperation and integration within the Americas, including forming a continental free trade area by 2005. Since then there have been periodic meetings with the aim of agreeing on better ways of achieving integration.

The potential of the FTAA seemed undeniable, because the region would represent a preferential market of 800 million people, accounting for a GDP of around $13 trillion. Benefits included the potential for higher direct investment in the region, the guarantee of preferential access to developed markets for smaller countries, and increased transparency of rules and regulations.

The integration of this union appeared to be in Brazil's interests, in light of the barriers the United States imposed against Brazilian goods. However, this view was not widely shared. Brazilian economists estimated that the FTAA would mean an increase in Brazilian imports from the United States of around 25%; whereas Brazil's exports to the United States would rise by only 8%.[61] In addition, Brazil's interests diverged as much from those of the United States as they did from the smaller countries within the region. Small countries heavily geared to exports could benefit from a free trade area that included the United States, provided that their exports would not face significant competition within the United States. But countries with more complex economies, such as Brazil, could face greater difficulties. Many Brazilian products would suffer fierce competition from more efficient U.S. rivals. However, the question of whether Brazilian firms would modernize without the "threat" of competition remained.

The United States

As Brazil's single largest trading partner, the United States received about 23% of Brazilian exports. The trade balance with the United States had traditionally been unfavorable to Brazil. Before the 1999 devaluation, trade imbalances between the United States and Brazil had been attributed by the U.S. government to the so-called "Brazil cost" and to the overvaluation of the real relative to the U.S. dollar. According to Rubens A. Barbosa, Brazilian Ambassador to the United States, after the devaluation, "...the persistent asymmetry in our bilateral trade, however, points [to the fact] that the U.S. trade barriers—and not merely the intrinsic circumstances of our export performance—are still among the major factors responsible for the asymmetries in the commercial transactions with the United States."[62]

Brazil had probably suffered the most antidumping and countervailing-duty investigations by the United States. Between 1980 and 1999, the United States conducted 42 antidumping investigations and 31 investigations against Brazilian exports that had been "unfairly" subsidized by the Brazilian government.[63] The list of products included, among others, orange juice, iron, rubber, cotton, and steel. According to Brazilian officials, U.S. antidumping rules and countervailing procedures were arbitrary and simply a disguised form of protectionism.[64] Barbosa noted the example of Brazilian steel, which had been subject to antidumping investigations, countervailing duties, and safeguard measures.

Under WTO regulations, antidumping duties can be imposed against a country if a company exports a product at a price lower than the price it normally charges on its own home market, if producers are selling below the cost of production, or if their selling price in the importing country's market is below that in other destinations. Countries are allowed to charge an extra duty—known as a countervailing duty—on subsidized imports found to be hurting domestic producers. Finally, a WTO member can temporarily restrict imports of a product (take "safeguard" actions) if its domestic industry is injured or threatened by a surge in imports. [65] However, the WTO allows governments to act only where there is a genuine ("material") injury to the domestic industry. Governments have to demonstrate that the violation takes place, show the extent of the violation, and show that it is causing injury. [66]

In 1998 the United States began a new set of investigations against Brazilian hot-rolled steel and carbon steel plates. The U.S. steel industry saw its position severely challenged as the demand for steel plummeted after reductions in investment and consumption in East Asia and as cheaper steel flooded the U.S. market after Russia and Brazil devalued their currencies. Prices reached all time lows. The *U.S. Steel Report* argued that non-competitive market structures in these countries and other structural problems that had led to unfair trade over the years also contributed to the problem.[67] Brazil objected to the assumption held in Washington that past subsidies paid to state-owned firms provided a continuing unfair benefit to their now privatized firms.[68] The U.S. Steel Manufacturing Association contended that the protection was necessary: "The United States needs a strong steel industry. That is inarguable...."[69] Barbosa

commented, "...trade restrictions and countervailing duties continued to be collected [by the U.S.] on imports of Brazilian hot-rolled steel and carbon steel plates, although WTO had condemned the U.S. practices on which those duties were based."[70]

Another trade conflict that caused great concern to Brazilian officials was the United States' request to the WTO, in January 2001, to form a dispute panel against the 1997 Brazilian patent law. The United States claimed the law violated WTO rules because it forced companies to produce in Brazil after a certain period of time.[71] "This is really about a specific portion of law, and the question is: Who owns the patent?" a U.S. Embassy official in Brazil said. [72] However, Brazilian officials feared it might affect Brazilian production of anti-AIDS drugs.[73] Brazil had earned international praise for its anti-AIDS campaign.[74] Since 1997 virtually every AIDS patient in Brazil received—for free—a triple cocktail that not only helped stabilize the epidemic but cut the death rate by 50%. Brazilian companies produced seven of the 12 anti-AIDS drugs administered in the free drug program. This cut the cost of the triple therapy to around $3,000 from around $10,000.[75]

Brazil's 1997 patent law, passed to comply with the WTO (every country joining WTO must pass laws with respect to patents), ended the non-patentability of food, chemical, pharmaceutical, and biotechnology products. However, Brazil's law entitled the government, when it deemed necessary, to issue a license to a local firm, and the legislation prohibited retroactive imposition of royalties on products already produced or sold in Brazil.

Thus, under the new law, anything commercialized anywhere in the world by May 15, 1997, remained forever un-patented in Brazil. This aspect of the law covered most first generation anti-AIDS drugs.[76] Among those not copied, Merck's and Roche's drugs, patented after 1997, represented around 36% of Brazil's $310 million expenditures on AIDS medication in the year 2000. Brazilian officials were concerned about the increasing costs of the AIDS drug program. One solution was for these companies to sell the drugs at a lower price.[77] Another option was to produce the drugs locally. Brazilian officials argued that this move would be consistent with WTO regulations because members were allowed to make copies of patented items under certain situations, including national emergencies—the Brazilian government had already declared the AIDS crisis a national emergency. [78] Pharmaceutical companies challenged this approach. [79]

Other U.S. industries and sectors insisted on protection as well. Several important Brazilian exports were penalized with high tariffs or quotas. Sugar faced a 236% equivalent tariff, tobacco a 350% equivalent tariff, and frozen orange juice concentrate, a 44.7% tariff. Although a greater number of U.S. products were subject to significant tariffs (i.e., above 10%), Brazilian import tariffs were generally less onerous, ranging from 3% on certain computer chips and aircraft parts to 35% on vehicles [see **Exhibit 6.8**].

A Brazilian Embassy study indicated that the removal of U.S. barriers affecting orange juice, steel products, sugar, footwear, tobacco, gasoline, shrimp, ethyl alcohol, and crude soy bean oil would correspond to an annual gain in GDP for Brazil of about $831 million. According to Ambassador Ruben Barbosa, "...whether in negotiations regarding dumping and subsidies or in seeking to liberalize market access, the course of action pursued by Brazil up to this point, in all economic sectors, has produced either no results whatsoever or minimal results." [80]

Brazil's Frustration

Although the WTO was created to lower trade barriers throughout the world, developing countries have regarded it with some suspicion. Most developing countries have come to believe that this multinational forum simply reflected U.S. and European interests. Indeed, at the WTO conference in Seattle, Brazil, backed by several developing countries, fought to restrain the efforts by various industrialized countries to impose stricter labor standards on poorer countries. [81] In addition, several countries questioned the effectiveness of WTO enforcement mechanisms against the "big countries." Nevertheless, a major concern was the view that multilateral trade progress was paralyzed after the failure of the 1999 WTO trade conference to get a new round of negotiations off the ground.

In a speech delivered to the Mercosur region in Buenos Aires, Argentina, in November 1999,

the director-general of the WTO, Mike Moore, commented: "Globalization is the word on everyone's lips, yet regional agreements have never been so popular. A single regional market can help the poorer countries build on their competitive advantages, and increase their political commitment to an open economy. But regional accords can widen the trade divide between the industrialized and the developing countries." Furthermore, Moore warned that, "...regionalism alone leads not towards an open world economy, but an unbalanced system of hub and spokes, with rich countries at the center, holding all the cards, and developing countries on the periphery." [82] In 2000, there were 200 regional trade groupings, compared with 50 in 1990. [83]

On September 12, 2000, in a speech delivered at the 55th Session of the General Assembly of the United Nations, Brazil's Foreign Minister, Luiz Felipe Lampreia, said,

> As I stated at the World Trade Organization conference in Seattle, the name of this game is discrimination. We must reverse these grave distortions in international trade, especially as concerns agricultural products. It is inadmissible that the most prosperous nations, whose economies are strongly based in the manufacturing and service industries, should be legally entitled to restrict access to their markets for agricultural goods. While, at the same time, they call for the free flow of those goods in which they benefit from an enormous competitive advantage.... Mr. President, Nations must come increasingly to comprehend and respect differing realities, outlooks, and objectives among themselves. At the same time, they must recognize their commonalties and affinities; explore and enlarge areas of convergence and opportunities for cooperation; overcome suspicions, rivalries, and disputes. Nowadays it is above all through regional integration that this learning process takes place. [84]

| EXHIBIT 6.1 | **MAP OF BRAZIL** |

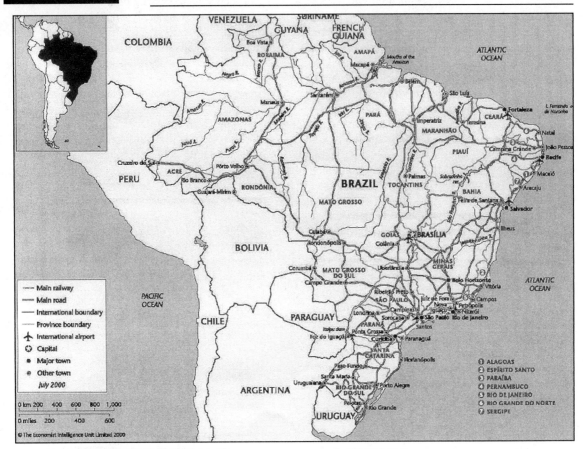

SOURCE: *The Economist.*

EXHIBIT 6.2 — NATIONAL INCOME ACCOUNTS (1981–1999)

	1981	1983	1985	1987	1989	1990	1991	1992	1993	1994	1995	1996	1997	1998	1999
GDP (1998 R$ billion)	595.3	582.7	662.4	737.2	760.0	728.3	735.8	731.8	767.8	812.8	847.1	869.6	898.3	900.1	907.3
Real GDP growth	-4.3	-1.1	6.6	5.5	1.5	-4.2	1.0	-0.5	4.9	5.9	4.2	2.7	3.3	0.2	0.8
GDP (current US$ billion)	258.6	189.5	211.1	282.4	415.9	469.3	405.7	387.3	429.7	543.1	705.4	775.5	807.8	787.5	529.4
Population (MM inhabitants)	121.2	126.6	132.0	137.3	142.3	144.1	146.4	148.9	150.9	153.1	155.3	157.5	159.6	161.8	163.9
Investment (% GDP)	23.1	18.6	16.9	22.2	24.8	20.7	18.1	18.4	19.3	20.8	20.5	19.1	19.9	19.9	19.1
Invest. Federal SOEs (% GDP)	5.2	4.1	3.3	3.7	3.0	1.9	2.3	2.4	2.0	1.6	1.4	1.6	1.7	1.3	1.5
Domestic savings (% GDP)	18.6	15.2	16.8	21.7	25.0	19.6	16.9	19.3	18.5	19.9	17.7	15.7	15.2	14.6	N/A
Public	-0.7	0.7	0.3	-1.5	-1.3	5.7	3.5	1.7	2.4	4.3	-1.6	-1.1	-1.9	N/A	N/A
Private	19.3	14.5	16.5	23.2	26.3	13.9	13.4	17.6	16.1	15.6	19.3	16.8	17.1	N/A	N/A

SOURCE: IPEA (Institute of Research and Applied Economics), www.ipeadata.gov.br; IBGE (Brazilian Institute of Geography and Statistics); Central Bank of Brazil.

EXHIBIT 6.3 — PRICES, MONETARY AND FINANCIAL SECTOR VARIABLES (1981–1999)

	1981	1983	1985	1987	1989	1990	1991	1992	1993	1994	1995	1996	1997	1998	1999
GDP deflator (%)	101.0	131.0	249.0	206.0	1,304.0	2,596.0	416.7	969.0	1,996.2	2,240.2	77.6	17.4	8.3	4.7	4.3
Annual interest rates (selic), (%)	89.3	193.2	225.9	353.0	2,407.3	1,153.2	536.8	1,549.4	3,060.0	1,153.6	53.0	23.9	42.0	31.2	18.9
M1/GDP (%)	7.7	5.1	3.5	4.2	2.0	3.3	2.8	1.8	1.3	4.3	4.1	3.7	5.3	5.6	6.8
M4/GDP (%)	25.4	24.7	27.9	27.0	24.8	15.6	15.5	25.6	27.5	32.6	36.0	39.8	44.1	50.0	59.9

SOURCE: IPEA (Institute of Research and Applied Economics), www.ipeadata.gov.br; IBGE (Brazilian Institute of Geography and Statistics); Central Bank of Brazil.

EXHIBIT 6.4 — UNEMPLOYMENT AND LABOR PRODUCTIVITY INDICATORS (1981–1999)

	1981	1983	1985	1987	1989	1990	1991	1992	1993	1994	1995	1996	1997	1998	1999
Rate of unemployment (%)	7.9	6.7	5.2	3.7	3.3	4.3	4.8	5.8	5.3	5.1	4.6	5.4	5.7	7.6	7.6
Labor productivity (1976=100)	122.5	125.2	147.9	147.5	149.1	144.7	156.6	166.2	182.6	200.9	208.9	239.3	266.5	288.4	N/A
Real wages index (1988=100)	90.3	90.0	95.6	97.7	96.9	83.9	77.6	88.5	97.4	107.7	118.9	126.4	134.0	136.9	N/A

SOURCE: IPEA (Institute of Research and Applied Economics), www.ipeadata.gov.br; Central Bank of Brazil.

EXHIBIT 6.5	SECTOR OF ECONOMIC ACTIVITY AS A % OF GDP (1960-1997)						
	1960	1970	1980	1990	1995	1999
Agriculture, value added	20.68	12.34	11.01	8.10	9.01	8.09
Industry, value added	37.07	38.22	43.73	38.69	36.67	35.23
Manufacturing	29.69	29.29	33.42	N/A	23.58	22.84
Services, etc., value added	42.26	49.44	45.26	53.21	54.32	56.68
Real GDP growth rates[a]	7.40	6.20	8.70	1.60	3.00	1.80

SOURCE: IPEA (Institute of Research and Applied Economics), www.ipeadata.gov.br.; IBGE (Brazilian Institute of Geography and Statistics).

[a]Numbers show the average growth per year of the previous decade. 1995 and 1999 columns show the average growth per year of the previous five- and four-year periods, respectively.

EXHIBIT 6.6	PUBLIC SECTOR INDICATORS AS A % OF GDP (1981-1999)																	
	1981	1983	1985	1987	1989	1990	1991	1992	1993	1994	1995	1996	1997	1998	1999
Gross tax collections	25.2	26.9	23.8	24.3	23.7	29.6	24.4	25.0	25.3	27.9	28.0	28.2	28.2	29.0	N/A
Operational deficit	6.5	3.1	4.4	5.7	6.9	-1.3	0.1	1.8	0.7	-1.1	5.0	3.8	4.3	7.5	3.5
Primary deficit[a]	N/A	N/A	-2.6	1.0	1.0	-4.6	-2.8	-1.6	-2.3	-5.1	-0.3	0.1	1.0	0.0	-3.1
Net public sector debt	23.7	49.5	50.1	47.3	38.9	38.5	35.3	35.7	32.2	26.0	27.3	30.9	30.9	42.4	46.9
Internal	8.8	16.6	19.5	17.3	20.3	15.5	12.0	17.0	17.8	17.6	21.8	27.0	26.6	36.1	37.0
External[b]	14.9	32.9	30.6	30.0	18.6	23.0	23.3	18.7	14.4	8.4	5.5	3.9	4.3	6.3	9.9

SOURCE: IPEA (Institute of Research and Applied Economics), www.ipeadata.gov.br; Central Bank of Brazil.

[a]The primary deficit does not include interest payments. Deficit (+), Surplus (-).

[b]Data includes debt defaults and renegotiation in 1989 and 1993–94.

| EXHIBIT 6.7A | BALANCE OF PAYMENTS AND SELECTED DATA, US$ BILLIONS (1981-2000) |

Balance of Payments	1981	1983	1985	1987	1989	1990	1991	1992	1993	1994	1995	1996	1997	1998	1999	2000P
Exports	23.2	21.9	25.6	26.2	34.4	31.4	31.6	35.8	38.6	43.5	46.5	47.7	53.0	51.1	48.0	55.1
Manufacturing exports	12.0	11.5	14.2	14.9	18.9	17.4	17.3	21.4	23.5	24.9	25.6	26.4	29.2	29.3	30.3	NA
Imports	22.1	15.4	13.2	15.1	18.3	20.7	21.0	20.6	25.3	33.1	49.9	53.3	59.9	57.7	49.2	55.8
Trade balance	1.1	6.5	12.4	11.1	16.1	10.7	10.6	15.2	13.3	10.4	-3.4	-5.6	-6.9	-6.6	-1.2	-0.7
Service balance	-4.0	-3.9	-3.3	-3.9	-5.7	-5.6	-4.9	-4.1	-7.3	-8.4	-10.4	-11.3	-15.9	-16.9	-10.6	-10.6
Interest payments	-9.2	-9.5	-9.6	-8.8	-9.6	-9.7	-8.6	-7.3	-8.3	-6.3	-8.2	-9.2	-10.4	-11.9	-15.3	-15.1
Current account balance	-11.7	-6.8	-0.2	-1.4	1.0	-3.8	-1.4	5.9	-0.4	-1.3	-18.0	-23.1	-30.9	-33.6	-25.1	-24.6
Foreign direct investment	1.8	0.9	0.8	0.6	0.7	0.6	0.6	1.4	0.6	1.9	4.6	15.5	20.7	20.5	30.1	29.6
Short-term capital	1.2	1.1	-1.4	0.7	0.7	-1.3	-4.1	1.7	3.2	0.9	18.8	5.4	-19.0	-31.6	-8.5	-6.4
Capital account balance	12.8	2.1	-2.6	-8.0	-11.4	-3.9	-4.3	5.9	8.6	14.3	29.4	34.0	25.9	20.6	14.2	30.2
Current account balance (% GDP)	-4.5%	-3.6%	-0.1%	-0.5%	0.2%	-0.8%	-0.3%	1.5%	-0.1%	-0.2%	-2.5%	-3.0%	-3.8%	-4.3%	-4.7%	NA
Foreign reserves	7.5	4.6	9.2	6.8	8.7	9.1	8.8	23.2	31.7	38.5	51.5	60.1	51.7	44.0	35.7	43.8
Gross external debt	73.9	93.5	105.1	121.1	115.5	123.4	123.9	136.0	145.7	148.3	159.3	179.9	200.0	243.2	241.1	232.8[a]
Gross external debt (% GDP)	28.6%	49.3%	49.8%	42.9%	27.8%	26.3%	30.5%	35.1%	33.9%	27.3%	22.6%	23.2%	24.8%	30.9%	45.5%	NA
Exchange rate (R$/US$) (end of year)	4.6E-11	3.6E-10	3.8E-09	2.6E-08	4.1E-06	1.0E-04	4.0E-04	4.5E-03	0.12	0.84	0.97	1.04	1.12	1.21	1.79	1.95
Devaluation rate (%)	76.7%	669.9%	966.4%	588.6%	15,620.8%	2,333.2%	300.0%	1,025.0%	2,535.6%	611.6%	15.2%	6.9%	7.4%	8.3%	48.0%	9.3%
Effective real exchange rate 06/94 = 100[b]	127.1	134.9	135.9	143.9	95.7	113.7	117.4	108.2	96.8	77.1	86.4	85.0	79.4	84.6	98.0	NA

SOURCE: IPEA (Institute of Research and Applied Economics), www.ipeadata.gov.br; Central Bank of Brazil.

P = Preliminary data.

[a] Data for September 2000.

[b] An increase in the index denotes real depreciation.

EXHIBIT 6.7B	**EXPORTS AND IMPORTS BY PRODUCT, % OF TOTAL (1999)**	

Imports (FOB)		**Exports (FOB)**	
Total (US$ Millions)	49,219	Total (US$ Million)	48,011
Total	100.0%	Total	100.0%
Consumer Goods	12.8	Primary Products	37.0
Foodstuffs	4.2	Coffee	5.1
Apparel	1.0	Soybeans	7.9
Others	7.5	Cocoa	0.2
		Sugar	4.0
Raw Materials	34.5%	Orange juice	2.6
Grains	2.9	Meat	4.0
Peeled wheat beans	1.7	Iron ore, manganese and other ores	6.1
Fertilizers	1.8	Tobacco	1.9
Chemical products	18.3	Others	5.3
Cast iron and steel	1.8		
Nonferrous metals	1.9	Industrialized Products	63.0%
Coal	1.2	Transport equipment and accessories	13.7
Others	6.7	Machines and mechanical instruments	6.1
		Electric and electronic equipment	3.8
Oil and Derivatives	9.8%	Metallurgical products	10.5
		Chemical products	7.2
Capital Goods *machinery parts*	43.0%	Wood and manufactured wood	2.9
		Footwear and leather products	2.9
		Oil derivatives	2.5
		Paper and pulp	4.5
		Textile products	2.1
		Others	6.9%

SOURCE: Central Bank of Brazil.

EXHIBIT 6.7c — BREAKDOWN OF BRAZILIAN TRADE FLOWS (US$ MILLION)

Region	Sector	1996 Exports	1996 Imports	1996 Balance	1997 Exports	1997 Imports	1997 Balance	1998 Exports	1998 Imports	1998 Balance
Latin America and the Caribbean	Basic products	749	4,731	-3,982	799	4,656	-3,857	917	3,879	-2,962
	Semi-manufactured goods	492	622	-130	561	688	-117	585	677	-92
	Manufactured goods	10,430	6,350	4,080	13,327	8,164	5,163	12,785	7,902	4,883
	Other	19	20	-1	24	--	24	26	46	-20
	Total	**11,690**	**11,723**	**-33**	**14,711**	**13,498**	**1,213**	**14,313**	**12,504**	**1,809**
Asia[a]	Basic products	3,025	1,757	1,268	3,568	1,322	2,246	3,072	892	2,180
	Semi-manufactured goods	2,937	54	2,883	2,904	69	2,835	2,202	63	2,139
	Manufactured goods	2,706	7,442	-4,736	2,284	9,191	-6,907	1,516	7,762	-6,246
	Other	11	10	1	9	1	8	5	7	-2
	Total	**8,679**	**9,263**	**-584**	**8,765**	**10,583**	**-1,818**	**6,795**	**8,724**	**-1,929**
European Union	Basic products	6,042	216	5,826	7,754	206	7,548	6,766	232	6,534
	Semi-manufactured goods	1,864	220	1,644	1,923	258	1,665	2,272	256	2,016
	Manufactured goods	4,892	13,460	-8,568	4,801	15,844	-11,043	5,672	16,271	-10,599
	Other	38	49	-11	35	8	27	34	60	-26
	Total	**12,836**	**13,945**	**-1,109**	**14,513**	**16,316**	**-1,803**	**14,744**	**16,819**	**-2,075**
NAFTA	Basic products	1,311	1,141	170	1,357	1,106	251	1,210	862	348
	Semi-manufactured goods	2,055	459	1,596	2,292	498	1,794	2,233	412	1,821
	Manufactured goods	7,076	12,271	-5,195	7,139	15,370	-8,231	7,942	14,533	-6,591
	Other	55	42	13	30	4	26	26	55	-29
	Total	**10,497**	**13,913**	**-3,416**	**10,818**	**16,978**	**-6,160**	**11,411**	**15,862**	**-4,451**
Other	Basic products	1,117	1,345	-228	1,076	1,741	-665	1,122	1,452	-330
	Semi-manufactured goods	1,133	267	866	886	312	574	933	292	641
	Manufactured goods	1,954	2,739	-785	2,334	3,086	-752	2,264	2,870	-606
	Other	518	26	492	713	--	713	540	1	539
	Total	**4,722**	**4,377**	**345**	**5,009**	**5,139**	**-130**	**4,859**	**4,615**	**244**

SOURCE: United Nations Trade Statistics.

[a]Includes Middle East.

EXHIBIT 6.7D	DIRECTION AND COMPOSITION OF TRADE, 1998 (US$ MILLION)

	United States	Argentina	Germany	Total
EXPORTS FOB				
Meat	1.0	134.0	56.7	1,247.8
Fruit and vegetables and preparations	353.7	48.7	14.4	1,667.0
Sugar and preparations	130.4	18.0	0.7	2,027.1
Coffee	368.0	76.7	370.3	2,333.6
Animal feeding stuffs	0.3	5.4	129.7	1,799.3
Tobacco and manufactures	117.1	12.5	150.9	1,558.9
Oilseeds, nuts, and kernels	8.8	0.6	262.4	2,204.9
Wood and manufactures	385.4	54.9	61.1	1,126.9
Pulp	278.1	12.0	47.8	1,049.4
Ores, slag, and ash	224.1	159.4	572.2	3,465.8
Of which:				
Iron ore	167.6	155.2	569.8	3,251.1
Mineral fuels	197.0	9.4	3.6	353.2
Animal and vegetable oils and fats	34.4	9.3	9.3	982.9
Chemicals[a]	445.5	853.5	201.1	3,444.8
Paper, etc., and manufactures	88.1	278.2	13.2	929.9
Textiles fibers and manufactures	134.6	292.9	39.9	935.2
Nonmetallic mineral manufactures[b]	506.6	97.8	66.8	1,233.7
Iron and steel and manufactures[c]	1,219.2	403.1	127.5	4,058.5
Aluminum and manufactures[c]	71.7	81.6	1.5	1,137.4
Tools, etc., and misc. metal manufactures	39.3	85.5	4.7	294.8
Machinery, excluding electrical	1,320.1	927.0	349.4	4,338.3
Electrical machinery	585.0	343.0	54.5	1,712.1
Road vehicles and tractors	424.2	2,036.8	181.3	4,975.2
Aircraft	947.0	2.5	1.0	1,317.6
Footwear	921.9	75.5	31.3	1,387.1
Scientific instruments, etc.	150.9	88.5	8.4	569.0
Total, including others	**9,888.9**	**6,747.1**	**3,005.7**	**51,119.9**
IMPORTS CIF				
Food	344.2	2,583.7	51.0	5,096.3
Of which:				
Cereals and preparations	150.4	1,454.0	22.5	2,261.3
Rubber and manufactures	229.2	80.0	63.1	959.9
Mineral fuels	520.2	760.6	16.2	5,615.9
Chemicals[a]	3,420.7	599.5	1,142.1	10,374.3
Paper, etc., and manufactures	334.2	56.7	73.7	982.8
Textile fibers and manufactures	244.0	341.4	25.3	1,691.7
Nonmetallic mineral manufactures[b]	110.3	26.6	66.3	615.5
Iron and steel and manufactures[c]	247.7	121.3	166.5	1,479.3
Nonferrous metals and manufactures[c]	329.7	31.7	134.5	1,134.8
Tools, etc., and misc. metal manufactures	123.0	15.7	101.8	488.5
Machinery, excluding electrical	3,542.2	398.7	1,789.7	11,014.5
Electrical machinery	2,425.0	148.9	740.1	8,192.9
Road vehicles and tractors	518.5	2,646.9	599.3	5,853.3
Aircraft	318.0	0.1	18.6	957.5
Scientific instruments, etc.	1,049.2	37.0	322.4	2,586.7
Total, including others	**14,318.7**	**8,421.2**	**5,462.9**	**57,732.0**

SOURCE: United Nations, Trade Statistics; EIU Country Profile 2000

[a]Including crude fertilizers and manufacture of plastics. [b]Including precious metals and jewelry. [c]Including scrap.

EXHIBIT 6.7E   **TRADE FLOWS BY REGION (1995-1999)**

	1995		1996		1997		1998		1999	
	Exports	Imports	Exports	Imports	Exports	Imports	Exports	Imports	Exports	Imports
Total (US$ millions)	46,506	49,972	47,747	53,346	52,994	59,837	51,140	57,734	48,011	49,222
Total (%)	100.0%	100.0%	100.0%	100.0%	100.0%	100.0%	100.0%	100.0%	100.0%	100.0%
Mercosur	13.2%	13.7%	15.3%	15.6%	17.1%	15.9%	17.4%	16.3%	14.1%	13.7%
Argentina	8.7%	11.2%	10.8%	12.8%	12.8%	13.4%	13.2%	13.9%	11.2%	11.8%
Paraguay	2.8%	1.0%	2.8%	1.0%	2.7%	0.9%	2.4%	0.6%	1.6%	0.5%
Uruguay	1.7%	1.5%	1.7%	1.8%	1.6%	1.6%	1.7%	1.8%	1.4%	1.3%
Chile	2.6%	2.2%	2.2%	1.7%	2.3%	1.6%	2.0%	1.4%	1.9%	1.5%
Mexico	1.1%	1.6%	1.4%	1.8%	1.6%	2.0%	2.0%	1.7%	2.2%	1.3%
Asia	16.8%	16.1%	15.8%	13.9%	13.9%	14.7%	10.5%	13.3%	11.5%	12.8%
China	2.6%	2.1%	2.3%	2.1%	2.1%	1.9%	1.8%	1.8%	1.4%	1.8%
Korea	1.8%	2.7%	1.8%	2.2%	1.4%	2.3%	0.9%	1.7%	1.3%	2.1%
Japan	6.7%	6.6%	6.4%	5.2%	5.8%	5.9%	4.3%	5.7%	4.6%	5.2%
Canada	1.0%	2.3%	1.1%	2.4%	1.1%	2.4%	1.1%	2.3%	1.1%	2.0%
European Union	27.8%	27.7%	26.9%	26.7%	27.4%	26.5%	28.8%	29.2%	28.6%	30.4%
Germany	4.6%	9.6%	4.4%	9.1%	4.9%	8.3%	5.9%	9.1%	5.3%	9.6%
France	2.2%	2.8%	1.9%	2.5%	2.1%	2.7%	2.4%	3.4%	2.5%	4.0%
Italy	3.7%	5.7%	3.2%	5.5%	3.2%	5.7%	3.8%	5.6%	3.8%	5.3%
United States	18.9%	21.3%	19.5%	22.4%	17.8%	23.2%	19.3%	23.7%	22.6%	24.1%

SOURCE: Central Bank of Brazil.

EXHIBIT 6.8 **TARIFF COMPARISON: BRAZIL AND THE UNITED STATES (1999)**

U.S. Tariffs for 15 Leading Brazil Global Exports	Ad Valorem Equivalent (%)	Brazilian Tariffs for 15 Leading U.S. Global Exports	Ad Valorem Equivalent (%)
Coffee, not roasted, not decaffeinated	0.0	New passenger transports W gt>15,000Kg	3.0
Iron ores and concentrates, not agglomerated	0.0	Parts for automatic data processing machines	24.0
Soybeans, whether or not broken	0.0	Chips, W frs digital monolithic integrated circuits	3.0
Oilcake and other solid residues from the extraction of soybean	0.8	Parts and accessories for vehicles	21.0
Turbojet airplanes, exceeding 7,000 kg but not 15,000 kg	0.0	Other parts of civil airplanes/helicopters	3.0
Orange juice, frozen	44.7	Other parts and accessories passenger vehicle	18.0
Chemical woodpulp	0.0	Parts of turbojet and turbopropeller A/C eng, civil	3.0
Cane sugar, raw	236.0	Control units of data processing machines	15.0[a]
Iron ores and concentrates	0.0	Passenger veh. new, >= 3000 cc, 6 cyl.	35.0
Women's leather footwear	10.0	Engines F road truck, bus, auto, ov 2000 cc	21.0
Aluminum	2.6	Soybeans, whether or not broken	11.0
Other semimanufactured articles of iron or steel	2.1	Monolithic integrated circuits digital	5.0
Other cane sugars in solid form	18.2	Vehicles, new, eng. exc. 1,500, exc. 3,000 cc <= 4 cyl.	35.0
Unmanufactured tobacco, processed for use in cigarettes	350.0	Gold bullion unwrought, nonmonetary	3.0
Soybean oil, crude	19.7	Digital processing units	30.0
Average tariff	**45.6**	**Average tariff**	**14.3**

Percent share of above items in total Brazil exports: 36.4

Percent share of above items in total U.S. exports: 18.1

SOURCE: Brazilian Embassy.

[a] Average.

EXHIBIT 6.9 **SOCIO-ECONOMIC DEVELOPMENT, VARIOUS COUNTRIES (1998)**

	Brazil	Mexico	Argentina	Chile	India	United States	Japan	Germany	China	Korea
GDP per capita (PPP 1998)	6,625	7,704	12,013	8,787	2,077	29,605	23,257	25,512	3,105	13,478
Life expectancy at birth (years)	67.0	72.3	73.1	75.1	62.9	76.8	80.0	77.3	70.1	72.6
Adult literacy rate (age 15 above)	84.5	90.8	96.7	95.4	55.7	99.0	99.0	99.0	82.8	97.5
Population without access (%):										
to safe water	24.0	15.0	29.0	9.0	19.0	N/A	N/A	N/A	33.0	7.0
to health services	N/A	9.0	N/A	5.0	25.0	N/A	N/A	N/A	N/A	0.0
to sanitation	30.0	28.0	32.0	N/A	71.0	N/A	N/A	N/A	76.0	0.0
Doctors/100,000 people	134.0	85.0	268.0	108.0	48.0	245.0	177.0	319.0	115.0	127.0
TVs/1,000 people	316.0	261.0	289.0	232.0	69.0	847.0	707.0	580.0	272.0	346.0
PCs/1,000 people	30.0	47.0	39.0	48.0	3.0	459.0	237.0	305.0	9.0	157.0
Main phone lines/1,000 people	121.0	104.0	203.0	205.0	22.0	661.0	503.0	567.0	70.0	433.0
Internet hosts/1,000 people	1.3	1.2	1.8	2.0	0.0	112.8	13.3	17.7	0.0	4.0

SOURCE: Human Development Report—United Nations Development Programme.

EXHIBIT 6.10A	INCOME DISTRIBUTION IN BRAZIL (1960-1996)

	Income Distribution		
Year	Lower 40%	Top 10%	Gini Coefficient
1960	11.3	39.6	0.50
1970	10.0	46.5	0.57
1980	9.7	47.9	0.59
1990	7.2	48.7	0.63
1996	8.0	47.6	0.60

SOURCE: World Bank, World Development Indicators, several years.

EXHIBIT 6.10B	INCOME DISTRIBUTION IN SELECT COUNTRIES, 1999

% Income Controlled by:	Brazil	Chile	Mexico	United States
Lowest 20%	2.5	3.5	3.6	4.8
Second 20%	5.7	6.6	7.2	10.5
Third 20%	9.9	10.9	11.8	16.0
Fourth 20%	17.7	18.1	19.1	23.5
Highest 20%	64.2	61.0	58.2	45.2
Highest 10%	47.9	46.1	42.8	28.5

SOURCE: World Bank, World Development Indicators, 1999.

Note: May not add up to 100% due to rounding.

EXHIBIT 6.11 INDICATORS OF ECONOMIC DEVELOPMENT—1998

Country	Population (millions)	Surface Area ('000 sq.miles)	GNP ($billions)	GNP per Capita ($)	PPP GNP per Capita ($)	Mean Tariff (%)	Trade in Goods (% of PPP GDP)	Value Added as a % of GDP				Total External Debt
								Agriculture	Industry	Manufacturing	Service	
Mercosur												
Argentina	36	2,780	290.3	8,030	11,728	13.5	12.9	7	37	25	56	144,050
Brazil	166	8,457	767.6	4,630	6,460	14.6	9.9	8	36	23	56	243,202
Paraguay	5	407	9.2	1,760	4,312[b]	9.5	34.7	25	22	15	53	2,304
Uruguay	3	177	20.0	6,070	8,451	12.2	22.7	8	27	18	64	7,600
Other Developing												
Chile	15	757	73.9	4,990	8,507	11.0	24.7	8	35	17	57	36,302
Mexico	96	1,958	368.1	3,840	7,450	13.3	32.9	5	27	20	68	159,959
China	1,239	9,597[c]	923.6	750	3,051	17.5	8.3	18	49	37	33	154,599
Developed												
Canada	30	9,971	580.9	19,170	22,814	7.5	59.0	--	--	--	--	--
France	59	552	1,465.4[d]	24,210[d]	21,214	--	46.3	2	26	19	72	--
Japan	126	387	4,089.1	32,350	23,592	5.7	21.3	--	--	--	--	--
United Kingdom	59	245	1,264.3	21,410	20,640	--	48.1	2	31	21	67	--
United States	270	9,364	7,903.0	29,240	29,240	5.2	19.9	2	27	18	71	--

SOURCE: World Bank, World Development Indicators

[a] PPP is purchasing power parity.

[b] The estimate is based on regression; others are extrapolated from the latest International Comparison Program benchmark estimates.

[c] Includes Taiwan, China.

[d] GNP and GNP per capita estimates include the French overseas departments of French Guiana, Guadeloupe, Martinique, and Reunion.

ENDNOTES

1   For an overview of the academic literature, see Jagdish Bhagwati, "Regionalism and Multilateralism: An Overview," in *Trading Blocs: Alternative Approaches to Analyzing Preferential Trade Agreements,* ed. Jagdish Bhagwati, Pravin Krishna and Arvind Panagariya (Cambridge, MA: MIT Press, 1999) pp. 3-31; Paul Krugman, "Is Bilateralism Bad?" *International Trade and Trade Policy,* ed. Elhanan Helpman and Assaf Razin (Cambridge: MIT Press, 1991) pp. 9-23; Jeffrey Frankel *Regional Trading Blocs* (Washington, D.C.: Institute for International Economics, 1997); Anne Krueger, "Introduction" in *The WTO as an International Organization,* ed. Anne Krueger (Chicago: The University of Chicago Press, 1998) pp. 1-30; T.N. Srinivasan, "Regionalism and the WTO: Is Nondiscrimination Passé?" in *The WTO as an International Organization,* ed. Anne Krueger (Chicago: The University of Chicago Press, 1998) pp. 329-352; Michael Finger and Alan Winters, "What Can the WTO Do for the Developing Countries?" in *The WTO as an International Organization,* ed. Anne Krueger (Chicago: The University of Chicago Press, 1998) pp. 365-400; On Mercosur, see Luigi Manzetti, "The Political Economy of Mercosur" in *Modern Political Economy and Latin America. Theory and Policy,* ed. Jeffry Frieden, Manuel Pastor Jr., and Michael Tomz (Boulder, CO: Westview Press, 2000); Barry Eichengreen "Does Mercosur Need a Single Currency?" Working Paper, University of California, Berkeley (1998); Alfonso Bevilaqua, Marcelo Catena, and Ernesto Talvi "Integration, Interdependence and Regional Goods: An Application to Mercosur," *Journal Economia,* vol. 2, no. 1 (Washington, D.C.: Brookings Institute Press, 2001) pp. 153-200.

2   Taken from Jose Roberto Mendonca de Barros, "A década do Brasil," *Examen,* 2000.

3   *Country Report: Brazil 2000.* Economist Intelligence Unit (EIU), <www.eiu.com, 2000>.

4   *Country Report: Brazil 2000.* Economist Intelligence Unit (EIU), <www.eiu.com, 2000>.

5   T. Lynn Smith, "The People of Brazil and Their Characteristics," *Modern Brazil: New Patterns and Development,* ed. John Saunders (Gainesville, FL: University of Florida, 1971).

6   Folha de São Paulo - 23 de abril de 2000. Poll by Data Folha.

7   See http://www.ipeadata.gov.br - Social Indicators.

8   Barros and Urani (1992) show that if wage differentials by education level are eliminated, labor income inequalities in Brazil would be reduced by almost 50%. See Eliana Cardoso, Ricardo Paes de Barros, and Andre Urani, "Inflation and Unemployment as Determinants of Inequality in Brazil: The 1980s," *Reform, Recovery and Growth: Latin America and the Middle East,* ed. Rudiger Dornbusch and Sebastian Edwards (Chicago, IL: University of Chicago Press, 1995).

9   Diane Jean Schemo, "Companies Pitch in Where Public Education Leaves Off," *New York Times,* July 16, 1998.

10   The bark of the tree "pau brasil" or Brazil-wood was used as dyestuff in Europe.

11   There were smaller cycles of cotton, cacao, and rubber.

12   Werner Baer, *The Brazilian Economy; Growth and Development* (Westport, CT: Praeger, 1995) p. 18.

13   In August 1931, the government suspended foreign debt payments and began to negotiate a debt consolidation agreement.

14   Baer, op. cit., p. 41.

15   See Paul R. Krugman and Maurice Obstfeld, *International Economics: Theory and Policy,* 5th ed. (New York, NY: Addison-Wesley, 2000) pp. 713-714.

16   Given the absence of adequate capital markets, the BNDE (currently the BNDES, the National Bank of Economic and Social Development), Brazil's development bank, was created in 1952 to help plan and finance infrastructure and industrial projects often at subsidized interest rates.

17   Peter Evans, *Embedded Autonomy: States and Industrial Transformation* (Princeton, NJ: Princeton University Press, 1995) p. 153.

18   According to the economist Albert O. Hirschman, one industry may facilitate the development of another by easing conditions of production in the other and by setting the pace for further rapid industrialization. A "forward linkage" industry is one that lowers the cost of production for another activity. A "backward linkage" raises the demand for another activity. Additionally, the protection of industries may encourage the learning and assimilation of new techniques of production (learning by doing). See Albert O. Hirschman, *The Strategy of Economic Development* (New Haven, CT: Yale University Press, 1958).

19   Baer, op. cit., p. 18.

20   An indexation or monetary correction on financial instruments was instituted. The principal and

interest were readjusted in accordance with the rate of inflation. Later, a monetary correction was applied to taxes and wages.

[21] Baer, op. cit., p. 80.

[22] Helen Shapiro, *Brazil – Managing Structural Change in the 90's*, Harvard Business School Case 391-206 (1993).

[23] Jorge Dominguez, "Order and Progress in Brazil," *Ideology and National Competitiveness: An Analysis of Nine Countries*, ed. George C. Lodge and Ezra F. Vogel (Boston, MA: Harvard Business School Press, 1987) p. 241.

[24] Authors' interview with Antônio Delfim Neto, Finance Minister of Brazil (1968 to 1973), São Paulo, August 2000.

[25] "Survey on Brazil," *The Economist*, March 25, 1999.

[26] Gustavo H.B. Franco, "O Desafio Brasileiro: Ensaios sobre Desenvolvimento, Globalizacão e Moeda," *Editora* 34, 1999, p. 68.

[27] Ibid., p. 73.

[28] In 1998, the telecommunications company Telebras was sold for $19 billion.

[29] The primary balance does not include interest payments.

[30] *Country Report: Brazil 2000*. Economist Intelligence Unit (EIU), <www.eiu.com, 2000>.

[31] "Survey on Brazil," *The Economist*, March 25, 1999.

[32] "A década do Brasil," *Examen*, 2000.

[33] World Bank Development Indicators (All figures are for 1998). OECD Revenue Statistics, 2001.

[34] *Country Report: Brazil 2001*. Economist Intelligence Unit (EIU), <www.eiu.com, 2001>.

[35] Set at R$180 in December 2000.

[36] J.S. Arbache, "Do Unions always Decrease Wage Dispersion? The Case of Brazilian Manufacturing," *Journal of Labor Research*. Working Paper, University of São Paolo (2000).

[37] Data form Mercado do Trabalho. Conjuntura e Analise no. 12, February 2000. National household surveys collected by Brazilian National Statistical Institute. Average data from 1992 to 1997.

[38] "Embargo à carne brasileira já foi superado, afirma Praini," *Estado do São Paolo*, March 13, 2001.

[39] Larry Rohter, "Brazil's Hot Commodity? Not Coffee, Not Soccer," *New York Times*, December 31, 2000.

[40] *Commerce Profile: Brazil 2001*. Economist Intelligence Unit (EIU), <www.eiu.com, 2001>.

[41] "Canada Gets WTO Approval for Sanctions against Brazil," *The Wall Street Journal,* December 13, 2000, p. A21.

[42] "US Joins Canada's Ban of Brazil Beef," *The Wall Street Journal*, February 5, 2001.

[43] "Brasil denuncia Canada em reunião da OMC," *O Estado do São Paolo*, March 15, 2001.

[44] On Mercosur, see Jeffrey Frankel, Ernesto Stein, Shang-jin Wei, "Trading Blocs and the Americas: The Natural, the Unnatural, and the Supernatural," *Journal of Development Economics,* vol. 47, no. 1 (1995) pp. 61-95; P. R. Almeida. "Brasil y el futuro del Mercosur: dilemas y opciones," *Integración y Comercio* (Washington, D.C.: Interamerican Development Bank, 1999); and A. Averbug "Brazilian Trade Liberalization and Integration in the 1990s," Working Paper BDS, 1999; Alfonso Bevilaqua, Marcelo Catena and Ernesto Talvi "Integration, Interdependence and Regional Goods: An Application to Mercosur," *Journal Economia,* vol. 2, no. 1 (Washington, D.C.: Brookings Institute Press, 2001) pp. 153-200.

[45] Wilson Suzigan and Annibal V. Villela, *Industrial Policy in Brazil* (Campinas, Brazil: UNICAMP, 1997) p. 169; Jeffrey Carson, "Democracy Looks South: Mercosur and the Politics of Brazilian Trade Strategy," *Democratic Brazil*, ed. Peter Kingstone and Timothy Power (Pittsburgh, PA: University of Pittsburgh Press, 2000) p. 205.

[46] Luigi Manzetti, "The Political Economy of Mercosur" *Modern Political Economy and Latin America. Theory and Policy*, ed. Jeffry Frieden, Manuel Pastor Jr. and Michael Tomz (Boulder, CO: Westview Press, 2000).

[47] J. Carson, op. cit., p. 208.

[48] For more details on Chile's trade strategy, see Robert Kennedy, *Chile: The Latin American Tiger* Harvard Business School Case 798-092 (1999).

[49] An additional bilateral accord allowed goods manufactured in Brazil's Manus free-trade zone or Argentina's Tierra del Fuego to be traded with full tariff exemptions within Mercosur.

[50] Based on Almeida, op. cit.

[51] On custom unions, see Jacob Viner, *The Customs Unions Issue* (New York, NY: Carnegie Endowment for International Peace, 1950); Richard Lipsey, "The Theory of Custom Unions: General Survey," *The Economic Journal*, vol. 70 (1960) pp. 496-513; Richard Baldwin and Anthony Venables, "Regional Economic Integration" *Handbook of International Economics*, ed. Gene Grossman and Kenneth Rogoff (Amsterdam, Netherlands: Elsevier, 1995) pp. 1597-1640.

52   See Barry Eichengreen, "Does Mercosur Need a Single Currency?" NBER Working Paper W6821, December 1998.

53   *Mercosur Report,* 2000.

54   *Mercosur Report,* 2000.

55   A. Averbug, "Brazilian Trade Liberalization and Integration in the 1990s," Working Paper BDS, 1999.

56   Ministerio de Desenvolvimento, Indústria e Comércio Exterior, "Barreiras externas às exportações Brasileiras," (www.mdic.gov.br, 1999).

57   Ibid.

58   The European Union agreed to begin negotiations on a free-trade area with Mercosur in July 2001, extending until 2005, the same period stipulated for the implementation of the Free-Trade Area of the Americas (FTAA). These deadlines nevertheless remain subject to change.

59   Calculations by Luiz V. Pereira, taken from A. Averbug, "Brazilian Trade Liberalization and Integration in the 1990s," Working Paper BDS, 1999.

60   Based on P. R. Almedia, "Brasil y el futuro del Mercosur: dilemas y opciones" *Integración y Comercio* (Washington, D.C.: Interamerican Development Bank, 1999) and A. Averbug, "Brazilian Trade Liberalization and Integration in the 1990s," Working Paper BDS, 1999.

61   Calculations by Marcelo P. Abreu , taken from A. Averbug, "Brazilian Trade Liberalization and Integration in the 1990s," Working Paper BDS, 1999.

62   Brazilian Ambassador to the U.S. Rubens Barbosa, "Brazil-U.S. Trade: The Export Challenge," *Gazeta Mercantil*, March 9, 2000.

63   Ministério do Desenvolvimento, Indústria e comércio exterior, "Barreiras Externas às exportações Brasileiras." (www.mdic.gov.br, 1999).

64   "O porrete do antidumping," *O Estado de São Paolo*, March 12, 2001.

65   Anne Krueger, "Introduction," *The WTO as an International Organization.* ed. Anne Krueger (Chicago, IL: University of Chicago Press, 1998).

66   Dumping refers to the practice of exporting a product at a price lower than that normally charged in the home market. Governments usually take action against dumping to protect local industries. Taken from www.wto.org.

67   *Report to the President-Global Steel Trade: Structural Problems and Future Solutions,* US Department of Commerce, International Trade Administration, <www.ita.doc.gov>, July 2000.

68   Frances Williams, "Brazil in US Steel Move," *Financial Times*, January 1, 2001.

69   Speech by the U.S. Steel Manufacturing Association, before Members of the Senate and Congressional Steel Caucuses, December 12, 2000.

70   Brazilian Ambassador to the U.S. Rubens Barbosa, "Brazil-U.S. Trade: The Export Challenge," *Gazeta Mercantil*, March 9, 2000.

71   Unless the patent holder can prove that it is economically non-viable to manufacture the product domestically.

72   "U.S., Brazil Clash over AIDS Drugs," *The Washington Post*, February 6, 2001.

73   Tina Rosenberg, "Look at Brazil," *New York Times,* January 28, 2001.

74   Stephen Buckley, "U.S., Brazil Clash over AIDS Drugs; 'Model' Treatment Program, Seen at Risk in Dispute on Patents and Pricing," *The Washington Post*, February 6, 2001; "Look at Brazil," *New York Times,* January 28, 2001.

75   Tina Rosenberg, "Look at Brazil," *New York Times,* January 28, 2001.

76   Stephen Buckley, "U.S., Brazil Clash over AIDS Drugs; 'Model' Treatment Program, Seen at Risk in Dispute on Patents and Pricing," *The Washington Post*, February 6, 2001; "Look at Brazil," *New York Times,* January 28, 2001.

77   "Brazil's AIDS Program Faces a New Threat," *Wall Street Journal Europe*, February 14, 2001.

78   Ibid.

79   "U.S., Brazil Clash over AIDS Drugs," *The Washington Post*, February 6, 2001.

80   Brazilian Ambassador to the U.S. Rubens Barbosa, "Brazil-U.S. Trade: The Export Challenge," *Gazeta Mercantil*, March 9, 2000.

81   Stephen Buckley, "Brazil Moves from Wings to Center Stage," *The Washington Post*, August 6, 2000.

82   "Regional Trade Pacts Thrive as the Big Players Fail to Act," *The New York Times*, December 28, 2000, p. 1.

83   Ibid.

84   Speech delivered by Luiz Felipe Lampreia, Brazil's Foreign Minister at the 55th Session of the General Assembly of the United Nations,

<www.brasilemb.org>, [Brazil's Embassy in US],
September 12, 2000.

The African Renaissance

The end of apartheid by peaceful revolution (between 1989 and 1994) is the turning point in this case. Out of a history of slavery, discrimination, and then brutal apartheid ("apartness"), South Africa finally emerged as a free and democratic state with a black majority-ruled government. At issue in early 1997 is how this government can turn around the decades of damage while simultaneously making South Africa competitive in an open-world economy.

The case describes South African economic performance during the 1990s, as well as the difficult social problems (e.g., unemployment, crime, education, and AIDS) it now faces. Students are expected to evaluate this situation and then consider the new strategy adopted by the African National Congress government in 1996. The GEAR (Growth, Employment and Redistribution) strategy, with its ambitious goals, is a political compromise. Is it feasible? Will it work?

But if not GEAR, then what? The case again provides opportunities to discuss other possible strategies for development—fiscal and monetary choices, industrial policies, trade policies, and others. But one must evaluate them in terms not only of political feasibility, but in the context of an already global world economy.

Finally, the case allows careful consideration of the factors that affect foreign direct investment: issues such as political stability, economic feasibility, growth and profitability. Is the African Renaissance now on a firm footing? Is this the right time to invest in South Africa?

CASE STUDY   SOUTH AFRICA: GETTING IN GEAR

RICHARD H. K. VIETOR

Don't ask the turkeys to vote for Christmas.
—Christopher Stals, Governor,
South African Reserve Bank

Introduction

It was a cool, midwinter evening in Johannesburg as Thabo Mbeki thumbed through the Reserve Bank's *Quarterly Bulletin* for June 1997.[1] The First Deputy President of the Government of National Unity, and likely successor to Nelson Mandela in 1999, wanted to see for himself the latest results of GEAR—the macroeconomic strategy for Growth, Employment and Redistribution that his government had adopted just one year earlier. Mbeki, with a Masters degree in economics from Sussex University, searched the report for signs of good news. Although immensely pleased that South Africa seemed to be politically stable and recovering from apartheid, he was looking for evidence of job creation, private investment, and disinflation. He wondered if Chris Stals was likely to lower interest rates soon to give the South African economy a needed boost.

GEAR was the political and economic culmination of a series of studies and plans undertaken since 1990—the beginning of the end of apartheid. First came the Change of Gears Scenario, proposed by an international team of analysts financed by Nedbank/Old Mutual.[2] Then there were Anglo-American's "High Road - Low Road" scenarios, the Platform for Investment in 1992, the African National Congress's (ANC) Reconstruction and Development Program in 1994, and Growth for All from the business community in 1995.[3] GEAR, released in June 1996, was produced by a technical team supervised by Trevor Manuel, the new Minister of Finance.

The GEAR strategy was designed to deliver real GDP growth of 6% by the year 2000, with job creation of 400,000 per annum. This was more than double the present growth trajectory, but was necessary to cut into structural unemployment, which had already surpassed 37%.[4] In the wake of apartheid the massive unemployment, primarily of black South Africans, underlay a wave of crime and violence that had reached epidemic proportions. Investment and savings, meanwhile, had dropped to record lows. Education, housing, and infrastructure desperately needed attention, while AIDS appeared to be spreading rapidly. With GEAR, the ANC acknowledged the limitations of government and recognized that the market would have to play a major role in rebuilding the economy. But first, to reduce inflation, the government would have to curb fiscal deficits and credit growth. Although the Reserve Bank's effort appeared to be working, it left too few funds for needed programs and had pushed real short-term interest rates to 12%.

As he looked over the figures, Mbeki wondered if macroeconomic growth would be rapid enough to ease South Africa's severe social problems and sustain the extraordinary political stability that currently prevailed. Perhaps, he thought, more was needed than macroeconomic reform—possibly a more aggressive microeconomic strategy—to reposition South Africa in the increasingly competitive global economy.

Historical Context

In total area, South Africa is nearly as large as Western Europe minus Spain, and is home to about 44 million people.[5] It is divided into two main regions: a relatively arid inland plateau, fringed by coastal plains on three sides. An escarpment, dominated by the Drakensberg Mountains, separates the two. Climatically, it is divided into a winter-rainfall area in the southwest and one of summer- rainfall in the east. [See **Exhibit 7.1**.] The zones were sufficiently different that relatively little interaction occurred between the pastoral people of the west (KhoiSan) and the iron-age cultivators (Bantu tribes) that occupied the east (Transvaal, Natal, Highveld) in the centuries prior to 1000 A.D.[6] There are relatively few rivers or lakes in South Africa, but the coastline stretches 2,900 kilometers. South Africa shares borders with Namibia, Botswana, Zimbabwe, Swaziland, and Mozambique, and completely surrounds Lesotho.

Conquest by Europeans

European settlers, representing the Dutch East India Company, established a fort and refueling station at Table Bay (Cape Town) in 1652. For the remainder of the century, immigrants gradually encroached on the grazing lands of Khoikhoi herders. Slave labor was imported from elsewhere in Africa, from Malaya, and from India. As colonial farmers penetrated northward, conflict between the Dutch and the Khoikhoi became endemic.[7] By the mid-eighteenth century, colonial settlers had begun extending control over indigenous laborers, enforcing travel passes for the "bastard hottentots" and indenturing women and children. The Europeans' dialect, a simplified form of Dutch, evolved into the Afrikaans language. By 1795, the Xhosa tribes in the east came increasingly into conflict with colonists to the south and with competing African tribes.[8] In the early 1800s, a series of inter-tribal wars broke out, in which the Zulus, headed by Shaka, dominated for almost a decade.

Meanwhile, the British had captured Cape Town from the Dutch and had established a crown colony in 1806. Two years later, the slave trade was curtailed and, before long, anti-slavery sentiment in Great Britain put increasing pressure on South African slave owners. In 1828, Parliament outlawed slave ownership. Two days later, the governor of the Cape Colony promulgated Ordinance 50—making "hottentots and other free people of colour" equal before the law with whites. The law, which was opposed by British settlers and Afrikaners, did not curtail discrimination, eliminate poverty, or usurp entrenched domination by whites.

Afrikaners who could not tolerate British domination picked up stakes and migrated northeast, to find new lands in territories they named Natal, the Orange Free State, and the Transvaal. "The Great Trek", between 1836 and 1854, brought Afrikaners into conflict with the Zulus, and western rifles invariably prevailed. Over the next 30 years, European expansion into the northeast was marked by near constant warfare with Zulu and other African tribes and the repeated reassertion of British colonial authority over new Afrikaner states.

As early as the 1860s, distinctions among four racial/ethnocultural groups were emerging in the Cape Colony. Census data in 1865 reported 180,000 Europeans (British and Afrikaners), 200,000 Hottentots and others collectively called "coloured," 100,000 Kaffirs—the black Africans who dominated eastern populations—and a few thousand Asians.[9]

In 1867, alluvial diamonds were found at the confluence of the Vaal and Harts rivers. Several years later, diamond-bearing formations were discovered, extending deep below the surface of what became Kimberly—the diamond city. As mining moved underground, masses of people were required to do manual labor. Skilled operatives, mostly white Europeans, commanded high wages, while manual labor, mostly black Africans, were paid far less. After a few chaotic years, the British high commissioner issued rules that *defacto* excluded black persons from owning mines. Gradually, a two-tiered, racially segregated workforce and migratory social system emerged. By 1887, a British immigrant named Cecil Rhodes had acquired control of the Kimberly mines, renamed deBeers Consolidated Mines.[10] About the same time, gold was discovered 30 miles from Pretoria—at what is today Johannesburg. Together, these discoveries, which inspired an immense immigration, changed the face of South Africa. Eventually, platinum, chrome, and other rare ores were discovered, making South Africa the world's leading producer of rare minerals [see **Exhibit 7.2**].

The mining boom in the Transvaal led to a rapid expansion of British immigration and growing friction with the established Afrikaner population. The quasi-autonomous Transvaal Republic was managed by an elective Volksraad and a president named Paul Kruger. Kruger's efforts during the 1890s to expand Transvaal were thwarted by Cecil Rhodes, then governor of the Cape Colony. An attempted insurrection by British settlers led to a clampdown by Kruger, the importation of arms, and a tighter alliance with the Orange Free State. When negotiations failed, the Boer War ensued, lasting three years—from 1899 to 1902. The British engaged in a scorched earth policy, leaving thousands of Afrikaner women and children to die in concentration camps.

British victory and the Peace of Vereeniging led to the establishment of British colonial rule. South Africa would be, in the words of Lord High Commissioner Alfred Milner, "a self-governing white community, supported by well-treated and justly-governed black labour from Cape Town to Zambesi."[11] Black Africans were disenfranchised, "pass laws" restricting travel were tightened, and labor conditions were enforced by the military. Colonial elections, held in 1907, resulted in Afrikaner victories for Louis Botha and Jan Smuts. Within two more years a constitution was drafted and in 1909, the British Parliament passed the South Africa Act. On May 31, 1910, the Union of South Africa became a self-governing dominion of the British Empire.

Segregation

The era of formal segregation—1910 to 1948—was a period dominated by racist assumptions in Africa, much of Asia, and America. In South Africa, where whites dominated the capitalist economy, race and class coincided, blacks were poor, unskilled, and uneducated and were generally subordinate to whites. Even in industrial relations, race mattered. White mineworkers earned 11 to 15 times as much as black mineworkers. And as the material gap between whites and other ethnic groups narrowed, it widened between whites and blacks. In the 1990s, the top 10% of South Africa's population earned 67 times that of the bottom 20%.[12]

During the 1910 to 1948 era, the United Party, lead by Botha and Smuts, ruled an increasingly racist state. In 1911, the Mines and Works Act granted white workers a monopoly on skilled positions. In 1913, the Natives Land Act prohibited Africans from purchasing land outside the reserves. Subsequent legislation set aside 12% of South Africa's lands as native reserves—areas that would eventually become the "homelands." As urbanization accelerated, the government tried to limit the flow of Africans into cities with complex pass laws. Permits were required to leave the farm where one lived or the town where one worked. A 1922 law authorized urban governments to establish and enforce locations for black residence.

Black South Africans resisted, but gradually adapted. They formed various political organizations; the most important turned out to be the African National Congress, established in 1912. The ANC, headed by lawyers, clergy, and journalists, elicited white support and used constitutional means to oppose racism. More radical organizations, such as the Industrial and Commercial Workers Union, were ruthlessly suppressed.[13] During World War II, a group of young ANC activists developed a platform against segregation: *Africans' Claims in South Africa*. Among these activists were young professionals from the best missionary schools and colleges, including Oliver Tambo, Walter Sisulu, and Nelson Mandela.

But World War II deepened Afrikaners' worries about race relations, because of the massive influx of black Africans into the cities. Literary and political debate ensued over the need for complete separation of races. A 1946 government report was torn between the appeal of complete segregation and the labor needs of the industrial economy. The word "apartheid" was coined by Afrikaner intellectuals to mean "apartness." When the National Party won the election of 1948, the prime minister appointed Hendrik Verwoerd to the Senate and then to Minister of Native Affairs. Over the next 16 years, the last eight of which Verwoerd was prime minister, apartheid was implemented in its most brutal form.

Apartheid

Four ideas, according to historian Leonard Thompson, were at the heart of apartheid:

> First, the population of South Africa comprised four "racial groups"—White, Coloured, Indian, and African—each with its own inherent culture. Second, Whites, as the civilized race, were entitled to have absolute control over the state. Third, white interests should prevail over black interests; the state was not obliged to provide equal facilities for the subordinate races. Fourth, the white racial group formed a single nation with Afrikaans and the English-speaking components, while Africans belonged to several (eventually 10) [geographically] distinct nations or potential nations—a formula that made the white nation the largest in the country.[14]

These ideas were shortly written into law: the Prohibition of Mixed Marriages Act, the Immorality Act, and the Population Registration Act. Pass laws were strengthened, and Africans were removed from farms to homelands and from urban neighborhoods to satellite townships. Under the Group Areas Act (1950), government divided cities into zones where members of only one race could live. An estimated 3 million people were forcibly resettled from farms, "black spots," and strategic development areas to the new townships. These were fenced and guarded. Working papers were needed for residents to come and go. The government took charge and severely constrained the education of black Africans. "If the native in South Africa today," testified Dr. Verwoerd in 1953, "is being taught to expect that he will live his adult life under a policy of equal rights, he is making a big mistake."[15] "Whites Only" notices appeared everywhere—taxis, buses, elevators, hearses, church halls, restaurants, cinemas, schools, and universities.

Repressive legislation continued to be approved: the Riotous Assemblies Act (1956), the Unlawful Organizations Act (1960), the Sabotage Act (1962), the Bantu Laws Amendment Act (1964), the General Law Amendment Act (1966), the Internal Security Act (1976), and so on. To enforce apartheid, the bureaucracy was expanded and a large Security Force operated with increasing impunity. By 1969, even white South Africans bluntly acknowledged the implications of apartheid. As C. M. Botha, the Minister of Bantu Administration, put it in Parliamentary debate,

> For whites and for each Bantu Nation separate development is the course. Bantu person can be present in the white areas solely for their labour—not for a stake or a share in the Parliament, or for anything else…. The Bantu cannot strive towards the top on an equal footing with the whites in our politics, social matters, labour, economy and education in white South Africa. This is our territory, and here there are only limited opportunities of that nature for them….In their homelands there are measureless and limitless opportunities for them….That is the morality of our policy.[16]

Under the combined weight of poverty, repression, and forced resettlement, black community structure broke down. In Soweto, with a population of over four million today, 8 to 20 people lived in typical four-room houses; many lived in two-room shacks, thrown together with cardboard, scrap lumber, and corrugated metal, that had sprung up after influx control laws collapsed in the mid-1980s. In Crossroads, outside of Cape Town, 25,000 people shared a single water tap. Uneducated children stole to survive and eventually acquired arms.

Opposition to apartheid swelled. The laws of the early 1950s were actively protested by the African National Congress. Marches and meetings were repeatedly broken up by police with thousands of volunteers arrested and jailed. In 1955, a huge meeting was organized in Kliptown, a village near Johannesburg. Three thousand delegates assembled as the Congress of the People, adopting the following charter:

> We the People of South Africa declare for our country and the world to know that South Africa belongs to all who live in it, black and white, and that no government can justly claim authority unless it is based on the will of all the people.[17]

As violence escalated, nonviolent protest became increasingly difficult to sustain. In 1960, when 5,000 people demonstrated peacefully against pass laws in Sharpeville, the police opened fire and killed 69, half of whom were women and children. This tragedy finally pushed the ANC leadership toward violence. Nelson Mandela organized Umkonto we Sizwe as a militant wing, with the following manifesto: "The time comes in the life of any nation when there remain only two choices—submit or fight. That time has come to South Africa." [18]

In 1963, the government arrested leaders of Umkonto we Sizwe. Among them, Nelson Mandela and Walter Sisulu received life sentences on Robben Island. A few years later, a 22-year-old student named Steve Biko formed the South African Students Organization and began developing the ideology of Black Consciousness. In 1976, when black schoolchildren demonstrated in Soweto, a police crackdown eventually led to the killing of 575 people. Dozens of black South Africans died in detention by the Security Force. Steve Biko was among those arrested, beaten, and killed in August 1977.[19]

Later that year, the UN Security Council imposed an arms embargo on South Africa, and Vice-President Walter Mondale told Prime Minister Vorster that America supported majority rule. During the next several years, South Africa's foreign relations deteriorated sharply, as more and more foreign powers denounced apartheid. The government, meanwhile, imported oil and invested heavily in the economy to duplicate imported sources of capital goods. In 1985, Chase Manhattan Bank precipitated a financial crisis by refusing to roll over its loans to South Africa. In the wake of intensive citizen action, and over President Reagan's veto, the U.S. Congress passed the Comprehensive Anti-Apartheid Act, imposing a wide-ranging boycott on commerce with South Africa.

GDP growth had long since begun to slow, from a high of 6.5% in the mid-1960s to zero by 1986. Total factor productivity, which had slowed during the 1960s, became negative in the 1970s. It did not help that the real exchange rate actually rose in the 1970s when the price of gold rose to $800/per ounce. Income per capita peaked in 1981, long before sanctions were applied. Appreciation of the rand made South African-manufactured exports less competitive, causing a decline of investment, turning the current account negative, and undermining job creation.[20]

As the domestic situation deteriorated, the government began searching for reform. Some of the worst segregation laws were amended and a series of dialogues commenced between ANC members in exile, church leaders, government officials, and business leaders. The economy, meanwhile, plunged into a deep recession, putting even greater pressure on the government. In 1989, when Prime Minister Botha resigned after a stroke, the National Party elected F.W. de Klerk in his place. De Klerk, nearly 20 years younger than Botha, realized that a negotiated settlement was the only feasible solution. On February 2, 1990, he lifted the bans on the ANC and the Pan African Congress, removed restrictions on 33 other organizations, suspended capital punishment, and freed political prisoners. Nine days later, after 27 years in prison, Nelson Mandela was released to a tumultuous public welcome.

Later that year, the basic apartheid laws were repealed. Two more years of talks led to an interim constitution endorsed by de Klerk, Mandela, and 18 political parties. In April 1994, South African citizens went to the polls in a surprisingly free and peaceful election and gave the ANC 63% of the vote. Nelson Mandela was inaugurated as president on May 10, 1994.

The New South Africa

The constitution, approved in December 1996, established a federal system of government: a two-house national parliament and nine provinces—each with a premier, regional legislature, and significant local authority. The parliament consisted of a 400-seat National Assembly, with direct elections and universal suffrage and a 90-seat Senate appointed proportionally by elected parties. President (Nelson Mandela) and Deputy President (T.M. Mbeki) represented the dominant party—the African National Congress (with 252 seats); the National Party (with 82 seats) was also represented by a Deputy President (F.W. de Klerk), until he resigned in 1996. The Zulu-dominated Inkatha Freedom Party (with 43 seats) was lead by M.G. Buthelezi, who occupied the Ministry of Home Affairs. A cabinet of 27 ministers ran the executive branch. The president appointed a supreme court to head a three-tiered court system. Other distinctive features included a Bill of Rights, a council of traditional leaders, recognition of 11 official languages, and such specialized institutions as a public protector and a commission on human rights.

Gauteng was the smallest of the nine new states, but it had the largest, most urban population (in Johannesburg, Soweto, and Pretoria), the largest share of disposable income, and the highest population growth. The Western Cape, with the second-largest city of Cape Town, also had a large share of disposable income, relatively low poverty, and a concentration of business. KwaZulu-Natal, where the city of Durban was located, was the third-largest province by population and disposable income.

Because of the government's relatively high investment during the 1970s, South Africa's infrastructure, primarily serving the white population, was unusually well-developed. Eskom, the state electric company, provided nearly 40,000 megawatts of power, at a mere 2.3 U.S. cents (compared to 7 cents, for example, in the United States) per kilowatt-hour. Twenty-one thousand kilometers of railroads, 58,000 km of highways, 5 million telephone connections, modern radio and television broadcasters, port facilities, and air transportation all made South Africa seem much like a European country. SASOL, the state petrochemical company, provided 45% of the nation's liquid fuel from coal, using unique liquefaction technology. A system of state-owned industrial and medical laboratories yielded a first-world health-care system (for whites) and a weapons industry that was globally competitive.

South Africa's private business sector was modern but relatively labor-intensive and high-cost compared to global competitors. The mining industry accounted for about 9% of South Africa's GDP, nearly 50% of foreign exchange earnings, and provided 600,000 jobs. Half a dozen ores led world production, with a host of others providing export revenues and most domestic needs. Agriculture (and forestry) was another successful sector, producing about 5% of GDP. South Africa was one of only six countries that was regularly a net food exporter. In addition to grains, meats, and most vegetables, South Africa also exported citrus fruits and fine wines. The timber industry provided 90% of South Africa's pulp and paper needs.

A third of South Africa's manufacturing sector was in metals refining and manufacturing. Ferroalloys and aluminum were exported, as were heavy fabrications. Electrical engineering and electronics were also successful sectors. Manufacturing contributed 24% of GDP and employed about 1.5 million. The finance sector—banks, insurance, brokerage firms, and building societies—was quite modern, although somewhat high-cost. The Johannesburg Stock Exchange was the twelfth-largest in the world, with market capitalization of $224 billion.[21]

Because of the years of inward-looking protectionism, South Africa's business structure was highly concentrated. Corporate acquisitions during apartheid (buy firms using their protected cash flows) resulted in a number of interlocking conglomerates, dominated by a few financial institutions. Old Mutual, Sanlam, SBIC, and ABSA each controlled more than R100 billion in assets; FNB, Anglo American, Liberty Life, Nedcor, and Investec followed with more than R50 billion. Eskom, the state electric utility, was tenth. Two dozen other financial companies, including three new black-owned conglomerates, and industrials, food companies, and mining houses followed—70 firms each with more than R4 billion in assets. There were also many large multinational firms—headed by Royal Dutch Shell, Daimler-Benz, Siemens, and Volkswagen—active in South Africa, although foreign investment still had not recovered from

the trough of the Apartheid era [see **Exhibit 7.3**].[22]

"Unbundling" and "black empowerment" were structural phenomena that had proceeded hand in hand since 1994. Unbundling referred to restructuring of business ownership by the selling off of diverse operating units owned by the large conglomerates. To ameliorate racial criticism, black empowerment encouraged the rise of black managers to senior executive positions, mostly in public-sector firms, and more specifically, the emergence of black-owned or black-controlled conglomerates. Through the use of pension funds from black unions, and leveraged buyouts, a series of increasingly large mergers had resulted in 18 black-controlled firms listed on the Johannesburg Stock Exchange[23] [see **Exhibit 7.4**]. Led by spin-offs from Anglo American of Johnic and JCI, more and more black-owned conglomerates had catapulted into the financial limelight. Metlife, New Africa Investment Ltd. (NAIL), and a dozen other firms controlled about R35 billion in assets.[24] A new black business leadership, headed by Cyril Ramaphosa, Dikgang Moseneke, and others was emerging. While they still had much to learn, their holding companies were at least performing satisfactorily.[25]

South Africa had a well-developed system of labor organizations. In 1996, there were some 200 unions, representing about 3.5 million workers. These were organized into several federations, the largest of which was the Congress of South African Trade Unions (COSATU, with 1.6 million members)—an ally of the ANC. After the 1994 election, organized labor negotiated with business and government in a trilateral forum—the National Economic Development and Labour Council (Nedlac). In the Labour Relations Act of 1995, the parliament promoted collective bargaining without compelling it. The Act created bargaining councils for wages, workplace forums for plant-level issues, and a Commission for Conciliation, Mediation, and Arbitration. In this format, large conglomerates of cartelized firms would settle on relatively generous terms, leaving small firms unable to make such concessions and thus unable to compete.[26]

In 1997, problems were deepening between COSATU, the business community, and the ANC government. A Basic Conditions of Employment Act was pending, which would reduce weekly hours worked (from 46 to 45), increase overtime pay, and provide paid maternity leave of up to four months. Two other amendments were pending that would provide a payroll tax to ensure training and an affirmative action scheme. Although both laws obviously were well intended, they would entail complex regulation and greater cost—neither of which the business community needed as it struggled to become competitive.[27] COSATU, moreover, had withdrawn its support of the GEAR and was beginning to agitate for more government spending to reduce unemployment.

Social Challenges

In the wake of the post-apartheid boom, South Africa faced severe social challenges. Among the most pressing of these were crime, education, unemployment, infrastructural expansion (housing, electrification, and water), internal migration, immigration (and emigration), and AIDS. Racial issues bound most of these problems together.

Crime

Crime in South Africa had become endemic. As recently as the 1970s, South Africa had been a fairly low-crime society. But family and community life became increasingly fragmented as an immense number of black South Africans migrated from the countryside to the cities. Unemployment, poverty, and the new urban environment broke down the values that had governed personal and family relationships. This situation was exacerbated by years of civilian resistance to authoritarian government in the wake of the Soweto uprising. It became increasingly acceptable for armed teenage dropouts to attack the systems that had oppressed them. Violence and theft escalated as the government liberalized the Group Areas Act after 1986. Criminal syndicates eventually developed to organize the drug trade, auto theft, and truck hijacking.

The most serious problems were murder, rape, motor vehicle theft, and robbery. Rapes had doubled over the past six years, and murder was up 51%. In 1996, 26,000 people were murdered in South Africa. This was more than eight times the rate in the United States, which itself had the highest rate of the developed countries. More than 96,000 motor vehicles were stolen (three times the rate, per-thousand-vehicle, of the

United States) and 13,000 hijacked (the driver was present); 3,700 trucks were hijacked.[28] Even political violence, while down from 1994, remained high—with 1,000 deaths and 1,600 injuries in a year.[29] A total of more than 2 million serious crimes was reported in 1996—about one for every 21 citizens.

Fear of crime had become palpable in some areas, such as Johannesburg, to the point where people had changed their behavior. Homes were surrounded by high walls with barbed wire fencing and elaborate alarm systems. People thought twice about going out in the evening, about where they parked, and about what belongings they carried. Security services proliferated. Law enforcement, meanwhile, was underfunded, understaffed, and corrupt. The South African Police Service had fewer than half as many officers per capita than did the United States, and they tended to be poorly trained. Some 45,000 officers did not have drivers' licenses and as many as 30,000 were functionally illiterate. Even worse, the judicial system had broken down. Courts were underfunded; prisons were full. Of 1,000 crimes committed, 450 were reported to the police, 230 solved, 100 prosecuted, 77 convicted, 36 imprisoned, and 1 rehabilitated.[30]

Education

The start of the school year in 1996 marked history in South Africa. For the first time in 50 years, discrimination in public schools was ended. A single national education department was now responsible for compulsory education for children ages seven to fifteen. The inequitable expenditures (e.g., R5,403 whites, R2,184 blacks per capita) would be rectified. But the task was sizable. An estimated 37% of the adult population was illiterate; approximately 5 million people over four years old had no education. To meet the needs of 12 million children, expenditures needed to be increased dramatically and redirected. Two thousand new schools, 65,000 new classrooms, and 50 million books would be needed. An average student-to-teacher ratio of 37 to 1 prevailed in primary schools. This ratio ranged as high as 60- or 70-to-1 in some areas.

Teacher training was also essential. About 40% of African teachers were unqualified or underqualified. Many of these teachers needed more basic education, as well as teacher training. State teaching colleges were fully enrolled but underfunded—despite the fact that 20% of the federal budget was being devoted to education.[31] Tertiary education in South Africa was much better, but suffered from the same imbalances of racial discrimination that plagued primary schools. Some 350,000 students were enrolled at South Africa's 21 universities, but the pass rate for black students was far below that for whites. Other issues that had recently arisen included the conversion to more Afro-centric university life and the nonpayment of bills.[32]

Labor

South Africa's labor market was severely distorted. Years of segregation and apartheid had rationed access to education, skills, jobs, housing, and health care according to skin color. To make matters worse, the state implemented various policies that directly undermined the opportunities for much of the population to earn income. As the South Africa Foundation noted, "Forced removals, Group Areas, the Land Act and assaults on the urban informal sector dispossessed millions of people of valuable assets and skills, and undermined the capacity of the economy to provide employment in rural areas…. The legacy of past labour and welfare inequalities is still powerful, and bedevils the efficient functioning of the labour market today."[33]

In the spring of 1997, the formal unemployment rate was 37.8%; the informal rate was estimated to be as high as 45%. The World Bank estimated that South African males aged 15 to 64 had one of the lowest labor force participation rates in the world.[34] The effects of this labor market on new entrants was devastating: only 1 in 30 new entrants could find a job in the formal economy. Thus, between 1980 and 1994, 97% of new workers—4.4 million—could find no work! Unemployment was worst among the unskilled [see **Exhibit 7.5**]. The economy seemed to have no capacity to create jobs. Recent figures suggested that as companies consolidated and modernized, they had actually cut employment by 71,000 in 1996.

A related problem was the efficacy of the labor market. Unskilled unionized workers were paid 20% to 40% more than non-unionized workers—an exceedingly high gap by world standards. And the formal-informal gap was probably the highest anywhere. One study, for example, showed semi-skilled, unionized

workers making R1,400 per month versus R650 in the informal sector.[35]

Long-term youth unemployment was abysmal. "About 2.3 million people in their teens and twenties, who have entered the labor market, have no gainful employment…most have been unemployed for more than four years."[36] And if something did not change, another 200,000 to 300,000 would be unemployed in each of the next few years. A final problem aggravated by unemployment was income inequality, which was among the most severe in the world [see **Exhibit 7.6**].

The high level of unemployment was a cumulative result of a macroeconomy that had not worked properly for many years. This was the problem that worried Chris Stals, governor of the Reserve Bank, more than any other. He did not see any way for the economy to create the 400,000 jobs annually that were necessary to prevent the unemployment rate from rising still further.[37] Most of South Africa's business and political leaders agreed. Land reform and government expenditures could provide some jobs, but if budget deficits were to be reduced, economic growth and a low-wage, flexible labor market would have to do most of the work. The business community supported a two-tier labor market—one tier for organized workers maintaining their benefits and rules, and a second tier with minimal regulation to encourage "outsiders" to enter the labor-intensive formal sector.[38]

Infrastructure

The inequitable provision of infrastructure had caused additional problems. Too many homes still lacked electricity and plumbing—indeed, there were far too few homes. The latest statistics showed about 73% of urban households, and just 15% of rural households, had electricity. Among black South Africans, the numbers were worse. Eskom, the national electric company, had undertaken a program to make 1.5 million new connections in five years; this endeavor helped, but was still not enough [see **Exhibit 7.7**].[39]

Perhaps even more fundamental problems were water and sewage services. In 1994, 54% of African homes in urban areas had running water, only 8% in rural areas. Others had water on or near their site or used tanks, wells, or public kiosks. The government had engaged in 12 huge water projects since 1994, but even when those were completed in 1998, many people would still not be served.[40] In urban areas, only 85% of the population (72% of Africans) had flush toilets. In rural areas, it was less than 12%. Chemical lavatories, latrines, and buckets were still widely used—even in cities.

Housing

Lack of adequate housing was another element of South Africa's infrastructural problem. While there were an estimated 8.3 million households in South Africa, the formal housing stock was about 3.4 million units. About 1.5 million urban households lived in "informal housing units"—service sites designated for water or electric service, where shacks had been constructed. There were also more than 1 million families living in squatters shacks and another 5% of households in hostels. In rural areas, another 17 million people lived in a mix of formal and informal structures. The backlog of housing needed was at least 1.5 million units, and this backlog was increasing (due to immigration and population growth) by about 180,000 units annually.

> "Housing the nation," read the preamble of a 1995 White Paper on Housing, "is one of the greatest challenges facing the Government of National Unity. The extent of challenge derives not only from the enormous size of the housing backlog and the desperation and impatience of the homeless, but stems also from the extremely complicated bureaucratic, administrative, financial and institutional framework inherited from the previous government."[41]

Although the 1994 Reconstruction and Development Programme targeted construction of one million homes in five years, the budget set aside R2.9 billion in the 1995/96 budget to support housing—an increase of 80% over the previous year. Households with incomes of R3,500 or less were eligible for state housing subsidies. Yet by the end of 1995, just 6% of the 50,000 loans targeted had been granted; just 10,000 homes were built. Only about 35,000 were built in 1996, leaving several billion rand of unused funds available.

There were many housing-related problems. The cost of a cheap, four-room home, with sewage and electricity, was about R65,000 to R70,000. Several large banks had agreed to provide fixed-rate mortgages for up to 80% of the value of the house, at about 22% interest. A severe problem, however, was that many would-be borrowers did not understand either the concept of a mortgage or the difference between the bank and the government. Thus, by early 1996, the Mortgage Indemnity Fund (set up by the government) reported that banks had repossessed 70,000 properties due to non-performing loans. In some of the townships, formal boycotts of mortgage payments had been organized by borrowers who did not have jobs.[42]

In the 1997/98 budget, R4 billion was allocated to housing—a 156% increase plus the roll-over of the unused R1.7 billion. The federal government had designated Provincial Task Teams to implement and streamline construction and housing delivery. For 1997/98, 192,000 new homes were planned.[43]

Immigration and Emigration

Official immigration to South Africa in the most recent year was about 6,400 people: 43% from Europe, 25% from Asia, and 25% from Africa. Emigration, which amounted to more than 10,000, went mostly to Australia, Canada, and Europe. A rising concern in South Africa was that a growing number of professionals—doctors, managers, engineers—was leaving, resulting in something of a brain drain.

But informal, or illegal, immigration was far greater. The coordinator of border control for the South African Police offered an estimate (in 1995) of nearly 5 million, costing taxpayers as much as R5 billion, annually. Deputy President Mbeki estimated the number of illegal immigrants still in the country as two million to three million.[44] The vast majority came from sub-Saharan Africa—Zimbabwe, Mozambique, Angola, and Botswana. Typically, males came to the townships around Johannesburg to find work, living with relatives or townsfolk already there. Eventually, their wives and children, and perhaps siblings and parents, would join them—severely aggravating the housing and services capacity of the township.

AIDS

These massive movements of people only aggravated South Africa's exposure to AIDS. During the 1980s, South Africa was relatively free of AIDS. But in the past three years, surveys conducted on women attending antenatal clinics revealed an epidemic of HIV infection. By October 1995, an estimated 1.8 million people, 90% of whom were African, were infected. The demographics reflected the heterosexual character of the epidemic in Africa. The highest rate of infection affected females in their teens or early twenties. Figures showed a doubling rate of 15 months, which explained the estimate of 2.5 million HIV positive cases by spring 1997. The official government estimate recently put the level of HIV infection at 5 million to 6 million by 2005—17% to 24% of the sexually active population. Although the government was expanding educational programs as quickly as possible, lack of funds, extreme poverty, congestion in the townships, and cultural prejudices of African men all interfered with progress.[45]

Growth, Employment and Redistribution (GEAR)

By 1996, South Africa had recovered from the stagnation that had prevailed since the early 1980s. GDP was growing at 3%, and inflation had declined to 8.5% [see **Exhibit 7.8**]. Much as this pleased both business and political leadership, the government's fiscal deficit was still 5.6%—an amount that resulted in too much additional borrowing, a growing current account deficit, and a depreciating currency. This became obvious in February, when a run on the rand drove its value down about 16%—or about 8% in real terms. Worse yet, growth was not enough to create new jobs. As previously mentioned, an estimated 71,000 jobs were actually lost in the year 1996. If nothing changed, the Ministry of Finance believed it faced the prospect of continuing slow growth with fiscal deficits causing higher inflation and interest rates and too little job creation.

It had become clear to almost everyone—including ANC leadership and the Government of National Unity—that the existing growth path would not reduce unemployment, provide revenues necessary for social services, or redistribute income. Something more was needed. So in June 1996, Financial Minister Trevor Manuel announced a new macroeconomic strategy—GEAR—that would hopefully accelerate non-gold exports, private sector investment, and infrastructural development. GEAR would push GDP growth to 6% and job creation to 400,000 by the year 2000. At the center of this program was deficit reduction—a change of heart for the ANC government.[46]

The GEAR's medium-term strategy was as follows:

1. an acceleration of fiscal reform, reducing the deficit to 3% of GDP by 2000, to help counter inflation; this included further revision of the tax structure and a more redistributive thrust of expenditures;
2. gradual relaxation of exchange controls while maintaining monetary policies consistent with inflation reduction;
3. trade and industrial policy reforms, including further reduction of tariffs, tax incentives to stimulate investment, small and medium business development, and a competitive policy with the development of industrial clusters;
4. public sector asset restructuring, including better governance and regulation of public corporations, the sale of nonstrategic assets, and public-private partnerships in transport and telecommunications;
5. an expansionary public infrastructure investment program;
6. a structured flexibility within the collective bargaining system to support a competitive and more labor-intensive growth path; reducing minimum wage schedules for young trainees, and increasing incentives for more shifts, job sharing, and employment flexibility;
7. a social agreement to facilitate wage and price moderation, accelerate investment and employment, and enhance public service delivery.[47]

When the strategy was initially announced, it was immediately attacked by some members of the ANC and the trade union leaders. There was a sense that it was produced by "eight white men" and did not represent the interests of South African labor.[48] But as the government's commitment to GEAR appeared to strengthen, business became increasingly enthusiastic. By March 1997, when Trevor Manual made his budget speech, there was general enthusiasm for the plan and for government's financial management.

Fiscal Policy

For the fiscal year ending in March 1997, the budget deficit stood at 5.6% of GDP. The budget proposed reducing it to 4% in 1998 [see **Exhibits 7.9a** and **7.9b**]. The primary balance (revenues minus expenditures, excluding debt service) was actually positive—2.4% of GDP. Direct taxes remained high, but there were plans to shift more revenue dependence to the value-added tax. Budgetary reform was making progress, with reduced defense expenditures and some privatization revenues allowing somewhat greater expenditures on housing and infrastructure. One clear problem, however, was the government wage bill. Government's real wages were up 4.9% in 1996 [see **Exhibit 7.10**].[49]

Monetary Policy

In March 1997, the Minister of Finance announced a series of exchange-rate liberalizations. Controls were to be lifted on capital outflows of up to R200,000 by individuals. Corporations could hold foreign currency earnings offshore for 30 days and could transfer up to R30 million for approved foreign investments. Local institutional investors could invest up to 10% of total assets offshore.[50]

Overall, the monetary policy of the South African Reserve Bank was to control the growth of M3, so that inflation would fall toward 4% or 5%; an additional goal was to maintain a constant real exchange rate for the rand. Chris Stals, the Bank's governor, felt he "didn't have much choice" regarding monetary policy, since global inflation rates were down to 2% to 3% in the economies with which South Africa competed. This had led to a very high short-term interest rate—about 17.75% for short-term bonds and 20.25% for the prime rate. Stals understood that rates this high dampened investment, but they reflected the high inflationary expectations. As he put it, "You can't lower rates by creating more money."[51]

Real exchange rates were the other important reflection of monetary policy. The sharp fall in the value of the rand in 1996 reflected a loss of confidence by investors. Although nonmineral exports were stimulated, imports recovered after about nine months, and the effects had begun to wear off after a year. Stals did not think real depreciation worked—at least for the South African economy. Thus, his target, to the extent that it mattered, was a constant real exchange rate. If inflation came down, exchange rates should stabilize [see **Exhibit 7.11**].

Although sympathetic to the need to reduce unemployment, Stals seemed firm in his commitment to reduce inflation. The real problem, he thought, was the structural inflexibility of labor markets. He had recently spoken out on this point and caused quite a political stir. But he believed real wages simply had to stop rising if South Africa were to effectively control inflation and if it were to expand nonmineral exports without further devaluation.[52]

Trade and Industrial Policy

Another important change due to GEAR was a focus on supply-side policies to make South Africa's economy more competitive and productive. South Africa had already begun to lower tariffs (from an average of 15% to 9%) and proposed to go further in 1997. Export incentives, moreover, that did not comply with WTO rules were to be phased out.

The GEAR also offered several new policies. The National Infrastructure Investment Framework had identified R170 billion in needed capital spending. The 1997/98 budget provided R14.5 billion for capital and social infrastructure—mostly housing, water and sanitation, and municipal infrastructure. Two new programs included the Spatial Development Initiative (SDI) and small business development. The former designated 10 development corridors in which industries could be concentrated to achieve external economies—industrial areas, metro-service corridors, agri-tourism areas, etc. Most SDIs were designated along the coast of the Indian Ocean, but an additional 10 had been identified for development inland.[53] For Small, Medium, and Micro Enterprises (SMMEs), a program of wholesale loans and loan guarantees was established to help broaden and deepen the structure of enterprise in South Africa.[54]

Most business executives and bureaucrats recognized the need for South African business to reduce costs and become more competitive. In some sectors, such as defense, metals, electronics, and petro-chemicals, there was potential for exporting more in competition with developed countries.[55] But there also needed to be some effort to grow labor intensive businesses—for South Africa's own market and for markets throughout Africa and the Indian Ocean rim. These neighboring economies were now growing at 5% annually and created a market that South African business could potentially tap [see **Exhibit 7.12a**].

Public Sector Asset Restructuring

Because the government was so heavily invested in the economy (i.e., 30% of GDP), there was a sense that public corporations needed a stronger, clearer set of principles to guide their behavior. The government was working on governance programs, including dividend and tax policies for government-owned corporations, a National Empowerment Fund to deepen employee ownership, treatment of pension and medical-aid fund deficits, and a more competitive and transparent bidding system.

The heart of this initiative, however, was privatization. But progress was slow, with opposition from labor unions intensifying. Six radio stations had been privatized, and restructuring committees were looking at sales of various airlines, airports, resorts, and so forth. Public-Private Partnerships, a related initiative, had begun with the sale of 30% of Telkom to Southwestern Bell/Telekom Malaysia for $1.3 billion. According to Dikgang Moseneke, the chairman of Telkom, this provided an infusion of not only capital but also management skills, technology, and especially training. More than 300 engineers were currently receiving specialized training and would eventually spend time in Malaysia or the United States. Moseneke planned to double Telkom's network in four years, at a cost of R53 billion. Doing so would indeed require an immense injection of capital and skilled labor.[56]

Flexible Wage and Labor Structure

In many ways, the flexible wage and labor structure was the element of GEAR on which the rest depended. The level of unemployment was intolerable and had to improve if political stability were to be maintained. GEAR envisioned creation of about 400,000 jobs annually by the year 2000, to reduce unemployment to 32%. Unlike previous plans, GEAR depended on the economic growth of 6% to accomplish at least 30% of this job creation; another 25% could be achieved by the infrastructural and public works expenditures of government; and 30% needed to come from

institutional reforms in the labor market—skill development, wage moderation, and strategies to enhance flexibility through collective bargaining.[57]

These policies echoed the private sector's call for a dual wage strategy. In other words, as new jobs were created, younger workers were trained (either by government or by the private sector) and employed; they had to be willing to accept lower wages and benefits inferior to those guaranteed to unionized workers. Real wages could not rise significantly, nor faster than productivity, if South Africa were to become more competitive. Unfortunately, organized labor could see the problem domestically, but was less familiar with working conditions elsewhere—especially in India, China, and Indonesia, where wages were one-fifth as high. Thus, its willingness to tolerate low wages and harsh working conditions was increasingly doubtful.

A National Social Agreement

The final aspect of GEAR was its call for social cooperation. The government was committing to a tougher fiscal policy, with monetary restraint and constant fixed exchange rates. In return, it promised to deliver better income distribution and social policies; "orderly collective bargaining between organized labor and employers must remain the foundation of industrial relations."[58] Nedlac, the tripartite organization for discussions between business, government, and labor, was the primary vehicle for achieving this social pact. Yet the Nedlac mechanism was not working very well, and COSATU had recently opted out.

The Challenge

In the three years since its first democratic election, South Africa had remained incredibly peaceful and had grown, albeit slowly. But now the South African Chamber of Business concluded, "The challenge for the authorities lies in their political will to harness the economy's potential, and set the economy on the growth high road as set out in their GEAR strategy."[59] Although the economy had slowed during the last two quarters of 1996 and the first quarter of 1997, it appeared to be ready to expand again, with a more realistic budget, a somewhat depreciated currency, and stable inflation. The

Department of Finance was projecting growth of 2.25%, with inflation of 8.5% and an increase in real wages of 2.5% [see **Exhibit 7.13**].[60]

Even though growth was somewhat less than that which the GEAR had called for, most South African business executives were satisfied. It had, after all, been only a year since the GEAR was announced. Government was working hard to implement these various proposals, yet it would take some time to affect the real economy. Some people faulted the program for not reducing deficits fast enough.[61] Others felt that unemployment had to be addressed immediately, either by public works or by reducing hours worked per employee.[62]

Delivery, as one economist put it, was the key, not strategy. The GEAR was fine, but its implementation through the political process over the next two years was crucial.[63] This, of course, would be the prime responsibility of Thabo Mbeki during the months running up to the election in April 1999. But as he dealt with one or another interest group, Mbeki had to wonder if the GEAR was adequate for dealing with South Africa's institutional weaknesses, and if it was doable. As the ANC's candidate for the next presidency, and with Nelson Mandela's endorsement, Mbeki was almost certain to win. Yet, if the economy didn't improve soon, organized labor would just be one of the interests abandoning ship.

EXHIBIT 7.1   SOUTH AFRICAN MAPS

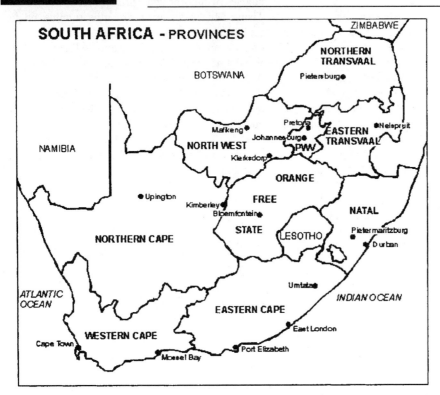

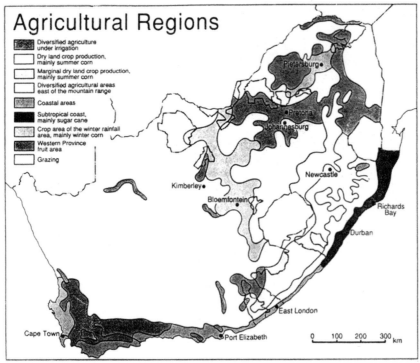

SOURCE: Case writer.

EXHIBIT 7.2   SOUTH AFRICA'S SHARE OF WORLD MINERAL PRODUCTION, 1994

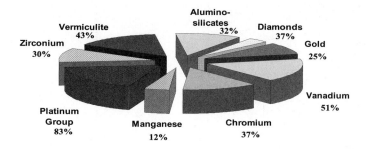

SOURCE: *South Africa at a Glance, 96–97* (Editors, Inc., 1997), 102–103.

EXHIBIT 7.3A   ANNUAL FOREIGN DIRECT INVESTMENT IN SOUTH AFRICA, 1994–1997*

Millions Rand

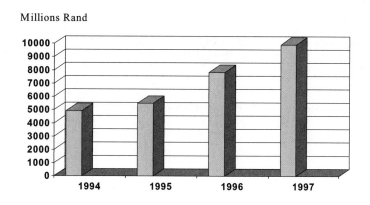

SOURCE: "FDI Essential for Economic Growth," *Financial Mail, Special Survey of Top Companies*, June 27, 1997, 314.

* May 1994 thru April 1997

EXHIBIT 7.3B **FOREIGN DIRECT INVESTMENT IN SOUTH AFRICA, BY SOURCE**

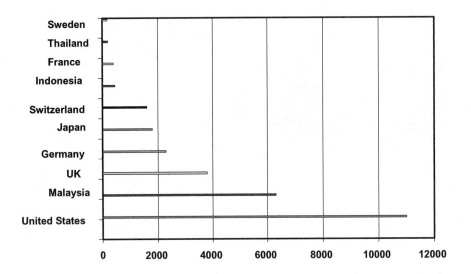

SOURCE: "FDI Essential for Economic Growth," *Financial Mail*, June 1997, 315.

Total FDI in Millions of Rand, 5/94–4/97

EXHIBIT 7.3C **FOREIGN DIRECT INVESTMENT IN SOUTH AFRICA, BY SECTOR**

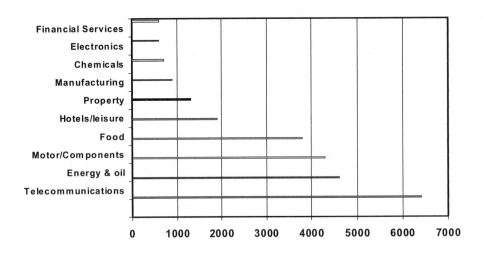

SOURCE: "FDI Essential for Economic Growth," *Financial Mail*, June 1997, 314.

Total FDI in Millions of Rand, 5/94–4/97

EXHIBIT 7.4	TOP BLACK-CONTROLLED FIRMS IN SOUTH AFRICA IN 1996

Ranked by Assets	Company	Sector	Total Assets (Rm)
1	Metlife	Insurance	10,910
2	Johnnic	Industrial Holdings	10,435
3	JCI	Mining	8,515
4	New Africa Inv.	Industrial Holdings	1,247
5	Saflife	Insurance	1,112
6	Aflife	Insurance	1,089
7	Cap Alliance	Insurance	1,059
8	Real Africa Inv.	Industrial Holdings	894
9	Real Africa Hld.	Industrial Holdings	890
10	Botswana Rst.	Copper	828

SOURCE: "Black Economic Empowerment," *Financial Mail, Special Survey,* June 1997, 174

EXHIBIT 7.5	AVERAGE POPULATION, GROWTH RATE, AND UNEMPLOYMENT RATE, 1991, 1994

	Population in 1991 (000)	Population in 1994 (000)	Average annual growth rate	Unemployment rate
African	28,383	30,475	2.4%	41.1%
Asian	987	1,027	1.3%	17.1%
Coloured	3,280	3,424	1.4%	23.3%
White	5,061	5,165	0.7%	6.4%
Total/aver.	37,771	40,091	2.05%	32.6%

SOURCE: *South Africa Survey, 1995/96,* 12.262.

EXHIBIT 7.6	INCOME DISTRIBUTION BY POPULATION GROUP—1993

	Population share	Income share	Per capita income (R)	Disparity ratio*
African	76.2%	29.3%	2,717	11.8
Asian	2.6%	4.8%	12,963	2.5
Coloured	8.3%	7.4%	6,278	5.1
White	12.9%	58.5%	32,076	1
Total/aver.	100.0%	100.0%	7,062	4.5

SOURCE: *South Africa Survey, 1995/96,* 12.262.
* White to other.

EXHIBIT 7.7	ELECTRICITY, WATER, TELEPHONE AVAILABILITY, 1994

	African	Coloured	Indian	White	Total
Electricity for lighting					
Urban	67%	90%	99%	99%	82%
Rural	16%	60%	74%	93%	21%
Telephone in dwelling					
Urban	25%	51%	73%	88%	51%
Rural	2%	7%	47%	83%	5%
Flush toilet					
Urban	72%	93%	98%	100%	85%
Rural	7%	45%	63%	99%	12%

SOURCE: *South Africa Survey, 1995/96,* 12.262.
* White to other.

EXHIBIT 7.8	NATIONAL INCOME ACCOUNTS								
	1989	1990	1991	1992	1993	1994	1995	1996	1997Q1[a]
Nominal GDP (R billion)	240.6	276.1	310.1	341.0	383.7	431.7	485.8	543.0	559.6
Real GDP (1990 prices)	276.9	276.1	273.2	267.3	270.7	278.1	287.5	296.5	293.9
Real GDP growth (%)	n/a	-0.3%	-1.0%	-2.2%	1.3%	2.7%	3.4%	3.1%	-1.0%
Real Values									
Private consumer expenditures	n/a	159.5	158.7	156.4	156.9	161.7	169.4	175.8	n/a
Gross domestic fixed investment	n/a	54.1	50.1	47.5	46.2	50.2	55.4	59.1	n/a
Govt. consumer expenditures	n/a	52.7	53.9	54.7	56.3	58.6	58.8	61.8	n/a
Exports of goods	n/a	70.7	70.7	72.5	76.0	76.7	83.9	90.4	n/a
Imports of goods	n/a	54.0	55.2	58.2	62.2	72.3	84.2	90.6	n/a
Change in inventories	n/a	-7.0	-4.9	-5.7	-2.4	3.1	4.3	-0.1	n/a
Gross domestic savings as a % of GDP	n/a	n/a	n/a	n/a	n/a	n/a	17.2	16.9	13.5
C/GDP %	n/a	57.8%	58.1%	58.5%	58.0%	58.1%	58.9%	59.3%	n/a
I/GDP %	n/a	19.6%	18.3%	17.8%	17.1%	18.0%	19.3%	19.9%	n/a
G/GDP %	n/a	19.1%	19.7%	20.5%	20.8%	21.1%	20.5%	20.8%	n/a
X/GDP %	n/a	25.6%	25.9%	27.1%	28.1%	27.6%	29.2%	30.5%	n/a
Im/GDP %	n/a	-22.1%	-22.0%	-23.9%	-23.9%	-24.9%	-27.8%	-30.6%	n/a
Nominal GDP per capita (US$)	n/a	n/a	2,957.0	3,079.0	2,955.0	2,955.0	3,201.0	2,977.0	n/a

SOURCE: *South Africa, A Country Report 1997*, ABSA Bank Internal Data.

[a]Q1 Annualized data

EXHIBIT 7.9A	SOUTH AFRICAN GOVERNMENT—REVENUES 1997/98 BUDGET

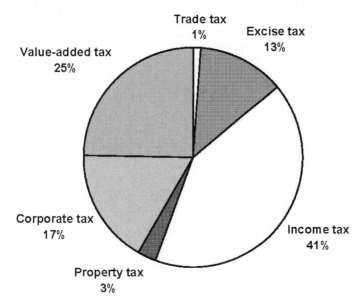

SOURCE: Department of Finance, *Budget Review*, 1997.

EXHIBIT 7.9B	SOUTH AFRICAN GOVERNMENT—EXPENDITURES 1997/98 BUDGET

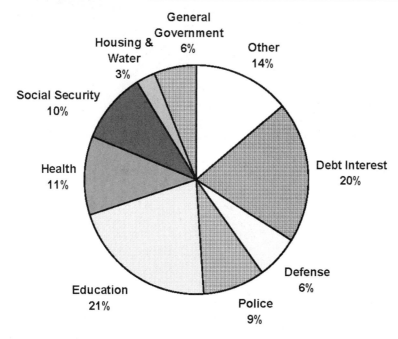

SOURCE: Department of Finance, *Budget Review*, 1997.

EXHIBIT 7.10A   **GNP PER CAPITA, REAL WAGES, AND PRICES**

(Pct. change from previous year)

Year	GNP per capita	Average Real Wages Private	Public	CPI	PPI	GDP Deflator
1985	-3.2	-3.7	-4.3	16.3	16.9	16.2
1986	-1.7	-2.4	-2.7	18.6	19.6	16.3
1987	1.2	1.0	2.3	16.1	13.9	14.2
1988	1.7	2.7	-0.9	12.9	13.2	15.1
1989	-1.2	-0.6	3.7	14.7	15.2	17.2
1990	-3.8	0.0	0.7	14.4	12.0	15.1
1991	-2.7	0.7	2.1	15.3	11.4	13.5
1992	-4.5	1.5	1.4	13.9	8.3	12.4
1993	-0.5	0.1	-1.5	9.7	6.6	11.1
1994	2.0	1.4	6.0	9.0	8.2	9.5
1995	0.8	2.5	-1.9	8.7	9.6	8.9
1996	1.6	1.8	0.6	7.4	6.9	8.4

SOURCE: Republic of South Africa, Department of Finance, *Budget Review*, 1997, p. 2.10.

EXHIBIT 7.10B   **PRODUCTIVITY**

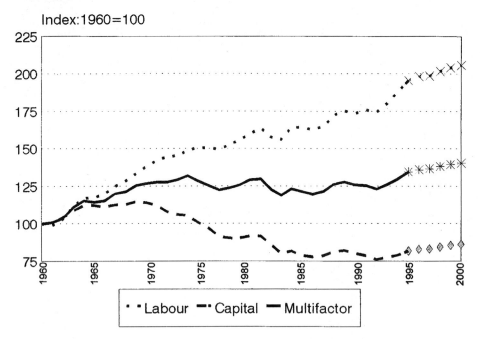

SOURCE: A. J. Jacobs, Chief Economist, ABSA Bank, "Economy Presentation," July 1997.

EXHIBIT 7.10C   **AVAILABILITY OF NET SAVINGS**

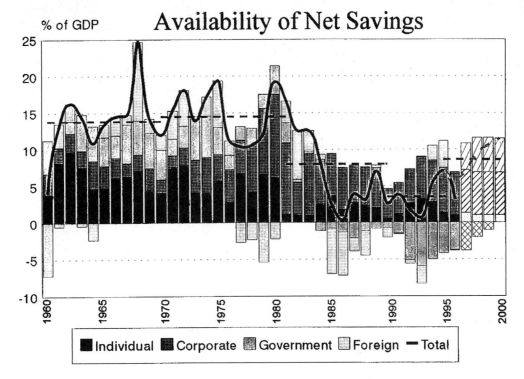

SOURCE: A. J. Jacobs, Chief Economist, ABSA Bank, "Economy Presentation," July 1997.

EXHIBIT 7.11   **EXCHANGE RATE AND MONEY SUPPLY**

Year	Nominal Exchange Rate 1990 = 100	Pct. change	Real Exchange Rate 1990 = 100	Pct. change	US $ Exchange Rate Rand per $	Pct. change	M3 Pct. change	Domestic Credit Pct. change	Prim Rate Pct.
1985	151.8	-32.4	82.0	-22.6	2.228	-33.8	12.3	15.9	N/A
1986	127.8	-15.8	85.6	4.3	2.283	-2.4	9.3	8.3	N/A
1987	131.6	3.0	99.8	16.7	2.036	12.2	17.6	15.0	N/A
1988	114.7	-12.8	95.8	-4.1	2.273	-10.4	27.3	26.5	N/A
1989	103.3	-9.9	95.4	-0.4	2.622	-13.3	22.3	17.4	N/A
1990	100.0	-3.2	100.0	4.8	2.588	1.3	12.0	19.4	21.0
1991	94.0	-6.0	103.0	3.0	2.761	-6.3	12.3	12.3	20.2
1992	89.5	-4.8	104.8	1.8	2.852	-3.2	8.0	10.4	18.9
1993	81.2	-9.2	100.2	-4.4	3.267	-12.7	7.0	9.4	16.2
1994	73.7	-9.3	97.1	-3.0	3.550	-8.0	15.7	19.9	15.6
1995	69.5	-5.7	97.4	0.2	3.627	-2.1	15.2	13.2	17.9
1996	60.5	-13.0	89.4	-8.2	4.292	-15.6	13.6	16.1	19.7
1997 Q1a	59.6	-9.4	91.1	6.9	4.441	-14.6	12.9	17.1	20.25

SOURCE: Republic of South Africa, Department of Finance, *Budget Review*, 1997, p. 2.11.

[a] Rates of change for Q1 are annualized.

EXHIBIT 7.12ᴬ	SOUTH AFRICA BALANCE OF PAYMENTS, MILLIONS OF RAND									
	1988	1989	1990	1991	1992	1993	1994	1995	1996	1997 Q1ᵃ
Merchandise exports (excluding gold)	32,125	38,384	42,735	44,709	49,010	56,512	64,952	81,289	98,818	105,610
Net gold exports	19,701	19,140	18,177	19,587	19,391	22,449	23,671	22,537	26,294	26,816
Service receipts	8,884	11,543	11,346	12,386	13,310	14,525	17,970	20,118	21,978	26,670
Merchandise imports	(39,408)	(44,266)	(43,408)	(47,385)	(51,883)	(59,869)	(76,251)	(97,962)	(116,326)	(122,913)
Service payments	(18,011)	(21,539)	(23,711)	(23,312)	(25,153)	(27,997)	(31,709)	(36,259)	(39,060)	(43,681)
Direct investment payments	(1,750)	(2,105)	(2,227)	(2,195)	(2,466)	(2,127)	(2,204)	(2,392)	n/a	n/a
Interest	(4,615)	(5,588)	(6,118)	(5,594)	(5,228)	(6,046)	(6,531)	(7,555)	n/a	n/a
Current account balance	3,383	3,467	5,324	6,187	4,975	6,049	(1,207)	(10,157)	(8,479)	(7,940)
Long term capital movements	n/a	(606)	(102)	(1,730)	(1,511)	(272)	3,503	15,125	4,885	n/a
Public authorities	n/a	(469)	511	1,051	3,142	(2,886)	4,102	6,854	6,913	n/a
Non-monetary private sector	n/a	(15)	(650)	(2,657)	(3,964)	2,675	775	6,448	(826)	n/a
Basic balance	n/a	2,861	5,222	4,457	3,464	5,777	2,296	4,968	(3,594)	n/a
Short-term capital movements not related to reserves	n/a	(2,830)	(1,670)	(424)	(3,197)	(14,969)	825	4,109	(1,029)	n/a
Total capital movements not related to reserves	n/a	(3,436)	(1,772)	(2,154)	(4,708)	(15,241)	4,328	19,234	3,856	n/a
Change in net gold and other foreign reserves	n/a	31	3,552	4,033	267	(9,192)	3,121	9,077	(4,623)	n/a

SOURCE: South African Reserve Bank, *Quarterly Bulletin*, June 1997.

ᵃ Annualized data

EXHIBIT 7.12B		SOUTH AFRICA CURRENT ACCOUNT BALANCE IN MILLIONS OF U.S. DOLLARS						

	1988	1989	1990	1991	1992	1993	1994	1995
Total Imports	(17,210)	(16,810)	(16,778)	(17,156)	(17,216)	(18,287)	(21,452)	(27,001)
Total Exports	22,432	22,399	23,560	23,289	24,009	21,438	24,947	28,611
Trade Balance	5,222	5,589	6,783	6,134	5,794	5,850	3,494	1,610
Net Services	(899)	(926)	(680)	(764)	(1,222)	(1,530)	(1,494)	(1,971)
Net Income	(3,281)	(3,286)	(4,096)	(3,183)	(2,925)	(2,577)	(2,369)	(2,476)
Net Transfers	161	186	60	56	94	130	50	16
Current Account Balance	1,204	1,564	2,065	2,243	1,741	1,873	(319)	(2,820)

SOURCE: IMF, International Financial Statistics Yearbook, 1997.

EXHIBIT 7.12C		TRADE AS A PERCENTAGE OF GROSS DOMESTIC PRODUCT

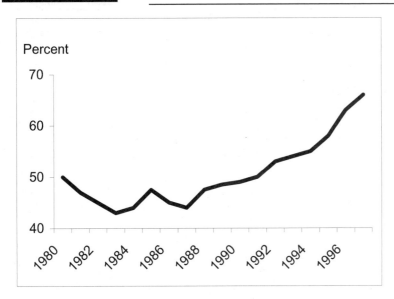

SOURCE: South African Reserve Bank, *Annual Economic Report*, 1998.

EXHIBIT 7.13			GEAR, INTEGRATED SCENARIO PROJECTION			
Model characteristics	**1996**	**1997**	**1998**	**1999**	**2000**	**Average**
Fiscal deficit (% of GDP, fiscal year)	5.1	4	3.5	3	3	3.7
Real government consumption (% of GDP)	19.9	19.5	19	18.5	18.1	19
Average tariff (% of imports)	10	8	7	7	6	7.6
Average real wage growth, private sector	-0.5	1	1	1	1	0.8
Average real wage growth, government sector	4.4	0.7	0.4	0.8	0.4	1.3
Real effective exchange rate (% change)	-8.5	-0.3	0	0	0	-1.8
Real bank rate	7	5	4	3	3	4.4
Real government investment growth	3.4	2.7	5.4	7.5	16.7	7.1
Real parastatal investment growth	3	5	10	10	10	7.6
Real private sector investment growth	9.3	9.1	9.3	13.9	17	11.7
Real non-gold export growth	9.1	8	7	7.8	10.2	8.4
Additional foreign direct investment (US$m)	155	365	504	716	804	509
Results	**1996**	**1997**	**1998**	**1999**	**2000**	**Average**
GDP growth	3.5	2.9	3.8	4.9	6.1	4.2
Inflation (CPI)	8	9.7	8.1	7.7	7.6	8.2
Employment growth (non-agricultural formal)	1.3	3	2.7	3.5	4.3	2.9
New jobs per year ('000)	126	252	246	320	409	270
Current account deficit (% of GDP)	2.2	2	2.2	2.5	3.1	2.4
Real export growth, manufacturing	10.3	12.2	8.3	10.5	12.8	10.8
Gross private savings (% of GDP)	20.5	21	21.2	21.5	21.9	21.2
Government dissavings (% of GDP)	3.1	2.3	1.7	0.7	0.6	1.9

SOURCE: *Growth, Employment and Redistribution: A Macroeconomic Strategy*, 14 June '96, p. 7–8.

EXHIBIT 7.14   INTERNATIONAL COMPARATIVE EXHIBITS

Country	GNP per capita in dollars	Purchasing power parity of GNP per capita, 1995 int'l $	Pct. share of income (lowest 20%)	Pct. share of income (highest 10%)	Gini Index[1]	% with access to sanitation	Population growth rate	Electricity production, kwh per capita, 1994	Telephone mainlines per 1,000 people	Adult illiteracy percentage
South Africa	3,160	5,030	3.3	47.3	58.4	46	2.2	4,617	95	18
Argentina	8,030	8,310	-	-	-	89	1.3	1,885	160	4
Brazil	3,640	5,400	2.1	51.3	63.4	73	1.5	1,640	75	17
China	620	2,920	5.5	30.9	41.5	-	1.1	773	34	19
Ghana	390	1,990	7.9	27.3	33.9	29	2.8	360	4	-
India	340	1,400	8.5	28.4	33.8	29	1.8	416	13	48
Indonesia	980	3,800	8.7	25.6	31.7	55	1.6	277	17	16
Kenya	280	1,380	3.4	47.7	57.5	43	2.7	131	9	22
Mexico	3,320	6,400	4.1	39.2	50.3	70	1.9	1,608	96	10
Nigeria	260	1,220	4.0	31.3	45.0	63	2.9	140	4	43
Pakistan	460	2,230	8.4	25.2	31.2	30	2.9	450	16	62
Uganda	240	1,470	6.8	33.4	40.8	60	3.2	-	2	38
Zimbabwe	540	2,030	4.0	46.9	56.8	58	2.4	667	14	15

All data as of 1995, unless otherwise indicated. Income distribution data is from various surveys in the 1990s

1. The Gini index measures the difference between a perfectly equal distribution of income and the actual distribution. Index values range from zero (perfect equality in income distribution) to 100 (representing perfect inequality).

SOURCE: The World Bank, *World Development Report* 1997.

ENDNOTES

1. South African Reserve Bank, *Quarterly Bulletin,* June 1997, No. 204.

2. Bob Tucker and Bruce Scott, eds., *South Africa: Prospects for Successful Transition* (Cape Town: Juta & Co., Ltd., 1992).

3. South African Foundation, *Growth for All: An Economic Strategy for South Africa* (Johannesburg, February 1996).

4. Mike Brown, "The GEAR Economy," Societe Generale Frankel Pollak, May 1997, 24.

5. While various sources list the population at 43–44 million, a new census reported in July 1997 a population of 38 million. Most observers feel that this figure grossly understates population, especially in the black townships.

6. Merton Dagut, ed., *South Africa: The New Beginning* (London: Euromoney Publications, 1991), 16, 40–41.

7. Nigel Worden, *The Making of Modern South Africa: Conquest, Segregation and Apartheid* (Oxford: Blackwell Publishers, 1994), 8–9.

8. Leonard Thompson, *A History of South Africa* (New Haven: Yale University Press, 1995), chapter 2.

9. Ibid., 50–66.

10. William H. Worger, *South Africa's City of Diamonds: Mine Workers and Monopoly Capitalism in Kimberley, 1867–1895* (New Haven: Yale University Press, 1987).

11. Alfred Milner, quoted in L. Thompson, *A History of South Africa,* (New Haven: Yale University Press, 1995), 144.

12. South African Foundation, *Growth for All,* (ANC Press Statement, 12 March 1996), 2.

13. L. Thompson, *A History of South Africa,* (1995), 176.

14. Ibid., 190.

15. Quoted in Fatima Meer, *Higher than Hope,* (New York: Harper & Rowe, 1988), 67

16. *House of Assembly Debates,* 3 February 1969, quoted in *Racism and Apartheid in South Africa* (Paris: The Unesco Press 1974), 75.

17. Quoted in *Ibid.,* 90.

18. Quoted in *Ibid.,* 96.

19. Donald Woods, *Biko: The Revised Edition* (New York: Henry Holt, 1987).

20. Peter Fallon and Loiz De Silva, *South Africa: Economic Performance and Policies,* discussion paper #7, World Bank, South African Department, Washington DC, 1994, 31–37, 43–51; R. Tucker, D. Scott, *South Africa: Prospects for Successful Transition,* 50–53.

21. *SA 96–97: South Africa at a Glance,* 103–110.

22. "Top Companies - Special Survey," *Financial Mail,* June 27, 1997, 330.

23. "Black Economic Empowerment," in *Financial Mail,* 1997, 173–178.

24. Marinus Daling, interview with the author, July 1997.

25. "Unbundling and Black Empowerment"; and "Johnic Makes Determined Play for Small Black Investor," *Sunday Independent,* April 27, 1997; and "Blacks Will Need to be Proactive," *Business Daily,* January 18, 1997.

26. Duncan Innes, interview with the author, July 1997.

27. Ibid.

28. South African Foundation, *Growth For All,* pp. 32–33.

29. Criminal Information Management Center, *1996 Report on Crime* (http://196.33.208.55/miovs.html); South African Institute of Race Relations, *Fast Facts,* April 1997, p.2.

30. South African Institute of Race Relations, "The Story of a Good Law, Its Bad Application, and the Ugly Results," Number 1, July 1997, 22–23.

31. South African Institute of Race Relations, *South African Survey, 1995/96,* 95–123.

32. *SA 96–97,* 51–55.

33. South African Foundation, *Growth for All,* 84.

34. World Bank, *World Development Report 1995* (Oxford: Oxford University Press, 1995).

35. Peter Moll, *Wage Developments in South Africa in the 1990's* Geneva: ILO, 1995

36. South African Foundation, *Growth for All,* 88–90.

37. Chris Stals, interview with the author, July 1997.

38. South African Foundation, *Growth for all,* 101–103

39. Eskom, *Statistical Yearbook, 1995; Annual Report 1996.*

40. South African Institute of Race Relations, *South Africa Survey, 1995/96,* 403–410.

41. Department of Housing, *White Paper on Housing,* 1995, preamble, 1.

42. South African Institute of Race Relations, *South African Survey, 1995/96,* 335–342.

43. Republic of South Africa, Department of Finance, *Budget Review 1997,* 8.9.

44. Department of Home Affairs, *Annual Report 1995.*

45. Department of Health, *Health Trends in South Africa 1994* (April 1995).

46. Department of Finance, *Growth, Employment and Redistribution: A Macroeconomic Strategy,* June 14, 1996, 2.

47. Ibid.,5.

48. Renee Grawitzky, "Cosatu "Will Not Help Implement Gear Strategy," *Business Times,* July 1, 1997.

49. Mike Brown, "The 'GEAR' Economy," Societe Generale Frankel Pollak, May 1997, 6.

50. *GEAR,* 10–11.

51 Chris Stals, interview.

52 Ibid.

53 Alan Hirsh, Ministry of Trade and Industry, interview with the author, July 1997.

54 *GEAR*, 13.

55 Alan Jacobs, Chief Economist, ABSA, interview with the author, July 1997.

56 Dikgang Moseneke, chairman Telekom, interview with the author, July 1997.

57 *GEAR*, 16–17.

58 Ibid., 19.

59 South African Chamber of Commerce, "Prospects for the South African Economy in 1997," 4.

60 Department of Finance, *Budget Review 1997*, 6.2.

61 Ben van Rensburg, economist, South African Chamber of Commerce, interview with the author, July 1997.

62 Cheryl Carolus, executive director, ANC, interview with the author, July 1997.

63 Jac Laubscher, Chief Economist, Sanlam, interview with the author, July 1997.

CHAPTER

Islamic Resurgence

Once again in the spring of 2002, Crown Prince Abdullah of Saudi Arabia stands at a crossroads. Domestically, he contemplates the need for social reform, control of terrorism, and a new strategy for economic development. Externally, he reassesses his strategic relationship with the United States, his oil export policy, and his region's stance with respect to Israel. Yet it is difficult to take decisive action, in part because of an unclear succession.

The case, written in the aftermath of September 11, is designed to help develop some familiarity with economic and political circumstances in the Arab world, to consider the problem associated with natural resource wealth, and to consider U.S.-Arab relations in the wake of the profound terrorist shock. The case describes Islamic history, the basic precepts of the Muslim faith and its interactions with Arab culture in Saudi Arabia, an absolute monarchy committed to "Wahhabi" fundamentalism.

Yet Saudi Arabia is blessed with the world's largest petroleum reserve. Thus, since 1974, Saudi Arabia has had huge, albeit unstable revenue flows from its oil exports, allowing it to modernize quickly and grow. But per capita income has decreased from $18,000 to $7,800 over the past two decades, and growth has stagnated at about 1.8% annually. The case provides the opportunity for examining the costs and benefits of a huge natural resource, both politically and economically.

Aware of these problems, the Crown Prince wants to diversify the economy and open it to globalization—yet given his cultural and religious commitments, he needs to do so without merely succumbing to westernization. Is this possible and, if so, how?

CASE STUDY   **SAUDI ARABIA: GETTING THE HOUSE IN ORDER**

RICHARD H. K. VIETOR

REBECCA EVANS

> *The age of abundance is over...we must get used to a new lifestyle that does not rely entirely on the state.*
> —Crown Prince Abdullah, 1998

> *The Kingdom has no alternative but to diversify and develop the sources of the national income by expanding investment channels, opening doors for international companies, and offering them lucrative incentives.*
> —Crown Prince Abdullah, 2001

Introduction

On August 27, 2001, Saudi Arabia's Crown Prince Abdullah mailed U.S. President George W. Bush a cautionary letter. In it, he discussed his disapproval of America's strong support for Israel and its failure to stop Israeli-Palestinian violence. Acknowledging the fragility of U.S.-Saudi relations, he wrote, "We are at a crossroads. It is time for the United States and Saudi Arabia to look at their separate interests. Those governments that don't feel the pulse of the people and respond to it will suffer the fate of the Shah of Iran."[1] By promoting Arab and Muslim interests, Crown Prince Abdullah hoped to avoid a repeat of the Islamic revolution that had sent Iran's King Reza Pahlavi into exile in 1979.

Since the early 1930s, Saudi Arabia had forged a strategic partnership with the United States. Saudi Arabia supplied the energy-hungry United States with oil from its 259 billion barrels of proven reserves (with sustainable production capacity of 10.5 million barrels per day). In exchange, the U.S. provided the kingdom with weapons and military support to protect its precious reserves. Following the 1990–91 Gulf War, the U.S. military remained in Saudi Arabia, outraging radical Islamic fundamentalists, who rejected the Westernization of their country. In his *Declaration of War,* Saudi-born terrorist

Osama Bin Laden wrote, "The presence of the USA Crusader military forces on land, sea and air of the states of the Islamic Gulf is the greatest danger threatening the largest oil reserve in the world. The existence of these forces in the area will provoke the people of the country and induce aggression on their religion, feelings and prides..."[2]

When King Fahd suffered a debilitating stroke in 1995, his half-brother, Crown Prince Abdullah, had assumed the daily responsibilities of the king. Following the 1998 oil crisis, when oil prices plummeted to just $8 per barrel, Crown Prince Abdullah pledged to introduce economic reforms that would diversify Saudi Arabia's oil-dependent economy. But as oil prices rose, and Saudis protested against modernization initiatives, economic reform once again became less of a priority. Then in 2001, oil prices dropped again, contributing to low revenues and a huge public debt. Increased output from non-OPEC oil producers threatened to take away Saudi Arabia's price-setting control.

On September 11, 2001, 19 terrorists hijacked four passenger jets and crashed them into the World Trade Center in New York City and the Pentagon in Washington, D.C. More than 3,000 people died. The hijackers were believed to be members of al Qaeda, an Islamic militant group led by Osama bin Laden.[3] In the weeks following the September 11th attacks, U.S.-Saudi ties weakened. Wary of strong anti-U.S. sentiment among radical Islamic fundamentalists, Saudi officials hesitated to join the international coalition against terrorism (organized by the U.S. government). Crown Prince Abdullah was also reluctant to allow the United States to launch attacks against Afghanistan from its airbases.

In the U.S., the press reported that some members of the royal Al Saud family were guilty of funding terrorist organizations. With 15 of the 19 terrorists of Saudi origin, many Americans grew critical of Saudi Arabia's government and culture. In an editorial published in the *Wall Street Journal* in January 2002, one American wrote, "Anti-women, anti-meritocratic, anti-democracy, anti-education in any meaningful, liberating sense, racist and profoundly anti-freedom, Saudi-sponsored religious extremism, funded by all drivers of those oversized SUVs [Sports Utility Vehicles] on American roads, is the most destructive vision in the world today."[4] Crown Prince Abdullah feared that the negative press would discourage foreign investment just as Saudi Arabia was beginning to open its economy. As he outlined his agenda for economic reform, the Crown Prince considered how he would balance economic diversification, the structure of established economic interests, and Islamic values.

Islam

Mecca (*Makkah* in Arabic) and Medina (*Madinah*), located in Saudi Arabia, are extremely holy sites for the followers of the Islamic faith, called Muslims.[*] In 2001, there were more than one billion Muslims worldwide. Their holy book—the Quran—contains the words of God (*Allah*) as spoken to His messenger Muhammad through the Angel Gabriel. Muhammad first promulgated the religion of Islam in Mecca in A.D. 610. As a result of persecution, Muhammad moved to Medina in 622, where he remained until his death in 632. [5] Muslims follow the Islamic religious law (*Shari'a*, meaning "the right path")*,* which is based on the Quran, the sayings of the prophet (*Hadith*), the studies of Muslim scholars (*fiqh*), and the studies of the interpretation of Quranic verses (*tafsir*).

As both a religious and socio-political system, Islam includes five obligatory acts, known as the five pillars of Islam: (i) affirming to no god but God, and Muhammad as His messenger, (ii) praying five times daily, (iii) paying a welfare tax to care for the needy, (iv) fasting during the daylight hours of the month of Ramadan (with the exception of pregnant women, soldiers on duty, etc.), and (v) making a pilgrimage (the *Hajj*) to Mecca, once in a person's lifetime. Another duty, sometimes called the sixth pillar, is that of *jihad*, or "struggle." There are two definitions of jihad. The "greater" jihad refers to a spiritual struggle for moral perfection. The "lesser" jihad refers to

a war fought against non-Muslim faiths. It is this concept of "lesser" jihad that has been misused by extremists to justify acts of terror against non-Muslims. Islam also includes six pillars of faith: the belief in (i) the one God, (ii) the angels, (iii) the sacred books, (iv) the messengers, (v) the day of judgment, and (vi) the divine will or events both good and evil.[6]

An important minority sect of Islam, the *Shiites*, coalesced around the belief that Muhammad had a true spiritual leader (*Imam*) as successor. The Imam was the source of authoritative interpretation of Islamic law as well as the leader of the polity. Shiite Muslims were concentrated in Iran, Iraq, Lebanon, and Yemen. Only 10 percent of Saudis were Shiites. The "traditionalists," who called themselves *Sunnis,* made up 90% of the Saudi population.

The Wahhabi movement greatly influenced the practice of Islam in Saudi Arabia. During the 18th century, Muhammad Ibn Abd Al Wahhab spoke out against the growing popularity of polytheistic practices and lax interpretations of Islamic law. He condemned such acts as votive and sacrificial offerings, praying to saints, and the building of shrines. Wahhabi religious scholars practiced a strict interpretation of the Quran and rejected modern reinterpretations of gender relations, family law, and participatory democracy.

In Saudi Arabia, religion pervaded every aspect of one's life.[†] Five times a day, businesses and shops shut down to allow for prayer. Muslims monitored each other closely to make sure that they followed dress codes, prayer rituals, and other Islamic laws, including the ban on alcohol consumption.[7] The state-financed religious police (*mutawwa)* harassed women who were not dressed properly and punished those who broke Islamic laws. In his book, *To Be a Saudi*, Hani A. Z. Yamani wrote that the "real effects of Islam on Saudi society are much more important and profound. It shapes our family relations, our education system, our social fabric, our future aspirations, and the manner in which we view life itself."[8]

---

* Technically, "Islam" is the act of submission to God's will (as revealed by God in the Quran) and a Muslim is one who submits to God's will.

† Saudi Arabians practiced a stricter form of Islam than most Islamic countries in the Middle East. In more liberal countries such as Egypt or Turkey, religion had less influence on law, politics, and women's rights, etc.

Country Background

Saudi Arabia's oil-rich desert kingdom occupies an estimated area of around 2.15 million square kilometers, about one-fourth the area of the United States.[9] Located on the Arabian Peninsula in the Middle East, Saudi Arabia shares borders with Jordan, Iraq, Kuwait, Bahrain, Qatar, United Arab Emirates, Oman, and Yemen. [See Map, **Exhibit 8.1**.] Arabs make up 90 percent of the population, while the remaining 10 percent are Afro-Asian.[10] Most of the population had been nomadic or semi-nomadic until the 1960s. But with rapid economic development and urban growth, more than 95 percent of the population settled by 2001.[11] The male literacy rate is 84 percent, while the female literacy rate is 67 percent.[12] Arabic is the official language.

Government

Saudi Arabia is a monarchy, ruled by the sons of the kingdom's founder, Abdul Aziz Ibn Andulrahman Al Saud (commonly known as Ibn Saud). The king rules in accordance with the Shari'a. Saudi kings and high-ranking princes hold weekly informal meetings for citizens to air their grievances. In 1953, King Saud Ibn Abdul Aziz introduced the kingdom's first form of collective government, the Council of Ministers. Responsible for executive matters, the family-dominated Council members are appointed by the king. However, the king remains autonomous and can veto any of the Council's decisions within thirty days.

Since the ruling family's legitimacy is tied to Islam, rulers look to the religious establishment to support its policy decisions. Senior religious scholars form the Council of Senior Ulema, an official body that serves as a forum for regular consultation between the king and religious leaders.[13] During times of controversy, the ulema issues opinions (*fatwas*) on any points in doubt.[14] Fatwas have been issued against the children's video game Pokémon, telephones that played recorded music on hold, and the sending of flowers to hospital patients, as well as the killing of non-Muslims and suicide terrorism.[15]

The Consultative Council acts as the legislative branch and an advisory forum for the king. Founded as part of King Fahd's 1992 Basic System of Government, the Consultative Council was originally composed of 60 appointed representatives who served four-year terms, including former senior government officials, community leaders, university professors, and members of the business community.[16] In 1997, King Fahd increased the Council's membership from 60 to 90 members. Crown Prince Abdullah expanded the Council to 120 members in 2001. In addition, a regional government system had been established in 1992 and was composed of 13 councils that were led by tribal leaders and prominent merchants.

The legal system is based on Islamic law and Royal Decrees issued by the king or the Council of Ministers. Judges, who spend years studying Islamic law, rule the kingdom's system of over 300 Shari'a courts. The king appoints the judges based on the recommendation of the Supreme Judicial Council. Many of the court's decisions uphold the Shari'a. The courts impose corporal punishment, including amputations of hands and feet for robbery and floggings for crimes such as "sexual deviance" and drunkenness. Capital punishment has at times been applied for crimes such as murder, rape, armed robbery, drug smuggling, and sodomy. After a lengthy trial, the condemned were decapitated in public squares.[17]

Early History

In the six centuries following Muhammad's revelations, the Saudi Arabian peninsula was ruled by a number of competing empires. The most powerful empires were the Byzantines centered in Constantinople and the Sassanids based in Persia. Science and mathematics flowered in the Middle East under the Abbasid caliphate, even as the territory it controlled declined steadily; learning, meanwhile, stagnated in Western Europe. During the sixteenth century, the Ottoman empire assumed control over most of the peninsula, but allowed local rulers a great deal of autonomy.

The real growth of modern Saudi Arabia began in the mid-eighteenth century with the rise of Muhammad Ibn Saud, the leader of the Al Saud family and the central state of Diriya. In 1744, he joined forces with Muhammad Ibn Abd Al Wahhab, leader of the puritanical Wahhabis. The two men vowed to establish a state ruled according to strict Islamic principles. Using Wahhabi religious fervor, they united the many tribes and families that ruled the various regions of the Arabian Peninsula. Clerics were sent throughout the region to teach the reformed Wahhabi movement to backsliding Muslims. In this power-sharing arrangement, Muslims were also obligated to swear an oath of allegiance to the legitimate Al Saud ruler. In return for complete sovereignty, the ruler was responsible for making sure that the people knew God's laws and conformed to them. Although the unification strategy met with initial success, rivalry between the tribes—encouraged by the Ottomans—threatened the dominance of the Al Saud family. By 1818, the Al Sauds, defeated by the Ottomans, had lost control of most of their territory.

In 1924, Abdul Aziz Ibn Andulrahman Al Saud (Ibn Saud) reasserted control over the country after leading a series of military conquests. Appealing once again to the Wahhabi doctrine, Ibn Saud made strategic and martial alliances with other tribes. In 1932, he proclaimed the kingdom of Saudi Arabia and declared himself king. Extraction of Saudi Arabia's vast oil reserves began in 1938 and later funded the kingdom's economic development.

The Al Saud Dynasty

When Ibn Saud died in 1953, he left over thirty sons. The eldest son, Saud, assumed the role of king and ruled for eleven years. Under his rule, Saudi Arabia co-founded the Organization of Petroleum Exporting Countries (OPEC), a cartel of oil-producing nations committed to controlling oil prices. In 1964, King Saud was deposed on grounds of incompetence by his half-brother, Faisal. Upon taking the throne, King Faisal introduced the kingdom's first economic reforms and used oil revenues to modernize the state. Reforms included increased education and healthcare expenditures, infrastructure development, and the introduction of television and other forms of Western technology that offended some devout Saudis.[18]

With the outbreak of the Arab-Israeli War in October 1973, U.S.-Saudi relations deteriorated. When the U.S. refused to stop aiding Israeli forces, Saudi Arabia joined the other Arab producers and imposed an oil embargo on the U.S. and the Netherlands. Then OPEC members agreed to cut production, sending oil prices up to an unprecedented $12 per barrel. With spare production capacity exhausted in the United States, this event transferred oil-pricing power from multinational companies to OPEC nations. Six years later, the Iranian Revolution sparked a second oil shock. OPEC fixed prices at $34 per barrel and revenues soared. By 1981, Saudi Arabia's oil revenues had reached $113 billion per year.[19]

When a young prince assassinated King Faisal in 1975, Prince Khalid became king. During his six-year reign, Saudi Arabia's oil wealth continued to finance the kingdom's economic development. In just a few years, desert villages were transformed into modern cities with air-conditioned skyscrapers and paved highways. Petrodollars helped build new airports, hotels, hospitals, power plants, oil refineries, mosques, and schools. Sectoral development programs granted loans and subsidies to nearly every sector of the economy. With huge government contracts, businesses flourished. While the oil boom greatly increased the wealth of Saudi princes, it also created a powerful new middle class of merchants.[20] Saudi citizens enjoyed a rise in per capita income and received numerous benefits from the state's generous social welfare system. When Khalid died in 1982, he was succeeded by his half-brother, King Fahd. Another half-brother, Prince Abdullah, was named the Crown Prince. To reassert his power and express his deep commitment to Islam, King Fahd assumed the title of the Custodian of the Two Holy Mosques.

Faced with falling oil prices, King Fahd led the kingdom through a deep recession in the mid-1980s. Hoping to boost non-oil revenues, King Fahd introduced an economic liberalization program that included the gradual reduction of electricity, water, and gasoline subsidies and the introduction of corporate taxes. However, the business community resisted many of the proposed reforms. Saudi politicians, who shared a special relationship with business leaders, quickly capitulated to their demands and promised to consider the interests of the business community in their liberalization program.[21] Turning his attention toward regional politics, King Fahd helped orchestrate a cease-fire between Iraq and Iran in 1988 and acted as a mediator in the Lebanese civil war. He also played a key role in the formation of the Gulf Cooperation Council (GCC), a coalition of six Arabian Gulf states that fostered regional economic cooperation and peaceful development.

The Gulf War and Beyond

When Iraq invaded Kuwait on August 2, 1990—triggering the Gulf War—King Fahd called on the United States to liberate Kuwait and protect the kingdom. The U.S. responded by sending more than 600,000 troops to Saudi Arabia. By allowing non-Muslim troops on the land of the two holy mosques, King Fahd angered Islamic fundamentalists and some conservative factions of the ulema. Ultimately, the U.S. troops, aided by a coalition of Western and Arab allies, defeated Iraq and reestablished Kuwait's sovereignty.

After King Fahd suffered a stroke, Crown Prince Abdullah became the de-facto ruler of the kingdom. Popular among Saudis, Crown Prince Abdullah was committed to economic and social reform. As a staunch supporter of Arab and Islamic causes, he was highly critical of the United States' pro-Israel position in the Arab-Israeli conflict.

In 2002, the advanced ages of 81-year old King Fahd and 79-year old Crown Prince Abdullah sparked some debate over the kingdom's next successor. Traditionally, the throne was passed from brother to brother among the sons of Ibn Saud. The 1992 Basic Law of Government codified the process of royal succession. The reigning king should nominate his heir, choosing the "most upright" of Ibn Saud's descendants, of which there are now more than 7,000. Among Saud's sons are the so-called "Sudairi Seven"—seven sons of his favorite wife. Kind Fahd is one of these, along with Prince Sultan, Abdel Rahman, Nayef, Turki, Salmon, and Ahmed. Crown Prince Abdullah is the son of another wife and has no brothers. The Sudairi Seven hold considerable power, limiting Abdullah's freedom of action. Several of their children are being groomed for power, as are some of Abdullah's. The choice of successor, however, will not be made until Abdullah succeeds Fahd. [22]

The Economy in 2002

The souring of the global economy coincided with the September 11th terrorist attacks, lowering oil demand and driving oil prices down in the fourth quarter of 2001. Crude oil prices fell $10 per barrel between August and October.[23] Despite the downturn, economists estimated that Saudi Arabia's economy grew 2.2 percent in 2001. Although the kingdom had a budget surplus of $6 billion in 2000, low oil prices and high government spending contributed to a budget deficit of $6.7 billion in 2001. The public debt rose to $160 billion, or 99 percent of GDP. Since 1995, Saudi Arabia had generally enjoyed surpluses on the current account (except in 1998). For 2001 it measured $8.3 billion. Saudi oil production for the year averaged a little over 8 million barrels per day (bl/d), while oil prices averaged $21.80 per barrel ($24.30 Brent). [24] [See **Exhibits 8.2**, **8.3**, and **8.4**.]

In 2001, Saudi Arabia's central bank, the Saudi Arabian Monetary Agency (SAMA), followed a monetary policy that aimed to maintain the stability of prices and the Saudi riyal exchange rate.[25] After posting a negative 1.0 percent inflation rate in 2000, inflation remained low, recording a rate of negative 0.8 percent in 2001. The stock market continued to grow, rising 43 percent in 1999, 11.3 percent in 2000, and 7.6 percent in 2001. "Monetary conditions are sound and well managed— liquidity is ample in the banking system, money supply growth is supportive of GDP growth, inflation is in check, and interest rates are low," reported the Saudi American Bank (SAMBA).[26] Since June 1986, the Saudi riyal had been pegged against the U.S. dollar at a rate of SR3.75:US$1. Yet, "the currency is not overvalued," affirmed Brad Bourland, Chief Economist at SAMBA. "It had to be defended during the 1998 oil price collapse, but it has been stable ever since."[27]

The economic outlook for 2002, however, looked bleak. Some officials expected GDP growth to remain flat, while others predicted it would contract by 2 percent. Even if the world economy recovered, stimulating oil demand, Saudi oil production would only expand from 7.0 million bl/d to 7.4 million bl/d because of increased output by non-OPEC producers. Growth in the non-oil sector was forecast at 4 percent. The budget deficit would measure close to $12 billion, given a 32 percent decline in revenues and a 21 percent cut in spending. Saudi Arabia's public debt was expected to swell to $180 billion or 109 percent of GDP. Inflation would likely remain under 1 percent. [28] [See **Exhibits 8.6 and 8.7**.]

Saudi Arabia hoped to join the World Trade Organization by 2004. To gain admittance, Saudi Arabia would need to increase market access to its banking, finance, communications, and tourism sectors. Other trade-liberalizing steps would include lowering tariffs, eliminating tax differentials between foreign and domestic service firms, and improving commitments for legal, health, education, and environmental services.[29] The business community spoke in favor of the goal of WTO membership, saying it would lead to an open economy and a more transparent financial and legal system.

The Economic Reform Agenda

During the high-price environment of the 1970s, Saudi oil revenues subsidized education, utilities, healthcare, and housing. However, when oil prices fell during the 1980s and 1990s, government funds ran dry. Saudi Arabia's oil-dependent economy could no longer support lavish welfare programs. Volatile oil prices contributed to persistent budget deficits. Between 1986 and 1994, budget deficits averaged nearly $2.5 billion per year.[30] As the debt burden increased, economic reform and diversification became a priority. Reform advocates pushed for the sale of government-owned industries and the removal of subsidies that hampered the development of a free market system. [See **Exhibit 8.5**.]

"The days of the oil boom are over," declared Crown Prince Abdullah in a 1996 speech. Assembling a new cabinet, he announced a multi-year reform program dedicated to fiscal discipline, privatization, and the gradual elimination of deficits.[31] The new Minister of Finance and National Economy, Dr. Ibhrahim Al Assaf, supported Crown Prince Abdullah's efforts to grow Saudi Arabia's non-oil economy. "The economic atmosphere is appropriate for the private sector to play a higher role in the national economy, given the opportunities presented by a strong and modern infrastructure and liberalization," assured Al Assaf.[32]

The price collapse of 1998 undermined Crown Prince Abdullah's initial attempts to rein in the public debt and eliminate the budget deficit. By the end of the year, decreased revenues contributed to a deficit of over $12 billion. The Crown Prince, however, remained committed to economic reform. In August 1999, he issued a Royal Decree announcing the formation of the Supreme Economic Council (SEC). The new eleven-member Council met weekly to discuss how to boost investment, create jobs for Saudi nationals, and increase the role of the private sector. In April 2000, the Council passed the historic Foreign Investment Act (FIA). The new code represented "the most significant reform in Saudi Arabia's investment

climate" by allowing foreign companies to own 100% of local entities and permitting non-Saudis to own real estate.[33] Previously, foreign holdings of 49% barred companies "from qualifying for tax holidays, soft loans from the Saudi Industrial Development Fund (SIDF) and equal treatment in competition for government contracts."[34] The SEC also established the Saudi Arabian General Investment Authority (SAGIA), responsible for promoting foreign investment and streamlining the application process by creating a one-stop shop facility.[35]

Diversification in 2002

Despite the SEC's diversification efforts, Saudi Arabia's economy remained largely dependent on oil revenues at the end of 2001. Since 1991, the oil sector had accounted for an average of 35% of nominal GDP, about 75 percent of government revenues and 85 percent of export receipts.[36] Critics blamed Crown Prince Abdullah for the state's continued involvement in the economy. Many were frustrated with the slow pace of reform. "We're becoming a nation of great talks and no action," complained one businessman.[37] Saudi Arabia's rigid legal system hindered many reform efforts. "The government is slow to change because the old laws provide no mechanisms to review," explained Prince Mohammed al Faisal. "The government must set up a Committee to make a change, and this takes forever."[38] Reformers faced opposition from some members of the royal family who did not want to curb their extravagant spending habits. In order to honor Islamic values, reformers had the difficult task of modernizing without introducing Western values. "We are proud Arab Muslims. We have thousands of years of history and culture, and we like to modernize, but not necessarily Westernize, and we are different," stated Prince Bandar Bin Sultan, Saudi Arabia's ambassador to the United States.[39]

Although the oil industry dominated Saudi Arabia's economy, the non-oil sector grew throughout the 1990s. Officials estimated that private sector growth averaged between 4 and 5 percent in 2001. Growth in the agriculture, manufacturing, construction, and financial services sectors contributed to the rising importance of the non-oil economy. [See **Exhibits 8.8** and **8.9**.] In the 1980s, the government pursued a policy of greater self-sufficiency in agriculture. A decade later, Saudi Arabia became a top wheat exporter and was self-sufficient in poultry, egg farming, and certain fruits and vegetables. Agriculture was also an important source of employment. Private sector participation in the manufacturing industry expanded in the 1990s. Large investments were made in chemicals, construction materials, rubber, plastics, ceramics, and glassware. The construction sector accounted for an estimated 8.7% of GDP in 1999 and was a large employer of non-Saudi workers. With its role in commissioning infrastructure projects, the government was the construction industry's biggest client. Saudi Arabia's 10 commercial banks operated in the markets for foreign exchange, inter-bank deposits, government debt, and equity. Saudi Arabia's stock market was an over-the-counter market in which commercial banks bought and sold shares through an electronic trading system, established by SAMA in 1990. With few issuers and a narrow investor base, the stock market remained relatively illiquid.[40]

Intent on diversifying the economy, Crown Prince Abdullah continued to propose reforms, using the seventh five-year economic plan as his guide. The 2000–2004 plan set infrastructural targets and provided a spending framework. The plan emphasized job creation for Saudis, foreign investment, and non-oil GDP growth. Despite past reform failures, many Saudis were confident that this time, Crown Prince Abdullah would break the kingdom from its oil dependency. Outlining the latest program of reforms, Dr. Fawaz Al Alami, the Deputy Minister of Commerce, assured that "these reforms [would] help Saudi Arabia compete and prosper in a globalized economy."[41]

Infrastructure Development

By 2002, Saudi Arabia's infrastructure—built during the 1970s oil boom—was in need of repair. While the intricate highway system remained in good condition, the country's water, power, and telephone systems required significant investment. In the big cities of Riyadh and Jeddah, water rationing often occurred during the hot summer months, when temperatures reached 109 degrees Fahrenheit. To support Saudi Arabia's growing population, the government would need to spend an estimated $100 billion to meet electricity demand over the next fifteen years and $27 billion on water treatment facilities.[42] Other development projects included the construction of new schools and

healthcare facilities, a coast-to-coast railway network, and a $350 million expansion of King Abdulaziz International Airport in Jeddah.

Foreign Investment

In order to protect against volatile oil prices and spur job creation, the government hoped to encourage a steady stream of foreign investment. Already, the FIA had eliminated several key barriers to foreign investment, opening up the gas, water, electricity, petrochemicals, and other sectors of the economy. Showing his commitment to economic liberalization, Crown Prince Abdullah proposed the opening of the kingdom's upstream gas sector to foreign companies. He established the Supreme Council for Petroleum and Mineral Affairs to negotiate with independent oil companies. In May 2001, the government selected ExxonMobil, Shell, BP, Phillips, Occidental, Marathon, TotalFinaElf, and Conoco to develop the upstream gas sector. The Saudi Gas Initiative was expected to bring an estimated $25 billion in foreign investment into the kingdom. However, nine months after the preliminary agreements were signed, officials had yet to close the deal. Disputes over access to gas resources and the proper rate of return stalled negotiations, and the March 2, 2002, deadline passed without an official agreement. [See World Oil Markets note.]

Privatization

Increasing budget deficits made the privatization of state-owned companies a priority. Despite resistance from bureaucrats, Crown Prince Abdullah announced that he was "keen to progress with privatization in a way that would not negatively impact on the welfare of citizens, especially the less privileged."[43] Given the high unemployment rate, Crown Prince Abdullah hoped to avoid massive layoffs. Nevertheless, he urged privatization efforts to continue in the telecommunications, electricity, airline, postal service, and railway sectors.

Although the telecommunications and electricity industries had been prepared for privatization, no shares had been sold to the private sector. In April 1998, the Council of Ministers approved the formation of the Saudi Telecommunications Company. The first group of shares were to be sold in early 2000, eventually reducing the state's share to zero. However, when talks with the U.S.-owned SBC

Communications broke down, the Saudi government decided to focus on restructuring, postponing the telecommunications privatization until 2003.[44]

In February 2000, Saudi Arabia's ten electricity companies consolidated into a single joint-stock company, the Saudi Electricity Company (SEC). The state had yet to release the schedule for the divestment of its 85% holding. Ultimately, the new power company was to be self-supported and independent from the government. The SEC would be responsible for increasing total capacity from 17, 000 megawatts per year in 2000 to 70,000 megawatts per year by the year 2020.[45]

In 1995, Saudi Arabian Airlines (Saudia) initiated a modernization campaign to prepare the largest airline in the Middle East for privatization. However, reform efforts to eliminate free ticket allocations to government officials, lower-than-cost domestic airfares, government subsidies, and other inefficiencies dragged on for several years. By 2002, there were still no concrete plans to privatize. Investors would not be interested in buying a stake in the airline until it became profitable.[46]

Banks

There were ten commercial banks in Saudi Arabia, of which three were wholly Saudi-owned. The Al Rajhi Banking and Investment Company followed the Shari'a, which outlawed the payment of interest. At the other nine banks, only a small, but quickly growing, portion of business was conducted along Islamic principles. Most banking was conducted along traditional lines, with payment and collection of interest, despite uncertain legal support. However, since banks were not legally protected in recovering faulty loans on real estate collateral, few provided mortgage loans to homebuyers and real estate investors, thus creating a severe financing shortage.[47] There were reports that the banking sector was looking into setting up separate non-religious courts to handle business and commercial disputes.[48]

Tourism

There were three categories of Saudi Arabian tourists: pilgrims making the *Hajj* to the holy cities of Mecca and Medina, business visitors, and recreational tourists from Saudi Arabia and other Gulf Corporation Council (GCC) states. In April 2000, Crown Prince Abdullah established the Supreme Council on Tourism. The Council's vision statement read, "As the cradle of Islam, we the Kingdom of Saudi Arabia aim to develop sustainable tourism for the socio-cultural, environmental and economic benefit of all, reflecting our cherished Islamic values, heritage and traditional hospitality."[49] To increase non-oil revenues, the Council planned to develop the domestic tourism industry. The Union of Industrial and Trade Chambers estimated that domestic tourism expenditure averaged $17 billion annually. Statistics showed that the number of domestic tourists—which increased from 2.4 million in 1998 to 3.3 million in 2000—was growing at an annual rate of 17%. The Council's Sustainable Tourism Development Plan focused on family-oriented tourism that cultivated Islamic values. The Council identified 10,000 potential historical, cultural, and natural sites; organized state, city, and town tourism boards; and was prepared to submit official proposals by April 2002.[50]

Social Issues and Reform

Demographics and Unemployment

The Saudi government's official population estimate of 22 million included 5.3 million foreign nationals.* Saudi Arabia's fertility rate of 5.5 infants per woman was much higher than the world average of 2.7. By the end of 2001, more than 45% of the population was below the age of 15.[51] [See **Exhibit 8.12**.] To accommodate the large youth population, Saudi Arabia would have to build more schools, increase health care spending, and create employment opportunities.

The Saudi population was expected to nearly double to 29.7 million in 2020, increasing the labor force from 3.3 million in 2000 to 8.3 million in 2020. Already, young Saudis had difficulty finding suitable employment. The Saudi American Bank estimated that the unemployment rate of male Saudis in 2001 was 15 percent. [See **Exhibit 8.11**.] Others estimated that the unemployment rate was closer to 20 percent. Each year, an estimated 163,000 Saudis

---

* Some scholars believed that the government overestimated the population for defense purposes. These scholars estimated that the actual population figure was closer to 13 million, including 4 million foreign nationals.

entered the labor force, while the private sector generated about 50,000 jobs and the public sector generated about 30,000 jobs.[52] Women made up just 15% of the workforce.[53] Although the poor received social benefits, unemployed Saudis were not granted any direct government support. Many became burdens for their extended families, which provided support until jobs were secured.

During the oil boom, Saudis had lived quite comfortably. After receiving a free college education, Saudis were guaranteed a high-paying job in the public sector, where they often worked a 4-hour day.[54] When oil revenues fell, some Saudis were reluctant to seek work in the private sector. Most of the unemployed Saudis were in their twenties and thirties. The younger Saudis longed for the laid-back lifestyle that their parents had enjoyed. But government salaries had changed little over the past fifteen years, and young Saudis could not afford to live extravagantly.[55] Per-capita income had fallen from $18,000 at the height of the oil boom in 1981 to $7,500 in 2001.* Still, many Saudi youths believed that certain jobs, usually held by non-Saudis, were beneath them. "They do not want to get their hands dirty," commented one expatriate business manager. "Until young Saudis change their attitudes, the country is going to remain overdependent on foreign labor."[56]

Many Saudis lacked the specialized skills of foreign workers, who made up one-third of the population, two-thirds of the workforce, and 80 percent of the private workforce.[57] University graduates, who tended to major in Islamic, Arabic, and other studies that were not in high demand in the workplace, often lacked practical experience. [See **Exhibit 8.13**.] Employers argued that foreign workers were cheaper and more dependable. "Most Saudis are spoiled," explained one investment banker. "They won't work. They believe that by their birthright, they deserve this or that." [58] Often, the most efficient workers were non-Saudis.[59]

In an effort to increase Saudi employment, the government introduced the Saudization policy. The goal of the policy was to replace foreign workers with Saudi nationals. Since 1995

---

* The Saudi American Bank argued that despite the drop in GDP per capita the quality of life in Saudi Arabia had improved as a result of cumulative government investment in public infrastructure and services.

the government raised the administrative expenses of hiring expatriates. Another resolution required firms with a minimum of 20 employees to Saudize 5% of its workforce per year. However, many private firms continued to hire expatriates because of weak law enforcement and the availability of cheaper foreign labor.[60] In 1996–97, average monthly salaries for professional and technical jobs held by Saudis were SR8,390 compared to SR3,987 for non-Saudis. For jobs that required higher educational degrees, salaries were around SR18,454 for Saudis and SR9,139 for non-Saudis.[61]

Education

In 2000, 60% of eligible Saudi boys were enrolled in both primary and secondary schools. For girls, enrollment rates were 58% and 52%, respectively.[62] Saudi Arabia's ulema had substantial control over the state's education system. As a result, primary, secondary, and, often, tertiary school curriculums were focused on Islamic studies. In the lower schools, one-third of the curriculum was dedicated to Islamic studies; one-third to Arabic; and one-third to other subjects, usually minimizing social sciences, math, and physical sciences.[63] Many parents complained that the religious-intensive lessons, which were based on rote learning, bored students. Some were concerned that the education system encouraged Saudi youth to join radical Islamic fundamentalist groups. "The education system is a disaster," argued one parent. "Religious fanatics control the curriculum...It is very radical and anti-West."[64]

During the 1970s and 1980s, the government funded university education abroad for many Saudis. By the 1990s, eight universities had been established in the kingdom. The government continued to pay for higher education, but generally for attendance at domestic universities. Many seeking doctoral and master degrees abroad were still funded by the government. Only 30% of university students were females, who were allowed to only enroll in six of the eight universities. There were two Islamic universities and six traditional universities. Even at the more technical universities, religion dominated the curriculum. In his book, Yamani wrote, "Our universities should emphasize technical specializations, as religious guidance is to be confined to the home, the mosque, and the elementary school. It is ludicrous that an engineer's degree is dependent on his knowledge of the holy Quran."[65]

Crown Prince Abdullah aimed to improve the weak education system. Despite expenditure cutbacks, the 2002 budget allocated SR54.3 billion (26.9% of the total budget) to education. This represented a 2.5% increase over the 2001 budget, which allocated SR53 billion (24.7% of the total budget).[66] Other reform efforts included the hiring of 86,000 new teachers and the construction of new schools.

Women

The role of women in Saudi society was controversial. Saudi culture placed restrictions on where and how women traveled, worked, dined, studied, shopped, dressed, married, and divorced. Although Islamic law allowed polygamy, it had become less common.[67] Women, including foreign women, were not allowed to drive and, when traveling, had to be escorted by a male relative. They could be admitted to hospitals only with the consent of a male relative. In public, women were required to wear the *abaya*, a black robe and veil that covered the entire body, exposing only the eyes. When a fire at a girls' school in Jeddah left fifteen students dead, the religious police were accused of stopping the girls from leaving the burning building because they were not wearing the *abaya*. The incident fueled debate over the restrictions placed on Saudi women.[68]

Although women were permitted to work, only 5% of them held jobs. They received less pay and fewer benefits than males. Female workers were not allowed to have contact with their male co-workers. Most women worked as teachers, physicians, or nurses. However, some female entrepreneurs had taken advantage of a 1977 law granting women licenses to run private businesses. Working their way around restrictive customs, many of these women established competitive companies and shops. The arrival of the Internet helped many females run their businesses more efficiently. Event planners, fashion merchants, and travel agents were able to make online sales and transactions that would have been more complicated in person.[69]

Some progressive Saudis believed that women's rights should be expanded. "When will we start showing the trust that our mothers, wives, sisters, and daughters justly deserve?" questioned Hani Yamani.[70] Others believed that women's rights were protected by the Shari'a.

"The Islamic faith has given women rights that are equal to or more than the rights given them in the Old Testament and the Bible," explained Crown Prince Abdullah. "There is no inherent discrimination against women and no limitation to how far women can go in our society."[71] Saudi women's rights included owning property, receiving financial support from husbands or male relatives, and gaining access to free, though segregated, education through the university level. Recently, two private girls' colleges had been established. One student at the Dar-Al-Hikma College for Girls commented, "From this college, I think lots of women will have a role in changing the country."[72]

Over the years, Saudi women lobbied for increased civil rights. On November 6, 1990, more than seventy women drove through the streets of Riyadh protesting the ban on female driving. When Islamic fundamentalists condemned their behavior, the government fired the female demonstrators from their jobs. In December 2001, Saudi women's rights expanded when interior minister Prince Nayef bin Abdul-Aziz agreed to issue female citizens their own identity cards. The new cards included a picture of the woman's unveiled face. Previously, women carried family identity cards, which listed them as dependents of their fathers or husbands. "The problem is the picture [of a woman's face]. They don't want us to show our pictures," explained a Saudi woman. "It is not Islam, it is cultural."[73] The new identity cards would help prevent fraud and give women more control over their bank accounts and business transactions.[74]

Radical Fundamentalism

Those who believe, and those who are Jews, and the Christians, and the Sabians, whoever believes in Allah and the Last day and does good, they shall have their reward from their Lord, and there is no fear for them, nor shall they grieve.

—Quran, 2.62*

---

* The Quran was revealed as a list of teachings in response to a specific question, situation, or historical event. Therefore, many Muslims discourage interpreting Quranic verses out of context.

Do not take the Jews and Christians for friends; they are friends of each other; and whoever amongst you takes them for a friend, then surely he is one of them; surely Allah does not guide the unjust people

—Quran, 5.51 [*]

Since the 1920s, radical Islamic fundamentalists challenged the ruling Al Saud family's legitimacy. The leaders of the opposition movement in Saudi Arabia were religious scholars (*ulema*). Some were angry at the monarchy for assuming control over political and economic reform. To appease the clerics, the Al Sauds accommodated their authority in religion, education, and the judiciary. However, the ulema demanded a greater role in political and economic decision-making in order to preserve Islamic traditions. They also protested against modernization efforts that helped the wealthy and excluded the poor. As scholar Nazih Ayubi explained in *Political Islam,* "The Islamists are not angry because the airplane has replaced the camel; they are angry because they cannot get on the airplane."[75]

In November 1979, a Sunni Muslim extremist and 250 armed followers seized the Grand Mosque in Mecca. After several weeks, the Saudi military successfully removed the dissidents. More than 200 soldiers and radicals died in the standoff, while the remaining radicals were publicly executed.[76] In the same year, Iranian fundamentalists overthrew the Shah of Iran. The Iranian revolution mobilized the Saudi radical fundamentalist movement. When oil prices fell in the mid-1980s, the ulema recruited disgruntled low-income citizens. They condemned the Al Sauds for continuing to live extravagantly during the recession. The Gulf War crisis of the early-1990s further mobilized political activists, who took advantage of the kingdom's instability to recruit more followers. Iraq's sudden invasion of Kuwait shocked the kingdom. The radicals felt betrayed when the

royal family called on non-Muslim foreigners to defend Saudi Arabia's oil fields.[77]

When King Fahd announced his plans to initiate political reforms in November 1990, the radical ulema responded by issuing a petition, entitled The Letter of Demands. The document listed a set of political reforms that would increase the power of religious leaders. The demands included the establishment of an independent consultative council, the repeal of laws and regulations that did not conform to Islamic law, and a requirement for all government officials to be moral. Public wealth was to be evenly distributed. Banks were to be cleansed of usury. And, foreign policy could not rely on alliances that were not sanctioned by Islamic law.[78]

Two years later, the King Saud University Committee for Reform and Advice submitted a second letter of demands, entitled The Memorandum of Exhortation. The letter, which was signed by more than one hundred professors and ulema, listed grievances such as military overspending, government aid to non-Islamic governments, and the airing of television programs that glorified "decadent Western lifestyles." This time, the petitioners demanded that both the government and the ulema be released from their roles as the sole arbiters of Islam. They sought to return to the more decentralized religious system that had existed before Ibn Saud. In response, King Fahd denounced the radicals and their petition over national television, while reaffirming the state's deep commitment to Islam.[79]

On November 13, 1995, a bomb placed in a pickup truck exploded outside the U.S. Army headquarters in Riyadh, killing five Americans and two Indians. Several others were wounded. Although five Saudi citizens confessed on television and were publicly executed, there were rumors that others were responsible for the bombing. A second terrorist attack against U.S. soldiers based in Saudi Arabia occurred in June 1996. The car bombing at the air base in Khobar killed 19 U.S. servicemen and wounded 64 others. Saudi militant Osama Bin Laden was suspected to be linked to the bombing, though U.S. investigators eventually blamed the attack on a senior member of the Iranian Revolutionary Guard.[80]

Following the September 11th terrorist attacks, the U.S. press published controversial stories that questioned the future stability of the

---

[*] There are many different translations of the Quran. One version uses "allies" instead of "friends," thus altering the meaning of this quotation. According to most commentators, this verse is taken to mean that each of these communities, the Jews and the Christians, extend genuine friendship to other adherents of the same faith, and that the Muslim should not expect the same genuine friendship from these communities.

Al Saud regime. The articles revealed bitter power struggles among the princes, corruption scandals, human rights abuses, and the growing membership of fundamentalist groups. Some Saudis agreed that the Saudi government was becoming increasingly unstable. "The government is not solid," warned one Saudi. "In ten years or less, if the government can't solve the kingdom's problems, the existing government will be overthrown." Some feared that continued public dissent could lead to an Islamic uprising, reminiscent of the Iranian revolution.

Upset by the U.S. media, Crown Prince Abdullah defended the regime and criticized foreign journalists for misinterpreting Saudi society. "It might seem paradoxical to Western observers that a royal family who denies democracy, basic freedoms, and accountability could enjoy widespread public support—but a paradox in the West is politics in the Middle East," wrote Nawaf E. Obaid. In his article, "In Al-Saud We Trust," Obaid compared Saudi Arabia with pre-revolutionary Iran, concluding that the Saudi government was more stable and had greater popular support. Many Saudis agreed that while some corrupt royals were disliked, others, like Crown Prince Abdullah, were extremely popular. [81] These Saudis believed that the radical Islamic fundamentalist movement had weakened in recent years. Crown Prince Abdullah's efforts to include the ulema in political and economic decision-making combined with higher oil prices had helped appease many radicals. "No, I don't think the government is fragile," commented Brad Bourland. "There's really no terrorism in Saudi Arabia, and the government is stable." [82]

Fragile Ties with the United States

Following the Palestinian uprising (*intifada*) of October 2000, the Saudi media (which was tightly controlled by the government) aired Israel's violent response on national television. Saudis watched as Israelis attacked rock-throwing Palestinians with tanks, helicopters, and guns supplied by the United States. Many Saudis could not understand why the U.S. continued to support the Israeli army. "It is strange given the number of people in Palestine who suffer and die, that the West sees Islam as a problem," remarked Saleh A. Kamel of Arab Radio and Television. [83] Crown Prince Abdullah continued to openly criticize the United States' role in the Israeli-Palestinian conflict. "When you look at your own nation and how it was founded, the principles were justice, righteousness, equity and concern for eliminating evil and decadence and corruption," he said. "As a member of my community, it is very difficult for me to accept what is happening in the territories because it is inhumane and violates basic principles and tenets." [84]

After the events of September 11th, many Saudis believed that the kingdom would break ties with the U.S. if it maintained what the Saudis saw as a pro-Israel position. "The Israeli-Palestine problem is central to U.S.-Saudi relations," warned Prince Mohammed al Faisal. [85] There were rumors that Saudi officials had threatened to remove U.S. troops from Saudi Arabia if the violence in the West Bank and Gaza Strip continued. But Crown Prince Abdullah denied the rumors and remained silent on the issue. "Our relationship over the years has been based on equity and based on common interests and a shared worldview," he explained. "In the current environment, we find it very difficult to defend America, and so we keep our silence." [86] [See **Exhibit 8.10**.]

Saudi Arabia's connections to the September 11th suicide bombings had also strained its relationship with the United States. In late 2001, NATO authorities who raided the Sarajevo office of the Saudi High Commissioner for Aid to Bosnia discovered computer files containing photographs of terrorist attacks and street maps of Washington, D.C. Also found was "a computer program explaining how to use crop duster aircraft to spread pesticide[s], and materials used to make fake U.S. State Department identification badges and credit cards...." [87]

On January 28, 2002, Crown Prince Abdullah invited U.S. journalists from *The New York Times* and *The Washington Post* to speak with him about the status of U.S.-Saudi relations. In contrast to his August letter, Crown Prince Abdullah assured his audience that the relationship was strong and secure. "I don't believe there is a change in the relationship between the United States and Saudi Arabia," he explained. "Our relationship has been strong for over six decades, and I don't see any reason why there should be a change." [88] Although he remained critical of America's Middle East policy, Crown Prince Abdullah challenged those who questioned the stability of the kingdom and its close ties with the U.S.

Lessons from September 11th

Following the Gulf War, King Fahd had struggled to balance modernization with Islamic tradition. Trying to explain Islam to the Western world had also proved to be a major challenge. In a televised speech in March 1991, King Fahd had stated, "We are never interested in any way, shape or form with those who want to say that this country is a backward country…Why are we backward or underdeveloped? Because we hold fast to the Book of God and the Sunna of His Prophet? This is a strength and an honor. We take pride in it…I promise before God that the Islamic faith is our basis, our foundation, our starting point. What contradicts it we are not interested in and will not follow."[89]

After the September 11th terrorist attacks, Saudis felt an urgency to explain their religion to the rest of the world. Since many of the terrorists had Saudi origins, the kingdom feared that people would assume that all followers of Islam were violent. "Radicals take pieces of Islam, focus on them and ignore other facets of the religion. You have to take the whole thing as a package," asserted Prince Mohammed al Faisal. "The September 11th killers betrayed Islam."*[90]*

Proving his commitment to political reform, Crown Prince Abdullah attacked corruption in the Al Saud family. He took away lavish privileges like free telephone calls and travel on private airlines and criticized family members for demanding large commissions on international business deals. In his quest to liberalize the oil-dependent economy, Crown Prince Abdullah wooed international oil giants to invest in the oil sector; cut import taxes from 12% to 5% in two months, and pushed for WTO membership.

While supporting modernization efforts, Crown Prince Abdullah remained a devout Muslim. He took steps to open the economy to foreigners without disrupting Islamic traditions. As an Arab nationalist, he pushed for the formation of a Palestinian state and criticized those who supported Israel.[91] Striving to end the conflict, Crown Prince Abdullah proposed that Saudi Arabia and its Arab neighbors establish normal relations with Israel if it agreed to withdraw to its pre-1967 borders.[92] "I tell the Israeli people," said Crown Prince Abdullah at the Arab League summit in Beirut, "that if their government gives up the policy of force and suppression and accepts genuine peace, we will not hesitate in accepting the Israeli people's right to live in security with the rest of the people in the region."[93] On Thursday, March 28, 2002, the Arab League voted to adopt its first pan-Arab initiative for peace in the Middle East.[94]

In the post-September 11th world, pressure to reform Saudi Arabia's economy mounted. Though Crown Prince Abdullah had laid the groundwork for change, it would take years before Saudis felt the benefits of economic diversification. With a high unemployment rate, depressed oil prices, and a lower standard of living, Saudi youth were growing impatient. Fanatical religious groups, who rebelled against the status quo, economic inequality, social injustices, and closed politics, appealed to some disillusioned citizens. "Before we come to [the United States] for help, let's get our own house in order," concluded Prince Bandar Bin Sultan.[95]

EXHIBIT 8.1 **MAP OF SAUDI ARABIA**

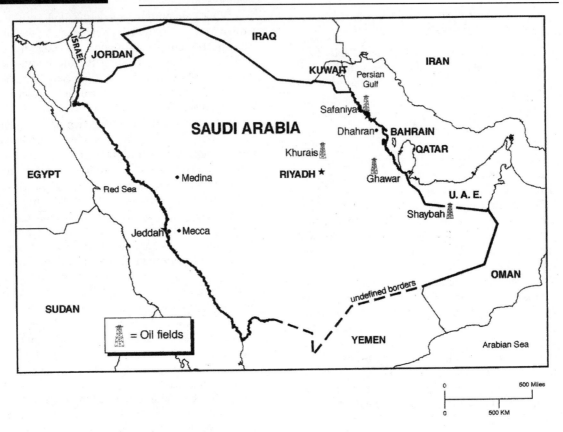

SOURCE: Created by Case writer.

| EXHIBIT 8.2 | **HISTORICAL SUMMARY, 1990–2001** |

	1990	1991	1992	1993	1994	1995	1996	1997	1998	1999	2000	2001
GDP and Components:												
Nominal GDP (SR billion)	391.9	442.0	461.4	443.8	450.0	478.7	529.3	548.4	481.2	535.0	648.9	*635.2*
Real GDP (SR billion at 1970 prices)	56.2	60.9	62.7	62.3	61.8	62.0	62.9	64.6	65.6	65.9	68.8	*69.5*
Real GDP per capita (US dollars)	N/A	N/A	N/A	N/A	6,594	6,789	7,294	7,313	6,208	6,689	7,863	*7,483*
Real GDP growth rate (%)	10.7	8.4	2.8	-0.6	-0.7	0.3	1.4	2.7	1.5	0.4	4.5	*1.0*
Employment and Other:												
Labor Force (millions)	5.6	5.8	6.2	6.7	6.9	6.7	6.9	7.3	7.8	8.2	8.6	*8.8*
Unemployment Rate (% of Saudi labor force)	N/A	N/A	N/A	N/A	N/A	N/A	N/A	N/A	N/A	N/A	14	*15*
Population (millions)	N/A	N/A	N/A	N/A	18.2	18.8	19.4	20.0	20.7	21.3	22.0	*22.7*
Saudi	N/A	N/A	N/A	N/A	13.2	13.6	14.1	14.6	15.1	15.7	16.2	*16.8*
Non-Saudi	N/A	N/A	N/A	N/A	5.0	5.2	5.3	5.4	5.6	5.6	5.8	*5.9*
Population Growth Rate (% change)	N/A	N/A	N/A	N/A	N/A	3.3	3.2	3.1	3.5	2.9	3.3	*3.2*
Gross National Savings (% GDP)	15.6	-2.1	7.8	9.7	11.4	16.5	18.5	19.9	11.1	19.2	24.6	*20.3*
Financial Indicators:												
Exchange Rate (SR/US dollar)	3.745	3.745	3.745	3.745	3.745	3.745	3.745	3.745	3.745	3.745	3.745	*3.745*
Stock of M1 (SR billion)	102	120	123	122	126	125	133	141	140	157	166	*181*
M1 growth rate (%)	11.6	17.7	2.9	-1.6	3.4	-0.2	6.1	6.1	-0.6	11.7	5.7	*9.2*
CPI (% change)	2.2	4.8	-0.1	1.1	0.6	4.8	1.2	0.1	-0.4	-1.6	-1.0	*-0.8*
3-month Saudi riyal deposit rate	N/A	5.83	3.65	3.52	5.10	6.18	5.47	5.79	6.21	6.14	6.67	*N/A*
Budget Deficit (% of GDP)	N/A	-16.9	-9.0	-10.5	-7.7	-5.7	-3.7	-2.9	-10.3	-6.9	3.6	*-3.9*
Public Debt (% GDP)	N/A	N/A	N/A	N/A	76.0	83.0	84.0	87.0	116.0	119.0	95.0	*99.0*
Oil Prices:												
Arabian Light (US dollars/barrel)	20.82	17.43	17.94	15.68	15.39	16.73	19.91	18.71	12.20	17.45	26.81	*N/A*

SOURCE: Compiled from Saudi American Bank, *The Saudi Economy in 2002*. February 2002; Saudi Arabian Monetary Authority, *Thirty-Seventh Annual Report*, September 2001; The Economist Intelligence Unit.

N/A = not available.

Italics = estimate.

EXHIBIT 8.3	BALANCE OF PAYMENTS, 1990–2000 (MILLIONS OF U.S. DOLLARS)										
	1990	1991	1992	1993	1994	1995	1996	1997	1998	1999	2000
Current account balance	**-4,152**	**-27,546**	**-17,740**	**-17,268**	**-10,487**	**-5,325**	**681**	**305**	**-13,150**	**412**	**15,567**
Trade balance	22,889	21,818	20,039	16,522	21,289	24,390	35,370	34,362	11,287	25,039	51,176
Exports of goods	44,414	47,789	50,287	42,395	42,614	50,041	60,729	60,731	38,822	50,757	78,973
Of which, oil*	39,960	43,462	46,396	38,505	38,024	43,416	54,109	53,183	32,472	44,745	72,037
Imports of goods	-21,525	-25,971	-30,248	-25,873	-21,325	-25,650	-25,358	-26,370	-27,535	-25,717	-27,797
Net services	-19,383	-35,896	-28,816	-21,181	-14,546	-15,603	-21,523	-21,706	-12,152	-13,476	-20,469
Services—credit	3,031	2,908	3,466	3,283	3,347	3,480	2,772	4,257	4,730	5,380	4,798
Services—debit	-22,414	-38,804	-32,282	-24,464	-17,893	-19,083	-24,295	-25,963	-16,882	-18,856	-25,267
Net income	7,979	6,767	5,434	3,908	1,472	2,803	2,446	2,785	2,769	2,924	370
Income—credit	9,199	8,700	7,378	6,208	4,032	4,987	5,127	5,756	5,810	5,811	3,338
Income—debit	-1,220	-1,933	-1,944	-2,300	-2,560	-2,184	-2,681	-2,971	-3,041	-2,887	-2,968
Net transfers	-15,637	-20,235	-14,397	-16,517	-18,702	-16,916	-15,613	-15,134	-15,053	-14,076	-15,511
Capital account balance	**-1,224**	**27,595**	**12,075**	**18,763**	**10,341**	**6,542**	**5,069**	**343**	**12,431**	**2,403**	**-12,902**
Net direct investment flows	1,864	160	-79	1,369	350	-1,877	-1,129	3,044	4,289	-782	-1,460
Net portfolio investment	-3,342	471	-6,500	8,213	-2,527	4,057	-2,642	-7,362	6,941	11,712	-9,394
Other investment assets	1,437	27,562	18,446	6,885	12,022	4,221	9,115	2,688	1,983	-10,674	-5,596
Other investment liabilities	-1,183	-598	208	2,296	497	142	-275	1,973	-782	2,147	3,549
Overall Balance**	-5,376	49	-5,665	1,495	-146	1,217	5,750	648	-719	2,815	2,665

SOURCE: Compiled from International Monetary Fund, *International Financial Statistics Yearbook, 2001*; Saudi Arabian Monetary Authority, *Thirty-Seventh Annual Report*, September 2001.

*Oil export revenues are consistent with trade figures but not necessarily with Saudi Arabia's budget figures. Saudi Aramco does not publish its income statement and is not consolidated with the Saudi budget.

**Saudi Arabian balance of payments contains no "errors and omissions."

EXHIBIT 8.4A	GROSS DOMESTIC EXPENDITURE (% SHARE)				
	1996	**1997**	**1998**	**1999**	**2000***
Government Consumption	26.5	27.6	32.6	29.2	27.0
Private Consumption	39.0	37.6	41.3	38.5	32.9
Gross Capital Formation	18.0	19.7	21.4	18.9	16.3
Net Exports	16.5	15.1	4.8	13.4	23.8

SOURCE: Saudi Arabian Monetary Agency, *Thirty-Seventh Annual Report*, September 2001.

EXHIBIT 8.4B	GROSS DOMESTIC EXPENDITURE (AT CURRENT PRICES)

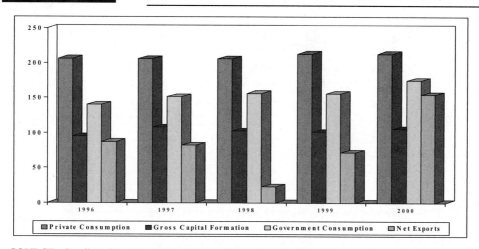

SOURCE: Saudi Arabian Monetary Agency, *Thirty-Seventh Annual Report*, September 2001.

EXHIBIT 8.5	TREND IN ACTUAL OIL AND NON-OIL GOVERNMENT REVENUE, 1975–2000

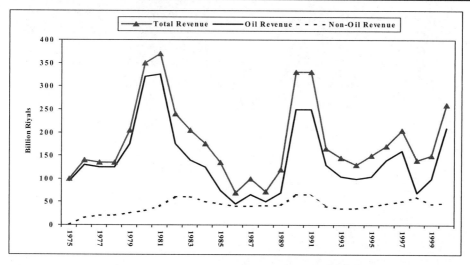

SOURCE: Compiled from Saudi Arabian Monetary Agency, *Thirty-Seventh Annual Report*, September 2001.

EXHIBIT 8.6	**BUDGET ALLOCATIONS BY MAJOR SECTORS, 1998–2002 (BILLIONS OF US DOLLARS)**				
	1998	**1999**	**2000**	**2001**	**2002**
Budgeted Revenues	47.47	32.27	41.87	57.33	41.86
Budgeted Expenditures	52.57	44.01	49.33	57.18	53.86
[As % of GDP]	40.9%	30.8%	28.5%	33.7%	N/A
Education	12.13	11.41	13.17	14.13	14.48
Health	4.37	4.05	5.31	4.82	6.08
Water/Municipal Services	1.73	1.44	1.89	1.92	2.53
Infrastructure/Transport/Communications	2.86	1.84	3.92	2.19	4.42
Subsidies/Social Programs	2.08	1.38	1.47	1.64	N/A
Defense and Security	20.85	18.32	19.95	21.02	N/A
Other	8.55	5.57	N/A	11.46	26.35
Budget Balance	**-5.10**	**-11.74**	**-7.46**	**0.15**	**-12.00**
Actual Total Revenue	**37.76**	**39.33**	**68.83**	**N/A**	**N/A**
Of which oil	21.33	27.87	57.07	N/A	N/A
Actual Total Expenditures	**50.67**	**49.14**	**62.75**	**N/A**	**N/A**
Actual Balance	**-12.91**	**-9.68**	**6.08**	**-6.70**	**N/A**

SOURCE: Compiled from for 1998–2000, Saudi Arabian Monetary Authority, *Annual Report, 2000, 2001*; for 2001–2002, Saudi American Bank, *The Saudi Economy in 2002*. February 2002.

EXHIBIT 8.7	**BUDGET ALLOCATIONS FOR 2001 (PERCENT OF TOTAL)**

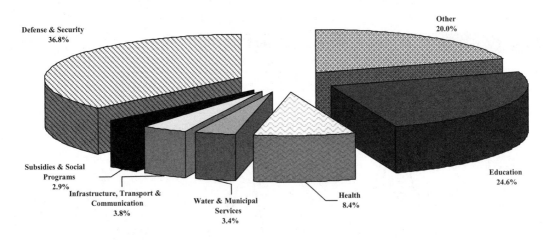

SOURCE: Saudi American Bank, *The Saudi Economy in 2002*. February 2002.

EXHIBIT 8.8 — NON-OIL EXPORTS BY COMMODITY GROUP (MILLIONS OF US DOLLARS)

	1995	1996	1997	1998	1999^
Petrochemicals	2,715	2,786	2,947	2,660	2,454
Construction	723	791	959	731	750
Agricultural, animal & food products	424	358	443	444	472
Other*	2,663	2,521	3,040	2,418	2,163
Total	6,494	6,457	7,389	6,253	5,839

SOURCE: Compiled from The Economist Intelligence Unit. *Country Profile: Saudi Arabia*, 2001.

^preliminary estimate; *including re-exports

EXHIBIT 8.9 — TOP TEN PRIVATE SAUDI COMPANIES IN 2001 (RANKED BY TURNOVER/SALES, SR MILLION)

Company Name	Rank	Turnover/Sales	Assets	Capital	Employees
Saudi Basic Industries Corp.	1	26,664	89,132	15,000	13,944
Kingdom Holding Co.	2	25,300	72,100	70,050	45
Dallah Al-Baraka Group	3	16,868	46,567	3,750	37,600
Saudi Aramco Mobil Refinery	4	14,102	5,910	2,050	856
Saudi American Bank	5	5,927	80,688	4,000	2,319
Consolidated Contractors Int'l Co.	6	5,126	3,743	375	40,408
Riyad Bank	7	4,974	65,523	4,000	3,299
Olayan Financing Company	8	4,000	8,000	10	8,800
Al-Rajhi Banking & Investment Corp.	9	3,718	48,680	2,250	N/A
The Saudi British Bank	10	3,169	43,922	1,600	1,992

SOURCE: Compiled from *The Arab News.* "Top 100 Saudi Companies, 2000." January 2002.

EXHIBIT 8.10A — GALLUP POLL: DO YOU HAVE A FAVORABLE OPINION OF THE U.S.?

Country	Favorable	Unfavorable	Neither
Lebanon	41%	40%	19%
Turkey	40%	33%	25%
Kuwait	28%	41%	31%
Indonesia	27%	30%	43%
Jordan	22%	62%	16%
Morocco	22%	41%	19%
Saudi Arabia	**16%**	**64%**	**19%**
Iran	14%	63%	14%
Pakistan	9%	68%	23%
Total	22%	53%	23%

SOURCE: www.usatoday.com.

EXHIBIT 8.10B	ZOGBY INTERNATIONAL POLL: % WITH FAVORABLE ATTITUDE TOWARD AMERICANS VS. U.S. POLICY

	Americans	**U.S. Policy**
Egypt	35%	4%
Iran	34%	2%
Saudi Arabia	**42%**	**8%**
Kuwait	50%	5%
Lebanon	62%	9%
Pakistan	68%	20%

SOURCE: Zogby International Poll in Jim VandeHei, "Islam's Split-Screen View of the U.S." *The Wall Street Journal.* April 12, 2002.

EXHIBIT 8.11	UNEMPLOYMENT CALCULATION FOR 2001

Unemployment base, year-end 1994

Saudi Labor Force	2,400,000
Unemployment Rate (at structural low of 4 %)	4.00%
Number of Unemployed, 1994	96,000

Employment developments, 1995–1999

Entrants to Labor Force	659,900
Private sector jobs created (Net)	−270,000
Government civilian jobs created	−148,570
Addition to unemployed	241,330
Unemployed, 1994	96,000
Total unemployed, year-end 1999	337,300
Saudi Labor Force, year-end 1999	*2,890,000*
Unemployment rate, 1999	*11.67%*

Employment developments, 2000 & 2001

Entrants to the Labor Force	326,000
Private sector jobs created (Net)	−100,000
Government civilian jobs created	− 60,000
Addition to unemployed	166,000
Total unemployed, year-end 1999	337,300
Total unemployed, year-end 2001	503,300
Saudi Labor Force, year-end 2001	*3,300,000*
Unemployment rate, 2001	*15.25%*

SOURCE: Compiled from Saudi American Bank, *The Saudi Economy in 2002.* February 2002.

EXHIBIT 8.12 RELATIVE DISTRIBUTION OF SAUDI POPULATION BY SEX AND AGE GROUP, 2000

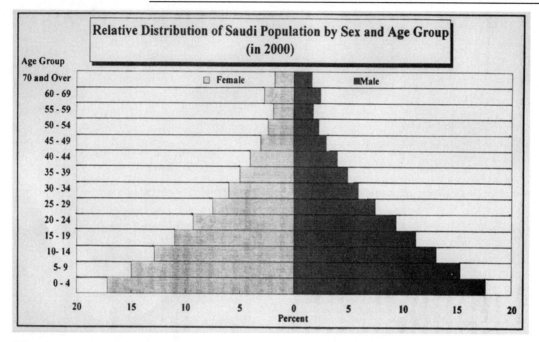

SOURCE: Saudi Arabian Monetary Agency, *Thirty-Seventh Annual Report*, September 2001.

EXHIBIT 8.13 AREAS OF SPECIALIZATION OF SAUDI POST-SECONDARY GRADUATES, 1995–1999

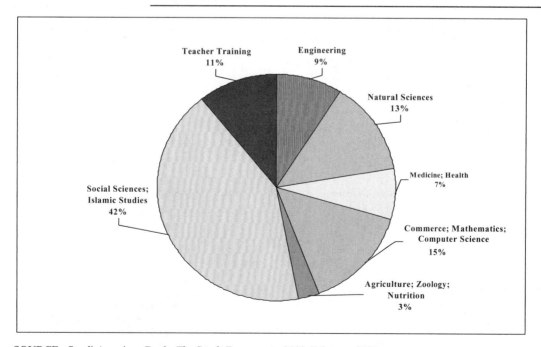

SOURCE: Saudi American Bank, *The Saudi Economy in 2002*, February 2002.

ENDNOTES

1 James M. Dorsey, "Saudi Leader Warns U.S. of 'Separate Interests,'" *The Wall Street Journal,* October 29, 2001.

2 Osama Bin Laden, "Declaration of War," August 23, 1996.

3 Bill Gertz, "CIA Warns of New Al Qaeda Threat," *The Washington Times,* February 7, 2002.

4 Ralph Peters, "The Saudi Threat," *The Wall Street Journal,* January 4, 2002.

5 Much of the material in this section draws upon "Crisis in the Gulf," Harvard Business School Case no. 9-391-178.

6 Interview with Prince Mohammed K.A. al-Faisal, Vice President, Al Faisaliah Group.

7 Federal Research Division, Library of Congress, *Saudi Arabia: A Country Study* (Washington D.C., 1993).

8 Hani A. Z. Yamani, *To Be a Saud.* (London: Janus Publishing Company, 1997).

9 Energy Information Administration, *Saudi Arabia,* (January, 2002).

10 Central Intelligence Agency. *The World Factbook 2000, Saudi Arabia.*

11 U.S. Department of State. *Background Note: Saudi Arabia.* September, 1998.

12 United Nations Educational, Scientific and Cultural Organization (UNESCO).

13 Federal Research Division, Library of Congress, *Saudi Arabia: A Country Study* (Washington D.C., 1993).

14 Frank E. Vogel and Samuel L. Hayes, III, *Islamic Law and Finance,* (Boston: Kluwer Law International, 1998).

15 *The Economist,* "Saudi Arabian Justice: Cruel, or Just Unusual?" June 14, 2001.

16 Interview with Prince Mohammed K.A. al-Faisal, Vice President, Al Faisaliah Group.

17 Human Rights Watch, *World Report 2001, Saudi Arabia.*

18 PBS Frontline, "Saudi Arabia: A Chronology of the Country's History and Key Events in the U.S.-Saudi Relationship," November 2001.

19 F. Gregory Gause III, "Saudi Arabia over a Barrel," *Foreign Affairs,* May/June 2000.

20 Kiren Aziz Chaudhry, *The Price of Wealth* (Ithaca: Cornell University Press, 1997).

21 Kiren Aziz Chaudhry, "Economic Liberalization and the Lineages of the Rentier State," *Comparative Politics,* October 1994.

22 The Economist Intelligence Unit, *Country Profile : Saudi Arabia, 2002.*

23 Saudi American Bank, *The Saudi Economy in 2002.*

24 Ibid.

25 Interview with Muhammad S. al-Jasser, Vice Governor, Saudi Arabian Monetary Agency.

26 Saudi American Bank, *The Saudi Economy in 2002.*

27 Interview with Brad Bourland, Chief Economist, Saudi American Bank.

28 Saudi American Bank, *The Saudi Economy in 2002.*

29 Ibid.

30 The Economist Intelligence Unit, *Country Profile: Saudi Arabia,* 2001.

31 Nawaf E. Obaid, *The Oil Kingdom at 100.* (Washington, D.C.: The Washington Institute for Near East Policy, 2000).

32 Ibid.

33 Dr. Saud Al-Ammari. "Recent Legal and Economic Reforms in Saudi Arabia." *Middle East Economic Survey,* March 20, 2002.

34 Ibid.

35 "Saudi Arabia Approves New Foreign Investment Law," *Embassy of Saudi Arabia, Press Release,* April 10, 2001.

36 The Economist Intelligence Unit, *Country Profile: Saudi Arabia,* 2001.

37 Jeddah Economic Forum, January 2002.

38 Interview with Prince Mohammed K.A. al-Faisal, Vice President, Al Faisaliah Group.

39 PBS Frontline, "Interview with Bandar Bin Sultan," September 2001.

40 The Economist Intelligence Unit, *Country Profile: Saudi Arabia,* 2001.

41 Speech by Dr. Fawaz Al Alami, Deputy Minister of Commerce. Jeddah Economic Forum, January 2002.

42 Neil MacFarquhar, "Leisure Class to Working Class in Saudi Arabia," *The New York Times,* August 26, 2001.

43 *The Financial Times,* "Regal Reformer," June 25, 2001.

44 The Economist Intelligence Unit. *Country Profile: Saudi Arabia*, 2001.

45 The US-Saudi Business Council, "The Saudi Arabian Electricity Sector," 2000.

46 Nawaf E. Obaid, *The Oil Kingdom at 100* (Washington, D.C.: The Washington Institute for Near East Policy, 2000).

47 Interview with Hani A. Z. Yamani, Executive Chairman, Air Harbour Technologies.

48 Interview with Prince Mohammed K.A. al-Faisal, Vice President, Al Faisaliah Group.

49 Kingdom of Saudi Arabia Supreme Commission for Tourism, *Sustainable Tourism Development Plan, Draft Version 7.*

50 Ibid.

51 Saudi American Bank. *The Saudi Economy in 2002.*

52 Ibid.

53 Programme on Governance in the Arab Region. "Saudi Arabia: Women in Public Life," August 2000.

54 Neil MacFarquhar, "Leisure Class to Working Class in Saudi Arabia," *The New York Times*, August 26, 2001.

55 Interview with Prince Mohammed K.A. al-Faisal, Vice President, Al Faisaliah Group.

56 K.S. Ramkumar and Michel Cousins, "Saudization: The Battle Ahead," *Arab News*, January 2002.

57 The Economist Intelligence Unit, *Country Profile: Saudi Arabia*, 2001.

58 Interview with Taher M. O. Agueel, Head, Structured Finance, The National Commercial Bank.

59 Ibid.

60 The Economist Intelligence Unit, *Country Profile: Saudi Arabia*, 2001.

61 Ibid

62 Ibid.

63 Anthony H. Cordesman, "The Islamic Extremism in Saudi Arabia and the Attack on Al Khobar: Review Draft," *Center for Strategic and International Studies*, June 2001.

64 Interview with Hani A. Z. Yamani, Executive Chairman, Air Harbour Technologies.

65 Hani A. Z. Yamani, *To be a Saudi* (London: Janus Publishing Company, 1997).

66 Saudi American Bank, *The Saudi Economy in 2002.*

67 Anthony H. Cordesman, "Islamic Extremism in Saudi Arabia and the Attack on Al Khobar," *Review Draft for the Center for Strategic and International Studies*, June 2001.

68 James M. Dorsey, "Fire Sparks Rare Saudi Outcry at Regime," *The Wall Street Journal*, March 20, 2002.

69 *The Economist*, "How Women Beat the Rules," September 30, 1999.

70 Hani A. Z. Yamani, *To Be a Saudi*, (London: Janus Publishing Company, 1997).

71 *The New York Times*, "Interview with Crown Prince Abdullah of Saudi Arabia," January 28, 2002.

72 National Public Radio, *Morning Edition: Saudi Women*, February 25, 2002.

73 Ibid.

74 Ward Pincus, "Saudi Women Issued Identity Cards for the First Time," *The Boston Globe*. December 5, 2001.

75 Joshua Teitelbaum, *Holier Than Thou: Saudi Arabia's Islamic Opposition* (Washington D.C.: The Washington Institute for Near East Policy, 2000).

76 PBS Frontline, "Saudi Arabia: A Chronology of the Country's History and Key Events in the U.S.-Saudi Relationship," November 2001.

77 Joshua Teitelbaum, *Holier Than Thou: Saudi Arabia's Islamic Opposition* (Washington D.C.: The Washington Institute for Near East Policy, 2000).

78 Ibid.

79 Ibid.

80 The Economist Intelligence Unit, *Country Profile: Saudi Arabia*, 2001.

81 Nawaf E. Obaid, "In Al-Saud We Trust," *Foreign Affairs*. February, 2002.

82 Interview with Brad Bourland, Chief Economist, Saudi American Bank.

83 Speech by Saleh A. Kamel, Arab Radio and Television, Jeddah Economic Forum, January 2002.

84 *The New York Times*, "Interview with Crown Prince Abdullah of Saudi Arabia," January 28, 2002.

85 Interview with Prince Mohammed K.A. al-Faisal, Vice President, Al Faisaliah Group.

86 *The New York Times*, "Interview with Crown Prince Abdullah of Saudi Arabia," January 28, 2002.

87 Aida Cerkez-Robinson, "Terror Targets Found in Bosnia Raid," *Associated Press*, February 21, 2002.

88 Ibid.

89 F. Gregory Gause III, *Oil Monarchies* (New York: Council on Foreign Relations Press, 1994).

90 Ibid.

91 James M. Dorsey, "Saudi Prince Tries to Reshape Kingdom," *The Wall Street Journal,* February 5, 2002.

92 *The Economist,* "Could It Be a Turning Point?" February 28, 2002.

93 CNN.com, "Excerpts from Saudi Crown Prince's Speech," March 28, 2002.

94 CNN.com, "Arab Summit Adopts Saudi Peace Initiative,"March 28, 2002.

95 PBS Frontline, "Interview with Bandar Bin Sultan," September 2001.

INDUSTRY NOTE   WORLD OIL MARKETS

RICHARD H. K. VIETOR

REBECCA EVANS

In 2002, the world depended on oil. Fears of global warming had increased consumption of natural gas, nuclear power, and other alternative fuels; still, oil was expected to maintain its 40% market share through 2020.[1]

World oil consumption, which measured 76 million barrels per day (mm bl/d) in 2000, was forecast to increase to 120 mm bl/d by 2020. Oil demand would grow faster in developing countries, especially in Asia and Central and South America. By 2020, developing nations were expected to consume as much oil as industrialized nations. However, in the short term, oil demand would grow slowly. The global economic downturn and the September 11 terrorist attacks had weakened demand. The International Energy Agency (IEA) estimated that demand increased by a meager 100 thousand barrels per day (m bl/d) in 2001. Oil consumption was expected to rebound in 2002 as the world economy recovered. In 2002, the IEA expected demand to rise by 600 m bl/d.[2]

Total proven world oil reserves stood at an estimated 1.03 trillion barrels.[3] With production of 76.7 mm bl/d, the IEA estimated that the world had a spare crude capacity of 4.7 mm bl/d.[4] The rise in demand over the 2000–2020 period would require an increase in world oil supply of 45 mm bl/d. Although both OPEC and non-OPEC producers would gain from production increases, the OPEC nations would be the primary beneficiaries. In the short term, oil supplies remained vulnerable to political, economic, and environmental shocks.

The Petroleum Industry

Petroleum or oil was a dark substance, composed of compressed organic compounds containing carbon and hydrogen. Oil fueled automobiles, heated and cooled homes, and provided the building blocks for thousands of consumer products. Formed millions of years ago, oil deposits were located in the earth's crust along fault lines and cracks in rocks. The Middle East region held the world's largest oil reserves, followed by Central and South America, Africa, Eastern Europe, and North America. [See **Exhibit 8N.2.**]

The oil industry was broadly divided in two sectors: upstream and downstream development. Drilling, production, and other upstream activities were located closer to the source, while downstream activities, such as refining and marketing, were generally closer to the consumer. Although upstream oil development involved more investment risk than downstream activities, it often yielded greater profits and a higher return on investment.

To locate deposits, oil producers performed seismic tests. Producers then drilled wells to estimate the size of oil reservoirs. Many oil wells also contained gas, which was dissolved in the oil and later extracted. Two different processes helped remove oil from underground. In the Middle East, oil was produced through natural lift measures, whereby built-up reservoir pressures forced oil to the surface. In North America and other parts of the world, oil was extracted by artificial lifts or electric and gas powered pumps. Natural-lift production was cheaper, costing Middle East producers as little as $1.50 per barrel. In contrast, artificial lifting costs were as high as $15 per barrel in some U.S. oil fields.

Oil pipelines and tankers transported crude oil from the major oil producing nations to the top consuming nations in North America, Asia, and Europe. Pipelines helped move landlocked oil across continents and were cheaper than alternative methods such as rail, barge, and truck. Tankers were a low cost, efficient, and flexible means of intercontinental transport. The volume of oil and the distance of the shipping route determined the size of the vessel and the transportation costs. Ideally, oil was transported to the closest market in order to minimize costs. The remaining oil was then shipped to the next closest market, and so on, until all the oil had been placed. However, refinery configurations, product demand mix, product quality specifications, international politics, tariffs, and other restrictions altered the flow of oil.

Refining and other downstream activities were usually located in consuming nations because it was cheaper to ship crude oil than refined products. North America held the world's largest refining capacity, followed by Asia and Europe. Through different refining processes, crude oil was manufactured into a mix of finished petroleum products including liquid petroleum gas, jet fuel, kerosene, gasoline, and diesel. Basic petrochemicals like aromatics and olefins were produced as by-products of petroleum refining. These chemicals were used to make detergents, fertilizer, medicines, paint, plastics, synthetic fibers, and hundreds of other products.[5]

The Origins of the Oil Industry

Colonel Edwin Drake made the first oil discovery in Titusville, Pennsylvania in 1859. Following his discovery, a small oil industry bloomed in western Pennsylvania. John D. Rockefeller entered the business in 1865 and established the Standard Oil Company, which soon controlled 10% of the U.S. oil industry. When disparate state regulations began to impede transcontinental oil transport, Rockefeller formed the Standard Oil Trust to act as a holding company to independent oil companies in different states. By 1900, Standard Oil companies dominated the U.S. oil industry and had a strong foothold in international markets. However, in 1911, the Supreme Court ruled that Standard Oil's monopoly violated the Sherman Anti-Trust Act of 1890. Forced to divest itself, Standard Oil split into 38 individual companies. Many of the Standard Oil companies continued to grow in size and importance. Standard Oil of New Jersey (Exxon), Standard Oil of New York (Mobil), and Standard Oil of California (Chevron) were numbered among the Seven Sisters, a group of international oil companies that controlled oil markets from 1915–1973.[6]

In 1901, an oil discovery at Spindletop had given birth to the Texas oil industry. The two oil majors, Gulf Oil and the Texas Oil Company (Texaco), built pipelines, refineries, and ships that exported Texas oil to European markets. The remaining Sisters, Royal Dutch/Shell and BP, also emerged at the turn of the century. In 1897, British entrepreneur Marcus Samuel built a fleet of tankers and storage installations throughout

the Far East, forming the Shell Transport and Trading Company. Nine years later, Shell merged with Royal Dutch to become the Royal Dutch/Shell Group. In 1908, British investors William Knox D'Arcy and G.B. Reynolds struck oil in Persia. A year later, the Anglo-Persian Oil Company was established. The new company would become Anglo-Iranian Oil, British Petroleum, and finally BP.[7]

Oil demand surged after the First World War. The United States and Britain desired greater access to foreign oil supplies, especially those in the Middle East. After the fall of the Ottoman Empire, the United States had urged Britain and France to share their rights to the Turkish Petroleum Company concession. Reaching a compromise in 1928, they granted five American oil companies a 25% stake in the newly renamed Iraq Petroleum Company. The parties also agreed to extend the Red Line agreement of 1914, which held that all companies working in a proscribed region (outlined in red pencil) of the Middle East must pursue joint concessions. Once the agreement was signed, all other companies were excluded from developing oil in the region. The consortium of Shell, BP, Exxon, Mobil, Compagnie Francaise des Petroles (CFP), and C.S. Gulbenkian cooperated to control output and sustain high oil prices.

In 1932, Standard Oil Company of California or Socal (Chevron), which was not hindered by the Red Line agreement, won a concession and found oil in Bahrain. In need of funds, Saudi Arabia's King Ibn Saud granted Socal a concession on its east coast. By 1938, Socal had uncovered Saudi Arabia's vast oil reserves. Texaco partnered with Socal, and production came on stream in early 1939. The operating company changed its name to the Arabian American Oil Company (Aramco) in 1944 and added two more partners, Standard Oil Company of New Jersey (Exxon) and Socony-Vacuum (Mobil), in 1946. These four U.S. companies maintained full control of Aramco until the 1970s.

After the Second World War, the Seven Sisters dominated the international oil market. Producing nearly all the oil outside of the United States, the seven oil majors controlled each step of the production chain. By the 1950s, the companies managed 96% of the world's reserves, 90% of production, 76% of refining capacity, and 74% of product sales.[8] The Seven

Sisters ruled world oil markets for several decades until producing nations began to exercise their intrinsic power.*

The OPEC Story

The Organization of Petroleum Exporting Nations (OPEC) was established in Baghdad on September 14, 1960, by the five major oil producing and exporting countries: Iran, Iraq, Kuwait, Saudi Arabia, and Venezuela. By 2000, OPEC's membership had grown to include Algeria, Indonesia, Libya, Nigeria, Qatar, and the United Arab Emirates (U.A.E.). Together, the OPEC nations controlled more than 75% of the world's proven oil reserves and 40% of total world oil production. OPEC's founding mission was to provide a fair and stable petroleum market for the benefit of both oil consumers and producers. Through consensual decision-making, the OPEC cartel aimed to maintain a steady stream of oil revenue to fund member countries' development plans.

In its first decade of operation, OPEC had little influence over world oil markets. With the United States producing most of its oil domestically, OPEC remained a marginal producer. In March 1959, President Eisenhower had instituted a program of mandatory quotas to insure a "vigorous, healthy petroleum industry in the United States."[9]

Seeking greater market influence, OPEC severed the link between the member countries' oil revenues and world oil prices, which had been falling since the late 1950s. A system of posted prices, which had little market significance, was established to determine the per barrel income to the governments and the after-tax cost to the companies. However, as late as 1970, OPEC was still not regarded as a significant factor in world oil markets. There were several sources of downward pressure on the price of oil, including large-scale Russian oil exports and increased competition from aggressive new oil companies such as Italy's

state-owned ENI. Despite declining prices, taxes on oil continued to rise, with a corresponding decline in the profit margins of producing companies.

OPEC came into its own during the early 1970s. Distorted reserve inventories had triggered a major oil and gas shortage in the United States. In just 40 months, U.S. spare capacity, which had averaged as much as 4 mm bl/d in 1967, was exhausted.[10] Once spare capacity was gone, the U.S. oil companies lost control of oil prices. OPEC countries— particularly Saudi Arabia—now held most of worldwide spare capacity. When the Arab-Israeli War unfolded in October 1973, the United States was exceptionally vulnerable. Using oil as a weapon, the Arab producers imposed an embargo on the United States and other nations supporting Israel. At the October 16 OPEC meeting, oil ministers agreed to unilaterally raise prices to $5 per barrel, an effective increase of more than 60%.[11] Their unanimous decision to restrict output marked the beginning of a new era in which price-setting power shifted from the Seven Sisters to the OPEC producers. As oil prices shot up to $12 per barrel, OPEC's coffers swelled. Member countries celebrated revenues of about $120 billion in 1974.[12]

The Iranian revolution sparked a second oil shock in 1979 when Iran's oil production temporarily ceased. Spot prices soared to $40 per barrel, climbing higher after Iraq invaded Iran. Fearing a substitution away from oil, OPEC agreed to fix official prices at $34 per barrel. Still, revenues continued to climb, reaching $280 billion in 1980.[13]

The 1986 Price Collapse

In response to the high price environment of the 1970s, many non-OPEC countries invested in domestic oil production. But as the world's oil supply expanded during the mid-1980s, demand lagged due to conservation and a deep recession. Desperate to boost prices, Saudi Arabia, the swing producer, made dramatic production cuts. Between 1981 and 1985, Saudi producers lowered output from 10 mm bl/d to 3.5 mm bl/d, and revenues shrank from $113 billion to $25.9 billion.[14] Still, prices refused to rally. Saudi officials blamed other OPEC members for cheating or exceeding their production quotas. The Saudis "were losing $20 billion a year because of the swing producer role even though other OPEC countries were cheating," explained

---

* In the late 1990s, a wave of mega-mergers changed the face of the oil industry. In 1998, BP acquired Amoco for $48 billion to become BP-Amoco. This was followed by the $80 billion merger of Exxon and Mobil. In October 2001, Chevron and Texaco merged to form ChevronTexaco Corp.

one observer.[15] Seeking greater market share, Saudi Arabia abandoned its traditional oil policy and increased production from 2 to 5 mm bl/d. OPEC crumbled as Nigeria, Indonesia, Venezuela, U.A.E., and Iran raced to match Saudi Arabia's price discounting scheme. The ensuing oil glut sent prices plummeting. In 1986, oil prices dropped to $8 per barrel, returning in real terms to 1974 levels.

Faced with low revenues, OPEC producers renewed their commitment to collaborative price setting. After months of heated debate, OPEC again agreed to reduce daily output, this time from 20.5 to 16.7 mm bl/d during a two-month trial period. Although several countries continued to cheat on their production quotas, the new policy proved successful. Oil prices rose from $8 per barrel to $16 per barrel. In 1987, Saudi Arabia pushed for a fixed price system, and OPEC members agreed on a fixed price of $18 per barrel. However, consistent quota-busting and disputes over production adjustments undermined OPEC's ability to maintain the fixed price. [See **Exhibit 8N.5**.]

OPEC in the 1990s

By mid-1990, OPEC was producing 1.5 million barrels above its quota of 24 mm bl/d. Supply exceeded demand by nearly 2 million barrels despite production cutbacks by non-OPEC countries. The new glut suggested once again that the major producers were more interested in gaining market share than in cooperating to force prices higher.

After the Iraqi invasion of Kuwait in August 1990, oil prices skyrocketed from $18 per barrel to $30 per barrel in just a few days. In a highly political move, Saudi Arabia's King Fahd increased production to cover the loss of Iraqi and Kuwaiti oil. Prices dropped back to $20 per barrel as the market stabilized. Saudi revenues might have been higher had prices stayed at $30 per barrel. But by increasing production, King Fahd had spared the U.S. economy and secured U.S. military support. Following the Gulf Crisis, OPEC held prices around $21 per barrel. The market remained stable until 1993, when overproduction pushed prices down to $15 per barrel. Over the next few years, oil prices remained volatile as quota disputes continued to destabilize OPEC.

In 1997, OPEC increased its production ceiling by 10% just as the Asian markets collapsed. The global economy slipped into recession, and oil demand slumped. Prices dropped 30% to just $10 per barrel in 1998. Dependent on oil revenues, the Arab economies floundered. Yet the crisis helped rebuild OPEC. Reunited by economic misfortune, OPEC members agreed to slash production. Both OPEC and non-OPEC producers reduced output in 1999. Aided by the early recovery of Asian markets, oil prices returned to normal levels by the end of the year.

The Price Band Mechanism

In March 2000, OPEC adopted a price band mechanism aimed at keeping oil prices in a $22–$28 per barrel range. Under the new system, quotas would automatically adjust when prices moved beyond the band. The slowdown of the United States economy tested the system: As demand waned, a series of automatic production cuts kept prices within the band. For most of the year, prices averaged $25 per barrel. But as the global economy soured in 2001, oil prices dipped below the bottom of the band. Then in September, terrorist attacks against the United States pushed prices down to a two-year low of $17 per barrel. Some officials feared that the U.S.-led retaliation against Afghanistan would spark a supply shock and force prices upward. However, the negative economic impact of the terrorist attacks sent oil prices in the opposite direction.

At OPEC's 117th meeting on September 26, leaders had planned to make production cuts to boost prices to $25 per barrel. Given the uncertain economic and political climate, OPEC members decided to postpone the cutbacks. By November, oil prices were still hovering around $18 per barrel. As government revenues tumbled, OPEC leaders grew anxious and agreed to reduce supply by 1.5 mm bl/d, effective January 1, 2002. OPEC warned that the cutbacks were contingent on production cuts by the major non-OPEC producers. Without their cooperation, oil prices would remain below the desired price band. Hoping to avoid a price war, Saudi Arabia's oil minister, Al Naimi, traveled to Russia, Mexico, and Norway to persuade oil ministers to cut oil production by a total of 500,000 barrels per day. "Everyone should heed the lessons of the past, and that means that going after market share just creates losses," said Naimi. "We are in a crisis mode and we need help. This is a serious appeal."[16] After initial resistance, Mexico agreed to shave production by

100,000 barrels per day, while Norway consented to cuts of 100,000 to 200,000 barrels per day. But Russia refused to kowtow to OPEC, choosing instead to forgo profits for greater market share.

The Emerging Non-OPEC Producers

OPEC started losing market share to non-OPEC countries in the early 1980s. The high price environment of the l970s had encouraged non-OPEC exploration and production. Security issues had prompted consuming nations to invest in domestic oil production. Originally, the growth of non-OPEC producers had not threatened OPEC members. Most assumed that limited resources and high production costs would inhibit future production. However, technological advances, cost-reduction programs, and efforts to attract outside investment made production economically viable in many non-OPEC countries. Production in these countries increased every year from 1993 to 2000.[17] [See **Exhibit 8N.3**.]

In 2000, non-OPEC countries supplied 60% of the world's oil but held less than 20 percent of the world's proven reserves. Seven of the top ten oil producers were non-OPEC nations. Non-OPEC production, which had grown by 1.8 mm bl/d in 2000–2001, was expected to increase by 800,000 barrels per day in 2002.[18] Non-OPEC output was forecast to grow in the future, with the greatest production increase coming from the former Soviet Union. The United States, Russia, Mexico, Norway, the United Kingdom, China, and Canada were among the top non-OPEC producers. [See **Exhibits 8N.4, 8N.9,** and **8N.10**.]

United States

The United States, with proven oil reserves of only 21.8 billion, was the world's third largest oil producer and the largest consumer. In 2000, the United States imported an estimated 11.5 mm bl/d of oil, satisfying 58% of U.S. oil demand. Top suppliers included Canada, Saudi Arabia, Venezuela and Mexico, with OPEC nations supplying 45% of U.S. imports. Following the September 11 terrorist attacks, President Bush ordered the Energy Department to increase the Strategic Petroleum Reserve to full capacity.[19] In

the future, the United States hoped to become less dependent on Middle East imports.[20]

Russia

With oil reserves around 50 billion barrels, Russia was the second largest oil producer and exporter. Although production had been stagnant during the early to mid-1990s, investment increased when oil prices rose in 1999. During the next two years, production grew by 10.6%, and exports surged. Oil revenues rallied Russia's flagging economy and boosted GDP growth to a record 8.3% in 2000. Russia's willingness to cooperate with OPEC cutbacks dissipated in 2001. As OPEC called for production cuts, Russia continued to increase production. Ignoring OPEC's threats to raise production and induce a price war, Russia remained intent on growing its 7% market share. As its relations with the United States improved, Russia hoped to export oil to its former adversary.[21]

Mexico

A net oil importer until 1976, Mexico developed its oil industry during the presidency of Jose López Portillo (1976–1982). By 2000, Mexico had emerged as the seventh largest world oil producer and the tenth largest oil exporter. On a daily basis, Mexico produced 3.0 mm bl/d and exported 1.5 mm bl/d. Oil accounted for a third of government revenue. Pemex, the state-owned oil and gas monopoly, dominated Mexican oil production. Although privatization plans had been rejected, the government maintained its commitment to modernize the oil giant. The EIA estimated that production would continue to grow, reaching 4 mm bl/d by 2010. Mexico had a history of cooperating with OPEC nations. During the 1998 price collapse, Mexico was the only non-OPEC producer to make significant output cuts.[22]

Norway

As the world's sixth largest oil producer and third largest oil exporter, Norway played an influential role in the world oil market. Large oil discoveries in the North Sea during the 1980s and 1990s contributed to some of the highest current account surpluses in Norway's history. Norway's political stability and proximity to Western Europe offset its high production costs, allowing the country to expand its market share.

With 9.4 billion barrels of proven reserves, Norway was expected to produce 3.4 mm bl/d in 2001, an increase of 130,000 barrels per day from 2000. Production would likely peak in 2006 at 3.7 mm bl/d.[23]

United Kingdom

The largest oil producer and exporter in the European Union, the United Kingdom ranked ninth in world oil production and thirteenth in net exports. The U.K. held an estimated 5 billion barrels of proven oil reserves, mostly located in the North Sea. Production, which measured 2.47 mm bl/d in 2000, was expected to shrink to 1.9 mm bl/d in 2001. With British oil production in the hands of private oil majors Royal Dutch/Shell and British Petroleum, government revenues would be unaffected by the production decline.[24]

China

With the world's largest population, China was the fifth largest oil producer and one of the world's fastest growing consumers. China produced more than 3.2 mm bl/d, with 1 mm bl/d coming from the Daqing field alone. As onshore oil fields matured, China had begun to invest in offshore exploration and development on the Bohai Sea. Fearing dependence on oil imports, China had acquired oil concessions in Kazakhstan, Venezuela, Sudan, Iran, Iraq, and Peru.[25]

Canada

Ranked tenth among the world's top oil producers, Canada held proven oil reserves of only 4.7 billion barrels. Close to 60% of Canadian oil was produced in the western province of Alberta. The Athabasca Oil Sands Deposit, with 1.7 trillion to 2.5 trillion barrels of bitumen, was one of the world's largest petroleum resources.[26] Canada exported 30% of its oil and was the largest supplier of U.S. oil.[27] In 2000, the United States imported 1.81 mm bl/d from Canada, 1.57 mm bl/d from Saudi Arabia, 1.55 mm bl/d from Venezuela, and 1.37 mm bl/d from Mexico.[28]

Saudi Arabia's Oil Empire

With 259 billion barrels of proven oil reserves, Saudi Arabia was the world's largest oil producer and exporter. Europe, Asia and the United States were Saudi Arabia's main export markets.[29] In 2000, Saudi Arabia produced 8.4 mm bl/d, withholding excess capacity of around 2 mm bl/d. Plans were underway to increase capacity to 12.5 mm bl/d. In Saudi Arabia, production costs were $1.50 per barrel compared to the world average of $5 per barrel. Discovery costs were equally low—less than $0.10 per barrel compared with $4 per barrel in other parts of the world.[30] More than one-fourth of the world's total oil reserves were located in Saudi Arabia. Ghawar was the largest onshore oilfield and held estimated reserves of 70 billion barrels. The largest offshore oilfield, Safaniya, contained estimated reserves of 19 billion barrels.[31] [See **Exhibit 8N.1**.]

Saudi Aramco

The Saudi Arabian Oil Company, or Saudi Aramco, managed nearly all of Saudi Arabia's oil and gas operations. In 1976, Saudi Arabia's King Faisal had nationalized Aramco but retained U.S. executives to run the company. Twelve years later, King Fahd officially established the Saudi Arabian Oil Company by royal decree and placed the company under Saudi management. In 2000, Oil Minister Ali Al Naimi headed the board of directors that managed the company and its 56,500 employees.[32] [See **Exhibits 8N.7 & 8N.8**.]

As the world's largest oil producing company, Saudi Aramco invested heavily in exploration and development. Most of Saudi Arabia's oilfields were located in the east, in the politically unstable Persian Gulf region. Following the Gulf War in 1990–91, Saudi Arabia followed a diversification strategy that aimed to develop oilfields south of Riyadh. The development of the Shaybah field in the southwest Empty Quarter region was expected to yield reserves of 7 billion barrels. Other pending development projects included the Qatif field, which had an expected capacity of 500,000 barrels per day, and the Khurais field, with an expected capacity of 800,000 barrels per day. The newly formed Supreme Council for Petroleum and Mineral Affairs had approved $15 billion per year to increase oil and gas output during the 2000–2004 period.[33]

There were seven oil refineries in Saudi Arabia, with combined capacity of 1.75 mm bl/d. Saudi Aramco's overseas refineries had an additional capacity of 1.6 mm bl/d. Downstream development plans included a $1.2 billion upgrade of the 300,000 barrels per day Ras Tanura refinery. Another project would boost capacity at the Rabigh refinery to 400,000 barrels per day. Saudi Arabia also had ambitious plans to expand its petrochemical sector.[34]

The Natural Gas Sector

Saudi Arabia held the world's fourth largest natural gas reserves, estimated at 204.5 trillion cubic feet.[35] The government pledged to increase gas production in order to satisfy growing domestic demand. New water desalination and power generation plants were to be powered by natural gas. In 1999, Saudi Aramco had announced that it would invest $45 billion over the next 25 years on upstream gas development and processing facilities. But foreign investment was crucial for meeting development goals. In May 2001, the Saudi government selected ExxonMobil, Shell, BP, Phillips, Occidental, Marathon, TotalFinaElf, and Conoco to develop the kingdom's upstream gas sector. In June, oil executives met with Saudi officials in Jeddah to sign preliminary agreements for the historic Saudi Gas Initiative, which marked the first reopening of the gas sector since its nationalization in the 1970s. However, the March 2, 2002, deadline passed without an official agreement after disputes over access to gas fields and the proper rate of return stalled the deal. [See **Exhibits 8N.6, 8N.11**, and **8N.12**.]

Hoping to position themselves for the opening of the upstream oil sector, the eight oil giants agreed to invest $25 billion on upstream gas development. The Initiative was divided into three core ventures. ExxonMobil, Shell, BP, and Phillips would oversee core venture one in South Ghawar. This project would include exploration, pipelines, two gas-fired power plants, two petrochemical plants, and two desalination units. Core venture two, led by ExxonMobil and Occidental, included exploration in the Red Sea, development of the Barqan and Midyan fields, and the construction of petrochemical, power, and desalination plants. In core venture three, Shell, TotalFinaElf, and Conoco would explore the Shaybah field, development in the Kidan field, and lay pipelines from Shaybah to the Haradh and Hawiyah gas treatment plants.[36]

The Future of Saudi Arabian Oil

Over the past 25 years, Saudi Arabia had followed a price moderating policy. As the swing producer, Saudi Arabia bore the brunt of production cuts in order to maintain stable oil prices. As government revenues fell in 2001, Saudi Arabia had refused to cut production to accommodate OPEC cheaters. To maintain the welfare state that had emerged during the high price environment of the 1970s, Saudi officials recognized that future policy decisions would be driven by revenue needs.[37] While price moderation would remain important, Saudi Arabia would focus on growing its market share.

As OPEC headed into the new millennium, the future of the organization looked uncertain. Disputes over quota-busting threatened to break up the cartel. In October 2001, OPEC members produced 800,000 barrels per day more than the agreed ceiling of 23.2 mm bl/d (OPEC's spare capacity was estimated at 4.5 mm bl/d).[38] Like a Band-Aid, the price band mechanism had held the warring factions of the cartel together and had kept oil prices stable. However, the terrorist attacks and global recession had proved the band's ineffectiveness in the face of macroeconomic events. Meanwhile, OPEC continued to lose market share to non-OPEC producers. Officials reported that OPEC's market share had slipped from 60% in the late 1970s to 30% in 2001.[39] OPEC's production decisions had become reliant on cooperation from non-OPEC producers. In November 2001, Russia announced that it would reduce oil production by just 50,000 barrels per day. OPEC had pushed for a 150,000 barrels per day reduction. As January approached, OPEC questioned whether it should proceed with its planned production cuts of 1.5 mm bl/d. This would require Saudi Arabia to hold its production at just 7.0 mm bl/d.

EXHIBIT 8N.1	MAP OF SAUDI ARABIA AND OIL FIELDS

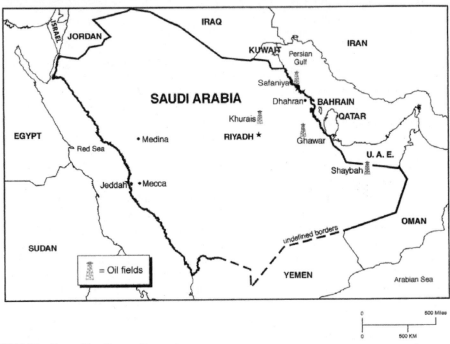

SOURCE: Created by Case writer.

EXHIBIT 8N.2	WORLD CRUDE OIL AND NATURAL GAS RESERVES, JANUARY 1, 2000

	Crude Oil (billion barrels)	Natural Gas (trillion cubic feet)
North America	**55.1**	**261.3**
Canada	4.9	63.9
Mexico	28.4	30.1
United States	21.8	167.4
Central & South America	**89.5**	**222.7**
Brazil	7.4	8.0
Venezuela	72.6	142.5
Western Europe	**18.8**	**159.5**
Norway	10.8	41.4
United Kingdom	5.2	26.7
Eastern Europe & Former U.S.S.R.	**58.9**	**1,999.2**
Russia	48.6	1,700.0
Middle East	**675.6**	**1,749.2**
Iran	89.7	812.3
Iraq	112.5	109.8
Kuwait	96.5	52.7
Saudi Arabia	263.5	204.5
United Arab Emirates	97.8	212.0
Africa	**74.9**	**394.2**
Algeria	9.2	159.7
Angola	5.4	1.6
Libya	29.5	46.4
Nigeria	22.5	124.0
Far East & Oceania	**44.0**	**363.5**
China	24.0	48.3
Indonesia	5.0	72.3
World Total	**1,016.8**	**5,149.6**

SOURCE: Compiled from *Oil and Gas Journal*.

EXHIBIT 8N.3 WORLD OIL PRODUCTION, 1970–2000

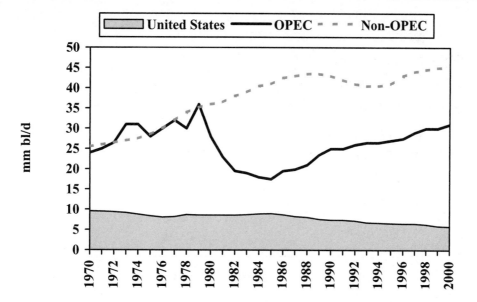

SOURCE: Energy Information Administration: www.eia.doe.gov.

EXHIBIT 8N.4A TOP WORLD CRUDE OIL PRODUCERS (INCLUDES LEASE CONDENSATE), 2000

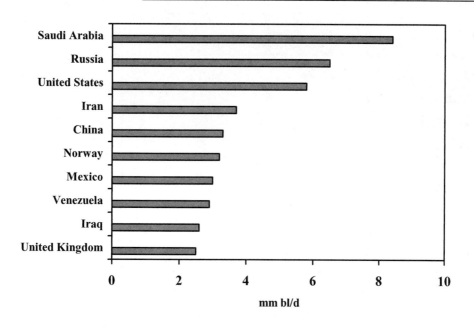

SOURCE: Energy Information Administration, www.eia.doe.gov.

EXHIBIT 8N.4b   TOP WORLD OIL NET EXPORTERS, 2000

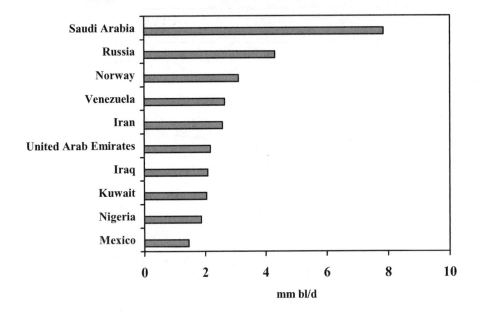

SOURCE: Energy Information Administration, www.eia.doe.gov.

EXHIBIT 8N.4c   TOP WORLD OIL NET IMPORTERS, 2000

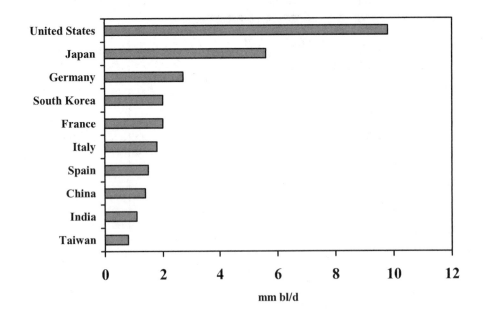

SOURCE: Energy Information Administration, www.eia.doe.gov.

EXHIBIT 8N.4D   OPEC SPARE PRODUCTION CAPACITY

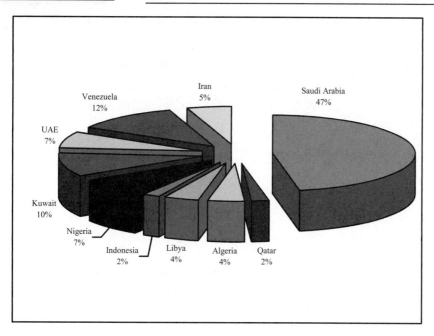

SOURCE: Adapted from Nawaf E. Obaid. *The Oil Kingdom at 100*. Washington, D.C.: The Washington Institute for Near East Policy, 2000, pg. 133.

EXHIBIT 8N.5   REAL AND NOMINAL CRUDE OIL PRICES, 1970–2001

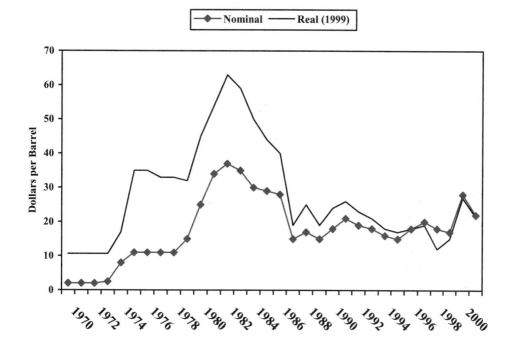

SOURCE: Energy Information Administration, www.eia.doe.gov.

EXHIBIT 8N.6 RESIDENTIAL NATURAL GAS PRICES, 1970–2001

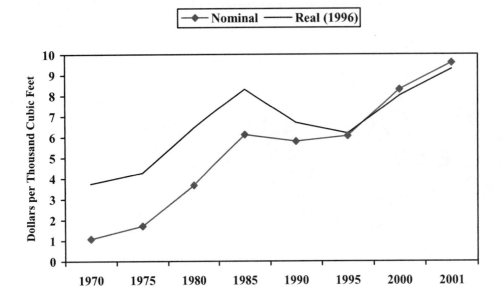

SOURCE: Energy Information Administration, www.eia.doe.gov.

EXHIBIT 8N.7 SAUDI ARAMCO, CRUDE OIL PRODUCTION (EXCLUDES LEASE CONDENSATE), 1996–2001

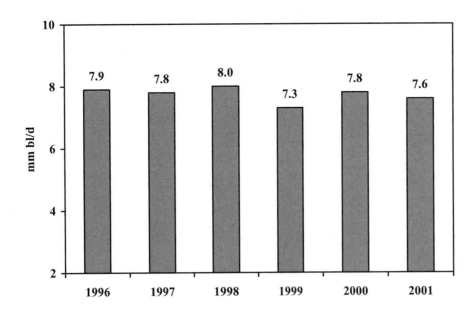

SOURCE: Adapted from *Saudi Aramco*, www.saudiaramco.com.

EXHIBIT 8N.8   SAUDI ARAMCO, RAW GAS TO GAS PLANTS, 1996–2000

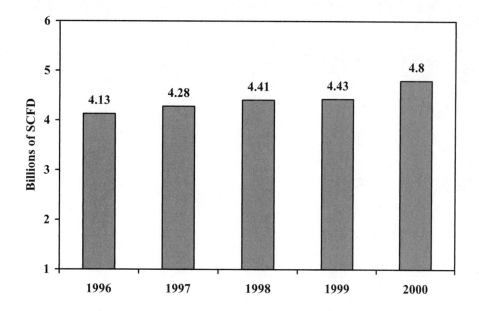

SOURCE: Adapted from *Saudi Aramco*, www.saudiaramco.com.

EXHIBIT 8N.9	WORLD CRUDE OIL PRODUCTION (INCLUDES LEASE CONDENSATE), 1980–2000 (THOUSAND BARRELS PER DAY)																				
Country	1980	1981	1982	1983	1984	1985	1986	1987	1988	1989	1990	1991	1992	1993	1994	1995	1996	1997	1998	1999	2000
North America	**11,968**	**12,170**	**12,668**	**12,733**	**13,097**	**13,187**	**12,589**	**12,432**	**12,268**	**11,693**	**11,461**	**11,644**	**11,446**	**11,199**	**11,093**	**10,982**	**11,156**	**11,396**	**11,303**	**10,694**	**10,814**
Canada	1,435	1,285	1,271	1,356	1,438	1,471	1,474	1,535	1,616	1,560	1,553	1,548	1,605	1,679	1,746	1,805	1,837	1,922	1,981	1,907	1,980
Mexico	1,936	2,313	2,748	2,689	2,780	2,745	2,435	2,548	2,512	2,520	2,553	2,680	2,669	2,673	2,685	2,618	2,855	3,023	3,070	2,906	3,012
United States	8,597	8,572	8,649	8,688	8,879	8,971	8,680	8,349	8,140	7,613	7,355	7,417	7,171	6,847	6,662	6,560	6,465	6,452	6,252	5,881	5,822
Central & South America	**3,647**	**3,656**	**3,457**	**3,432**	**3,612**	**3,602**	**3,813**	**3,700**	**3,950**	**3,995**	**4,318**	**4,535**	**4,621**	**4,817**	**5,059**	**5,481**	**5,848**	**6,326**	**6,435**	**6,293**	**n/a**
Brazil	182	213	260	339	475	564	572	566	554	596	631	630	626	643	671	695	795	841	969	1,132	n/a
Venezuela	2,168	2,102	1,895	1,801	1,798	1,677	1,787	1,752	1,903	1,907	2,137	2,375	2,371	2,450	2,588	2,750	2,938	3,280	3,167	2,826	2,899
Western Europe	**2,531**	**2,705**	**3,026**	**3,399**	**3,660**	**3,847**	**3,983**	**4,028**	**4,001**	**3,947**	**4,125**	**4,326**	**4,676**	**4,873**	**5,543**	**5,878**	**6,299**	**6,300**	**6,275**	**6,349**	**n/a**
Norway	528	501	520	614	697	788	870	1,022	1,158	1,554	1,704	1,890	2,229	2,350	2,521	2,768	3,104	3,143	3,017	3,018	3,200
United Kingdom	1,622	1,811	2,065	2,291	2,480	2,530	2,539	2,406	2,232	1,802	1,820	1,797	1,825	1,915	2,375	2,489	2,568	2,518	2,616	2,684	2,470
Eastern Europe & Former U.S.S.R.	**12,038**	**12,185**	**12,269**	**12,336**	**12,203**	**11,909**	**12,221**	**12,366**	**12,339**	**11,989**	**11,216**	**10,191**	**8,727**	**7,764**	**7,131**	**7,017**	**6,917**	**7,054**	**7,066**	**7,416**	**n/a**
Former U.S.S.R.	11,706	11,850	11,912	11,972	11,861	11,585	11,895	12,050	12,053	11,715	10,975	9,992	7,632	6,730	6,135	5,995	5,850	5,920	5,854	6,079	0
Russia	0	0	0	0	0	0	0	0	0	0	0	0	7,632	6,730	6,135	5,995	5,850	5,920	5,854	6,079	6,479
Middle East	**18,442**	**15,766**	**12,641**	**11,624**	**11,369**	**10,307**	**12,462**	**12,936**	**14,513**	**16,013**	**16,545**	**16,130**	**17,373**	**18,265**	**18,669**	**18,979**	**19,174**	**19,923**	**21,178**	**20,502**	**n/a**
Iran	1,662	1,380	2,214	2,440	2,174	2,250	2,035	2,298	2,240	2,810	3,088	3,312	3,429	3,540	3,618	3,643	3,686	3,664	3,634	3,557	3,684
Iraq	2,514	1,000	1,012	1,005	1,209	1,433	1,690	2,079	2,685	2,897	2,040	305	425	512	553	560	579	1,155	2,150	2,508	2,566
Kuwait	1,656	1,125	823	1,064	1,157	1,023	1,419	1,585	1,492	1,783	1,175	190	1,058	1,852	2,025	2,057	2,062	2,007	2,085	1,898	2,126
Saudi Arabia	9,900	9,815	6,483	5,086	4,663	3,388	4,870	4,265	5,086	5,064	6,410	8,115	8,332	8,198	8,120	8,231	8,218	8,362	8,389	7,833	8,404
United Arab Emirates	1,709	1,474	1,250	1,149	1,146	1,193	1,330	1,541	1,565	1,860	2,117	2,386	2,266	2,159	2,193	2,233	2,278	2,316	2,345	2,169	2,268
Africa	**6,125**	**4,772**	**4,733**	**4,751**	**5,121**	**5,371**	**5,175**	**5,232**	**5,581**	**5,962**	**6,432**	**6,721**	**6,755**	**6,638**	**6,674**	**6,954**	**7,112**	**7,368**	**7,340**	**7,296**	**n/a**
Algeria	1,106	1,002	987	968	1,014	1,037	945	1,048	1,040	1,095	1,175	1,230	1,214	1,162	1,180	1,202	1,242	1,277	1,246	1,202	809
Libya	1,787	1,140	1,150	1,105	1,087	1,059	1,034	972	1,175	1,150	1,375	1,483	1,433	1,361	1,378	1,390	1,401	1,446	1,390	1,319	1,410
Nigeria	2,055	1,433	1,295	1,241	1,388	1,495	1,467	1,341	1,450	1,716	1,810	1,892	1,943	1,960	1,931	1,993	2,001	2,132	2,153	2,130	2,140
Far East & Oceania	**4,848**	**4,822**	**4,687**	**4,980**	**5,426**	**5,758**	**5,984**	**5,972**	**6,085**	**6,264**	**6,468**	**6,660**	**6,615**	**6,680**	**6,822**	**7,043**	**7,205**	**7,323**	**7,324**	**7,319**	**n/a**
China	2,114	2,012	2,045	2,120	2,296	2,505	2,620	2,690	2,730	2,757	2,774	2,835	2,845	2,890	2,939	2,990	3,131	3,200	3,198	3,195	3,250
Indonesia	1,577	1,605	1,339	1,343	1,412	1,325	1,390	1,343	1,342	1,409	1,462	1,592	1,504	1,511	1,510	1,503	1,547	1,520	1,518	1,472	1,286
World Total	**59,600**	**56,076**	**53,481**	**53,256**	**54,489**	**53,982**	**56,227**	**56,666**	**58,737**	**59,863**	**60,566**	**60,207**	**60,213**	**60,236**	**60,991**	**62,335**	**63,711**	**65,690**	**66,921**	**65,870**	**68,200**

SOURCE: Energy Information Administration, www.eia.doe.gov.

EXHIBIT 8N.10 **WORLD OIL CONSUMPTION, 1980–2000 (THOUSAND BARRELS PER DAY)**

Country	1980	1981	1982	1983	1984	1985	1986	1987	1988	1989	1990	1991	1992	1993	1994	1995	1996	1997	1998	1999	2000
North America	20,204	19,229	18,354	18,034	18,655	18,701	19,277	19,739	20,532	20,706	20,364	20,036	20,404	20,639	21,245	21,208	21,873	22,354	22,715	23,432	23,800
Mexico	1,270	1,399	1,476	1,350	1,452	1,466	1,486	1,520	1,550	1,640	1,679	1,695	1,723	1,710	1,795	1,724	1,763	1,872	1,935	1,975	2,073
United States	17,056	16,058	15,296	15,231	15,726	15,726	16,281	16,665	17,283	17,325	16,988	16,714	17,033	17,237	17,718	17,725	18,309	18,620	18,917	19,519	19,701
Central & South America	3,573	3,517	3,375	3,192	3,217	3,185	3,407	3,518	3,565	3,576	3,591	3,654	3,748	3,887	4,050	4,248	4,455	4,645	4,859	4,949	n/a
Brazil	1,148	1,085	1,061	980	1,033	1,079	1,238	1,263	1,300	1,317	1,339	1,346	1,369	1,429	1,511	1,596	1,718	1,823	1,915	1,950	n/a
Venezuela	400	433	427	400	379	383	402	404	397	388	396	405	414	427	440	448	444	455	457	470	n/a
Western Europe	14,322	13,169	12,723	12,379	12,413	12,385	12,785	12,927	13,084	13,159	13,246	13,660	13,841	13,731	13,815	14,347	14,525	14,726	14,985	14,800	n/a
Eastern Europe & Former U.S.S.R.	10,707	10,550	10,621	10,474	10,417	10,461	10,463	10,508	10,383	10,190	9,725	9,434	7,910	6,710	5,885	5,681	5,173	5,045	4,968	4,912	n/a
Russia	0	0	0	0	0	0	0	0	0	0	0	0	4,423	3,750	3,179	2,976	2,619	2,562	2,449	2,396	n/a
Middle East	2,058	2,199	2,352	2,612	2,673	2,854	2,977	3,055	3,154	3,283	3,377	3,376	3,581	3,778	3,941	4,067	4,081	4,238	4,339	4,424	n/a
Africa	1,474	1,577	1,660	1,698	1,758	1,826	1,827	1,844	1,905	1,985	2,076	2,131	2,169	2,207	2,243	2,303	2,359	2,432	2,463	2,523	n/a
Far East & Oceania	10,729	10,662	10,417	10,350	10,699	10,679	11,024	11,408	12,196	13,017	13,595	14,269	15,105	16,044	17,108	18,024	18,945	19,617	19,312	19,865	n/a
China	1,765	1,705	1,660	1,730	1,740	1,885	2,000	2,120	2,275	2,380	2,296	2,499	2,662	2,959	3,161	3,363	3,610	3,916	4,106	4,320	4,600
Hong Kong	124	128	125	119	115	110	113	116	121	124	127	133	152	158	180	186	183	138	184	229	n/a
India	643	729	737	773	824	895	947	988	1,084	1,150	1,168	1,190	1,275	1,311	1,413	1,575	1,681	1,765	1,844	1,930	n/a
Indonesia	408	455	479	470	470	465	470	493	524	583	651	695	707	765	778	814	886	1,003	954	990	n/a
Japan	4,960	4,848	4,582	4,395	4,576	4,384	4,439	4,484	4,752	4,983	5,140	5,284	5,446	5,401	5,674	5,711	5,867	5,711	5,512	5,572	5,528
Korea, South	537	536	534	561	587	569	607	639	731	843	1,025	1,202	1,456	1,690	1,856	2,027	2,183	2,392	1,973	2,040	2,146
Singapore	202	214	222	220	235	227	257	285	304	329	363	389	420	469	503	512	541	620	599	592	n/a
Taiwan	380	340	330	337	384	378	405	420	483	521	542	545	557	616	659	737	780	775	808	825	n/a
World Total	63,067	60,903	59,503	58,739	59,831	60,091	61,759	62,999	64,819	65,917	65,974	66,559	66,758	66,996	68,286	69,878	71,411	73,057	73,642	74,905	75,525

SOURCE: Energy Information Administration, www.eia.doe.gov.

EXHIBIT 8N.11 WORLD DRY NATURAL GAS PRODUCTION, 1980–1999 (TRILLION CUBIC FEET)

Country	1980	1981	1982	1983	1984	1985	1986	1987	1988	1989	1990	1991	1992	1993	1994	1995	1996	1997	1998	1999
North America	**23.06**	**22.82**	**21.59**	**19.68**	**21.26**	**20.50**	**19.81**	**20.62**	**21.58**	**21.90**	**22.56**	**22.65**	**23.24**	**23.95**	**25.06**	**25.16**	**25.70**	**25.92**	**26.02**	**26.17**
Canada	2.76	2.67	2.72	2.56	2.79	3.04	2.86	3.10	3.57	3.73	3.85	4.06	4.52	4.91	5.27	5.60	5.78	5.86	6.05	6.26
United States	19.40	19.18	17.82	16.09	17.47	16.45	16.06	16.62	17.10	17.31	17.81	17.70	17.84	18.10	18.82	18.60	18.85	18.90	18.71	18.62
Central & South America	**1.23**	**1.36**	**1.43**	**1.49**	**1.70**	**1.75**	**1.78**	**1.74**	**1.87**	**2.13**	**2.01**	**2.15**	**2.14**	**2.30**	**2.44**	**2.58**	**2.76**	**2.92**	**3.12**	**3.32**
Western Europe	**7.46**	**7.29**	**6.73**	**6.99**	**7.15**	**7.38**	**7.21**	**7.43**	**7.06**	**7.31**	**7.24**	**7.83**	**7.92**	**8.33**	**8.44**	**8.80**	**10.09**	**9.71**	**9.64**	**9.90**
Netherlands	3.40	3.15	2.69	2.85	2.88	3.01	2.76	2.77	2.45	2.67	2.69	3.04	3.06	3.11	2.95	2.98	3.37	2.99	2.84	2.65
Norway	0.92	0.92	0.90	0.91	0.97	0.94	0.99	1.04	1.05	1.09	0.98	0.97	1.04	0.97	1.04	1.08	1.45	1.62	1.63	1.76
United Kingdom	1.32	1.33	1.36	1.40	1.36	1.52	1.60	1.68	1.62	1.58	1.75	2.01	1.96	2.31	2.47	2.67	3.18	3.03	3.14	3.49
Eastern Europe & Former U.S.S.R.	**17.06**	**18.15**	**19.50**	**20.79**	**22.59**	**24.52**	**26.05**	**27.18**	**28.96**	**29.71**	**30.13**	**29.85**	**28.58**	**27.98**	**26.47**	**25.93**	**26.28**	**24.85**	**25.16**	**25.41**
Former U.S.S.R.	15.37	16.43	17.68	18.93	20.74	22.71	24.19	25.36	27.19	28.11	28.78	28.62	0.00	0.00	0.00	0.00	0.00	0.00	0.00	0.00
Romania	1.20	1.24	1.35	1.40	1.34	1.27	1.34	1.32	1.28	1.13	1.00	0.88	0.78	0.75	0.69	0.68	0.63	0.61	0.52	0.50
Russia	0.00	0.00	0.00	0.00	0.00	0.00	0.00	0.00	0.00	0.00	0.00	0.00	22.62	21.81	21.45	21.01	21.23	20.17	20.87	20.83
Turkmenistan	0.00	0.00	0.00	0.00	0.00	0.00	0.00	0.00	0.00	0.00	0.00	0.00	2.02	2.29	1.26	1.14	1.31	0.90	0.47	0.79
Uzbekistan	0.00	0.00	0.00	0.00	0.00	0.00	0.00	0.00	0.00	0.00	0.00	0.00	1.51	1.59	1.67	1.70	1.70	1.74	1.94	1.96
Middle East	**1.42**	**1.45**	**1.37**	**1.52**	**2.00**	**2.38**	**2.63**	**3.03**	**3.31**	**3.69**	**3.72**	**3.84**	**4.14**	**4.43**	**4.69**	**4.99**	**5.53**	**6.22**	**6.60**	**6.81**
Iran	0.25	0.21	0.25	0.31	0.48	0.60	0.54	0.57	0.71	0.78	0.84	0.92	0.88	0.96	1.12	1.25	1.42	1.66	1.77	1.87
Qatar	0.18	0.16	0.19	0.17	0.21	0.19	0.19	0.20	0.21	0.22	0.28	0.33	0.40	0.48	0.48	0.48	0.48	0.61	0.69	0.85
Saudi Arabia	0.33	0.56	0.43	0.42	0.62	0.72	0.89	0.95	1.03	1.05	1.08	1.13	1.20	1.27	1.33	1.34	1.46	1.60	1.65	1.63
United Arab Emirates	0.20	0.23	0.20	0.27	0.34	0.48	0.54	0.68	0.66	0.81	0.78	0.92	1.02	0.94	0.91	1.11	1.19	1.28	1.31	1.34
Africa	**0.69**	**1.04**	**1.24**	**1.69**	**1.80**	**1.86**	**1.88**	**2.10**	**2.24**	**2.39**	**2.46**	**2.69**	**2.77**	**2.81**	**2.72**	**3.01**	**3.23**	**3.52**	**3.70**	**4.10**
Algeria	0.41	0.77	0.94	1.31	1.36	1.36	1.33	1.52	1.63	1.71	1.79	1.93	1.97	1.90	1.81	2.05	2.19	2.43	2.60	2.90
Far East & Oceania	**2.44**	**2.62**	**2.69**	**2.99**	**3.54**	**4.00**	**4.22**	**4.50**	**4.78**	**4.98**	**5.44**	**5.76**	**6.06**	**6.55**	**7.11**	**7.50**	**8.13**	**8.47**	**8.55**	**8.98**
Indonesia	0.63	0.66	0.67	0.78	1.06	1.23	1.18	1.29	1.34	1.42	1.53	1.72	1.79	1.97	2.21	2.24	2.35	2.37	2.27	2.34
Malaysia	0.06	0.06	0.06	0.15	0.33	0.44	0.53	0.55	0.58	0.61	0.65	0.75	0.80	0.88	0.92	1.02	1.23	1.36	1.37	1.45
World Total	**53.35**	**54.73**	**54.56**	**55.15**	**60.05**	**62.39**	**63.57**	**66.61**	**69.80**	**72.13**	**73.57**	**74.78**	**74.84**	**76.36**	**76.93**	**77.96**	**81.71**	**81.61**	**82.79**	**84.69**

SOURCE: Energy Information Administration, www.eia.doe.gov.

EXHIBIT 8N.12 WORLD DRY NATURAL GAS CONSUMPTION, 1980–1999 (TRILLION CUBIC FEET)

Country	1980	1981	1982	1983	1984	1985	1986	1987	1988	1989	1990	1991	1992	1993	1994	1995	1996	1997	1998	1999
North America	**22.56**	**22.11**	**20.80**	**19.64**	**20.91**	**20.44**	**19.23**	**20.22**	**21.26**	**22.11**	**22.01**	**22.38**	**23.10**	**23.99**	**24.56**	**25.41**	**26.07**	**26.12**	**25.41**	**26.06**
Canada	1.88	1.84	1.86	1.86	2.02	2.17	2.13	2.11	2.33	2.43	2.38	2.40	2.60	2.74	2.82	2.79	3.00	2.98	2.87	3.10
Mexico	0.80	0.87	0.94	0.95	0.95	0.99	0.88	0.89	0.90	0.88	0.92	0.95	0.96	0.98	1.03	1.04	1.10	1.18	1.28	1.26
United States	19.88	19.40	18.00	16.84	17.95	17.28	16.22	18.03	18.80	18.72	19.04	19.54	19.54	20.28	20.71	21.58	21.96	21.97	21.26	21.70
Central & South America	**1.24**	**1.32**	**1.42**	**1.42**	**1.70**	**1.75**	**1.78**	**1.74**	**1.87**	**2.13**	**2.02**	**2.15**	**2.14**	**2.30**	**2.44**	**2.58**	**2.76**	**2.92**	**3.12**	**3.25**
Venezuela	0.52	0.57	0.60	0.58	0.61	0.62	0.67	0.66	0.66	0.77	0.76	0.79	0.76	0.82	0.88	0.89	0.96	0.99	1.11	1.09
Western Europe	**8.66**	**8.51**	**8.36**	**8.52**	**9.17**	**9.48**	**9.68**	**10.07**	**9.89**	**10.41**	**10.50**	**11.29**	**11.23**	**11.67**	**11.89**	**12.76**	**13.80**	**13.60**	**14.00**	**14.64**
Belgium	0.37	0.34	0.28	0.30	0.31	0.31	0.27	0.30	0.30	0.33	0.34	0.36	0.37	0.39	0.40	0.44	0.49	0.47	0.52	0.55
France	0.98	1.00	0.98	1.00	1.08	1.11	1.13	1.04	0.96	0.98	1.00	1.13	1.15	1.16	1.16	1.18	1.31	1.30	1.31	1.35
Germany	0.00	0.00	0.00	0.00	0.00	0.00	0.00	0.00	0.00	0.00	0.00	2.78	2.74	2.83	2.97	3.17	3.16	3.01	3.03	3.04
Germany, East	0.00	0.00	0.00	0.50	0.59	0.58	0.60	0.56	0.60	0.59	0.36	0.00	0.00	0.00	0.00	0.00	0.00	0.00	0.00	0.00
Germany, West	2.13	2.02	1.84	1.90	2.00	1.97	1.99	2.18	2.11	2.25	2.31	0.00	0.00	0.00	0.00	0.00	0.00	0.00	0.00	0.00
Italy	0.97	0.94	0.94	0.97	1.13	1.15	1.22	1.35	1.46	1.58	1.67	1.78	1.76	1.80	1.75	1.92	1.98	2.05	2.20	2.40
Netherlands	1.49	1.42	1.51	1.45	1.54	1.62	1.62	1.67	1.51	1.55	1.54	1.72	1.67	1.71	1.65	1.70	1.87	1.76	1.75	1.70
Spain	0.06	0.07	0.07	0.08	0.07	0.08	0.09	0.10	0.13	0.17	0.19	0.22	0.23	0.22	0.24	0.30	0.33	0.44	0.45	0.51
United Kingdom	1.70	1.74	1.74	1.81	1.85	1.99	2.02	2.08	1.97	1.95	2.06	2.22	2.17	2.41	2.54	2.69	3.18	3.01	3.07	3.26
Eastern Europe & Former U.S.S.R.	**15.86**	**16.97**	**18.23**	**19.59**	**21.28**	**23.11**	**24.48**	**25.44**	**26.94**	**27.49**	**27.83**	**27.56**	**26.08**	**25.99**	**23.92**	**23.04**	**23.46**	**22.22**	**22.21**	**22.32**
Belarus	0.00	0.00	0.00	0.00	0.00	0.00	0.00	0.00	0.00	0.00	0.00	0.00	0.65	0.60	0.50	0.45	0.49	0.53	0.54	0.61
Former U.S.S.R.	13.33	14.44	15.52	16.82	18.51	20.30	21.52	22.46	24.09	24.53	24.96	25.01	0.00	0.00	0.00	0.00	0.00	0.00	0.00	0.00
Russia	0.00	0.00	0.00	0.00	0.00	0.00	0.00	0.00	0.00	0.00	0.00	0.00	16.48	16.18	15.21	14.51	14.50	13.43	14.04	14.01
Ukraine	0.00	0.00	0.00	0.00	0.00	0.00	0.00	0.00	0.00	0.00	0.00	0.00	3.50	3.87	3.33	2.97	2.93	2.83	2.61	2.75
Uzbekistan	0.00	0.00	0.00	0.00	0.00	0.00	0.00	0.00	0.00	0.00	0.00	0.00	1.09	1.54	1.23	1.35	1.43	1.45	1.41	1.42
Middle East	**1.31**	**1.30**	**1.21**	**1.43**	**1.90**	**2.27**	**2.53**	**2.93**	**3.28**	**3.58**	**3.60**	**3.60**	**4.02**	**4.27**	**4.54**	**4.74**	**5.27**	**5.85**	**6.24**	**6.34**
Africa	**0.74**	**0.61**	**0.82**	**1.00**	**1.10**	**1.07**	**1.14**	**1.24**	**1.31**	**1.34**	**1.35**	**1.51**	**1.48**	**1.54**	**1.61**	**1.69**	**1.79**	**1.79**	**1.84**	**1.97**
Far East and Oceania	**2.52**	**2.69**	**2.78**	**3.03**	**3.63**	**4.12**	**4.28**	**4.67**	**5.00**	**5.26**	**5.61**	**5.89**	**6.31**	**6.80**	**7.41**	**7.79**	**8.50**	**8.91**	**9.08**	**9.62**
Japan	0.90	0.92	0.96	1.02	1.37	1.47	1.49	1.54	1.62	1.73	1.85	1.98	2.02	2.03	2.18	2.21	2.39	2.44	2.53	2.65
World Total	**52.89**	**53.51**	**53.63**	**54.63**	**59.69**	**62.24**	**63.12**	**66.31**	**69.55**	**72.32**	**72.91**	**74.38**	**74.35**	**76.58**	**76.36**	**78.02**	**81.65**	**81.41**	**81.90**	**84.20**

SOURCE: Energy Information Administration, www.eia.doe.gov.

ENDNOTES

1   Energy Information Administration, *International Energy Outlook*, 2001.

2   Energy Information Administration, *January's Oil Market Report Highlights*. January 18, 2002.

3   Standard & Poor's, *Oil &Gas: Production & Marketing Industry Survey*, October 18, 2001.

4   Hart's Petroleum Finance Week, "IEA's Oil Demand Growth Outlook for 2002 Is Even More Bearish than EIA's," October 22, 2001.

5   Energy Information Administration, *Oil Market Basics*, 2001.

6   Peter Ellis Jones, *Oil: A Practical Guide to the Economics of World Petroleum* (New York: Nichols Publishing, 1988).

7   Ibid.

8   Dag Harald Claes, *The Politics of Oil-Producer Cooperation* (Boulder: Westview Press, 2001).

9   Richard H. K. Vietor, *Energy Policy In America since 1945* (New York: Cambridge University Press, 1984).

10   Ibid.

11   Peter Ellis Jones, *Oil: A Practical Guide to the Economics of World Petroleum* (New York: Nichols Publishing, 1988).

12   Energy Information Administration, *OPEC Revenues Fact Sheet*, December 2001.

13   Ibid.

14   Gause, F. Gregory, "Saudi Arabia over a Barrel," *Foreign Affairs*, May/June 2000.

15   Harvard Business School Case, *Crisis in the Gulf*, 9-391-178.

16   William Drozdiak, "Cheap Oil Comes at a Price," *The Washington Post*, November 21, 2001.

17   Energy Information Administration, *International Energy Outlook, 2001*.

18   Ibid.

19   Neela Banerjee, "Bush Orders Increased Emergency Supply of Oil," *The New York Times*, November 14, 2001.

20   Energy Information Administration, *United States*, October, 2001.

21   Energy Information Administration, *Russia*, October 2001.

22   *The New York Times*, "Oil Sinks to 2-Year Low amid Showdown among Producers," November 15, 2001.

23   Energy Information Administration, *Norway*, August 2001.

24   Energy Information Administration, *United Kingdom*, September 2001.

25   Energy Information Administration, *China*, April 2001.

26   Syncrude Canada Ltd.

27   Energy Information Administration, *Canada*, February 2001.

28   Energy Information Administration, *United States*, October 2001.

29   APS Review Oil Market Trends, "Saudi Arabia-Costs to Produce Oil," October 22, 2001.

30   The Economist Intelligence Unit, *EIU Country Profile: Saudi Arabia*, 2001.

31   Energy Information Administration, *Saudi Arabia*, June 2001.

32   Nawaf E. Obaid, *The Oil Kingdom at 100*, (Washington, D.C.: The Washington Institute for Near East Policy, 2000).

33   Energy Information Administration, *Saudi Arabia*, June 2001.

34   Ibid.

35   The Economist Intelligence Unit, *EIU Country Profile: Saudi Arabia*, 2001.

36   Ibid.

37   Nawaf E. Obaid, *The Oil Kingdom at 100* (Washington D. C.: The Washington Institute for Near East Policy, 2000).

38   Thaddeus Herrick and Bhushan Bahree, "Saudis Propose Deeper-Than-Expected OPEC Cuts," *The Wall Street Journal*, November 9, 2001; *Hart's European Fuels News*, "OPEC Looks for Stability," October 31, 2001.

39   *Hart's European Fuels News*, "OPEC Looks for Stability," October 31, 2001; Alexei Barrionuevo, "OPEC Cutback May Help Prices, Erode Its Clout," *The Wall Street Journal*, December 31, 2001.

Regional Integration

This case examines the leading edge of globalization. Fifteen European countries are joined in an organization designed to create a single integrated market and 11 of them (today 12 including Greece) have entered monetary union.

There are several issues to consider here. First, one ought to think about why the Europeans are doing this; what problems are they trying to solve? And is this the appropriate solution? Then one should think about the extra-national form of government; how does it work? But the centerpiece of the case is the process of market integration since the passage of the Single European Act in 1985. At the time, the Europeans agreed to a program of reducing internal barriers to the movement of people, goods, and capital. Although its initiatives were originally planned for implementation in seven years, it has taken much longer and is still far from complete.

This case provides data for an evaluation of how far Europe has come and how far it still has to go in integrating product markets, capital markets, and labor markets. The exhibits provide important evidence that should be studied carefully.

The second part of the case explores monetary union—i.e., the adoption of a single currency and a single central bank, beginning in January 1999. Here, one must think carefully about what monetary integration means. What are its costs and benefits? And what does it mean for fiscal and social autonomy? The case also provides data for consideration of four of the larger issues facing the Union: (1) budgetary problems, vis-a-vis the countries that contribute and the countries that are subsidized; (2) the Stability and Growth Pact, requiring member states to balance budgets by 2003 (which, as of this writing, has proven impossible for at least four nations); (3) the challenges of bringing three to eight East European states into the Union; and (4) continuing problems with immigration.

Finally, students are asked to think broadly about Europe's future trajectory. Is it likely to grow in an integrated fashion (i.e., all the parts converging to the same levels of GDP/capita), and is the whole likely to grow at the same overall rates as its largest competitor, the United States?

EUROPEAN MONETARY UNION

RICHARD H. K. VIETOR

> *To achieve growth and further employment we need to improve the efficiency of the European economy by making our markets more flexible and improving manufacturing and service sector performance. To do this we must improve the regulatory framework in which our firms operate; develop a more entrepreneurial European economy, with more efficient capital markets and fewer barriers to easy entry/exit to markets; open protected markets to competition while securing affordable access to services of general interest and eliminate anti-competitive behavior by firms or by the public sector.*[1]
> —The European Commission (1998)

Introduction

In the spring of 1999, Romano Prodi, newly designated chairman of the European Commission, prepared to help create an economically integrated Europe. Since the introduction of the euro on January 1, Europe had been operating with a single currency—at least for business-to-business transactions. Despite some technical problems with the changeover and an 8% depreciation of the euro against the dollar, this extraordinary step toward integration had gone fantastically well. Western Europe continued to experience healthy growth—in excess of 2% annually—and the Commission was expanding its plans to further integrate Europe's markets.

But before real integration could be achieved, many more reforms would be needed. While the Commission recently concluded that "thanks to the Single Market Programme, today's European product markets work much better than they did in the 1970s,"[2] they still exhibited wide price differentials, diverse regulations, and a lack of inter-European investment and competition. Capital markets had moved further, as members of the European

Union had dropped regulations and encouraged competition across national borders. But even here, prices and margins remained high, and inter-European rationalization had only just begun. Finally, the markets for labor had barely begun to integrate. High minimum wages, payroll taxes, unemployment benefits, and diverse restrictions on flexibility had pushed Europe toward an employment crisis. Unemployment for the EU-11 had exceeded 11% for more than six years [see **Exhibit 9.1**].

In little more than three years, at least 11 European countries planned to adopt the common currency for all their economic transactions. Transparency then should force more integration on these fragmented markets and on their macroeconomic policies, which varied as much as European cultures. The question on Prodi's mind was whether Europeans could really sustain the extraordinary pace of change. Tax systems, pensions, health care, work rules, agricultural subsidies, and fiscal budgets all needed significant adjustment and integration, while pressures mounted for the Commission to liberalize its own decision-making process and reform its generous budget. In the East, meanwhile, 13 more nations were seeking admittance to the Union—a pressure that was sure to make integration all the more challenging.

The Postwar Background of European Economic Integration

The destruction wrought by the Second World War gave rise to an outpouring of sentiment in favor of European unification. In 1946, Winston Churchill called for a "United States of Europe." Others talked of the need for some type of European federation. Yet all efforts to create political unity, such as the Council of Europe in 1949, failed because most governments would not surrender political sovereignty.

Economic integration proved more tractable. In 1951, France, West Germany, Belgium, Luxembourg, the Netherlands, and Italy established the European Coal and Steel

---

Professor Richard H. K. Vietor prepared this case. HBS cases are developed solely as the basis for class discussion. Cases are not intended to serve as endorsements, sources of primary data, or illustrations of effective or ineffective management.

Community (ECSC). The ECSC was essentially a customs union in coal and steel. It served to enhance efficiency and profitability in these two industries and, equally important, it fostered cooperation between former adversaries like France and Germany.

Treaty of Rome

In 1957, the six ECSC members signed the Treaty of Rome, which established the European Economic Community (EEC). The Treaty laid out a timetable by which its members would remove all internal tariffs and establish a common external tariff by 1970 (an objective that was reached two years ahead of schedule). It also provided for the creation of a common agricultural policy and the removal of some nontariff barriers to the free movement of people, services, and capital. Finally, the Treaty sought to "lay the foundations of an even closer union among the people of Europe and to preserve and strengthen peace and liberty."

Economic integration proceeded, albeit haltingly. In 1967, the European Economic Community, the European Coal and Steel Community, and the European Atomic Energy Community adopted a unified institutional structure. EEC membership also increased. Britain, Ireland, and Denmark joined in 1973, Greece in 1981, Spain and Portugal in 1986, and Austria, Finland, and Sweden in 1995, bringing the total number of member states to 15.[3]

Institutions of the European Community

Four principal institutions comprised the European Community (EC): the Commission, the Council of Ministers, the European Parliament, and the Court of Justice. Some of their responsibilities defined by the Treaty of Rome were amended by subsequent regulations. In particular, the Amsterdam Treaty of 1997 (effective May 1, 1999) increased the power of both the Council and the Parliament, relative to the Commission.

The Commission was the executive arm of the EC, directed by a president and 19 commissioners. The president was selected by member countries (for a five-year renewable term); the commissioners were appointed by national governments and the president-designate (two from each of the five large countries—France, Great Britain, Italy, Germany, and Spain—and one from each of the

smaller EC countries). The Amsterdam Treaty mandated that the European Parliament approve the appointment of the entire commission and its president. Commission members were supposed to represent the interest of the EC as a whole. A staff of approximately 14,000 serving in 24 directorates supported these Commission members [see **Appendix A**].

The Commission performed three main functions: it initiated EC proposals, represented the EC in international trade negotiations, and managed the EC budget. It was also responsible for the management of some EC policies (agriculture, anti-trust) and for overseeing national policies to ensure they were consistent with EC policy. It investigated violations of EC treaties, issued decisions when violations were found, and had the option of referring violations to the Court of Justice.

The Council of Ministers served as the EC's main decision-making body; it could not initiate legislation, but it had the power to approve, amend, or reject Commission proposals. It consisted of representatives from each government but was not a permanent group. Agricultural ministers sat on the Council when it dealt with agricultural policy, trade ministers sat on the Council when it dealt with trade matters, and so on. The Council presidency was responsible for setting the agenda, and it rotated among member states every six months. Decisions were mostly adopted by a qualified-majority (62 votes out of a total of 87). Here too the Amsterdam Treaty had broadened the Council's range of qualified-majority voting to include many of the EC's new provisions, such as initiatives on jobs, public health, social exclusion, transparency, and customs cooperation, but not taxation, which still needed unanimity.

The European Parliament comprised 626 members, directly elected by voters in each nation since 1979. It had offices in Brussels but gathered for meetings in Strasbourg. Parliament's role in the legislative process allowed it to help draft directives and regulations. In 1992, Parliament began to share joint decision-making powers with the Council on issues such as freedom of movement of workers, free circulation of products, freedom to set up business, and freedom to provide services. The Amsterdam Treaty extended Parliament's co-decision powers with the Council to include such areas as public health, transport policy, free movement of people, and social and economic policy. Together with the Council, Parliament had the power to adopt or reject the Commission's budget proposal. Parliament could also turn out the Commission through a vote of no-confidence.

The Court of Justice interpreted EC treaties and directives and sought to apply Community law in a uniform way. Fifteen judges sat on the Court, one from each nation. The Amsterdam Treaty allowed the Court to rule on issues affecting peoples' freedom and security. Court decisions had precedence over national rulings, but in numerous cases companies and states disregarded the Court.[4]

EC regulations and directives began as Commission proposals. The process for approving proposals typically took from two to five years. Proposals were initiated by the Commission and then sent to Parliament for study and debate. Review by Parliament was followed by approval (or amendment) by the Council. A proposal was sent to the Parliament for a second reading. Once both Parliament and the Council accepted a proposal, it became a directive. Member states were then obligated to change ("transpose") their national laws to conform to it.

European Monetary System

Another step toward economic integration was taken with the formation of the European Monetary System (EMS) in 1979. Proposed by German Chancellor Helmut Schmidt and French President Valery Giscard d'Estaing in 1978, the EMS established a system of "fixed but adjustable" exchange rates, designed to insulate intra-European trade from the effects of floating exchange rates and to promote greater macroeconomic convergence.

Eight European states (Germany, France, Belgium, Netherlands, Luxembourg, Denmark, Ireland, and Italy) joined the EMS on March 1, 1979. The basis of its Exchange Rate Mechanism (ERM) was the existing ("parity") exchange rates between member nations. While the parity rates were fixed, the system left room for some variability. Currencies could fluctuate within a band of +/- 2.25% from initial parity.[5] Central banks of member nations were required to use their foreign exchange reserves to maintain currencies within these bands. In addition, member nations could borrow from other ERM members whenever their currencies reached the lower end of the allowed band. Parity rates and exchange rates could be changed by unanimous agreement.

During the 1980s, the EMS seemed to work, haltingly, to reduce inflation differentials and foster convergence in economic cycles [see **Exhibit 9.3**]. The relative success of the system eventually prompted Spain (1989) and the United Kingdom (1990) to join.

Single European Act

In 1985, the Commission released a *White Paper* that outlined a program to complete the internal market by December 31, 1992. It proposed 282 targets of growth, covering a variety of issues, products, services, and industries, each with its own timetable for implementation. The measures were designed to eliminate many of the costs and constraints facing European firms and thereby increase their efficiency and competitiveness (**Appendix B** lists the major elements of the 1992 program). This "adventure in deregulation," as *The Economist* put it, would create a stronger and more prosperous Europe.[6]

The Single European Act amended key parts of the original Treaty of Rome and aimed to remove three types of obstacles: (1) physical barriers, which included intra-EC border stoppages, customs controls, and associated paperwork; (2) technical barriers, which involved meeting divergent national product standards, technical regulations, conflicting business laws, and the opening of national protected public procurement markets; and (3) fiscal barriers, which mainly dealt with rates of VAT (value-added taxes) and excise duties.

Border Controls

A key component of the 1992 agenda was the elimination of border controls. These controls included tax collection (aggravated by differences in value-added tax [VAT] and excise rates), agricultural checks (such as applications for adjustments to farm product prices), veterinary checks (which were necessitated by differing national health standards), and transportation controls. Such measures created delays and added considerably to costs. Smaller companies suffered the most. Customs cost per consignment was estimated to be up to 30%–45% higher for companies with fewer than 250 employees than they were for larger firms.[7]

Standardization

More than 100,000 different regulations and standards existed in the EC in the 1980s. These included regulations affecting health, safety, the environment, and technical standards within industries. EC countries set their own national standards for a wide range of industries, from automobiles to food processing, from electrical products to telecommunications. Firms were required to vary products and testing for each different national market; this increased marketing difficulties and added significantly to costs.

In the past, the Commission had sought to solve the problem of divergent standards and regulations by harmonizing national legislation throughout the EC (i.e., establishing similar laws in all member states). But given the entrenched interests in each country, this approach was scarcely feasible. The Court of Justice, in the Cassis de Dijon case, actually introduced a new approach, based on the principle of "mutual recognition": the practices, regulations, and other forms of control in one member state could be accepted in other countries, even if such regulations did not apply there. Thus, products lawfully produced or marketed in one EC nation, if legal at home, would have access to all other EC markets.

National Procurement

Public procurement amounted to some 12% of the EC's GDP. The 1992 program sought to end national protectionism for all public procurement contracts. In particular, the Commission aimed to open the four previously excluded sectors (energy, transport, telecommunications, and water supply) to competitive bidding. However, the Commission's proposal allowed national governments to give preference to products with at least 50% European content.

VAT Harmonization

The Commission intended to end the divergence in national indirect tax rates, which encompassed both the value-added tax (VAT) and excise taxes. Divergent VAT rates, from 1% to 38% (for very different types of goods), distorted trade flows by encouraging consumers to buy goods in low VAT countries and ship them home without paying the higher VAT. One of the problems confronted by the Commission in considering changes in the VAT was that most EC countries had two, if not three, tiers of VAT rates. The *White Paper* proposed abolishing the highest tier of VAT rates (applied in only six countries). Two tiers would then remain: a reduced rate for basic necessity goods and a standard rate for all other products. The *White Paper's* plan was to reduce the differences within each of these two tiers—to a band of 4% to 9% for the reduced rate and a band of 14% to 20% for the standard rate—over several years.

To reduce the need for border controls, the *White Paper* also proposed that the VAT should be applied in the country where a sale took place rather than collected at the border. Companies would report the value of their exports to their own governments, which would then seek reimbursement of the VAT from the government of the country where the good was sold.

Services

In the view of the Commission, "the establishment of a common market in services [was] one of the main preconditions for a return to economic prosperity."[8] Services encompassed a variety of activities, including finance, transportation, and telecommunications. It was one of the fastest-growing and most heavily regulated sectors in Europe.

In the three key areas of finance—banking, insurance, and securities—member states agreed that some regulation was justified on the grounds of consumer protection. The Single Market program placed a high priority on creating a common financial market. A central element in the 1992 program was the liberalization of capital movements—what one Commission official referred to as "the life-blood of cross-frontier trade in financial services."[9]

The second thrust of the 1992 banking program aimed to eliminate two other significant barriers found in most states: restrictions on the right of establishment (the right to set up branches or subsidiaries in another country) and on the freedom to provide services across frontiers (marketing and advertising of financial services). Finally, the Commission proposed that the principles of home country rule and mutual recognition should also govern banking supervision.

The Maastricht Treaty

Leaders of all twelve EC member nations gathered in the small Dutch town of Maastricht in December 1991 to discuss proposals for the creation of a European economic and monetary union (EMU). Together, they drafted the Maastricht Treaty. On the political side, the Maastricht agreement provided added powers for the European Parliament, increased regional funds for the poorer EC countries, and created a framework for a common foreign policy. More significantly, Maastricht established a clear timetable for achieving monetary union by January 1, 1997, or if that proved infeasible, by January 1, 1999. The Council of Ministers would decide (by qualified majority) whether a majority of countries had met five convergence requirements:

- **Price stability** Inflation must be within 1.5 percentage points of the average of the three EC countries with the lowest inflation rates.

- **Interest rates** Long-term interest rates must be within two percentage points of the average of the three countries with the lowest inflation rates.

- **Deficits** National budget deficits must not exceed 3% of GDP.

- **Debt** Public debt must not exceed 60% of GDP.

- **Currency stability** A currency must not have been devalued in the previous two years and should have remained within a normal fluctuation band (originally 2.25%) of its central parity rate in the exchange rate mechanism.

Once monetary union took effect, the exchange rates of member nations would be irrevocably fixed and a new European currency (euro) would be substituted over a three-year period. A European Central Bank in Frankfurt would set Europe's monetary policy. Independent of national authorities, its principal task would be the maintenance of price stability.

Maastricht represented one of the most significant milestones in European history. Soon after the December 1991 agreement, each member state had to approve the agreement by referendum. Denmark initially voted it down, but subsequently approved it (with an opting-out clause). So did the rest of the EC nations. But the convergence criteria proved more difficult to achieve. After the German reunification in 1991, the Bundesbank raised interest rates under pressure from immense subsidies to rebuild East Germany. When the mark rose in value, EMU countries raised interest rates sharply to maintain the currency band. But they quickly gave up and devalued their currencies as Europe plunged into recession.

EURO TIMELINE

Stage 1: July 1990–December 1993

- Co-ordination of economic policies

- Liberalization of capital markets

Stage 2: Phase A, January 1994-December 1998

- Adaptation of legal and administrative framework for conversion

- Establishment of the European Monetary Institution

- (From Early 1998): Decision on the starting date of Stage 3

- Decision as to the participating countries

- Establishment of the European Central Bank (ECB)

Stage 3: Phase B, January 1999

- Introduction of the euro for non-cash transactions

- Irrevocable fixing of exchange rate to six significant figures for participating countries

- ECB adopts responsibility for centralized policy

Phase C January 2002-July 2002

- Euro bank notes

- All remaining assets converted into euro

- Disappearance of national currencies

SOURCE: Nat West, *A Guide for Business,* December 1997, section 1.1.

In little more than two years though, the European Monetary System was redesigned, with 15% fluctuation bands, new parity rates, and a new target of 1999 for monetary union. Member states began moving again to achieve the convergence criteria. Recovery helped these efforts, and by May of 1998, low inflation, low interest rates, and reduced deficits had been substantially achieved by all but Greece. The stage was set [see **Exhibit 9.4**].

Market Integration

Over the last 13 years, the Commission had issued nearly 1,400 directives. **Exhibit 9.5** indicates that all but 13.2% of these had been implemented by national governments. Finland, with only .7% left to transpose, had done the most, while Portugal, with 5.5% of the directives left to implement, slightly lagged behind Ireland and Belgium. **Exhibit 9.6** shows where the problems lay. Telecommunications, until recently, remained dominated by state enterprises, which were inefficient and monopolistic. For similar reasons, public procurement had remained a problem, although some progress had been made. And rules affecting social policies, not surprisingly, had difficulty getting implemented.

Diverse cultures appeared to remain the biggest barrier to market integration—by far. As one executive who ran an auto leasing company said, "Cultural barriers and language barriers were huge. Americans think integration will take one or two years, when really it is a process of hundreds of years." Thus, his organization did purchasing, maintenance, contracts, programs, accounting, and taxes locally; only finance was Europe-wide. A trade industry official agreed, but added that differences in tax systems and labor laws were nearly as problematic. A third executive suggested that culture overwhelmed much else. "Netherlands," he said, "is closer to the USA culturally than to France." This explained the slow progress in retail integration—in food, clothes, professional services, retail banking, and so on. Even branding had a long way to go.[10]

Product Markets

The Single Europe Act's first objective, to facilitate the free movement of people, goods, and services, had been substantially achieved.

Border checks of passports and shipping invoices had been virtually eliminated. Most external tariffs had been liberalized, with the exception of some sensitive imports (automobiles, textiles, consumer electronics, and agricultural products). The voluntary import restriction negotiated with Japan in 1991 (holding Japanese market share in automobiles to a ceiling of 10.5%) was still in effect, although due to expire by the end of 1999.[11]

The standardization of diverse regulation had made significant progress, although it still needed to improve considerably [see **Exhibit 9.7**]. The process of mutual recognition helped for consumer durables and capital goods, but ran into problems with foodstuffs, pesticides, or drugs, where national regulatory authorities feared foreign risks. Here, the Commission developed another mechanism, the adoption of "essential requirements." Once those were agreed upon, European standards organizations were charged with harmonizing the standards. Some 17% of European trade was facilitated by this method.[12]

Despite the progress on regulatory harmonization, national governments had been balking at the newly agreed-upon rules and were creative at inventing new regulatory barriers. The number of "notifications," by which a member state notifies its intention to regulate a specific field, rose fairly steadily during the 1990s. Telecommunications, food products, transportation, and mechanical engineering engendered most of these notifications [see **Exhibit 9.8**].

All of this harmonization was intended to force rationalization of inefficient assets, increase competition, and drive down costs. If one considers cross-border, intra-EU mergers and intra-EU foreign direct investment, it appeared this process was indeed underway. After intensifying sharply in the late 1980s, intra-EU mergers peaked at about 4,000 annually between 1989 and 1991 and then receded somewhat during the remainder of the 1990s. Most of the mergers were intra-country tie-ups (Krupp/Thyssen) rather than EU-wide (Hoechst/Rhone-Poulenc), much less international. The Netherlands and the United Kingdom showed merger activity disproportionate to their relative size [see **Exhibits 9.9a** and **9.9b**]. However, by 1997 international mergers were picking up in both number and size. At the top of the list were the mergers of Daimler-Chrysler and of Deutsche Bank-Bankers Trust. It remained to be seen if concentration would increase competition and lower prices, and if combination would increase the quality of management.[13]

To make sure that increasing integration and cross-border investment served the interests of economic efficiency, competition policy in Europe was intensifying. Stronger antitrust laws had recently been enacted—in Denmark and the Netherlands in 1997, and in Germany, Finland, and the United Kingdom in 1998. Across Europe, competition authorities had been strengthened, with at least nine countries enforcing the competition provisions (Articles 85–86) of the Treaty of Rome.[14]

Cross-border investment had also heated up. For the EU-15, intra-EU foreign direct investment had averaged .8% of GDP per year since 1992. Ireland, the Netherlands, and Belgium/Luxembourg had the most investment activity—generally three to four times this average. Among the large countries, only the United Kingdom exceeded the average. Most of the intra-EU FDI during the 1990s was in services; manufacturing's share dropped appreciably. In 1997, member states of the EU had invested 172 billion euros in other countries; of that, 42% was invested in other EU states. FDI inflows amounted to 99 billion euros—57.5 billion from other EU states. Net outflows increased by 8% from the previous year.[15]

Price dispersion With deregulation and the intensification of competition, dispersion of prices across Europe should have narrowed. Indeed, this had happened in some areas. The OECD estimated that price variation decreased between 1985 and 1996, from a coefficient of 20% to about 16% [see **Exhibit 9.10**]. A more careful examination by sector showed that in industries with relatively low productivity (e.g., pharmaceuticals, beverages, tobacco products, fabricated metals), price dispersion still exceeded 20% and ranged as high as 35%. However, where Europe's productivity was relatively higher (e.g., shipbuilding, rubber and plastic, mechanical engineering), price dispersion had shrunk to 11% or less [see **Exhibit 9.11**].[16]

Among the most important products (from a consumer-purchasing perspective) were automobiles, the retail prices of which were carefully tracked. Price differentials had declined for most models since 1995. In 1995, a Ford Fiesta sold for 48% more in one EU country than

another. By November 1998, the largest gap was down to 34.6% (a Ford Mondeo). However, price differentials on a dozen models still ranged from 16% to 32%. It appeared that manufacturers raised prices in cheap markets rather than lowering prices in less-competitive ones [see **Exhibit 9.12**].[17] The United Kingdom exhibited the most expensive prices, while Portugal, Spain, and the Netherlands tended to have the cheapest.

Prices for consumer goods still varied significantly due to various factors—"structural (member states' differences in living standards and tastes, transport costs), regulatory (consumption and other taxes, nontariff barriers), and firm strategies (concentration, differentiated products, advertising, etc.)."[18] Thus, Lacoste shirts could vary from $63 to $80, Levi's 501 jeans from $66 to $88, and a Swatch watch by as much as 50%—from $30 to $45. Even the price of a Coca Cola (1.5 litre bottle) ranged 100%, from .77 euros in Spain to 1.57 euros in Germany. A Big Mac, which *The Economist* had long used as a currency standard, varied from 1.85 euros in Greece to 3.47 euros in Finland.[19]

Still, the Commission was hopeful that "by enhancing price transparency, in combination with competition policy . . . the euro's introduction should put pressure on firms seeking to segment markets."[20]

Value-added tax Another factor that artificially segmented markets was the dispersion of value-added tax rates. Dispersion of these rates by as much as 20% of price had long caused significant distortions in distribution channels, sourcing, and even manufacturing location. These imposed costs on enterprises, on consumers, and on governmental collection agencies.[21] The Single Europe Act's initial package resulted in a narrowing of tax bands into "normal" rates on most goods, but with broader rates for exceptions. These normal rates varied by 17% in 1992. Six years later, this spread had shrunk to 10%. Likewise, the gap for exceptional rates was reduced from 37% to 24%. But with the collection system still based on sales destination (and with a variety of special regimes), the Commission did not think market forces would force any further reduction in the remaining divergence.[22] The marginal tax rate on consumption still varied by almost 100%, from 12.3% in Spain to 21.2% in Denmark.[23] Thus, the Commission was preparing to propose an entirely new, Europe-wide tax system with collection at the point of origin.

State aid and procurement The Commission remained particularly concerned about distortions to competition caused by government procurement and state aid. Because government purchases and subsidies were so important in Europe—averaging 12% of GDP—they significantly disrupted competition. Since the mid-1980s, privatization had made significant progress. In the United Kingdom, state enterprises had been thoroughly privatized. Progress was also made in France and Italy, but little had changed elsewhere. During the 1990s, a 20% increase in total procurement had been accompanied by somewhat larger increases in bid notices and awards. Yet local preference and unwillingness to change suppliers persisted.[24]

State aid, although shrinking a bit since 1990, remained a problem. Nonagricultural aid represented 1.4% of the Community's GDP, and was especially high in Italy (2.1%) and Germany (1.9%).[25] In 1997, aid to the manufacturing sector alone amounted to 38 billion euro annually. "Current levels are still too high," said Karl Van Miert, the Commissioner for competition policy. "This level of spending continues to distort competition and trade and thus undermines the advantages offered by Economic and Monetary Union."[26]

Capital Markets

The Single Europe Act had clearly viewed capital markets, then diffusely regulated and fragmented, as an important barrier to integration and global competitiveness. Thus, one of the EC's principal thrusts had been to lower regulatory barriers in banking, securities, and insurance, and foster a deeper, more modern finance system in Europe. The progress here, perhaps fostered by global competition and technological innovation, was less ambiguous.

Harmonization by the Commission had begun even before 1985, with the First Banking Coordination Directive (1977). But it was a series of directives after 1986 that really opened up European banking to competition and rationalization. Especially important was the Second Banking Directive in 1989, which established the principle of mutual recognition of a single banking license. Home country regulation would govern a bank's foreign branches for some product offerings and interest

rates, while supervisory standards, capital requirements, and limitations to participation in the nonfinancial sector were harmonized. A few months later, a directive on solvency ratios sought to harmonize credit risk. In the early 1990s, these measures were followed by directives on capital adequacy, deposit guarantees, and liberalization of capital flows [see **Exhibit 9.13**].[27]

The impact of this deregulation was dramatic. The value of EU bonds, equities and bank loans exceeded those of the U.S. by 1995, and wholesale banking had grown more integrated. Prices and costs fell as a significant merger movement ensued. **Exhibit 9.14a** summarizes the changes in loan prices and mortgages. Not surprisingly, assorted evidence shows that commercial products benefited most in countries that had relatively less sophisticated financial systems. Fees and deposit prices showed similar trends, with Ireland and Denmark leading the way [see **Exhibits 9.14b and 9.14c**]. Part of this trend was due to a significant increase in branching across borders, while the number of domestic branches shrank [see **Exhibit 9.14d**].

The opening of competition across member states' retail markets had gone slowly, to date. There were few cross-border sales of life insurance, for example. Non-life insurance fared better, though cross-border sales merely ranged from .13% in Germany to 4.13% in Belgium. The price of credit cards in Belgium was more than twice that of the Netherlands. Mortgages in France cost 50% more than in the United Kingdom, more than 100% more than in Denmark, and another 100% more than in the Netherlands. At least through 1998, the need to "ensure a high-level of consumer protection" was "used as an excuse to hinder cross-border business." Yet as long as differences among member states persisted on bankruptcy provision, security, and pensions, developing Pan-European markets for retail financial products would remain difficult.[28]

The volume of mergers and acquisitions in the financial sector had clearly accelerated during the 1990s. **Exhibit 9.8b** shows more than 500 mergers occurring annually, most of which involved domestic firms. Perhaps a third as many mergers involved firms crossing borders. "It is very difficult to merge across borders because of legal barriers," said one senior banker at Deutsche Bank.[29] The data also indicated more moves by EU banks outside of Europe, as well as some limited increase in entry. The average size of assets more than doubled in the 1990s, as firms attempted to consolidate and achieve economies of scale. Still, five-firm concentration ratios have remained in the range of 40% to 45% for most of Europe (except in Denmark and the Netherlands), and had actually fallen during the 1990s in France, Greece, and Luxembourg.[30]

Despite this substantial progress, significant obstacles to integration still remained. These included differences in implementation of financial market legislation, the absence of harmonization in areas such as pension funds, differences in national fiscal regimes, and technical barriers. Poorly functioning financial markets especially affected small and medium-sized enterprises. These firms were obviously more dependent on banks, yet paid higher interest rates and were subject to credit rationing due to lack of collateral. Private equity and venture capital markets for smaller firms remained underdeveloped through most of Europe. One senior banker in Germany opined that it might take 50 years for European banking to achieve the degree of integration experienced in the United States.[31]

Labor Markets

Everyone seemed to agree that labor markets remained fragmented in Europe and required the most extensive reform. Executives in Amsterdam said this, bankers in Germany said it, and regulators in Brussels nodded, sadly. Although the migration of workers across member states had increased by 33%, the total numbers involved were pitifully small—311,000 in 1996, up from 233,000 previously. Once again, culture and language remained a huge barrier to movement.[32]

The low employment rates and high and persistent levels of structural unemployment suggest that labor markets function relatively poorly in the EU. However, the problems differed immensely between regions, among member states, between declining industries and new high-tech sectors, and between categories of labor.[33] The employment rate in Austria, Denmark, Sweden, and the United Kingdom was about 70% or higher; but in Spain and Italy, employment was barely 50%. Unemployment had fallen sharply in Ireland and the Netherlands, while remaining high in Spain, Italy, France, and Germany. And regional differences were

striking, especially in Italy, Spain, and Germany. These variations reflected, in part, differences in efforts at structural reform. But most people in Europe were not willing to work outside their own country.

The structure of employment varied significantly from the United States. In Europe, there was more farming, more industry, and less service than in the U.S. For adult males, the unemployment rates were similar; but for youth, women, and older people, the rates in Europe far exceeded those of the United States.

The sources of these problems could be found in relative productivity differentials, in education and training, in geographic mobility, in minimum wage levels, in benefit levels, and in taxation. [These issues are treated carefully elsewhere, in HBS, "Unemployment in France," HBS No. 795–065]. Recently, the Commission called more stridently for efforts at major reform of labor markets. The 1999 Employment Guidelines advised member states to implement tax reforms and curb expenditure growth, dependency, and social protection. "Flexibility criteria have been tightened, with stricter definitions of availability for work and tougher sanctions on those refusing to take up a job." The duration of benefits had been slightly reduced to curb disincentives to work, and several states had lowered high marginal effective tax rates [see **Exhibits 9.15a** and **9.15b**].[34]

Another area of reform related to work organization and work-time flexibility. A few member states were experimenting with work sharing, part-time work, and work-hour flexibility. In 1998, for example, it became possible for social partners to agree on the annualization of work hours in Belgium, Spain, and France. In Austria, one could exchange overtime for time off. In the Netherlands, where barriers to part-time work were eliminated, 35% of total employment was now part-time [see **Exhibit 9.16**]. Perhaps the biggest change in European labor markets was the reduction of the working week. If designed well, such reductions might redistribute work—but there were many difficult conditions to meet if unemployment was to be reduced.

Finally, the EC pointed to the importance of an "employment-friendly" regulatory environment. This pertained especially to employment protection. As the Commission urged, "workers, management, the social partners [unions and employer associations] and policy makers alike [must] strike the right balance between *flexibility* and *security*." Where employment protection was strict—in Italy and Spain—unemployment was especially high. Where it was less strict—the United Kingdom and the Netherlands—unemployment had recently fallen. [35]

Monetary Union

In May 1998, the European Council selected 11 member states to participate in the EMU: Germany, France, Italy, Spain, Belgium, Netherlands, Portugal, Austria, Ireland, Finland, and Luxembourg. While Greece wanted to be a part of the "Euro-zone," it had failed to meet the convergence criteria. On the other hand, Britain, Denmark, and Sweden were qualified to join EMU in its first wave, but decided to opt out for the time being.

EMU began on January 1, 1999. Yet as one senior economist noted, "EMU is not a revolution but an evolution." [36] While the EMU participants maintained control over their fiscal policy, the European Central Bank (ECB) was responsible for setting monetary policy for the entire Euro-zone. The ECB combined with the 15 national central banks (NCBs) to form the European System of Central Banks (ESCB), modeled after Germany's Bundesbank. While the national banks conducted banking activities for their respective countries, they were no longer directly involved in decision making for monetary policy, except through their membership on the Governing Board of the ECB. [37]

The primary objective of the ESCB was a "stability-oriented monetary policy strategy." Price stability was to be maintained over the mid-term and was defined as "a year-on-year increase in the Harmonised Index of Consumer Prices (HICP) for the euro area of below 2%." According to one ECB economist, "We're given one tool and one objective and told to get on with it and that we shouldn't veer from it. We do the best we can do by maintaining price stability, and countries should know what we will do because that is our goal. We're serious about maintaining price stability. There are a lot of very serious people here." [38] Driven by the central goal to maintain price stability, the ESCB had four key tasks: (1) define and implement the EC's monetary policy, (2) conduct foreign exchange operations, (3) hold and manage member states' official foreign reserves, and (4) ensure a smoothly operating payments system. Its monetary policy instruments included open market operations, "standing facilities" (e.g., overnight lending capacity), and minimum reserves.

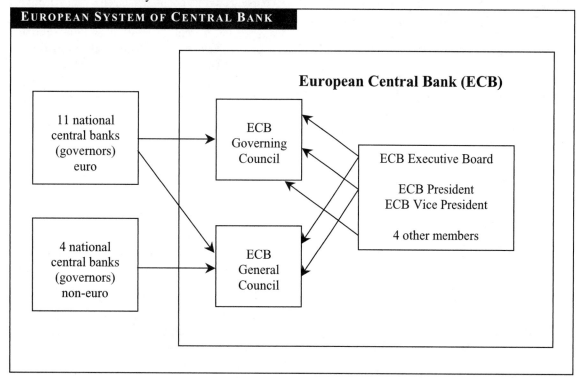

EUROPEAN SYSTEM OF CENTRAL BANK

European Central Bank (ECB)

11 national central banks (governors) euro

4 national central banks (governors) non-euro

ECB Governing Council

ECB General Council

ECB Executive Board

ECB President
ECB Vice President

4 other members

Three decision-making bodies governed the ESCB: the Governing Council, the Executive Board, and the General Council. While the Governing Council made monetary decisions for the Euro-zone, the Executive Board implemented monetary policy. The General Council carried out such tasks as the collection of statistical data and the preparation of the ECB's annual reports. The Maastricht Treaty intended to free the ESCB from political pressures by mandating that "neither the ECB, nor a national central bank, nor any member of their decision-making bodies shall seek or take instructions from Community institutions of a Member State or from any other body."[39]

However, while the ECB represented one of the most independent central banks in the world, it seemed difficult for it not to be influenced by a country's political will. The economic cycles of the EMU participants varied widely, making it impossible to set a single interest rate that would be ideal for each member state. At one end of the spectrum was Germany whose slow growth favored lower interest rates. At the opposite end, Ireland and Spain had rapid growth and tended to view Euro-zone interest rates differently. As economist Martin Feldstein put it, "The fall in demand in a country could not be offset, as it could be with an individual national currency, by an automatic decline in the exchange value of the currency . . . and the decline in its interest rates."[40] Interest rates had remained unchanged since the 11 EMU central banks simultaneously lowered their rates by at least .3% on December 4, 1998. Until his resignation on March 11, 1999, German Finance Minister Oskar LaFontaine had fought ardently for a cut in interest rates. Finally, after keeping interest rates constant for over three months, the ECB on April 8 made a surprise cut in its benchmark interest rate from 3% to 2.5%. It was "an unexpectedly large fall," commented ECB President Willem Duisenberg, "but we want to add this is it. . . . We hope our goal to [get governments to] pursue a restructuring policy will be given a new incentive from the measures taken today. If they don't do that, monetary policy is no alternative." "We've done our bit," said another ECB economist, "[governments] can't wait for us to do it again. This is all."[41]

Making Firms Competitive

Although the Single Market Act had certainly begun to affect competition, it was the single currency regime that most businesses anticipated, some warily, some eagerly. Monetary integration entailed fairly clear-cut costs, but offered significant, though less concrete, benefits. Harris Opinion Research, having surveyed large European companies, estimated transition costs of $30 million per firm, or around $50 billion (for companies with over 5,000 employees). *The Financial Times* had estimated total costs at $150 billion.[42]

Changes in accounting systems, pricelists and invoices, bank accounts, purchase orders, packaging, treasury operations (cash management, exposure management, cross-border cash pooling), and information technology systems loomed large on the cost side. Of course, these were one-time costs—any savings would be repeated annually. Lower interest rate differentials, a more coherent finance strategy, less currency hedging, and especially lower exchange-rate charges were among the immediate and obvious savings.[43]

But the real threats were loss of competitive advantage based on domestic market dominance, lower prices, and more intense competition—throughout all of Europe. These threats, of course, could be counterbalanced by an effective adjustment strategy. Firms simply had to adapt to a regional market of more than 300 million people. They had to reorganize themselves, reduce unnecessary costs, better develop their distribution systems and compete aggressively against a host of new competitors—from outside the EU as well as inside.

Issues Facing the European Union

In the spring of 1999, the EU was faced with many challenges. It was trying to enforce the Stability and Growth Pact, restructure its budget, and establish a plan for admitting new countries into the EU. The 1997 Stability and Growth Pact was designed to help maintain fiscal discipline in the Euro-zone [see **Exhibit 9.19**]. The Pact mandated that the deficits of EMU participants not exceed 3% of their GDP. In the case of noncompliant countries, sanctions in the form of a noninterest-bearing deposit with the Commission would be invoked within 10 months. If a country's excessive deficit persisted, it could face fines up to 0.5% of GDP. Sanctions required the Council's qualified majority vote. A country would not face sanctions if it had taken immediate corrective actions. Also, exceptions would be made for countries suffering from severe recession (a GDP decline of 2% or more in a given year).[44]

Failure to enforce properly measures outlined in the Stability Pact could lead to loose fiscal policy which could, in turn, interfere with the effectiveness of the ECB's monetary policy. Moreover, "The Stability Pact" claimed Feldstein, "tells governments that they can not run fiscal deficits above three percent. . . . Since national monetary and fiscal policies would be precluded, the most likely outcome of the shift to a single monetary policy would be the growth of substantial transfers from the EU to countries that experience cyclical increases in unemployment."[45] Also, if EMU participants did not follow the Pact's rules, they would be unlikely ever to achieve balanced budgets.

In terms of the EU's budget, there were plans to increase the efficiency of its revenues so as to allow for EU enlargement. In 1997, Agenda 2000 had set out to strengthen the Union in preparation for the addition of new EU members from Eastern and Central Europe. "We cannot think of pursuing agricultural reforms or the reform of structural policies without at the same time taking into account enlargement and the financial constraints," explained EU president Jacques Santer. "It is this mix of equations that the Commission has sought to solve in developing the communication, Agenda 2000."[46]

At its March 1999 meeting in Berlin, the European Council reached an overall agreement on Agenda 2000. When talks nearly collapsed, EU diplomats managed to arrive at a compromise that would eventually reduce farm expenditures and restrictive structural fund objectives [see **Exhibit 9.20**]. For the 2000–2006 period, they agreed to keep the EU budget close to its current level of 85 billion euros. Over the next seven years, the final accord aimed to bring farm spending down to an annual average of 40.5 billion euros. The EU planned to cut cereal price guarantees by 15% and beef price guarantees by 20%. However, plans to reduce direct aid to farmers were dropped toward the end of discussions, and reforms in the dairy sector were delayed until 2005. A total of 213 billion euros

was to be devoted to structural aid (programs to promote development of regions lagging behind).[47]

Finally, the Commission's mismanagement of the EU budget had placed the Union in a state of flux. After being accused of "chronic cronyism and corruption" by an independent panel of the European Parliament, the entire Commission resigned on March 15, 1999. The Parliament accused commissioner Edith Cresson of basing her hiring decisions on favoritism; several other commissioners were also implicated in mismanagement. At the Berlin meeting less than two weeks later, EU diplomats chose former Italian Prime Minister Romano Prodi as the new Commission president. While Prodi's five-year term would not begin until the end of the year, it was hoped that his appointment would help bring order to the EC's crisis situation. In the meantime, the fired commissioners continued working in a "caretaker capacity." A new 626-member European Parliament would also be elected in early June.[48]

Meeting Twenty-First Century Objectives

Europe had taken a huge and decisive step toward preparing itself to compete in a globalized world. Monetary integration would either force the completion of a single market, with all the benefits that entailed, or would derail European growth by faltering on cultural and political issues. European leaders had to think seriously about the process of moving forward.

The incredibly powerful ECB had chartered a course of monetary stability above all else. **Exhibit 9.21** reflects the growth trajectory that Europe had followed since the late 1970s. If it were to revitalize growth of GDP per capita, the EU needed to traverse effectively the host of problems still blocking integration. The successful creation of a single European market would depend on President Prodi's ability to fix the Commission's administration, budgeting, and external barriers while trying to continue along the path of internal reform. Indeed, Prodi had a challenging job awaiting him.

EXHIBIT 9.1	EU COUNTRY PERFORMANCE

Country	Area (in square km)[1]	Population (in millions)	1998 GDP (in Euros)	Average Real GDP Growth 1990 Prices, 1991–1998 (%)	Real GDP/ Capita PPP Adjusted 1998 (US$)[2]	I/GDP 1998 (%)	Average Inflation Rate GDP Deflator 1991–1998 (%)	Average Unemployment Rate 1991–1998 (%)	Ratio of Top Decile Income to Bottom Decile[3]	Exports + Imports as a % of GDP[***] (1998)	Unit Labor Costs (National Currencies) 1998 (1991=100)	Current Account/ GDP Nominal 1998 (%)	Gross Savings/ GDP 1998 (%)
Belgium	30,260	10,222	222.8	1.7	23,137	18.2	2.3	9.0	4.8	141.9	112.3	5.1	22.9
Germany	349,270	82,150	1,906.2	1.6	22,210	19.5	2.4	8.5	3.1	53.4	109.9	.2	21.6
Spain	499,440	39,418	493.8	2.0	16,129	21.1	4.0	21.5	6.0	58.4	122.3	.1	21.5
France	550,100	59,145	1,283.4	1.7	21,502	17.1	1.6	11.8	4.5	50.7	108.4	2.9	20.2
Ireland	68,890	3,721	74.5	8.4	NA	19.3	2.3	12.6	5.9	149.5	98.0	3.6	23.9
Italy	294,060	57,754	1,044.9	1.2	20,817	16.8	4.0	11.2	5.4	51.6	113.7	3.1	20.9
Luxembourg	2,560	433.7	14.8	4.7	NA	22.7	2.2	2.7	4.8	172.2	NA	14.1	40.2
Netherlands	33,920	15,783	337.9	2.7	22,193	20.0	2.0	6.0	3.5	105.5	110.2	5.8	27.0
Austria	82,730	8,121	189.3	1.9	22,416	24.1	2.4	4.0	4.9	89.1	108.7	-1.9	24.3
Portugal	91,950	9,896	95.8	2.5	14,095	25.7	5.3	6.3	7.1	73.7	137.2	-2.1	20.0
Finland	337,030[1a]	5,171	110.9	2.8	20,906	17.5	1.6	14.7	NA	72.7	92.2	5.8	24.0
EU-11	2,340,210	291,814	5,774.2	1.8	NA	19.1	2.7	11.2	NA	62.8	110.3[*]	1.9	21.7
Denmark	42,430	5,319	156.4	2.6	23,390	21.0	1.9	7.3	3.1	66.6	110.9	-.9	21.2
Greece	128,900	10,623	107.1	1.7	NA	21.8	10.1	9.0	6.6	39.0	194.7	-2.4	19.1
Sweden	411,620	8,954	204.4	1.3	20,170	14.5	1.9	8.7	NA	82.9	110.3	1.5	16.4
United Kingdom	241,600	59,399	1,252.3	2.6	20,061	17.1	2.8	8.6	NA	54.5	115.6[**]	.2	18.0
EU-15	3,164,760	376,109	7,494.6	1.9	NA	18.5	2.8	10.5	5.5[*]	61.6	111.6[**]	1.5	20.9
United States	9,573,110	272,745	7,538.0	3.1	29,405	18.1	2.2	5.8	11.2[3a]	24.7	115.5	-2.5	16.3
Japan	377,835	126,643	3,320.7	0.8	22,805	26.4	0.4	3.1	NA	20.9	104.1	3.3	29.8

SOURCE: Compiled from European Commission, *Statistical Annex of European Economy.*

[1] SOURCE: World Bank, *World Data 1995.*

[1a] SOURCE: CIA, *1996 World Fact Book.*

[2] SOURCE: OECD, 1998.

[3] SOURCE: *Eurostat Press Release no. 6996,* September 14, 1998.

[3a] SOURCE: US Census Bureau.

[*] Does not include Finland, Sweden and the United Kingdom.

[**] Does not include Luxembourg.

[***] Includes intra-EU trade.

EXHIBIT 9.2   EU COUNTRIES

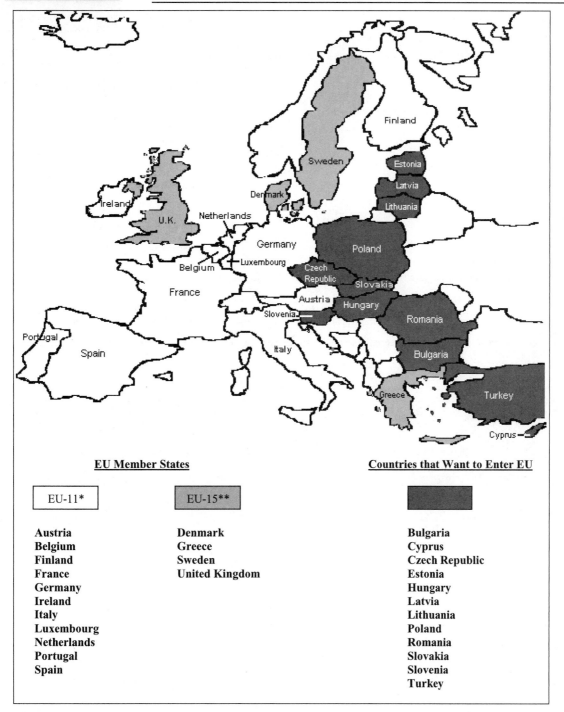

SOURCE: Case writer.

* EU-11 member states use the euro.

** EU-15 member states do not use the euro.

| EXHIBIT 9.3 | | INFLATION RATES FOR EMS AND OTHER COUNTRIES |

			Inflation Rates				Average Annual Inflation Differentials[a]	
	EMS 8[b]	Non-EMS Europe[c]	United States	Germany	France	Italy	EMS 8	Non-EMS[d]
1979	8.7	12.3	11.2	4.1	10.7	14.7	5.3	8.5
1980	12.0	14.7	13.6	5.4	13.3	21.3	7.4	6.9
1981	12.2	14.2	10.4	6.3	13.3	19.5	7.0	6.6
1982	10.8	12.3	6.2	5.3	12.0	16.5	5.7	7.7
1983	7.9	10.7	3.2	3.3	9.5	14.7	5.0	9.4
1984	6.5	10.7	4.3	2.4	7.7	10.8	3.5	9.8
1985	4.9	9.3	3.6	2.2	5.9	9.2	2.8	7.3
1986	2.5	7.7	1.9	-0.1	2.5	5.9	2.6	8.1
1987	2.3	6.7	3.7	0.2	3.3	4.7	2.5	5.3
1988	2.5	6.4	4.1	1.3	2.7	5.1	2.0	4.1
1989	3.7	7.5	4.8	2.8	3.5	6.3	2.0	4.4
1990	3.7	8.2	5.2	2.7	3.4	6.6	1.6	4.6
1991	3.6	NA	4.2	3.9	3.2	6.8	NA	NA

SOURCE: K. Froot and K. Rogoff, "The EMS, the EMU and the Transition to a Common Currency," *NBER Macroeconomics Annual 1991* and IMF, *International Financial Statistics.*

[a]Computed by taking a simple average of the absolute value of all pairwise inflation differentials in each period.

[b]EMS 8 is comprised of Belgium, Denmark, France, Germany, Italy, the Netherlands, Ireland, and Luxembourg.

[c]Non-EMS Europe is comprised of Greece, Norway, Portugal, Spain, Sweden, Switzerland, and the United Kingdom.

[d]Non-EMS is comprised of non-EMS Europe and the United States.

| EXHIBIT 9.4 | | CONVERGENCE |

	Inflation (CPI) (%)			Long-term Interest Rate (%)			Government Deficit/GDP			Debt/GDP		
	1997	1998[a]	1999[a]	1997	1998[a]	1999[a]	1997	1998[a]	1999[a]	1997	1998[a]	1999[a]
Belgium	1.8	1.1	1.4	5.8	4.8	4.7	2.0	1.3	1.2	121.9	117.2	113.7
Germany	1.7	1.0	1.1	5.7	4.6	4.5	2.7	2.6	2.3	61.5	61.3	61.0
Spain	2.5	2.3	2.1	6.4	4.9	4.8	2.6	2.1	1.6	68.9	67.7	66.0
France	1.1	0.6	1.2	5.6	4.7	4.5	3.0	2.9	2.3	58.1	58.3	58.6
Ireland	0.9	2.7	3.3	6.3	4.8	4.6	-0.9	-2.1	-3.4	63.4	53.3	44.1
Italy	2.5	2.2	2.0	6.7	4.9	4.8	2.7	2.6	2.3	121.6	118.8	115.3
Luxembourg	1.1	1.4	1.7	5.6	4.8	4.5	-3.0	-2.2	-2.0	6.7	7.1	7.5
Netherlands	2.0	2.2	2.3	5.6	4.6	4.5	0.9	1.4	1.4	71.4	68.6	66.6
Austria	2.0	1.1	1.3	5.7	4.7	4.5	1.9	2.2	2.1	64.3	64.0	63.6
Portugal	2.5	2.6	2.4	6.4	4.9	4.8	2.5	2.3	2.0	61.5	57.4	55.3
Finland	1.5	1.5	1.6	6.0	4.8	4.7	1.1	-0.7	-1.8	55.1	52.9	50.2
EU-11	1.9	1.4	1.5	6.0	4.7	4.6	2.5	2.3	2.0	75.1	73.8	72.5
Denmark	2.2	1.9	2.4	6.2	5.0	5.0	-0.5	-1.3	-2.7	64.1	58.8	54.3
Greece	5.5	4.8	2.9	9.3	8.5	6.7	4.0	2.4	2.1	109.5	108.7	107.0
Sweden	2.2	1.3	1.8	6.7	5.1	5.0	0.8	-0.9	-1.4	76.9	74.0	69.5
UK	2.6	2.0	2.2	7.0	5.6	5.2	2.1	.01	-0.1	53.5	51.5	49.9
EU-15	2.1	1.6	1.7	6.2	4.9	4.7	2.3	1.8	1.4	72.0	70.3	69.0

SOURCE: European Commission, *Statistical Annex of European Economy*, November 1998.

[a]Forecast.

EXHIBIT 9.5 **PROGRESS IN IMPLEMENTATION OF SINGLE-MARKET DIRECTIVES, DECEMBER 2, 1998**

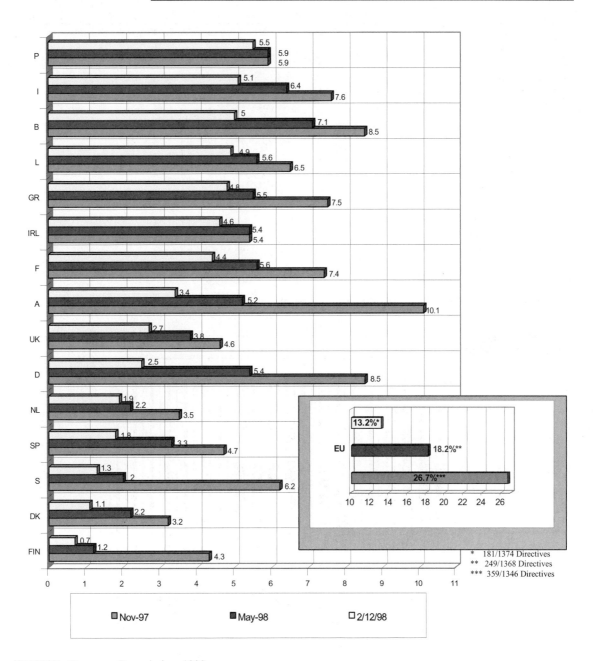

SOURCE: European Commission, 1998.

EXHIBIT 9.6   BREAKDOWN BY AREA AND MEMBER STATE OF NON-TRANSPOSED DIRECTIVES, OCTOBER 15, 1998

	%	B	DK	GER	GR	SP	F	IRL	I	L	NL	A	P	FIN	S	UK
Telecommunications (15)	66.7	4	na	na	10	na	2	1	2	6	4	na	4	na	3	na
Public Procurement (10)	60	1	1	1	5	4	1	1	2	1	1	1	4	na	na	1
Transport (48)	52.1	12	7	4	5	7	9	17	12	9	8	9	11	3	3	9
Intellectual and Industrial Property (7)	42.9	na	na	na	2	na	na	3	1	1	1	na	1	na	na	na
Social Policy (38)	26.3	2	na	3	5	na	3	1	8	9	na	2	4	na	na	2
Chemical Products (74)	21.6	9	1	5	6	2	7	11	6	7	1	7	6	1	na	2
Veterinary Checks (193)	18.1	10	2	8	13	7	23	14	19	14	4	17	17	2	6	13
Environment (92)	17.4	11	3	4	7	5	6	6	6	4	4	3	5	2	3	6
Cosmetic Products (38)	15.8	1	na	na	2	na	3	4	1	3	1	3	2	na	1	na
Food Legislation (101)	14.8	3	1	4	4	3	4	10	7	3	na	6	11	1	na	2
Capital Goods (99)	12.1	8	2	2	2	1	3	4	7	4	na	2	2	1	1	1
Motor Vehicles (146)	8.2	na	1	1	1	1	3	1	na	7	1	1	1	1	1	11
Plant-Health Checks (172)	6.4	1	1	1	2	1	3	1	2	10	1	4	5	1	na	3
Total	na	64	20	33	64	32	67	76	74	80	26	55	74	12	18	50

SOURCE: European Commission.

(#) number of Directives concerned in each sector.

EXHIBIT 9.7   PROGRESS OF STANDARDIZATION ACTIVITIES BY THE EU

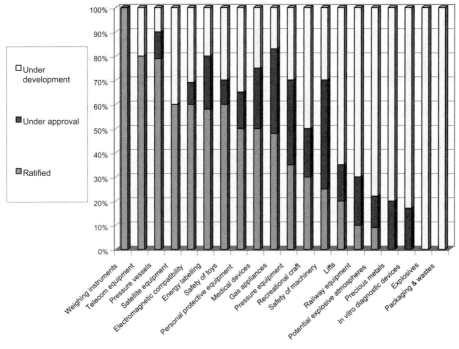

SOURCE: European Commission, "Economic Reform: Report on the Functioning of Community Product and Capital Markets," 1999.

| EXHIBIT 9.8A | EVOLUTION OF NUMBERS OF NOTIFICATIONS AND DETAILED OPINIONS (1992–1998)[A] |

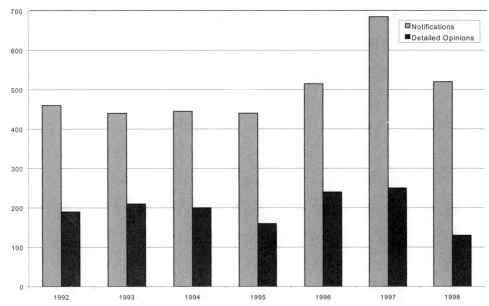

SOURCE: European Commission.

[a]These figures do not include 230 notifications from the Netherlands following from the case "CIA Securities" (1996) in the ECJ. Furthermore, the figures reflect the situations up to 11 November 1998.

| EXHIBIT 9.8B | NUMBER OF MERGERS AND ACQUISITIONS INVOLVING EU FIRMS IN BANKING |

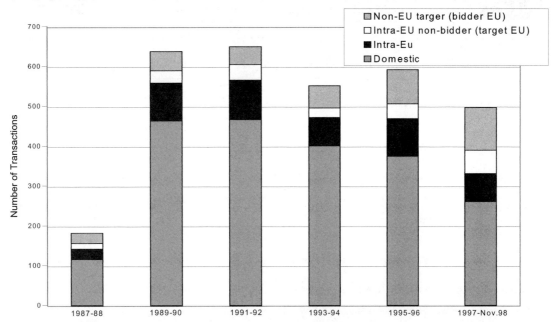

SOURCE: Compiled from *Acquisitions Monthly*, "European Community, Economic Reform: Report on the Functioning of Community Product and Capital Markets," 1998, p. A.12.

EXHIBIT 9.9A	CROSS-BORDER MERGERS AND ACQUISITIONS INVOLVING EU FIRMS

Percentage shares of each Member State, compared to shares of EU GDP, 1995–1998

Member State	Target[a] (acquired company)	Bidder[b] (acquired)	GDP as % of EU total (1996)
Belgium	4.4	3.3	3.1
Denmark	3.2	4.7	2.0
Germany	20.8	14.3	27.4
Greece	0.4	0.2	1.4
Spain	5.6	1.7	6.8
France	14.4	14.6	17.8
Ireland	1.3	3.3	0.8
Italy	7.5	3.2	14.1
Luxembourg	0.6	1.0	0.2
Netherlands	7.2	12.4	4.6
Austria	2.2	1.6	2.7
Portugal	1.1	0.4	1.3
Finland	3.8	3.1	1.5
Sweden	4.9	8.1	2.9
United Kingdom	22.6	28.4	13.4
EU	100.0	100.0	100.0

SOURCE: European Commission, *Cardiff II*, p. 30.

[a]Takeovers of EU firms, by another Member State or non-EU firms, classified by nationality of the acquired company.

[b]Takeovers by EU firms, of firms in another Member State or outside the EU, classified by nationality of the acquired company.

EXHIBIT 9.9B	NUMBER OF COMPLETED MERGERS INVOLVING EU FIRMS (1986–1997)

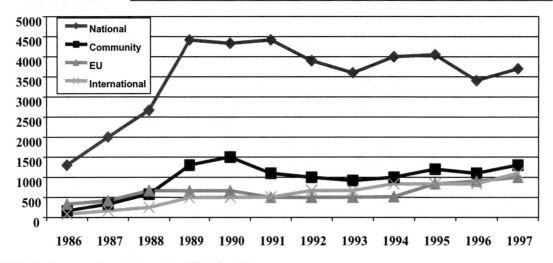

SOURCE: European Commission, "Cardiff I," fig A10.

National: mergers between firms based in the same Member State.

Community: firms of different Member States.

EU: non-EU firms acquired by EU firms.

| EXHIBIT 9.10 | DEVELOPMENTS OVER TIME IN EU PRICE DISPERSION (COEFFICIENT OF VARIATION) |

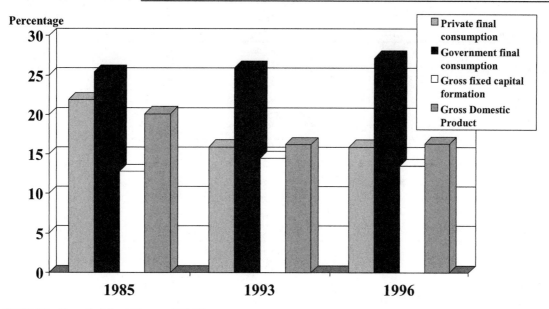

SOURCE: Compiled from Eurostat/OECD.

Unweighted, included excise and value-added taxes.

| EXHIBIT 9.11 | EU PRODUCTIVITY AND PRICE DISPERSION IN MANUFACTURING SECTORS (1996) |

| Sector | Relative Productivity (total manufacturing=100) | | | Coefficient of Price Variation |
	EU	USA	EU/USA	EU
Pharmaceuticals	165	277	0.60	32.1%
Food, beverage, tobacco	98	131	0.75	15.9%
Chemical industry	162	203	0.80	15.9%
Transport equipment	97	115	0.85	13.1%
Precision instruments	99	114	0.87	8.6%
Electrical engineering	102	118	0.87	10.9%
Motor vehicles	114	125	0.91	15.3%
Office machinery and computers	151	157	0.96	14.2%
Paper and printing	106	94	1.13	16.6%
Mechanical engineering	98	85	1.14	8.3%
Metal articles	83	69	1.21	16.2%
Rubber and plastic	91	73	1.25	11.4%

SOURCE: European Commission, *Eurostat*.

The "EU" column shows sectoral productivity levels in index relative to the EU's average manufacturing productivity level (=100); the "USA" column does the same for the USA. The "EU/USA" column divides the EU's relative productivity levels by those of the USA—the result indicates in which sector the EU is relatively more productive than the USA. The final column provides a measure of price dispersion around the EU.

EXHIBIT 9.12	PRICE DISPERSION FOR AUTOMOBILES IN THE EU MARKET, 1997–98 (% DIFFERENCE, HIGHEST AND LOWEST, INCLUDING LOCAL VAT)		
	1/11/98	**1/5/98**	**1/11/97**
Small Segments A and B			
Opel Corsa	16.2%	(24.0%)	(43.5%)
Ford Fiesta	28.8%	(44.7%)	(26.9%)
Renault Clio	27.7%	(33.8%)	(30.4%)
Peugeot 106	14.3%	(21.1%)	(35.8%)
VW Polo	32.0%	(36.7%)	(54.3%)
Medium Segment C			
VW Golf	31.0%	(43.5%)	(40.1%)
Opel Astra	19.5%	(26.0%)	(25.3%)
Ford Focus	27.8%	(33.8%)	(45.4%)[a]
Renault Mégane	19.8%	(27.9%)	(31.7%)
Peugeot 306	30.6%	(46.2%)	(44.2%)
Large Segments D, E, and F			
BMW 318 I	18.7%	(12.0%)	(30.9%)[b]
Audi A 4	19.1%	(13.0%)	(12.5%)
Ford Mondeo	34.6%	(58.5%)	(34.7%)
Opel Vectra	17.1%	(18.2%)	(15.6%)
VW Passat	24.0%	(36.4%)	(33.5%)

SOURCE: European Commission, "Car Prices in the European Union on 1 November 1999—Differences Decrease Sharply," February 1, 1999.

[a]Ford Escort/Orion, being replaced by Ford Focus.

[b]November 1, 1997: BMW 316i.

EXHIBIT 9.13	THE TIMING OF FINANCIAL SERVICES DEREGULATION

Measure	B	G	IRL	F	DK	GR	NL	I	L	P	SP	UK
73/183 Freedom of Establishment	1983	1974	1977	1975	1976	1986		1975	1975	1992	1987	1976
First Banking Directive	1993	1980	1989	1980	1978	1981	1978	1985	1981	1992	1987	1979
83/350 Consol. Surveillance	1985	1985	1985	1985	1984	1986	1986	1986	1986	1986	1985	1979
86/635 Consol. Accounts	1992	1990	1992	1991	1992	1994	1993	1992	1992	1992	1991	1994
89/117 Branches /HQ outside EU	1992	1990	1992	1991	1992	1994	1992	1992	1992	1992	1993	1993
89/299 92/16 Own Funds	1994	1990	1991	1990	1992	1992	1991	1993	1992	1993	1993	1992
Second Banking Directive	1994	1991	1992	1992	1992	1992	1992	1992	1993	1992	1994	1993
Solvency Ratio Directives	1994	1990	1991	1991	1992	1992	1991	1993	1993	1992	1993	1992
Money Laundering Directive	1995	1993	1995	1992	1993	1993	1994	1993	1993	1993	1993	1993
Large Exposures Directive	1994	1993	1994	1993	1995	1994	1993	1994	1993	1992	1993	1993
Deposit Insurance Directive	1994		1995	1995	1995	1995	1995			1995		1995
Interest Rate Deregulation	1990	1988	1993	1990	1981	1993	1981	1990	1990	1992	1992	1979
Liberalization of Capital Flows	1991	1982	1985	1990	1967	1994	1980	1983	1990	1992	1992	1979

SOURCE: EC, Single Market Review: Credit Institutions and Banking (Brussels, 1997), p. 12.

EXHIBIT 9.14A   PRICE CHANGES FOR DIFFERENT TYPES OF LOANS SINCE THE FULL IMPLEMENTATION OF THE SMP

Product Area	IRL	UK	F	G	SP	P	B	NL	GR	DK	I	EU
Corporate customer deposits (large firms)	-44	-22	-47	-32	-42	-19	-27	-22	-39	-36	-25	-29
Corporate customer deposits (small firms)	-43	-22	-41	-26	-41	-18	-25	-23	-25	-21	-16	-24
Retail customer loans	-43	-25	-37	-8	-36	-4	-21	-24	-26	-25	-12	-21
Retail customer deposits	-26	-29	-41	-19	-45	-30	-23	6	-39	-31	-18	-16

SOURCE: Postal survey.

NB: Price defined as margin between rate charged to customer and money market rate.

Changes in the margin due to business cycles effect excluded.

-50 is 'large decrease,' -25 is 'small decrease,' 0 is 'no change,' 25 is 'small increase,' and 50 is 'large increase.'

EXHIBIT 9.14B   PRICE CHANGES FOR CORPORATE AND RETAIL CUSTOMER DEPOSITS SINCE THE FULL IMPLEMENTATION OF THE SMP

Product Area	IRL	UK	F	G	SP	P	B	NL	GR	DK	I	EU
Corporate customer deposits (large firms)	-40	-21	-42	-31	-26	-29	-27	-22	-28	-18	-11	-25
Corporate customer deposits (small firms)	-37	-19	-35	-29	-29	-30	-27	-30	-30	-13	-8	-24
Retail customer deposits	-37	-11	-35	-30	-28	-25	-27	-32	-30	-31	-4	-23

SOURCE: Postal survey.

NB: Prices defined as margin between rate paid to customer and money market rate.

Changes in margin due to business cycle effects excluded.

-50 is 'large decrease,' -25 is 'small decrease,' 0 is 'no change,' 25 is 'small increase,' and 50 is 'large increase.'

EXHIBIT 9.14C   THE EXTENT TO WHICH THE FEES CHARGED TO CUSTOMERS HAS CHANGED SINCE THE FULL IMPLEMENTATION OF THE SMP

Customer Type	IRL	UK	F	G	SP	P	B	NL	GR	DK	I	EU
Corporate customer (large firms)	-25	-14	-17	-22	-2	17	-3	-8	-5	15	4	-10
Corporate customer (small firms)	-23	-15	-5	-21	11	22	2	-8	-3	18	11	-6
Retail customers	-18	-3	12	-15	18	34	3	-6	0	25	18	0

SOURCE: Postal survey.

NB: -50 is 'large decrease,' -25 is 'small decrease,' 0 is 'no change,' 25 is 'small increase,' and 50 is 'large increase.'
'The last three years' was used as a proxy for the post-SMP period.

EXHIBIT 9.14D   CHANGES IN THE NUMBER OF BRANCHES SINCE THE FULL IMPLEMENTATION OF THE SMP

Market	IRL	UK	F	G	SP	P	B	NL	GR	DK	I	EU
Domestic market	4	-18	-7	-1	19	39	-4	-44	26	-39	46	-1
Market of other EU countries	25	19	-7	34	6	30	11	31	26	0	12	21

SOURCE: European Commission and Postal survey.

NB: -50 is 'large decrease,' -25 is 'small decrease,' 0 is 'no change,' 25 is 'small increase,' and 50 is 'large increase.'

EXHIBIT 9.15A	MAIN FEATURES OF THE UNEMPLOYMENT IN THE EU 1997				
	Unemployment Rate of Total Labour Force	Share of Long-Term Unemployed Among all Unemployed (12 Months)	Unemployment Rate of Those with Low Educational Level	Share of Unemployed with Low Educational Level Among Total Unemployed	Unemployment Rate for Youth (15-24)
	(1)	(2)	(3)	(4)	(5)
Belgium	9.2	60.5	13.4	50.2	21.3
Denmark	5.5	27.2	14.6	37.3	8.1
Germany	10.0	50.1	13.3	26.5	10.7
Greece	9.6	55.7	6.3	37.3	31.0
Spain	20.8	51.8	20.6	62.6	39.2
France	12.4	39.6	14.0	45.1	29.0
Ireland	10.1	57.0	16.4	63.7	15.9
Italy	12.1	66.3	9.1	55.6	33.6
Luxembourg	2.6	34.6	3.8	71.5	7.3
Netherlands	5.2	49.1	7.9	49.4	9.7
Austria	4.4	28.7	5.7	34.7	7.6
Portugal	6.8	55.6	6.2	76.6	14.1
Finland	13.1	29.8	21.6	38.2	35.4
Sweden	9.9	34.2	10.1	31.9	21.9
UK	7.0	38.6	12.2	55.0	13.6
EURO-Zone	11.6	50.9	N.A.	47.0	23.5
EU-15	10.7	49.0	13.7	47.2	21.2
USA	4.9	8.7	10.0	N.A.	11.3
Japan	3.4	21.8	N.A.	N.A.	6.6

SOURCE: EC, *Cardiff II*, Brussels, February 17, 1999, pp. 33, 36.

(1) Harmonized unemployment rates, *EUROSTAT*.

(2) *Labour Force Survey, EUROSTAT.* For USA and Japan, *OECD Employment Outlook 1998.*

(3) Educational level lower than upper secondary, persons aged 25 to 64 years old (1995), *OECD Employment Outlook 1998.*

(4) Educational level lower than upper secondary (lower secondary and less); persons aged 25-59 (1997 2Q), *LFS, EUROSTAT.*

(5) *Labour Force Survey, EUROSTAT.* For USA and Japan, *OECD Employment Outlook 1998.*

EXHIBIT 9.15B	IMPLICIT TAX RATES ON LABOUR AND CAPITAL (%)—1996				
	Implicit Tax Rate on Employed Labour	Taxes on Low-Skilled Workers	Implicit Tax Rate on Consumption	Total Tax Wedge	Implicit Tax Rate on Other Factors
	(1)	(2)	(3)	(4)	(5)
Belgium	44.8	50.5	13.7	48.2	38.6
Denmark	47.1	41.3	21.2	54.2	35.8
Germany	43.3	46.5	13.7	45.6	36.1
Greece	44.9	34.9	16.6	34.5	9.7
Spain	38.3	34.4	12.3	37.4	24.0
France	44.9	44.3	14.6	51.1	47.6
Ireland	29.1	26.5	18.9	36.6	21.4
Italy	50.1	48.3	13.4	45.4	33.1
Luxembourg	30.2	29.1	17.9	44.8	49.8
Netherlands	46.7	39.3	15.4	48.4	37.0
Portugal	42.0	30.6	15.9	34.2	18.0
UK	27.3	26.8	14.6	33.1	36.8
Austria	45.8	37.4	15.6	49.9	38.9
Finland	55.3	45.3	19.0	55.6	24.1
Sweden	57.6	48.6	16.1	56.3	47.4
EURO-Zone*	44.8	44.2	14.1	46.4	35.6
EU-15	42.6	41.8	14.4	44.8	35.6
USA	23.2	29.2	5.5	27.9	45.3
Japan	24.7	18.4	5.1	27.1	52.3

SOURCE: EC, *Cardiff II*, Brussels, February 17, 1999, pp. 33, 36.

*EURO-Zone includes 11 countries: Belgium, Germany, Spain, France, Ireland, Italy, Luxembourg, Netherlands, Portugal, Austria and Finland

(1) The ratio of taxes directly borne by the employed labour to the total compensation of employees. Employed labour taxes include: social security contributions paid to the employers and the employees, the taxes on payroll and workforce, and personal income tax on employed labour.

(2) Tax benefit of singles with no children (wage level 67% of APW). Employees' and employers' SSC and personal income tax less transfer payments (% of gross labour costs: gross wage earnings plus employer's SSC).

(3) The ratio of consumption taxes to the after-tax value of consumption.

(4) The tax wedge includes all taxes borne by labour (social security contributions and personal taxes on labour income) plus the part of consumption taxes paid when spending labour income. The tax wedge is the difference between the producer wage and the consumer wage as a percentage of the former.

(5) Social security contributions and other taxes paid by the self-employed, plus taxes on capital income expressed as a percentage of the capital income (total operating surplus).

EXHIBIT 9.16	EMPLOYMENT RATE, EU

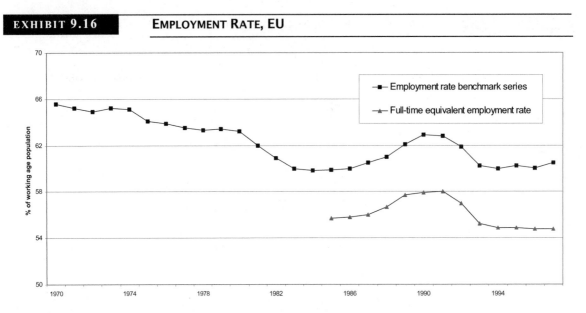

SOURCE: EC, "Commission Recommendation for the Broad Guidelines of the Economic Policies of the Member States and the Community," Brussels (CB-CO-99-152-EN-C), March 3, 1999, p.15

EXHIBIT 9.17	NET REPLACEMENT RATE OF UNEMPLOYMENT BENEFITS IN 1995

Country	Net Replacement Rates[3]			
	2/3 of APW[2]		APW[2]	
	1st month	60th month	1st month	60th month
Belgium	79	86	61	58
Denmark	93	82	70	74
Germany	74	85	72	66
Greece[1]	N.A.	N.A.	57	N.A.
Spain	72	49	74	35
France	86	57	76	46
Ireland	60	60	49	49
Italy	41	7	42	5
Luxembourg	87	84	87	66
Netherlands	87	92	79	71
Austria	65	62	63	61
Portugal	88	3	78	2
Finland	87	95	75	81
Sweden	80	109	78	82
UK	81	85	61	64

SOURCE: OECD, Benefit Systems and Work Incentives, 1998 and European Commission, Cardiff II, p. 37.

Note: The summary measure of net replacement rates and tax rates have been calculated as a simple average of the rates for three family types (single person, couple without children, and couple with two children). The net replacement for the 60th month of unemployment includes the possible topping-up of social assistance.

[1] The Greek net replacement rate is from the study of the Central Planning Bureau for 1993.

[2] APW = Average Production Wage.

[3] This shows the percentage of a low-wage worker's (2/3 of APW) wage recovered from unemployment benefits, and the same for an average wage worker (APW).

EXHIBIT 9.18	**AVERAGE ANNUAL WORKED HOURS PER EMPLOYEE IN THE NETHERLANDS AND IN SELECTED OECD COUNTRIES**

	1973	1979	1983	1990	1996[a]
Netherlands	1,724	1,591	1,530	1,433	1,372
West Germany	1,804	1,699	1,686	1,562	1,508
France	1,771	1,667	1,558	1,539	1,529
SW [a]	1,557	1,451	1,453	1,480	1,554
United Kingdom[a]	1,929	1,821	1,719	1,773	1,732
United States	1,896	1,884	1,866	1,936	1,951

SOURCE: OECD, "Employment Outlook 1997, Paris: Organisation of Economic Cooperation and Development," July 1997, Table G.

[a]Total employment.

EXHIBIT 9.19	**GENERAL GOVERNMENT NET LENDING/BORROWING (% OF GDP) STABILITY AND CONVERGENCE PROGRAMME PROJECTIONS**

	Date[1]	1998	1999	2000	2001	2002
		Stability Programmes				
Belgium	12/98	-1.6	-1.3	-1.0	-0.7	-0.3
Germany	01/99	-2.5	-2.0	-2.0	-1.5	-1.0
Spain	12/98	-1.9	-1.6	-1.0	-0.4	0.1
France	01/99	-2.9	-2.3	-2.0	-1.6	-1.2[2]
Ireland	12/98	-2.6	-2.0	-1.5	-1.0	-
Italy	12/98	-2.6	-2.0	-1.5	-1.0	-
Luxembourg	02/99	2.1	1.1	1.2	1.3	1.7
Netherlands[3]	10/98	-1.3	-1.3	-	-	-1.1
Austria	11/98	-2.2	-2.0	-1.7	-1.5	-1.4[4]
Portugal	12/98	-	-2.0	-1.5	-1.2	-0.8
Finland	09/98	-1.1	2.4	2.2	2.1	2.3
		Convergence Programmes				
Denmark	10/98	1.1	2.5	2.8	2.6	-[5]
Greece	6/98	-2.4	-2.1	-1.7	-0.8	-
Sweden	12/98	-1.5	0.3	1.6	2.5	-
United Kingdom[6]	12/98	0.8	-0.3	-0.3	-0.1	0.2[7]

SOURCE: EC, "Commission Recommendation for the Broad Guidelines of the Economic Policies of the Member States and the Community," Brussels (CB-CO-99-152-EN-C), March 3, 1999, p. 10.

(1) Date when programme was adopted.

(2) Prudent scenario, favorable scenario projection: -1.7, -1.2 and -0.8% of GDP, respectively, in the years 2000 to 2002.

(3) No annual data provided for years 2000/01.

(4) Cautious scenario, middle and favorable scenario projections: -0.25 and 0.25% of SDP, respectively, in the year 2002.

(5) Projection for the year 2005: 3.5% of GDP.

(6) Data for the financial years beginning in each for the calendar years indicated.

(7) Projection in the financial year 2003/04: 0.1% of GDP.

EXHIBIT 9.20 **AGENDA 2000 EUROPEAN UNION BUDGET**

Euro million—1999 Prices Appropriations for Commitments	2000	2001	2002	2003	2004	2005	2006
1. Agriculture	40,920	42,800	43,900	47,770	42,760	41,930	41,660
CAP expenditure (excluding rural development)	36,620	38,480	39,570	39,430	38,410	37,570	37,290
Rural development and accompanying measures	4,300	4,320	4,330	4,340	4,350	4,360	4,370
2. Structural Operations	32,045	31,455	30,865	30,285	29,595	29,595	29,170
3. Internal Policies	5,900	5,950	6,000	6,050	6,100	6,150	6,200
4. External Action	4,550	4,560	4,570	4,580	4,590	4,600	4,610
5. Administration	4,560	4,600	4,700	4,800	4,900	5,000	5,100
6. Reserves	900	900	650	400	400	400	400
7. Pre-Accession Aid	3,120	3,120	3,120	3,120	3,120	3,120	3,120
Total Appropriations for Commitments	91,995	93,385	93,805	93,005	91,465	90,795	90,260
Total Appropriations for Payments	89,590	91,070	94,130	94,740	91,720	89,910	89,310
Appropriations for payments as % of GNP	1.13%	1.12%	1.13%	1.11%	1.05%	1.00%	0.97%
Available for Accession (appropriations for payments)	na	na	4,140	6,710	8,890	11,440	14,220
Ceiling on Appropriations for Payments	89,590	91,070	98,270	101,450	100,610	101,350	103,530

SOURCE: Berlin European Council, "Presidency Conclusions," March 24 and 25, 1999.

EXHIBIT 9.21 **GDP PER CAPITA, 1970–1998 FOR THE U.S., JAPAN, AND THE EC (PPP ADJUSTED)[A]**

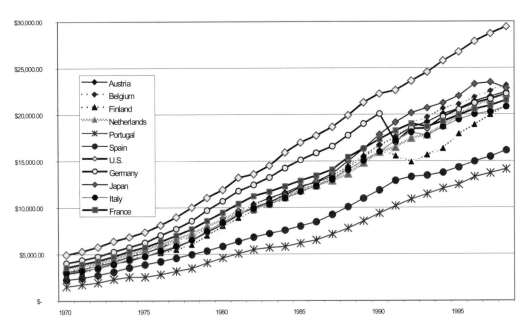

SOURCE: Bruce Scott, manuscript, 1999.

[a]Data for Germany represents unified East and West Germany beginning in 1991.

EXHIBIT 9.22	CONTRIBUTIONS TO EU BUDGET OF EU MEMBER STATES

	1995				1986	
	Net Contribution					
	Total	Per Head		GDP per head as	Total	Net Contributions
	m ecu	ecu	Rank	% of EC Average[a]	m ecu	Per Head Ecu
Germany	13,431	164.6	(1)	106.7	3,742	61.3
Britain	4,720	80.7	(6)	98.2	1,438	25.3
Netherlands	2,005	129.7	(2)	100.4	-217	-14.9
France	1,727	29.6	(9)	107.2	561	10.1
Sweden	937	105.5	(5)	95.3	--	--
Austria	905	112.9	(3)	109.3	--	--
Italy	614	10.7	(10)	101.7	195	3.4
Belgium	311	30.6	(8)	110.4	284	28.7
Finland	165	32.3	(7)	92.5	--	--
Luxembourg	45	110.6	(4)	128.2	59	160.3
Denmark	-306	-58.6	(11)	112.0	-421	82.2
Ireland	-1,887	-526.8	(15)	85.3	-1,230	-374.4
Portugal	-2,381	-241.8	(13)	67.9	-319	-22.1
Greece	-3,489	-333.0	(14)	60.0	-1,273	-127.8
Spain	-7,218	-184.0	(12)	76.1	-95	-2.5

SOURCE: Court of Auditors Report; European Commission.

[a]Based on PPP.

EXHIBIT 9.23	COUNTRY DATA FOR PROSPECTIVE EU MEMBERS

Country	Population (millions)[a]	1995 GDP[a] (in bn US$)[b]	Real Per Capita GDP, PPP Adj. ($)[c]	5 yr. Avg. Inflation Rate (%)[d]	% of 1995 X + M with EC Countries	1994 Agri. As % of GDP[f]
Norway	4.4	146.1	15,518	2.67	75.5	2.92[3]
Switzerland	7.2	306.1	15,887	3.35	70.0	3 .00[3]
Cyprus	0.7	N.A	9,203	4.7	47.5	4.97
Malta	0.4	N.A	6,627[1]	3.24	76.8	2.52
Turkey	61.4	169.3	3,807	76.14	48.7	15.46
Poland	38.6	115	3,826	129.6	269.5	6.29
Hungary	10.1	43.7	4,645	25.96	63.5	6.01
Czech Republic	10.3	47.3	4,095[2]	19.53	62.6	4.99[4]

[1]1989 data, [2]1990 data, [3]1991 data, [4]1995 data.

[a] Source: U.S. Bureau of the Census, International Data Base; CIA, *1996 World Factbook*.

[b] Source: Organization for Economic Cooperation and Development, *National Accounts of the OECD Countries, 1996* Vol.1; Countries, submissions to the OECD and Secretariat estimates; CIA Directorate of Intelligence, *Handbook of International Economic Statistics*, 1996.

[c] Real GDP per capita in constant dollar using Chain index (1985 international prices); Penn World Tables.

[d] Source: International Monetary Fund, *International Financial Statistics Yearbook*, February 1997.

[e] Source: *International Monetary Fund, Direction of Trade Statistics Quarterly,* March 1997 and December 1996.

[f] Source: United Nations Statistics Division.

APPENDIX A	**THE DIRECTORATES GENERAL**

DGI	External Relations: Commercial Policy and relations with North America, the Far East, Australia, and New Zealand
DGIA	External Relations: Europe and the New Independent States, Common Foreign and Security Policy and External Missions
DGIB	External Relations: Southern Mediterranean, Near East, Latin America, South and South-east Asia, and North-South Cooperation
DGII	Economic and Financial Affairs
DGIII	Industry
DGIV	Competition
DGV	Employment, Industrial Relations, and Social Affairs
DGVI	Agriculture
DGVII	Transport
DGVIII	Development
DGIX	Personnel and Administration
DGX	Audiovisual Media, Information, Communication, and Culture
DGXI	Environmental, Civil Protection, and Nuclear Safety
DGXII	Science, Research, and Development
DGXIII	Telecommunications, Information Market, and Exploitation of Research
DGXIV	Fisheries
DGXV	International Markets and Financial Services
DGXVI	Regional Policies and Cohesion
DGXVII	Energy Policies
DGXIX	Budgets
DGXXI	Customs and Indirect Taxation
DGXXII	Education, Training, and Youth
DGXXIII	Enterprise Policy, Distributive Trades, Tourism, and Cooperatives
DGXXIV	Consumer Policy and Consumer Health Protection

SOURCE: Frank McDonald and Steven Dearden, *European Economic Integration* (Great Britain: Henry Ling Ltd., 1999), p. 17.

APPENDIX B	MAJOR ELEMENTS OF THE 1992 PROGRAM

In standards, testing, certification
Harmonization of standards for:
Toys
Automobiles, trucks, and motorcycles and their emissions
Telecommunications
Construction products
Machine safety
Measuring instruments
Medical devices
Gas appliances
Cosmetics
Quick frozen foods
Flavorings
Food preservatives
Instant formula
Fruit juices
Food inspection
Definition of spirited beverages and aromatized wines
Tower cranes (noise)
Household appliances (noise)
Tire pressure gauges
Detergents
Fertilizers
Lawn mowers (noise)
Medicinal products and medical specialties
Radio interferences

New rules for harmonizing packing, labeling, and
processing requirements
Ingredients and labels for food and beverages
Nutritional labeling
Classification, packaging, labeling of dangerous preparations

Harmonization of regulations for health
Harmonization of an extensive list of rules
Medical specialties
Pharmaceuticals
Veterinary medical products
High technology medicines
Implantable electromedical devices
Single-use devices (disposable)
In-vitro diagnostics

Changes in government procurement regulations
Coordination of procedures on the award of public works and
supply contacts
Extension of EC law to telecommunications, utilities,
transport

Services

Harmonization of regulation of services
Banking
Mutual funds
Broadcasting
Tourism
Road passenger transport
Railways
Information services
Life and nonlife insurance
Securities
Maritime transport
Air transport
Electronic payment cards

Liberalization of capital movements
Long-term capital, stocks
Short-term capital

Consumer protection regulations
Misleading definition of products
Indication of prices

Harmonization of laws regulating company behavior
Mergers and acquisitions
Trademarks
Copyrights
Cross-border mergers
Accounting operations across borders
Bankruptcy
Protection of computer programs
Transaction taxes
Company law

Harmonization of taxation
Value-added taxes
Excise taxes on alcohol, tobacco, and other

Harmonization of veterinary and phytosanitary controls
industry (including marketing)
Covering items such as:
Antibiotic residues
Animals and meat
Plant health
Fish and fish products
Live poultry, poultry meat, and hatching eggs
Pesticide residues in fruit and vegetables

Elimination and simplification of national transit
documents and procedures for intra-EC trade
Introduction of the Single Administrative Document (SAD)
Abolition of customs presentation charges
Elimination of customs formalities and the introduction of
common boarder posts

Harmonization of rules pertaining to the free movement
of labor and professions within the EC
Mutual recognition of higher educational diplomas
Comparability of vocational training qualifications
Training of engineers and doctors
Activities in the field of pharmacy
Elimination of burdensome requirements related to residence
permits

SOURCE: *Business America*, August 1, 1988, p.2.

ENDNOTES

1. The European Commission, "Economic Reform: Report on the Functioning of Community Product and Capital Markets," (Brussels: EC, 1998).

2. The European Commission, "Economic and Structural Reform in the EU (Cardiff II)," Brussels, February 17, 1999, p. 2.

3. Norway applied to join the EC, but in two national referenda (1973, 1994) its citizens voted against membership.

4. Michael Calingaert, *The 1992 Challenge from Europe: Development of the European Community's Internal Market* (Washington, DC: National Planning Association, 1988), p. 36; and Pascal Fontaine, *Europe in 10 Points* (Luxembourg: Office for Official Publications of the European Communities, 1998), pp. 9-13.

5. Because of its tenuous monetary position, Italy was given a wider band of +/- 6%.

6. "A Survey of Europe's Internal Market," *The Economist,* July 9, 1988, p. 8.

7. Paola Cecchini et al., *The Benefits of a Single Market* (Aldershot, England: Gower, 1988), pp. 8-10.

8. Commission of the European Communities, *Completing the Internal Market, White Paper from the Commission to the European Council,* Brussels, June 14, 1985.

9. European Community, *News,* No. 7/89, March 14, 1989.

10. Interviews by the authors in Amsterdam, April 7, 1999.

11. European Commission, "European Automobile Industry," Brussels, July 10, 1996; and Peter Holmes and Alasdair Smith, "Automobile Industry," in Pierre Buigues et al., eds., *European Policies on Competition, Trade and Industry: Conflict and Complementarities* (Aldershot: Edward Elgar, 1995), pp. 132-147.

12. Mario Monti, *The Single Market and Tomorrow's Europe* (England: Clays Ltd., St Evives PLC, 1996), p. 31.

13. Duetshce Bank Research, *EMU Watch,* No. 67 (March 15, 1999), pp. 3-4.

14. EC, "Economic and Structural Reform," *Economic and Structural Reform in the EU (Cardiff II),* Brussels, February 17, 1999, p. 10.

15. EC, "Economic Reform: Report on the Functioning of Community Product and Capital Markets" (Brussels, 1998), figure A.6; and Eurostat, "News

16. Release, "EU Member States Investment 46% More Abroad," August 3, 1998 (No. 59/98), p. 2.

16. Fabienne Ilzkovitz and Adriaan Dierx, "From the Single Market to the Single Currency: New Challenges for European Companies," IL/748/98-EN, Table A-1, pp. 17-18.

17. European Commission, "Car Prices in the European Union on 1 November, 1998 — Differences Decrease Sharply," Brussels [IP/99/60], February 1, 1999, p. 2.

18. EC, "Economic and Structural Reform," *Economic and Structural Reform in the EU (Cardiff II),* Brussels, February 17, 1999, p. 10.

19. Bureau Europeen des Unions des Consommateurs, "The Impact of the Euro on Price Transparency," 1998. It should be noted that the most recent issue of the "hamburger standard" in *The Economist,* April 3, 1999, reported a price variance of just 18%, as Greece and Finland were not included.

20. European Commission, "Economic and Structural Reform," *Economic and Structural Reform in the EU (Cardiff II),* Brussels, February 17, 1999, p. 10.

21. European Commission, "A Common System of VAT — A Programme for the Single Market," XXI/1156/96-EN, July 1996, p. 3.

22. European Commission, "Economic Reform: Report on the Function of Community Produce and Capital Markets" [Cardiff I], 1998, p. 21.

23. European Commission, "Economic and Structural Reform," p. 36.

24. European Commission, "Economic Reform," *Economic Reform: Report on the Functioning of Community Product and Capital Markets* (Brussels, 1998p. 20 and figure B.12.

25. European Commission, "Economic and Structural Reform," p. 11.

26. Karle Van Miert, Brussels, March 30, 1999, quoted in Erik Berggren memorandum, April 2, 1999.

27. European Commission, *The Single Market Review: Impact on Services — Credit Institutions and Banking* (Brussels: European Community, 1997), vol. III, pp. 19-23.

28. EC, "Financial Services: Building a Framework for Action," (Brussels, COM (1998) 625), October 28, 1998, pp. 11-12; EC, "Implementing the Framework for Financial Markets: An Action Plan," May 11, 1998.

29   Interview with the authors at Deutsche Bank, Frankfurt, April 8, 1999.

30   European Commission, *The Single Market Review: Impact on Services,* p. 75.

31   Interview with the authors at Deutsche Bank, April 8, 1999.

32   European Commission, "Economic Reform: Report on the Function of Community Produce and Capital Markets" [Cardiff I], p. 6.

33   European Commission, "Economic Reform," p. 4.

34   Ibid., p. 21.

35   Ibid., p. 22.

36   Interview with the authors at Deutsche Bank, Frankfurt, April 8, 1999.

37   "The Euro: A Stable Currency for Europe," Deutsche Bank Research and http://www.ecb.int/.

38   Interviews with the authors at the ECB, Frankfurt, April 19, 1999.

39   "The European System of Central Banks," Federal Reserve Bank of Dallas, *Economic Review,* First Quarter 1999 and http://www.ecb.int/.

40   Martin Feldstein, "EMU and International Conflict," *Foreign Affairs,* November/December 1997, 76,6, p. 66.

41   Interview; "The European System of Central Banks," Federal Reserve Bank of Dallas, *Economic Review,* First Quarter 1999; Edmund L. Andrews, "European Banks, Acting in Unison, Cut Interest Rate," *The New York Times,* December 4, 1998; and "ECB Makes Surprise Half-Point Cut in Main Interest Rate," *Financial Times,* April 9, 1999.

42   "After the Euro…Now What?" *Chief Executive,* December 1998, p. 34.

43   William Hjerpe, in Peter Marsh, "When Transparency Leads to Added Value," *Financial Times,* January 26, 1999.

44   NatWest Markets, "Preparations for Economic and Monetary Union: A Guide for Business," December 1997.

45   M. Feldstein, "EMU and International Conflict," *Foreign Affairs,* November/December 1997, p. 66.

46   http://europa.eu.int/comm/agenda2000.

47   "Presidency Conclusions, Berlin European Council," 24 and 25 March 1999, and "EU Reaches Accord on Farm Aid, Budget Scandal Spurs Leaders to Protect Credibility," *The Globe and Mail,* March 27, 1999.

48   "Group Running European Union Quits en Masse," *The New York Times,* March 16, 1999, and "Former Italian Premier Chosen to Head European Commission," *The New York Times,* March 25, 1999.

Monetary Union and Microeconomic Competitiveness

We have an opportunity to think about the implication of integration for an individual country—with real political parties, businesses, labor unions, and students.

Italy, after decades of rapid growth stimulated by fiscal deficits, had fallen into a corrupt political mire by 1992. Just when things looked worst, the Maastricht agreement committed Italy to competitive, macroeconomic performance by 1997 or, failing that, 1999. Under a succession of "technici" governments, Italy adjusted its monetary and fiscal policy, bringing down inflation, interest rates, fiscal deficits, and government debt. So it succeeded in entering the monetary union in 1999, although its macroeconomic institutions had not adjusted to the demands of open, global competitiveness.

Silvio Berlusconi, an affluent businessman and one-time prime minister, was again elected with a significant majority to foster the adjustment Italy needed. Privatization sectors needed to be regulated, or made competitive. Government spending needed to be curtailed and taxes reduced; pensions needed reform, as did education; labor unions had to become more responsive to business needs. And all of this had to be accomplished in the face of more open competition as part of Europe, but with a world economy slumping into recession. As Berlusconi acknowledged, this would require "the work of a Titan."

CASE STUDY   ITALY: A NEW COMMITMENT TO GROWTH

RICHARD H. K. VIETOR

REBECCA EVANS

Italy is a very conservative place. People don't want to change what is comfortable.
—Boris Biancheri, President, ANSA; Former Italian Ambassador to the United States

We cannot go on like this, fatalistically. We can change policy, reverse the trend, go from decline to growth. A new "economic miracle" is possible.
—Silvio Berlusconi, Prime Minister of Italy

Introduction

"This month is crucial for me," observed Silvio Berlusconi, the prime minister of Italy.[1] In July 2002, the media tycoon turned politician would learn if his economic and labor reform proposals would be approved by Italy's parliament and labor unions. So far, his efforts to reform Italy's stagnant economy had been blocked by fiscal deficits and union protests. After taking office in June 2001, Berlusconi had signed a contract with the Italian people pledging to eliminate Italy's structural problems by cutting taxes, increasing pensions, creating new jobs, reducing crime, and launching major infrastructure projects. Berlusconi had vowed to leave the political arena if he failed to deliver on at least four of these five objectives.[2]

Despite a weak economy, Italy had signed the Maastricht Treaty in 1992 and committed to meet the strict convergence requirements needed to join the European Monetary Union (EMU). Over the next seven years, Italy succeeded in improving its public finances. The budget deficit dropped from 9.6% of gross domestic product (GDP) in 1992 to 2.8% in 1998, and the public debt was reduced. Inflation and interest rates fell dramatically. However, the exchange rate depreciated relative to the required band of the exchange rate mechanism. By pursuing tight fiscal and monetary policies, Italy managed to meet the requirements and joined the EMU in May 1998. But throughout the 1990s, the economy barely grew. In Berlusconi's opinion, Italy's slow growth was "principally attributable to political and institutional problems, to the long and unfinished transition from the First to the Second Republic, and to the permanence of a still statist left."[3] He argued that the rigid labor market, the large bureaucratic government, high taxes, and other remnants of the former welfare state hampered competitiveness. Economic and cultural differences between Italy's North and South also hindered the development of a market economy.

As the leader of Italy's 59th government since World War II, Berlusconi aimed to deliver both economic growth and political stability. His center-right coalition, led by the Forza Italia party, held a majority in both houses of Parliament, clearing the way for major reform. A month into office, Berlusconi presented Parliament with an economic growth program called "the 100-day package." The three-pronged growth strategy included measures to reform the labor market and the welfare state, reduce taxes, and modernize the public administration. On October 10, 2001, Parliament approved the package, passing several laws that simplified tax and bureaucratic procedures. However, the pace of reform had slowed in the wake of the September 11 terrorist attacks and the ensuing global downturn. Inheriting a higher-than-anticipated budget deficit for 2001, the Berlusconi administration was forced to postpone tax cuts. As for moving ahead with labor reform, Berlusconi's efforts to change rigid labor laws were strongly opposed by labor unions. The conflict culminated in the assassination of labor economist Marco Biagi and a nationwide strike.

Despite the delays to his reform package, the prime minister remained optimistic. "In one year, I can't influence the deep structure of the state," he explained. "But I can expect to go a full five

Research Associate Rebecca Evans prepared this case under the supervision of Professor Richard H. K. Vietor. It is a rewritten version of an earlier case, "Italy: From Welfare State to Market Economy," HBS Case No. 700-129. HBS cases are developed solely as the basis for class discussion. Cases are not intended to serve as endorsements, sources of primary data, or illustrations of effective or ineffective management.

years."[4] Others were more skeptical of Berlusconi's political longevity. Some pointed to conflict-of-interest issues, saying that the prime minister used his political position to increase his many business holdings. Although the courts cleared Berlsuconi of an array of corruption charges, he still faced accusations of false accounting and bribery.[5] Meanwhile, some feared that he was overextending himself by also serving as foreign minister. Berlusconi shrugged off their concerns, focusing his attention on revitalizing the Italian economy. Recognizing the enormity of Italy's structural problems, he remarked, "I have the work of a titan to accomplish."[6]

Country Background

Demographics

Italy occupies a central position in the northern Mediterranean, which allows for easy access to Europe, northern Africa, and the Middle East. [See **Exhibit 10.1**.] Located in southern Europe, the boot-shaped peninsula has an area of 301,000 square miles. Northern Italy shares borders with France, Switzerland, Austria, and Slovenia. Italy is home to the Mediterranean islands of Sardinia and Sicily, as well as two independent states, Vatican City and the Republic of San Marino.

Italy was divided into two main socioeconomic regions: the North and the South. The North was the industrial heart of the country. This region boasted low unemployment rates and a well-built infrastructure. The economy was comprised of a few large corporations and thousands of small to medium family-owned manufacturing companies. The South, also known as the Mezzogiorno, suffered from high crime rates, high unemployment, and a poor infrastructure. The state still maintained a large presence in this area. In 1999, the government established the Southern Italy Development Programme (PSM). Through an increase in public investment, the PSM aimed to boost productivity and employment, closing the gap between the North and South.

The Italian population was relatively homogeneous. About 98% of the population was Italian; 99% was Roman Catholic.[7] Most people spoke Italian, the official language. Italians had very strong family ties. Many children did not leave home until their late 20s or early 30. Married couples often moved within one kilometer of their parents' homes.[8] Bound by their roots, most Italians were unwilling to relocate even when offered higher paying jobs. "Many people don't want to move because of regional differences," explained Kristien Michoel of NOMISMA. "They fear leaving the safety of their local region. It is a cultural thing."[9]

Immigration

Italy's immigration rate grew substantially in the 1990s. By 2000, there were 1.7 million immigrants in Italy. Many came from Morocco, the former Yugoslavia, Tunisia, Albania, Egypt, Ethiopia, and the Philippines. An estimated 200,000 immigrants were illegal. Italy's large Adriatic border was difficult to police, allowing many immigrants to slip into the "black hole of the southern economy."[10] Determined to crack down on illegal immigration, Berlusconi ordered a two-day roundup of illegal aliens in May 2002. More than 200 were caught and arrested. In July, Parliament passed a controversial anti-immigration bill. The new law required non-European immigrants to be fingerprinted and prevented unemployed immigrants from seeking residence permits. All illegal immigrants were to be expelled immediately.[11]

Population Growth

By 2001, Italy had a population of 57.5 million. Despite a high population density, Italy had the lowest birthrate in Europe.[12] Population projections showed that Italy would soon have a negative population growth rate. [See **Exhibit 10.2**.] "The population is not growing. It is dreadful," commented Professor Dino Piero Giarda. "How is this country going to grow if the population isn't growing?"[13] Italy's rapidly aging population posed another problem. ISTAT, Italy's national statistical institute, predicted that by 2010 the population aged 57 and above would equal 61% of the population between 20 and 56.[14] Already, the government spent 15% of GDP on state-funded pensions. Because active workers' contributions paid for current pensioners, many feared that the future workforce would not be able to support the growing number of retirees.[15]

Income Distribution

There were three distinct phases of income distribution during Italy's post-war era. Income inequality remained stable during the 1950s and 1960s. In the 1970s, inequality fell sharply but rebounded in the 1980s and fluctuated around a flattened trend up through the early 1990s. [See **Exhibit 10.3a**.] In 1994, the top decile held 22.9% of post-tax household income, while the bottom decile had 2.4%[16]. [See **Exhibit 10.3b**.]

Crime

Organized crime groups, an increase in illegal immigrants, and a resurgence of terrorist groups such as the leftist Red Brigades contributed to Italy's high crime rates. In the South, where organized crime was concentrated, crime rates were the highest. The major ring of organized crime groups included the Mafia in Sicily, the Camorra in Campania, and the 'Ndrangheta in Calabria. These gangs took advantage of the South's high unemployment rate and recruited workers, including young children, to participate in the drug trade and other illicit enterprises. The Mafia's use of violence and intimidation discouraged legitimate investment in the South. In the 1920s, Mussolini had nearly eradicated the Mafia. However, when the Allies landed in Sicily in 1943, they exploited the Mafia's territorial know-how to defeat the Italian and German armies. Following World War II, the Mafia gained control of Sicily's political and legal systems.[17] For many years, some politicians had tolerated and even colluded with the Mafia. Political instability, moreover, made it difficult to sustain an effective battle against organized crime groups. After the corruption investigations of 1992, the government finally began enforcing strict anti-Mafia measures.[18]

A Brief History

In the eighth century B.C., Greeks settled in the southern tip of Italy and introduced new forms of art and architecture. They also developed a strong agricultural-based economy. At the same time, the Etruscans moved into central Italy, where they established a sophisticated community. In the North, the Gauls of Celtic origin migrated from the Alps into the fertile Po Valley.

Rome was founded on the banks of the Tiber River in the middle of the eighth century B.C. During the sixth century, the powerful Romans conquered the Etruscans and established the Roman Republic. The formation of the republic marked an important social transformation in which the plebeians gained political power and the first written laws were recorded. In the fifth and fourth centuries, the republic expanded its empire into southern Italy. The expansion inevitably led to a series of battles—the Punic Wars—between Rome and Carthage. In 146 B.C., Rome defeated Carthage and became the elite Mediterranean military power.

In the fifth century A.D., the Western Roman Empire, weakened by political instability and poor economic conditions, collapsed after a series of foreign invasions. Political unity was lost, and in the following centuries Italy became "an oft-changing succession of small states, principalities, and kingdoms which fought among themselves and were subject to ambitions of foreign powers."[19] The influence of the Christian Church grew during the tumultuous years of the early medieval period. Under Pope Gregory the Great (590–684), the Church assumed greater political and administrative powers as it acquired more territory throughout central Italy.

The Renaissance of the fourteenth century marked the point at which Italy moved out of the Middle Ages. Economic prosperity in Italy's northern and central regions fueled the rebirth of classical art, literature, and science. The textile industry flourished in Florence and Milan, while Venice and Genoa controlled the spice trade. France and Spain competed for territorial control of Italy during the sixteenth century. Only the Papal States and Venice remained independent during this time. With the successful campaigns in 1796 and 1800, Napoleon conquered the entire Italian peninsula and established a republic.

After Napoleon's fall, the Austrians assumed control of Italy. However, Italy's intellectuals and middle class desired more democratic institutions. In 1848, Giuseppe Mazzini and Giuseppe Garibaldi led a revolution against the Austrians and established the Roman Republic and the Republic of San Marco.

In 1861, Italy united under a constitutional monarchy with a parliamentary government. Victor Emmanel II of the House of Savoy was crowned the first king of Italy. However, despite the facade of a unified nation, Italy remained deeply fragmented. Class distinctions, especially in the South, continued to divide Italy. Meanwhile, the Church viewed the new state as a challenge to the Vatican's authority. The Vatican issued a *non expedit* decree that forbade Catholics and their religious leaders from participating in national elections. The Church's opposition to secularization, and its refusal to recognize the state, remained "an open sore that delayed and complicated the development of popular political participation in Italy."[20]

The House of Savoy maintained a monarchy until the end of World War I in 1918. Italy fought the war on the side of the Allies. Although the victory expanded Italy's northeastern borders, it left the Italian economy in ruins. The king invited Benito Mussolini, the leader of the National Fascist Party (Partito Nazionale Fascista), to form a government. Mussolini increased the power of the head of government, abolished all other political parties, and established a fascist dictatorship in 1926. Although fascism took control of nearly every arm of the state, the Church prevented the fascists from being fully totalitarian. Mussolini signed the Concordant of 1929, a compromise agreement that pronounced that the Church and the state were to both be "independent and sovereign."[21]

In 1940, Mussolini's ties with Hitler brought Italy into World War II on the German side. On July 10, 1943, the Allies invaded Sicily and triggered an anti-fascist movement, the Resistance, led by the Partito D'Azione (which broke up soon after liberation), the communists (who later formed the Partito Comunista Italiano, PCI), the Partito Socialista Italiano (Socialist Party, PSI), and the Partito Popolare Italiano (the Christian Democrat faction, or Democrazia Cristiana, DC). Following the invasion, the king replaced Mussolini with Marshall Pietro Badoglio, who signed an armistice with the Allies on September 2, 1943. In 1945, the Germans surrendered, and Mussolini was shot and killed.

On June 2, 1946, Italy held its first popular referendum, in which the people voted to replace the monarchy with a democratic republic. However, the election results revealed the existence of a North-South division: the North and Center voted for the republic, while the South voted in favor of the monarchy. A constituent assembly composed of members from the DC, PSI, and PCI was elected to plan the new republic. On January 1, 1948, the constitution, a compromise between Catholic and communist ambition, gained approval. The new constitution outlined the framework for a bicameral parliamentary system.

The Italian Political System

The 1948 constitution established a democratic system composed of three levels: the executive, the judiciary, and a bicameral parliament. The president of the republic was elected for a seven-year term by an electoral college composed of Parliament and 58 regional delegates. The president's powers included the promulgation of all government decrees and laws, any of which could be referred back to Parliament if deemed unconstitutional. The president determined the dates for general elections and referendums and appointed the prime minister and one of the Constitutional Court judges.

The executive branch was composed of a Council of Ministers headed by a president—the prime minister. Both the council and the prime minister had to maintain a vote of confidence in Parliament. The executive branch could initiate legislation and introduce decree laws and legislative decrees.

The judicial system was based on a civil law system derived from the Savoy monarchy and influenced by ecclesiastical law. The Constitutional Court consisted of 15 judges. Judicial appointments were made by the president, Parliament, and the other ordinary and administrative supreme courts.

The Senate and the Chamber of Deputies, the two houses of Parliament, formed the legislative arm of the government. The two houses shared equal powers. Bills needed to win a majority in both houses before they could become laws. There were 326 seats in the Senate, of which 315 were elected. The other seats were held by former presidents and a few senators who had been elected for life. The Chamber of Deputies had 630 elected members. Both houses were elected for five years.

The Rise and Fall of the Christian Democrats

Despite massive destruction of its infrastructure, Italy rebounded from WWII and moved quickly through the restoration period. The 1950s gave birth to the "Italian miracle," an industrial boom that brought prosperity to the northern and central regions. The industrial revolution shifted Italy's economic focus from agriculture to manufacturing. Large funds were not available to support big capital concerns such as energy, steel, and chemicals. Instead, family-owned businesses became the mainstay of the Italian economy. Entrepreneurs established small companies that focused on textiles, machinery, and food processing. These businesses took advantage of Italy's proximity to the water by exporting goods around the world.[22]

The state established the Cassa per il Mezzogiorno (Funds for the Development of the South) to bridge the economic gap between the North and the South. However, a great migration of southern workers spoiled the success of the program. Although most Italians were reluctant to move, the depressed conditions of the South forced many struggling workers to flee to the North. The labor flight left the southern economy in poor shape and widened the gap between the two regions.

The Christian Democrat Party (DC) rose to power after gaining its first parliamentary majority in 1945. The PPI, the first party to gain "tacit approval" from the Church, was the predecessor of the DC.[23] Fears of becoming marginalized had led the Church to acknowledge its support of the PPI's socialist goals. The Church shared the PPI's belief that wealth should be spread equally among the people. In the eyes of the Church, excessive wealth was ungodly. This Catholic attitude influenced the politics of the DC during its 50-year dominance of the Italian government.

As the Cold War unfolded in Europe, the DC also gained the support of the United States. In Italy, the PCI had emerged as the most powerful communist party in the West. Fearing that the communists would take control of Italy, the United States poured money into the DC and threatened to withdraw its financial support if the PCI were to enter the government.[24]

The post-war governments of the centrist DC, led by Alcide de Gasperi, followed policies of reconstruction and economic development that included strict anti-inflation measures and the re-launch of the Institute for the Industrial Reconstruction (IRI), a state-owned holding company that purchased shares in steel, iron, and other industries.[25] Italy's industrial success during this period helped to build the country's

international reputation. On March 25, 1957, Italy signed the Treaty of Rome and became one of the six founding members of the European Economic Community (EEC). The treaty aimed to remove all internal tariffs and establish a common market in goods and services in just 10 years.

Italy's industrial boom continued into the early 1960s. With one of the fastest-growing economies in the world, Italy became a leading international exporter of manufactured goods. Growth slowed in 1964, however, and Italy entered a recession. The PSI formed a coalition government with the DC and launched a nationalization initiative. The opening of the Italian government to the left had important socioeconomic consequences. This coalition, led by the DC's Aldo Moro, improved economic growth "by nationalizing certain corporations in the electrical and chemical sectors, including many public services, and starting a program for far-reaching reforms and modernization of the Italian administrative, fiscal and financial structures."[26]

In the South, the state attempted to bridge the economic gap by building "cathedrals in the desert." Taking advantage of cheap labor, state enterprises multiplied in the South. Large plants were constructed for companies in the transportation, telecommunications, utilities, steel, coal, and petrochemical industries. The system created ENI, ENEL, SIP (Telecom Italia), and other state-owned monopolies. Over 70% of the industry in the South was in the hands of the state. "The positive results of state-owned enterprises were the building up of high-tech know-how and the improvement of the South's infrastructure," explained Fernando Napolitano, vice president and managing partner of Booz Allen Hamilton Italia. "However, the negative results included the establishment of artificial jobs [not market driven] and a lack of focus on western management styles."[27]

Near the end of the 1960s, social tensions escalated. Violent protests erupted across the country as trade unions and university students grew restless with the political establishment. The increasing social unrest was reflected in the election results of 1968. The PCI and extreme leftist parties gained a larger share of the popular vote, and it became harder for the DC to form strong coalitions. Pressure from the left helped pass some of the world's most advanced social legislation in the early 1970s.[28]

The Italian economy, which imported 85% of its energy, foundered in 1973 when oil prices skyrocketed. The energy crisis sent inflation rates soaring to 20% per year, and Italy entered yet another recession.[29] As wages increased, companies were forced to make cutbacks and the nation's unemployment rate rose dramatically. The economic crisis was compounded by an increase in political corruption. Organized crime helped to make the *anni di piombo*, or years of lead, a time of extreme terrorism led by the leftist Red Brigades (Brigate Rosse), which intended to destabilize the country.

In an attempt to restore order to the economy and the government, the DC was forced to invite the PCI to support a government of national unity in 1976. The *compromesso storico*, or historic compromise, between the communists and the DC marked the first moment of cooperation between the two political groups. The PCI agreed not to vote against the government. However, this peaceful union was short-lived. On March 16, 1978, Moro, president of the DC, was kidnapped and murdered by the Red Brigades.

Despite the political unrest at home, Italy continued to make progress toward its goal of European integration. In 1979, Italy became one of eight European states to form the European Monetary System (EMS). The new system of "fixed but adjustable" exchange rates aimed to protect intra-European trade from the effects of floating exchange rates.

The 1980s brought renewed stability to Italy's government and economy. The PSI experienced a comeback in the early 1980s. In the 1983 general election, the DC's share of the popular vote dropped from 38.3% to 32.9%.[30] With a plan to increase government efficiency via institutional reforms, Bettino Craxi, the leader of the PSI, became the next prime minister. Craxi maintained power for the next four years, during which he passed important anti-inflation measures that stabilized the economy. During the mid-1980s, productivity growth and an increase in foreign investment revitalized Italy's export-driven economy. This second "economic miracle" was led by an army of small to medium-sized companies.

In 1986, Italy took another major step toward European unification when it signed the Single European Act (SEA). The SEA amended the Treaty of Rome and outlined specific measures to liberalize the free movement of goods, services, and people within the European Community (EC). In addition, the SEA made a commitment to complete the internal market by December 31, 1992. As the end of the decade approached, Italians were enjoying a higher standard of living. In 1986, Italy's GDP per capita was 9% greater than Great Britain's. It was becoming clear to the world that "the Italians [were] doing something right, and doing it despite a political and administrative system that [remained] the least adapted to the requirements of modern, efficient government in western Europe."[31]

The Fall of Communism

The collapse of the Berlin Wall in 1989 rocked the foundation of the Italian political system. Democracy and capitalism triumphed after the fall of the East European communist bloc. Since its first days as a republic, Italy's political system had been built around the fear of Soviet communism. Once the threat to democracy was removed, the need for a strong anticommunist government slipped away. The political dominance of the DC crumbled as people realized that the "automatic collusion in the corrupt practices of the DC and its coalition partners could no longer be perceived as a requirement for the survival of liberal democracy in Italy."[32] Italy's economy also felt the impact of the collapse of communism. For years, the Soviet Union had been an important trade partner, especially in Emilia-Romagna and Italy's other communist "red regions." The Soviets had also been a major contributor to the PCI. As the rest of the world celebrated the end of communism, Italy scrambled to stabilize its fragile political system.

Operation "Clean Hands"

The corruption investigations of 1992, known as *Tangentopoli,* brought about the demise of the coalition led by the DC. Operation *Mani Pulite* (Clean Hands) uncovered a web of corruption between political leaders, local authorities, and major corporations. Italian magistrates uncovered an "institutionalized system of bribes" through which profits from state-owned enterprises had flowed directly into the hands of political officials.[33] Many of Italy's large private businesses had given money to the ruling political parties in exchange for public contracts. With the majority of Italy's ruling political class under investigation, paralysis spread through the country. "From the smallest town to the biggest city, from the peripheral public officials to the general managers of the ministries, everyone closed down, looking to evade responsibility," observed Berlusconi.[34]

The corruption scandals led to the death of the First Republic, a 50-year span of centrist governments dominated by the DC. Although many outsiders had interpreted the frequent turnover of governments as a sign of instability, the DC's continuous control of Parliament throughout the post-war period had lent a high degree of stability to the Italian political system. Mario Carlo Ferrario, president of Redifin, explained, "There were new governments each year, but it was the most stable country in Europe, because the same coalition was always in power with the same people." [35]

Disillusioned voters attempted to simplify the multiparty system by voting for electoral reform in the 1993 referendum. The new first-past-the-post electoral system forced the creation of two opposing poles. In the elections of the 1990s, voters chose between the center-right and the center-left coalitions. Unfortunately, the reforms only complicated Italian political life. In Berlusconi's opinion, "The consequence [of the new system] was further political fragmentation which rendered it impossible to achieve a unified direction in the economic action of the government in power."[36] Although the reforms had succeeded in creating two separate coalitions, there was still an abundance of small parties that slowed legislation and could easily disrupt a government's stability by defecting from the ruling coalition.

Economic Gloom in the Early 1990s

The Italian economy presented a paradox. On the surface, the economy was booming due to increased productivity and surging exports. But the façade of economic prosperity hid the real truth about Italy's sick macroeconomy, which "continued to be plagued by high unemployment, high interest rates, high labor costs, high inflation, vast public expenditures, and a staggering public deficit." [37] Italy's large fiscal imbalances were the legacy of inefficient economic policies, the high cost of the welfare system, and years of political corruption. In 1985, the budget deficit had risen to 12% of GDP and then leveled off to about 10% of GDP

for the remainder of the decade.[38] Growth deteriorated during the second half of the 1980s, and Italy's GDP growth differential in relation to the other EU nations became negative for the first time.[39] Meanwhile, the productivity gap between Italy's North and South continued to expand.

The gloomy state of Italy's economy continued into the early 1990s. In 1991 and 1992, Italy ran trade and current account deficits [see **Exhibit 10.6a**]. Large budget deficits and growing public debt drew the attention of Italy's skeptical European neighbors, which questioned Italy's commitment to market integration. As growth declined, the growth gap between Italy and the rest of the EU widened [see **Exhibit 10.8**]. Inflation rates and interest rates remained high, and industries struggled to adapt to rising wages. The system of wage indexation and bargaining made the labor market very rigid. In 1992, the budget deficit equaled 9.6% of GDP, the public sector debt ballooned to 124.9% of GDP, and GDP growth slowed to 0.6% [see **Exhibits 10.5** and **10.7**].

The March to Monetary Union

In 1992, Italy and the eleven other EC nations signed the Maastricht Treaty. The treaty established convergence requirements and set a timetable for achieving monetary union by January 1, 1997, or January 1, 1999, at the latest. The criteria for membership in the EMU included a budget deficit less than or equal to 3% of GDP, a public debt below 60% of GDP or declining at a satisfactory pace, an inflation rate within 1.5% of the average of the three EC nations with the lowest rates, long-term interest rates within two percentage points of the average of the three countries with the lowest rates, and a currency that had not been devalued in the previous two years and that had remained within a normal currency band. The Maastricht commitments challenged Italy to address its huge fiscal imbalances.

Amato's Reforms

After the fall of the First Republic, Giuliano Amato, a leader of the PSI and a former Treasury minister, formed Italy's first government of *tecnici,* or nonparty academics, managers, and senior civil servants[40] [see **Exhibit 10.12**]. Although his government lasted for less than a year, Amato introduced major economic and institutional reforms that put Italy on course to meet the Maastricht deadlines. Once in office, Amato passed Italy's most austere post-war budget, which included large tax and excise increases as well as a 0.6% levy on money held in bank deposits and on residential real estate.[41] Amato initiated pension reform that increased the retirement age of male and female workers covered by pension plans to 65 years. The Treasury reduced future expenditures by ending its support of the universal health-care system. Under Amato's leadership, a historic agreement between unions and employers led to the abolishment of the inflationary system of wage indexation. The Amato government also passed important anti-Mafia measures.[42]

Privatization

Amato launched an aggressive privatization program that abolished the Ministry for State Owned Participated Enterprises and slowly opened Italy to competition. Almost overnight, he converted the four largest state holding companies—Instituto per la Ricostruzione Industriale (IRI), Ente Nazionale Idrocarburi (ENI), Instituto Nazionale delle Assicurazioni (INA), and Ente Nazionale per l'Energia Elettrica (ENEL)—into joint-stock companies that were placed under the control of the Treasury. Amato's plan aimed to reduce the budget deficit by raising 27 trillion lire (L) through privatization of the holding companies between 1993 and 1995[43] [see **Exhibit 10.16**].

Devaluation

Due to high inflation and interest rates, the lira was forced out of the exchange rate mechanism in September 1992, leading to a 30% devaluation. Although the devaluation boosted Italy's exports, it was soon followed by a recession. Frustrated with the weak economy, labor blamed Amato and his rigid economic programs. After the four party leaders of his coalition were charged with bribery, Amato resigned as prime minister.

Ciampi's Government

Carlo Azeglio Ciampi formed a "caretaker government" of *tecnici* in April 1993,[44] continuing Amato's program of institutional reform. The Incomes Policy Agreement of July 1993 established a framework for wage negotiations. "In the 1970s and 1980s, Italy had dreamed of a Politica della Concertazione where government, unions, and businessmen would sit around the same table and decide how much to increase salaries for that year," explained Sergio Romano. "The unions finally acquired the right to participate in this way."[45] The new income agreement kept wages within the projected inflation rate, businesses were allowed to introduce profit-related and performance-related pay, and companies gained flexibility with regard to starting salaries and temporary labor agreements. The Ciampi government led Italy through the privatization of IRI's two commercial banks. In December 1993, Credito Italiano floated on the stock exchange, and Banca Commerciale Italia followed in March 1994. Ciampi also initiated the privatization of the smaller state-owned companies in the steel, food-processing, and chemical sectors.[46]

Berlusconi's New Party

Berlusconi, a powerful businessman, surprised Italians in 1994 by announcing that he had formed a new conservative party, Forza Italia, and was running for prime minister. "We found ourselves with the elimination of the Christian Democrats and the possibility of the communists coming into the government," said Berlusconi. "I was then the only Italian person with the necessary credibility and the support of the public. I came to the decision that I would become a political figure, and I set up the new party in two months."[47] Berlusconi's dynamic personality and large media presence attracted voters, who were encouraged by his promise to lower taxes, increase jobs, and open Italy to competition. In May 1994, the right-wing Freedom Pole alliance formed a coalition government, and Berlusconi was elected prime minister.

Critics accused Berlusconi of a conflict of interest between his ownership of the Fininvest holding company and his role of prime minister. Berlusconi's business empire included three private television networks, publishing houses, supermarket chains, and insurance companies. Many suspected that Berlusconi had entered politics in order to rescue Fininvest, which had an estimated debt of L6,000 billion in 1993.[48] In November 1994, he was investigated concerning bribes that Fininvest companies had paid to the tax police.[49]

During Berlusconi's short-lived government, public sector spending declined, and the GDP grew for seven months before falling over the issue of pension reform. The shaky alliance between the numerous coalition parties reflected the shortcomings of the first-past-the-post system, which still allowed 25% of Parliament to be elected through proportional representation. In December 1994, the Northern League joined a parliamentary vote of no confidence, leading to Berlusconi's resignation.

Prodi's Leadership

In January 1995, Lamberto Dini, the Treasury minister, formed a temporary government of *tecnici*. A year later, a general election was called and two distinct coalitions emerged: the center-left Ulivo, or Olive Tree, and the center-right Polo per le Liberta, or Freedom Pole. Prodi, an economics professor and former head of IRI, had founded the Olive Tree alliance. Prodi became prime minister in May 1996 when his coalition defeated the Freedom Pole. For the first time in Italy's history, a center-left alliance, composed of many former communists, ruled the government.

Prodi passed tight budgetary measures in order to prepare Italy for its entrance into the EMU. The government continued to open Italy to competition by further reducing state holdings in ENI and privatizing Telecom Italia in 1997. As a result of budget cuts and increased tax revenue, Italy's budget deficit fell to 2.7% of GDP in 1997, just inside the limits of the Maastricht treaty. With a reduced deficit and a declining public debt, Italy was accepted into the EMU in May 1998. On January 1, 1999, exchange rates were locked, monetary policy fell under the control of the European Central Bank (ECB), and the euro was adopted as the single currency.

The Dual Economy

Italy's dual economy was dominated by two tiers of private companies. The first tier consisted of a few large family-owned companies. Many of the families "exerted control through holding companies and cross shareholdings with industrial and financial allies."[50] Some of the most influential family businesses were the Agnelli family's FIAT, Italy's largest conglomerate, which produced cars, tractors, steel, machine tools, and airplane engines; Pirelli, a tire company that manufactured industrial rubber products and telecom cables; and Olivetti, a computer and telecommunications business.[51] Other conglomerates were run by the Benetton, Romiti, Marzotto, Del Vecchio, Ferrero, and Gardini families. For more than 50 years, the powerful Mediobanca, a private merchant bank, financed the "narrow cartel of northern entrepreneurs"[52] [see **Exhibit 10.10**]. Close ties to the state had helped FIAT and other companies secure large contracts through public procurement. In the late 1990s, the family conglomerates increased their international competitiveness through mergers and increased productivity.[53]

The second tier of Italy's dual economy was made up of clusters of family-owned small and medium-sized companies (SMEs). These *distretti,* or industrial districts, were described as "geographic concentrations of interconnected firms, specialized suppliers, service providers, firms in related industries and associated institutions . . . [that] all contribute to a system that produces the goods that are characteristic of the district."[54] For example, the leather footwear industry in Verona spawned a cluster of interrelated businesses (tanneries, footwear machinery, leather clothing, athletic footwear, etc.) whose proximity facilitated the sharing of knowledge and resources. Other clusters included ceramic tiles in Sassuolo, silk in Como, textiles in Prato, factory automation equipment in Turin, and packaging machinery in Bologna [see **Exhibit 10.1**]. While the industrial districts were largely concentrated in the North, a few successful clusters had developed in the South.

SMEs formed the backbone of the Italian economy. Small firms thrived in Italy, where 98% of manufacturing firms had fewer than 50 workers and 83% had fewer than 10. SMEs accounted for more than a third of Italy's export revenues. These firms were an important source of job creation; they provided over two million jobs in the manufacturing sector.[55] Italy had the highest percentage of SMEs among the EU countries. Many pointed to the success of its clusters, claiming that Italy had shown that "to have a highly developed economy, it [was] not necessarily true that it must be based on large firms."[56]

Several characteristics seemed essential to the development of a strong cluster: geographic concentration, close family ties, domestic rivalry, specialization, and cooperation and knowledge transfer between firms and suppliers. In *The Competitive Advantage of Nations,* Michael E. Porter explained that in Italy, "constant competitive advantage was present, due to sophisticated and demanding local buyers, strong and unique distribution channels, and intense rivalry among local firms."[57] Families performed an important role of educating young workers. "The real uniqueness of Italy, however, [was] the out-of-school learning process in particular industries," wrote Porter. "Highly specialized knowledge and skills [were] passed within families and from generation to generation."[58] Specialization was a crucial element of the districts, allowing small firms to focus their limited resources on what they did best.[59] In addition, specialization helped reduce quality-control problems. Gucci's network of specialized suppliers contributed to the success of its leather handbag business. Gucci, part of the leather goods cluster in the Tuscany region, had about 160 hardware, raw material, and other small suppliers within a 10-kilometer radius of its Florence plant. This system of production provided maximum flexibility, in that Gucci could let demand dictate how much work was outsourced to its suppliers.[60]

The packaging machinery cluster in Bologna offered an example of cooperation and knowledge transfer between firms and suppliers. Nearly 75% of the packaging machinery industry was near Bologna in the industrial Emilia-Romagna region. The cluster included 20 medium-sized firms with fewer than 100 employees and about 100 smaller firms. Many of the SMEs in this district specialized in different types of packaging machinery. Industria Macchine Automatiche S.p.A. (IMA) was a world leader in tea bagging and pharmaceutical packaging machines. Although IMA did not collaborate directly with its competitors, its suppliers passed along innovative ideas. "Our network of over 200 suppliers is extremely important for the transfer of information," said Giuseppe Bussolari, director of IMA's Tea Division. "Our suppliers usually work with three or more different companies, and we learn about new techniques from them. "[61]

Bologna's packaging cluster was supported by numerous industry associations, state-funded agencies, local banks, and cooperative programs [see **Exhibit 10.9**]. These service centers helped "SMEs by offering services that the internal resources of smaller firms [had] trouble handling."[62] The Instituto Aldini Valeriani in Bologna trained mechanical engineers and other students for jobs in the packaging cluster. Porter noted the importance of trade associations in the Prato's textile cluster: "Through five industry associations in different but related fields, there [was] joint research on new technologies, construction of a central depurator (purifier), cooperation in the purchases of services, raw materials and equipment, operation of a general warehouse, and an ongoing effort to influence local infrastructure."[63]

The Slow-Growth Economy

Although Italy succeeded in cleaning up its messy public finances, the economy continued to grow slowly. GDP growth fell from 2.0% in 1997 to 1.6% in 1999. Economists blamed Italy's growth problems on EMU adjustments and a slowdown in world markets, especially in Asia. But as Italy's economy slumped, the other EU countries enjoyed significant growth. From 1990 to 1999, the Italian economy expanded 13.2%, compared with 23.8% for the EU.[64]

In 2000, European growth boosted consumer demand. Italy's economy surged, growing 2.9%. As a consequence, the budget deficit decreased to 0.5%. The public debt continued to decline, reaching 107.5% of GDP. However, the rally was short-lived. In 2001, rising energy prices, international uncertainties, and a sharp slowdown in world trade depressed growth, which slowed to 1.8%. The deficit widened to 1.4%. The projected 2002 deficit of 1.5% in 2002 was higher than the Stability and Growth Pact target. While temporary factors had affected short-term growth, it was clear that deeply rooted performance and institutional problems threatened Italy's long-term growth potential.

Foreign Investment

Throughout the 1990s, outward direct investment was substantially greater than inward direct investment. Italy's inward investment flows were consistently below those of the other EU nations[65] [see **Exhibits 10.6a** and **10.6b**]. Poor infrastructure, rigid labor laws, low labor productivity levels, and the fear of organized crime discouraged many foreign companies from investing in Italy. "Italy suffers from a stereotype," explained Elio Catania, CEO of

IBM Italia. "Italy is considered to be a closed country. There is a lack of flexibility, capital is not efficient, the infrastructure is not efficient, and there is corruption in some areas. But all this is beginning to change."[66] There were also cultural explanations for Italy's FDI imbalance. "The culture sees foreign investment as a threat to the existing system because they will have to apply the market economy and work harder," reasoned Renato Ruggiero, vice chairman of Salomon Smith Barney. "American or German investment will force market standards on Italian business."[67] In addition, Italy's industrial districts, which had deep familial ties, were opposed to foreign investment. "Small firms are linked to families like lovers," commented Maurizio Sella, chairman of the Italian Banking Association (ABI). "Selling them is impossible. They won't at any cost borrow and give up control to outsiders."[68]

Taxation

Corporate taxes were high in Italy. Taxes on corporate income ranged from 46% to 54% and were higher than in most Organization for Economic Cooperation and Development (OECD) nations [69] [see **Exhibit 10.14a**]. Many Italians believed that the high level of taxation was a legacy of the *Catto-Comunisti* (Catholic-Communist) mentality. "In Italy, there are two religions," explained Fedele Confalonieri, president of Mediaset. "The Catholics and the communists both think that if you own property it is a sin."[70] Tax revenues were used to pay interest on Italy's huge public debt. "My theory is that the amount of public debt is equal to the tax evasion of the last 10 years. I would say that we lose about L250 trillion in tax evasion each year," commented investment banker Guido Roberto Vitale. "If people paid taxes, we would have a surplus."[71] High corporate taxes dampened investment and perpetuated the growth of small firms (those with fewer than 15 employees), which enjoyed both tax and labor-law advantages.

Financial Markets

Italy suffered from inefficient financial markets that were just beginning to open up. Italy had a minimal stock exchange that brought in very little capital because the government still maintained a 50% stake in several public companies. [72] Pier Giorgio Romiti, CEO of

Impregilo S.p.A., explained that Italy had evolved from an economy where more than half the GDP came from state-owned companies. "That is not real capitalism," he said. "All the state-owned companies are on the market, and the other half is the family-owned businesses."[73]

Politicians controlled Italy's banks for years. "In Italy, our banking system is a disaster," said Marco Spinedi of NOMISMA.[74] "It is public, oligopolistic, and there are very high rates." In the early 1990s, there were over 600 banks in Italy. A wave of mergers and acquisitions at the end of the decade triggered the consolidation of the banking sector. By 2001, the five biggest banks accounted for 54% of the banking system's total assets, compared with 36% in 1995.[75] Bank privatization also accelerated. In May 2001, government-controlled banks held just 12% of funds.[76] Consolidation and privatization greatly reduced the influence of Mediobanca. After the death of founder Enrico Cuccia in June 2000, Mediobanca struggled to compete in the changing banking environment.[77]

Unemployment

At 9.4%, Italy had the second-highest unemployment rate in the EU. The country's "hard core of long-term, hard-to-place workers" consisted of new workers, women, younger workers, and the aged[78] [see **Exhibit 10.4**]. Italy's recorded unemployment rate had reached a high of 11.7% in 1997, but in recent years employment had increased. Females accounted almost entirely for the net gain in employment.[79] Although an increase in part-time and temporary work contracts had helped to create more jobs, the persistent unemployment of the disadvantaged category of labor remained a problem.[80]

While unemployment had fallen in the North, it remained persistently high in the South. Unemployment rates in this region were especially high among women and youths. "The lack of working women in the South is mainly a cultural phenomenon," said Enzo Giustino, former vice president of Confindustria. "In the past, it was not even conceived that a woman could work."[81] Despite regional differences in labor demand and cost of living, wages were the same throughout Italy. There were plans to lower wages in the South in an effort to attract investment and boost employment.

Some argued that unemployment statistics were unreliable and did not reflect those employed in the South's black-market economy. Underground workers received low wages and no employment benefits.[82] "There is high unemployment because the system is too generous," explained Vitale. "It is easy to stay on the unemployment list, get your subsidy, and work on the black market. That way people can get two salaries, and they are very happy."[83]

Italy's tax wedge was among the highest of the EU nations [see **Exhibit 10.14b**]. The growth of the tax wedge during the 1990s was believed to have contributed to Italy's high unemployment and lack of competitiveness.[84] Although unit labor costs in the manufacturing industry declined after 1998, Italy's productivity growth still lagged in comparison with that of the EU. Italy's pension system also contributed to the rigidity of the labor market. Generous early-retirement pensions discouraged people over the age of 50 from participating in the workforce. While on-the-job protections were strong, unemployment benefits were less than spectacular. As a result, job mobility among younger workers remained low because of the high value placed on job security.[85]

Unions

After WWII, the labor movement had split into three major trade unions: the Italian General Confederation of Labor (CGIL), representing many communists and socialists; the Italian Confederation of Workers' Unions (CISL), composed mostly of Christian Democrats; and the Italian Union of Labor (UIL), representing Republicans and Social Democrats. During the workers' movement of the 1960s, the unions began to loosen their ties with the political parties and rules were changed so that union leaders could no longer be members of Parliament.[86] Before the collapse of the Christian Democrats, the unions had been aligned with parties of the DC-led coalition. When the coalition fell in 1992, the unions acted together as a single political force that represented over 10 million workers.[87]

Some employers blamed Italy's unions for creating a rigid labor market. The historic *Patto Di Natale* ("Christmas Pact") had been signed on December 15, 1998. The pact formalized the 1992–1997 Concertazione agreements between unions, the government, and business. The labor market grew increasingly rigid as unions were given more negotiating power. Employers found it nearly impossible to hire and fire employees.

"The firing restriction is very frustrating," remarked Franco Tatò, former CEO of ENEL.[88] "If you fire an employee, you end up in court, where the judge can oblige you to rehire a fired employee." Union leaders countered that the labor market was more flexible. "The rules are the same in the North and the South. How can you say the system is too rigid when there is practically full employment in the North?" questioned Sergio D'Antoni, former leader of the CISL.[89]

Bureaucracy

Business leaders complained that Italy's huge public administration and pervasive regulation hindered business development. The government had announced a major restructuring in which the number of ministries would be reduced from 22 to 12 by 2001.[90] The influence of the bureaucracy made it difficult to finance growth, and many companies chose to remain small. "One of the real tragedies of business life in Italy is that the authority's procedure for doing anything is unbelievable. There is terrible difficulty in establishing what you need, how much you need, and who to ask," said Tatò.[91]

Umberto Bossi, the controversial leader of the Northern League Party, believed a move toward federalism would help streamline Italy's highly centralized, bureaucratic government. Backed by Berlusconi, Bossi proposed a series of controversial amendments that would increase the financial power of regional governments. The new laws, which were passed in a referendum in October 2001, entitled regions to establish and collect their own taxes and granted them "financial autonomy in connection with the expenditure of their resources and the determination of their revenues."[92] Critics argued that federalism was a risky solution that could increase the gap between the North and South economies. "Federalism is a new way to avoid fixing the government," commented Corrado Passera, CEO of Banca Intesa.[93]

Privatization

A strong commitment to privatization during the 1990s helped reduce the state's involvement in the economy. From 1993–1999, the Italian government raised about 100 billion euros (€) through its privatization program. Main privatizations included the sale of significant stakes in Banca Nazionale del Lavoro (BNL);

IRI, a holding company; ENEL, the electricity giant; and ENI, an oil and gas behemoth [see **Exhibit 10.15**]. Privatization proceeds helped the government improve Italy's public finances, especially by reducing the debt-to-GDP ratio.

After 1999, the number of privatizations slowed due to a weak stock market and the government's desire to hold on to assets of strategic economic importance.[94] Italy continued to suffer from "an underdevelopment of free-market capitalism."[95] Little competition had been introduced in the utilities, energy, and telecommunications sectors. The government maintained holdings in ENI and ENEL. Telecom Italia continued to monopolize the markets for fixed telephones. A *Financial Times* survey reported that "when it comes to the liberalisation of markets—exposing public and private utilities to competition—the pace of change in Italy has been modest at best."[96] Depending on the health of the stock market, the 2002–2006 Privatization Plan called for the sale of stakes in Telecom Italia, ENEL, Alitalia, ENI, and ETI, a tobacco monopoly.

In the South, privatization of state-owned enterprises disrupted the structure of the economy by removing the foundation upon which it had been built. "Liberalization is getting rid of the state, and the South is not doing well as a result," explained Giustino.[97] "In theory, it is good, but in practice it leads to unemployment and decreased revenues."

Education

In Italy, educational attainment at the secondary and tertiary levels was well below that of other OECD nations [see **Exhibit 10.16**]. In 1998, only 34% of adults between the ages of 25 and 64 had obtained the *maturità* (high school) diploma or an advanced degree.[98] Investment in the education system remained low, and there was a scarcity of schools in the South. At the university level, a focus on trade-specific skills usually excluded the teaching of basic management practices. Business owners complained that there was a lack of science and technology graduates. The mostly public universities suffered from overcrowding due to low admission standards.[99] As a result, many students left Italy to attend universities elsewhere in Europe or the United States. Few returned to Italy to work.

Technology

Italy was slow to adapt to the new digital economy. For years, its export-driven economy had specialized in the manufacturing of low-tech, low-value-added products [see **Exhibit 10.11**]. The country's weak financial markets contributed to an absence of venture capital funds. Poor infrastructure, especially in the South, hampered the development of e-commerce. A 2000 study by the EU revealed that it took an average of 13.2 minutes to place an order on Italy's Internet and an average of 15.7 days to deliver the product, while in the United Kingdom it took 8.4 minutes to make a purchase and 4.1 days to deliver it.[100]

In 2001, the government created the Ministry of Innovation and Technology. The role of the new ministry was to create an e-government program that would increase the transparency and effectiveness of the Italian government. "By interjecting IT systems across other ministries and into local governments and schools, the government will run more efficiently," stated Minister Lucio Stanca of the Ministry for Innovation and Technology.[101]

Globalization

During the 1990s, the growth of total-factor productivity in Italy, which had been higher than the EU average in earlier decades, dropped below that of the large EU nations[102] [see **Exhibit 10.13**]. Italy's declining productivity caused concern that its dual economy could not compete effectively in a global economy. "The industrial structure is too fragmented," explained Paolo Scaroni, CEO of ENEL. "There are very few mergers and not many midsized businesses that could become multinational companies."[103] While industrial districts compensated for a number of weaknesses of small firms, they could not provide the same support as multinational distributors.[104] As a result, Italy's small firms lacked scale efficiencies, access to capital, managerial education, distribution capacity, and significant research and development investment.

The First 100 Days

In October 1998, the Prodi government fell after narrowly losing a vote of confidence. Massimo D'Alema, the leader of the Democratic Left (DS), formed a new government and pledged to continue Prodi's political and economic reform initiatives. However, divisions over policy issues prevented the passage of important reform legislation. After resigning in December 1999, D'Alema formed a second center-left government. The short-lived coalition fell apart in April, and Treasury Minister Giuliano Amato put together a solid center-left coalition that ruled until the June 2001 general election.

Disillusioned by a string of failed center-left governments, Italians voted for Berlusconi and his center-right Casa delle Liberta coalition. Winning a majority in both houses, Berlusconi's coalition defeated Francesco Rutelli and his Olive Tree coalition. "Those who have voted have shown their desire for change," said Berlusconi in his televised victory address. "We will not let them down and will govern with stability for a full five years."[105]

In his "100-day package," Berlusconi proposed immediate changes to Italy's administrative, tax, judiciary, education, and labor laws. By October 2001, Parliament had approved over 50 reforms, including:

- Elimination of 700 administrative laws
- Pardon for black-market economy companies, allowing them to enter the official sector by paying tax and national insurance contributions at reduced rates
- Reintroduction of the Tremonti Law, offering lower corporate tax rates for companies that reinvest profits
- Lower tax rates for low-income families with children
- Abolition of inheritance and gift taxes
- Amnesty for repatriated offshore accounts
- Elimination of required permission to renovate houses
- Introduction of fixed-term employment contracts
- Increase in minimum pensions for those over 70 years old
- Higher salaries for teachers, policemen, and soldiers
- Mandatory education from early kindergarten through age 18 (an increase of two years), language requirement for high school students, and increased computer usage at all schools

At a year-end conference in December, Berlusconi reviewed the success of his reform program. "No other government, in the entire history of the republic, has produced as many measures in its first six months in power," he said. Yet critics argued that the new laws had done little to stimulate growth. "He's tried to reform with lots of little pieces, but so far, he has achieved next to nothing," stated Passera.[106]

Berlusconi's controversial fiscal and labor reform proposals were less successful. During his campaign, Berlusconi had promised to lower income taxes from 43% to 33%. But after discovering hidden deficits for 2001 (as much as $18 billion), the government was forced to postpone the highly anticipated tax cuts. Labor unions opposed Berlusconi's plans to privatize the pension system and amend rigid labor laws. To ease firing restrictions, the government had proposed the suspension of Article 18 of the Workers' Charter. The law gave workers who were employed in companies with over 15 employees the right to be reinstated if they were fired without just cause. However, unions were infuriated when the new plan was announced without mention of its intended purpose: to increase competitiveness and encourage the hiring of new employees. Claiming that the removal of Article 18 violated workers' fundamental rights, the labor unions organized Italy's first general strike in 20 years. On April 16, 2002, more than two million workers gathered in Rome to protest, bringing labor negotiations to a halt.

A Future of Growth?

On July 5, 2002, Berlusconi overcame two legislative battles, jump-starting his reform agenda. After months of heated negotiations, the CISL and UIL unions signed a watered-down labor pact that would ease rigid hiring and firing rules. The Pact for Italy would suspend Article 18 for a three-year trial period. CGIL, the country's largest union, refused to sign the deal on the grounds that it would lead to lower employment. The same day, the cabinet adopted the government's Economic and Financial Planning Document for 2003–2007. The approved budget forecasts included income tax cuts, greater unemployment benefits, a significant public works program, and specific measures to improve infrastructure in the South.[107]

Though dependent on the recovery of the world economy, government projections showed GDP growth of 1.3% for 2002 and 2.9% for 2003 and 2004. Increased public spending and tax cuts totaling €5.5 billion were expected to contribute to budget deficits of 0.8% in 2003 and 0.5% in 2004. According to budget forecasts, a balanced budget would not be achieved until 2005. Meanwhile, the public debt was predicted to fall to 108.5% of GDP in 2002 and 104.5% in 2003.

The European Commission disapproved of Italy's new planning document, since failure to achieve a balanced budget by 2003 would breach the Stability and Growth Pact. Although the EC had prolonged deadlines for France, Germany, and Portugal, it had yet to offer Italy an extension. Threatening to impose sanctions against Italy, Ernst Welteke, president of Bundesbank and a member of the ECB's governing council, explained, "You have to force budget discipline . . . sanctions should be employed when good conditions are not used to reduce debts."[108]

Despite complaints from the EC, Berlusconi was determined to proceed with pension reform, increased public spending, and the biggest tax cut in Italy's history. In his mind, Italy had already achieved sufficient macroeconomic stability. In order for Italy to compete in a global economy, economic growth would have to be the top priority. In the fall, the government would need to submit its stability program to the EC, explaining how the country intended to honor its commitments. Berlusconi, in the meantime, would pressure the EC to change the focus and purpose of the Stability and Growth Pact. "Now we must move to another phase, one which maintains stability but also puts emphasis on growth and flexibility," concluded Finance Minister Giulio Tremonti.[109]

EXHIBIT 10.1   **MAP OF ITALY AND INDUSTRIAL CLUSTERS**

SOURCE: Case writer.

EXHIBIT 10.2   **POPULATION PROJECTIONS, 2010–2050 (MILLIONS OF PEOPLE)**

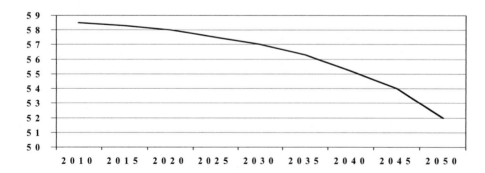

SOURCE: Italian National Statistical Institute (ISTAT).

EXHIBIT 10.3A	GINI INDEX OF CONCENTRATION OF HOUSEHOLDS' DISPOSABLE INCOME IN POST-WAR ITALY

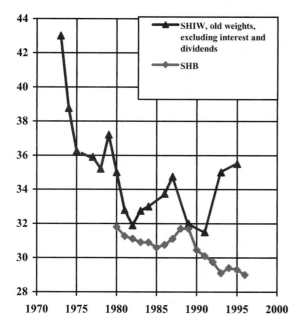

SOURCE: Andrea Brandolini, "The Distribution of Personal Income in Post-War Italy," Bank of Italy, April 1999.

SHIW = Bank of Italy's Survey of Household's Income and Wealth.

SHB = ISTAT's Survey of Household Budgets.

EXHIBIT 10.3B	INCOME INEQUALITY (%)

	First Decile	Second Decile	Third Decile	Fourth Decile	Fifth Decile	Sixth Decile	Seventh Decile	Eighth Decile	Ninth Decile	Tenth Decile
1947a	2.2	3.8	4.9	5.8	6.4	8.1	9.2	11.2	14.2	34.2
1993b	2.0	4.0	6.0	7.0	8.0	9.0	11.0	12.0	16.0	26.0
1994b	2.4	4.7	5.9	7.0	8.2	9.5	11.1	12.9	15.4	22.9

SOURCE: Luzzatto Fegiz (1949, p. 15, Table 2.4); Eurostat (1997, p. 2, Table 1); 1998b, p. 2.

[a]Distribution of Household Incomes by Decile, Doxa Survey, 1947–1948.

[b]Distribution of Post-tax Household Equivalent Incomes: Decile shares, ECHP, 1993–1994.

EXHIBIT 10.4	UNEMPLOYMENT RATES, 2000 (%)

	Italy	Center-North	South	Germany	France	Nether-lands	Spain	United Kingdom	United States	Japan
Total Unemployment	10.7	5.8	21.3	8.1	10.1	3.5	14.1	5.6	4.0	5.0
Youths (15–24)	31.1	16.8	55.0	7.7	20.8	7.0	25.5	11.8	9.3	9.2
Men (25–54)	6.3	3.0	12.9	7.7	8.9	2.5	9.2	5.6	3.3	4.7
Women (25–54)	12.1	7.0	26.0	9.0	13.0	4.2	20.5	4.7	3.8	5.4
Older (55–64)	4.4	2.9	7.3	11.4	7.6	2.7	9.0	4.3	2.5	4.7

SOURCE: OECD, ISTAT

EXHIBIT 10.5   HISTORICAL SUMMARY, 1989–2002

	1989	1990	1991	1992	1993	1994	1995	1996	1997	1998	1999	2000	2001	2002
GDP and Components														
Nominal GDP (bil Euro)	795	867	936	948	848	863	839	971	1,029	1,068	1,108	1,165	1,217	1,271
Real GDP (bil Euro, 1995 prices)	776	793	802	807	798	815	839	848	865	881	895	920	937	952
Real GDP growth rate (%)	2.9	2.2	1.1	0.6	-1.2	2.2	2.9	1.1	2.0	1.8	1.6	2.9	1.8	1.7
GDP per capita (USD at PPP)	14,875	15,825	17,342	18,278	17,876	18,834	20,100	20,943	21,061	22,277	23,353	24,470	25,450	26,360
Private Consumption (% of GDP)	58.0	57.4	57.8	58.6	58.2	58.5	58.3	57.9	58.5	59.0	59.7	60.0	59.7	59
Government Consumption (% of GDP)	19.2	20.1	20.1	20.2	20.2	19.6	18.3	18.5	18.6	18.4	18.5	18.7	18.9	18.8
Gross Fixed Investment (% of GDP)	21.9	21.9	21.4	20.7	18.3	18.0	18.3	18.3	18.3	18.5	19.1	19.8	19.8	20.1
Stockbuilding (% of GDP)	1.1	0.5	0.6	0.3	-0.2	0.5	1.0	0.3	0.6	0.8	0.6	0.5	-0.1	0.2
Exports (% of GDP)	20.1	20.1	18.8	19.2	22.4	23.9	27.0	25.8	26.4	26.4	25.5	28.4	28.3	28.3
Imports (% of GDP)	-20.3	-20.0	-18.8	-19.0	-18.9	-20.4	-23.0	-20.9	-22.3	-22.9	-23.5	-27.4	-26.7	-26.3
Prices, Wages, and Other														
Consumer Price Index (% change)	6.3	6.5	6.3	5.1	4.5	4.0	5.2	4.0	2.1	1.9	1.7	2.5	2.8	2.2
Nominal Average Wages (% change)	6.0	7.3	9.7	5.4	3.7	3.4	3.1	3.1	3.8	3.0	1.8	2.0	1.9	2.6
Nominal Unit Labor Costs (% change)	1.0	22.8	4.3	3.3	-20.0	-5.7	-3.9	10.0	-10.1	1.4	-2.0	-15.8	-0.8	2.8
Gross National Saving (% GDP)	21.5	21.0	19.9	18.6	18.9	19.8	21.6	21.9	21.6	21.0	20.5	19.8	19.9	20.0
Population (millions)	n/a	n/a	n/a	56.9	57	57.3	57.4	57.4	57.4	57.6	57.5	57.5	57.5	57.5
Population Growth Rate (%)	n/a	n/a	n/a	0.2	0.3	0.4	0.1	0.0	0.1	0.4	-0.3	0.1	0.0	0.0
Labor Force Participation Rate (%)	n/a	n/a	n/a	n/a	n/a	n/a	n/a	57.7	57.9	58.7	59.3	59.9	60.4	n/a
Recorded Unemployment Rate (%)	9.7	8.9	8.5	8.8	10.1	11.0	11.5	11.5	11.7	11.6	11.2	10.4	9.5	9.4
Financial Indicators														
Government Expenditure (% of GDP)	50.3	52.9	54.0	53.2	55.4	52.7	51.1	51.3	48.5	47.3	46.7	44.4	45.3	45.3
M2 (bil Euro)	n/a	n/a	n/a	n/a	n/a	n/a	n/a	n/a	599	619	651	665	639	658
M2 growth rate (%)	n/a	n/a	n/a	n/a	n/a	n/a	n/a	n/a	n/a	3.2	5.1	2.3	-4.0	3.0
3-Month T-Bill Rate (%)	12.7	12.3	12.7	14.5	10.5	8.8	10.7	8.6	6.4	5.0	2.7	4.1	4.1	n/a

SOURCE: EIU Country Data.

Italics = Estimates; n/a = not available.

EXHIBIT 10.6A BALANCE OF PAYMENTS, 1989–2001 ($ MILLIONS)

	1989	1990	1991	1992	1993	1994	1995	1996	1997	1998	1999	2000	2001
Current account balance	-10,886	-12,733	-21,432	-29,217	7,802	13,209	25,076	39,999	32,403	19,998	8,111	-5,670	1,591
Trade balance	-2,167	723	-896	-200	28,889	31,568	38,729	54,118	39,878	35,631	23,437	10,717	17,813
Exports of goods	140,118	169,940	168,790	178,155	169,153	191,421	233,998	252,039	240,404	242,572	235,856	238,736	242,292
Imports of goods	-142,285	-169,216	-169,086	-178,355	-140,624	-159,854	-195,269	-197,921	-200,527	-206,941	-212,420	-228,019	-224,480
Net services	1,978	2,831	3,070	411	3,345	5,443	6,569	8,055	7,764	4,170	1,081	-56	-32
Services—credit	33,863	35,649	51,675	58,545	52,284	53,681	61,619	65,660	66,991	67,549	58,788	56,116	59,580
Services—debit	-31,885	-32,818	-48,605	-58,134	-48,939	-48,238	-55,050	-57,605	-59,227	-63,379	-57,707	-56,172	-59,612
Net income	-8,467	-13,908	-17,576	-21,887	-17,218	-16,690	-15,644	-14,959	-11,202	-12,317	-11,050	-12,004	-10,933
Income—credit	14,867	21,685	25,157	28,757	31,844	28,599	34,168	40,142	45,734	51,319	46,361	38,763	38,763
Income—debit	-23,334	-35,593	-42,733	-50,644	-49,062	-45,289	-49,812	-55,101	-56,936	-63,636	-57,411	-50,677	-48,928
Net transfers	n/a	n/a	n/a	-7,541	-7,215	-7,112	-4,579	-7,215	-4,036	-7,485	-5,356	-4,328	-5,257
Capital account balance	24,552	38,885	24,084	12,357	6,919	-13,182	-1,218	-7,916	-3,444	-15,716	-14,451	10,384	-2,546
Net direct investment	n/a	n/a	n/a	-1,043	-3,580	-3,040	-2,182	-5,151	-6,714	-9,772	220	1,100	1,211
Direct investment outflows	n/a	n/a	n/a	-4,148	-7,329	-5,239	-7,024	-8,697	-10,414	-12,407	-6,723	-12,075	-13,814
Direct investment inflows	n/a	n/a	n/a	3,105	3,749	2,199	4,842	3,546	3,700	2,635	6,943	13,175	15,025
Net portfolio investment	3,256	-394	-6,170	8,155	74,064	-7,108	40,872	49,320	11,674	3,114	-25,017	-23,243	-7,125
Portfolio investment assets	n/a	n/a	n/a	-16,975	12,178	-37,631	-5,790	-26,607	-62,975	-109,913	-129,624	-80,262	-33,836
Portfolio investment liabilities	n/a	n/a	n/a	25,130	61,886	30,523	46,662	75,927	74,649	113,027	104,607	57,019	26,711
Other investment assets	n/a	n/a	n/a	-28,863	-44,197	2,092	-28,947	-68,358	-25,541	-21,232	-33,573	241	-15,308
Other investment liabilities	n/a	n/a	n/a	33,301	-21,027	-6,152	-12,632	16,206	13,703	9,816	39,085	27,077	18,275
Other capital movements	n/a	n/a	n/a	807	1,659	1,026	1,671	66	3,434	2,358	4,834	5,209	2,823
Errors & Omissions	-2,552	-15,764	-9,059	-7,132	-17,856	1,547	-21,054	-20,176	-15,810	-25,754	-1,711	-1,466	364
Change in reserves[a]	-11,114	-10,388	6,407	23,992	3,135	-1,575	-2,804	-11,907	-13,150	21,472	8,051	-3,248	-591

SOURCE: *International Financial Statistics Yearbook*, International Monetary Fund 2000, 2001, July 2002.

[a] Negative sign indicates an increase.

EXHIBIT 10.6B | FOREIGN DIRECT INVESMENT INFLOWS, 1995–2000 (% OF GDP)

	1995	1996	1997	1998	1999	2000
Finland	0.82	0.87	1.73	9.41	3.59	7.31
France	1.52	1.41	1.65	2.13	3.27	3.41
Germany	0.56	0.24	0.58	1.13	2.66	9.44
Ireland	0.57	0.79	0.73	10.28	19.50	21.73
Italy	**0.44**	**0.29**	**0.43**	**0.36**	**0.59**	**1.25**
Netherlands	2.96	4.04	2.95	9.40	10.38	14.69
Portugal	0.61	1.32	2.33	2.82	0.99	5.89
Spain	1.08	1.12	1.14	2.01	2.62	6.53
United Kingdom	1.92	2.30	2.81	5.24	6.01	9.00

SOURCE: OECD.

| EXHIBIT 10.7 | GENERAL GOVERNMENT FINANCES, 1992–2001 |

	1992	1993	1994	1995	1996	1997	1998	1999	2000	2001
	billions of lire								*millions of euros*	
Revenue	698,893	749,454	748,812	814,468	871,073	955,235	962,623	998,503	515,683	534,628	557,203
Current revenue	665,110	735,339	741,239	799,132	862,814	935,628	948,233	987,719	510,114	529,523	553,959
Direct taxes	221,506	250,835	244,854	263,494	290,923	318,466	296,914	321,587	166,086	170,440	183,348
Indirect taxes	167,660	186,611	192,173	215,935	224,852	247,286	318,303	326,421	168,582	175,160	176,722
Social contributions	226,188	240,615	244,267	263,809	286,166	304,631	266,65	270,819	139,867	148,074	154,519
Income from capital	9,412	9,177	8,516	10,921	11,728	12,507	11,455	14,217	7,342	5,599	6,095
Other	40,344	48,101	51,429	44,973	49,145	52,738	54,896	54,675	28,237	30,250	32,775
Capital revenue	33,783	14,115	7,573	15,336	8,259	19,607	14,390	10,784	5,569	5,105	3,244
Expenditure	842,547	896,373	898,962	950,164	1,006,120	1,008,953	1,020,967	1,039,014	536,606	540,891	574,817
Current expenditure	772,376	819,456	831,148	867,179	933,834	938,692	943,014	955,321	493,382	511,432	533,057
Compensation of employees	190,248	193,121	197,446	200,521	218,559	229,935	221,571	227,262	117,371	122,810	129,028
Intermediate consumption	75,608	79,923	82,371	120,962	128,908	134,675	141,820	150,803	77,883	59,276	61,720
Social services	290,578	302,873	319,464	298,752	320,665	344,137	351,185	370,367	191,279	221,274	231,217
Subsidies to firms	27,032	33,915	32,864	26,256	28,251	24,286	27,539	28,038	14,480	13,923	13,950
Interest payments	172,662	187,800	179,927	205,991	218,701	186,509	167,552	145,726	75,261	75,265	77,111
Other	16,288	21,824	19,076	14,697	18,750	19,150	33,347	33,125	17,108	18,884	20,031
Capital expenditure	70,171	76,917	67,814	82,985	72,286	70,261	77,953	83,693	43,224	29,459	41,760
Gross investment	45,538	41,049	37,855	38,109	42,111	44,557	49,795	54,301	28,044	28,021	27,122
Investment grants	23,410	26,616	24,387	22,700	23,040	17,253	19,155	20,815	10,750	13,090	15,607
Other	1,223	9,252	5,572	22,106	7,135	8,451	9,003	8,577	4,430	-11,652	-969
Government Deficit	-143,654	-146,919	-150,150	-135,696	-135,047	-53,718	-58,344	-40,511	-20,922	-6,263	-17,614
Government Deficit (% of GDP)	-9.6	-9.5	-9.2	-8.6	-7.1	-2.7	-2.8	-1.8	-1.8	-0.5	-1.4
Government Debt (% of GDP)	124.9	124.2	123.8	123.2	122.5	120.3	116.8	115.1	110.5	107.5	104.3

SOURCE: *Annual Reports*, Bank of Italy, 1999–2001.

EXHIBIT 10.8 REAL GDP GROWTH IN ITALY VS. THE EURO AREA, 1995–2001 (% CHANGE OVER PREVIOUS SEMESTER)

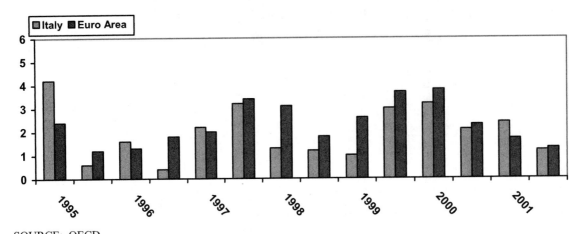

SOURCE: OECD.

EXHIBIT 10.9 BOLOGNA AUTOMATIC PACKAGING MACHINERY DISTRICT

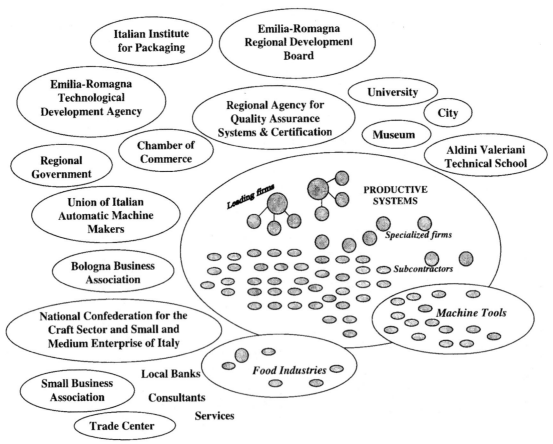

SOURCE: "The Italian SME Experience and Its Transferability to Developing Countries," UNIDO/NOMISMA and United Nations Industrial Development Organization, August 1996.

EXHIBIT 10.10   ECONOMIC POWER

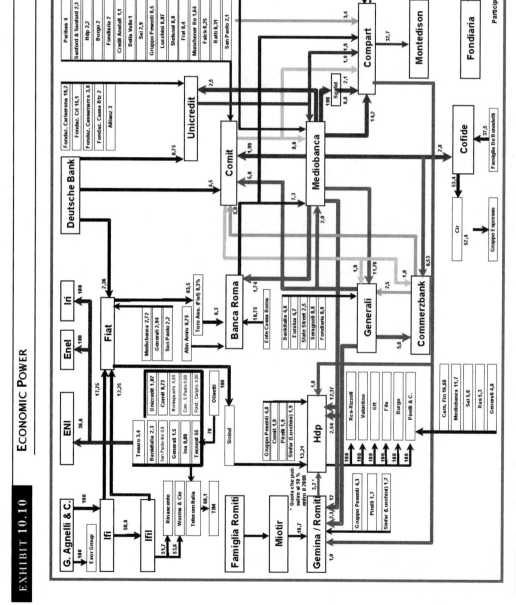

Participation is in % of capital

SOURCE: Fernando Napolitano, vice president and managing partner of Booz Allen Hamilton Italia.

| EXHIBIT 10.11 | IMPORTS AND EXPORTS BY ACTIVITY SECTOR, 1999–2000 (% VOLUMES) |

	Imports		Exports	
	1999	2000	1999	2000
Agriculture & fishing	4.2%	3.5%	1.7%	1.5%
Energetic ores	6.5%	10.7%	0.0%	0.0%
Non-energetic ores	0.8%	0.9%	0.2%	0.2%
Food, beverages & tobacco	7.5%	6.6%	5.5%	5.0%
Textiles & clothing	5.2%	4.9%	10.6%	10.3%
Leather & leather products	1.9%	2.1%	5.0%	5.1%
Wood and wood products	1.4%	1.3%	0.6%	0.6%
Paper products & publishing	3.0%	2.8%	2.3%	2.3%
Refined oil products	1.5%	2.1%	1.2%	2.0%
Chemicals & artificial fibers	13.6%	12.9%	8.8%	9.3%
Rubber & plastics	2.3%	2.1%	3.7%	3.6%
Non-metallic ore products	1.2%	1.1%	3.8%	3.5%
Metals & metal products	9.8%	10.2%	7.9%	8.1%
Machinery & mechanical equipment	8.5%	7.8%	20.4%	19.5%
Electric & precision instruments	15.0%	14.8%	9.8%	10.1%
Transportation means	15.0%	13.6%	11.4%	11.6%
Other manufactured products	1.7%	1.6%	6.7%	6.7%
Electric power, gas and water	0.7%	0.6%	0.0%	0.0%
Other products	0.1%	0.4%	0.5%	0.6%
Total (billions lire at current prices)	**400,837**	**495,499**	**427,994**	**498,201**

SOURCE: ISTAT.

| EXHIBIT 10.12 | ITALIAN GOVERNMENTS, 1989–2001 |

Prime Minister	Coalition (Major Parties)	Political Alignment	Begin	End
Giulio Andreotti	DC,PSI,PSDI,PLI	center-left	22-Jul-89	29-Mar-91
Giulio Andreotti	DC,PSI,PSDI,PLI	center-left	14-Apr-91	24-Apr-92
Giuliano Amato	PSI,PSDI,PLI	tecnici	28-Jun-92	28-Apr-93
Carlo Azeglio Ciampi	PSI, PSDI, PLI	tecnici	28-Apr-93	16-Apr-94
Silvio Berlusconi	Polo per le Liberta: Forza Italia, Lega Nord, AN, CCD	center-right	10-May-94	22-Dec-94
Lamberto Dini	PDS,PPI, AD, Lega Nord, Greens	tecnici, center-left	17-Jan-95	11-Jan-96
Romano Prodi	Ulivo: PDS,RC, PPI, I Verdi, Rinnovamento Italiano	center-left	17-May-96	09-Oct-98
Massimo D'Alema	Ulivo: PDS, PPI,UDR, PDCI	center-left	21-Oct-98	18-Dec-99
Massimo D'Alema	Ulivo: DS, PPI, Democratici per l'Ulivo, RI, I Verdi	center-left	22-Dec-99	19-April-00
Giuliano Amato	Ulivo: DS, PPI, Democratici per l'Ulivo, RI, SDI, PDCI, Udeur, I Verdi	center-left	25-April-00	11-June-01
Silvio Berlusconi	Casa delle Liberta : Forza Italia, AN, Lega Nord, CCD, CDU	center-right	11-June-01	To date

SOURCE: Case writer.

EXHIBIT 10.13	**INDEX OF TOTAL-FACTOR PRODUCTIVITY, 1964–2001 (INDICES, 1995=100; % CHANGE ON PREVIOUS YEAR)**

	Italy		U.S.A.		Germany		France	
	Index	**%**	**Index**	**%**	**Index**	**%**	**Index**	**%**
1964	66.37	-0.55	78.3	3.18	90.46	0.80	56.33	5.90
1980	88.71	1.09	85.0	-2.29	98.42	-1.65	85.71	0.09
1989	96.39	1.54	94.57	1.39	105.06	1.74	97.19	2.51
1990	96.13	-0.27	94.62	0.05	107.89	2.69	98.05	0.88
1991	95.61	-0.54	94.03	-0.62	96.10	-10.93	98.03	-0.02
1992	95.48	-0.14	96.23	2.34	98.17	2.15	98.97	0.96
1993	95.34	-0.15	97.28	1.09	97.01	-1.18	98.13	-0.85
1994	97.7	2.48	99.16	1.93	98.86	1.91	99.37	1.26
1995	100.0	2.35	100.0	0.85	100.0	1.15	100.0	0.63
1996	99.6	-0.40	101.72	1.72	100.61	0.61	100.42	0.42
1997	101.1	0.50	103.49	1.74	102.07	1.45	101.43	1.01
1998	99.79	-0.31	105.74	2.17	103.37	1.27	103.39	1.93
1999	99.22	-0.57	107.8	1.95	103.98	0.59	104.2	0.78
2000[a]	99.98	0.77	110.17	2.20	106.06	2.00	105.53	1.28
2001[b]	101.0	1.05	111.17	0.91	108.02	1.85	106.19	0.63

SOURCE: OECD; Datastream.

[a]projection; [b]forecast

EXHIBIT 10.14A	**INCOME TAXES (TAX AS % OF GDP)**

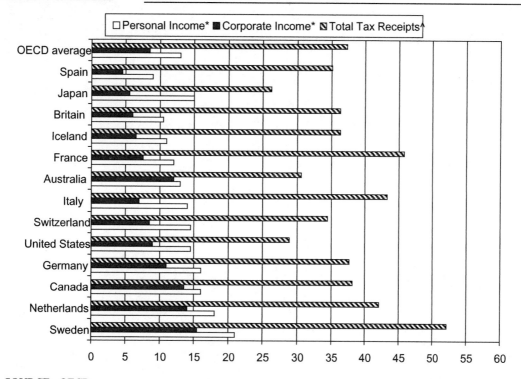

SOURCE: OECD.

*1997 data; ^1999 data

| EXHIBIT 10.14B | TAX WEDGE (2000)[a] AND IMPLICIT TAX RATE ON CONSUMPTION (1996)[b] |

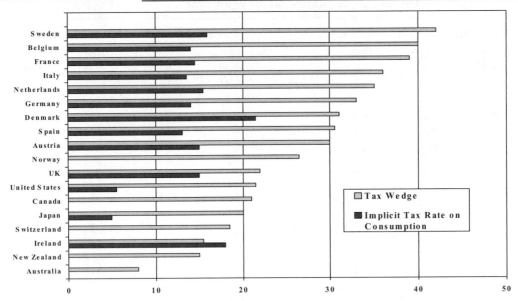

SOURCE: European Commission Services estimates.

[a] Income tax plus employee and employer social security contributions minus cash benefits, as % of labor costs (one-earner family with two children).

[b] Data unavailable for five countries.

EXHIBIT 10.15	MAIN PRIVATIZATIONS IN THE 1990S

Year	Corporation	Percentage Sold	Gross Proceeds in Billions of Lire
1993	Credito Italiano	58.09	1,801.10
	Other		951.80
1994	IMI—1st tranche	32.89	1,794.00
	COMIT (IRI)	54.35	2,891.20
	INA—1st tranche	47.25	4,530.00
	Other		3,133.00
1995	Italtel (IRI)	40.00	1,000.00
	Ilva Laminati Piani (IRI)	100.00	2,514.00
	IMI—2nd tranche	19.03	913.00
	INA—2nd tranche	18.37	1,687.00
	ENI—1st tranche	15.00	6,299.00
	Other		1,347.40
1996	Nuova Tirrena	91.14	548.00
	INA—3rd tranche	31.08	4,200.00
	IMI—3rd tranche	6.94	501.20
	ENI—2nd tranche	15.82	8,872.00
	Other		870.00
1997	ENI—3rd tranche	17.60	13,231.00
	Telecom Italia	39.54	22,883.00
	SEAT editoria	61.27	1,653.00
	Banca di Roma (IRI)	36.50	1,898.00
	Other		880.00
1998	SAIPEM (ENI)	18.75	1,140.00
	ENI—4th tranche	14.83	12,995.00
	BNL	67.85	6,707.00
1999	ENEL	31.70	32,045.00
	Autostrade (IRI)	82.40	13,016.00
	Mediocredito Centrale	100.00	3,944.00
	Other		141.00
2000	Aeroporti di Roma	51.20	2,569.00
	Finmeccanica	43.70	10,660.00
	Other		2,132.00
Total Proceeds :			169,746.70

SOURCE: "Regulatory Reform in Italy," OECD, 2001.

EXHIBIT 10.16	EDUCATIONAL ATTAINMENT IN 1999 (% OF POPULATION)

	Upper Secondary					Tertiary (Type A & Advanced Research)				
	25–64	25–34	35–44	45–54	55–64	25–64	25–34	35–44	45–54	55–64
France	62	76	65	56	42	11	15	10	10	7
Germany	81	85	85	81	73	13	13	15	14	10
Italy	42	55	50	37	21	9	10	11	10	5
Japan	81	93	92	79	60	18	23	25	16	9
Spain	35	55	41	25	13	15	22	16	12	7
United Kingdom	62	66	63	60	53	17	19	17	16	12
United States	87	88	88	88	81	27	29	27	30	23

SOURCE: OECD.

ENDNOTES

1 Interview with Prime Minister Silvio Berlusconi, June 2002.

2 Fernando Napolitano, vice president and managing partner of Booz Allen Hamilton Italia, arranged interviews with Italian government officials and business leaders that were essential to the development of this case.

3 Interview with Berlusconi, February 2000.

4 Interview with Berlusconi, June 2002.

5 "He's Not Safe Yet," *The Economist*, January 17, 2002.

6 Interview with Berlusconi, June 2002.

7 "Background Notes: Italy," U.S. Department of State, Bureau of European Affairs, October 1999.

8 *1998 Report Synthesis*, ISTAT.

9 Interview with Kristien Michoel, project manager at NOMISMA, February 2000.

10 Interview with Ambassador Sergio Romano, historian and journalist, February 2000.

11 "Key Provisions of Italy's Anti-Immigration Legislation," *Agence France-Presse*, May 29, 2002.

12 Fred Kapner, "Rome Tries to Balance Pension Reform with Popular Demands," *Financial Times*, July 2, 2002.

13 Interview with Professor Dino Piero Giarda, undersecretary of state, Treasury Ministry, February 2000.

14 *Annual Report 1998*, Bank of Italy, p. 117.

15 Kapner.

16 Andrea Brandolini, "The Distribution of Personal Income in Post-War Italy: Source Description, Data Quality, and the Time Pattern of Income Inequality," Bank of Italy, April 1999.

17 Interview with Fernando Napolitano, vice president and managing partner of Booz Allen Hamilton Italia.

18 Mario B. Mignone, *Italy Today: At the Crossroads of the New Millenium* (New York: Peter Lang Publishing, 1998).

19 "Background Notes: Italy," U.S. Department of State, Bureau of European Affairs, October 1999.

20 Hilary Partridge, *Italian Politics Today* (Manchester: Manchester University Press, 1998).

21 Ibid.

22 Interview with Mario Carlo Ferrario, president of Redifin, February 2000.

23 Partridge, p. 10.

24 Ibid., p. 67.

25 Ibid., p. 21.

26 Mignone, p. 144.

27 Interview with Napolitano, February 2000.

28 Mignone, p 147.

29 "Windows on Italy: The History," Embassy of Italy in the United States.

30 Partridge, p. 102.

31 Mignone, p. 155.

32 Partridge, p. 81.

33 "EIU Country Profile: Italy 1999–2000," *The Economist Intelligence Unit*.

34 Interview with Berlusconi, February 2000.

35 Interview with Ferrario, February 2000.

36 Interview with Berlusconi, February 2000.

37 Mignone, p. 149.

38 "EIU Country Profile: Italy 1999–2000," *The Economist Intelligence Unit*.

39 "Italy's Slow Growth in the 1990s: Facts, Explanations, and Prospects," European Commission, Office for Official Publications, 1999.

40 "EIU Country Profile: Italy 1999–2000," *The Economist Intelligence Unit*.

41 Mignone, p. 167.

42 "EIU Country Profile: Italy 1999–2000," *The Economist Intelligence Unit*.

43 Lisa Bannon, "Italy's Privatization Plan Outlines Sweeping Changes," *The Wall Street Journal Europe*, November 16, 1992, p. 2.

44 Partridge, p. 77.

45 Interview with Romano, February 2000.

46 "EIU Country Profile: Italy 1999–2000," *The Economist Intelligence Unit*.

47 Interview with Berlusconi, February 2000.

48 Partridge, p. 160.

49 Partridge, p. 157.

50 "EIU Country Profile: Italy 1999–2000," *The Economist Intelligence Unit.*

51 Ibid.

52 Mignone, p. 149.

53 Ibid., p. 150.

54 Italian Institute for Foreign Trade, "Spotlighting Italy: Focus on Clusters," *The Economist,* February 5, 2000.

55 Ibid.

56 "The Italian SME Experience and Its Transferability to Developing Countries," UNIDO/NOMISMA and United Nations Industrial Development Organization, August 1996.

57 Michael E. Porter, *The Competitive Advantage of Nations* (New York: Free Press, 1980).

58 Ibid., p. 437.

59 "The Italian SME Experience and Its Transferability to Developing Countries," UNIDO/NOMISMA and United Nations Industrial Development Organization, August 1996.

60 Interview with Gucci managers, February 2000.

61 Interviews with Alberto Vacchi, managing director of IMA S.p.A., and Giuseppe Bussolari, director of the Tea Division at IMA S.p.A, February 2000.

62 "The Italian SME Experience and Its Transferability to Developing Countries," UNIDO/NOMISMA and United Nations Industrial Development Organization, August 1996.

63 Porter, p. 443.

64 "EIU Country Profile, 2001," *The Economist Intelligence Unit.*

65 "Italy's Slow Growth in the 1990s: Facts, Explanations, and Prospects," European Commission, 1999.

66 Interview with Elio Catania, CEO of IBM Italia, February 2000.

67 Personal interview with Renato Ruggiero, vice chairman of Salomon Smith Barney and former president of the World Trade Organization, February 2000.

68 Interview with Maurizio Sella, chairman of the Associazione Bancaria Italiani, June 2002.

69 Interviews with Diana Bracco, CEO of Bracco Pharmaceuticals, and Elio Catania, CEO of IBM, February 2000.

70 Interview with Fedele Confalonieri, president of Mediaset, February 2000.

71 Interview with Guido Roberto Vitale, former head of Lazard, Vitale, and Borghese, February 2000.

72 Interview with Ferrario, February 2000.

73 Interview with Pier Giorgio Romiti, CEO of Impregilo S.p.A., February 2000.

74 Forza Italia Press Office.

75 "The Governor's Concluding Remarks at the Ordinary General Meeting of Shareholders," Banca D'Italia, May 31, 2001.

76 "EIU Country Profile, 2001," *The Economist Intelligence Unit.*

77 "EIU Country Profile: Italy, 1999–2000," *The Economist Intelligence Unit.*

78 "Italy's Slow Growth in the 1990s: Facts, Explanations, and Prospects," European Commission, 1999.

79 *Economic Bulletin- No. 28,* Bank of Italy, February 1999.

80 *Eurostatistics Yearbook, 1999,* European Commission.

81 Interview with Enzo Giustino, vice president of Confindustria, South Italy, February 2000.

82 "Background Notes: Italy," U.S. Department of State, Bureau of European Affairs, October 1999.

83 Interview with Vitale, February 2000.

84 *Annual Report 1998,* Bank of Italy, p. 107.

85 "EIU Country Forecast, 2000," *The Economist Intelligence Unit.*

86 Partridge, p. 98.

87 Interview with Napolitano, February 2000.

88 Interview with Franco Tatò, former CEO of ENEL, February 2000.

89 Interview with Sergio D'Antoni, former leader of CISL, February 2000.

90 Interview with Vincenzo Maria Vita, former undersecretary of state for the Ministry of Communications, February 2000.

91 Interview with Tatò, February 2000.

92 "Federalism in Italy: What Are the Changes for Regions?" *International Financial Law Review,* December 1, 2001.

93 Interview with Corrado Passera, CEO of Banca Intesa, June 2002.

94   "EIU Country Report: Italy, April 2002," *The Economist Intelligence Unit.*

95   "Italy: Review 1999," *Europe Review World of Information*, November 11, 1999.

96   James Blitz, "Chipping away at Tip of Institutionalised Icebergs," *Financial Times Survey: Italian Industry & Finance*, December 16, 1998.

97   Interview with Giustino, February 2000.

98   *Annuario Statistico Italiano 1999*, ISTAT, and interview with Paola Vaglica, Booz Allen Hamilton Italia.

99   "EIU Country Profile : Italy, 2001," *The Economist Intelligence Unit.*

100 "Italy: Race to Reduce the 'Net Lag,'" *Financial Times*, February 1, 2000.

101 Interview with Minister Lucio Stanca, Ministry for Innovation and Technology, June 2002.

102 *Policy Brief: Economic Survey of Italy, 2001*, OECD, January 2002.

103 Interview with Paolo Scaroni, CEO of ENEL, June 2002.

104 Interview with Passera, June 2002.

105 "Victorious Berlusconi Says Stability Is Priority," *The Independent*, June 15, 2001.

106 Interview with Passera, June 2002.

107 "Italy Government Aims for 2003 Deficit of 0.8 Pct of GDP, O.5 Pct in 2004," *AFX News*, July 7, 2002.

108 "Solbes Warns Portugal, France, Italy and Germany on Public Debt," *Agence France-Presse*, July 10, 2002.

109 "Italy's Tremonti Wants Stability Pact Overhaul," *Dow Jones Newswires*, June 25, 2002.

The Limits of Managed Growth

After growing at 10.1% annually for 17 years prior to 1971, Japan finally staggered in the face of oil shocks, Nixon shocks, and *"endaka"* (era of high yen). With Japan's resource costs rising sharply at the same time as did the value of the yen, remaining competitive internationally was an immense challenge. Yet the Japanese rose to that challenge, growing at 4.1% annually for another two decades until finally sinking into a deep, lasting recession.

This case deals with the stagnation of Japan after 1991. Since then, Japan has had four recessions and has managed growth of barely one percent annually. What has gone wrong? The case tries to provide the facts necessary for students to consider the reasons for stagnation. What is wrong with monetary policy? With fiscal policy? With crucial institutions, such as MITI and the Ministry of Finance? And what are the problems with labor relations, with education, with corporate governance, and with pension obligations? Why won't the Japanese spend more, and how is deflation affecting them?

Two governments have offered substantial plans for structural adjustment. First, the Hashimoto government in 1996 offered "Free, Fair and Global," a five part plan for structural adjustment. While some parts were eventually implemented, Hashimoto left office and Japan has not recovered. More recently, Junichiro Koizumi has offered to re-engage reform, but thus far, to little avail.

Students are asked to consider the causes of Japan's problems, to assess reforms, and to consider whether or not the conditions can persist much longer, in a global economy that continues to evolve.

JAPAN: BEYOND THE BUBBLE

RICHARD H. K. VIETOR

REBECCA EVANS

Since the 1990s the Japanese economy has struggled for a long time, people have lost faith in politics and there is an air of stagnation in the society. It is becoming clear that the system that worked in the past may not necessarily be suited to 21st century society.
—Prime Minister Junichiro Koizumi

Introduction

Following his party's victory in the June 2001 Tokyo municipal elections, Prime Minister Junichiro Koizumi unveiled a bold economic reform strategy aiming to bolster Japan's flagging economy. In late April, the ruling Liberal Democrat Party (LDP) had appointed Koizumi prime minister following the resignation of the highly unpopular Yoshiro Mori. Koizumi's unprecedented 85% public approval rating had given the LDP a much-needed boost. After its overwhelming success in the municipal elections, the LDP anticipated another victory in the July upper-house elections. Still, nobody knew if Koizumi's popularity would be short-lived, given that Japan's economy was slipping back into recession. In order to secure his job and restore the nation's economic glory, the self-proclaimed reformer needed to rescue the economy from the stagnation that had plagued Japan for over a decade.

Breaking with tradition, Koizumi announced his cabinet appointees without first consulting with party leaders. He chose Heizo Takenaka as Economics Minister and Makiko Tanaka, one of five female appointees, as Foreign Minister. Financial Affairs Minister Jakuo Yanagisawa was one of seven ministers retained from the Mori administration.

Over the last twelve years, eleven different prime ministers had governed Japan. Following the LDP's poor performance in the upper-house elections of July 1998, Ryutaro Hashimoto resigned as prime minister. The LDP chose Foreign Minister Keizo Obuchi as his successor. After implementing a series of fiscal stimulus packages that failed to jump-start Japan's ailing economy, Obuchi suffered a stroke and was hospitalized. At a backroom meeting in April 2000, LDP party leaders handpicked Yoshiro Mori as the country's next prime minister. The Mori administration drew criticism for its numerous corruption scandals and weak economic policies. As the LDP's popularity waned, party leaders urged Mori to step down, but Mori resisted. Finally, after the New Komeito and New Conservative Party threatened to withdraw from their coalition with the LDP, Mori agreed to resign.

Like his predecessors, Koizumi faced the daunting task of instituting structural reform in order to stimulate economic growth. The collapse of Japan's "bubble economy" in 1990 and 1991 had thoroughly deflated asset and land prices, and few companies had been able to restore profitability to anything like western levels. Over the following decade, Japan's economy remained in the doldrums, as the government futilely attempted to restore growth both through monetary and fiscal stimulus. Since the collapse of the asset bubble, the government had introduced ten fiscal stimulus packages worth ¥100trn. [See **Exhibit 11.15**.] However, heavy fiscal spending had failed to produce self-sustaining growth and contributed, instead, to a debt of almost 140% of GDP. As a result, Japan boasted the highest public-debt burden of the 29 members of the Organisation for Economic Co-Operation and Development (OECD).

Fruits of the Miracle

Although the Japanese economic miracle ended in 1971, the country reaped the benefits of its rapid growth for the next two decades, despite severe supply-side shocks. Reinvestment and productivity made Japan's export business incredibly efficient. The nation was able to

---

Research Associate Rebecca Evans prepared this case under the supervision of Professor Richard H. K. Vietor. It is a substantially revised version of HBS No. 798-083 prepared by Research Associate Stephen Lynaugh under the supervision of Professor Richard H. K. Vietor. HBS cases are developed solely as the basis for class discussion. Cases are not intended to serve as endorsements, sources of primary data, or illustrations of effective or ineffective management.

achieve its goal of catching the United States—surpassing the United States in GDP per capita by 1989 (although purchasing power was still only 72% that in the United States). [See **Exhibit 11.1a**.]

Continued Economic Growth

At an average annual rate of 4.4%, economic growth from 1971 to 1991 was consistently strong. In only four of those years did the rate drop below 3%, generally when some sort of shock was experienced. These shocks demonstrated both the exposure of Japan's system and its ability to make economic reforms. (Details of Japan's growth and spending are in **Exhibits 11.1 to 11.7**.)

Nixon shocks On August 15, 1971, U.S. President Richard Nixon ended the Bretton Woods system of fixed exchange rates, in effect since 1944. Under that agreement, the price of gold was fixed to the U.S. dollar, at $35 per ounce. All other currencies were pegged to the dollar; for Japan, the rate was ¥360/$1. When Nixon made his announcement, the dollar dropped and the yen rose to ¥308/$1. Nixon also imposed a 10% surcharge on imports, trying to push the Japanese into opening their markets.[1]

Within a year, President Nixon visited China. The Japanese were again caught unaware by this sudden realignment of world powers and were embarrassed by their lack of foreknowledge. The event reinforced Japanese sensitivity to their limited political connections in Washington and their overdependence on the United States.[2]

Oil shocks Late in 1973, the first oil shock hit the world, as OPEC countries enforced an oil embargo and quadrupled prices. Japan, which relied almost exclusively on imported oil, was forced to pay significantly more. Inflation skyrocketed in 1974, imports rose by 40%, and growth vanished. After a year, trade was back in balance, and Japan took advantage of the gap created between the ¥/$ exchange rate and the country's purchasing power parity (PPP) based on export prices. The following years saw big trade surpluses as Japan continued to pursue energy conservation.

Again, at the end of the 1970s, the Iranian Revolution forced oil prices to double, provoking another round of inflation, a slump in the balance of trade, and conservation.[3] Japan was also reaching technological equality with the rest of the industrialized world, forcing a slowdown of its advantageous productivity growth.

Nonetheless, during the early 1980s, Japanese exports in a few industries began to swamp American production. The depreciation of the yen due to the second oil shock reopened the gap between the ¥/$ exchange rate and the ¥ cost of manufacturing, allowing extensive export growth. In cars and car parts, steel, consumer electronics, and machine tools, Japan was gaining U.S. market share annually. In response, the United States threatened Japan with "reciprocity" legislation that could close U.S. markets to asymmetrical trade. A series of U.S. trade complaints brought temporary and "voluntary" limitations to Japan's export onslaught, while the United States tried to adjust.

With the Reagan plan, U.S. real interest rates rose sharply in 1981 and the value of the dollar eventually climbed 63%. The yen weakened, which only reasserted Japan's export competitiveness. By 1985, the U.S. trade balance was negative $122 billion, while Japan's surplus rose to $56 billion. In September 1985, industrial countries decided that these currency trends had gone too far. G-5 finance ministers met at the Plaza Hotel in New York and announced their agreement that the dollar had appreciated too much. Within weeks, the dollar began falling, reaching ¥128/$1 by 1988. This initiated the period of endaka—or "high yen." [See **Exhibit 11.7b**.]

Endaka Now Japan came under increasing pressure, as the dollar prices of its exports rose sharply. If they were to prevent a balance of trade crisis, Japanese firms would have to cut costs, lower prices, and eventually reinvest in more modern plant and equipment. This they did with a vengeance. They benefited, of course, from the massive drop (yen terms) in the prices of their raw materials imports. Returns on equity, never much higher than 8%, plunged to just 3% by 1991. As the Bank of Japan lowered interest rates to 2.5% by February 1987, real investment skyrocketed—from 27% to 32% of GDP by 1991—an unprecedented level for a developed country. Japan virtually rebuilt its industrial system.

As the trade surplus soared to more than $90 billion annually, the Japanese invested in their stock market, foreign equities, real estate, and foreign debt. Savings were immense, but there was no clear end to investment possibilities.

Land prices in Tokyo and Osaka more than tripled, and the Nikkei stock market average rose from 11,000 to 39,000 points. Japanese banks and investment funds bought U.S. Treasury bills, and Japanese businesses bought nearly $140 billion of U.S. equities and real estate such as Columbia Pictures, Pebble Beach Golf, and New York's Rockefeller Center. Japan's manufacturers built plants in the United States, Europe, and southeast Asia to gain market access and avoid protectionism, to gain access to technology, or to lower labor costs, which were high at home.

Adjustment to the Bursting Bubble and Globalization

Eventually, endaka caught up with Japan. Under the pressure of asset speculation, and a threat of inflation in 1989, a new governor of the Bank of Japan moved to raise interest rates and cool off the economy. Rates rose further in 1990, and by 1991, Japan was in recession. Economic growth fell below 1% annually by 1993 and had barely recovered to 3% in 1996, when it fell once more. Following yet another recession in 1998, the economy grew slowly, posting a real GDP growth rate of 0.8% in 1999 and 1.7% in 2000. The Nikkei hit a low of 12,607 in July 2001, and real estate values dropped. Economists warned that the Japanese economy was headed into recession. Meanwhile, the unemployment rate jumped to a record high of 4.9%. [See **Exhibit 11.7c.**]

After a long struggle to balance its budget, the government attempted fiscal stimulus by 1992. For three years, through 1995, deficit spending rose dramatically. Although this drove government debt and debt service to record levels, it did little to stimulate growth. Then the government lowered interest rates, down to 0.5% by 1995. Unfortunately, with asset prices still falling and bad debt plaguing the books of the nation's banks, even these low rates could not stimulate much borrowing.

Hoping to restore confidence in the nation's struggling banks and weak economy, the Bank of Japan introduced a zero-interest rate policy in February 1999. When banks failed to pay off their bad loans, the frustrated Bank of Japan governor, Masaru Hayami, raised interest rates slightly in August 2000. But as the economy lost steam in 2001, Hayami was forced to reinstate the zero-interest rate policy in an attempt to end price deflation. Proponents of this controversial policy, known as "quantitative easing," believed that lowering interest rates to zero would flood the economy with enough cash to raise prices. Critics argued that the policy could lead to a disastrous wave of hyperinflation. After announcing the rate cut, Hayami urged the government to introduce much-needed structural change. "The Bank of Japan strongly hopes that comprehensive steps will proceed rapidly on all fronts toward structural reform under the government's decisive leadership," he stated.[4]

Institutional Concerns

There was no simple explanation for Japan's continuing stagnation. But to the extent that many Japanese viewed westernization as part of the solution, they tended to cite traditional institutions as part of the problem. Although labor and capital markets, the strong bureaucracy, corporate governance, and unique social arrangements had worked well in the past, they now seemed to fit less well with the imperatives of globalization.

Labor Markets

Job security was paramount for the Japanese: most people would choose a lower-paying, permanent employment position in a prestigious company rather than work for a higher-paying startup company that did not guarantee job security. These more secure positions generally were offered by medium- and larger-sized employers and accounted for about one-third of all positions; smaller employers did not strictly adhere to this policy.[5] For many years, this business practice was admired—companies garnered tremendous employee loyalty, and their substantial growth required increasing numbers of employees. Japan had a low unemployment rate relative to its industrial counterparts.

Japanese corporations promoted from within, following primarily a seniority system. Tax advantages even encouraged this policy; the longer employees worked for a company, the less tax was imposed on their retirement allowance.[6] Some people believed the seniority system was being slowly revised, and the Ministry of Labor reported a slight increase in wage disparity;[7] the gradual introduction of merit-based compensation could add to the disparity. But overall the seniority system was still intact, with few senior executives under the age of 55. Labor costs kept steadily rising.

Many Japanese were shocked in the late 1990s when major firms such as Yamaichi Securities declared bankruptcy, forcing their employees to find alternative positions. However, most Japanese companies maintained large payrolls through the slow growth period; few firms issued layoffs. Instead, companies instituted hiring freezes and offered some early retirement packages, reducing payrolls through attrition. These policies "worked well when the economy was constantly growing," said a president of a major research center. "But now companies cannot expect higher growth, so they must change the system."[8]

Capital Markets

Japanese banks dominated the country's financial markets, limiting equity market development. After the occupation, Japanese companies had a great need for funds, but individuals were risk-averse and had little money. As individuals stored their assets in banks, banks were tapped to take the funding risks by loaning to companies. As a result, companies were financed predominantly through debt, not equity. Investors continued accumulating personal financial assets, which they then deposited in savings accounts. By March 1999, personal financial assets had accumulated to $12.74 trillion, mostly in banks or postal savings. [See **Exhibit 11.8**.]

Because banks played such a vital role in funding businesses, the relationship between businesses and their banks became increasingly mutually dependent. To protect themselves, the banks and businesses had formed interlocking relationships, holding equity in each other.[9] Moreover, restrictions on the security of a bank's portfolio were comparatively weak; until 1998, Japanese banks could lend up to 20% of their capital to a single borrower (excluding bond and equity holdings), versus 10% in the United States. Furthermore there were no legal restrictions on the use of real estate as collateral, although banks could not hold real estate on their balance sheets.[10] [See **Exhibit 11.13**.] Now total exposure is limited to 25%.

Many Japanese institutions kept balance sheets based on book values rather than market values. In some situations this created hidden profits, as an asset's market value was much

higher than its book value. However, in a large number of cases, this method of accounting held hidden losses; the dramatic decline in asset and land prices following the bubble forced financial institutions to hold on to depressed assets or to sell them at a significant loss. Beginning in September 2001, financial institutions would be subject to a new system of marked-to-market accounting standards. The new accounting system would force institutions to value shareholdings according to prevailing market prices rather than book values.[11]

The collapse of the bubble also affected the massive bad debt problem. Many firms were leveraged beyond their means; as companies' collateral plummeted, they defaulted on their loans, turning worthless assets over to banks. In turn, the banks needed to face their own paper losses. Banks suffered additional losses in Southeast Asia due to financial crisis. But writing off bad debt was complicated, because land and buildings used as collateral for bad loans were sometimes owned by yakuza, the organized crime syndicates, which refused to write down their share.

April 1998 saw the introduction of "prompt corrective action" to protect a bank's capital adequacy ratio. Internationally active banks were required to meet the 8% minimum set by the Bank of International Settlements (BIS). Banks operating solely within Japan were forced to have at least a 4% ratio. Failure to meet these standards would require a management improvement plan or, in more severe cases, restructuring. Additionally, banks began to use marked-to-market accounting systems to increase their transparency. To meet these standards, many banks closed their international offices; in March 1998 the Ministry of Finance classification listed only 45 international and 102 domestic banks, compared with earlier figures of 80 and 67 respectively.

For a long time, the government would not allow banks to fail, either injecting funds to prevent a bank from defaulting or encouraging a merger with a healthier bank. This policy changed dramatically when the government allowed Hokkaido Takushoku to collapse in November 1997. An even greater shock occurred when Yamaichi Securities collapsed a few weeks later, facing ¥260 billion in off-the-book debts.

Individuals had limited opportunities in the capital markets. The bulk of personal financial savings was held in commercial savings accounts (or in postal savings), which earned a nominal interest rate of 0.4% for deposits between one and two years. The postal accounts helped fund the Fiscal Investment and Loan Program, an off-budget fund financing public infrastructure. Individuals were also limited in reporting foreign exchange transactions. As a result, few people held U.S. Treasury Bills, foreign equity, mutual fund holdings, or derivative securities.

Bureaucratic Power

Japan was a representative democracy. There was a parliament (the Diet), which consisted of a 500-member House of Representatives and a 252-member House of Councillors. In the House of Representatives, elections occurred at least every four years. Members of the House of Councillors were elected to six-year terms. The Diet elected a prime minister, whose primary executive duty was to select a cabinet to oversee the bureaucracy. The legal system was headed by a U.S.-style Supreme Court, appointed by the cabinet, which sat over a system of lesser courts.[12]

The Diet had traditionally been controlled by LDP factions—groups of powerful, senior politicians within the party. Kakuei Tanaka, who was prime minister for almost two years, was perhaps the best example. In 1974, Tanaka was forced to resign as prime minister due to financial improprieties. Thereafter, he built a faction of more than 100 Diet members and acted as "kingmaker" in Japanese politics for more than a decade. Relying heavily on Tanaka's leadership, the Japanese political system suffered in the years after his death. No one stepped forward to replace Tanaka, and Japanese politics stagnated. Problems merely festered until eventually the LDP splintered in 1992 and briefly fell from power.

Besides the legislature there was the bureaucracy, which many people argued held the real power in Japanese politics. The bureaucracy consisted of 22 ministries or cabinet-level agencies. The head of each ministry, a member of the Diet, sat in the cabinet. All cabinet decisions had to be unanimous; effectively each minister had veto power over cabinet activity. Yet the true decision makers for each ministry were the vice-ministers, who began competing to head their ministry from the time they entered, usually just out of college. If the prime minister wanted to address policy, he needed the entire cabinet's permission, whose members in turn required the support of the vice-ministers in each of their ministries.[13] This desire for consensus was popular in Japan, as the people felt achieving harmony, or wa, was worth almost any cost.

Ministry of Finance

The Ministry of Finance (MOF) held power in all areas of the financial world. The ministry had managed government fiscal policy and tariffs. In conjunction with the Bank of Japan (BOJ), MOF was the linchpin for much financing of big business. Large city banks needed MOF consent for their lending policies.[14] And because the Ministry controlled the tax code, maintaining tax advantages for its policies was simple, further securing MOF control.

MOF had also held influence over monetary and securities policy. Although the head of the Bank of Japan was officially appointed by the prime minister and cabinet, MOF officials were often involved in the selection process, and a MOF representative could attend BOJ policy meetings. Ministry officials managed restrictions throughout the capital markets, including limiting the scope of foreign exchange, derivative, or individual stockholding transactions. In the United States, these responsibilities were spread throughout Congress, the Office of Management and Budget, the Treasury Department, the Federal Reserve Board, the Securities and Exchange Commission, and the Internal Revenue Service. MOF power was further augmented, like other Japanese ministries, by control over its own appointments and promotions.

The MOF responsibility for watching each bank's reserve capital led to scandals. Some ministry officials notified banks prior to inspections, allowing problem loans to be concealed. Also serious was the revelation that the MOF might have helped some banks and securities firms hide losses to prevent them from failing. These scandals forced Finance Minister Hiroshi Mitsuzuka to resign in March 1998 and led to continued arrests in both the ministry and several major banks.

The ministry was slow to take responsibility for the continuing stagnation, despite its clearly ineffective policies. Numerous officials called for changes in fiscal policy and in the structure of the ministry, but its leaders were loathe to make that adjustment.

Ministry of International Trade and Industry

One of the crucial components of the Japanese economic miracle was the Ministry of International Trade and Industry (MITI). After the occupation, MITI used its control over trade and investment to "pick" and support a handful of industries for leading Japan's export-oriented growth. Its success continued into the 1970s, as MITI set its sights on the semiconductor and computer industries. [See **Exhibit 11.14**.]

But while MITI still had considerable influence in the business community, much of its original power had dissipated. So MITI shifted its focus away from the heavy industries, toward the service sector and telecommunications. Recently, a subcommittee of the Industry Structure Council had urged MITI to focus on more structural measures for achieving economic reform—especially deregulation, promotion of competition, and acceleration of intellectual-capital formation.[15] Because MITI was "exposed to the outside world," commented Shijuro Ogata, approvingly, "it grew smarter and more aware as an organization."[16]

Bureaucracies like MITI often vied for power among themselves. One such conflict occurred between the Ministry of Posts and Telecommunications and MITI over telecommunications development. With the digital revolution, telecommunications became increasingly important, and MITI officials felt it should be the ministry's next focus. However, the Ministry of Posts and Telecommunications held more sway over the Diet members, so in 1998 the Diet conferred the development of that industry on Posts and Telecommunications—a rare defeat for the once-powerful MITI.

Corporate Governance

Intertwined in the system of government and bureaucracy was Japan's business sector. Government officials often retired to a life of business when their government responsibilities ended, usually around age 50. This process was called amakudari, or "descent from heaven," and bureaucrats could move from company to company as distinguished advisors, receiving large paychecks each step along the way. Playing a critical role in the business sector were the keiretsu, or business groups, which were giant conglomerations centered around a major bank. The keiretsu descended from the zaibatsu, industrial combines dominated by old industrial families, which were dissolved after World War Two. Instead of being centered around a family, the keiretsu were centered around large city banks, which re-emerged in the late 1950s.

Initially, the main bank in each keiretsu played a crucial role in financing the businesses within the enterprise group. Businesses borrowed three or four times their net worth. With thin earnings and high interest coverage ratios, they essentially acceded management control to the group's main bank. The main bank then overborrowed from the Bank of Japan. Because the central bank held the ultimate responsibility for the system, it also had the ultimate control over lending decisions of dependent banks. By the 1980s, many of the larger companies had grown independent enough to generate funding on their own.

This debt-financing system permitted Japanese businesses to focus on long-term issues, as opposed to the shorter-term concerns of western-style shareholders. Taking the long view allowed Japanese businesses to acquire market share, which could eventually be mined for profit. Tax incentives encouraged borrowing over equity funding.[17]

Business groups with a strong main bank were known as "horizontal" keiretsu. Six large horizontal keiretsu dominated Japanese business: Mitsubishi, Mitsui, Sumitomo, Fuyo, DKB, and Sanwa. The Mitsubishi group, the largest of these with $392 billion in 1996 sales, included about 30 companies in businesses as diverse as heavy industries, electricity, aluminum, paper production, beer, and automobiles. [See **Exhibit 11.16**.] While the business group had played a critical role creating partnerships between companies in the past, leaders explained the relationship was less important in the 1990s. Under equal conditions, members would choose to deal with other group members, but given a better deal with an outside company, the outsider would likely be selected.[18]

A smaller group of "vertical" keiretsu had also emerged. These groups typically included a large manufacturer with its suppliers and distributors as subsidiaries. A prominent example of the vertical business group was the Toyota Motor Corporation. These groups were called vertical because they were managed in a rough pyramid structure, with the parent company maintaining a long-term relationship with the subsidiaries. This type of business structure was best suited for mass production of industrial products.

A third type of keiretsu was the "satellite" group, in which a core company formed subsidiaries to perform after-market functions or to engage in new ventures. Hitachi and NTT were this type of "satellite" group.

Cross-holding of shares was another distinctive feature of Japanese corporate governance. Much of the limited equity of Japanese firms was held by other members of the same group—especially the banks. The amount of cross-holding had generally risen, despite the Anti-Monopoly Act of 1977, reaching a high of 52% by the early 1990s.[19] Although it had shrunk to 36% in 1999/2000, it continued to accommodate an environment of low equity earnings.[20] [See **Exhibit 11.9**.] In other words, corporations felt little pressure from shareholders, or "the market." Company priorities placed value on labor market issues and long-term market share. Thus while the Mitsubishi Corporation had 46 board members, all but two were insiders; the two outsiders were the chairman of Mitsubishi Heavy Industries and the president of Mitsubishi Electric.[21]

Finally, Japan's corporations increasingly faced scandals involving organized crime. Periodically reports would break about arrests in a sokaiya scandal, in which business would pay off criminals, known as sokaiya, with huge sums of money to prevent them from disclosing embarrassing information about the company, thereby disrupting its annual shareholders meeting. These scandals were widespread, affecting, among others, all four major securities houses: Daiwa Securities, Nikko Securities, Nomura Securities, and the now-bankrupt Yamaichi Securities.[22] Shijuro Ogata summed up the corporate climate by saying, "Corporate leaders became arrogant, thinking they had nothing to learn from outsiders because outsiders were coming to them to learn. The usefulness of the old-style corporate practice is over, and a revised approach might be necessary."[23]

Social Issues

A number of social issues had been developing during the past two decades. Demographics played a major role, with the rapidly aging population posing huge issues for government policy and personal savings. While women had a growing presence in government and business, vast numbers of women maintained traditional roles in society. Quality of life was still a major concern, as prices were exceedingly high, salarymen worked long hours each week, while others lacked some basic facilities. Education levels were high, but creativity and innovation seemed to suffer.

Aging problem   Like many industrial nations, Japan faced a serious aging problem. High life expectancy, partly due to the country's universal medical care, and low fertility made the Japanese problem especially severe. At the end of 1996, 15.1% of the Japanese population was elderly (aged 65 and older)—about 19 million people. Over the next 25 years, this percentage was expected to increase sharply, while the overall population stayed around 125 million. By 2049, the elderly population would comprise 32.3% of the population.[24] [See **Exhibit 11.19b**.]

Medical care   Since 1961, Japan's outstanding health insurance had covered everyone. The Health Insurance Law, periodically revised, adjusted individual cost-sharing proportions and coverage issues to fit social needs. The Gold Plan for elderly medical care was last revised in 1994. This plan attempted to allow all elderly people to maintain their dignity and live independently as well as to provide care to everyone who needed it—the most serious concern for the elderly.[25]

Pensions   The Japanese pension structure was reorganized to be more equitable and stable. The core of this system was the Basic National Pension, which covered the entire population. As of March 1996, it provided an average monthly benefit of ¥45,000, although people did not receive benefits until age 65. In addition to this basic pension, private sector retirees could collect from the Employees' Pension and public sector retirees from the Mutual Aid Pension, both of which were paid in proportion to the beneficiaries' wages and salaries prior to retirement.

Japanese social security costs had expanded rapidly over the previous 25 years, rising from ¥4 trillion in 1971 to ¥60 trillion in 1994. As a percentage of national income, total social security expenditure (including public health care and some welfare services) was still only 16.2%, compared to 19.4% in the United States and 31.5% in Germany.[26] Yet, due to rapid aging, Japan was facing a sizable increase in social security costs. The Ministry of Health and Welfare estimated total social security expenditures to rise to between 29% and 35.5% of national income by 2025, depending on economic growth rates. Its most optimistic prediction was based on a nominal growth rate of 3.5% until 2000 and 3.0% thereafter: its least optimistic prediction still assumed nominal growth of 1.75% until 2000 and 1.5% thereafter.[27] [See **Exhibit 11.19a**.]

The elderly saved relatively little, expecting previous savings and government pensions to support their retirement. Thus, the budget deficit was predicted to rise, as the government struggled to meet public pension obligations that were even less adequately funded than those in the United States. Stemming from this activity, it seemed likely that the personal savings rate would decline from its level of 12% to 15% of income. The trade surplus was expected to turn into a deficit eventually, as the declining pool of workers would limit the output that could be exported.

Role of women   The role of women in Japan had improved since the economic miracle, but was still nowhere near western standards and norms. In January 1970, women comprised 2.9% of the Diet; by the end of 1996, that number had risen to 7.6%, although it was only 4.6% of the more powerful House of Representatives. Ms. Hisako Takahashi became the first woman named Justice of the Supreme Court in 1994, but by April 1996, female judges throughout the country numbered 257, 8.9% of the total.

More than 27 million women sought work in 1996, over 40% of the total labor force. Women were especially prominent in education, comprising over 61% of teaching staff at elementary schools, 11% of the teaching staff at universities and 41% of the teachers at junior colleges. Over 97% of girls advanced to upper secondary school, and 46% continued to junior college or university—both figures higher than the ones for boys.[28]

Yet, despite the educational gains, few women held important positions in major corporations. Women had an easier time getting positions at smaller companies, many of which were apparel or retail-focused. Several of these companies had relatively high profits, which activists argued encouraged opening companies to women.[29]

Standard of living   Costs in Japan were extremely high. This was due in part to the fact that many items needed to be imported and that space was at a premium in an island nation of only 378,000 square kilometers (146,000 sq. miles, about the size of California with five times the population). However, part of this problem was also attributed to the lack of competition and extensive regulations on business activity.

Japanese workers historically worked long weeks, often more than five days per week, totaling over 2,200 hours per year in the 1980s. By 1996 that number had declined to around 1,900 hours per year, but that figure did not include the after-work dinners and entertainment in which salarymen traditionally participated.[30] Several nights each week, workers stayed out until late at night, only to get up early the next morning and begin the cycle again.

Finally, while the per capita GNP in dollars was substantially higher than in the United States or Germany, in terms of purchasing power parity it still lagged behind. Retail prices for food and clothes were almost twice as high in Tokyo as they were in either New York or London. Electricity cost 50% more in Japan than in the United States or France. And the 1994 average price of residential land in Tokyo was ¥560,000 per sq. meter, while the average house cost ¥132 million. By comparison, land costs in New York were only ¥10,000 per sq. meter and ¥33 million per house.[31]

Education   Japanese students scored well by international standards. In the Third International Mathematics and Science Study, Japanese eighth graders ranked third out of 41 countries in both mathematics and science. All of Japan's eighth grade students had studied algebra, compared to only 25% in the United States, yet math instruction accounted for only 117 hours per year in Japan, instead of the 143 hours in the United States.[32] This success lay partly in the Japanese style of teaching. Students learned much through memorization and were periodically tested through competitive examination. By the time they finished university studies, they had an extensive command of facts, figures, languages (at least two), and history at their fingertips.

But the factors favoring the Japanese educational dominance also contributed to some of the difficulties its leaders felt they faced. Students had little creativity, stifled by the rote learning. Critics argued that despite the strong educational statistics, Japan had only five citizens who received Nobel prizes in scientific fields; two of them worked predominantly in the United States.

The Hashimoto Era and Structural Reform

To regain governmental control, the LDP allied with the Social Democratic Party (SDPJ) in 1994, allowing Social Democrat Tomiichi Murayama to serve as prime minister. When support for the Murayama government collapsed in January 1996, Ryutaro Hashimoto, a prominent LDP politician and the Minister of International Trade and Industry, ascended to the post of prime minister. Hashimoto was a political lone wolf but was hardly viewed as radical upon entering office. However, he surprised the country when he proposed radical reforms to the traditional Japanese system, ideas that even surpassed the Maekawa Report of 1986 that proposed restructuring the Japanese economy.[33]

In November 1996, Hashimoto announced a grand plan to restructure administration, deregulation, education, the financial system, fiscal policy, and social security. The cornerstone to this plan was financial market reform, dubbed the "Big Bang". Modeled after British reforms in the 1980s, the Big Bang was to liberate the Japanese capital market by 2001. If all went according to plan, Japan's new capital market would be "Free"—completely following market principles; "Fair"—totally transparent and reliable; and "Global"—used by the entire world.

Administrative Structure

"The ministries have a tremendous amount of power," complained a director at the Bank of Japan. "This centralized system must be decentralized to make changes for the future."[34] A year earlier, Hashimoto had formed a 15-member Administrative Reform Council, with himself as the head. The council of political outsiders was charged with reorganizing the governing structure to be more efficient and more responsive to the needs of the people. The council issued a report that recommended strengthening the powers of the prime minister and the cabinet, reducing the number of ministries, and limiting the number of bureaucrats and civil servants.[35]

The Basic Law outlining the intentions of the reform would be introduced in the Diet by June 1998, and specific proposals would be introduced in the following years. Administrative Reform Council member Ken Moroi defended the plan's importance: "We have now entered the era of megacompetition. Unless we do away with many of the regulations we currently have, the Japanese nation, industries, and companies won't survive."[36]

The plan's critics felt the proposal merely reorganized the current bureaucracy and did not cut enough government functions. There were also doubts over the speed with which the administrative reforms would occur. Many argued that the ministries would not easily give up their power.

Economic Structure

By the time of Hashimoto's formal reform package, significant inroads had already been made. Restrictions on large-scale retailers were reduced. Several foreign retailers had increased their presence—the most successful was Toys 'R' Us, with over 60 stores nationwide. Telephone deregulation dated back to 1985, with the partial privatization of Nippon Telephone and Telegraph (NTT), although the company remained a monopoly. In late 1997, the Ministry of Posts and Telecommunications announced its plans for the NTT breakup, which would occur by the end of 1999.

These changes had improved pricing on non-regulated goods but, overall, they had not opened the Japanese economy—in 1995, foreign direct investment outflows surpassed inflows by a ratio of 15.5:1. [See **Exhibit 11.17**.] Explanations for this situation included language difficulties, especially in grasping detailed information on business and the nuances of Japanese laws and regulations (and worse, the marked shortage of professional experts, such as lawyers and CPAs, to provide support for business people); the limited supply of employees due to the employment appeal of Japanese companies; and the high taxes and fixed costs companies faced. A favorable environment for new business activities would be pursued through mass deregulation. MITI's focus had shifted from developing industries to developing the means to bolster economic growth.[37]

An Action Plan for Economic Structural Reform listed fifteen growth fields to pursue: medical care and welfare, quality of life and culture, information and telecommunications, new manufacturing technology, distribution and logistics, environment, business support, ocean, biotechnology, improvement of the urban surroundings, aviation and space (civil demand), new energy and energy conservation, human resources, economic globalization, and housing.

MITI's deregulation plan covered five main areas. In the logistics area, controls on supply-demand adjustments would be abolished in areas of road cargo transport, rail, coastal shipping, and port transport. In the energy sector, regulatory reforms aimed to increase competition in the electricity market by allowing for competition from Independent Power Providers. Additionally, there would be a revision of electricity rates. Market principles would be further introduced in both the petroleum and natural gas markets. With regard to information and telecommunications, MITI proposed a fair and effective competitive environment by eliminating remaining tariffs and diversifying services. Incentive regulations such as price caps and yardsticks would be introduced in FY1999. In subsequent years, the ministry would revise connection rules and long-term incremental cost calculations. In terms of finance, the "Big Bang" would enable the Japanese financial market to grow to a size similar to that of New York and London.[38]

MITI had simulated the effects of these deregulatory measures and found a potential benefit to real GDP of 6.0%. Specific benefits included an increase in plant and equipment investment of ¥39 trillion (2.6 GDP percentage points), a drop in consumer prices of 3.4%, and a consumer surplus increase of ¥365,000 per household.[39]

Education Structure

To improve the Japanese educational system, the proposed reforms aimed to introduce greater flexibility in the educational process, with the hope of boosting creativity in students. The Program for Educational Reform outlined five main goals to achieve by 2003. The first goal included the reform of the educational system and the cultivation of a rich humanity. Here, reformers proposed reducing the school week to five days, unifying the lower and upper secondary school system, encouraging autonomous learning instead of rote memorization, increasing computer training, and improving teacher quality and administration of schools.[40] The second goal focused on eliciting prompt responses to changing social needs. The educational system needed to be more flexible with respect to the changing face of Japan. This flexibility included adjusting to the aging population, adapting to the information-oriented society, and keeping pace with cultural changes.

A third goal aimed to increase schools' cooperation with students' families and communities. Towards a fourth goal of increased international exposure, the program called for promoting more exchange programs and improved foreign language education. The final goal was the establishment of a forum with the business community for the expansion of the educational reform movement.

Financial Structure

Two themes dominated this program: the financial market reform and the disposal of the massive bad debts accumulated over the previous decade. The market reform revolved around the "Free, Fair, and Global" principles. Critical to this effort was the efficient disposal of banks' bad debt. Upon fruition, this reform would make Tokyo a financial center to rival New York and London.

Reformers developed several categories of changes to advance such a system. First, they planned to expand the choice of means for investors and borrowers. The ban on derivative securities was lifted, increased use of asset-backed securities was proposed to increase liquidity, and banks were authorized to sell securities, investment trusts, and insurance.[41] Secondly, they aimed to improve the quality of intermediaries' services and to promote competition. An amended Anti-Monopoly Law would allow holding companies. Stock trading commissions were to be liberalized fully by the end of 1999. To support weak banks, the government announced a ¥30 trillion stabilization package in January 1998. Seventeen trillion yen would protect investor deposits in potentially unstable banks. The remaining ¥13 trillion would recapitalize banks, although it would be possible for smaller banks to fail in the future. Most bankers felt if the estimates of problem loans were accurate, this package would be sufficient to stave off further problems, allowing financial reforms to continue.

Fiscal Structure

While the Japanese economy had been the strongest fiscally in the Group of Seven from 1985 to 1992, by 1996 it was performing the worst. Its budget deficit had ballooned to 7% and showed few signs of improving. Hashimoto's fiscal reform plan followed five major principles. First, he set a goal to reduce the budget deficit to no more than 3% of GDP by FY2003 (two years ahead of the original deadline). Next, he announced that the years 1998 through 2000 would be devoted to fiscal reform. Third, reformers intended to implement year-on-year reductions in general expenditures, with no area spared. The fourth goal was to reduce all current long-term spending programs, such as the ¥630 trillion in public works over 10 years. Finally, they planned to maintain the ratio of taxes, social welfare premiums, and government deficit to national income, also known as the national burden, below 50%.

In June 1997, the Cabinet announced its policies to achieve these goals including: coordination with the social security reform plan, a three-year extension of the public works program in conjunction with reducing total spending to ¥470trn, a 10% reduction (¥920bn) in defense spending, up to a 10% reduction in Official Development Assistance expenditures, and settlement of the ¥28 trn debt in the former Japan National Railways.[42]

The Japanese economy had not recovered by the end of 1997, and businessmen were deeply concerned over the lack of government fiscal stimulus. Without this stimulus, they feared Japan would never emerge from its slow growth period. But Hashimoto risked losing great face if he offered a stimulus package, expanding the budget deficit beyond the previous year's level. Instead, he raised the national sales tax from 3% to 5% to offset income tax reductions. Though Hashimoto's much-criticized move was intended to rein in the bloated deficits, the tax hike stifled consumer demand, business investment, and imports, triggering a major recession. Taking blame for the economic disaster, Hashimoto watched helplessly as the yen took a nose-dive, the stock market plummeted, unemployment soared, and bad loans piled up in Japanese banks.

By the end of April 1998, fiscal stimulus was unavoidable. The government unveiled the details of an economic stimulus package, worth ¥16.65 trillion ($128 billion). The package included one-time ¥2 trillion tax cuts for 1998 and 1999, ¥7.7 trillion in public-works spending, ¥2.3 trillion to improve liquidity in the real estate market, ¥2 trillion in increased lending to small and medium-sized companies, and a much smaller sum in tax credits for investment and housing.[43]

Social Security Structure

The social security structural reform aimed to address Japan's changing demographics. Much of the reform was intertwined with the other proposals; the fiscal structural reform planned to limit the burden of government to 50% of national income. Also, continued economic growth would facilitate the social security system's stability.

The Ministry of Health and Welfare felt its decision concerning this issue was of such importance that it created an education plan for the Japanese people, so individuals could register their opinions before any action was taken on the five proposals under consideration. The first proposal aimed to maintain the current benefit level. To accomplish this, premiums would have to rise to 34.3% of income to overcome the additional costs with the elderly population. Another proposed keeping the premium below 30%. To do so could involve raising the retirement age and increasing premiums slightly.[44] Under this proposal, the benefits would decline by 10%. A third proposed to maintain the premium at 20% of income and tax employee bonuses. These bonuses would be taxed at the same rate as monthly employee salary—currently bonuses were exempt from such taxation. This proposal would result in a total benefit reduction of 20%. Some reformers pushed to maintain the premium at the status quo, the fourth proposal. By 2025, benefits would be reduced by 40%. The final proposal would abolish the social insurance system for employees. Citizens would still have the universal coverage portion of their social security, but the secondary part of social insurance would be completely privatized.

Ultimately, the ministry would design a pension reform based on these proposals, in addition to its plan to eliminate waste in medical care, current pension plans, and welfare policy. The complete reform of the pension system was scheduled to occur by 2000.

Hashimoto's Legacy

Punished for the disastrous state of the economy, the LDP performed poorly in the July 1998 upper-house elections. Hashimoto resigned as prime minister. Although his term ended abruptly, he continued to play a key role in implementing many of the structural reforms of his 1996 agenda. Several of these reforms were enacted during the Keizo Obuchi (Jul. 1998–Apr. 2000) and Yoshiro Mori (Apr. 2000–Apr. 2001) administrations.

As intended, Hashimoto's Big Bang financial reforms increased competition between financial institutions and opened up more opportunities for household savings. The April 1998 revision to the Foreign Exchange and Foreign Trade Control Law completely dismantled the foreign exchange banking system. Before this change, currency transactions had been limited to authorized banks and a few securities. By the end of 1999, stock trading commissions were completely liberalized; restrictions on the stock brokerage business of banks' securities were lifted; and insurance companies were finally permitted to enter the banking business through subsidiaries.[45]

In response to Japan's rapidly aging population, the Diet passed a major pension reform bill in March 2000. Officials hoped to relieve the burgeoning pension burden by cutting benefits and increasing the retirement age. The pension reform bill included the following provisions[46]:

- Earnings-related benefits would be cut by 5% for new retirees as of April 1, 2000, though a grace period would delay the actual reduction until FY2004.

- Increases in earnings-related pensions payments would be indexed to the CPI instead of disposable income.

- The eligibility age for earnings-related pensions would be gradually increased from 65 to 70 between 2013 and 2025 for men and between 2018 and 2030 for women. The eligibility age for reduced basic pensions would also be raised from 60 to 65, beginning in FY 2001. The reduction in monthly benefits would be 30%.

- Employees between the ages of 65 and 70 would have to pay pension contributions starting in April 2002 and would receive a reduction in benefits if their combined income from pension and salary exceeded certain limits.

- As of April 2003, a uniform pension contribution rate would be applied to both monthly wages and bonuses. Under the current system, the contribution rate applied to bonuses was 1%. The change was designed to be revenue-neutral, with an initial combined rate of 13.58%.

The reorganization of Japan's bloated bureaucracy commenced in January 2001, when 22 central government agencies were reduced to just 12 ministries. [See **Exhibit 11.18**.] The massive restructuring curbed the powers of the Ministry of Finance (MOF), giving the new Financial Services Agency the authority to introduce financial sector regulation. Responsibility for drawing up the budget shifted from the MOF to a special committee within the Cabinet.[47]

In accordance with Hashimoto's original proposal, the administrative reform program included measures to increase the authority of the prime minister and his cabinet. The new arrangement granted the prime minister the right to submit policy proposals to the Cabinet. Previously, the prime minister had presided over cabinet meetings or "autograph sessions" in which his sole function was to sign bills drafted by top bureaucrats. In addition, a new Cabinet Office was established to advise the prime minister in policy-making decisions. Finally, the administrative reform assigned an additional five aides to the Cabinet Secretariat to assist the prime minister in carrying out state affairs.[48]

Structural Reform under Koizumi

When Prime Minister Koizumi took office in April 2001, one of the biggest economic challenges facing Japan was the accumulation of bad loans in the nation's banks. Over the past few years, Japan's financial crisis had forced many banks to merge in an effort to pool resources and cut costs. Following the mergers, Mizuho Holdings Inc., which included Dai-Ichi Kangyo Bank, Fuji Bank, Industrial Bank of Japan, and Yasuda Trust, became the biggest bank in the world with estimated assets of $1.3trn.[49] The mergers forced banks to share the increasing burden of non-performing loans (NPLs). While the government estimated the number of NPLs still at ¥33trn, the Democratic Party of Japan (DPJ) believed that the real number of NPLs was closer to ¥150trn.[50] The United Sates and other developed nations pressured Japan to clean up its bad loans. However, Japanese workers feared that the clean-up would lead to an increase in unemployment. A wave of corporate bankruptcies had contributed to Japan's high unemployment level: More than 18,926 companies had collapsed in 2000, causing 199,280 employees to lose their jobs.[51] [See **Exhibits 11.10** to **11.13**.]

Pressured to rally Japan from its decade-long economic slump, Prime Minister Koizumi announced an ambitious economic strategy in early May. "I want to carry out reforms that could be called the 'New Century Restoration,'" explained Koizumi in his first policy speech to the Diet, "We want to establish a new economic and social system that's appropriate for the twenty-first century."[52] Though short on details, Koizumi's radical policy proposals reflected his strong commitment to structural reform and fiscal discipline.

The new reform agenda included plans to force banks to write off all NPLs in two to three years. Unclear whether the government would use public funds to bail out banks, Koizumi commented, "On the use of public funds, I think the reality is that it can go either way. There is a possibility of using them but it might not happen." Critics warned that efforts to eliminate all NPLs would lead to another wave of bankruptcies and increased unemployment.

As part of his strategy, Koizumi aimed to increase economic competition through rapid deregulation. He advocated the privatization of the postal savings system (the savings bank run by the post office), which held $2trn in deposits. For years, politicians and bureaucrats had used the savings bank to finance lavish government projects. Koizumi, who spent much of his political life advocating the privatization of the postal system, intended to break the existing postal savings system into regional savings funds that would later be privatized as individual banks.[53]

To halt the growth of Japan's $5.6trn debt, Koizumi proposed a cap on government borrowing at $245bn per year. Reducing Japan's ballooning deficits would require major spending cuts, but Koizumi, who promised not to raise taxes, had yet to offer any specifics regarding how he planned to cut government spending.

Aware that workers would shoulder the burden of structural reform, Koizumi pushed for a government-subsidized unemployment plan. He proposed jobless benefits that would pay up to 100% of worker's pay for up to twelve months. With Japan's tight labor laws, such reforms would make it easier for companies to lay off workers and restructure.[54]

A Looming Recession

A few months into Koizumi's term, the economic climate had worsened. The government reported that GDP had shrunk an unexpected 0.2% during the first three months of 2001—an annualized rate of 0.8%.[55] Industrial production had fallen 8.5% in the six months to June.[56] It seemed inevitable that Japan would soon slide back into recession. Some officials argued that the recession had already begun. "Personally, I think the chances are high that we have now entered a recession phase," remarked Economics Minister Heizo Takenaka on June 14th.[57] As reports of Japan's deteriorating economy surfaced, several economists questioned the timing of Koizumi's proposed structural reforms. While most agreed that the reforms would improve the economy over the long term, many realized that enforcing a tight fiscal policy in the short term might spark an even deeper recession.

Before Koizumi took office in April, the LDP, damaged by the mishaps of the Mori administration, was not favored to win the upper-house elections scheduled for July. But Koizumi's radical image helped bolster new support for the party. "The fact that I was selected as prime minister is proof that the LDP has changed," explained Koizumi.[58] But despite his popularity, Koizumi lacked the support of the largest party faction of the LDP. Some voters feared that an LDP victory in the July elections would revitalize the power of the LDP's Old Guard. This line of thinking could lead the DJP to gain control of the upper-house and call a general election in the early fall. With the threat of a severe economic recession looming on the horizon, two questions remained; Would Koizumi be in office long enough to enact the necessary economic reforms? If so, would Koizumi be able to implement his structural reform agenda during a time of recession?

EXHIBIT 11.1A GDP AND COMPONENTS, 1971-2000

Year	Nominal GDP (trillions of yen)	Private Consumption (% of GDP)	Government Consumption (% of GDP)	Gross Fixed Investment (% of GDP)	Exports (% of GDP)	Imports (% of GDP)	Real GDP (1990 prices) (trillions of yen)	GDP growth rate	Real GDP per capita ($US)
1971	81	53.6%	11.7%	32.0%	11.7%	9.0%	190.7	4.3%	5,145
1972	92	54.0%	11.9%	31.8%	10.6%	8.3%	206.2	8.1%	6,346
1973	113	53.6%	12.0%	34.4%	10.0%	10.0%	222.1	7.7%	7,519
1974	134	54.3%	12.8%	33.6%	13.6%	14.3%	220.9	-0.6%	6,864
1975	148	57.1%	13.7%	28.4%	12.8%	12.8%	227.1	2.8%	6,859
1976	167	57.5%	13.6%	28.1%	13.6%	12.8%	236.7	4.2%	7,078
1977	186	57.7%	13.5%	27.2%	13.1%	11.5%	247.9	4.7%	8,107
1978	204	57.7%	13.4%	27.2%	11.1%	9.4%	259.9	4.9%	10,749
1979	222	58.7%	13.4%	28.8%	11.6%	12.5%	277.4	6.7%	10,923
1980	243	55.2%	13.3%	31.7%	13.5%	14.4%	287.4	3.6%	10,853
1981	261	54.4%	13.6%	30.7%	14.5%	13.8%	297.7	3.2%	11,474
1982	274	55.4%	13.8%	29.6%	14.3%	13.6%	307.1	3.1%	10,408
1983	285	56.0%	14.1%	28.2%	13.7%	12.0%	315.4	2.3%	11,132
1984	305	55.2%	13.9%	27.9%	14.7%	12.1%	328.9	3.8%	11,531
1985	325	54.5%	13.7%	27.6%	14.2%	10.8%	345.3	4.3%	11,979
1986	341	54.2%	13.9%	27.5%	11.2%	7.3%	354.4	3.1%	17,308
1987	356	54.3%	13.9%	28.6%	10.2%	7.2%	368.9	4.5%	20,890
1988	381	53.5%	13.6%	30.0%	9.8%	7.6%	391.8	6.5%	24,936
1989	409	53.3%	13.4%	30.9%	10.3%	8.8%	410.3	5.4%	24,155
1990	442	53.0%	13.3%	32.2%	10.4%	9.4%	430.0	5.3%	24,042
1991	469	52.6%	13.3%	31.8%	10.0%	8.3%	446.4	3.0%	26,740
1992	482	53.5%	13.7%	30.5%	9.8%	7.7%	451.0	0.9%	28,643
1993	487	54.4%	14.2%	29.2%	9.1%	6.9%	452.3	0.5%	32,629
1994	492	55.4%	14.5%	28.2%	9.0%	7.0%	455.3	1.0%	35,644
1995	502	57.9%	14.4%	26.5%	9.0%	7.6%	461.5	1.6%	39,190
1996	511	55.1%	15.1%	28.6%	9.7%	9.2%	477.9	3.3%	37,397
1997	522	55.0%	15.2%	28.1%	10.7%	9.6%	482.2	1.9%	34,312
1998	516	55.6%	15.6%	26.9%	10.7%	8.8%	479.8	-1.1%	31,278
1999	513	56.3%	16.1%	26.2%	10.0%	8.4%	482.2	0.8%	35,669
2000	513	55.9%	16.6%	26.1%	10.8%	9.3%	489.4	1.7%	37,592

SOURCE: Ministry of Finance, *The Budget in Brief,* 1997, Table 1.3; Bank of Japan, *Economic Statistics Monthly,* January 1998; The Economist Intelligence Unit.

EXHIBIT 11.1B SHARE OWNERSHIP: PERCENT OF CORPORATION'S EQUITY HELD BY TYPE OF OWNER

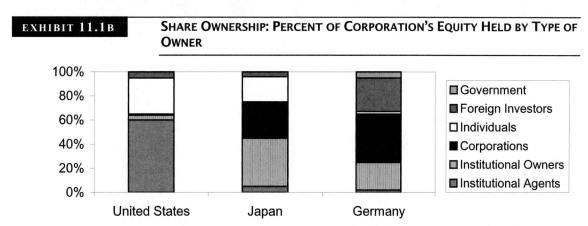

SOURCE: *The Economist*, January 25, 1992, p. 74.

Notes: *Institutional Owners* are institutions that hold equity for their own accounts (e.g., banks in Japanese *keiretsu*). *Institutional Agents* hold equity as agents for other investors (e.g., pension funds).

EXHIBIT 11.2A	**GENERAL GOVERNMENT BALANCES (% OF GDP)**

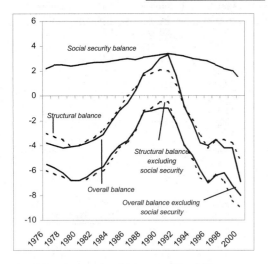

SOURCE: International Monetary Fund, "Japan Economic and Policy Developments," IMF Staff Country Report No. 00/143, November 2000.

EXHIBIT 11.2B	**GENERAL GOVERNMENT DEBT (% OF GDP)**

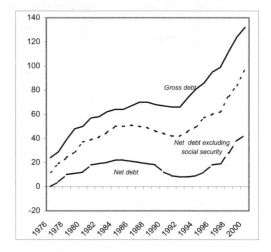

SOURCE: International Monetary Fund, "Japan Economic and Policy Developments," IMF Staff Country Report No. 00/143, November 2000.

EXHIBIT 11.3	**GENERAL EXPENDITURES BY MAJOR EXPENDITURE PROGRAM**

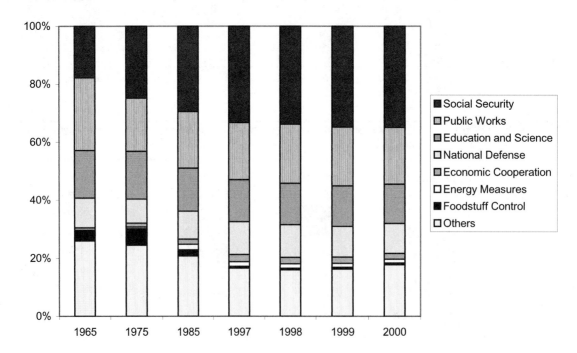

SOURCE: Ministry of Finance, *The Budget in Brief, 1997*, 2000.

Note: The above figures are calculated on an initial budget basis.

EXHIBIT 11.4 — BALANCE OF PAYMENTS (US$ BILLIONS)

	1977	1978	1979	1980	1981	1982	1983	1984	1985	1986	1987	1988
Current Account	10.9	16.5	-8.7	-10.8	4.8	6.9	20.8	35.0	49.2	85.8	87.0	79.6
Exports	79.2	95.3	101.1	126.7	149.5	137.7	145.5	168.3	174.0	205.6	224.6	259.8
Imports	-62.0	-71.0	-99.4	-124.6	-129.6	-119.6	-114.0	-124.0	-118.0	-112.8	-128.2	-164.8
Trade Balance	17.2	24.3	1.7	2.1	20.0	18.1	31.5	44.3	56.0	92.8	96.4	95.0
Net Services	-5.9	-8.0	-11.3	-12.1	-12.8	-11.5	-12.1	-11.9	-11.9	-14.2	-22.1	-31.9
Net Income	0.1	0.9	2.0	0.8	-0.8	1.6	2.9	4.2	6.7	9.3	16.4	20.6
Net Transfers	-0.4	-0.7	-1.1	-1.5	-1.6	-1.4	-1.6	-1.5	-1.7	-2.1	-3.7	-4.1
Financial Account	-5.0	-6.7	-6.8	18.9	-1.6	-16.2	-21.3	-36.6	-53.5	-73.5	-45.4	-66.2
Direct investment	-1.6	-2.4	-2.7	-2.1	-4.7	-4.1	-3.2	-6.0	-5.8	-14.3	-18.4	-34.7
Portfolio investment	0.8	0.8	-0.9	-6.3	-6.2	-2.7	-6.8	3.6	-0.3	8.7	26.0	-9.8
Other capital (net)	-4.1	-5.1	-3.3	27.3	9.3	-9.4	-11.3	-34.2	-47.4	-67.9	-53.0	-21.7
Errors & Omissions	0.5	0.1	2.4	-3.1	0.4	4.7	2.1	3.7	3.8	2.5	-3.7	3.1
Reserve assets	-6.5	-10.0	13.1	-5.0	-3.6	4.7	-1.6	-2.1	0.6	-14.8	-37.9	-16.5

	1989	1990	1991	1992	1993	1994	1995	1996	1997	1998	1999	2000
Current Account	57.0	35.9	68.2	112.6	131.6	130.3	111.0	65.9	92.6	120.7	106.9	116.9
Exports	269.6	280.4	308.2	332.6	352.7	385.7	428.7	400.3	400.9	374.0	403.7	459.5
Imports	-192.7	-216.8	-212.1	-207.8	-213.2	-241.5	-296.9	-316.7	-301.1	-251.7	-280.4	-342.8
Trade Balance	76.9	63.6	96.1	124.8	139.4	144.2	131.8	83.6	99.8	122.4	123.3	116.7
Net Services	-38.6	-44.7	-41.8	-44.0	-43.1	-48.1	-57.4	-62.2	-52.8	-49.4	-54.1	-47.6
Net Income	23.0	22.5	26.0	35.6	40.4	40.2	44.3	53.6	54.3	56.7	49.8	57.6
Net Transfers	-4.3	-5.5	-12.0	-3.8	-5.1	-6.1	-7.7	-9.0	-8.7	-8.8	-12.1	-9.8
Financial Account	-47.9	-21.5	-67.7	-100.3	-102.2	-85.1	-64.0	-28.1	-124.8	-116.8	-31.1	-75.5
Direct investment	-45.2	-46.3	-30.3	-14.6	-13.7	-17.2	-22.5	-23.2	-22.2	-21.4	-10.0	-23.3
Portfolio investment	-24.9	7.0	-50.3	-5.9	-35.1	-63.0	-50.5	-57.6	29.6	-39.2	-27.5	-36.0
Other capital (net)	22.2	17.8	12.9	-79.8	-53.4	-5.0	9.0	52.8	-132.1	-56.2	6.4	-16.2
Errors & Omissions	-21.8	-20.9	-7.7	-10.4	-0.5	-18.0	13.8	0.6	41.3	4.4	17.0	16.9
Reserve assets	12.8	6.6	7.2	-1.9	-28.9	-27.1	-60.8	-38.4	-9.1	-8.4	-92.8	-58.3

SOURCE: International Monetary Fund, International Financial Statistics, July 2001, 1997, and 1994; Balance of Payments of 1997, Ministry of Finance.

EXHIBIT 11.5		**MONEY SUPPLY (TRILLIONS OF YEN)**				
Year	**M1**	**Time Deposits**	**M2**	**M2 Growth Rate**	**CPI**	**Inflation Rate**
1971	27.7	39.7	67.4	24.3%	36.8	6.4%
1972	34.5	49.5	84	24.7%	38.5	4.6%
1973	40.3	57.9	98.2	16.8%	43.0	11.7%
1974	45	64.5	109.5	11.5%	53.0	23.3%
1975	50	75.4	125.3	14.5%	59.2	11.7%
1976	56.2	86.1	142.3	13.5%	64.8	9.5%
1977	60.8	97.3	158	11.1%	70.1	8.2%
1978	68.9	109.8	178.7	13.1%	73.0	4.1%
1979	71	122.7	193.7	8.4%	75.7	3.7%
1980	69.6	137.4	207.0	6.9%	81.6	7.8%
1981	76.5	152.7	229.2	10.7%	80.0	4.9%
1982	80.9	165.7	246.6	7.6%	82.2	2.8%
1983	80.8	182.8	263.6	6.9%	83.8	1.9%
1984	86.4	195.4	281.8	6.9%	85.7	2.2%
1985	89.0	217.8	306.8	8.9%	87.4	2.0%
1986	98.2	237.1	335.3	9.3%	88.0	0.6%
1987	103.0	269.7	372.7	11.2%	88.1	0.1%
1988	111.8	297.5	409.4	9.8%	88.7	0.7%
1989	114.5	343.2	457.6	11.8%	90.7	2.2%
1990	119.6	375.4	495.0	8.2%	93.5	3.1%
1991	131.0	375.5	506.5	2.5%	96.5	3.3%
1992	136.1	370.7	506.8	-0.1%	98.2	1.7%
1993	145.6	372.6	518.2	2.2%	99.4	1.2%
1994	151.7	382.4	534.1	3.1%	100.1	0.7%
1995	171.5	377.4	549.0	2.7%	100.0	-0.1%
1996	188.2	373.0	561.7	2.3%	100.1	0.1%
1997	194.3	374.1	566.5	3.1%	101.9	1.7%
1998	214.0	387.9	602.0	4.1%	102.5	0.6%
1999	240.0	383.3	623.0	3.4%	102.2	-0.3%
2000	248.0	381.8	630.0	1.1%	101.5	-0.2%

SOURCE: The Economist Intelligence Unit; International Monetary Fund, *International Financial Statistics*, May 2001; and International Monetary Fund, *Japan: Economic and Policy Developments*, November 2000.

EXHIBIT 11.6		**BOND YIELD AND NIKKEI STOCK PRICE INDEX**

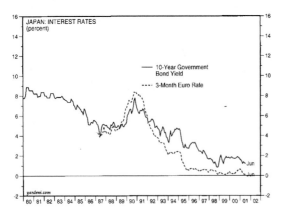

SOURCE: www.yardeni.com.

| EXHIBIT 11.7A | OFFICIAL DISCOUNT RATE (%) |

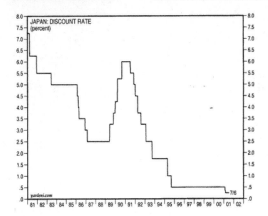

SOURCE: www.yardeni.com.

| EXHIBIT 11.7B | EXCHANGE RATE |

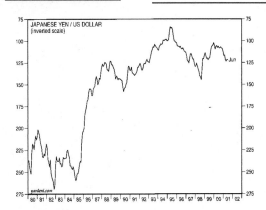

SOURCE: www.yardeni.com.

| EXHIBIT 11.7C | UNEMPLOYMENT (%) |

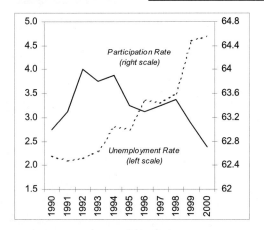

SOURCE: International Monetary Fund, *Japan: Economic and Policy Developments*, November 2000.

EXHIBIT 11.7D   **EMPLOYMENT AND HOURS WORKED (1990=100, 3-MONTH MOVING AVG)**

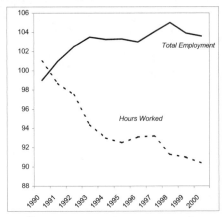

SOURCE: International Monetary Fund, *Japan: Economic and Policy Developments*, November 2000.

EXHIBIT 11.7E   **CONSUMPTION AND SAVING (%)**

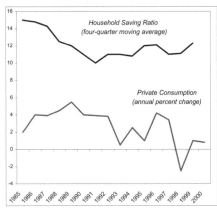

SOURCE: International Monetary Fund, *Japan: Economic and Policy Developments*, November 2000.

EXHIBIT 11.7F   **HOUSEHOLD NET WORTH AND LIABILITIES (% OF DISPOSABLE INCOME)**

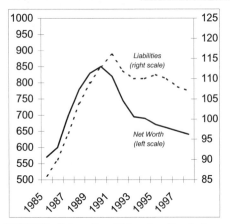

SOURCE: International Monetary Fund, *Japan: Economic and Policy Developments*, November 2000.

EXHIBIT 11.8A	PERSONAL FINANCIAL ASSETS (TRILLIONS OF $US, CONVERTED FROM YEN AT CURRENT RATE)

	March '95	March '99
Total personal financial assets	10.81	12.74
Postal savings	1.91	2.44
All other cash and deposits	4.23	4.56
Postal insurance	0.72	1.02
All other insurance	2.06	1.34

SOURCE: Bank of Japan, Post Office.

Note: All insurance figures and policy reserves; 1999 figures include more categories of assets

EXHIBIT 11.8B	SHARE OF HOUSEHOLDS USING FINANCIAL INSTITUTIONS

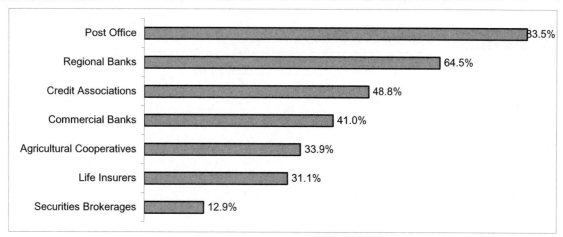

SOURCE: 1997 Ministry of Posts and Telecommunications Survey of 3,298 Households.

EXHIBIT 11.9A	PERCENT RETURN ON EQUITY FOR JAPANESE COMPANIES IN JANUARY OF EACH YEAR

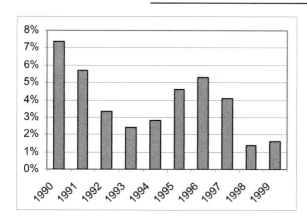

SOURCE: Analysts' Guide, Daiwa Shoken Chosabu.

EXHIBIT 11.9B	PERCENT. OF JAPAN'S LISTED STOCKS HELD IN CROSS-SHAREHOLDING ARRANGEMENTS

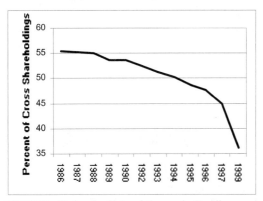

SOURCE: Daiwa Institute of Research, Baseline.

EXHIBIT 11.10	MAJOR BANK MERGERS

Pre-Merger	Post-Merger	Total Assets ($bn)
Bank of Tokyo-Mitsubishi Mitsubishi Trust Nippon Trust	*Mitsubishi Tokyo Financial Group*	835
Sumitomo Bank Sakura Bank	*Sumitomo Mitsui Banking*	960
Dai-Ichi Kangyo Bank Fuji Bank Industrial Bank of Japan Yasuda Trust	*Mizuho Holdings*	1,300
Sanwa Bank Tokai Bank Toyo Trust	*UFJ Holdings*	823
Mitsui Trust Chuo Trust	*Chuo Mitsui Trust*	152

SOURCE: Case writer created using data from Phred Dvorak, "For Japanese Banks, A New Vulnerability to Weak Stocks," *The Wall Street Journal,* April 16, 2001.

EXHIBIT 11.11	MAJOR BANKS' PROFITS, FY1990–99 (TRILLIONS OF YEN)

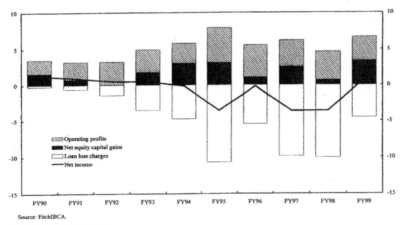

SOURCE: FitchIBCA.

EXHIBIT 11.12	LOAN CATEGORIZATIONS AND VALUES AS OF SEPTEMBER 2000

Loan Category	Description	Total Value (¥ trillion)	Total Value ($ billion @ ¥124)
Category 1 (standard)	Credit exposures which banks have not classified as categories 2, 3, or 4.	¥467.1 trillion	$3,767
Category 2 (substandard)	Credit exposures on which banks have judged adequate risk management on an exposure-by-exposure basis will be needed.	¥ 61.2 trillion	$ 493.7
Category 3 (doubtful)	Credit exposures on which banks have serious concerns in terms of their ultimate collection and thus are likely to incur losses, but have difficulties with rational estimation of when or how much losses will actually occur.	¥ 2.7 trillion	$ 21.8
Category 4 (loss)	Credit exposures which banks have judged to be non-collectable or of no value.	¥0.014 trillion	$ 0.1

SOURCE: Financial Services Agency of Japan

EXHIBIT 11.13	BANK LENDING (TWELVE-MONTH PERCENT CHANGE)

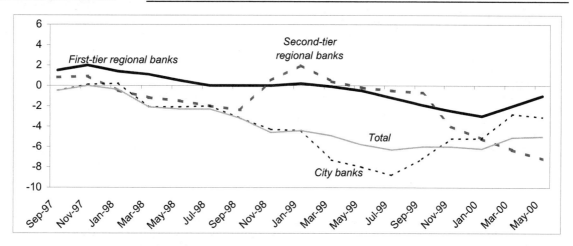

SOURCE: International Monetary Fund, *Japan: Economic and Policy Developments,* November 2000.

EXHIBIT 11.14A	GROWTH IN IT INVESTMENT

	1980–1985		1985–1990		1990–1994	
	Real	Nominal	Real	Nominal	Real	Nominal
Japan	18.5%	16.8%	16.1%	9.4%	1.8%	-0.8%
United States	9.5%	12.0%	5.8%	3.8%	17.0%	9.5%

SOURCE: Shinozaki, Akihiko. "Analysis of the Primary Causes and Economic Effects of Information." *The Japan Development Bank Research Report*, August 1996, p.35.

Note: The figures for Japan were deflated using "Wholesale Price Index" prepared by the Bank of Japan for each product item. The base year is 1990.

EXHIBIT 11.14B	**INFORMATION TECHNOLOGY STATISTICS**	
	1995/1996	**1999/2000**
No. of mobile phones (10,000 contracts)[a]	1,061	5,114
No. of ISDN lines	519,846	5,141,175[b]
Domestic personal computer shipments ('000 units)	5,704	9,941
No. of Japanese companies linked to the Internet (%)[c]	12	86
No. of Japanese domains allocated on the Internet	2,625	143,373[d]

SOURCE: The Economist Intelligence Unit.

[a]End-year [b]September 30, 1999 [c]Companies with 300 or more [d]March 1, 2000

EXHIBIT 11.15	**SUMMARY OF ECONOMIC STIMULUS PACKAGES, 1993–1999**						
	1993		**1994**	**1995**	**1998**		**1999**
	April	**September**	**February**	**September**	**April**	**November**	**November**
Total package	13.2	6.2	15.3	14.2	16.7	23.9	18.1
% of GDP	2.8	1.3	3.2	3.0	3.3	4.8	3.6
Tax reductions	0.2	0.0	5.9^	0.0	4.6^	6.0^^	0.0
% of GDP	0.0	0.0	1.2	0.0	0.9	1.2	0.0
Public investment^^^	7.6	2.0	1.5	6.5	7.7	8.1	6.8
% of GDP	1.6	0.4	0.9	1.4	1.5	1.6	1.4
Land purchases*	1.2	0.3	2.0	3.2	1.6	…	…
% of GDP	0.3	0.1	0.4	0.7	0.3	…	…
Increased lending by Housing Loan Corp**	1.8	2.9	1.2	0.5	0.0	1.2	2.0
% of GDP	0.4	0.6	0.3	0.1	0.0	0.2	0.4
Increased lending by government-affiliated financial institutions	2.4	1.0	1.5	2.6***	2.0	6.9	7.4
% of GDP	0.5	0.2	0.3	0.5	0.4	1.4	1.5
Other	0.0	0.0	0.2	2.6	0.8	1.7	1.9
% of GDP	0.0	0.0	0.0	0.0	0.2	0.3	0.4

SOURCE: International Monetary Fund, *Japan: Economic and Policy Developments,* November 2000.

^Temporary measures; ^^Later increased to 9.3 trillion yen (1.9% of GDP); ^^^Public investment comprises general public works (including land purchases), disaster reconstruction, buildings and equipment and independent public works projects by local government;* Excludes land acquisition for public works projects, which is included in public spending; **Includes loans by the Pension Welfare Service Public Corporation; ***Includes 1.3 trillion yen in lending by the Japanese Corporation for small businesses.

EXHIBIT 11.16 — DISTRIBUTION OF COMPANIES IN HORIZONTAL BUSINESS GROUPS

	MITSUBISHI	MITSUI	SUMITOMO	FUYO	DKB	SANWA
Financial Services	Mitsubishi Bank Mitsubishi Trust & Banking Meiji Mutual Life Tokio Marine & Fire	Mitsui Taiyo Kobe Bank Mitsui Trust & Banking Mitsui Mutual Life Taisho Marine & Fire	Sumitomo Bank Sumitomo Trust & Banking Sumitomo Life Sumitomo Marine & Fire	Fuji Bank Yasuda Trust & Banking Yasuda Mutual Life Yasuda Fire & Marine	Dai-Ichi Kangyo Bank Asahi Mutual Life Taisei Fire & Marine Fukoku Mutual Life Nissan Fire & Marine Kankaku Securities Orient	Sanwa Bank Toyo Trust & Banking Nippon Life Orix
Computers, Electronics & Electrical Equipment	Mitsubishi Electric	Toshiba	NEC	Oki Electric Industry Yokogawa Electric Hitachi[1]	Fujitsu Fuji Electric Yaskawa Electric Mfg. Nippon Columbia Hitachi[1]	Iwatsu Electric Sharp Nitto Denko Kyocera Hitachi[1]
Cars	Mitsubishi Motors	Toyota Motor[1]		Nissan Motor	Isuzu Motors	Daihatsu Motor
Trading & Retailing	Mitsubishi	Mitsui Mitsukoshi	Sumitomo	Marubeni	C. Itoh Nissho Iwai[1] Kanematsu Kawasho Seibu Department Stores	Nissho Iwai[1] Nichimen Iwatani International Takashimaya
Food & Beverages	Kirin Brewery	Nippon Flour Mills		Nisshin Flour Milling Sapporo Breweries Nichirei		Itoham Foods Suntory
Construction	Mitsubishi Construction	Mitsui Construction Sanki Engineering	Sumitomo Construction	Taisei	Shimizu	Toyo Construction Obayashi Sekisui House Zenitaka
Metals	Mitsubishi Steel Mfg. Mitsubishi Materials Mitsubishi Aluminum Mitsubishi Cable Industries	Japan Steel Works Mitsui Mining & Smelting	Sumitomo Metal Industries Sumitomo Metal Mining Sumitomo Electric Industries Sumitomo Light Metal Industries	NKK	Kawasaki Steel Kobe Steel[1] Japan Metals & Chemicals Nippon Light Metal Furukawa Furukawa Electric	Kobe Steel[1] Nakayama Steel Works Hitachi Metals Nisshin Steel Hitachi Cable
Real Estate	Mitsubishi Estate	Mitsui Real Estate Development	Sumitomo Realty & Development	Tokyo Taternono	Tokyo Dome	
Oil & Coal	Mitsubishi Oil			Tonen	Showa Shell Sekiyu	Cosmo Oil
Rubber & Glass	Asahi Glass		Nippon Sheet Glass		Yokohama Rubber	Toyo Tire & Rubber
Chemicals	Mitsubishi Kasei Mitsubishi Petrochemical Mitsubishi Gas Chemical Mitsubishi Plastics Industries Mitsubishi Kasei Polytec	Mitsui Toatsu Chemicals Mitsui Petrochemical Industries	Sumitomo Chemical Sumitomo Bakelite	Showa Denko Nippon Oil & Fats Kureha Chemical Industry	Kyowa Hakko Kogyo Denki Kagaku Kogyo Nippon Zeon Asahi Denka Kogyo Sankyo Shiseido Lion	Ube Industries Tokuyama Soda Hitachi Chemical Sekisui Chemical Kansai Paint Tanabe Seiyaku Fujisawa Pharmaceuticals
Fibers & Textiles	Mitsubishi Rayon	Toray Industries		Nisshinbo Industries Toho Rayon	Asahi Chemical Industry	Unitika Teijin
Pulp & Paper	Mitsubishi Paper Mills	Oji Paper		Sanyo-Kokusaku Pulp	Honshu Paper	
Mining & Forestry		Mitsui Mining Hokkaido Colliery & Steamship	Sumitomo Forestry Sumitomo Coal Mining			
Industrial Equipment	Mitsubishi Heavy Industries Mitsubishi Kakoki	Mitsui Engineering & Shipbuilding	Sumitomo Heavy Industries	Kubota Nippon Seiko	Niigata Engineering Iseki Ebara Kawasaki Heavy Industries Ishikawajima-Harima Heavy Industries	NTN Hitachi Zosen Shin Meiwa Industry
Cameras & Optics	Nikon			Canon	Asahi Optical	Hoya
Cement		Onoda Cement	Sumitomo Cement	Nihon Cement	Chichibu Cement	Osaka Cement
Shipping & Transportation	Nippon Yusen Mitsubishi Warehouse & Transportation	Mitsui OSK Lines Mitsui Warehouse	Sumitomo Warehouse	Showa Line Keihin Electric Express Railway Tobu Railway	Kawasaki Kisen Shibusawa Warehouse Nippon Express[1]	Navix Line Hankyu Nippon Express[1]

[1] Companies affiliated with more than one group.

SOURCE: Brown & Company Ltd., in *Fortune*, July 15, 1991, p. 81.

EXHIBIT 11.17	FOREIGN DIRECT INVESTMENT ($USBN)

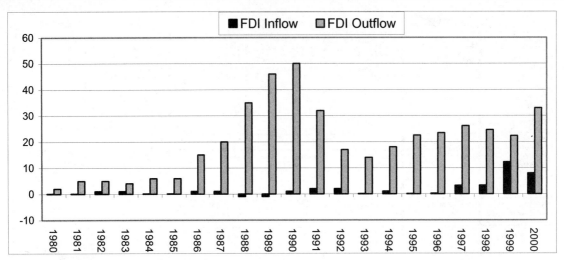

SOURCE: The Economist Intelligence Unit

EXHIBIT 11.18	REORGANIZATION OF MINISTRIES FOR 2001

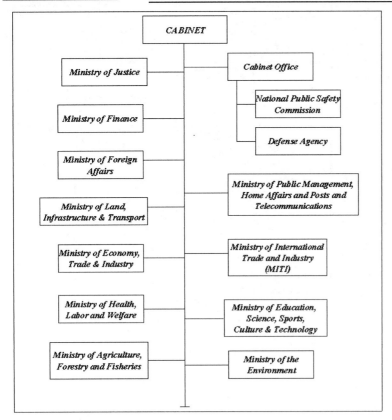

SOURCE: Government of Japan.

| EXHIBIT 11.19A | PROJECTIONS OF SOCIAL SECURITY COSTS (AS % OF NATIONAL INCOME) |

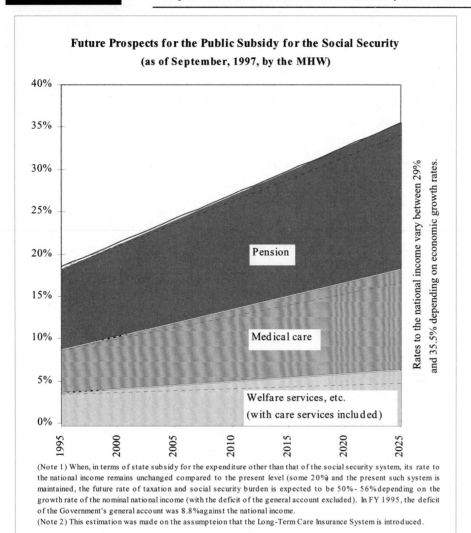

Future Prospects for the Public Subsidy for the Social Security

(as of September, 1997, by the MHW)

(Note 1) When, in terms of state subsidy for the expenditure other than that of the social security system, its rate to the national income remains unchanged compared to the present level (some 20%) and the present such system is maintained, the future rate of taxation and social security burden is expected to be 50%- 56% depending on the growth rate of the nominal national income (with the deficit of the general account excluded). In FY 1995, the deficit of the Government's general account was 8.8% against the national income.

(Note 2) This estimation was made on the assumpteion that the Long-Term Care Insurance System is introduced.

SOURCE: Japan International Corporation of Welfare Services, *Textbook for the 7th Study Programme for the Asian Social Insurance Administrators*, Tokyo, Japan, October 1997.

EXHIBIT 11.19B   **PERCENTAGE OF POPULATION OVER SIXTY YEARS OLD, 1990-2050**

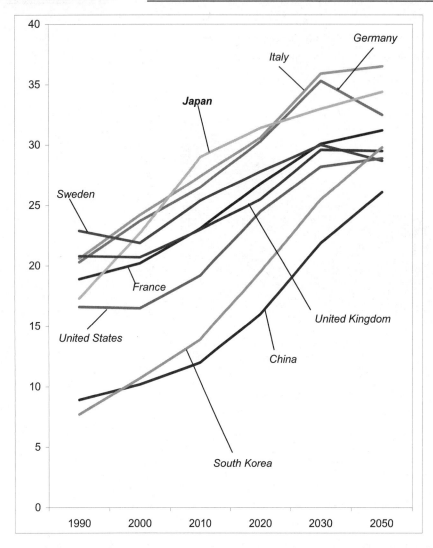

SOURCE: The World Bank, *Averting the Old Age Crisis* (New York: Oxford University Press, 1994.)

ENDNOTES

1 W.G. Beasley, *The Rise of Modern Japan,* 2nd Edition (New York: St. Martin's Press, 1995), pp. 263-4.

2 Takatoshi Ito, *The Japanese Economy* (Cambridge, Mass.: The MIT Press, 1992), p. 70.

3 Takatoshi Ito, *The Japanese Economy* (Cambridge, Mass.: The MIT Press, 1992), p. 71.

4 P. Landers and P. Dvorak, "Deflation Fighter: Japan's Central Bank Issues Wakeup Call on Flagging Economy," *The Wall Street Journal,* March 20, 2001.

5 Karel Van Wolferen, *The Enigma of Japanese Power* (New York: Alfred A. Knopf Inc., 1989), p. 170.

6 Yasuhiko Hibata, Yomiuri Research Institute, *The Daily Yomiuri,* February 4, 1998, p. 5.

7 The Japan Institute of Labour, Ministry of Labour, "White Paper on Labour 1997," p. 91.

8 Personal interview with Mr. Yoshio Suzuki, President, Asahi Research Center, Co. Ltd.

9 Banks in Japan were allowed to own equity positions of up to 10% of the total outstanding shares in other businesses. The Anti-Monopoly Law Reform of 1977 reduced this number to 5%, effective in 1987.

10 Eisuke Sakakibara and Robert A. Feldman, "The Japanese Financial System in Comparative Perspective," *Journal of Comparative Economics,* 7, (1983): 1-24.

11 *The Yomiuri Shimbun.* "Economic Forum: Measure to Counter Asset Deflation." March 28, 2001.

12 The Economist Intelligence Unit, *EIU Country Report,* Japan, 3rd quarter 1997, p. 4.

13 Personal interview with Administrative Reform Council member Mr. Ken Moroi.

14 Karel Van Wolferen, *The Enigma of Japanese Power* (New York: Alfred A. Knopf Inc., 1989), pp. 121-124.

15 "Regarding the Report of The Subcommittee for Long-Range Issues of the Industrial Structure Council." News from MITI, October 1995.

16 Personal interview with Mr. Shijuro Ogata, former Deputy Governor of the Bank of Japan.

17 Chalmers Johnson, *MITI and the Japanese Miracle* (Stanford, Calif.: Stanford University Press, 1982), pp. 203-7.

18 Personal interview with Mitsubishi Corporation President Minoru Makihara.

19 Takatoshi Ito, *The Japanese Economy* (Cambridge, Mass.: The MIT Press, 1992), pp. 180-192.

20 The Economist Intelligence Unit. *Japan: Country Profile, 2001.*

21 Personal interview with Mitsubishi Corporation President Minoru Makihara.

22 Bill Spindle and Norihiko Shirouzu, "Mitsubishi Racketeering Probe Widens," *The Wall Street Journal,* October 27, 1997, p. A19.

23 Personal interview with Mr. Shijuro Ogata, former Deputy Governor of the Bank of Japan.

24 Statistics Bureau and Statistics Center, Management and Coordination Agency, Japan in Figures 1998, Section 2: Population, Tables 1 and 2. Internet address: http://www.stat.go.jp/ 1611m.htm.

25 Health and Welfare Bureau for the Elderly, Ministry of Health and Welfare, "New Gold Plan," December 1994, p. 32.

26 Health and Welfare Bureau for the Elderly, Ministry of Health and Welfare, "New Gold Plan," December 1994, p. 44.

27 Japan International Corporation of Welfare Services, *Textbook for the 7th Study Programme for the Asian Social Insurance Administrators,*(Tokyo, Japan, October 1997 pp. 76-80).

28 "Women in Japan Today" website. URL: http://www.sorifu.go.jp/danjyo/index2.html.

29 Nihon Keizai Shinbun, February 9, 1998, p. 7.

30 The Japan Institute of Labour, Ministry of Labour, "White Paper on Labour, 1997," p. 19.

31 Japan Institute for Social and Economic Affairs, *Japan 1998: An International Comparison,* (Washington, DC, 1998 pp. 99-100).

32 *Facts on File World News Digest,* "Math, Science Education Study Released," December 5, 1996.

33 An advisory committee headed by former Bank of Japan Governor Haruo Maekawa proposed restructuring the Japanese economy to be less dependent on exports for growth. However, its report floundered in the bureaucracy and its ideas were never implemented.

34 Personal interview with Mr. Koichi Koike, Director, Administration Department, Bank of Japan.

35   Final Report of the Administrative Reform Council (Provisional Translation), December 3, 1997.

36   Personal interview with Administrative Reform Council member Mr. Ken Moroi.

37   Personal interview with Mr. Akihiko Shinozaki, Deputy Director, Loan Division, Japan Development Bank.

38   "The Action Plan for Economic Structure Reform," Ministry of International Trade and Industry, May 1997.

39   "Estimated Economic Effects of Deregulation," Summary of Report of the Study Group on the Economic Effects of Deregulation.

40   "Program for Educational Reform," Ministry of Education, Science, Sports and Culture, revised August 5, 1997.

41   "Financial System Reform," Ministry of Finance, June 13, 1997.

42   "On the Promotion of Fiscal Structural Reform," Cabinet decision, June 3, 1997.

43   David P. Hamilton, "Japan Renews Blitz to Sell Its Stimulus Plan," *The Wall Street Journal*, April 27, 1998.

44   Personal interview with Mr. Nobuyuki Takakura, Senior Policy Coordinator, Policy Planning and Evaluation Division, Minister's Secretariat, Ministry of Health and Welfare.

45   The International Monetary Fund, *Japan: Economic and Policy Developments*, November 2000.

46   The International Monetary Fund, *Japan: Economic and Policy Developments*, November 2000.

47   The Economist Intelligence Unit. *Country Profile: Japan*, 2001.

48   *The Yomiuri Shimbun*, "New Government Setup Vital to Keep Nation Vibrant," January 4, 2001.

49   P. Dvorak, "For Japanese Banks, A New Vulnerability to Weak Stocks," *The Wall Street Journal*, April 2, 2001.

50   G. Tett, "Japan's Bad Loans Put at $1,200bn," *Financial Times.*, April 19,2001.

51   P. Dvorak, "Corporate Bankruptcies in Japan Hit Record High," *The Wall Street Journal*, April 16, 2001, Yumiko Ono, "The Long Goodbye," *The Wall Street Journal*, July 5, 2001.

52   CNN.com, "Short on Detail, Koizumi Pledges Deep Reforms," May 7, 2001.

53   B. Bremner and R. Neff, "Japan's Reformer," *Business Week*, May 7, 2001; G. Tett, "Japan's New Finance Chief Determined to Push Reform," *Financial Times*. May 7, 2001.

54   B. Bremner and R. Neff, "Japan's Reformer," *Business Week*. May 7, 2001; G. Tett, "Japan's New Finance Chief Determined to Push Reform," *Financial Times*. May 7, 2001.

55   Akiko Kashiwagi, "Japan Fears It's Back in Recession," *The Washington Post*, June 15, 2001.

56   Gillian Tett and Bayan Rahman. "Japan Is Heading for Sharp Slowdown, Figures Suggest," *The Financial Times*, June 29, 2001.

57   Akiko Kashiwagi, "Japan Fears It's Back in Recession," *The Washington Post*, June 15, 2001.

58   Linda Sieg, "Japan's PM Koizumi Keeping Political Powder Dry," Reuters, July 9, 2001.

Deficits, Debt, and Defense

We conclude this book with the United States, the world's largest economy, and President George Bush's strategy for moving forward. By excerpting *The Economic Report of the President*, from February 2003, we provide the most recent look at what Bush is doing with fiscal policy, monetary policy, defense policy, and trade.

The numbers in the case allow students to evaluate U.S. economic performance over the past two decades since the Reagan Revolution, when President Ronald Reagan boldly put the U.S. on a new growth trajectory. One can examine GDP growth, the components of growth, inflation, productivity, and unemployment. One can assess fiscal and monetary developments, under Reagan and Bush, under President Bill Clinton, and again under the younger George Bush. One can look at America's performance internationally, by examining exchange rates and the balance of payments. Using all these numbers, one can build a fairly good assessment of the economic effectiveness of each administration's programs.

The case provides a wonderful opportunity to understand the macroeconomics of globalization through the relationship between America's fiscal deficits and its trade deficits.

Finally, as the text reports, George Bush has engaged in two wars (Afghanistan and Iraq) and cut taxes three times since taking office in 2001. Alan Greenspan, meanwhile, has lowered interest rates twelve times, to a record low. Students are asked to contemplate the effectiveness of these policies for dealing with America's problems and to consider likely alternatives. They can also think about the likely future path of America's current trajectory.

| CASE STUDY | U.S. DEFICITS & DEBT: EXCERPTS FROM THE ECONOMIC REPORT OF THE PRESIDENT, FEBRUARY 2003 |

EDITED BY: RICHARD H. K. VIETOR

To the Congress of the United States

The economy is recovering from the effects of the slowdown that began in the middle of 2000 and led to the subsequent recession. The American economy has been hit hard by the events of the past three years, most tragically by the effects of the terrorist attacks of September 11, 2001. Our economy and investor confidence were hurt when we learned that some corporate leaders were not playing by the rules. The combined impact of these events, along with the three-year decline in stock values that impacted business investment, slowed growth in 2002. Despite these challenges, the economy's underlying fundamentals remain solid—including low inflation, low interest rates, and strong productivity gains. Yet the pace of the expansion has not been satisfactory; there are still too many Americans looking for jobs. We will not be satisfied until every part of our economy is vigorous and every person who wants a job can find one.

We are taking action to restore the robust growth that creates jobs. In January, I proposed a growth and jobs plan to add needed momentum to our economic recovery. We will accelerate the tax relief already approved by Congress and give it to Americans now, when it is most needed. Lowering tax rates and moving more Americans into the lowest tax bracket will help our economy grow and create jobs. Faster marriage tax relief and a faster increase in the child tax credit will especially help middle-class families, and should take effect now. We will take steps to encourage small business investment, helping them to expand and create jobs. We will end the unfair double taxation of corporate income received by individuals. By putting more money back in the hands of shareholders, strengthening investor confidence in the market, and encouraging more investment, we will have more growth and job creation. These steps will allow Americans to keep more of their own money to spend, save, or invest. They will boost the economy, ensure that the recovery continues, and

provide long-term economic benefits through higher productivity and higher incomes.

As our economy recovers, we also have an obligation to help Americans who have lost their jobs. That is why we extended unemployment payments for workers who lost their jobs and improved incentives for investment to create new jobs. I also proposed a bold new program of reemployment accounts to help workers searching for jobs.

Our commitment to a strong economy does not stop with these important steps. We will continue to strengthen investor confidence in the integrity of our markets. We will develop better ways to train workers for new jobs. We will make the Nation's regulation and tax code less onerous and more reflective of the demands of a dynamic economy, and expand opportunities for open trade and stronger growth in all nations, especially for emerging and developing economies.

Our Nation's economic progress comes from the innovation and hard work of Americans in a free market that creates opportunities no other system can offer. Government does not create wealth, but instead creates the economic environment in which risk takers and entrepreneurs create jobs. With the right policies focused on growth and jobs, strong economic fundamentals—and hard work—I am confident we will extend economic opportunity and prosperity to every corner of America.

THE WHITE HOUSE
FEBRUARY 2003

Macroeconomic Policy and the Budget Outlook

The U.S. economy has suffered a number of serious setbacks in the past three years, including the terrorist attacks of September 2001, the significant loss of stock market wealth since 2000, and the recent corporate accounting

---

Professor Richard H. K. Vietor excerpted this text and these exhibits from a publicly available document, *Economic Report of the President, February 2003.*

scandals. Yet the contraction of 2001 was one of the mildest on record, with recovery proceeding steadily, if modestly, in 2002. One reason for the economy's stability in the face of these adverse developments was the stance of macroeconomic policy, both monetary (set by the Federal Reserve) and fiscal (set by the President and the Congress). This section analyzes the effects of monetary and fiscal policy in detail, illustrating their likely impact on macroeconomic performance in 2002 as well as the fiscal outlook for the years ahead.

Monetary Policy

In 2001, faced with signs of a slowing of economic activity, the Federal Reserve reduced its policy interest rate, the Federal funds rate, 11 times during the year, from 6.50 percent to 1.75 percent. The Federal Reserve then held the funds rate steady through most of 2002, until a further half-percentage-point cut on November 6 brought it down to 1.25 percent. Although the Federal funds rate thus remained constant for most of 2002, earlier rate reductions continued to stimulate the economy throughout the year. Understanding the reasons for this lag requires an understanding of the channels through which monetary policy affects the economy. A lowering of interest rates stimulates demand through four main channels: encouraging consumption (particularly of durables), stimulating business investment (by lowering the cost of capital), promoting residential investment (as seen from the booming housing sector), and lowering the foreign exchange value of the dollar (which tends to raise exports and lower imports). All of these effects take time to be felt. Consumers must plan how best to take advantage of lower borrowing costs, firms must plan new investments, and importers and exporters must determine how any change in the dollar's exchange value will affect their prices and costs.

Measuring the size of these effects as well as the time needed for them to be fully expressed is an active area of macroeconomic research. One method for measuring the effect of monetary policy uses formal models of the economy, in which the behavioral relationships governing consumption, investment, imports, and exports are fully specified. After the researcher specifies a time path for the Federal funds rate, the model supplies the likely path for each component of aggregate demand, based on the behavioral

relationships embedded in the model's equations. In contrast to this model-based method, a more data-based method for measuring the effects of monetary policy omits any formal modeling of behavioral relationships, instead using statistical techniques to measure the past effect of funds rate changes on a few key variables, such as output and the price level. An important goal of this method is to take account of other factors, such as changes in fiscal policy and temporary shocks to aggregate demand and prices, which may also have affected the economy when a given change in monetary policy was taking place. Although the precise channels of monetary policy are not specified in the data-based method, it is hoped that the answers are less sensitive to particular assumptions, which can differ across large behavioral models.

Results from both model-based and data-based methods suggest that monetary policy changes take effect only after a lag of several months, but that these effects are long-lasting, so that the rate reductions in 2001 are likely to have stimulated the economy throughout 2002. To gain a sense of the magnitudes involved, one well-known model of the economy predicts that, holding other factors constant, a 1-percentage-point decrease in the Federal funds rate raises real GDP by 0.6 percent above its baseline level after one year. This effect of monetary stimulus on real GDP rises to 1.7 percent after two years. Data-based methods broadly concur with this assessment: one study shows that the typical decrease in the funds rate raises output steadily in subsequent quarters, reaching a maximum effect on output after about 18 months. Both methods therefore imply that interest rate cuts in 2001 continued to exert considerable economic stimulus in 2002.

Fiscal Policy

An important goal of fiscal policy is to promote growth by limiting the share of output commanded by the government. In 2001 the Congress and the Administration made major progress along these lines with passage of the Economic Growth and Tax Relief Reconciliation Act (EGTRRA), which featured a broad-based cut in marginal tax rates. The long-term benefits of such a policy are clear, as high marginal tax rates discourage the entrepreneurship and risk taking on which the strength of the U.S. economic system depends. Yet although the goal of EGTRRA was to improve long-term living standards and limit the size of the government, the legislation conferred important short-term benefits as well, thanks to the way in which the tax rate reductions were set in place and the timing of the act's passage. A new lower tax rate of 10 percent was introduced at the bottom range of the previous 15 percent bracket, and taxpayers in 2001 were given an advance rebate on their likely savings due to this reduction.

Rebate checks ($300 for most single taxpayers, $600 for most married couples filing jointly) arrived in mailboxes in the summer of 2001. The timing of the resulting $36 billion infusion of spendable income into the economy could not have been more favorable. Although the depth of the 2001 recession would not be known until revised GDP figures were announced the next year, GDP had already declined by 0.6 percent at an annual rate in the first quarter of 2001 and by 1.6 percent in the second quarter. As estimated from the traditional relationship between overall GDP and current income, the tax plan added about 1.2 percentage points of growth at an annual rate in the third quarter. As a result, without the checks, third-quarter GDP would have declined at an annual rate of 1.5 percent rather than the 0.3 percent rate actually observed. In the fourth quarter, tax relief continued to add 12 percentage points to the annual rate of real GDP growth, so that instead of rising at an annual rate of 2.7 percent, GDP would have risen by only 1.5 percent in the absence of the rebates.

The rebate checks mailed in 2001 represented only a small fraction of the tax relief from the EGTRRA package. In addition to lower marginal tax rates, EGTRRA increases the incentives for saving, for making bequests to heirs, and for investment. As a result, tax relief from EGTRRA probably helped the private sector create 800,000 jobs by the end of 2002 relative to the baseline level without tax relief, while raising GDP growth by about 0.5 percentage point over the course of that year.

In March 2002 the President signed the Job Creation and Worker Assistance Act, which implemented a tax policy especially appropriate for the fledgling recovery. The act promoted investment by allowing firms to immediately write off (that is, expense) 30 percent of the value of qualified investments in the year of purchase for investments made through September 11, 2004. Government policies can significantly improve growth by removing tax distortions that penalize investment or other productive activities. For example, introducing expensing lowers the cost of capital, thereby making more investment opportunities profitable on an after-tax basis. The act stimulates investment by allowing partial expensing through most of 2004. In addition to reducing the tax-adjusted cost of investment, the act extended unemployment benefits to workers who have exhausted their regular benefits. This enhanced the role of unemployment insurance as one of the economy's most important automatic stabilizers.

The Federal Budget

After four years of surplus, the unified Federal budget recorded a deficit of $158 billion in fiscal 2002, or about 1.5 percent of GDP. The return of the deficit was primarily due to four factors: the lingering effects of the recession of 2001, the stock market plunge, increased Federal expenditure necessitated by the war on terrorism, and the costs of homeland security. Recessions tend to increase budget deficits because they lead to higher outlays (for unemployment insurance, for example) at the same time that they reduce tax receipts (because taxable income fails). The decline in receipts during the most recent downturn in the business cycle has been especially pronounced. Total receipts in fiscal 2002 were $1,853 billion, having fallen $138 billion, or about 7 percent from their level in fiscal 2001. This represented a much larger percentage decrease in receipts than in previous, far more severe recessions. One of the most important reasons for the dramatic decline in receipts given the mildness of the 2001 contraction was the coincident decline in the stock market. The stock market's decline reduced capital gains receipts in addition to reducing taxes on wage and salary income for workers whose jobs are closely tied to equity markets. More detailed information on the precise sources of the decline in receipts will not be available until the Treasury completes its regular annual examination of individual tax returns. Even with the decline in receipts, however, the budget deficit was relatively small as a fraction of GDP compared with those seen in previous periods of war and recession.

The President's Jobs and Growth Initiative

On January 7, 2003, the President proposed a plan to enhance the long-term growth of the economy while supporting the emerging recovery. At the start of 2003 the consensus of private forecasters predicted accelerating growth in real GDP over the course of the year, which would raise investment, reduce unemployment, and increase job growth. This consensus view is reflected in the Administration's outlook, discussed below. Yet the recovery in investment could be delayed by weaker-than-expected profit growth, higher required rates of return arising from geopolitical and other risks, or a prolonged period during which companies focus on repairing their balance sheets. More general risks to recovery in 2003 include an increased sense of caution, which could lead households to pull back on their spending plans, and the potential for further terrorist attacks. To insure against these near-term risks while boosting long-term growth, the President has proposed a focused set of initiatives. Specifically, the President's plan would:

- Accelerate to January 1, 2003, many features of the 2001 tax cut that are currently scheduled to be phased in over several years. These include the reductions in marginal income tax rates, additional marriage penalty relief, a larger child credit, and a wider 10 percent income tax bracket
- Eliminate the double taxation of corporate income by excluding dividends from individual taxable income
- Increase expensing limits for small business investment, raising to $75,000 the amount that small businesses may deduct from their taxable income in the year the investment takes place
- Provide $3.6 billion to the States to fund personal Reemployment Accounts for unemployed workers. These accounts would allow eligible workers to spend up to $3,000 to defray the costs of finding or training for a new job. Workers could keep any unspent balance in their account if they find work within 13 weeks of going on unemployment.

Accelerating the marginal tax rate reductions would insure against a softening of consumption by putting more money in consumers' pockets through long-term tax cuts, which have been shown to be more effective than temporary cuts in boosting near-term spending. Ending the double tax on corporate income would increase the ability of corporations to raise equity capital, providing near-term support to investment while improving the long-term efficiency of capital markets. The provisions also support investment by small firms. Higher expensing limits would make it easier for small firms to expand by reducing the tax-adjusted cost of capital; lower marginal tax rates would increase growth incentives for small business owners whose business income is taxed at individual rates. Finally, Personal Reemployment Accounts would provide unemployed workers with a new set of incentives as they look for work. Accounts of this type, which reward unemployed workers for finding jobs quickly, have been shown in experiments in several States to increase the speed with which unemployed workers find new jobs. Moreover, by allowing workers a choice between using the funds to support their job search and using them for job training expenses, the accounts are well suited for the dynamic U.S. labor market.

The Effect of Tax Relief on Interest Rates

One of the most widely discussed issues in fiscal policy concerns the effect of tax relief on interest rates. It is widely agreed that, in the immediate aftermath of a permanent tax cut, consumption increases because consumers have more disposable income. This increase to consumption raises GDP in the near term, especially if the economy is operating below its potential, with large amounts of unused labor and capital. In the long run, lower tax rates have somewhat complicated, offsetting effects on GDP. On the negative side, if the reduction in tax rates is not accompanied by spending reductions, it will increase the budget deficit and may reduce national saving. Lower national saving, in turn, will shrink the pool of loanable funds available in capital markets, which increases interest rates and reduces investment. Ultimately, lower investment leads to a smaller stock of productive capital, resulting in lower wages, lower productivity, and lower output. Offsetting this, however, is the positive effect of tax relief that operates through improved incentives to work and take risks, for example by creating a new firm or by making a new investment. Incentives to undertake these activities improve after a cut in marginal tax rates, because the tax reduction allows more of the rewards to be captured by workers, entrepreneurs, and investors and not by the government. When tax relief extends to capital income (such as dividends), as proposed in the President's most recent jobs and growth initiative, an additional positive effect arises through stronger incentives to save. These positive effects on GDP operating through improved incentives also have an impact on future budget deficits and investment, because deficits will be less onerous if the economy grows in response to the improved investment climate.

Developments in the Rest of the World

Growth in many of the United States' major trading partners was even more disappointing in 2002 than was growth at home. Although growth in Canada, America's largest trading partner, was a surprisingly robust 4.0 percent during the four quarters ending in the third quarter of 2002, growth elsewhere lagged far behind. The economy of the United Kingdom grew only 2.1 percent over the same period; growth rates in Germany (0.4 percent), Italy (0.5 percent), France (1.0 percent), Japan (1.3 percent), and Mexico (1.8 percent) were even lower. Low demand for U.S. exports continued with the emerging recovery in the United States (which increased U.S. demand for imports) and sent the U.S. trade deficit to a record high in 2002.

Discussion of the U.S. position in international markets is often framed in terms of the current account, a broader measure of international transactions. In addition to the trade balance in goods and services, the current account includes net investment income, net compensation of resident alien workers, and net unilateral transfers. Because the trade component is by far the largest in the current account balance, the widening in the trade deficit in 2002 contributed strongly to the widening in the current account deficit. The latter reached a record 4.9 percent of GDP in the second quarter of 2002 before falling slightly to 4.8 percent in the third quarter.

One advantage of framing international finance discussions in terms of the current account is that, as a matter of national accounting, the current account balance equals the difference between net national saving and net national investment. For example, if U.S. saving were smaller than U.S. investment in a given period, the difference—the excess of investment over saving—must have been financed by foreigners. In the process of financing U.S. investment, foreign investors obtain U.S. assets, either in portfolio form (that is, as stocks, bonds, or other financial securities) or through direct controlling ownership of physical capital. These assets then generate investment income in the form of dividends, interest payments, and profits that can be repatriated to the investors abroad. Balance of payments data therefore resemble a "sources and use of funds" statement for the Nation as a whole, providing useful information on the amounts of internal and external investment financing. High levels of investment in the late 1990s meant that past current account deficits require an increasing portion of the income earned by the capital to flow abroad. Over the past year, the U.S. current account deficit has widened because net investment has been essentially flat while net saving has fallen [see **Exhibit 12.1**].

The relationship between the current account deficit and net investment by foreigners in U.S. assets also makes clear how changes in international demand for U.S. assets can affect the trade balance, and vice versa. Consider an increase in foreigners' demand for U.S. assets. Their resulting accumulation of U.S. assets can affect international trade flows through an appreciation of the dollar, because foreigners must obtain dollars in order to purchase U.S. assets. Appreciation of the dollar tends to make imports cheaper for U.S. residents and U.S. exports more expensive to consumers abroad; both these effects move the trade balance (and the current account) toward deficit.

In light of the large number of trade-related and financial forces operating on the current account, it is impossible to label a current account deficit of a given magnitude either good or bad. As noted above, recent current account deficits result from U.S. investment outpacing domestic saving. One factor contributing to high U.S. investment relative to saving is the rapid increase in U.S. productivity relative to that in many other major countries, which makes the United States a good place to invest. Because productivity growth is ultimately responsible for rising living standards, the current account deficit reflects at least in part some very good news about the American economy.

Even so, a current account deficit indicates that the United States is consuming and investing more than it is producing. As **Exhibit 12.1** shows, the U.S. current account has typically been in deficit for the past two decades. As a result, the net international investment position in the United States (the value of U.S. investment holdings abroad less that of foreign holdings in the United States) has moved from an accumulated surplus of slightly less than 10 percent of GDP in the late 1970s to a deficit of almost 20 percent of GDP in 2001 [see **Exhibit 12.2**]. Recent increases in the current account deficit have led to some concerns that continued current account deficits (and the increase in the United States' international debt that would result) might not be sustainable. Clearly, debt cannot increase without limit. Because debt has to be serviced by the repatriation of capital income abroad, the ratio of a country's debt to its income has to stabilize at some point.

Yet the United States today is far from the point at which servicing its international debt becomes an onerous burden. In fact, until last year, more investment income was generated by U.S. investment in foreign countries than by foreign investments inside the United States, even though the net international investment position of the United States moved into deficit almost two decades ago [see **Exhibit 12.2**]. Given the United States' negative international investment position, the fact that, until 2002, more investment income flowed into the United States than flowed out of it implies that the rates of return on U.S. investment abroad were higher than the returns enjoyed by foreign investors in the United States.

The Economic Outlook

The economy continues to display supply-side characteristics favorable to long-term growth. Productivity growth remains strong, and inflation remains low and stable. Real GDP is expected to grow faster than its 3.1 percent potential rate during the next four years, and then to grow at a 3.1 percent annual rate during the balance of the budget window. The Administration's projections are shown in **Exhibit 12.3**.

Near-Term Outlook

The Administration expects that aggregate economic activity will have weathered a quarter of weakness at the end of 2002, following which it will gather strength during 2003, with real GDP growing 3.4 percent during the four quarters of the year. The unemployment rate, which was 5.9 percent in the fourth quarter of 2002, is projected to edge down about 0.3 percentage points by the fourth quarter of 2003.

Real exports, which turned up in 2002, are projected to improve further during 2003, reflecting the widely held expectation of stronger growth among the United States' trading partners and the lagged effects of the past year's decline in the dollar. Although real imports and exports are expected to grow at similar rates during the four quarters of 2003, the United States imports more than it exports, and therefore the dollar value of imports is expected to increase more than the dollar value of exports. As a result, net exports are likely to become more negative during the course of 2003.

Less change is expected for the largest component of aggregate demand, consumption, which is expected to remain robust in 2003. The negative influence of the stock market decline on household wealth, and thus on consumption, is expected to wane as this decline recedes into history. Consumption growth will also be supported by fiscal stimulus and the lagged effects of recent interest rate cuts. Finally, low interest rates will continue to support the purchase of consumer durables, just as they did for much of 2002.

Inflation Forecast

As measured by the GDP price index, inflation fell to 0.8 percent during the four quarters ending in the third quarter of 2002—down from 2.6 percent during the same period a year earlier. This broad-based index of prices of goods and services produced in the United States is expected to rise somewhat faster, at 1.4 percent during 2003, as the restraining effects of falling energy prices and low food price inflation subside and the economy strengthens. Inflation is expected to remain low, however, as the unemployment rate is now above the level that the Administration considers to be the center of the range consistent with stable inflation, and capacity utilization in the industrial sector is substantially below its historical average. Inflation by the GDP measure is projected to edge up to 1.8 percent by 2007 and to stay there for the remainder of the budget window.

As measured by the CPI, inflation during the 12 months ended in December 2002 was 2.4 percent; core inflation was 1.9 percent. The CPI, which differs from the GDP price index both in its methodology and in that it includes only consumer goods and services, is projected to rise 2.0 percent in 2003, close to last year's core rate.

The Administration expects nonfarm labor productivity to grow at a 2.1 percent annual average pace over the forecast period, virtually the same as that recorded from the business cycle peak in 1990 through the third quarter of 2002. This projection is notably more conservative than the nearly 2 3/4 percent average rate actually recorded since 1995.

As productivity growth has stayed high since 1995, the productivity improvement has increasingly come to be seen as lasting. Data from 2001 and 2002 only strengthen this conclusion. During the seven quarters ending in the third quarter of 2002—a period that includes a recession and a recovery—labor productivity grew at an annual rate of 3.2 percent, somewhat higher than the annual rate of 2.5 percent form 1995 to 2000 and much higher than the 1.4 percent trend from 1973 to 1995. An improvement of only about 2 percentage points in productivity growth may not sound impressive, but over time even a small increase in productivity growth brings about a large improvement in living standards. For example,

growth in productivity of 1.4 percent a year implies that productivity doubles every 50 years, but growth of 2.5 percent implies a doubling every 28 years.

Strong productivity growth also helps to keep inflation down, by allowing real wages to grow without an increase in unit labor costs, which would drive up firms' costs of production and therefore push output prices upward. Indeed, another bright spot in 2002 was the behavior of inflation and real wages. The consumer price index (CPI) rose 2.4 percent in 2002 (December to December), close to its 1.6 percent rate of increase in 2001. The core CPI, which does not include the volatile food and energy components, rose 1.9 percent.

Interest Rate Outlook

Following a large decline in 2001, the interest rate on 91-day treasury bills fell an additional 50 basis points in 2002 and ended the year at 1.2 percent. These reductions reflected the Federal Reserve's efforts to stimulate the economy, which left real short-term rates (that is, nominal rates less expected inflation) close to zero. Real rates are not expected to remain this low once the recovery becomes firmly established, and nominal rates are projected to increase gradually to 4.3 percent by 2007, which would leave the real interest rate on Treasury bills close to its historical average.

EXHIBIT 12.1   SAVING, INVESTMENT, AND THE CURRENT ACCOUNT BALANCE

Chart 1-10 **Saving, Investment, and the Current Account Balance**
The current account deficit narrowed in 2001 as net domestic investment fell more quickly than saving, but it widened in 2002.

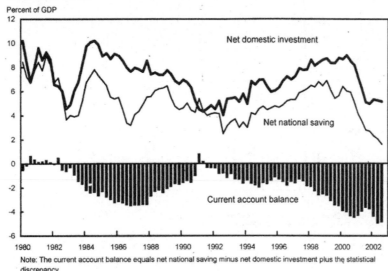

Note: The current account balance equals net national saving minus net domestic investment plus the statistical discrepancy.
Source: Department of Commerce (Bureau of Economic Analysis).

SOURCE: Department of Commerce, Bureau of Economic Analysis.

EXHIBIT 12.2   INTERNATIONAL INVESTMENT POSITION AND INVESTMENT INCOME

Chart 1-11 **International Investment Position and Investment Income**
Although the Nation's net international investment position became negative in the mid-1980s, net investment income remained positive until 2002.

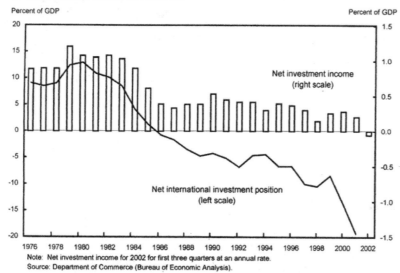

Note: Net investment income for 2002 for first three quarters at an annual rate.
Source: Department of Commerce (Bureau of Economic Analysis).

SOURCE: Department of Commerce, Bureau of Economic Analysis.

EXHIBIT 12.3	ADMINISTRATION FORECAST

TABLE 1-1.— *Administration Forecast*[1]

Year	Nominal GDP	Real GDP (chain-type)	GDP price index (chain-type)	Consumer price index (CPI-U)	Unemploy-ment rate (percent)	Interest rate, 91-day Treasury bills (percent)	Interest rate, 10-year Treasury notes (percent)	Nonfarm payroll employ-ment (millions)
	Percent change, fourth quarter to fourth quarter				Level, calendar year			
2001 (actual)	2.0	0.1	2.0	1.9	4.8	3.4	5.0	131.9
2002	4.2	2.9	1.2	2.3	5.8	1.6	4.6	130.8
2003	4.8	3.4	1.4	2.0	5.7	1.6	4.2	132.5
2004	5.2	3.6	1.5	2.1	5.5	3.3	5.0	135.2
2005	5.0	3.4	1.6	2.1	5.2	4.0	5.3	137.9
2006	5.0	3.3	1.7	2.2	5.1	4.2	5.4	140.4
2007	4.9	3.1	1.8	2.2	5.1	4.2	5.5	142.6
2008	5.0	3.1	1.8	2.3	5.1	4.3	5.6	144.7

[1] Based on data available as of November 29, 2002.

Sources: Council of Economic Advisers, Department of Commerce (Bureau of Economic Analysis), Department of Labor (Bureau of Labor Statistics), Department of the Treasury, and Office of Management and Budget.

SOURCE: Council of Economic Advisers, Department of Commerce (Bureau of Economic Analysis), Department of Labor (Bureau of Labor Statistics), Department of the Treasury, and Office of Management and Budget.

EXHIBIT 12.4	NEW MEASURES OF CONSUMER PRICE INFLATION

Box 1-3. New Measures of Consumer Price Inflation

Following through on a request from the Congress, the Bureau of Labor Statistics has developed a new measure of consumer price inflation. Unlike the current official Consumer Price Index for Urban Consumers, the new measure not only adjusts for consumer substitution between goods in response to movements in relative prices, but also uses current expenditure weights rather than weights that are several years out of date. The fact that weights from different adjoining years are "chained" together gives the new measure of inflation its name: the chained CPI, or C-CPI. The chained CPI is a supplemental series and is not intended to replace the official CPI, versions of which are used to index Social Security benefits, pensions, Federal tax brackets, and many private contracts.

Any consumer price index must somehow aggregate the many prices faced by consumers into a single number. The official CPI aggregates prices by using a fixed market basket. (Currently the basket reflects consumption shares in 1999-2000 for 211 major categories of goods and services.) The disadvantage of using a fixed-weight basket is that the resulting price index is unable to reflect the reallocations that consumers make when relative prices change. For example, if the price of chicken were to rise while that of steak held steady, consumers might well buy more steak; then the use of fixed weights would overstate the increase in the cost of meat generally, caused by the increase in the cost of chicken. The new chained index reflects this substitution, but at some cost. Specifically, the new index requires data on consumer expenditure before *and after* these substitutions have occurred. But whereas prices are relatively easy to measure on a real-time basis, expenditure shares are not, which means that current expenditure shares must be estimated for the most recent periods.

Because it reflects substitution by consumers, the new measure uses expenditure weights that are constantly changing as consumption patterns change. As a result, the expenditure weights do not get out of date as they do with a fixed-weight index. The difference that this use of up-to-date weights makes is particularly important to the contribution of computers to the cost of living, because the relative price of computers has fallen during the past two decades even as the expenditure share of computers has risen. A fixed-weight basket would tend to understate the weight of computers in current consumption, because its expenditure weights are typically years out of date. As the price of computers has fallen over time, the underweighting of computers in a fixed-weight index causes this index to overstate the increase in the cost of living. The chained CPI does not suffer from this problem, because its weights are constantly being updated.

SOURCE: Economic Report of the President, February 2003, p. 50.

EXHIBIT 12.5	THE PRESIDENT'S TEN-POINT PLAN FOR IMPROVING CORPORATE GOVERNANCE COMPARED TO CONGRESS' PROPOSED SARBANES-OXLEY ACT

Principle	Ten-Point Plan	Sarbanes-Oxley
Information accuracy and accessibility	1. Each investor should have quarterly access to information needed to judge a firm's financial performance, condition, and risk.	Pro forma accounting statements must be reconciled with generally accepted accounting principles (GAAP) in company reports. Material off-balance-sheet transactions must be disclosed in company reports.
	2. Each investor should have prompt access to critical information.	Filing deadlines are accelerated.
Management accountability	3. CEOs should personally vouch for the veracity, timeliness, and fairness of their companies' public disclosures, including their financial statements.	CEOs and CFOs must verify fairness and accuracy of company reports. Individuals committing "knowing and willful" violations of this requirement are subject to 20 years in prison.
	4. CEOs and other officers should not be allowed to profit from erroneous financial statements.	Following a restatement of earnings, executives must forfeit bonuses, incentive-based compensation, and profits from stock sales for the previous year.
	5. CEOs or other officers who clearly abuse their power should lose their right to serve in any corporate leadership position.	The SEC may bar individuals from serving as officers and directors.
	6. Corporate leaders should be required to tell the public promptly whenever they buy or sell company stock for personal gain.	Management and principal stockholders must report transactions by end of second business day.
Auditor independence	7. Investors should have complete confidence in the independence and integrity of companies' auditors.	The audit committee hires and oversees accounting firms. Companies must disclose whether one member of the audit committee is a "financial expert." Auditors disclose all critical accounting practices to audit committee.
		Auditors may not provide any of at least eight specified services for audit clients and must obtain prior approval from the audit committee for any services provided.
	8. An independent regulatory board should ensure that the accounting profession is held to the highest ethical standards.	The Public Company Accounting Oversight Board ("the Board") is funded by accounting support fees assessed on public companies.
		The SEC will appoint five full-time members in consultation with the Federal Reserve Chairman and the Treasury Secretary.
		Only two members may be or have been certified public accounts (CPAs). The Chair may not have been a CPA for 5 years prior to service.
		The Board may compel information from registered accounting firms and their clients in some circumstances.
	9. The authors of accounting standards must be responsive to the needs of investors.	The Board shall include in its auditing standards the requirement that firms employ GAAP.
	10. Firms' accounting systems should be compared with best practices, not simply against minimum standards.	The auditor's report to audit committee must compare company's audit practices with the auditor's preferred treatment.

Sources: The White House and the Congress.

SOURCES: The White House; Congress.

EXHIBIT 12.6	CONSUMPTION PROPENSITY

During the past four decades, net worth and the propensity to consume out of disposable income have tended to move together in aggregate data.

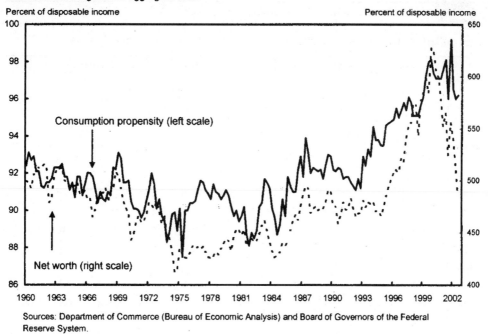

Sources: Department of Commerce (Bureau of Economic Analysis) and Board of Governors of the Federal Reserve System.

SOURCE: Department of Commerce (Bureau of Economic Analysis) and Board of Governors of the Federal Reserve System.

National Income or Expenditure

GROSS DOMESTIC PRODUCT, 1959–2002

[Billions of dollars, except as noted; quarterly data at seasonally adjusted annual rates]

Year or Quarter	Gross Domestic Product	Personal Consumption Expenditures				Gross Private Domestic Investment						
							Fixed Investment					
								Nonresidential				
		Total	Durable Goods	Non-durable Goods	Services	Total	Total	Total	Struc-tures	Equip-ment and Soft-ware	Resi-dential	Change in Private Invent-tories
1959	507.4	318.1	42.7	148.5	127.0	78.5	74.6	46.5	18.1	28.4	28.1	3.9
1960	527.4	332.3	43.3	152.9	136.1	78.9	75.7	49.4	19.6	29.8	26.3	3.2
1961	545.7	342.7	41.8	156.6	144.3	78.2	75.2	48.8	19.7	29.1	26.4	3.0
1962	586.5	363.8	46.9	162.8	154.1	88.1	82.0	53.1	20.8	32.3	29.0	6.1
1963	618.7	383.1	51.6	168.2	163.4	93.8	88.1	56.0	21.2	34.8	32.1	5.6
1964	664.4	411.7	56.7	178.7	176.4	102.1	97.2	63.0	23.7	39.2	34.3	4.8
1965	720.1	444.3	63.3	191.6	189.5	118.2	109.0	74.8	28.3	46.5	34.2	9.2
1966	789.3	481.8	68.3	208.8	204.7	131.3	117.7	85.4	31.3	54.0	32.3	13.6
1967	834.1	508.7	70.4	217.1	221.2	128.6	118.7	86.4	31.5	54.9	32.4	9.9
1968	911.5	558.7	80.8	235.7	242.3	141.2	132.1	93.4	33.6	59.9	38.7	9.1
1969	985.3	605.5	85.9	253.2	266.4	156.4	147.3	104.7	37.7	67.0	42.6	9.2
1970	1,039.7	648.9	85.0	272.0	292.0	152.4	150.4	109.0	40.3	68.7	41.4	2.0
1971	1,128.6	702.4	96.9	285.5	320.0	178.2	169.9	114.1	42.7	71.5	55.8	8.3
1972	1,240.4	770.7	110.4	308.0	352.3	207.6	198.5	128.8	47.2	81.7	69.7	9.1
1973	1,385.5	852.5	123.5	343.1	385.9	244.5	228.6	153.3	55.0	98.3	75.3	15.9
1974	1,501.0	932.4	122.3	384.5	425.5	249.4	235.4	169.5	61.2	108.2	66.0	14.0
1975	1,635.2	1,030.3	133.5	420.7	476.1	230.2	236.5	173.7	61.4	112.4	62.7	-6.3
1976	1,823.9	1,149.8	158.9	458.3	532.6	292.0	274.8	192.4	65.9	126.4	82.5	17.1
1977	2,031.4	1,278.4	181.2	497.2	600.0	361.3	339.0	228.7	74.6	154.1	110.3	22.3
1978	2,295.9	1,430.4	201.7	550.2	678.4	436.0	410.2	278.6	91.4	187.2	131.6	25.8
1979	2,566.4	1,596.3	214.4	624.4	757.4	490.6	472.7	331.6	114.9	216.7	141.0	18.0
1980	2,795.6	1,762.9	214.2	696.1	852.7	477.9	484.2	360.9	133.9	227.0	123.2	-6.3
1981	3,131.3	1,944.2	231.3	758.9	954.0	570.8	541.0	418.4	164.6	253.8	122.6	29.8
1982	3,259.2	2,079.3	240.2	787.6	1,051.5	516.1	531.0	425.3	175.0	250.3	105.7	-14.9
1983	3,534.9	2,286.4	281.2	831.2	1,174.0	564.2	570.0	417.4	152.7	264.7	152.5	-5.8
1984	3,932.7	2,498.4	326.9	884.7	1,286.9	735.5	670.1	490.3	176.0	314.3	179.8	65.4
1985	4,213.0	2,712.6	363.3	928.8	1,420.6	736.3	714.5	527.6	193.3	334.3	186.9	21.8
1986	4,452.9	2,895.2	401.3	958.5	1,535.4	747.2	740.7	522.5	175.8	346.8	218.1	6.6
1987	4,742.5	3,105.3	419.7	1,015.3	1,670.3	781.5	754.3	526.7	172.1	354.7	227.6	27.1
1988	5,108.3	3,356.6	450.2	1,082.9	1,823.5	821.1	802.7	568.4	181.6	386.8	234.2	18.5
1989	5,489.1	3,596.7	467.8	1,165.4	1,963.5	872.9	845.2	613.4	193.4	420.0	231.8	27.7

EXHIBIT B.1   CONTINUED

Year or Quarter	Net exports of goods and services			Government Consumption Expenditures and Gross Investment						Final Sales of Domestic Product	Gross Domestic Purchases[1]	Adden- dum: Gross National Product[2]	Percent change from Preceding Period	
					Federal									
	Net Exports	Exports	Imports	Total	Total	Na- tional Defense	Non- Defense	State and Local					Gross Domestic Product	Gross Domestic Pur- chases[1]
1959	-1.7	20.6	22.3	112.5	67.4	56.0	11.4	45.1	503.5	509.1	510.3	8.4	8.9
1960	2.4	25.3	22.8	113.8	65.9	55.2	10.7	47.9	524.1	525.0	530.6	3.9	3.1
1961	3.4	26.0	22.7	121.5	69.5	58.1	11.3	52.0	542.7	542.3	549.3	3.5	3.3
1962	2.4	27.4	25.0	132.2	76.9	62.8	14.1	55.3	580.4	584.1	590.7	7.5	7.7
1963	3.3	29.4	26.1	138.5	78.5	62.7	15.8	59.9	613.1	615.4	623.2	5.5	5.4
1964	5.5	33.6	28.1	145.1	79.8	61.8	18.0	65.3	659.6	658.9	669.4	7.4	7.1
1965	3.9	35.4	31.5	153.7	82.1	62.4	19.7	71.6	710.9	716.2	725.5	8.4	8.7
1966	1.9	38.9	37.1	174.3	94.4	73.8	20.7	79.9	775.7	787.4	794.5	9.6	9.9
1967	1.4	41.4	39.9	195.3	106.8	85.8	21.0	88.6	824.2	832.6	839.5	5.7	5.7
1968	-1.3	45.3	46.6	212.8	114.0	92.2	21.8	98.8	902.4	912.7	917.6	9.3	9.6
1969	-1.2	49.3	50.5	224.6	116.1	92.6	23.5	108.5	976.2	986.5	991.5	8.1	8.1
1970	1.2	57.0	55.8	237.1	116.4	90.9	25.5	120.7	1,037.7	1,038.5	1,046.1	5.5	5.3
1971	-3.0	59.3	62.3	251.0	117.6	89.0	28.6	133.5	1,120.3	1,131.6	1,136.2	8.6	9.0
1972	-8.0	66.2	74.2	270.1	125.6	93.5	32.2	144.4	1,231.3	1,248.4	1,249.1	9.9	10.3
1973	0.6	91.8	91.2	287.9	127.8	93.9	33.9	160.1	1,369.7	1,384.9	1,398.2	11.7	10.9
1974	-3.1	124.3	127.5	322.4	138.2	99.7	38.5	184.2	1,487.0	1,504.2	1,516.7	8.3	8.6
1975	13.6	136.3	122.7	361.1	152.1	107.9	44.2	209.0	1,641.4	1,621.6	1,648.4	8.9	7.8
1976	-2.3	148.9	151.1	384.5	160.6	113.2	47.4	223.9	1,806.8	1,826.2	1,841.0	11.5	12.6
1977	-23.7	158.8	182.4	415.3	176.0	122.6	53.5	239.3	2,009.1	2,055.1	2,052.1	11.4	12.5
1978	-26.1	186.1	212.3	455.6	191.9	132.0	59.8	263.8	2,270.1	2,322.0	2,318.0	13.0	13.0
1979	-24.0	228.7	252.7	503.5	211.6	146.7	65.0	291.8	2,548.4	2,590.4	2,599.3	11.8	11.6
1980	-14.9	278.9	293.8	569.7	245.3	169.6	75.6	324.4	2,801.9	2,810.5	2,830.8	8.9	8.5
1981	-15.0	302.8	317.8	631.4	281.8	197.8	84.0	349.6	3,101.5	3,146.3	3,166.1	12.0	12.0
1982	-20.5	282.6	303.2	684.4	312.8	228.3	84.5	371.6	3,274.1	3,279.8	3,295.7	4.1	4.2
1983	-51.7	277.0	328.6	735.9	344.4	252.5	92.0	391.5	3,540.7	3,586.6	3,571.8	8.5	9.4
1984	-102.0	303.1	405.1	800.8	376.4	283.5	92.8	424.4	3,867.3	4,034.7	3,968.1	11.3	12.5
1985	-114.2	303.0	417.2	878.3	413.4	312.4	101.0	464.9	4,191.2	4,327.2	4,238.4	7.1	7.2
1986	-131.9	320.3	452.2	942.3	438.7	332.2	106.5	503.6	4,446.3	4,584.7	4,468.3	5.7	6.0
1987	-142.3	365.6	507.9	997.9	460.4	351.2	109.3	537.5	4,715.3	4,884.7	4,756.2	6.5	6.5
1988	-106.3	446.9	553.2	1,036.9	462.6	355.9	106.8	574.3	5,089.8	5,214.6	5,126.8	7.7	6.8
1989	-80.7	509.0	589.7	1,100.2	482.6	363.2	119.3	617.7	5,461.4	5,569.8	5,509.4	7.5	6.8

EXHIBIT B.1   **CONTINUED**

Year or Quarter	Gross Domestic Product	Personal Consumption Expenditures				Gross Private Domestic Investment						
							Fixed Investment					
								Nonresidential				
		Total	Durable Goods	Non-durable Goods	Services	Total	Total	Total	Struc-tures	Equip-ment and Soft-ware	Resi-dential	Change in Private Invent-tories
1990	5,803.2	3,831.5	467.6	1,246.1	2,117.8	861.7	847.2	630.3	202.5	427.8	216.8	14.5
1991	5,986.2	3,971.2	443.0	1,278.8	2,249.4	800.2	800.4	608.9	183.4	425.4	191.5	-0.2
1992	6,318.9	4,209.7	470.8	1,322.9	2,415.9	866.6	851.6	626.1	172.2	453.9	225.5	15.0
1993	6,642.3	4,454.7	513.4	1,375.2	2,566.1	955.1	934.0	682.2	179.4	502.8	251.8	21.1
1994	7,054.3	4,716.4	560.8	1,438.0	2,717.6	1,097.1	1,034.6	748.6	187.5	561.1	286.0	62.6
1995	7,400.5	4,969.0	589.7	1,497.3	2,882.0	1,143.8	1,110.7	825.1	204.6	620.5	285.6	33.0
1996	7,813.2	5,237.5	616.5	1,574.1	3,047.0	1,242.7	1,212.7	899.4	225.0	674.4	313.3	30.0
1997	8,318.4	5,529.3	642.5	1,641.6	3,245.2	1,390.5	1,327.7	999.4	255.8	743.6	328.2	62.9
1998	8,781.5	5,856.0	693.2	1,708.5	3,454.3	1,538.7	1,465.6	1,101.2	282.4	818.9	364.4	73.1
1999	9,274.3	6,246.5	755.9	1,830.1	3,660.5	1,636.7	1,577.2	1,173.5	283.7	889.8	403.7	59.5
2000	9,824.6	6,683.7	803.9	1,972.9	3,906.9	1,755.4	1,691.8	1,265.8	314.2	951.6	426.0	63.6
2001	10,082.2	6,987.0	835.9	2,041.3	4,109.9	1,586.0	1,646.3	1,201.6	324.5	877.1	444.8	-60.3
1998: I	8,627.8	5,719.9	666.8	1,675.8	3,377.3	1,528.7	1,422.0	1,074.8	273.2	801.6	347.2	106.7
II	8,697.3	5,820.0	689.3	1,697.2	3,433.5	1,498.4	1,457.5	1,099.9	284.9	815.0	357.6	40.9
III	8,816.5	5,895.1	691.7	1,716.7	3,486.7	1,538.6	1,469.1	1,098.6	283.9	814.7	370.5	69.5
IV	8,984.5	5,989.1	725.1	1,744.4	3,519.6	1,589.3	1,513.9	1,131.7	287.5	844.2	382.2	75.4
1999: I	9,092.7	6,076.6	728.7	1,773.1	3,574.8	1,618.0	1,543.3	1,150.0	285.5	864.5	393.3	74.7
II	9,171.7	6,195.6	749.9	1,814.4	3,631.3	1,597.8	1,570.1	1,167.7	283.0	884.7	402.4	27.7
III	9,316.5	6,299.4	765.1	1,841.3	3,693.1	1,637.9	1,591.1	1,184.5	279.9	904.6	406.5	46.8
IV	9,516.4	6,414.5	779.9	1,891.7	3,742.9	1,693.2	1,604.3	1,191.9	286.3	905.5	412.5	88.9
2000: I	9,649.5	6,552.2	808.4	1,926.9	3,816.9	1,711.4	1,664.6	1,236.6	299.5	937.1	428.0	46.8
II	9,820.7	6,638.7	799.3	1,964.9	3,874.5	1,786.3	1,697.1	1,268.3	308.5	959.8	428.8	89.2
III	9,874.8	6,736.1	810.6	1,988.9	3,936.6	1,766.4	1,705.2	1,283.4	320.9	962.5	421.8	61.1
IV	9,953.6	6,808.0	797.2	2,011.1	3,999.7	1,757.4	1,700.4	1,274.8	328.0	946.8	425.6	57.1
2001: I	10,028.1	6,904.7	816.8	2,031.5	4,109.9	1,671.1	1,698.3	1,258.3	333.7	924.6	440.0	-27.2
II	10,049.9	6,959.8	820.3	2,044.8	4,094.7	1,597.2	1,654.3	1,210.0	329.9	880.2	444.2	-57.1
III	10,097.7	6,983.7	824.0	2,044.3	4,115.4	1,574.9	1,635.5	1,188.1	332.0	856.1	447.4	-60.6
IV	10,152.9	7,099.9	882.6	2,044.4	4,172.9	1,500.7	1,597.2	1,149.8	302.3	847.4	447.4	-96.5
2002: I	10,313.1	7,174.2	859.0	2,085.1	4,230.1	1,559.4	1,589.4	1,126.8	288.3	838.5	462.6	-29.9
II	10,376.9	7,254.7	856.9	2,108.2	4,289.5	1,588.0	1,584.6	1,115.8	275.2	840.7	468.7	3.4
III	10,506.2	7,360.7	897.8	2,116.9	4,346.0	1,597.3	1,579.7	1,109.8	259.4	850.4	469.9	17.6

EXHIBIT B.1   CONTINUED

Year or Quarter	Net exports of goods and services			Government Consumption Expenditures and Gross Investment					Final Sales of Domestic Product	Gross Domestic Purchases[1]	Addendum: Gross National Product[2]	Percent change from Preceding Period	
	Net Exports	Exports	Imports	Total	Federal			State and Local				Gross Domestic Product	Gross Domestic Purchases[1]
					Total	National Defense	Non-Defense						
1990	-71.4	557.2	628.6	1,181.4	508.4	374.9	133.6	673.0	5,788.7	5,874.7	5,832.2	5.7	5.5
1991	-20.7	601.6	622.3	1,235.5	527.4	384.5	142.9	708.1	5,986.4	6,006.9	6,010.9	3.2	2.3
1992	-27.9	636.8	664.6	1,270.5	534.5	378.5	156.0	736.0	6,303.9	6,346.8	6,342.3	5.6	5.7
1993	-60.5	658.0	718.5	1,293.0	527.3	364.9	162.4	765.7	6,621.2	6,702.8	6,666.7	5.1	5.6
1994	-87.1	725.1	812.1	1,327.9	521.1	355.1	165.9	806.8	6,991.8	7,141.4	7,071.1	6.2	6.5
1995	-84.3	818.6	902.8	1,372.0	521.5	350.6	170.9	850.5	7,367.5	7,484.8	7,420.9	4.9	4.8
1996	-89.0	874.2	963.1	1,421.9	531.6	357.0	174.6	890.4	7,783.2	7,902.1	7,831.2	5.6	5.6
1997	-89.3	966.4	1,055.8	1,487.9	538.2	352.6	185.6	949.7	8,255.5	8,407.7	8,325.4	6.5	6.4
1998	-151.7	964.9	1,116.7	1,538.5	539.2	349.1	190.1	999.3	8,708.4	8,933.3	8,778.1	5.6	6.3
1999	-249.9	989.3	1,239.2	1,641.0	565.0	364.3	200.7	1,076.0	9,214.8	9,524.2	9,297.1	5.6	6.6
2000	-365.5	1,101.1	1,466.6	1,751.0	589.2	374.9	214.3	1,161.8	9,761.1	10,190.1	9,848.0	5.9	7.0
2001	-348.9	1,034.1	1,383.0	1,858.0	628.1	399.9	228.2	1,229.9	10,142.5	10,431.0	10,104.1	2.6	2.4
1998: I	-122.6	974.1	1,096.7	1,501.8	526.1	338.4	187.7	975.8	8,521.1	8,750.4	8,634.5	7.2	8.0
II	-154.9	959.2	1,114.1	1,533.8	542.9	348.8	194.2	990.9	8,656.4	8,852.2	8,700.3	3.3	4.7
III	-165.3	946.7	1,112.0	1,548.1	539.5	354.7	184.8	1,008.6	8,747.0	8,981.8	8,802.1	5.6	6.0
IV	-164.1	979.7	1,143.8	1,570.3	548.4	354.7	193.7	1,021.9	8,909.1	9,148.6	8,975.4	7.8	7.6
1999: I	-196.4	959.2	1,155.6	1,594.6	550.0	354.0	196.0	1,044.5	9,018.0	9,289.1	9,112.7	4.9	6.3
II	-241.8	970.2	1,212.0	1,620.1	556.1	355.1	201.0	1,064.0	9,144.0	9,413.5	9,195.9	3.5	5.5
III	-274.6	996.8	1,271.4	1,653.9	569.0	368.7	200.3	1,084.8	9,269.7	9,591.2	9,333.6	6.5	7.8
IV	-286.7	1,031.2	1,317.9	1,695.4	584.9	379.5	205.5	1,110.5	9,427.5	9,803.1	9,546.0	8.9	9.1
2000: I	-330.6	1,055.9	1,386.5	1,716.5	575.7	365.5	210.2	1,140.8	9,602.6	9,980.1	9,670.5	5.7	7.4
II	-353.2	1,098.0	1,451.1	1,748.8	598.5	379.1	219.4	1,150.3	9,731.5	10,173.9	9,846.4	7.3	8.0
III	-384.9	1,130.9	1,515.8	1,757.2	589.7	375.0	214.7	1,167.4	9,813.6	10,259.7	9,892.5	2.2	3.4
IV	-393.2	1,119.8	1,513.0	1,781.4	592.9	380.0	213.0	1,188.5	9,896.6	10,346.8	9,982.8	3.2	3.4
2001: I	-372.7	1,100.0	1,472.8	1,825.0	613.3	391.4	221.9	1,211.7	10,055.3	10,400.8	10,038.0	3.0	2.1
II	-365.7	1,059.7	1,425.3	1,858.5	624.8	395.2	229.6	1,233.7	10,107.0	10,415.5	10,081.0	0.9	0.6
III	-312.6	1,005.8	1,318.4	1,851.7	627.4	400.3	227.2	1,224.3	10,158.3	10,410.4	10,109.3	1.9	-0.2
IV	-344.5	971.1	1,315.6	1,896.8	646.9	412.8	234.1	1,249.8	10,249.4	10,497.4	10,188.1	2.2	3.4
2002: I	-360.1	977.5	1,337.5	1,939.5	672.0	431.7	240.3	1,267.5	10,343.0	10,673.1	10,314.9	6.5	6.9
II	-425.6	1,018.1	1,443.7	1,959.8	688.2	442.1	246.1	1,271.6	10,373.5	10,802.4	10,356.8	2.5	4.9
III	-432.9	1,038.6	1,471.5	1,981.1	697.7	451.2	246.5	1,283.3	10,488.7	10,939.1	10,495.3	5.1	5.2

SOURCE: Department of Commerce, Bureau of Economic Analysis.

[1] Gross domestic product (GDP) less exports of goods and services plus imports of goods and services.

[2] GDP plus net income receipts from rest of the world.

| EXHIBIT B.2 | REAL GROSS DOMESTIC PRODUCT, 1959–2002 |

[Billions of chained (1996) dollars, except as noted; quarterly data at seasonally adjusted annual rates]

Year or Quarter	Gross Domestic Product	Personal Consumption Expenditures				Gross Private Domestic Investment						
							Fixed Investment					Change in Private Inventories
								Nonresidential				
		Total	Durable Goods	Nondurable Goods	Services	Total	Total	Total	Structures	Equipment and Software	Residential	
1959	2,319.0	1,470.7	......	......	......	272.9	......	......	......	......	......	......
1960	2,376.7	1,510.8	......	......	......	272.8	......	......	......	......	......	......
1961	2,432.0	1,541.2	......	......	......	271.0	......	......	......	......	......	......
1962	2,578.9	1,617.3	......	......	......	305.3	......	......	......	......	......	......
1963	2,690.4	1,684.0	......	......	......	325.7	......	......	......	......	......	......
1964	2,846.5	1,784.8	......	......	......	352.6	......	......	......	......	......	......
1965	3,028.5	1,897.6	......	......	......	402.0	......	......	......	......	......	......
1966	3,227.5	2,006.1	......	......	......	437.3	......	......	......	......	......	......
1967	3,308.3	2,066.2	......	......	......	417.2	......	......	......	......	......	......
1968	3,466.1	2,184.2	......	......	......	441.3	......	......	......	......	......	......
1969	3,571.4	2,264.8	......	......	......	466.9	......	......	......	......	......	......
1970	3,578.0	2,317.5	......	......	......	436.2	......	......	......	......	......	......
1971	3,697.7	2,405.2	......	......	......	485.8	......	......	......	......	......	......
1972	3,898.4	2,550.5	......	......	......	543.0	......	......	......	......	......	......
1973	4,123.4	2,675.9	......	......	......	606.5	......	......	......	......	......	......
1974	4,099.0	2,653.7	......	......	......	561.7	......	......	......	......	......	......
1975	4,084.4	2,710.9	......	......	......	462.2	......	......	......	......	......	......
1976	4,311.7	2,868.9	......	......	......	555.5	......	......	......	......	......	......
1977	4,511.8	2,992.1	......	......	......	639.4	......	......	......	......	......	......
1978	4,760.6	3,124.7	......	......	......	713.0	......	......	......	......	......	......
1979	4,912.1	3,203.2	......	......	......	735.4	......	......	......	......	......	......
1980	4,900.9	3,193.0	......	......	......	655.3	......	......	......	......	......	......
1981	5,021.0	3,236.0	......	......	......	715.6	......	......	......	......	......	......
1982	4,919.3	3,275.5	......	......	......	615.2	......	......	......	......	......	......
1983	5,132.3	3,454.3	......	......	......	673.7	......	......	......	......	......	......
1984	5,505.2	3,640.6	......	......	......	871.5	......	......	......	......	......	......
1985	5,717.1	3,820.9	......	......	......	863.4	......	......	......	......	......	......
1986	5,912.4	3,981.2	......	......	......	857.7	......	......	......	......	......	......
1987	6,113.3	4,113.4	455.2	1,274.5	2,379.3	879.3	856.0	572.5	224.3	360.0	290.7	29.6
1988	6,368.4	4,279.5	481.5	1,315.1	2,477.2	902.8	887.1	603.6	227.1	386.9	289.2	18.4
1989	6,591.8	4,393.7	491.7	1,351.0	2,546.0	936.5	911.2	637.0	232.7	414.0	277.3	29.6

EXHIBIT B.2   CONTINUED

Year or Quarter	Net Exports of Goods and Services			Government Consumption Expenditures and Gross Investment						Final Sales of Domestic Product	Gross Domestic Pur-chases[1]	Adden-dum: Gross National Product[2]	Percent Change from Preceding Period	
	Net Exports	Exports	Imports	Total	Federal			State and Local					Gross Domestic Product	Gross Domestic Pur-chases[1]
					Total	National Defense	Non-defense							
1959	......	72.4	106.6	661.4	......	......	......	......	2,317.4	2,377.2	2,332.8	7.2	7.6
1960	......	87.5	108.0	661.3	......	......	......	......	2,378.5	2,417.5	2,391.9	2.5	1.7
1961	......	88.9	107.3	693.2	......	......	......	......	2,435.5	2,471.5	2,448.8	2.3	2.2
1962	......	93.7	119.5	735.0	......	......	......	......	2,569.5	2,626.9	2,598.0	6.0	6.3
1963	......	100.7	122.7	752.4	......	......	......	......	2,683.6	2,734.7	2,710.8	4.3	4.1
1964	......	114.2	129.2	767.1	......	......	......	......	2,844.1	2,883.0	2,868.5	5.8	5.4
1965	......	116.5	142.9	791.1	......	......	......	......	3,008.5	3,079.1	3,051.7	6.4	6.8
1966	......	124.3	164.2	862.1	......	......	......	......	3,191.1	3,292.3	3,248.9	6.6	6.9
1967	......	127.0	176.2	927.1	......	......	......	......	3,288.2	3,382.6	3,330.4	2.5	2.7
1968	......	136.3	202.4	956.6	......	......	......	......	3,450.0	3,555.9	3,489.8	4.8	5.1
1969	......	143.7	213.9	952.5	......	......	......	......	3,555.9	3,664.5	3,594.1	3.0	3.1
1970	......	159.3	223.1	931.1	......	......	......	......	3,588.6	3,659.6	3,600.6	0.2	-0.1
1971	......	160.4	235.0	913.8	......	......	......	......	3,688.1	3,791.1	3,722.9	3.3	3.6
1972	......	173.5	261.3	914.9	......	......	......	......	3,887.7	4,003.8	3,925.7	5.4	5.6
1973	......	211.4	273.4	908.3	......	......	......	......	4,094.3	4,196.6	4,161.0	5.8	4.8
1974	......	231.6	267.2	924.8	......	......	......	......	4,080.7	4,136.5	4,142.3	-0.6	-1.4
1975	......	230.0	237.5	942.5	......	......	......	......	4,118.5	4,085.2	4,117.7	-0.4	-1.2
1976	......	243.6	284.0	943.3	......	......	......	......	4,288.8	4,354.2	4,351.4	5.6	6.6
1977	......	249.7	315.0	952.7	......	......	......	......	4,478.8	4,586.4	4,556.6	4.6	5.3
1978	......	275.9	342.3	982.2	......	......	......	......	4,722.9	4,834.8	4,805.3	5.5	5.4
1979	......	302.4	347.9	1,001.1	......	......	......	......	4,894.4	4,956.3	4,973.9	3.2	2.5
1980	......	334.8	324.8	1,020.9	......	......	......	......	4,928.1	4,863.8	4,962.3	-0.2	-1.9
1981	......	338.6	333.4	1,030.0	......	......	......	......	4,989.5	4,990.0	5,075.4	2.5	2.6
1982	......	314.6	329.2	1,046.0	......	......	......	......	4,954.9	4,916.6	4,973.6	-2.0	-1.5
1983	......	306.9	370.7	1,081.0	......	......	......	......	5,154.5	5,194.1	5,184.9	4.3	5.6
1984	......	332.6	461.0	1,118.4	......	......	......	......	5,427.9	5,646.6	5,553.8	7.3	8.7
1985	......	341.6	490.7	1,190.5	......	......	......	......	5,698.8	5,883.1	5,750.9	3.8	4.2
1986	......	366.8	531.9	1,255.2	......	......	......	......	5,912.6	6,096.2	5,932.5	3.4	3.6
1987	-156.2	408.0	564.2	1,292.5	597.8	450.2	146.5	695.6	6,088.8	6,286.2	6,130.8	3.4	3.1
1988	-112.1	473.5	585.6	1,307.5	586.9	446.8	138.9	721.4	6,352.6	6,489.5	6,391.1	4.2	3.2
1989	-79.4	529.4	608.8	1,343.5	594.7	443.3	150.5	749.5	6,565.4	6,674.6	6,615.5	3.5	2.9

EXHIBIT B.2   **CONTINUED**

Year or Quarter	Gross Domestic Product	Personal Consumption Expenditures				Gross Private Domestic Investment						Change in Private Inventories
						Total	Fixed Investment					
							Total	Nonresidential			Residential	
		Total	Durable Goods	Nondurable Goods	Services			Total	Structures	Equipment and Software		
1990	6,707.9	4,474.5	487.1	1,369.6	2,616.2	907.3	894.6	641.7	236.1	415.7	253.5	16.5
1991	6,676.4	4,466.6	454.9	1,364.0	2,651.8	829.5	832.5	610.1	210.1	407.2	221.1	-1.0
1992	6,880.0	4,594.5	479.0	1,389.7	2,729.7	899.8	886.5	630.6	197.3	437.5	257.2	17.1
1993	7,062.6	4,748.9	518.3	1,430.3	2,802.5	977.9	958.4	683.6	198.9	487.1	276.0	20.0
1994	7,347.7	4,928.1	557.7	1,485.1	2,886.2	1,107.0	1,045.9	744.6	200.5	544.9	302.7	66.8
1995	7,543.8	5,075.6	583.5	1,529.0	2,963.4	1,140.6	1,109.2	817.5	210.1	607.6	291.7	30.4
1996	7,813.2	5,237.5	616.5	1,574.1	3,047.0	1,242.7	1,212.7	899.4	225.0	674.4	313.3	30.0
1997	8,159.5	5,423.9	657.3	1,619.9	3,147.0	1,393.3	1,328.6	1,009.3	245.4	764.2	319.7	63.8
1998	8,508.9	5,683.7	726.7	1,686.4	3,273.4	1,558.0	1,480.0	1,135.9	262.2	875.4	345.1	76.7
1999	8,859.0	5,964.5	812.5	1,765.1	3,395.4	1,660.5	1,595.2	1,228.4	258.6	975.9	368.3	62.8
2000	9,191.4	6,223.9	878.9	1,833.8	3,524.5	1,762.9	1,691.9	1,324.2	275.5	1,056.0	372.4	65.0
2001	9,214.5	6,377.2	931.9	1,869.8	3,594.9	1,574.6	1,627.4	1,255.1	270.9	988.2	373.5	-61.4
1998: I	8,396.3	5,576.3	692.5	1,656.3	3,228.4	1,543.3	1,431.4	1,099.5	255.7	845.0	333.0	113.1
II	8,442.9	5,660.2	719.7	1,680.5	3,262.3	1,516.8	1,471.4	1,132.3	264.8	868.6	340.5	42.0
III	8,528.5	5,713.7	727.1	1,693.6	3,295.2	1,559.7	1,485.4	1,136.6	263.0	875.1	349.5	71.8
IV	8,667.9	5,784.7	767.3	1,715.3	3,307.6	1,612.1	1,531.7	1,175.4	265.1	912.9	357.4	80.0
1999: I	8,733.2	5,851.4	777.6	1,736.1	3,343.6	1,640.3	1,560.5	1,197.5	262.4	939.1	364.1	80.0
II	8,775.5	5,932.8	804.2	1,756.7	3,379.7	1,620.5	1,587.6	1,220.4	258.9	967.1	368.4	31.2
III	8,886.9	6,000.1	824.1	1,767.7	3,417.4	1,663.4	1,610.6	1,243.3	254.7	996.1	369.2	47.6
IV	9,040.1	6,073.6	844.2	1,799.9	3,440.7	1,717.8	1,622.2	1,252.4	258.5	1,001.2	371.7	92.2
2000: I	9,097.4	6,151.9	879.5	1,809.7	3,477.7	1,727.8	1,673.6	1,297.1	267.0	1,038.0	379.1	45.3
II	9,205.7	6,198.2	871.3	1,831.6	3,508.2	1,798.1	1,700.9	1,329.1	272.3	1,065.3	376.2	91.5
III	9,218.7	6,256.8	888.5	1,840.9	3,541.7	1,770.3	1,701.7	1,340.7	280.2	1,067.7	367.2	63.1
IV	9,243.8	6,288.8	876.5	1,853.1	3,570.6	1,755.2	1,691.3	1,329.9	282.7	1,053.1	367.2	59.9
2001: I	9,229.9	6,326.0	900.6	1,863.7	3,576.3	1,661.8	1,682.1	1,311.4	280.4	1,036.1	374.5	-26.9
II	9,193.1	6,348.0	912.4	1,862.3	3,589.3	1,583.5	1,633.5	1,261.0	274.4	989.9	374.0	-58.3
III	9,186.4	6,370.9	922.6	1,868.3	3,597.5	1,562.7	1,615.7	1,241.7	276.3	966.4	374.3	-61.8
IV	9,248.8	6,464.0	992.0	1,885.0	3,616.6	1,490.3	1,578.4	1,206.4	252.7	960.3	371.0	-98.4
2002: I	9,363.2	6,513.8	975.9	1,921.4	3,642.2	1,554.0	1,576.4	1,188.4	243.2	953.7	383.6	-28.9
II	9,392.4	6,542.4	980.7	1,920.9	3,666.2	1,583.9	1,572.6	1,181.1	231.7	961.4	386.1	4.9
III	9,485.6	6,609.9	1,032.4	1,925.8	3,687.0	1,598.0	1,571.6	1,178.7	218.2	977.2	387.1	18.8

EXHIBIT B.2   CONTINUED

Year or Quarter	Net Exports of Goods and Services			Government Consumption Expenditures and Gross Investment					Final Sales of Domestic Product	Gross Domestic Purchases[1]	Addendum: Gross National Product[2]	Percent Change from Preceding Period	
					Federal								
	Net Exports	Exports	Imports	Total	Total	National Defense	Non-defense	State and Local				Gross Domestic Product	Gross Domestic Purchases[1]
1990	-56.5	575.7	632.2	1,387.3	606.8	443.2	163.0	781.1	6,695.6	6,764.9	6,740.0	1.8	1.4
1991	-15.8	613.2	629.0	1,403.4	604.9	438.4	166.0	798.9	6,681.5	6,688.4	6,703.4	-0.5	-1.1
1992	-19.8	651.0	670.8	1,410.0	595.1	417.1	177.9	815.3	6,867.7	6,896.4	6,905.8	3.0	3.1
1993	-59.1	672.7	731.8	1,398.8	572.0	394.7	177.3	827.0	7,043.8	7,120.6	7,087.8	2.7	3.3
1994	-86.5	732.8	819.4	1,400.1	551.3	375.9	175.5	848.9	7,285.8	7,434.2	7,364.3	4.0	4.4
1995	-78.4	808.2	886.6	1,406.4	536.5	361.9	174.6	869.9	7,512.2	7,621.8	7,564.0	2.7	2.5
1996	-89.0	874.2	963.1	1,421.9	531.6	357.0	174.6	890.4	7,783.2	7,902.1	7,831.2	3.6	3.7
1997	-113.3	981.5	1,094.8	1,455.4	529.6	347.7	181.8	925.8	8,095.2	8,271.7	8,168.1	4.4	4.7
1998	-221.1	1,002.4	1,223.5	1,483.3	525.4	341.6	183.8	957.7	8,431.8	8,721.3	8,508.4	4.3	5.4
1999	-320.5	1,036.3	1,356.8	1,540.6	537.7	348.8	188.8	1,002.4	8,793.9	9,160.2	8,883.7	4.1	5.0
2000	-398.8	1,137.2	1,536.0	1,582.5	544.4	348.7	195.6	1,037.4	9,121.1	9,561.2	9,216.2	3.8	4.4
2001	-415.9	1,076.1	1,492.0	1,640.4	570.6	366.0	204.4	1,069.4	9,258.4	9,600.7	9,237.3	0.3	0.4
1998: I	-180.8	1,003.4	1,184.2	1,456.1	515.0	332.0	183.0	940.8	8,286.6	8,571.6	8,405.4	6.1	7.9
II	-223.1	993.1	1,216.2	1,482.6	530.1	342.0	188.0	952.4	8,397.2	8,657.0	8,448.7	2.2	4.0
III	-241.2	987.6	1,228.9	1,489.9	524.9	346.5	178.4	964.7	8,454.9	8,759.7	8,517.6	4.1	4.8
IV	-239.2	1,025.6	1,264.8	1,504.8	531.7	345.8	185.8	972.8	8,588.5	8,896.6	8,662.0	6.7	6.4
1999: I	-283.2	1,007.5	1,290.7	1,515.9	527.2	341.2	185.9	988.3	8,654.3	9,002.1	8,755.5	3.0	4.8
II	-319.6	1,018.1	1,337.7	1,526.7	530.6	341.0	189.5	995.7	8,741.0	9,076.2	8,801.8	2.0	3.3
III	-339.6	1,044.1	1,383.7	1,546.5	540.1	352.4	187.7	1,006.0	8,833.6	9,204.9	8,906.4	5.2	5.8
IV	-339.5	1,075.6	1,415.2	1,573.2	553.0	360.8	192.1	1,019.8	8,946.6	9,357.7	9,071.1	7.1	6.8
2000: I	-368.8	1,095.8	1,464.6	1,568.3	533.8	341.3	192.3	1,033.8	9,042.9	9,440.8	9,119.7	2.6	3.6
II	-394.6	1,133.9	1,528.5	1,586.1	554.0	353.4	200.3	1,031.8	9,111.1	9,571.9	9,233.0	4.8	5.7
III	-413.1	1,165.5	1,578.6	1,582.2	543.7	347.9	195.6	1,037.8	9,150.4	9,600.9	9,238.2	0.6	1.2
IV	-418.5	1,153.7	1,572.2	1,593.4	546.4	351.9	194.3	1,046.3	9,179.8	9,631.0	9,274.0	1.1	1.3
2001: I	-404.5	1,135.8	1,540.3	1,615.7	559.0	359.0	199.8	1,056.2	9,243.8	9,604.6	9,241.7	-0.6	-1.1
II	-414.8	1,098.8	1,513.6	1,638.0	567.2	361.4	205.6	1,070.2	9,234.3	9,577.1	9,224.3	-1.6	-1.1
III	-419.0	1,048.0	1,467.0	1,633.3	568.9	365.5	203.2	1,064.1	9,230.5	9,575.8	9,199.8	-0.3	-0.1
IV	-425.3	1,021.8	1,447.2	1,674.5	587.2	378.0	209.1	1,087.1	9,324.9	9,645.3	9,283.5	2.7	2.9
2002: I	-446.6	1,030.6	1,477.1	1,697.3	597.8	388.5	209.3	1,099.3	9,379.4	9,778.2	9,367.5	5.0	5.6
II	-487.4	1,065.5	1,552.9	1,703.3	608.7	395.8	212.9	1,094.7	9,377.9	9,840.8	9,376.7	1.3	2.6
III	-488.0	1,077.7	1,565.7	1,715.6	615.1	402.5	212.7	1,100.6	9,457.2	9,934.7	9,477.9	4.0	3.9

SOURCE: Department of Commerce, Bureau of Economic Analysis.

[1] Gross domestic product (GDP) less exports of goods and services plus imports of goods and services.

[2] GDP plus net income receipts from rest of the world.

EXHIBIT B.32	GROSS SAVING AND INVESTMENT, 1959–2002

[Billions of dollars, except as noted; quarterly data at seasonally adjusted annual rates]

Year or Quarter	Gross Saving													
	Total	Gross Private Saving						Gross Government Saving						
		Total	Personal Saving	Gross Business Saving				Total	Federal			State And Local		
				Total[1]	Undistributed Corporate Profits[2]	Corporate Consumption of Fixed Capital	Noncorporate Consumption of Fixed Capital		Total	Consumption of Fixed Capital	Current Surplus or Deficit (-)	Total	Consumption of Fixed Capital	Current Surplus or Deficit (-)
1959	105.8	84.2	26.5	57.7	17.5	23.7	16.5	21.6	13.6	10.4	3.2	8.0	4.2	3.8
1960	110.9	84.4	26.4	58.1	16.3	24.7	17.1	26.5	17.8	10.7	7.1	8.7	4.4	4.3
1961	113.9	91.5	31.9	59.6	16.8	25.2	17.6	22.5	13.5	11.0	2.5	9.0	4.7	4.3
1962	124.6	100.4	33.5	66.9	22.6	26.2	18.1	24.2	14.0	11.6	2.4	10.2	5.0	5.2
1963	132.8	104.3	33.1	71.2	25.2	27.2	18.7	28.5	17.5	12.3	5.2	11.0	5.4	5.7
1964	143.0	117.6	40.5	77.1	28.6	28.7	19.7	25.5	13.4	12.5	0.8	12.1	5.7	6.4
1965	158.1	129.4	42.7	86.6	34.9	30.8	21.0	28.8	16.0	12.8	3.2	12.7	6.2	6.5
1966	169.1	138.5	44.5	94.0	37.6	33.7	22.6	30.7	16.1	13.3	2.7	14.6	6.9	7.7
1967	171.1	150.8	54.0	96.9	35.4	37.1	24.3	20.3	5.8	14.2	-8.3	14.5	7.5	7.0
1968	183.3	153.7	52.7	101.1	33.6	41.1	26.4	29.6	13.8	15.1	-1.3	15.8	8.3	7.5
1969	199.8	157.0	52.6	104.3	29.8	45.6	29.0	42.8	25.5	15.9	9.6	17.3	9.3	8.0
1970	194.3	174.3	69.5	104.8	23.0	50.5	31.4	20.0	2.3	16.7	-14.4	17.6	10.6	7.1
1971	211.4	202.6	80.1	122.5	32.4	55.4	34.4	8.8	-9.5	17.4	-26.8	18.2	11.8	6.4
1972	241.6	217.0	76.9	140.1	41.1	60.9	38.5	24.6	-3.8	18.7	-22.5	28.4	12.9	15.6
1973	294.6	256.4	102.5	153.9	44.8	66.8	42.3	38.2	8.3	19.5	-11.2	30.0	14.3	15.7
1974	304.0	270.7	114.3	156.4	29.5	78.5	48.4	33.3	6.4	20.2	-13.9	27.0	17.7	9.3
1975	298.4	323.5	125.2	198.3	49.1	94.0	55.2	-25.1	-47.7	21.6	-69.3	22.7	20.2	2.4
1976	342.7	344.0	122.1	221.9	57.3	104.5	60.0	-1.3	-29.9	23.2	-53.0	28.6	21.3	7.3
1977	398.2	383.1	125.6	257.5	73.1	117.5	66.9	15.1	-20.6	24.6	-45.2	35.7	22.6	13.1
1978	481.6	439.1	145.4	293.6	82.9	134.5	76.2	42.5	-0.6	26.3	-26.9	43.1	24.4	18.7
1979	544.9	487.8	165.8	321.9	77.0	156.4	88.5	57.1	16.6	28.0	-11.4	40.5	27.4	13.0
1980	555.5	537.8	205.6	332.2	49.6	181.1	101.5	17.7	-22.8	30.9	-53.8	40.6	31.7	8.8
1981	656.5	631.7	243.7	387.9	64.1	210.1	113.7	24.8	-18.9	34.7	-53.7	43.8	36.3	7.5
1982	625.7	681.6	262.2	419.4	61.9	233.4	124.0	-55.9	-93.1	39.5	-132.6	37.2	39.5	-2.3
1983	608.0	693.8	227.8	466.0	93.2	244.4	128.3	-85.7	-131.5	42.4	-173.9	45.7	40.9	4.8
1984	769.4	824.8	306.5	518.3	124.7	260.2	133.4	-55.4	-121.6	46.4	-168.1	66.2	42.4	23.8
1985	772.5	833.4	282.6	550.8	128.3	280.9	141.7	-60.9	-127.9	49.3	-177.1	67.0	44.7	22.3
1986	735.9	806.5	267.8	538.7	88.0	302.1	148.7	-70.5	-139.2	52.9	-192.1	68.7	47.9	20.8
1987	810.4	838.3	252.8	585.5	107.3	320.8	157.4	-27.9	-91.6	56.3	-147.9	63.7	51.5	12.2
1988	936.2	943.0	292.3	650.6	138.3	344.3	168.1	-6.7	-77.2	60.2	-137.4	70.5	54.9	15.6
1989	967.6	955.1	301.8	653.2	99.2	370.6	183.4	12.5	-65.6	64.4	-130.0	78.1	58.8	19.3

EXHIBIT B.32   CONTINUED

Year or Quarter	Total	Gross Investment			Statistical Discre-pancy	Addenda:	
		Gross Private Domestic Invest-ment	Gross Govern-ment Invest-ment [3]	Net Foreign Invest-ment [4]		Gross Saving as a Percent of Gross National Product	Personal Saving as a Percent of Disposable Personal Income
1959	106.7	78.5	29.3	-1.2	0.8	20.7	7.6
1960	110.4	78.9	28.3	3.2	-0.6	20.9	7.2
1961	113.8	78.2	31.3	4.3	-0.2	20.7	8.3
1962	125.3	88.1	33.3	3.9	0.7	21.1	8.3
1963	132.4	93.8	33.6	5.0	-0.4	21.3	7.8
1964	144.2	102.1	34.6	7.5	1.2	21.4	8.8
1965	160.0	118.2	35.6	6.2	1.9	21.8	8.6
1966	175.6	131.3	40.4	3.9	6.4	21.3	8.3
1967	175.9	128.6	43.8	3.5	4.8	20.4	9.4
1968	187.6	141.2	44.7	1.7	4.3	20.0	8.4
1969	202.7	156.4	44.4	1.8	2.9	20.1	7.8
1970	201.2	152.4	44.8	4.0	6.9	18.6	9.4
1971	222.7	178.2	44.0	0.6	11.3	18.6	10.0
1972	250.3	207.6	46.3	-3.6	8.7	19.3	8.9
1973	302.6	244.5	49.4	8.7	8.0	21.1	10.5
1974	314.0	249.4	57.4	7.1	10.0	20.0	10.7
1975	316.1	230.2	64.5	21.4	17.7	18.1	10.6
1976	367.2	292.0	66.4	8.9	24.5	18.6	9.4
1977	419.8	361.3	67.5	-9.0	21.6	19.4	8.7
1978	502.6	436.0	77.1	-10.4	21.0	20.8	9.0
1979	580.6	490.6	88.5	1.4	35.7	21.0	9.2
1980	589.5	477.9	100.3	11.4	33.9	19.6	10.2
1981	684.0	570.8	106.9	6.3	27.5	20.7	10.8
1982	628.2	516.1	112.3	-0.2	2.5	19.0	10.9
1983	655.0	564.2	122.8	-32.0	47.0	17.0	8.8
1984	787.9	735.5	139.4	-87.0	18.6	19.4	10.6
1985	784.2	736.3	158.8	-110.9	11.7	18.2	9.2
1986	779.8	747.2	173.2	-140.6	43.9	16.5	8.2
1987	813.8	781.5	184.3	-152.0	3.3	17.0	7.3
1988	894.0	821.1	186.2	-113.2	-42.2	18.3	7.8
1989	983.9	872.9	197.7	-86.7	16.3	17.6	7.5

[1] Includes private wage accruals less disbursements not shown separately.
[2] With inventory valuation and capital consumption adjustments.

EXHIBIT B.32   **CONTINUED**

	Gross Saving													
		Gross Private Saving							Gross Government Saving					
				Gross Business Saving						Federal			State And Local	
Year or Quarter	Total	Total	Personal Saving	Total[1]	Undistributed Corporate Profits[2]	Corporate Consumption of Fixed Capital	Noncorporate Consumption of Fixed Capital	Total	Total	Consumption of Fixed Capital	Current Surplus or Deficit (-)	Total	Consumption of Fixed Capital	Current Surplus or Deficit (-)
1990	977.7	1,016.2	334.3	681.9	102.4	391.1	188.4	-38.6	-104.3	68.7	-173.0	65.7	63.1	2.6
1991	1,015.8	1,098.9	371.7	727.3	119.2	411.2	196.8	-83.2	-142.3	73.0	-215.3	59.1	66.9	-7.8
1992	1,007.4	1,164.6	413.7	750.9	124.4	427.9	214.3	-157.2	-222.2	75.4	-297.5	65.0	69.9	-4.9
1993	1,039.4	1,159.4	350.8	808.6	142.0	448.5	211.6	-120.0	-195.4	78.7	-274.1	75.4	73.9	1.5
1994	1,155.9	1,199.3	315.5	883.8	151.6	482.7	231.9	-43.4	-130.9	81.4	-212.3	87.5	78.9	8.6
1995	1,257.5	1,266.0	302.4	963.6	203.6	512.1	231.5	-8.5	-108.0	84.0	-192.0	99.4	84.1	15.3
1996	1,349.3	1,290.4	272.1	1,018.3	232.7	543.5	238.5	58.9	-51.5	85.3	-136.8	110.4	88.9	21.4
1997	1,502.3	1,343.7	252.9	1,090.8	261.3	581.5	250.9	158.6	33.4	86.8	-53.3	125.1	94.2	31.0
1998	1,647.2	1,375.0	301.5	1,073.5	189.9	620.2	264.2	272.2	132.0	88.2	43.8	140.2	99.5	40.7
1999	1,704.1	1,356.1	174.0	1,182.0	229.6	665.5	281.8	348.1	203.4	91.5	111.9	144.7	106.4	38.3
2000	1,807.9	1,372.1	201.5	1,170.5	152.6	721.1	296.8	435.8	302.8	95.9	206.9	133.0	115.0	18.0
2001	1,662.4	1,399.3	169.7	1,229.5	122.7	789.1	317.7	263.1	170.7	98.7	72.0	92.4	123.7	-31.3
1998: I	1,610.0	1,369.0	307.9	1,061.0	198.1	605.1	258.5	241.1	107.0	87.4	19.6	134.1	97.4	36.7
II	1,617.2	1,366.0	309.1	1,056.9	181.4	614.2	262.0	251.2	120.7	87.8	33.0	130.5	98.4	32.0
III	1,681.7	1,391.8	311.4	1,080.4	190.0	625.1	266.0	289.9	154.1	88.5	65.7	135.8	100.2	35.6
IV	1,679.8	1,373.4	277.6	1,095.8	190.1	636.2	270.2	306.4	146.1	89.1	57.0	160.3	101.9	58.4
1999: I	1,743.0	1,412.5	253.9	1,158.6	233.1	646.4	274.0	330.5	178.6	89.9	88.7	151.9	103.5	48.4
II	1,692.7	1,352.2	179.9	1,172.3	232.3	657.1	277.7	340.6	203.8	90.9	112.9	136.8	105.5	31.3
III	1,671.2	1,320.8	133.3	1,187.5	217.4	675.0	290.0	350.4	209.4	92.0	117.4	141.0	107.2	33.8
IV	1,709.7	1,338.8	129.0	1,209.8	235.6	683.4	285.7	370.9	221.9	93.2	128.8	149.0	109.3	39.6
2000: I	1,815.7	1,353.7	179.4	1,174.3	185.7	698.6	290.0	462.0	317.7	94.5	223.2	144.2	111.5	32.7
II	1,813.6	1,386.5	207.5	1,179.0	170.4	714.1	294.6	427.1	292.8	95.5	197.2	134.3	114.1	20.2
III	1,828.9	1,383.7	211.5	1,172.2	144.2	728.9	299.1	445.2	309.7	96.5	213.2	135.4	116.3	19.2
IV	1,773.4	1,364.4	207.7	1,156.7	110.2	742.8	303.7	409.0	291.0	97.2	193.8	118.0	118.1	-0.2
2001: I	1,699.0	1,324.1	173.7	1,150.4	86.3	755.9	308.2	374.9	271.5	97.7	173.8	103.4	119.9	-16.5
II	1,670.6	1,338.4	141.6	1,196.8	101.9	772.3	322.6	332.2	243.0	98.6	144.4	89.2	121.5	-32.3
III	1,665.6	1,535.6	302.2	1,233.4	79.5	835.6	318.2	130.0	47.3	99.0	-51.7	82.7	128.9	-46.2
IV	1,614.4	1,399.0	61.5	1,337.5	223.0	792.6	321.9	215.3	121.1	99.7	21.3	94.3	124.5	-30.2
2002: I	1,603.2	1,578.3	270.4	1,307.9	171.0	808.3	328.6	24.9	-45.2	100.6	-145.8	70.1	125.9	-55.8
II	1,604.0	1,616.1	314.3	1,301.8	140.5	826.1	335.1	-12.1	-94.3	101.3	-195.6	82.2	127.3	-45.1
III	1,573.7	1,596.4	303.0	1,293.4	118.6	836.1	338.7	-22.7	-98.4	102.2	-200.7	75.8	128.3	-52.5

EXHIBIT B.32   **CONTINUED**

Year or Quarter	Gross Investment				Statistical Discrepancy	Addenda:	
	Total	Gross Private Domestic Invest-ment	Gross Govern-ment Invest-ment [3]	Net Foreign Invest-ment [4]		Gross Saving as a Percent of Gross National Product	Personal Saving as a Percent of Disposable Personal Income
1990	1,008.2	861.7	215.8	-69.2	30.6	16.8	7.8
1991	1,035.4	800.2	220.3	14.9	19.6	16.9	8.3
1992	1,051.1	866.6	223.1	-38.7	43.7	15.9	8.7
1993	1,103.2	955.1	220.9	-72.9	63.8	15.6	7.1
1994	1,214.4	1,097.1	225.6	-108.3	58.5	16.3	6.1
1995	1,284.0	1,143.8	238.2	-98.0	26.5	16.9	5.6
1996	1,382.1	1,242.7	250.1	-110.7	32.8	17.2	4.8
1997	1,532.1	1,390.5	264.6	-123.1	29.7	18.0	4.2
1998	1,616.2	1,538.7	277.1	-199.7	-31.0	18.8	4.7
1999	1,665.4	1,636.7	304.7	-276.0	-38.8	18.3	2.6
2000	1,679.4	1,755.4	319.8	-395.8	-128.5	18.4	2.8
2001	1,545.1	1,586.0	335.8	-376.7	-117.3	16.5	2.3
1998: I	1,638.5	1,528.7	265.3	-155.5	28.5	18.6	4.9
II	1,580.0	1,498.4	274.1	-192.5	-37.2	18.6	4.9
III	1,600.0	1,538.6	284.1	-222.7	-81.7	19.1	4.9
IV	1,646.2	1,589.3	284.9	-228.0	-33.6	18.7	4.3
1999: I	1,689.7	1,618.0	292.7	-221.0	-53.3	19.1	3.9
II	1,636.5	1,597.8	302.9	-264.2	-56.2	18.4	2.7
III	1,639.7	1,637.9	306.1	-304.2	-31.5	17.9	2.0
IV	1,695.6	1,693.2	317.1	-314.7	-14.1	17.9	1.9
2000: I	1,677.0	1,711.4	322.5	-356.9	-138.7	18.8	2.6
II	1,726.8	1,786.3	317.5	-377.1	-86.8	18.4	2.9
III	1,664.9	1,766.4	317.7	-419.1	-164.0	18.5	2.9
IV	1,648.9	1,757.4	321.5	-430.0	-124.5	17.8	2.9
2001: I	1,593.2	1,671.1	331.6	-409.5	-105.7	16.9	2.4
II	1,557.7	1,597.2	343.0	-382.5	-112.9	16.6	1.9
III	1,547.8	1,574.9	323.7	-350.8	-117.8	16.5	4.0
IV	1,481.8	1,500.7	345.0	-363.9	-132.6	15.8	0.8
2002: I	1,493.2	1,559.4	355.5	-421.7	-110.0	15.5	3.5
II	1,439.0	1,588.0	348.2	-497.2	-165.0	15.5	4.0
III	1,453.4	1,597.3	351.7	-495.6	-120.3	15.0	3.8

Source: Department of Commerce, Bureau of Economic Analysis.

[3] For details on government investment, see Table B-20.
[4] Net exports of goods and services plus net income receipts from rest of the world less net transfers.

EXHIBIT B.42 CIVILIAN UNEMPLOYMENT RATE, 1955-2002

[Percent;[1] monthly data seasonally adjusted]

Year or Month	All Civilian Workers	Males			Females			Both Sexes 16-19 Years	White	Black and Other	Black	Experienced Wage and Salary Workers	Married Men, Spouse Present	Women who Maintain Families
		Total	16-19 Years	20 Years and Over	Total	16-19 Years	20 Years and Over							
1955	4.4	4.2	11.6	3.8	4.9	10.2	4.4	11.0	3.9	8.7	......	4.8	2.6	......
1956	4.1	3.8	11.1	3.4	4.8	11.2	4.2	11.1	3.6	8.3	......	4.4	2.3	......
1957	4.3	4.1	12.4	3.6	4.7	10.6	4.1	11.6	3.8	7.9	......	4.6	2.8	......
1958	6.8	6.8	17.1	6.2	6.8	14.3	6.1	15.9	6.1	12.6	......	7.3	5.1	......
1959	5.5	5.2	15.3	4.7	5.9	13.5	5.2	14.6	4.8	10.7	......	5.7	3.6	......
1960	5.5	5.4	15.3	4.7	5.9	13.9	5.1	14.7	5.0	10.2	......	5.7	3.7	......
1961	6.7	6.4	17.1	5.7	7.2	16.3	6.3	16.8	6.0	12.4	......	6.8	4.6	......
1962	5.5	5.2	14.7	4.6	6.2	14.6	5.4	14.7	4.9	10.9	......	5.6	3.6	......
1963	5.7	5.2	17.2	4.5	6.5	17.2	5.4	17.2	5.0	10.8	......	5.6	3.4	......
1964	5.2	4.6	15.8	3.9	6.2	16.6	5.2	16.2	4.6	9.6	......	5.0	2.8	......
1965	4.5	4.0	14.1	3.2	5.5	15.7	4.5	14.8	4.1	8.1	......	4.3	2.4	......
1966	3.8	3.2	11.7	2.5	4.8	14.1	3.8	12.8	3.4	7.3	......	3.5	1.9	......
1967	3.8	3.1	12.3	2.3	5.2	13.5	4.2	12.9	3.4	7.4	......	3.6	1.8	4.9
1968	3.6	2.9	11.6	2.2	4.8	14.0	3.8	12.7	3.2	6.7	......	3.4	1.6	4.4
1969	3.5	2.8	11.4	2.1	4.7	13.3	3.7	12.2	3.1	6.4	......	3.3	1.5	4.4
1970	4.9	4.4	15.0	3.5	5.9	15.6	4.8	15.3	4.5	8.2	......	4.8	2.6	5.4
1971	5.9	5.3	16.6	4.4	6.9	17.2	5.7	16.9	5.4	9.9	......	5.7	3.2	7.3
1972	5.6	5.0	15.9	4.0	6.6	16.7	5.4	16.2	5.1	10.0	10.4	5.3	2.8	7.2
1973	4.9	4.2	13.9	3.3	6.0	15.3	4.9	14.5	4.3	9.0	9.4	4.5	2.3	7.1
1974	5.6	4.9	15.6	3.8	6.7	16.6	5.5	16.0	5.0	9.9	10.5	5.3	2.7	7.0
1975	8.5	7.9	20.1	6.8	9.3	19.7	8.0	19.9	7.8	13.8	14.8	8.2	5.1	10.0
1976	7.7	7.1	19.2	5.9	8.6	18.7	7.4	19.0	7.0	13.1	14.0	7.3	4.2	10.1
1977	7.1	6.3	17.3	5.2	8.2	18.3	7.0	17.8	6.2	13.1	14.0	6.6	3.6	9.4
1978	6.1	5.3	15.8	4.3	7.2	17.1	6.0	16.4	5.2	11.9	12.8	5.6	2.8	8.5
1979	5.8	5.1	15.9	4.2	6.8	16.4	5.7	16.1	5.1	11.3	12.3	5.5	2.8	8.3
1980	7.1	6.9	18.3	5.9	7.4	17.2	6.4	17.8	6.3	13.1	14.3	6.9	4.2	9.2
1981	7.6	7.4	20.1	6.3	7.9	19.0	6.8	19.6	6.7	14.2	15.6	7.3	4.3	10.4
1982	9.7	9.9	24.4	8.8	9.4	21.9	8.3	23.2	8.6	17.3	18.9	9.3	6.5	11.7
1983	9.6	9.9	23.3	8.9	9.2	21.3	8.1	22.4	8.4	17.8	19.5	9.2	6.5	12.2
1984	7.5	7.4	19.6	6.6	7.6	18.0	6.8	18.9	6.5	14.4	15.9	7.1	4.6	10.3
1985	7.2	7.0	19.5	6.2	7.4	17.6	6.6	18.6	6.2	13.7	15.1	6.8	4.3	10.4
1986	7.0	6.9	19.0	6.1	7.1	17.6	6.2	18.3	6.0	13.1	14.5	6.6	4.4	9.8
1987	6.2	6.2	17.8	5.4	6.2	15.9	5.4	16.9	5.3	11.6	13.0	5.8	3.9	9.2
1988	5.5	5.5	16.0	4.8	5.6	14.4	4.9	15.3	4.7	10.4	11.7	5.2	3.3	8.1
1989	5.3	5.2	15.9	4.5	5.4	14.0	4.7	15.0	4.5	10.0	11.4	5.0	3.0	8.1
1990	5.6	5.7	16.3	5.0	5.5	14.7	4.9	15.5	4.8	10.1	11.4	5.3	3.4	8.3
1991	6.8	7.2	19.8	6.4	6.4	17.5	5.7	18.7	6.1	11.1	12.5	6.6	4.4	9.3
1992	7.5	7.9	21.5	7.1	7.0	18.6	6.3	20.1	6.6	12.7	14.2	7.2	5.1	10.0

EXHIBIT B.42   CONTINUED

Year or Month	All Civilian Workers	Males			Females			Both Sexes 16-19 Years	White	Black and Other	Black	Experienced Wage and Salary Workers	Married Men, Spouse Present	Women who Maintain Families
		Total	16-19 Years	20 Years and Over	Total	16-19 Years	20 Years and Over							
1993	6.9	7.2	20.4	6.4	6.6	17.5	5.9	19.0	6.1	11.7	13.0	6.6	4.4	9.7
1994	6.1	6.2	19.0	5.4	6.0	16.2	5.4	17.6	5.3	10.5	11.5	5.9	3.7	8.9
1995	5.6	5.6	18.4	4.8	5.6	16.1	4.9	17.3	4.9	9.6	10.4	5.4	3.3	8.0
1996	5.4	5.4	18.1	4.6	5.4	15.2	4.8	16.7	4.7	9.3	10.5	5.2	3.0	8.2
1997	4.9	4.9	16.9	4.2	5.0	15.0	4.4	16.0	4.2	8.8	10.0	4.7	2.7	8.1
1998	4.5	4.4	16.2	3.7	4.6	12.9	4.1	14.6	3.9	7.8	8.9	4.3	2.4	7.2
1999	4.2	4.1	14.7	3.5	4.3	13.2	3.8	13.9	3.7	7.0	8.0	4.0	2.2	6.4
2000	4.0	3.9	14.0	3.3	4.1	12.1	3.6	13.1	3.5	6.7	7.6	3.9	2.0	5.9
2001	4.8	4.8	15.9	4.2	4.7	13.4	4.1	14.7	4.2	7.7	8.7	4.6	2.7	6.6
2002	5.8	5.9	18.0	5.3	5.6	14.8	5.1	16.5	5.1	9.2	10.3	5.7	3.6	8.0
2001: Jan	4.2	4.2	14.8	3.6	4.1	12.5	3.5	13.7	3.6	7.0	8.2	4.0	2.3	6.4
Feb	4.2	4.2	15.0	3.5	4.1	11.9	3.6	13.5	3.7	6.7	7.5	4.1	2.3	6.0
Mar	4.3	4.4	14.3	3.8	4.2	13.3	3.6	13.8	3.7	7.2	8.4	4.2	2.4	6.1
Apr	4.5	4.6	15.1	3.9	4.3	13.2	3.8	14.2	3.9	7.1	8.2	4.3	2.5	6.3
May	4.4	4.5	15.4	3.9	4.3	12.1	3.8	13.8	3.9	7.1	8.0	4.3	2.6	6.2
June	4.6	4.7	15.8	4.1	4.4	13.0	3.9	14.4	4.0	7.4	8.4	4.5	2.6	6.3
July	4.6	4.7	15.6	4.0	4.6	14.0	4.0	14.8	4.1	7.3	8.1	4.5	2.7	6.3
Aug	4.9	5.1	17.4	4.4	4.8	14.1	4.2	15.8	4.3	8.1	9.0	4.8	2.8	6.8
Sept	5.0	5.0	16.0	4.3	5.0	13.6	4.4	14.9	4.3	8.0	8.8	4.8	2.8	7.1
Oct	5.4	5.5	17.2	4.8	5.3	13.6	4.8	15.4	4.7	8.6	9.6	5.3	3.1	6.8
Nov	5.6	5.9	17.7	5.2	5.4	13.7	4.9	15.7	5.0	8.8	9.9	5.5	3.3	8.0
Dec	5.8	5.8	17.2	5.2	5.8	15.1	5.2	16.2	5.1	9.1	10.2	5.7	3.4	8.0
2002: Jan	5.6	5.8	16.3	5.2	5.4	15.8	4.8	16.1	5.0	8.7	9.8	5.5	3.5	7.9
Feb	5.5	5.6	16.8	5.0	5.5	14.3	5.0	15.6	4.9	8.8	9.6	5.5	3.4	8.0
Mar	5.7	5.9	18.5	5.2	5.5	14.3	5.0	16.4	5.0	9.5	10.7	5.7	3.4	7.3
Apr	6.0	6.1	18.1	5.4	6.0	15.4	5.4	16.8	5.3	10.0	11.2	5.9	3.9	8.6
May	5.8	5.9	18.6	5.2	5.8	15.2	5.2	16.9	5.2	9.1	10.2	5.8	3.6	8.1
June	5.9	6.1	19.6	5.4	5.7	15.6	5.1	17.6	5.2	9.5	10.7	5.7	4.1	8.2
July	5.9	6.0	19.8	5.2	5.7	15.6	5.2	17.7	5.3	8.9	9.9	5.7	3.5	8.4
Aug	5.7	6.0	20.1	5.2	5.4	14.2	4.9	17.2	5.1	8.8	9.6	5.5	3.4	7.3
Sept	5.6	5.9	17.8	5.2	5.4	13.5	4.9	15.7	5.1	8.5	9.6	5.5	3.6	7.2
Oct	5.7	5.8	15.6	5.2	5.7	13.6	5.2	14.6	5.1	8.8	9.8	5.7	3.4	8.0
Nov	6.0	6.3	17.7	5.7	5.6	15.8	5.0	16.8	5.2	9.8	11.0	5.7	3.6	8.3
Dec	6.0	6.2	17.1	5.6	5.9	15.1	5.3	16.1	5.1	10.1	11.5	5.9	3.6	8.7

SOURCE: Department of Labor, Bureau of Labor Statistics.

[1] Unemployed as percent of civilian labor force in group specified.

Note.—Data relate to persons 16 years of age and over.

| EXHIBIT B.50 | CHANGES IN PRODUCTIVITY AND RELATED DATA, BUSINESS SECTOR, 1959-2002 |

[Percent change from preceding period; quarterly data at seasonally adjusted annual rates]

Year or Quarter	Output Per Hour of All Persons		Output[1]		Hours of All Persons[2]		Compensation Per Hour[3]		Real Compensation Per Hour[4]		Unit Labor Costs		Implicit Price Deflator[5]	
	Business Sector	Nonfarm Business Sector	Business Sector	Nonfarm Business Sector	Business Sector	Nonfarm Business Sector	Business Sector	Nonfarm Business Sector	Business Sector	Nonfarm Business Sector	Business Sector	Nonfarm Business Sector	Business Sector	Nonfarm Business Sector
1959	4.0	4.0	8.3	8.8	4.1	4.6	4.2	4.0	3.5	3.3	0.1	0.0	0.7	1.2
1960	1.9	1.3	1.9	1.7	0.0	0.4	4.3	4.5	2.6	2.7	2.4	3.1	1.1	1.2
1961	3.7	3.4	2.0	2.0	-1.7	-1.3	4.1	3.6	3.1	2.5	0.4	0.2	0.8	0.8
1962	4.6	4.5	6.4	6.8	1.7	2.2	4.5	4.0	3.4	3.0	-0.1	-0.5	1.0	1.0
1963	3.9	3.5	4.6	4.6	0.6	1.1	3.7	3.5	2.3	2.2	-0.2	0.0	0.6	0.7
1964	4.6	4.2	6.4	6.7	1.7	2.4	5.1	4.6	3.8	3.2	0.5	0.3	1.1	1.2
1965	3.6	3.1	7.0	7.1	3.3	3.8	3.8	3.3	2.1	1.7	0.2	0.2	1.6	1.4
1966	4.1	3.5	6.8	7.2	2.6	3.6	6.7	5.8	3.7	2.9	2.5	2.2	2.5	2.3
1967	2.2	1.7	1.9	1.7	-0.3	-0.1	5.7	5.9	2.6	2.7	3.5	4.1	2.7	3.2
1968	3.1	3.1	5.0	5.3	1.8	2.1	7.7	7.4	3.4	3.1	4.4	4.2	3.9	3.8
1969	0.5	0.1	3.0	3.0	2.5	2.9	7.0	6.8	1.5	1.3	6.5	6.7	4.5	4.4
1970	2.0	1.5	0.0	-0.1	-2.0	-1.6	7.7	7.2	1.9	1.4	5.6	5.6	4.4	4.5
1971	4.4	4.2	3.9	3.8	-0.4	-0.3	6.4	6.5	1.9	2.0	1.9	2.2	4.3	4.4
1972	3.3	3.4	6.6	6.9	3.3	3.4	6.2	6.4	2.9	3.0	2.8	2.9	3.3	2.9
1973	3.2	3.1	7.0	7.3	3.7	4.0	8.5	8.2	2.2	1.9	5.2	4.9	5.2	3.6
1974	-1.7	-1.6	-1.5	-1.5	0.1	0.1	9.7	9.8	-1.2	-1.1	11.6	11.6	9.6	10.2
1975	3.5	2.7	-1.0	-1.7	-4.3	-4.3	10.3	10.1	1.0	0.9	6.5	7.2	9.6	10.6
1976	3.6	3.7	6.8	7.2	3.1	3.4	8.8	8.6	2.9	2.7	5.1	4.7	5.2	5.4
1977	1.6	1.5	5.6	5.6	3.9	4.0	7.9	8.0	1.3	1.4	6.1	6.4	6.1	6.4
1978	1.1	1.3	6.2	6.5	5.0	5.1	8.8	8.9	1.8	1.9	7.6	7.6	7.2	6.8
1979	0.0	-0.4	3.3	3.2	3.4	3.6	9.7	9.5	0.3	0.1	9.8	10.0	8.5	8.5
1980	-0.3	-0.3	-1.1	-1.1	-0.9	-0.8	10.8	10.8	-0.2	-0.2	11.1	11.1	9.1	9.7
1981	1.9	1.2	2.7	2.0	0.7	0.8	9.5	9.7	0.1	0.3	7.4	8.3	9.2	9.5
1982	-0.4	-0.6	-2.9	-3.1	-2.6	-2.5	7.5	7.5	1.5	1.5	8.0	8.1	5.7	6.2
1983	3.6	4.5	5.4	6.4	1.6	1.8	4.2	4.3	0.1	0.1	0.6	-0.2	3.4	3.2
1984	2.8	2.2	8.8	8.3	5.8	6.0	4.4	4.3	0.4	0.3	1.5	2.1	2.9	2.8
1985	2.0	1.3	4.2	3.9	2.2	2.5	4.9	4.7	1.5	1.3	2.9	3.3	2.7	3.2
1986	3.0	3.0	3.7	3.8	0.7	0.8	5.2	5.2	3.3	3.3	2.1	2.1	1.6	1.7
1987	0.5	0.4	3.5	3.5	3.0	3.2	3.9	3.8	0.5	0.4	3.4	3.4	2.5	2.5
1988	1.2	1.3	4.3	4.5	3.0	3.2	4.8	4.6	1.1	0.9	3.5	3.2	3.1	3.0
1989	1.0	0.8	3.5	3.4	2.5	2.6	2.8	2.7	-1.4	-1.5	1.8	1.9	3.7	3.7
1990	1.3	1.1	1.5	1.4	0.2	0.3	5.7	5.5	0.7	0.5	4.3	4.3	3.5	3.6
1991	1.1	1.2	-1.2	-1.3	-2.3	-2.4	4.7	4.9	1.1	1.2	3.6	3.6	3.5	3.7

EXHIBIT B.50   CONTINUED

Year or Quarter	Output Per Hour of All Persons		Output[1]		Hours of All Persons[2]		Compensation Per Hour[3]		Real Compensation Per Hour[4]		Unit Labor Costs		Implicit Price Deflator[5]	
	Business Sector	Nonfarm Business Sector	Business Sector	Nonfarm Business Sector	Business Sector	Nonfarm Business Sector	Business Sector	Nonfarm Business Sector	Business Sector	Nonfarm Business Sector	Business Sector	Nonfarm Business Sector	Business Sector	Nonfarm Business Sector
1992	3.9	3.7	3.7	3.5	-0.2	-0.2	5.3	5.3	2.7	2.7	1.4	1.6	2.0	2.1
1993	0.5	0.5	3.1	3.3	2.6	2.9	2.5	2.2	0.0	-0.3	1.9	1.7	2.2	2.2
1994	1.3	1.3	4.9	4.7	3.5	3.3	2.0	2.1	-0.1	0.0	0.7	0.8	1.8	1.9
1995	0.7	0.9	3.1	3.4	2.4	2.4	2.1	2.1	-0.3	-0.3	1.4	1.2	2.0	2.0
1996	2.8	2.5	4.4	4.3	1.6	1.7	3.2	3.1	0.5	0.4	0.4	0.5	1.6	1.4
1997	2.3	2.0	5.2	5.1	2.9	3.1	3.1	3.0	0.9	0.8	0.8	0.9	1.8	2.1
1998	2.6	2.6	4.9	5.0	2.2	2.4	5.5	5.4	4.0	3.9	2.8	2.7	0.8	0.9
1999	2.6	2.4	4.7	4.6	2.0	2.2	4.6	4.4	2.4	2.2	1.9	2.0	1.0	1.2
2000	3.0	2.9	4.1	4.0	1.0	1.0	6.8	7.0	3.4	3.5	3.7	3.9	1.7	1.8
2001	1.1	1.1	-0.2	-0.1	-1.3	-1.2	2.9	2.7	0.2	-0.1	1.8	1.6	2.0	1.9
1998: I	5.1	4.9	7.5	7.8	2.2	2.8	7.3	7.0	6.5	6.2	2.1	2.0	0.5	0.6
II	0.1	0.6	1.9	2.1	1.9	1.4	5.4	5.8	4.2	4.6	5.3	5.1	0.5	0.4
III	2.3	1.9	4.4	4.3	2.0	2.4	4.7	4.6	3.1	3.0	2.3	2.7	0.9	1.2
IV	4.4	4.3	8.2	8.3	3.7	3.8	4.0	3.8	2.2	2.0	-0.4	-0.4	0.5	0.5
1999: I	3.1	2.4	3.4	3.3	0.2	0.9	8.2	7.3	6.5	5.5	5.0	4.8	1.3	1.4
II	-0.6	-0.8	2.1	1.9	2.7	2.6	0.5	0.6	-2.3	-2.2	1.1	1.3	1.0	1.5
III	3.8	3.7	5.9	6.0	2.0	2.2	3.7	3.7	0.8	0.8	-0.1	0.0	1.2	1.4
IV	5.8	6.3	8.4	8.3	2.4	1.9	5.1	5.8	1.7	2.5	-0.7	-0.5	1.1	1.3
2000: I	0.3	0.2	2.2	1.9	1.9	1.7	14.7	15.2	10.3	10.7	14.4	14.9	2.4	2.7
II	6.7	6.0	5.4	5.4	-1.2	-0.6	3.0	2.2	0.0	-0.7	-3.5	-3.6	2.2	1.9
III	0.4	0.6	0.4	0.2	0.0	-0.4	8.3	8.7	4.6	4.9	7.8	8.0	1.1	1.4
IV	2.1	1.7	0.9	1.1	-1.2	-0.6	3.7	3.1	0.7	0.2	1.6	1.4	1.9	1.6
2001: I	-1.5	-1.5	-1.0	-0.9	0.4	0.5	3.1	2.8	-0.6	-0.9	4.7	4.3	3.4	3.3
II	-0.2	-0.1	-2.8	-2.7	-2.6	-2.6	0.5	0.1	-2.6	-2.9	0.7	0.3	2.2	2.0
III	1.8	2.1	-0.9	-0.8	-2.6	-2.9	0.9	1.0	0.2	0.3	-0.9	-1.1	1.8	1.7
IV	7.6	7.3	3.5	2.9	-3.9	-4.1	1.4	1.5	1.7	1.8	-5.8	-5.4	-1.6	-1.0
2002: I	8.3	8.6	5.9	6.2	-2.2	-2.2	3.0	2.9	1.6	1.4	-4.9	-5.3	0.3	-0.2
II	1.8	1.7	0.6	0.9	-1.2	-0.7	4.2	3.9	0.8	0.5	2.4	2.2	0.7	1.4
III	5.4	5.1	5.2	5.1	-0.2	0.0	5.3	4.9	3.4	3.0	-0.1	-0.2	0.4	0.1

SOURCE: Department of Labor, Bureau of Labor Statistics.

[1] Output refers to real gross domestic product in the sector.
[2] Hours at work of all persons engaged in the sector. See footnote 2, Table B-49.
[3] Wages and salaries of employees plus employers' contributions for social insurance and private benefit plans. Also includes an estimate of wages, salaries, and supplemental payments for the self-employed.
[4] Hourly compensation divided by the consumer price index. See footnote 4, Table B-49.
[5] Current dollar output divided by the output index.
Note.—Percent changes are based on original data and may differ slightly from percent changes based on indexes in Table B-49.

Money Stock, Credit, and Finance

MONEY STOCK AND DEBT MEASURES, 1959–2002

[Averages of daily figures, except debt end-of-period basis; billions of dollars, seasonally adjusted]

Year and Month	M1 — Sum of Currency, Demand Deposits, Travelers Checks, and Other Checkable Deposits (OCDs)	M2 — M1 plus Retail MMMF Balances, Savings Deposits (including MMDAs), and Small Time Deposits	M3 — M2 Plus Large Time Deposits, RPs, Eurodollars, and Institution-Only MMMF Balances	Debt[1] — Debt of Domestic Nonfinancial Sectors	Percent change — From Year or 6 Months Earlier[2] M1	M2	M3	From Previous Period[3] Debt
December:								
1959	140.0	297.8	299.7	689.5	......	......	......	7.7
1960	140.7	312.4	315.2	724.2	0.5	4.9	5.2	5.0
1961	145.2	335.5	340.8	767.7	3.2	7.4	8.1	6.0
1962	147.8	362.7	371.3	820.6	1.8	8.1	8.9	6.9
1963	153.3	393.2	405.9	876.0	3.7	8.4	9.3	6.8
1964	160.3	424.7	442.4	939.9	4.6	8.0	9.0	7.3
1965	167.8	459.2	482.1	1,007.1	4.7	8.1	9.0	7.1
1966	172.0	480.2	505.4	1,074.6	2.5	4.6	4.8	6.7
1967	183.3	524.8	557.9	1,152.6	6.6	9.3	10.4	7.3
1968	197.4	566.8	607.2	1,242.7	7.7	8.0	8.8	7.9
1969	203.9	587.9	615.9	1,332.0	3.3	3.7	1.4	7.2
1970	214.3	626.4	677.0	1,422.3	5.1	6.5	9.9	6.9
1971	228.2	710.1	775.9	1,557.5	6.5	13.4	14.6	9.5
1972	249.1	802.1	885.8	1,713.5	9.2	13.0	14.2	10.0
1973	262.7	855.3	984.9	1,897.9	5.5	6.6	11.2	10.7
1974	274.0	901.9	1,069.7	2,072.3	4.3	5.4	8.6	9.2
1975	286.8	1,016.0	1,169.9	2,264.7	4.7	12.7	9.4	9.3
1976	305.9	1,151.7	1,309.7	2,508.3	6.7	13.4	11.9	10.8
1977	330.5	1,269.9	1,470.1	2,829.6	8.0	10.3	12.2	12.8
1978	356.9	1,365.6	1,644.2	3,214.5	8.0	7.5	11.8	13.8
1979	381.4	1,473.3	1,808.3	3,606.5	6.9	7.9	10.0	12.2
1980	408.1	1,599.4	1,995.1	3,957.9	7.0	8.6	10.3	9.5
1981	436.2	1,754.9	2,254.0	4,366.4	6.9	9.7	13.0	10.4
1982	474.3	1,909.8	2,460.2	4,788.3	8.7	8.8	9.1	10.1
1983	520.8	2,125.9	2,697.0	5,364.8	9.8	11.3	9.6	12.0
1984	551.2	2,309.6	2,990.5	6,151.2	5.8	8.6	10.9	14.7
1985	619.1	2,494.9	3,207.5	7,132.3	12.3	8.0	7.3	15.7
1986	724.0	2,731.6	3,498.7	7,975.1	16.9	9.5	9.1	11.9
1987	749.4	2,830.6	3,685.8	8,677.6	3.5	3.6	5.3	9.0
1988	786.1	2,993.8	3,928.2	9,461.7	4.9	5.8	6.6	9.1
1989	792.1	3,157.4	4,075.9	10,166.3	0.8	5.5	3.8	7.3
1990	824.1	3,276.8	4,151.9	10,850.6	4.0	3.8	1.9	6.5
1991	896.2	3,376.1	4,204.3	11,312.5	8.7	3.0	1.3	4.3
1992	1,024.0	3,430.3	4,215.4	11,839.9	14.3	1.6	0.3	4.6

| EXHIBIT B.69 | | CONTINUED | | | | | | |

Year and Month	M1 — Sum of Currency, Demand Deposits, Travelers Checks, and Other Checkable Deposits (OCDs)	M2 — M1 plus Retail MMMF Balances, Savings Deposits (including MMDAs), and Small Time Deposits	M3 — M2 Plus Large Time Deposits, RPs, Eurodollars, and Institution-Only MMMF Balances	Debt[1] — Debt of Domestic Nonfinancial Sectors	Percent change — From Year or 6 Months Earlier[2] M1	M2	M3	From Previous Period[3] Debt
1993	1,129.1	3,483.0	4,277.4	12,434.1	10.3	1.5	1.5	4.9
1994	1,149.7	3,496.0	4,360.1	13,001.5	1.8	0.4	1.9	4.5
1995	1,126.5	3,639.8	4,625.7	13,706.9	-2.0	4.1	6.1	5.4
1996	1,079.1	3,813.8	4,971.6	14,440.2	-4.2	4.8	7.5	5.3
1997	1,072.2	4,030.5	5,447.5	15,243.1	-0.6	5.7	9.6	5.6
1998	1,096.5	4,383.9	6,037.7	16,285.5	2.3	8.8	10.8	6.8
1999	1,124.4	4,654.2	6,539.6	17,377.6	2.5	6.2	8.3	6.5
2000	1,088.9	4,938.6	7,109.9	18,250.6	-3.2	6.1	8.7	4.9
2001	1,179.3	5,458.6	8,027.0	19,369.2	8.3	10.5	12.9	6.1
2002 [p]	1,219.1	5,815.6	8,541.2	......	3.4	6.5	6.4	......
2001: Jan	1,095.8	4,983.7	7,207.8	......	-1.7	7.6	10.5	......
Feb	1,098.9	5,022.8	7,274.0	......	-0.6	7.8	10.2	......
Mar	1,107.4	5,071.9	7,327.0	18,487.9	1.5	8.4	9.9	5.2
Apr	1,109.7	5,114.3	7,430.5	......	1.9	9.4	12.1	......
May	1,116.6	5,140.4	7,523.4	......	4.6	9.9	14.1	......
June	1,125.6	5,187.3	7,612.1	18,746.6	6.7	10.1	14.1	5.6
July	1,138.6	5,227.1	7,655.0	......	7.8	9.8	12.4	......
Aug	1,147.3	5,264.4	7,667.0	......	8.8	9.6	10.8	......
Sept	1,200.0	5,374.4	7,819.8	19,065.8	16.7	11.9	13.5	6.8
Oct	1,161.0	5,367.9	7,866.9	......	9.2	9.9	11.7	......
Nov	1,163.8	5,414.4	7,956.5	......	8.5	10.7	11.5	......
Dec	1,179.3	5,458.6	8,027.0	19,369.2	9.5	10.5	10.9	6.4
2002: Jan	1,182.9	5,468.2	8,018.8	......	7.8	9.2	9.5	......
Feb	1,184.8	5,498.8	8,057.0	......	6.5	8.9	10.2	......
Mar	1,187.8	5,493.0	8,051.8	19,601.0	-2.0	4.4	5.9	4.8
Apr	1,176.7	5,476.5	8,038.7	......	2.7	4.0	4.4	......
May	1,183.4	5,542.4	8,118.5	......	3.4	4.7	4.1	......
June	1,190.2	5,576.3	8,159.2	20,004.5	1.8	4.3	3.3	8.2
July	1,197.4	5,635.5	8,217.3	......	2.5	6.1	5.0	......
Aug	1,183.2	5,680.3	8,291.3	......	-0.3	6.6	5.8	......
Sept	1,191.2	5,705.5	8,326.7	20,336.8	0.6	7.7	6.8	6.6
Oct	1,199.8	5,754.6	8,348.7	......	3.9	10.2	7.7	......
Nov	1,201.0	5,802.4	8,485.9	......	3.0	9.4	9.1	......
Dec [p]	1,219.1	5,815.6	8,541.2	......	4.9	8.6	9.4	......

SOURCE: Board of Governors of the Federal Reserve System.

[1] Consists of outstanding credit market debt of the U.S. Government, State and local governments, and private nonfinancial sectors.

[2] Annual changes are from December to December; monthly changes are from 6 months earlier at a simple annual rate.

[3] Annual changes are from fourth quarter to fourth quarter. Quarterly changes are from previous quarter at annual rate.

| EXHIBIT B.73 | BOND YIELDS AND INTEREST RATES, 1929-2002 |

[Percent per annum]

Year and month	U.S. Treasury securities					Corporate bonds (Moody's)		High-grade municipal bonds (Standard & Poor's)	New home mortgage yields[4]	Commercial paper, 6 months[5]	Prime rate charged by banks[6]	Discount rate, Federal Reserve Bank of New York[6]	Federal funds rate[7]
	Bills (new issues)[1]		Constant maturities[2]			Aaa[3]	Baa						
	3-month	6-month	3-year	10-year	30-year								
1929	......	......	......	......	......	4.73	5.90	4.27	......	5.85	5.50-6.00	5.16	......
1933	0.515	......	......	......	......	4.49	7.76	4.71	......	1.73	1.50-4.00	2.56	......
1939	0.023	......	......	......	......	3.01	4.96	2.76	......	0.59	1.50	1.00	......
1940	0.014	......	......	......	......	2.84	4.75	2.50	......	0.56	1.50	1.00	......
1941	0.103	......	......	......	......	2.77	4.33	2.10	......	0.53	1.50	1.00	......
1942	0.326	......	......	......	......	2.83	4.28	2.36	......	0.66	1.50	1.00[8]	......
1943	0.373	......	......	......	......	2.73	3.91	2.06	......	0.69	1.50	1.00[8]	......
1944	0.375	......	......	......	......	2.72	3.61	1.86	......	0.73	1.50	1.00[8]	......
1945	0.375	......	......	......	......	2.62	3.29	1.67	......	0.75	1.50	1.00[8]	......
1946	0.375	......	......	......	......	2.53	3.05	1.64	......	0.81	1.50	1.00[8]	......
1947	0.594	......	......	......	......	2.61	3.24	2.01	......	1.03	1.50-1.75	1.00	......
1948	1.040	......	......	......	......	2.82	3.47	2.40	......	1.44	1.75-2.00	1.34	......
1949	1.102	......	......	......	......	2.66	3.42	2.21	......	1.49	2.00	1.50	......
1950	1.218	......	......	......	......	2.62	3.24	1.98	......	1.45	2.07	1.59	......
1951	1.552	......	......	......	......	2.86	3.41	2.00	......	2.16	2.56	1.75	......
1952	1.766	......	......	......	......	2.96	3.52	2.19	......	2.33	3.00	1.75	......
1953	1.931	......	2.47	2.85	......	3.20	3.74	2.72	......	2.52	3.17	1.99	......
1954	0.953	......	1.63	2.40	......	2.90	3.51	2.37	......	1.58	3.05	1.60	......
1955	1.753	......	2.47	2.82	......	3.06	3.53	2.53	......	2.18	3.16	1.89	1.78
1956	2.658	......	3.19	3.18	......	3.36	3.88	2.93	......	3.31	3.77	2.77	2.73
1957	3.267	......	3.98	3.65	......	3.89	4.71	3.60	......	3.81	4.20	3.12	3.11
1958	1.839	......	2.84	3.32	......	3.79	4.73	3.56	......	2.46	3.83	2.15	1.57
1959	3.405	3.832	4.46	4.33	......	4.38	5.05	3.95	......	3.97	4.48	3.36	3.30
1960	2.928	3.247	3.98	4.12	......	4.41	5.19	3.73	......	3.85	4.82	3.53	3.22
1961	2.378	2.605	3.54	3.88	......	4.35	5.08	3.46	......	2.97	4.50	3.00	1.96
1962	2.778	2.908	3.47	3.95	......	4.33	5.02	3.18	......	3.26	4.50	3.00	2.68
1963	3.157	3.253	3.67	4.00	......	4.26	4.86	3.23	5.89	3.55	4.50	3.23	3.18
1964	3.549	3.686	4.03	4.19	......	4.40	4.83	3.22	5.83	3.97	4.50	3.55	3.50
1965	3.954	4.055	4.22	4.28	......	4.49	4.87	3.27	5.81	4.38	4.54	4.04	4.07
1966	4.881	5.082	5.23	4.92	......	5.13	5.67	3.82	6.25	5.55	5.63	4.50	5.11
1967	4.321	4.630	5.03	5.07	......	5.51	6.23	3.98	6.46	5.10	5.61	4.19	4.22
1968	5.339	5.470	5.68	5.65	......	6.18	6.94	4.51	6.97	5.90	6.30	5.16	5.66
1969	6.677	6.853	7.02	6.67	......	7.03	7.81	5.81	7.81	7.83	7.96	5.87	8.20
1970	6.458	6.562	7.29	7.35	......	8.04	9.11	6.51	8.45	7.71	7.91	5.95	7.18
1971	4.348	4.511	5.65	6.16	......	7.39	8.56	5.70	7.74	5.11	5.72	4.88	4.66
1972	4.071	4.466	5.72	6.21	......	7.21	8.16	5.27	7.60	4.73	5.25	4.50	4.43
1973	7.041	7.178	6.95	6.84	......	7.44	8.24	5.18	7.96	8.15	8.03	6.44	8.73
1974	7.886	7.926	7.82	7.56	......	8.57	9.50	6.09	8.92	9.84	10.81	7.83	10.50
1975	5.838	6.122	7.49	7.99	......	8.83	10.61	6.89	9.00	6.32	7.86	6.25	5.82

EXHIBIT B.73   **CONTINUED**

Year and month	U.S. Treasury securities					Corporate bonds (Moody's)		High-grade muni-cipal bonds (Stan-dard & Poor's)	New home mort-gage yields[4]	Com-mercial paper, 6 months[5]	Prime rate charged by banks[6]	Discount rate, Federal Reserve Bank of New York[6]	Federal funds rate[7]
	Bills (new issues)[1]		Constant maturities[2]										
	3-month	6-month	3-year	10-year	30-year	Aaa[3]	Baa						
1976	4.989	5.266	6.77	7.61	......	8.43	9.75	6.49	9.00	5.34	6.84	5.50	5.04
1977	5.265	5.510	6.69	7.42	7.75	8.02	8.97	5.56	9.02	5.61	6.83	5.46	5.54
1978	7.221	7.572	8.29	8.41	8.49	8.73	9.49	5.90	9.56	7.99	9.06	7.46	7.93
1979	10.041	10.017	9.71	9.44	9.28	9.63	10.69	6.39	10.78	10.91	12.67	10.28	11.19
1980	11.506	11.374	11.55	11.46	11.27	11.94	13.67	8.51	12.66	12.29	15.27	11.77	13.36
1981	14.029	13.776	14.44	13.91	13.45	14.17	16.04	11.23	14.70	14.76	18.87	13.42	16.38
1982	10.686	11.084	12.92	13.00	12.76	13.79	16.11	11.57	15.14	11.89	14.86	11.02	12.26
1983	8.63	8.75	10.45	11.10	11.18	12.04	13.55	9.47	12.57	8.89	10.79	8.50	9.09
1984	9.58	9.80	11.89	12.44	12.41	12.71	14.19	10.15	12.38	10.16	12.04	8.80	10.23
1985	7.48	7.66	9.64	10.62	10.79	11.37	12.72	9.18	11.55	8.01	9.93	7.69	8.10
1986	5.98	6.03	7.06	7.68	7.78	9.02	10.39	7.38	10.17	6.39	8.33	6.33	6.81
1987	5.82	6.05	7.68	8.39	8.59	9.38	10.58	7.73	9.31	6.85	8.21	5.66	6.66
1988	6.69	6.92	8.26	8.85	8.96	9.71	10.83	7.76	9.19	7.68	9.32	6.20	7.57
1989	8.12	8.04	8.55	8.49	8.45	9.26	10.18	7.24	10.13	8.80	10.87	6.93	9.21
1990	7.51	7.47	8.26	8.55	8.61	9.32	10.36	7.25	10.05	7.95	10.01	6.98	8.10
1991	5.42	5.49	6.82	7.86	8.14	8.77	9.80	6.89	9.32	5.85	8.46	5.45	5.69
1992	3.45	3.57	5.30	7.01	7.67	8.14	8.98	6.41	8.24	3.80	6.25	3.25	3.52
1993	3.02	3.14	4.44	5.87	6.59	7.22	7.93	5.63	7.20	3.30	6.00	3.00	3.02
1994	4.29	4.66	6.27	7.09	7.37	7.96	8.62	6.19	7.49	4.93	7.15	3.60	4.21
1995	5.51	5.59	6.25	6.57	6.88	7.59	8.20	5.95	7.87	5.93	8.83	5.21	5.83
1996	5.02	5.09	5.99	6.44	6.71	7.37	8.05	5.75	7.80	5.42	8.27	5.02	5.30
1997	5.07	5.18	6.10	6.35	6.61	7.26	7.86	5.55	7.71	5.62	8.44	5.00	5.46
1998	4.81	4.85	5.14	5.26	5.58	6.53	7.22	5.12	7.07	......	8.35	4.92	5.35
1999	4.66	4.76	5.49	5.65	5.87	7.04	7.87	5.43	7.04	......	8.00	4.62	4.97
2000	5.85	5.92	6.22	6.03	5.94	7.62	8.36	5.77	7.52	......	9.23	5.73	6.24
2001	3.45	3.39	4.09	5.02	5.49	7.08	7.95	5.19	7.00	......	6.91	3.40	3.88
2002	1.62	1.69	3.10	4.61	......	6.49	7.80	5.05	6.43	......	4.67	1.17	1.67

SOURCES: Department of the Treasury, Board of Governors of the Federal Reserve System, Federal Housing Finance Board, Moody's Investors Service, and Standard & Poor's.

[1] Rate on new issues within period; bank-discount basis.

[2] Yields on the more actively traded issues adjusted to constant maturities by the Department of the Treasury. In February 2002, the Department of the Treasury discontinued publication of the 30-year series.

[3] Beginning December 7, 2001, data for corporate Aaa series are industrial bonds only.

[4] Effective rate (in the primary market) on conventional mortgages, reflecting fees and charges as well as contract rate and assuming, on the average, repayment at end of 10 years. Rates beginning January 1973 not strictly comparable with prior rates.

[5] Bank-discount basis; prior to November 1979, data are for 4–6 months paper. Series no longer published.

[6] For monthly data, high and low for the period. Prime rate for 1929–33 and 1947–48 are ranges of the rate in effect during the period.

[7] Since July 19, 1975, the daily effective rate is an average of the rates on a given day weighted by the volume of transactions at these rates. Prior to that date, the daily effective rate was the rate considered most representative of the day's transactions, usually the one at which most transactions occurred.

[8] From October 30, 1942, to April 24, 1946, a preferential rate of 0.50 percent was in effect for advances secured by Government securities maturing in 1 year or less.

Government Finance

FEDERAL RECEIPTS, OUTLAYS, SURPLUS OR DEFICIT, AND DEBT, SELECTED FISCAL YEARS, 1939–2004

[Billions of dollars; fiscal years]

Fiscal year or period	Total			On-budget			Off-budget			Federal debt (end of period)		Addendum: Gross domestic product
	Receipts	Outlays	Surplus or deficit(-)	Receipts	Outlays	Surplus or deficit(-)	Receipts	Outlays	Surplus or deficit(-)	Gross Federal	Held by the public	
1939	6.3	9.1	-2.8	5.8	9.2	-3.4	0.5	0.0	0.5	48.2	41.4	89.0
1940	6.5	9.5	-2.9	6.0	9.5	-3.5	0.6	0.0	0.6	50.7	42.8	96.7
1941	8.7	13.7	-4.9	8.0	13.6	-5.6	0.7	0.0	0.7	57.5	48.2	114.0
1942	14.6	35.1	-20.5	13.7	35.1	-21.3	0.9	0.1	0.8	79.2	67.8	144.2
1943	24.0	78.6	-54.6	22.9	78.5	-55.6	1.1	0.1	1.0	142.6	127.8	180.1
1944	43.7	91.3	-47.6	42.5	91.2	-48.7	1.3	0.1	1.2	204.1	184.8	209.0
1945	45.2	92.7	-47.6	43.8	92.6	-48.7	1.3	0.1	1.2	260.1	235.2	221.3
1946	39.3	55.2	-15.9	38.1	55.0	-17.0	1.2	0.2	1.0	271.0	241.9	222.7
1947	38.5	34.5	4.0	37.1	34.2	2.9	1.5	0.3	1.2	257.1	224.3	234.6
1948	41.6	29.8	11.8	39.9	29.4	10.5	1.6	0.4	1.2	252.0	216.3	256.4
1949	39.4	38.8	0.6	37.7	38.4	-0.7	1.7	0.4	1.3	252.6	214.3	271.5
1950	39.4	42.6	-3.1	37.3	42.0	-4.7	2.1	0.5	1.6	256.9	219.0	273.4
1951	51.6	45.5	6.1	48.5	44.2	4.3	3.1	1.3	1.8	255.3	214.3	321.0
1952	66.2	67.7	-1.5	62.6	66.0	-3.4	3.6	1.7	1.9	259.1	214.8	348.8
1953	69.6	76.1	-6.5	65.5	73.8	-8.3	4.1	2.3	1.8	266.0	218.4	373.4
1954	69.7	70.9	-1.2	65.1	67.9	-2.8	4.6	2.9	1.7	270.8	224.5	378.0
1955	65.5	68.4	-3.0	60.4	64.5	-4.1	5.1	4.0	1.1	274.4	226.6	395.2
1956	74.6	70.6	3.9	68.2	65.7	2.5	6.4	5.0	1.5	272.7	222.2	427.7
1957	80.0	76.6	3.4	73.2	70.6	2.6	6.8	6.0	0.8	272.3	219.3	450.7
1958	79.6	82.4	-2.8	71.6	74.9	-3.3	8.0	7.5	0.5	279.7	226.3	461.1
1959	79.2	92.1	-12.8	71.0	83.1	-12.1	8.3	9.0	-0.7	287.5	234.7	492.1
1960	92.5	92.2	0.3	81.9	81.3	0.5	10.6	10.9	-0.2	290.5	236.8	518.9
1961	94.4	97.7	-3.3	82.3	86.0	-3.8	12.1	11.7	0.4	292.6	238.4	531.8
1962	99.7	106.8	-7.1	87.4	93.3	-5.9	12.3	13.5	-1.3	302.9	248.0	568.5
1963	106.6	111.3	-4.8	92.4	96.4	-4.0	14.2	15.0	-0.8	310.3	254.0	599.7
1964	112.6	118.5	-5.9	96.2	102.8	-6.5	16.4	15.7	0.6	316.1	256.8	641.3
1965	116.8	118.2	-1.4	100.1	101.7	-1.6	16.7	16.5	0.2	322.3	260.8	687.9
1966	130.8	134.5	-3.7	111.7	114.8	-3.1	19.1	19.7	-0.6	328.5	263.7	754.2
1967	148.8	157.5	-8.6	124.4	137.0	-12.6	24.4	20.4	4.0	340.4	266.6	813.5
1968	153.0	178.1	-25.2	128.1	155.8	-27.7	24.9	22.3	2.6	368.7	289.5	868.4
1969	186.9	183.6	3.2	157.9	158.4	-0.5	29.0	25.2	3.7	365.8	278.1	949.2
1970	192.8	195.6	-2.8	159.3	168.0	-8.7	33.5	27.6	5.9	380.9	283.2	1,013.2
1971	187.1	210.2	-23.0	151.3	177.3	-26.1	35.8	32.8	3.0	408.2	303.0	1,081.4
1972	207.3	230.7	-23.4	167.4	193.8	-26.4	39.9	36.9	3.1	435.9	322.4	1,181.5
1973	230.8	245.7	-14.9	184.7	200.1	-15.4	46.1	45.6	0.5	466.3	340.9	1,308.1
1974	263.2	269.4	-6.1	209.3	217.3	-8.0	53.9	52.1	1.8	483.9	343.7	1,442.1
1975	279.1	332.3	-53.2	216.6	271.9	-55.3	62.5	60.4	2.0	541.9	394.7	1,559.8

EXHIBIT B.78   CONTINUED

Fiscal year or period	Total			On-budget			Off-budget			Federal debt (end of period)		Addendum: Gross domestic product
	Receipts	Outlays	Surplus or deficit(-)	Receipts	Outlays	Surplus or deficit(-)	Receipts	Outlays	Surplus or deficit(-)	Gross Federal	Held by the public	
1976	298.1	371.8	-73.7	231.7	302.2	-70.5	66.4	69.6	-3.2	629.0	477.4	1,736.7
Transition quarter	81.2	96.0	-14.7	63.2	76.6	-13.3	18.0	19.4	-1.4	643.6	495.5	454.8
1977	355.6	409.2	-53.7	278.7	328.5	-49.8	76.8	80.7	-3.9	706.4	549.1	1,971.3
1978	399.6	458.7	-59.2	314.2	369.1	-54.9	85.4	89.7	-4.3	776.6	607.1	2,218.6
1979	463.3	504.0	-40.7	365.3	404.1	-38.7	98.0	100.0	-2.0	829.5	640.3	2,503.8
1980	517.1	590.9	-73.8	403.9	476.6	-72.7	113.2	114.3	-1.1	909.0	711.9	2,732.1
1981	599.3	678.2	-79.0	469.1	543.0	-73.9	130.2	135.2	-5.0	994.8	789.4	3,061.6
1982	617.8	745.7	-128.0	474.3	594.3	-120.0	143.5	151.4	-7.9	1,137.3	924.6	3,228.6
1983	600.6	808.4	-207.8	453.2	661.3	-208.0	147.3	147.1	0.2	1,371.7	1,137.3	3,440.5
1984	666.5	851.9	-185.4	500.4	686.0	-185.6	166.1	165.8	0.3	1,564.6	1,307.0	3,839.4
1985	734.1	946.4	-212.3	547.9	769.6	-221.7	186.2	176.8	9.4	1,817.4	1,507.3	4,136.6
1986	769.2	990.4	-221.2	569.0	806.9	-237.9	200.2	183.5	16.7	2,120.5	1,740.6	4,401.4
1987	854.4	1,004.1	-149.7	641.0	810.2	-169.3	213.4	193.8	19.6	2,346.0	1,889.8	4,647.0
1988	909.3	1,064.5	-155.2	667.8	861.8	-194.0	241.5	202.7	38.8	2,601.1	2,051.6	5,014.7
1989	991.2	1,143.6	-152.5	727.5	932.7	-205.2	263.7	210.9	52.8	2,867.8	2,190.7	5,405.5
1990	1,032.0	1,253.2	-221.2	750.3	1,028.1	-277.8	281.7	225.1	56.6	3,206.3	2,411.6	5,735.6
1991	1,055.0	1,324.4	-269.3	761.2	1,082.7	-321.5	293.9	241.7	52.2	3,598.2	2,689.0	5,930.4
1992	1,091.3	1,381.7	-290.4	788.9	1,129.3	-340.5	302.4	252.3	50.1	4,001.8	2,999.7	6,218.6
1993	1,154.4	1,409.5	-255.1	842.5	1,142.9	-300.4	311.9	266.6	45.3	4,351.0	3,248.4	6,558.4
1994	1,258.6	1,461.9	-203.3	923.6	1,182.5	-258.9	335.0	279.4	55.7	4,643.3	3,433.1	6,944.6
1995	1,351.8	1,515.8	-164.0	1,000.8	1,227.1	-226.4	351.1	288.7	62.4	4,920.6	3,604.4	7,324.0
1996	1,453.1	1,560.5	-107.5	1,085.6	1,259.6	-174.1	367.5	300.9	66.6	5,181.5	3,734.1	7,694.6
1997	1,579.3	1,601.3	-22.0	1,187.3	1,290.6	-103.3	392.0	310.6	81.4	5,369.2	3,772.3	8,185.2
1998	1,721.8	1,652.6	69.2	1,306.0	1,336.0	-30.0	415.8	316.6	99.2	5,478.2	3,721.1	8,663.9
1999	1,827.5	1,701.9	125.6	1,383.0	1,381.1	1.9	444.5	320.8	123.7	5,605.5	3,632.4	9,137.7
2000	2,025.2	1,788.8	236.4	1,544.6	1,458.0	86.6	480.6	330.8	149.8	5,628.7	3,409.8	9,718.8
2001	1,991.2	1,863.9	127.3	1,483.7	1,517.1	-33.4	507.5	346.8	160.7	5,769.9	3,319.6	10,021.5
2002	1,853.2	2,011.0	-157.8	1,337.9	1,655.3	-317.5	515.3	355.7	159.7	6,198.4	3,540.4	10,336.6
2003 [1]	1,836.2	2,140.4	-304.2	1,304.7	1,772.3	-467.6	531.6	368.1	163.5	6,752.0	3,878.4	10,756.8
2004 [1]	1,922.0	2,229.4	-307.4	1,365.9	1,847.9	-482.1	556.2	381.5	174.7	7,320.8	4,166.1	11,303.1

SOURCES: Department of Commerce (Bureau of Economic Analysis), Department of the Treasury, and Office of Management and Budget.

[1] Estimates.

Note.—Through fiscal year 1976, the fiscal year was on a July 1-June 30 basis; beginning October 1976 (fiscal year 1977), the fiscal year is on an October 1-September 30 basis. The transition quarter is the 3-month period from July 1, 1976 through September 30, 1976.

Refunds of receipts are excluded from receipts and outlays.

See Budget of the United States Government, Fiscal Year 2004, for additional information.

EXHIBIT B.81	FEDERAL RECEIPTS, OUTLAYS, SURPLUS OR DEFICIT, AND DEBT, FISCAL YEARS 1999–2004

[Millions of dollars; fiscal years]

Description	Actual				Estimates	
	1999	2000	2001	2002	2003	2004
Receipts and Outlays						
Total receipts	1,827,454	2,025,218	1,991,194	1,853,173	1,836,218	1,922,025
Total outlays	1,701,891	1,788,773	1,863,895	2,010,975	2,140,377	2,229,425
Total surplus or deficit (-)	125,563	236,445	127,299	-157,802	-304,159	-307,400
On-budget receipts	1,382,986	1,544,634	1,483,675	1,337,852	1,304,653	1,365,857
On-budget outlays	1,381,113	1,458,008	1,517,057	1,655,313	1,772,280	1,847,924
On-budget surplus or deficit (-)	1,873	86,626	-33,382	-317,461	-467,627	-482,067
Off-budget receipts	444,468	480,584	507,519	515,321	531,565	556,168
Off-budget outlays	320,778	330,765	346,838	355,662	368,097	381,501
Off-budget surplus or deficit (-)	123,690	149,819	160,681	159,659	163,468	174,667
Outstanding Debt, End of Period						
Gross Federal debt	5,605,523	5,628,700	5,769,881	6,198,401	6,752,033	7,320,769
Held by Federal Government accounts	1,973,160	2,218,896	2,450,266	2,657,974	2,873,595	3,154,708
Held by the public	3,632,363	3,409,804	3,319,615	3,540,427	3,878,438	4,166,061
Federal Reserve System	496,644	511,413	534,135	604,191	......	......
Other	3,135,719	2,898,391	2,785,480	2,936,235	......	......
Receipts: On-Budget and Off-Budget	1,827,454	2,025,218	1,991,194	1,853,173	1,836,218	1,922,025
Individual income taxes	879,480	1,004,462	994,339	858,345	849,053	849,880
Corporation income taxes	184,680	207,289	151,075	148,044	143,186	169,060
Social insurance and retirement receipts	611,833	652,852	693,967	700,760	726,593	764,548
On-budget	167,365	172,268	186,448	185,439	195,028	208,380
Off-budget	444,468	480,584	507,519	515,321	531,565	556,168
Excise taxes	70,414	68,865	66,232	66,989	68,416	70,905
Estate and gift taxes	27,782	29,010	28,400	26,507	20,209	23,379
Customs duties and fees	18,336	19,914	19,369	18,602	19,052	20,713
Miscellaneous receipts	34,929	42,826	37,812	33,926	34,709	38,540
Deposits of earnings by Federal Reserve System	25,917	32,293	26,124	23,683	23,565	27,078
All other [1]	9,012	10,533	11,688	10,243	11,144	11,462
Adjustment for revenue uncertainty	......	......	......	......	-25,000	-15,000
Outlays: On-Budget and Off-Budget	1,701,891	1,788,773	1,863,895	2,010,975	2,140,377	2,229,425
National defense	274,873	294,495	305,500	348,555	376,286	390,419
International affairs	15,243	17,216	16,493	22,357	20,735	25,622
General science, space and technology	18,125	18,637	19,789	20,772	21,699	22,851
Energy	912	-1,060	39	483	708	918

EXHIBIT B.81   CONTINUED

Description	Actual				Estimates	
	1999	2000	2001	2002	2003	2004
Natural resources and environment	23,968	25,031	25,623	29,454	30,578	31,586
Agriculture	23,011	36,641	26,397	22,188	20,847	20,799
Commerce and housing credit	2,647	3,211	5,883	-385	1,262	-701
On-budget	1,626	1,182	3,581	266	5,500	2,344
Off-budget	1,021	2,029	2,302	-651	-4,238	-3,045
Transportation	42,533	46,854	54,449	61,862	64,228	63,449
Community and regional development	11,870	10,629	11,907	12,991	18,459	17,060
Education, training, employment, and social services	50,591	53,754	57,143	70,544	86,252	85,336
Health	141,074	154,533	172,270	196,545	223,068	246,579
Medicare	190,447	197,113	217,384	230,855	244,667	258,878
Income security	242,356	253,575	269,615	312,511	330,120	324,962
Social security	390,037	409,423	432,958	456,413	478,471	497,299
On-budget	10,824	13,254	11,701	13,988	13,067	14,032
Off-budget	379,213	396,169	421,257	442,425	465,404	483,267
Veterans benefits and services	43,212	47,083	45,039	50,984	57,070	62,022
Administration of justice	26,082	27,995	29,660	34,316	36,142	39,413
General government	15,599	13,273	14,589	17,385	18,998	20,503
Net interest	229,756	222,951	206,168	170,951	161,441	176,395
On-budget	281,827	282,747	274,979	247,771	245,017	265,093
Off-budget	-52,071	-59,796	-68,811	-76,820	-83,576	-88,698
Allowances	......	......	......	......	-368	-297
Undistributed offsetting receipts	-40,445	-42,581	-47,011	-47,806	-50,286	-53,668
On-budget	-33,060	-34,944	-39,101	-38,514	-40,793	-43,645
Off-budget	-7,385	-7,637	-7,910	-9,292	-9,493	-10,023

SOURCES: Department of the Treasury and Office of Management and Budget.

[1] Beginning 1984, includes universal service fund receipts.

Note.—See Note, Table B-78.

International Statistics

EXHIBIT B.103	U.S. INTERNATIONAL TRANSACTIONS, 1946-2002

[Millions of dollars; quarterly data seasonally adjusted. Credits (+), debits (-)]

Year or Quarter	Goods			Services				Income Receipts and Payments			Unilateral Current Transfers, Net [2]	Balance on Current Account
	Exports	Imports	Balance on Goods	Net Military Tran-sactions[2]	Net Travel and Trans-porta-tion	Other Services, Net	Balance on Goods and Services	Receipts	Payments	Balance on Income		
1946	11,764	-5,067	6,697	-424	733	310	7,316	772	-212	560	-2,991	4,885
1947	16,097	-5,973	10,124	-358	946	145	10,857	1,102	-245	857	-2,722	8,992
1948	13,265	-7,557	5,708	-351	374	175	5,906	1,921	-437	1,484	-4,973	2,417
1949	12,213	-6,874	5,339	-410	230	208	5,367	1,831	-476	1,355	-5,849	873
1950	10,203	-9,081	1,122	-56	-120	242	1,188	2,068	-559	1,509	-4,537	-1,840
1951	14,243	-11,176	3,067	169	298	254	3,788	2,633	-583	2,050	-4,954	884
1952	13,449	-10,838	2,611	528	83	309	3,531	2,751	-555	2,196	-5,113	614
1953	12,412	-10,975	1,437	1,753	-238	307	3,259	2,736	-624	2,112	-6,657	-1,286
1954	12,929	-10,353	2,576	902	-269	305	3,514	2,929	-582	2,347	-5,642	219
1955	14,424	-11,527	2,897	-113	-297	299	2,786	3,406	-676	2,730	-5,086	430
1956	17,556	-12,803	4,753	-221	-361	447	4,618	3,837	-735	3,102	-4,990	2,730
1957	19,562	-13,291	6,271	-423	-189	482	6,141	4,180	-796	3,384	-4,763	4,762
1958	16,414	-12,952	3,462	-849	-633	486	2,466	3,790	-825	2,965	-4,647	784
1959	16,458	-15,310	1,148	-831	-821	573	69	4,132	-1,061	3,071	-4,422	-1,282
1960	19,650	-14,758	4,892	-1,057	-964	639	3,508	4,616	-1,238	3,379	-4,062	2,824
1961	20,108	-14,537	5,571	-1,131	-978	732	4,195	4,999	-1,245	3,755	-4,127	3,822
1962	20,781	-16,260	4,521	-912	-1,152	912	3,370	5,618	-1,324	4,294	-4,277	3,387
1963	22,272	-17,048	5,224	-742	-1,309	1,036	4,210	6,157	-1,560	4,596	-4,392	4,414
1964	25,501	-18,700	6,801	-794	-1,146	1,161	6,022	6,824	-1,783	5,041	-4,240	6,823
1965	26,461	-21,510	4,951	-487	-1,280	1,480	4,664	7,437	-2,088	5,350	-4,583	5,431
1966	29,310	-25,493	3,817	-1,043	-1,331	1,497	2,940	7,528	-2,481	5,047	-4,955	3,031
1967	30,666	-26,866	3,800	-1,187	-1,750	1,742	2,604	8,021	-2,747	5,274	-5,294	2,583
1968	33,626	-32,991	635	-596	-1,548	1,759	250	9,367	-3,378	5,990	-5,629	611
1969	36,414	-35,807	607	-718	-1,763	1,964	91	10,913	-4,869	6,044	-5,735	399
1970	42,469	-39,866	2,603	-641	-2,038	2,330	2,254	11,748	-5,515	6,233	-6,156	2,331
1971	43,319	-45,579	-2,260	653	-2,345	2,649	-1,303	12,707	-5,435	7,272	-7,402	-1,433
1972	49,381	-55,797	-6,416	1,072	-3,063	2,965	-5,443	14,765	-6,572	8,192	-8,544	-5,795
1973	71,410	-70,499	911	740	-3,158	3,406	1,900	21,808	-9,655	12,153	-6,913	7,140
1974	98,306	-103,811	-5,505	165	-3,184	4,231	-4,292	27,587	-12,084	15,503	-9,249	1,962
1975	107,088	-98,185	8,903	1,461	-2,812	4,854	12,404	25,351	-12,564	12,787	-7,075	18,116
1976	114,745	-124,228	-9,483	931	-2,558	5,027	-6,082	29,375	-13,311	16,063	-5,686	4,295
1977	120,816	-151,907	-31,091	1,731	-3,565	5,680	-27,246	32,354	-14,217	18,137	-5,226	-14,335
1978	142,075	-176,002	-33,927	857	-3,573	6,879	-29,763	42,088	-21,680	20,408	-5,788	-15,143
1979	184,439	-212,007	-27,568	-1,313	-2,935	7,251	-24,565	63,834	-32,961	30,873	-6,593	-285

EXHIBIT B.103   CONTINUED

| Year or Quarter | Capital Account Transactions, Net | Financial Account | | | | | | | Statistical Discrepancy | |
| | | U.S.-Owned Assets Abroad, Net [Increase/Financial Outflow (-)] | | | | Foreign-Owned Assets in the U.S., Net [Increase/Financial Inflow (+)] | | | | |
		Total	U.S. Official Reserve Assets[3]	Other U.S. Govern- ment Assets	U.S. Private Assets	Total	Foreign Official Assets	Other Foreign Assets	Total (Sum of the Items with Sign Reversed)	Of Which: Seasonal Adjust- ment Discre- pancy
1946	......	......	-623	......	......	......	......	......	......	......
1947	......	......	-3,315	......	......	......	......	......	......	......
1948	......	......	-1,736	......	......	......	......	......	......	......
1949	......	......	-266	......	......	......	......	......	......	......
1950	......	......	1,758	......	......	......	......	......	......	......
1951	......	......	-33	......	......	......	......	......	......	......
1952	......	......	-415	......	......	......	......	......	......	......
1953	......	......	1,256	......	......	......	......	......	......	......
1954	......	......	480	......	......	......	......	......	......	......
1955	......	......	182	......	......	......	......	......	......	......
1956	......	......	-869	......	......	......	......	......	......	......
1957	......	......	-1,165	......	......	......	......	......	......	......
1958	......	......	2,292	......	......	......	......	......	......	......
1959	......	......	1,035	......	......	......	......	......	......	......
1960	......	-4,099	2,145	-1,100	-5,144	2,294	1,473	821	-1,019	......
1961	......	-5,538	607	-910	-5,235	2,705	765	1,939	-989	......
1962	......	-4,174	1,535	-1,085	-4,623	1,911	1,270	641	-1,124	......
1963	......	-7,270	378	-1,662	-5,986	3,217	1,986	1,231	-360	......
1964	......	-9,560	171	-1,680	-8,050	3,643	1,660	1,983	-907	......
1965	......	-5,716	1,225	-1,605	-5,336	742	134	607	-457	......
1966	......	-7,321	570	-1,543	-6,347	3,661	-672	4,333	629	......
1967	......	-9,757	53	-2,423	-7,386	7,379	3,451	3,928	-205	......
1968	......	-10,977	-870	-2,274	-7,833	9,928	-774	10,703	438	......
1969	......	-11,585	-1,179	-2,200	-8,206	12,702	-1,301	14,002	-1,516	......
1970	......	-8,470	3,348	-1,589	-10,229	6,359	6,908	-550	-219	......
1971	......	-11,758	3,066	-1,884	-12,940	22,970	26,879	-3,909	-9,779	......
1972	......	-13,787	706	-1,568	-12,925	21,461	10,475	10,986	-1,879	......
1973	......	-22,874	158	-2,644	-20,388	18,388	6,026	12,362	-2,654	......
1974	......	-34,745	-1,467	366	-33,643	35,341	10,546	24,796	-2,558	......
1975	......	-39,703	-849	-3,474	-35,380	17,170	7,027	10,143	4,417	......
1976	......	-51,269	-2,558	-4,214	-44,498	38,018	17,693	20,326	8,955	......
1977	......	-34,785	-375	-3,693	-30,717	53,219	36,816	16,403	-4,099	......
1978	......	-61,130	732	-4,660	-57,202	67,036	33,678	33,358	9,236	......
1979	......	-64,915	6	-3,746	-61,176	40,852	-13,665	54,516	24,349	......

EXHIBIT B.103   **CONTINUED**

Year or Quarter	Goods			Services			Balance on Goods and Services	Income Receipts and Payments			Unilateral Current Transfers, Net [2]	Balance on Current Account
	Exports	Imports	Balance on Goods	Net Military Tran-sactions[2]	Net Travel and Trans-porta-tion	Other Services, Net		Receipts	Payments	Balance on Income		
1980	224,250	-249,750	-25,500	-1,822	-997	8,912	-19,407	72,606	-42,532	30,073	-8,349	2,317
1981	237,044	-265,067	-28,023	-844	144	12,552	-16,172	86,529	-53,626	32,903	-11,702	5,030
1982	211,157	-247,642	-36,485	112	-992	13,209	-24,156	91,747	-56,583	35,164	-16,544	-5,536
1983	201,799	-268,901	-67,102	-563	-4,227	14,124	-57,767	90,000	-53,614	36,386	-17,310	-38,691
1984	219,926	-332,418	-112,492	-2,547	-8,438	14,404	-109,073	108,819	-73,756	35,063	-20,335	-94,344
1985	215,915	-338,088	-122,173	-4,390	-9,798	14,483	-121,880	98,542	-72,819	25,723	-21,998	-118,155
1986	223,344	-368,425	-145,081	-5,181	-8,779	20,502	-138,538	97,064	-81,571	15,494	-24,132	-147,177
1987	250,208	-409,765	-159,557	-3,844	-8,010	19,728	-151,684	108,184	-93,891	14,293	-23,265	-160,655
1988	320,230	-447,189	-126,959	-6,320	-3,013	21,725	-114,566	136,713	-118,026	18,687	-25,274	-121,153
1989	359,916	-477,665	-117,749	-6,749	3,551	27,805	-93,142	161,287	-141,463	19,824	-26,169	-99,486
1990	387,401	-498,435	-111,034	-7,599	7,501	30,270	-80,861	171,742	-143,192	28,550	-26,654	-78,965
1991	414,083	-491,020	-76,937	-5,274	16,561	34,516	-31,135	149,214	-125,084	24,130	10,752	3,747
1992	439,631	-536,528	-96,897	-1,448	19,969	41,918	-36,457	132,056	-109,101	22,954	-35,013	-48,515
1993	456,943	-589,394	-132,451	1,385	19,714	42,562	-68,791	134,159	-110,255	23,904	-37,637	-82,523
1994	502,859	-668,690	-165,831	2,570	16,305	50,278	-96,678	165,438	-148,744	16,694	-38,260	-118,244
1995	575,204	-749,374	-174,170	4,600	21,772	51,410	-96,388	211,502	-186,880	24,622	-34,057	-105,823
1996	612,113	-803,113	-191,000	5,385	25,015	58,757	-101,843	225,846	-201,743	24,103	-40,081	-117,821
1997	678,366	-876,485	-198,119	4,968	22,152	63,234	-107,765	260,558	-240,371	20,187	-40,794	-128,372
1998	670,416	-917,112	-246,696	5,220	10,145	64,398	-166,933	259,366	-251,751	7,615	-44,509	-203,827
1999	683,965	-1,029,987	-346,022	2,470	7,113	74,202	-262,237	290,536	-272,398	18,138	-48,757	-292,856
2000	771,994	-1,224,417	-452,423	421	2,472	70,849	-378,681	352,997	-331,215	21,782	-53,442	-410,341
2001	718,762	-1,145,927	-427,165	-2,978	-1,926	73,779	-358,290	283,771	-269,389	14,382	-49,463	-393,371
2000: I	184,486	-290,941	-106,455	-74	825	18,532	-87,172	84,083	-79,260	4,823	-11,749	-94,098
II	191,411	-303,581	-112,170	412	1,486	18,345	-91,927	90,183	-83,994	6,189	-12,349	-98,087
III	199,641	-314,779	-115,138	-199	-31	17,042	-98,326	88,129	-84,055	4,074	-12,925	-107,177
IV	196,456	-315,116	-118,660	282	189	16,931	-101,258	90,603	-83,909	6,694	-16,418	-110,982
2001: I	193,284	-306,316	-113,032	-742	903	15,711	-97,160	83,036	-81,990	1,046	-11,608	-107,722
II	184,846	-292,565	-107,719	-285	-1,219	15,899	-93,324	74,846	-68,840	6,006	-11,916	-99,234
III	173,274	-279,025	-105,751	-706	-255	26,934	-79,778	67,152	-66,345	807	-12,360	-91,331
IV	167,358	-268,021	-100,663	-1,245	-1,357	15,237	-88,028	58,737	-52,216	6,521	-13,579	-95,086
2002: I	164,649	-271,073	-106,424	-1,498	-544	12,974	-95,492	58,096	-59,042	-946	-16,016	-112,454
II	172,426	-294,893	-122,467	-1,679	-863	15,696	-109,313	60,722	-66,009	-5,287	-13,011	-127,611
III [p]	175,727	-298,903	-123,176	-2,083	-808	15,206	-110,861	63,472	-66,431	-2,959	-13,221	-127,041

EXHIBIT B.103   CONTINUED

Year or Quarter	Capital Account Transac-tions, Net	Financial Account							Statistical Discrepancy	
		U.S.-Owned Assets Abroad, Net [Increase/Financial Outflow (-)]				Foreign-Owned Assets in the U.S., Net [Increase/Financial Inflow (+)]				Of Which: Seasonal Adjust-ment Discre-pancy
		Total	U.S. Official Reserve Assets[3]	Other U.S. Govern-ment Assets	U.S. Private Assets	Total	Foreign Official Assets	Other Foreign Assets	Total (Sum of the Items with Sign Reversed)	
1980	......	-85,815	-7,003	-5,162	-73,651	62,612	15,497	47,115	20,886	......
1981	......	-113,054	-4,082	-5,097	-103,875	86,232	4,960	81,272	21,792	......
1982	199	-127,882	-4,965	-6,131	-116,786	96,589	3,593	92,997	36,630	......
1983	209	-66,373	-1,196	-5,006	-60,172	88,694	5,845	82,849	16,162	......
1984	235	-40,376	-3,131	-5,489	-31,757	117,752	3,140	114,612	16,733	......
1985	315	-44,752	-3,858	-2,821	-38,074	146,115	-1,119	147,233	16,478	......
1986	301	-111,723	312	-2,022	-110,014	230,009	35,648	194,360	28,590	......
1987	365	-79,296	9,149	1,006	-89,450	248,634	45,387	203,247	-9,048	......
1988	493	-106,573	-3,912	2,967	-105,628	246,522	39,758	206,764	-19,289	......
1989	336	-175,383	-25,293	1,233	-151,323	224,928	8,503	216,425	49,605	......
1990	-6,579	-81,234	-2,158	2,317	-81,393	141,571	33,910	107,661	25,208	......
1991	-4,479	-64,388	5,763	2,924	-73,075	110,808	17,389	93,420	-45,688	......
1992	612	-74,410	3,901	-1,667	-76,644	170,663	40,477	130,186	-48,350	......
1993	-88	-200,552	-1,379	-351	-198,822	282,040	71,753	210,287	1,123	......
1994	-469	-176,056	5,346	-390	-181,012	305,989	39,583	266,406	-11,220	......
1995	372	-352,376	-9,742	-984	-341,650	438,562	109,880	328,682	19,265	......
1996	693	-413,923	6,668	-989	-419,602	551,096	126,724	424,372	-20,045	......
1997	350	-487,599	-1,010	68	-486,657	706,809	19,036	687,773	-91,188	......
1998	704	-359,760	-6,783	-422	-352,555	423,569	-19,903	443,472	139,314	......
1999	-3,340	-477,569	8,747	2,750	-489,066	742,479	43,666	698,813	31,286	......
2000	837	-606,489	-290	-941	-605,258	1,015,986	37,640	978,346	7	......
2001	826	-370,962	-4,911	-486	-365,565	752,806	5,224	747,582	10,701	......
2000: I	210	-228,888	-554	-127	-228,207	240,723	22,711	218,012	82,053	7,951
II	206	-110,470	2,020	-570	-111,920	245,787	6,563	239,224	-37,436	-838
III	207	-93,029	-346	114	-92,797	244,933	12,904	232,029	-44,934	-10,675
IV	214	-174,104	-1,410	-358	-172,336	284,544	-4,538	289,082	328	3,566
2001: I	208	-215,815	190	77	-216,082	302,510	4,087	298,423	20,819	7,691
II	207	-80,036	-1,343	-783	-77,910	181,610	-20,831	202,441	-2,547	875
III	206	24,978	-3,559	77	28,460	17,889	16,882	1,007	48,258	-10,286
IV	205	-100,088	-199	143	-100,032	250,797	5,086	245,711	-55,828	1,721
2002: I	208	-25,918	390	133	-26,441	113,496	7,641	105,855	24,668	10,019
II	200	-131,079	-1,843	42	-129,278	204,307	47,252	157,055	54,183	1,256
III [p]	223	23,920	-1,416	172	25,164	148,510	9,319	139,191	-45,612	-14,063

SOURCE: Department of Commerce, Bureau of Economic Analysis.

[1] Adjusted from Census data for differences in valuation, coverage, and timing; excludes military.

[2] Includes transfers of goods and services under U.S. military grant programs.

[3] Consists of gold, special drawing rights, foreign currencies, and the U.S. reserve position in the International Monetary Fund (IMF).

EXHIBIT B.107	INTERNATIONAL INVESTMENT POSITION OF THE UNITED STATES AT YEAR-END, 1993-2001

[Billions of Dollars]

Type of investment	1993	1994	1995	1996	1997	1998	1999	2000	2001 ᵖ
Net International Investment Position of the United States									
With direct investment at current cost	-307.0	-311.9	-496.0	-521.5	-833.2	-918.3	-784.1	-1,350.8	-1,948.1
With direct investment at market value	-144.3	-123.7	-343.3	-386.5	-835.2	-1,094.2	-1,053.6	-1,583.2	-2,309.1
U.S.-Owned Assets Abroad									
With direct investment at current cost	2,753.6	2,998.6	3,452.0	4,012.7	4,567.9	5,091.1	5,959.0	6,191.9	6,196.1
With direct investment at market value	3,091.4	3,326.7	3,930.3	4,631.3	5,379.1	6,174.5	7,387.0	7,350.9	6,862.9
U.S. official reserve assets	164.9	163.4	176.1	160.7	134.8	146.0	136.4	128.4	130.0
Gold ¹	102.6	100.1	101.3	96.7	75.9	75.3	76.0	71.8	72.3
Special drawing rights	9.0	10.0	11.0	10.3	10.0	10.6	10.3	10.5	10.8
Reserve position in the International Monetary Fund	11.8	12.0	14.6	15.4	18.1	24.1	18.0	14.8	17.9
Foreign currencies	41.5	41.2	49.1	38.3	30.8	36.0	32.2	31.2	29.0
U.S. Government assets, other than official reserves	83.4	83.9	85.1	86.1	86.2	86.8	84.2	85.2	85.7
U.S. credits and other long-term assets	81.4	81.9	82.8	84.0	84.1	84.9	81.7	82.6	83.1
Repayable in dollars	80.7	81.4	82.4	83.6	83.8	84.5	81.4	82.3	82.9
Other	0.8	0.5	0.4	0.4	0.4	0.3	0.3	0.3	0.3
U.S. foreign currency holdings and U.S. short-term assets	1.9	2.0	2.3	2.1	2.1	1.9	2.6	2.6	2.5
U.S. private assets:									
With direct investment at current cost	2,505.3	2,751.3	3,190.9	3,765.9	4,346.9	4,858.3	5,738.4	5,978.4	5,980.5
With direct investment at market value	2,843.1	3,079.3	3,669.1	4,384.4	5,158.1	5,941.7	7,166.3	7,137.3	6,647.3
Direct investment abroad:									
At current cost	723.5	786.6	885.5	989.8	1,068.1	1,196.2	1,377.3	1,515.3	1,623.1
At market value	1,061.3	1,114.6	1,363.8	1,608.3	1,879.3	2,279.6	2,805.2	2,674.2	2,289.9
Foreign securities	853.5	948.7	1,169.6	1,468.0	1,751.2	2,052.9	2,583.3	2,389.4	2,110.5
Bonds	309.7	321.2	392.8	465.1	543.4	576.7	556.7	557.0	545.8
Corporate stocks	543.9	627.5	776.8	1,002.9	1,207.8	1,476.2	2,026.6	1,832.4	1,564.7
U.S. claims on unaffiliated foreigners reported by U.S. nonbanking concerns	242.0	323.0	367.6	450.6	545.5	588.3	677.5	821.6	830.1
U.S. claims reported by U.S. banks, not included elsewhere	686.2	693.1	768.1	857.5	982.1	1,020.8	1,100.3	1,252.1	1,416.8
Foreign-Owned Assets in the United States									
With direct investment at current cost	3,060.6	3,310.5	3,947.9	4,534.3	5,401.1	6,009.4	6,743.1	7,542.7	8,144.3
With direct investment at market value	3,235.7	3,450.4	4,273.6	5,017.8	6,214.3	7,268.6	8,440.5	8,934.0	9,172.1

EXHIBIT B.107   **CONTINUED**

Type of investment	1993	1994	1995	1996	1997	1998	1999	2000	2001 [P]
Foreign official assets in the United States	509.4	535.2	682.9	820.8	873.7	896.2	945.6	1,008.9	1,021.7
U.S. Government securities	381.7	407.2	507.5	631.1	648.2	669.8	693.8	749.9	798.8
U.S. Treasury securities	373.1	396.9	490.0	606.4	615.1	622.9	617.7	625.2	650.7
Other	8.6	10.3	17.5	24.7	33.1	46.8	76.1	124.7	148.1
Other U.S. Government liabilities	22.1	23.7	23.6	22.6	21.7	18.4	15.6	13.7	11.9
U.S. liabilities reported by U.S. banks, not included elsewhere	69.7	73.4	107.4	113.1	135.4	125.9	138.8	153.4	123.1
Other foreign official assets	35.9	31.0	44.4	54.0	68.4	82.1	97.3	91.8	87.9
Other foreign assets in the United States:									
With direct investment at current cost	2,551.2	2,775.3	3,265.1	3,713.5	4,527.3	5,113.2	5,797.5	6,533.8	7,122.5
With direct investment at market value	2,726.3	2,915.2	3,590.7	4,197.0	5,340.6	6,372.4	7,494.9	7,925.1	8,150.3
Direct investment in the United States:									
At current cost	593.3	618.0	680.1	745.6	824.1	919.8	1,100.8	1,374.8	1,498.9
At market value	768.4	757.9	1,005.7	1,229.1	1,637.4	2,179.0	2,798.2	2,766.0	2,526.7
U.S. Treasury securities	221.5	235.7	330.2	440.8	550.6	562.0	462.8	401.0	388.8
U.S. securities other than U.S. Treasury securities	696.4	739.7	969.8	1,165.1	1,512.7	1,903.4	2,351.3	2,623.6	2,856.7
Corporate and other bonds	355.8	368.1	459.1	539.3	618.8	724.6	825.2	1,076.0	1,392.6
Corporate stocks	340.6	371.6	510.8	625.8	893.9	1,178.8	1,526.1	1,547.6	1,464.0
U.S. currency	133.7	157.2	169.5	186.8	211.6	228.3	250.7	251.8	275.6
U.S. liabilities to unaffiliated foreigners reported by U.S. nonbanking concerns	229.0	239.8	300.4	346.8	459.4	485.7	564.9	729.3	804.4
U.S. liabilities reported by U.S. banks, not included elsewhere	677.1	784.9	815.0	828.2	968.8	1,014.0	1,067.2	1,153.4	1,298.2

SOURCE: Department of Commerce, Bureau of Economic Analysis.

[1] Valued at market price.

Note.—For details regarding these data, see *Survey of Current Business*, July 2002.

| EXHIBIT B.110 | FOREIGN EXCHANGE RATES, 1982-2002 |

[Foreign currency units per U.S. dollar, except as noted; certified noon buying rates in New York]

Period	Canada (dollar)	EMU Members (euro)[1][2]	Belgium (franc)[1]	France (franc)[1]	Germany (mark)[1]	Italy (lira)[1]	Nether-lands (guilder)[1]	Japan (yen)	Sweden (krona)	Switzer-land (franc)	United Kingdom (pound)[2]
Mar-73	0.9967	......	39.408	4.5156	2.8132	568.17	2.8714	261.90	4.4294	3.2171	2.4724
1982	1.2344	......	45.781	6.5794	2.4281	1,354.00	2.6719	249.06	6.2839	2.0319	1.7480
1983	1.2325	......	51.122	7.6204	2.5539	1,519.32	2.8544	237.55	7.6718	2.1007	1.5159
1984	1.2952	......	57.752	8.7356	2.8455	1,756.11	3.2085	237.46	8.2708	2.3500	1.3368
1985	1.3659	......	59.337	8.9800	2.9420	1,908.88	3.3185	238.47	8.6032	2.4552	1.2974
1986	1.3896	......	44.664	6.9257	2.1705	1,491.16	2.4485	168.35	7.1273	1.7979	1.4677
1987	1.3259	......	37.358	6.0122	1.7981	1,297.03	2.0264	144.60	6.3469	1.4918	1.6398
1988	1.2306	......	36.785	5.9595	1.7570	1,302.39	1.9778	128.17	6.1370	1.4643	1.7813
1989	1.1842	......	39.409	6.3802	1.8808	1,372.28	2.1219	138.07	6.4559	1.6369	1.6382
1990	1.1668	......	33.424	5.4467	1.6166	1,198.27	1.8215	145.00	5.9231	1.3901	1.7841
1991	1.1460	......	34.195	5.6468	1.6610	1,241.28	1.8720	134.59	6.0521	1.4356	1.7674
1992	1.2085	......	32.148	5.2935	1.5618	1,232.17	1.7587	126.78	5.8258	1.4064	1.7663
1993	1.2902	......	34.581	5.6669	1.6545	1,573.41	1.8585	111.08	7.7956	1.4781	1.5016
1994	1.3664	......	33.426	5.5459	1.6216	1,611.49	1.8190	102.18	7.7161	1.3667	1.5319
1995	1.3725	......	29.472	4.9864	1.4321	1,629.45	1.6044	93.96	7.1406	1.1812	1.5785
1996	1.3638	......	30.970	5.1158	1.5049	1,542.76	1.6863	108.78	6.7082	1.2361	1.5607
1997	1.3849	......	35.807	5.8393	1.7348	1,703.81	1.9525	121.06	7.6446	1.4514	1.6376
1998	1.4836	......	36.310	5.8995	1.7597	1,736.85	1.9837	130.99	7.9522	1.4506	1.6573
1999	1.4858	1.0653	......	......	......	......	......	113.73	8.2740	1.5045	1.6172
2000	1.4855	0.9232	......	......	......	......	......	107.80	9.1735	1.6904	1.5156
2001	1.5487	0.8952	......	......	......	......	......	121.57	10.3425	1.6891	1.4396
2002	1.5704	0.9454	......	......	......	......	......	125.22	9.7233	1.5567	1.5025
2001: I	1.5285	0.9220	......	......	......	......	......	118.25	9.7698	1.6636	1.4581
II	1.5411	0.8736	......	......	......	......	......	122.62	10.4477	1.7505	1.4212
III	1.5449	0.8908	......	......	......	......	......	121.63	10.5655	1.6930	1.4373
IV	1.5806	0.8951	......	......	......	......	......	123.74	10.5838	1.6473	1.4426
2002: I	1.5946	0.8770	......	......	......	......	......	132.42	10.4428	1.6802	1.4261
II	1.5552	0.9186	......	......	......	......	......	126.92	9.9831	1.5960	1.4615
III	1.5633	0.9842	......	......	......	......	......	119.27	9.3841	1.4872	1.5497
IV	1.5696	1.0003	......	......	......	......	......	122.52	9.0974	1.4664	1.5714

[1] European Economic and Monetary Union members include Austria, Belgium, Finland, France, Germany, Ireland, Italy, Luxembourg, Netherlands, Portugal, Spain, and beginning in 2001, Greece.

[2] U.S. dollars per foreign currency unit.

EXHIBIT B.110   **CONTINUED**

| | Trade-Weighted Value of the U.S. Dollar | | | | | | |
| | Nominal | | | | Real [7] | | |
Period	G–10 Index (March 1973=100) [3]	Broad Index (January 1997=100) [4]	Major Currencies Index (March 1973=100) [5]	OITP Index (January 1997=100) [6]	Broad Index (March 1973=100) [4]	Major Currencies Index (March 1973=100) [5]	OITP Index (March 1973=100) [6]
1982	116.6	44.2	114.2	5.3	105.9	109.0	99.1
1983	125.3	49.9	118.1	7.1	110.1	110.5	108.3
1984	138.2	57.0	125.8	9.4	117.1	117.7	114.9
1985	143.0	64.1	130.5	12.8	122.2	121.7	122.8
1986	112.2	59.9	107.2	16.0	107.0	99.2	126.7
1987	96.9	58.3	94.8	19.3	98.4	88.7	124.2
1988	92.7	59.0	88.2	23.4	91.8	83.5	113.7
1989	98.6	65.1	91.9	29.0	93.3	87.7	108.4
1990	89.1	70.2	87.9	39.5	92.0	84.7	111.3
1991	89.8	73.3	86.4	46.1	90.6	82.9	110.8
1992	86.6	76.1	84.9	52.6	88.7	81.8	107.3
1993	93.2	82.9	87.1	63.1	89.5	84.4	104.4
1994	91.3	90.4	85.6	80.6	89.2	84.0	104.3
1995	84.2	92.5	80.8	92.6	86.7	80.2	103.9
1996	87.3	97.4	84.6	98.3	88.7	85.3	100.8
1997	96.4	104.4	91.2	104.7	93.4	92.6	101.9
1998	98.8	116.5	95.8	126.0	101.6	97.7	115.3
1999	......	116.9	94.1	129.9	100.8	97.1	114.3
2000	......	119.7	98.3	130.3	104.3	103.2	114.5
2001	......	126.1	104.3	136.3	110.4	110.7	119.2
2002	......	127.3	103.1	141.2	110.9	109.7	121.9
2001: I	......	124.0	102.0	135.1	108.6	108.3	118.1
II	......	126.7	105.4	136.1	111.2	111.8	119.6
III	......	126.4	104.5	136.9	110.9	110.9	120.0
IV	......	127.2	105.4	137.3	111.0	112.0	119.0
2002: I	......	129.5	108.2	138.4	112.8	115.0	119.4
II	......	127.4	104.3	139.8	111.3	110.8	121.1
III	......	125.5	100.0	142.0	109.5	106.4	122.9
IV	......	126.6	100.0	144.7	110.2	106.5	124.2

SOURCE: Board of Governors of the Federal Reserve System.

[3] G-10 comprises the individual countries shown in this table. Discontinued after December 1998.

[4] Weighted average of the foreign exchange value of the dollar against the currencies of a broad group of U.S. trading partners.

[5] Subset of the broad index. Includes currencies of the euro area, Australia, Canada, Japan, Sweden, Switzerland, and the United Kingdom.

[6] Subset of the broad index. Includes other important U.S. trading partners (OITP) whose currencies are not heavily traded outside their home markets.

[7] Adjusted for changes in the consumer price index.

EXHIBIT 12.19	CBO's Baseline Budget Projections

The Budget and Economic Outlook: An Update
August 2003

CBO's Baseline Budget Projections

	Actual 2002	2003	2004	2005	2006	2007	2008	2009	2010	2011	2012	2013	Total, 2004-2008[a]
					In Billions of Dollars								
Revenues													
Individual income taxes	858	791	765	897	1,013	1,099	1,184	1,285	1,392	1,610	1,788	1,916	4,958
Corporate income taxes	148	125	161	221	259	266	270	274	280	291	303	316	1,177
Social insurance taxes	701	710	753	795	842	888	933	978	1,025	1,073	1,123	1,177	4,211
Other	146	144	147	151	162	168	177	185	184	192	216	225	804
Total	1,853	1,770	1,825	2,064	2,276	2,421	2,564	2,723	2,880	3,165	3,430	3,634	11,150
On-budget	1,338	1,247	1,276	1,487	1,667	1,780	1,889	2,012	2,135	2,383	2,610	2,774	8,099
Off-budget	515	523	549	577	609	641	675	710	746	782	820	860	3,051
Outlays													
Discretionary spending	735	826	900	931	948	969	996	1,022	1,048	1,080	1,100	1,134	4,745
Mandatory spending	1,105	1,188	1,250	1,289	1,333	1,401	1,482	1,570	1,665	1,776	1,854	1,984	6,755
Net interest	171	157	155	184	220	255	282	301	312	318	316	305	1,096
Total	2,011	2,170	2,305	2,404	2,501	2,624	2,761	2,893	3,025	3,174	3,269	3,422	12,595
On-budget	1,655	1,809	1,920	2,007	2,092	2,201	2,323	2,438	2,552	2,682	2,753	2,879	10,543
Off-budget	356	361	385	398	409	423	438	455	473	493	517	543	2,052
Deficit (-) or Surplus	-158	-401	-480	-341	-225	-203	-197	-170	-145	-9	161	211	-1,445
On-budget	-317	-562	-644	-520	-425	-421	-434	-426	-417	-298	-143	-105	-2,444
Off-budget	160	162	164	179	199	219	237	255	273	289	304	317	999
Debt Held by the Public	3,540	3,986	4,443	4,790	5,027	5,242	5,450	5,631	5,784	5,800	5,645	5,438	n.a.
Memorandum:													
Gross Domestic Product	10,337	10,730	11,245	11,869	12,536	13,219	13,920	14,640	15,375	16,122	16,901	17,729	62,789

SOURCE: Congressional Budget Office, *The Budget and Economic Outlook Update*, August 2003.

| EXHIBIT 12.20 | MONTHLY BUDGET REVIEW |

Monthly Budget Review

A Congressional Budget Office Analysis
November 7, 2003

FISCAL YEAR TOTALS
(In billions of dollars)

	2000	2001	2002	2003
Receipts	2,025	1,991	1,853	1,782
Outlays	1,789	1,864	2,011	2,157
Surplus or Deficit (-)	236	127	-158	-374
On-budget	86	-33	-317	-535
Off-budget	150	161	160	161
Surplus or Deficit (-) as a Percentage of GDP	2.4	1.3	-1.5	-3.5

SOURCES: Department of the Treasury; CBO.

TOTAL OUTLAYS
(In billions of dollars)

Major Category	Actual FY2002	Actual FY2003	Percentage Change Actual	Percentage Change Adjusted[a]
Defense--Military	332	389	17.1	16.0
Social Security Benefits	448	467	4.1	4.1
Medicare	256	277	8.2	6.9
Medicaid	148	161	8.9	8.9
Unemployment Insurance	55	58	6.0	6.0
Other Programs and Activities	593	644	8.5	9.1
Subtotal	1,832	1,994	8.9	8.7
Net Interest on the Public Debt	179	162	-9.6	-9.6
Total	2,011	2,157	7.2	7.1

SOURCES: Department of the Treasury; CBO.

a. Excludes the effects of payments that were shifted because of legislative action or changes in the accounting of certain health payments of the Department of Defense.

SOURCES: Department of the Treasury; CBO.